CAPITAL BUDGETING VALUATION

The *Robert W. Kolb Series in Finance* provides a comprehensive view of the field of finance in all of its variety and complexity. The series is projected to include approximately 65 volumes covering all major topics and specializations in finance, ranging from investments, to corporate finance, to financial institutions. Each volume in the *Kolb Series in Finance* consists of new articles especially written for the volume.

Each volume is edited by a specialist in a particular area of finance, who develops the volume outline and commissions articles by the world's experts in that particular field of finance. Each volume includes an editor's introduction and approximately thirty articles to fully describe the current state of financial research and practice in a particular area of finance.

The essays in each volume are intended for practicing finance professionals, graduate students, and advanced undergraduate students. The goal of each volume is to encapsulate the current state of knowledge in a particular area of finance so that the reader can quickly achieve a mastery of that special area of finance.

Please visit www.wiley.com/go/kolbseries to learn about recent and forthcoming titles in the Kolb Series.

CAPITAL BUDGETING VALUATION

Financial Analysis for Today's Investment Projects

H. Kent Baker

Philip English

The Robert W. Kolb Series in Finance

WILEY

John Wiley & Sons, Inc.

Published by John Wiley & Sons, Inc., Hoboken, New Jersey.
Published simultaneously in Canada.

For general information on our other products and services or for technical support, please contact our Customer Care Department within the United States at (800) 762-2974, outside the United States at (317) 572-3993 or fax (317) 572-4002.

Wiley also publishes its books in a variety of electronic formats. Some content that appears in print may not be available in electronic books. For more information about Wiley products, visit our web site at www.wiley.com.

Library of Congress Cataloging-in-Publication Data:

Baker, H. Kent (Harold Kent), 1944-
    Capital budgeting valuation : financial analysis for today's investment projects / H. Kent Baker and Philip English.
        p. cm. – (The Robert W. Kolb series in finance)
    Includes index.
    ISBN 978-0-470-56950-4 (cloth); ISBN 978-1-118-04456-8 (ebk); ISBN 978-1-118-04454-4 (ebk); ISBN 978-1-118-04455-1 (ebk)
    1. Capital budget.   2. Capital investments.   3. Value added.   I. English, Philip. II. Title.
        HG4028.C4B285 2011
        658.15′4–dc22

                                                                                    2010049527

Printed in the United States of America

10 9 8 7 6 5 4 3 2 1

Contents

Acknowledgments

C apital Budgeting Valuation—Financial Analysis for Today's Investment Projects reflects the involvement both directly and indirectly of many people. A distinguished group of academics and practitioners contributed their substantial talents to writing highly informative and useful chapters. Much of their work, however, relies upon numerous individuals who have contributed to the field of capital budgeting during the past five decades, many of whom are referenced specifically in each chapter. Special thanks go to Meghan Nesmith from American University, who edited the chapters and provided many helpful suggestions. The publishing team at John Wiley & Sons, Inc., including Evan Burton, Claire Wesley, Emilie Herman and many others, did a first-class job in bringing the book to final production. We also thank Bob Kolb for including this book in the Robert W. Kolb Series in Finance and the Kogod School of Business Administration at American University for providing support. Finally, we thank Linda Baker who provided not only encouragement but also reviewed parts of the manuscript.

CHAPTER 1

Capital Budgeting: An Overview

H. KENT BAKER
University Professor of Finance and Kogod Research Professor,
Kogod School of Business, American University

PHILIP ENGLISH
Assistant Professor of Finance, Kogod School of Business, American University

INTRODUCTION

Capital budgeting refers to the process that managers use to make decisions about whether long-term investments or capital expenditures are worth pursuing by their organizations. In other words, capital budgeting is the process of planning, analyzing, selecting, and managing capital investments. The basic notion is that managers use the capital, usually long-term funds, raised by their firms to invest in assets (also called *capital goods*) that will enable the firm to generate cash flows for at least several years into the future. Typical investments include replacements of existing assets and expansion of existing or new product lines. Capital budgeting is one of the most challenging tasks facing management because it concerns the *investment decision*, which deals with allocating funds over time in order to achieve a firm's objectives. For most companies, the investment decision has a greater impact on value than does the *financing decision*, which deals with acquiring needed funds. However, both investment and financing decisions are intertwined and at the heart of financial management.

Capital budgeting has a long-term focus that provides a link to an organization's *strategic plan*, which specifies how an organization expects to accomplish long-term strategic goals. Many capital investments require a substantial commitment of a firm's resources that directly affect firm performance, competitive position, and future direction. Because capital investments often commit a large amount of funds for lengthy periods, they are not only difficult or costly to reverse but also difficult to convert to more liquid assets (Migliore and McCracken, 2001). Also, errors in capital budgeting can affect the firm over a long horizon.

Capital Budgeting Process

The *capital budgeting process* is a system of interrelated steps for generating long-term investment proposals; reviewing, analyzing, and selecting them; and implementing and following up on those selected. This process is dynamic because changing factors in an organization's environment may influence the attractiveness of current or proposed projects. Although no universal consensus exists on the process, Baker and Powell (2005, p. 196) view capital budgeting as a six-stage process:

1. *Identify project proposals.* Develop and provide preliminary screening of project proposals.
2. *Estimate project cash flows.* Identify and estimate the incremental, after-tax cash flows for a proposed project.
3. *Evaluate projects.* Determine the financial viability of a project by evaluating the project's incremental after-tax cash flows.
4. *Select projects.* Choose the projects that best meet the selection criteria.
5. *Implement projects.* Determine the order of implementation, initiate, and track the selected projects.
6. *Perform a postcompletion audit.* Periodically compare the actual cash flows for the project to the prior estimates in the capital budgeting proposal.

All stages of the capital budgeting process are important. The failure to properly complete any stage of the capital budgeting process could have detrimental results. The process starts with the identification of investment opportunities and the preliminary screening of project proposals. Without having potentially viable projects that meet the firm's strategic concerns, the remainder of the capital budgeting process would be meaningless.

Arguably, the most challenging phase of this process is estimating project cash flows because no later stage in the process can fully overcome the inevitable forecasting errors resulting from managers dealing with an uncertain future. Miller (2000, p. 128) notes that "In the real world, virtually all numbers are estimates. The problem with estimates, of course, is that they are frequently wrong."

Despite the importance of estimating project cash flows, the financial literature tends to emphasize the evaluation and selection stages. Improper valuation can lead to incorrect decisions despite the identification of potentially viable projects and accurate estimation of their cash flows. Although many capital budgeting techniques are available for evaluating capital budgeting projects, the best methods typically recognize the amount, the time value, and the riskiness of a project's cash flows.

Selecting capital investments involves a unique set of challenges. Allocating funds among alternative investment opportunities is crucial to a firm's success and is especially important in terms of financial consequences. Capital assets represent a major portion of the total assets of many firms. The selection stage is particularly important in the face of limited investment funds, an area of capital budgeting known as *capital rationing*. While some organizations have sufficient resources available to fund all desirable projects, most face a scarcity of capital that enables them to fund some projects but not others. Capital rationing, whether internally or externally imposed, makes investment choices more difficult because the firm must reject some investments. However, capital rationing can also reduce and control agency costs. Capital rationing can avoid both overinvestment in low-return projects that occurs when managers have private information and incentives for controlling more assets and managerial understatement of current performance in order to lower their future performance targets.

After approving a capital investment, managers must implement and closely monitor the project. This stage involves raising capital to finance the project, authorizing expenditures, and monitoring projects in progress.

The final stage in the capital budgeting process is to conduct a postcompletion audit. Managers, however, do not engage in postcompletion auditing of all projects because doing so could be costly or impractical. Consequently, large capital budgeting projects tend to be the primary targets for such audits. The most important perceived benefits relate to the enhancement of organizational learning. Conducting postcompletion audits can provide important feedback for current and future investments, and consequently make capital investments more effective (Neale, 1991; Pierce and Tsay, 1992). For example, these audits may identify systematic biases in making cash flow estimates, which may lead to improved cash flow estimates and to better decision making in the future. Thus, postcompletion audits provide a means for holding managers accountable for their estimates and decisions involving capital investments.

Financial Objective of the Firm

Before carrying out the capital budgeting process, management should first define the organization's financial objective. The conventionally advocated capital investment objective, especially in large, listed corporations, is to make long-term investment decisions that will maximize owners' wealth. That is, senior managers of publicly held companies should select those projects that they believe will maximize the firm's value for its shareholders. As Jensen (2001, p. 8) notes, "This Value Maximization proposition has its roots in 200 years of research in economics and finance." Yet, this financial objective seems to be inconsistent with some empirical observations such those in Francis (1980).

The main contender to shareholder wealth maximization is *stakeholder theory*, which asserts that management decisions should consider stakeholder interests wider than those of the stockholders alone. This view contends that firms should pay attention to all their constituencies because many different classes of stakeholders contribute to their success. Beyond financial claimholders, stakeholders may include managers, employers, customers, suppliers, local communities, and the government. Survey evidence by Grinyer, Sinclair, and Ibrahim (1999) is consistent with the notion that some managers do not prefer maximization of stockholders' wealth as the main objective of the firm. Cloninger (1995) proposes the formal abandonment of a stockholder wealth maximizing criterion.

While stakeholder theory has intuitive appeal, recognizing a wide range of stakeholders introduces possible difficulties associated with multiple objectives. Trying to maximize multiple objectives, some of which may conflict, would leave the managers in a quandary about whose interests should take priority—stockholders or other stakeholders.

In theory, capital projects should be analyzed in terms of shareholder wealth maximization. Based on this assumption, managers should undertake all investment projects with a positive net present value (NPV) or an internal rate of return (IRR) higher than the prescribed hurdle rate. By so doing, managers should enhance firm market value and consequently increase owners' wealth. In practice, management should not necessarily accept a project just because it appears financially attractive. Achieving the financial objective of shareholder wealth maximization entails developing a business strategy. Success in capital investment affects the extent to which a company can achieve its strategic objectives. Investment decisions do not occur in a vacuum but are embedded in a company's strategy. Thus, strategy limits the set of investment projects available to managers. As Rumelt, Schendel, and Teece (1991) note, "There is no rule for riches." That is, no general rules in strategy exist that are guaranteed to create value.

According to Jensen and Meckling (1976), firms may experience conflicts of interest between owners and managers. What may be best for a firm's managers may not be in the best interests of its shareholders. Managers may desire to maximize their own wealth, which leads to various investment distortions. Further, some managers may want to build empires, maximize their compensation, secure their career, or shirk their responsibilities. Managerial overconfidence may lead them to pass up profitable projects, to undertake unprofitable ones, or to choose an investment with a suboptimal risk level. Thus, managers may not make suitable investment decisions. Corporate governance mechanisms such as managerial compensation contracts, the structure of the board of directors, and ownership structure can play an important role in reducing or eliminating such investment distortions.

Capital Investment Choice

As previously mentioned, the finance literature emphasizes the evaluation and selection stages of the capital budgeting process. Not surprisingly, many tools, techniques, methods, and mechanisms are available for making capital investment choices. Payne, Heath, and Gale (1999, p. 16) make the following observation: "According to theory, firms should use discounted cash flow methods to analyze capital budgeting alternatives. Within this theoretical frame, however, firms might evaluate somewhat similar projects differently." Survey research such as Graham and Harvey (2001) suggests that firms, especially large, listed firms, tend to evaluate projects using discounted cash flow (DCF) tools as the primary criterion and to compute weighted average cost of capital in the manner suggested by theory. Research also shows that the gap between traditional theory and capital budgeting practices has narrowed substantially. Managers are also placing increasing emphasis on the risk characteristics of projects. According to Stulz (1999, p. 8), "The reason why corporations do not enter gambles with volatile payoffs and small positive expected returns is that managers know that generally volatility matters."

When using DCF techniques, a major challenge of capital budgeting is correctly estimating the appropriate rate to use when discounting a project's cash flows. Although managers have a variety of sophisticated techniques at their disposal to estimate a firm's or project's cost of capital, each method involves potential complications. Although the capital asset pricing model (CAPM) and its competitor, the arbitrage pricing theory (APT), have come to dominate the asset pricing litera-ture, much debate remains about the validity of either model to estimate the cost of equity capital and determining the appropriate inputs for each. Estimating the cost of capital in an international context creates additional complexities. No agreement exists between academics and practitioners on the best approach to pursue.

Despite the abundance of capital budgeting techniques available, many schol-ars question the adequacy of DCF analysis in helping practitioners make decisions in a realistic business environment. Some, such as Myers (1977), who coined the term *real options,* suggest augmenting DCF analysis with real options analysis. For example, Trigeorgis (1988, 1993) and Van Putten and MacMillan (2004), among others, point out that traditional DCF methods may fail to consider the flexibility to revise decisions after a project begins. That is, the traditional DCF approach does not capture the realistic valuation of an investment because it does not explicitly account for the value of real options inherent in capital budgeting. Consequently, DCF techniques often fail to provide sound valuation when the business envi-ronment is uncertain and forgo the value created by flexibility in management decisions. According to Stout, Xie, and Qi (2008), managers should use real op-tions when making long-term investment decisions because such utilization can help optimize the capital budgeting process.

Survey evidence suggests that most companies have been slow to adopt real options (Graham and Harvey, 2001; Ryan and Ryan, 2002; Brounen, de Jong, and Koedijk, 2004). Based on their survey evidence, Baker, Dutta, and Saadi (2011) find a lack of expertise and knowledge is the primary reason preventing managers from using real options. Their evidence suggests that contrary to optimistic predictions, the use of real options appears disproportionate to their potential as a capital budgeting tool.

Purpose of the Book

The purpose of this book is to examine selected topics in capital budgeting in a clear and straightforward manner. Given the sheer volume of work written about capital budgeting, the book cannot cover every possible topic. However, it does provide a synthesis of the current state of capital budgeting. The coverage extends from discussing basic concepts, principles, and techniques to their application to increasingly complex and real-world situations. Throughout, the book emphasizes how financially sound capital budgeting facilitates the process of value creation.

Numerous books focus solely on capital budgeting. Additionally, corporate finance textbooks universally provide material on capital budgeting. Yet, few offer the scope of coverage and breadth of viewpoints contained in this volume. The book differs from its competition in several major ways. Perhaps the main feature distinguishing this book from others is its synthesis and discussion of empirical results from hundreds of studies. Although a single book cannot provide a detailed discussion of every paper written on capital budgeting, this book highlights what is known to date about important topics. An old adage is that there is nothing quite as practical as a good theory, that is, one that works in practice as well as on paper. The book takes a practical approach to capital budgeting by discussing why various theories make sense, the empirical support for them, and how firms use these theories to solve problems and to create wealth. The book also reports the results of numerous capital budgeting surveys that reveal the link between theory and practice.

Features of the Book

The book has four other distinguishing features.

1. It contains contributions from more than 30 different authors. Thus, the breadth of contributors assures a wide variety of viewpoints and a rich interplay of ideas.
2. The book offers a strategic focus so that readers can understand how the application of various techniques and approaches relates to a firm's overall strategy. This is because investment decisions help determine the firm's strategic position many years into the future.
3. The volume provides coverage of international topics on the premise that managers should view business from a global perspective.
4. The book discusses the potential benefits of using real options. Real options analysis has become important since the 1970s as option pricing models became more sophisticated. DCF methods essentially value projects as if they were risky bonds, with the promised cash flows known. Yet, managers still have many choices of how to increase future cash inflows or to decrease future cash outflows. That is, managers get to manage the projects, not simply accept or reject them. Further, capital budgeting is a dynamic process that unfolds as the project develops revealing new information as time elapses. Managerial flexibility is at the root of the real options approach, which enables traditional capital budgeting techniques to incorporate managerial flexibility and information revelation. In short, real options analysis tries to value the choices—the option value—that the managers will have in the future and adds these values to the net present value.

Intended Audience

The intended audience for this book includes academics, practitioners, students, and others interested in capital budgeting. For example, the book should suit researchers and financial managers given its scope of coverage. Nonfinancial executives should also find this volume relevant because capital budgeting theory has broad application to general management. This volume should also be appropriate as a stand-alone or supplementary text for advanced undergraduate and graduate students as well as for management training programs in capital budgeting. It should be especially useful in helping students develop the critical analytical skills required to assess potential investments. Finally, libraries should find this work to be suitable for reference purposes.

STRUCTURE OF THE BOOK

The remaining 23 chapters of this book are organized into seven parts. A brief synopsis of each chapter follows.

Part I. Foundation and Key Concepts

Chapters 2 and 3 discuss the role that corporate strategy and corporate governance can have in investment decisions.

Chapter 2 Corporate Strategy and Investment Decisions (Daniel Ferreira)

This chapter reviews the literature on business strategy and its relation to corporate investment decisions. It provides an overview of some important concepts and briefly discusses their practical implications. A selective review of empirical evidence is used to illustrate a few key ideas. The chapter offers an introductory discussion of topics such as competitive advantage, added value, industry analysis, the industry life cycle, firm scope, firm resources, and the trade-off between commitment and adaptation. Specific applications to the issue of corporate investment include corporate diversification, strategic investments, identifying and valuing synergies, mergers and acquisitions, cash flow forecasting, and interactions between investment and financing decisions.

Chapter 3 Corporate Governance and Investment Decisions (Fodil Adjaoud, Dorra Charfi, and Lamia Chourou)

The asymmetric information between managers and external financiers, the conflicts of interest between owners and managers, and the managerial overconfidence bias may lead managers to pass up profitable projects (underinvest), to undertake unprofitable ones (overinvest), or to choose an investment with a suboptimal risk level. Theoretically, corporate governance mechanisms such as the choice of capital structure, managerial compensation contracts, structure of the board of directors, and ownership structure play an important role in reducing or eliminating such investment distortions. However, the empirical literature is inconclusive as to whether managers of well-governed firms make better investment decisions than those of poorly governed firms.

Part II. Capital Investment Choice

The section contains six chapters involving capital investment choice. Chapters 4 and 5 examine various methods of evaluating capital investments. Chapter 6 explores the topic of capital budgeting under capital rationing while Chapter 7 provides a discussion of foreign investments. Chapter 8 focuses on the final stage of the capital budgeting process—postcompletion. Chapter 9 reviews some survey evidence involving both U.S. and non-U.S. firms about their reported use of capital budgeting techniques.

Chapter 4 Measuring Investment Value: Free Cash Flow, Net Present Value, and Economic Value Added (Tom Arnold and Terry Nixon)

This chapter focuses on issues involving the calculation of net present value (NPV) and closely related variants. Although relatively easy to understand conceptually, issues concerning the calculation of cash flow, assessment of risk, and project return relative to the cost of raising funds are not as clear. Two definitions of cash flow emerge in the literature: free cash flow (FCF) and cash flow from assets (CFA). These definitions differ due to the tax savings associated with interest. Although the numerical difference can be minimal, a clear impact exists on selecting the appropriate discount rate and assessing hurdle rates for comparison with internal rate of return (IRR). Economic value added (EVA) presents another measure of cash flow. Although EVA does not appear to produce project valuations that work well empirically, it provides a workable short-term metric for assessing management.

Chapter 5 Alternative Methods of Evaluating Capital Investments (Tom Arnold and Terry Nixon)

The primary focus of this chapter is to examine two metrics, payback period (PB) and the internal rate of return (IRR), including variations of each method. The PB is a simple metric that focuses on the time needed for short-term cash flows to recover the initial investment. Although the measure does not have any discounting element, its usage is still widespread and may potentially be the result of managers focusing on the short-term rather than on more valuable longer-term projects. Variations of PB include the discounted payback period (DPB) and the project balance method (PBL). The IRR is a rate of return metric that does not have an easy interpretation and, consequently, is often misinterpreted. The main difficulty in considering IRR is that intermediate cash flows do not typically appreciate at the IRR as the project continues through time. Related metrics are the modified internal rate of return (MIRR) and the profitability index (PI).

Chapter 6 Capital Rationing for Capital Budgeting (Alexander Brüggen)

This chapter describes the mechanism of capital rationing for capital budgeting. Capital rationing is the limitation of funds that are available for investments in an organization. With only limited funds available, different investment projects compete for capital. Managers can allocate these funds based on either a hurdle rate (every project beyond a certain threshold gets capital) or on a winner-picking method (the best ranked projects receive capital). This competition helps to control and reduce agency costs that occur due to overinvestment by managers or because managers understate their performance to lower their future performance targets. Negative side effects of capital rationing include competition that can put managers under pressure, which in turn can lead to misreporting. Research evidence on the effects of capital rationing is still mixed and depends on whether and how individuals derive a disutility from misreporting.

Chapter 7 Analyzing Foreign Investments (Wim Westerman and John Henry Hall)

Foreign investment can be very different from its domestic counterpart. Because the necessary analysis may have to be broader than for domestic investment, the financial valuation process is less straightforward, making the financial modeling of the investment generally more complex. This chapter demonstrates a phasing framework that outlines the investment process and discusses the design of a financial model. Complications in financial modeling tend to occur mainly due to asset and liability valuation differences, intracompany transfer pricing, different tax systems in different jurisdictions, incomplete transfer of results, exchange rate changes over time, political risks abroad, foreign financing conditions, and the parent versus subsidiary perspective. These problems are illustrated by applying a spreadsheet format with realistic numerical data to a specific case.

Chapter 8 Postcompletion Auditing of Capital Investments (Jari Huikku)
Postcompletion auditing (PCA) is a formal process that checks the outcomes of individual capital investment projects after the initial investment is completed and when the project is operational. The major reason for PCA and its most important perceived benefits are related to the enhancement of organizational learning. The appropriate design of a PCA system is crucial for such learning to take place. More specifically, communication-related issues such as appropriate filing and convenient access to PCA reports, improvement proposals and their systematic follow-up, and interactive forums for interpretation of results may enhance the effective conveyance of investment experiences to new investment projects. Alternative existing control mechanisms to achieve PCA benefits may discourage companies from adopting PCA or developing their PCA systems.

Chapter 9 Capital Budgeting Techniques in Practice: U.S. Survey Evidence
(Tarun K. Mukherjee and Naseem M. Al Rahahleh)
Numerous surveys over the last five decades have dealt with the capital budgeting practices of large U.S. firms. This chapter reviews the survey results with respect to the four stages of the capital budgeting process. The evidence shows that capital budgeting practices for the most part conform to traditional capital budgeting theory. Firms use cash flows as cost-benefit data and estimate them in a theoretically consistent manner. They use discounted cash flow (DCF) tools as the primary criteria with which to evaluate projects and compute weighted average cost of capital based on what theory suggests. Although the gap between conventional theory and capital budgeting practices has substantially narrowed, many scholars have challenged the adequacy of DCF analysis in helping practitioners make decisions in a realistic business environment and have suggested augmenting DCF analysis with real options analysis.

Part III. Project Cash Flows and Inflation

This section consists of two chapters. Chapter 10 discusses estimating project cash flows, which is perhaps the most important stage of the capital budgeting process. Chapter 11 examines how to adjust for inflation when evaluating capital budgeting projects.

Chapter 10 Estimating Project Cash Flows (Kyle Meyer and Halil Kiymaz)
Companies evaluate investment opportunities on a recurring basis. This process has various facets such as estimating the initial investment, forecasting future cash flows, and, when using discounted cash flow (DCF) methods, selecting the appropriate discount rate. This chapter discusses issues that firms should consider when estimating project cash flows and evaluating investment opportunities. In particular, this chapter examines factors related to estimating the initial investment and future cash flows during the project's life. Relatively little research has specifically addressed the methods used by firms to estimate project cash flows. Surveys of firm managers in various industries indicate that the use of DCF methods has increased over time. Additionally, many such surveys examine how firms impound project risk into the capital budgeting process. Results indicate that most firms adjust for risk by increasing the project's discount rate or through sensitivity analysis.

*Chapter 11 Capital Budgeting and Inflation (Ignacio Vélez-Pareja
and Joseph Tham)*
The purpose of this chapter is to discuss and show that conducting capital budgeting and investment appraisal based on financial statements with real or constant
prices is potentially misleading. Under certain circumstances, the adverse effects
of inflation could result in the selection of "bad" projects. The chapter also shows
that modeling with nominal prices is feasible and is a relatively simple task with a
spreadsheet program on a personal computer. Using a simple example, the chapter shows that using constant or real prices results in a bias because the real and
constant approaches overvalue cash flows. Thus, analysts should carry out capital
budgeting analysis using nominal prices.

Part IV. Risk and Investment Choice

This section of risk and investment choice contains four chapters. Chapter 12 highlights basic risk analysis techniques used in capital budgeting. Chapter 13 focuses
on several techniques for assessing political/country risk. In Chapter 14, attention
focuses on risk management in project finance. Chapter 15 examines simulation
concepts and methods.

*Chapter 12 Basic Risk Adjustment Techniques in Capital Budgeting
(John H. Hall and Wim Westerman)*
Firms can use various techniques to quantify the risk of capital investment projects
in order to improve their evaluation process. This chapter examines basic risk analysis techniques in capital budgeting, starting with judgment and shortening the
payback period. Both methods have merit and can be applied in certain circumstances. The overall principle of adjusting for a project's risk requires modifying
the cash flows or the discount rate. Adjusting the cash flows based on certainty
equivalents requires various assumptions, but may yield results useful in making
informed decisions. The risk-adjusted discount rate can be calculated using the
capital asset pricing model. Although this controversial method is problematic
due to certain assumptions, it arguably gives the best results in addressing the risk
of a project.

*Chapter 13 Capital Budgeting with Political/Country Risk (Yacine Belghitar
and Ephraim Clark)*
Political risk has a long and noble history in the theory and practice of foreign direct investment. A review of the literature indicates that no general consensus
exists about what constitutes political risk because of the multiplicity of the
sources of risk, the complexity of their interactions, and the variety of social sciences involved. As such, several techniques or methods have been considered to
assess political risk. Accounting for political risk in the capital budgeting process
can be summarized in three steps: (1) identify the risk, (2) assess the risk, and (3)
translate the assessment into consistent, concrete parameters compatible in theory and in practice with the discounted cash flow format of the modern capital
budgeting process.

Chapter 14 Risk Management in Project Finance (Stefano Gatti and Stefano Caselli)

This chapter analyzes the characteristics of project finance transactions in terms of a nexus of contracts and risk management tools. The capital budgeting of the special-purpose vehicle (SPV) created to design, build, operate, and finance the deal requires a preliminary assessment of the parties involved in the transaction and of the content of the contracts they sign with the vehicle. This step is necessary to highlight the main differences in capital budgeting for ongoing corporate entities compared to newly created vehicles. It is also crucial because contracts are the most effective risk management tool in such deals, enabling the SPV to carry out the risk pass-through and to limit the volatility and risk of project cash flows. An additional complication in capital budgeting for project finance is that the valuation of deal sustainability requires a joint satisfaction of standard profitability criteria such as net present value or internal rate of return along with financial covenants involving cover ratios.

Chapter 15 Risk Simulation Concepts and Methods (Tom Arnold and David North)

This chapter presents Monte Carlo simulation as a means to demonstrate numerically and visually the risk within the cash flows generated by a project. By allowing cash flow inputs to follow probability distributions rather than being static, trials or iterations can be generated by randomly drawing outcomes from the probability distributions of the input variables. After many iterations/trials, a probability distribution can be created for the project cash flows. The chapter also introduces the "compact" pro forma model as another potential means for performing Monte Carlo analysis to assess project cash flows. Further, other non-pro forma–related applications of Monte Carlo analysis are discussed.

Part V. Real Options and Project Analysis

Real options analysis is one of the newest and most rapidly growing areas of capital budgeting. It focuses on including managerial discretion and the impact of the evolution of information across time in the capital budgeting process. Chapter 16 introduces the concept of a real option and provides an extended numerical example of how including real options analysis affects decision making. Chapter 17 provides a description of the most commonly examined real options and their applications in capital budgeting.

Chapter 16 Real Options Analysis: An Introduction (Tom Arnold and Bonnie Buchanan)

The primary focus of this chapter is to provide an overview of how real options analysis considers the dynamic environment within a project rather than solely using forecasted expected values for future cash flows. The value of management interaction throughout the life of the project can be missed using static net present value techniques because these methods do not fully consider actions that can be taken to increase profits or cut losses. A numerical example demonstrates the value of recognizing a real option and the value of creating more real options within the example. Having demonstrated the benefit of real options analysis, the chapter continues by detailing how real options analysis emerged in the finance literature. Initially, financial economists realized a problem of "underinvestment" and attributed it to the debt structure of a firm requiring projects with short-term cash flows at the expense of longer-term projects that generated future growth options for the firm. Real options analysis emerged in response to the need for recognizing the value created by these longer-term, growth-oriented projects.

Chapter 17 Applications of Real Options Analysis (Tom Arnold and Bonnie Buchanan)
The primary focus of this chapter is to demonstrate the application of real option models in the finance literature. After demonstrating the benefit of risk-neutral pricing, seven different types of real options are discussed with examples of how and why such options are implemented. These options are as follows: (1) the option to wait or defer, (2) staged investment options, (3) the option to alter the scale of operations, (4) the option to abandon, (5) the option to switch inputs or outputs, (6) growth options, and (7) rainbow options. The common link between all of these applications is considering the behavior of management in light of a particular source of volatility and how the construct of a project can allow management the flexibility to use discretion while addressing volatility.

Part VI. Estimating the Project Cost of Capital

This section contains three chapters on estimating the appropriate discount rate for use in the capital budgeting process, which is a key part of project evaluation. Chapter 18 provides an introduction to estimating the discount rate using the firm's cost of capital. Chapter 19 covers the role of the capital asset pricing model (CAPM) and arbitrage pricing theory (APT) in determining the discount rate. Chapter 20 provides a discussion on adjusting the discount rate to reflect project risk.

Chapter 18 Cost of Capital: An Introduction (Octavian Ionici, Kenneth Small, and Frank D'Souza)
Although financial managers have many sophisticated techniques at their disposal to estimate a firm's cost of capital, understanding the power and nuances of each can be a daunting task. This chapter discusses current best practices regarding component costs of capital estimation. As an illustration, all major component costs of capital for a firm are estimated. The chapter discusses representative research on the cost of capital, the CAPM, and risk premium estimation, as well as estimating both a project's and firm's cost of capital in an international context.

Chapter 19 Using the Capital Asset Pricing Model and Arbitrage Pricing Theory in Capital Budgeting (S. David Young and Samir Saadi)
Over the past five decades, the CAPM and its competitor, APT, have come to dominate the asset pricing literature. But despite decades of research, considerable debate remains as to the validity of either model to estimate the cost of equity capital. This chapter provides an overview of this literature with particular emphasis on the relative merits and limitations of the CAPM and the APT in their application to capital budgeting decisions. The discussion reveals that the CAPM continues to be the dominant tool for corporate use in estimating the cost of equity.

*Chapter 20 Financing Mix and Project Valuation: Alternative Methods
and Possible Adjustments (Alex Pierru and Denis Babusiaux)*

Analysts can use various methods to value an investment project including the standard weighted average cost of capital (WACC) method, Arditti-Levy method, equity residual method, and adjusted present value. This chapter proposes a unique formulation from which these methods can be derived. This formulation permits demonstrating the equality of their net present values and the consistency of their internal rates of return in a straightforward manner when a predetermined debt ratio is targeted. The chapter contains a discussion of possible pitfalls when considering a project's financing mix. The adjustment of the standard WACC method for capitalized interest costs is also examined. Further, the chapter presents a generalized version of the standard WACC method that multinational firms should use when facing disparities in the tax treatment of interest paid across different taxing environments.

Part VII. Special Topics

The final four chapters of the book provide an examination of several areas of increasing importance in the modern capital budgeting process. Chapter 21 offers a discussion of capital budgeting for government entities. Chapter 22 focuses on the topic of behavioral finance, which examines the impact of bounded rationality and limited information on the decision-making process. Mergers and acquisitions (M&As) represent a particularly large and potentially risky category of capital budgeting decisions. Chapter 23 examines a new approach to capturing the effect of synergies on valuation and, hence, on the capital budgeting process for M&As. Chapter 24 concludes the book with an examination of multicriteria analysis in capital budgeting, an area that allows the incorporation of different stakeholder effects into the capital budgeting process.

Chapter 21 Capital Budgeting for Government Entities (Davina F. Jacobs)

This chapter provides an overview of the evolution of past and current budgeting practices by government for capital budgets. It also provides a comparison between the budget practices of low-income countries and more advanced countries, and highlights possible solutions for use by government entities wanting to ensure more efficient and effective capital budgeting practices. Also discussed are capital project appraisal methods, which could be considered as an economic analysis of the costs and benefits that might be generated by the proposed government investment options.

*Chapter 22 Decision Making Using Behavioral Finance for Capital Budgeting
(Yuri Biondi and Guiseppe Marzo)*

The accepted approach to capital budgeting leaves decision makers without appropriate guidance because it ignores the cognitive, organizational, and institutional dimensions of their decision-making process. This approach is based upon the unrealistic assumptions of neoclassical finance, where investors are assumed to be (or behave as if they are) fully rational and informed. This chapter explores the opportunity to analyze capital budgeting decisions within a more realistic context. To reach such an objective, it summarizes alternative perspectives addressing these specific dimensions: the cognitive, the organizational, and the institutional. All together, such dimensions suggest generalizing the current approach based on discounted cash flow analysis to provide decision makers with alternative ways to assess investment opportunities under more realistic approaches driven by behavioral and institutional finance.

Chapter 23 Merger and Acquisition Pricing: The Valuation of Synergy (Rainer Lenz)

Whether a company merger is successful often depends on realizing future synergies that are associated with a high level of uncertainty. Conventional valuation methods lack precision in their predictions of synergistic benefits. Inaccurate valuation of synergistic benefits helps to explain why mergers are often unsuccessful and destroy shareholder value. In this chapter, a new model is developed for estimating synergy effects related to merger activities. This approach combines traditional methods of capital budgeting with new elements of knowledge management and sociological system theory. The value of synergy is explicitly incorporated into a pricing model by using the system-specific knowledge of corporate business processes.

Chapter 24 Multicriteria Analysis for Capital Budgeting (Fernando R. Fernholz)

Multicriteria analysis (MCA) is a technique that formalizes the simultaneous consideration of different objectives and hence criteria in selecting among proposed investment projects. MCA expands the space for decision making for capital budgeting purposes. Three main methodologies—a weighted sum model, a weighted product method, and an analytical hierarchy process method—are discussed and examples are provided. The methodologies are robust and consistent in selecting the most desirable alternatives. The introduction and use of MCA in corporations and financial institutions has been facilitated by application, dissemination, and improvements in communication and data processing technology. Sustained and effective use of MCA requires the leadership of top management and decision support systems.

SUMMARY AND CONCLUSIONS

Today's capital investment decisions are more important than ever given rapid technological advances, shorter product life cycles, and global competition. Although survey evidence by Graham and Harvey (2001) and Brounen et al. (2004) among others shows a narrowing of the gap between the conventional theory and practice of capital budgeting, this gap is not entirely bridged. Managers face the difficult task of making capital investment decisions in an increasingly complex environment. Making errors could be costly because many capital investments involve large expenditures that may directly affect a firm's performance, sustainability, and future direction. When conducting project analysis, managers need to understand the underlying assumptions the techniques used, their advantages and disadvantages, and the real meaning of the results. The capital investments selected need to be consistent with the firm's strategic plan and contribute to achieving its financial objective, which is often held to be shareholder wealth maximization. Despite the plethora of approaches and methods, there is no one best way of accomplishing this task. Generally, however, in analyzing today's investment projects, a good decision model should consider all relevant cash flows, the time value of money, and risk as reflected in the project's required rate of return. Ultimately, investment decisions involve judgment. The following chapters offer a wealth of useful information that provides guidance in navigating through the complex maze involving capital investment decisions in the real world. Let's now begin this journey.

REFERENCES

Baker, H. Kent, Shantanu Dutta, and Samir Saadi. 2011. "Management Views on Real Options in Capital Budgeting." *Journal of Applied Finance*, forthcoming.

Baker, H. Kent, and Gary E. Powell. 2005. *Understanding Financial Management—A Practical Guide.* Malden, MA: Blackwell Publishing.

Brounen, Dirk, Abe de Jong, and Kees Koedijk. 2004. "Corporate Finance in Europe: Confronting Theory with Practice." *Financial Management* 33:4, 71–101.

Cloninger, Dale O. 1995. "Managerial Goals and Ethical Behavior." *Financial Practice and Education* 5:1, 50–59.

Francis, Arthur. 1980. "Company Objectives, Managerial Motivations and the Behavior of Large Firms: An Empirical Test of the Theory of Managerial Capitalism." *Cambridge Journal of Economics* 4:4, 349–361.

Graham, John R., and Campbell R. Harvey. 2001. "The Theory and Practice of Corporate Finance: Evidence from the Field." *Journal of Financial Economics* 60:2–3, 187–243.

Grinyer, John R., C. Donald Sinclair, and Daing Nasir Ibrahim. 1999. "Management Objectives in Capital Budgeting." *Financial Practice and Education* 9:2, 12–22.

Jensen, Michael C. 2001. "Value Maximization, Stakeholder Theory, and the Corporate Objective Function." *Journal of Applied Corporate Finance* 14:3, 8–21.

Jensen, Michael C., and William H. Meckling. 1976. "Theory of the Firm: Managerial Behavior, Agency Costs and Ownership Structure." *Journal of Financial Economics* 3:4, 305–360.

Migliore, R. Henry, and Douglas McCracken. 2001. "Tie Your Capital Budget to Your Strategic Plan." *Strategic Finance* 82:12, 38–43.

Miller, Edward M. 2000. "Capital Budgeting Errors Seldom Cancel." *Financial Practice and Education* 10:2, 128–135.

Myers, Stewart C. 1977. "Determinants of Corporate Borrowing." *Journal of Financial Economics* 5:2, 147–175.

Neale, Charles W. 1991. "The Benefits Derived from Post-auditing Investment Projects." *OMEGA International Journal of Management Science* 19:2/3, 113–120.

Payne, Janet D., Will Carrington Heath, and Lewis R. Gale. 1999. "Comparative Financial Practice in the US and Canada: Capital Budgeting and Risk Assessment." *Financial Practice and Education* 9:1, 16–24.

Pierce, Bethane J., and Jeffrey J. Tsay. 1992. "A Study of the Post-Completion Audit Practices of Large American Corporations: Experience from 1978 and 1988." *Journal of Management Accounting Research* 4, 131–155.

Ryan, Patricia A., and Glenn P. Ryan. 2002. "Capital Budgeting Practices of the Fortune 1000: How Have Things Changed?" *Journal of Business and Management* 8:4, 355–364.

Rumelt, Richard P., Dan Schendel, and David J. Teece. 1991. "Strategic Management and Economics." *Strategic Management Journal* 12 (Special Issue), 5–29.

Stout, David E., Yan Alice Xie, and Howard Qi, 2008, "Improving Capital Budgeting Decisions with Real Options." *Management Accounting Quarterly* 9:4, 1–7.

Stulz, René M. 1999. "What's Wrong with Modern Capital Budgeting?" *Financial Practice and Education* 9:2, 7–11.

Trigeorgis, Lenos. 1988. "A Conceptual Options Framework for Capital Budgeting." *Advances in Futures and Options Research* 3:1, 145–167.
Trigeorgis, Lenos. 1993. "Real Options and Interactions with Financial Flexibility." *Financial Management* 22:3, 202–224.
Van Putten, Alexander B., and Ian C. MacMillan. 2004. "Making Real Options Really Work." *Harvard Business Review* 82:12, 134–141.

ABOUT THE AUTHORS

H. Kent Baker is a University Professor of Finance and Kogod Research Professor in the Kogod School of Business at American University. He has held faculty and administrative positions at Georgetown University and the University of Maryland. Professor Baker has written or edited numerous books, the most recent including *Survey Research in Corporate Finance: Bridging the Gap between Theory and Practice* (Oxford University Press, 2011), *The Art of Capital Restructuring: Creating Shareholder Value through Mergers and Acquisitions* (Wiley, 2011), *Capital Structure and Financing Decisions: Theory, Evidence, and Practice* (Wiley, 2011), *Behavioral Finance: Investors, Corporations, and Markets* (Wiley, 2010), *Corporate Governance: A Synthesis of Theory, Research, and Practice* (Wiley, 2010), *Dividends and Dividend Policy* (Wiley, 2009), and *Understanding Financial Management: A Practical Guide* (Blackwell, 2005). He has more than 230 publications in academic and practitioner outlets including the *Journal of Finance, Journal of Financial and Quantitative Analysis, Financial Management, Financial Analysts Journal, Journal of Portfolio Management,* and *Harvard Business Review.* Professor Baker ranks among the most prolific authors in finance during the past half century. He has consulting and training experience with more than 100 organizations and has presented more than 750 training and development programs in the United States, Canada, and Europe. Professor Baker holds a BSBA from Georgetown University; M.Ed., MBA, and DBA degrees from the University of Maryland; and MA, MS, and two PhDs from American University. He also holds CFA and CMA designations.

Philip English is an Assistant Professor of Finance and Real Estate at the Kogod School of Business, American University. He currently serves as Director of the M.S. in Finance and M.S. in Real Estate. Before pursuing a doctorate, he worked as the primary financial officer and director of product development for Campbell Classics, a Virginia-based manufacturing firm. Professor English's research interests focus on the role of the legal environment in emerging markets, corporate governance, and mutual fund regulation. He has published in the *Journal of Law and Economics, Journal of Investing, Journal of Financial Research, Journal of Corporate Finance,* and *Emerging Markets Review.* While at Texas Tech, he won the Hemphill-Wells award, the highest university-level teaching award available to a faculty member of less than five years' tenure, and the President's Award for Teaching Excellence, also a university-level teaching award. He has also garnered teaching honors at the department and college level. He received a B.S. in Management, a B.S. in Finance, and an MBA from Virginia Tech. He earned a Ph.D. from the University of South Carolina. Professor English holds the CFA designation.

PART I

Foundation and Key Concepts

CHAPTER 2

Corporate Strategy and Investment Decisions

DANIEL FERREIRA
Associate Professor (Reader), London School of Economics

INTRODUCTION

Real investment decisions are not made in a vacuum; they are embedded in a company's strategy. By determining the scope of the company, the strategy limits the set of investment projects available to managers. By identifying the company's competitive advantages, the strategy helps assess the sources of synergies in mergers and acquisitions (M&As). Understanding the nature of competition and the business landscape is also useful for forecasting sales and advertising, identifying real options, and coordinating financing and investment opportunities.

A *strategy* is the formulation and implementation of a company's key decisions. A well-designed strategy should include a statement of the company's goals, some criteria to decide which activities a company should and should not do, and a view on how the company should be organized internally and how it should deal with the external environment. Furthermore, a strategy must also contain an explanation for its logic, that is, an explanation for why the goals will be achieved by adhering to the strategy.

This chapter presents an overview of the main ideas in *strategic management*, which is a management discipline that derives most of its intellectual foundations from economics. The focus of this chapter is on the role of strategic considerations for corporate investment decisions and the valuation of projects and companies. As an introductory chapter, it emphasizes general principles and ideas and does not discuss detailed applications and examples.

The main focus of the chapter is on *corporate strategy*. Corporate strategy studies the relevant strategic issues concerning the corporation as a whole, rather than a specific business unit. A corporation may operate in a single industry or in many different ones. A common use of the term corporate strategy denotes the study of strategy for the multimarket corporation, in contrast to *business unit strategy*, which applies to single-industry corporations and narrowly defined divisions within a corporation (Porter, 2008). Because the starting point for the analysis of corporate strategy is the company's portfolio of resources, rather than the products that it sells, this chapter applies the term corporate strategy to both single and multiple industry companies. By focusing on what companies can do particularly well, the analysis of corporate strategy can identify factors that allow these companies to create value in different markets and industries. Thus, understanding corporate strategy is useful even when a company is currently operating in a single, narrowly defined industry.

The chapter also provides a selective review of the academic literature on corporate investment and its relation to business strategy. Examples include the study of corporate behavior over the firm's life cycle, investment in conglomerate firms, the boundaries of the firm, and interactions between financing and investment decisions. These examples provide case-based and statistical evidence of the importance of strategy for investment decisions.

THE IMPORTANCE OF STRATEGY FOR INVESTMENT DECISIONS

Methods for evaluating project investment decisions are usually discussed without reference to corporate strategy issues. The typical capital budgeting method (directly or indirectly) involves three steps: (1) estimating cash flows generated by the project, (2) finding an adequate discount rate for each cash flow, and (3) estimating the initial cost of the investment (including opportunity costs). The main example of this is discounted cash flow (DCF) analysis, which is widely used in practice and occupies central stage in corporate finance and valuation textbooks.

In DCF analyses, much attention is devoted to the estimation of discount rates; not nearly as much is devoted to the estimation of cash flows (and even less to the cost of initial investment, which is usually simply assumed to be known). Explicit models of financial asset markets such as the capital asset pricing model (CAPM) commonly infer the discount rates to be used in valuation models. However, the approach to estimating cash flows is usually ad hoc and informal.

Sensitivity analyses usually reveal the importance of assumptions concerning the evolution of cash flows, especially the ones implicit in the project's terminal value. Small differences in growth rates for operating cash flows can lead to valuation differences that often dwarf those associated with changes in discount rates. So what explains the asymmetry between the treatment of discount rates and that of cash flows?

There is at least one practical reason. Financial asset markets are often modeled as markets in which the law of one price holds. In such frictionless financial markets, the price of a given asset reflects the market value of the asset's characteristics, which are summarized by its expected rate of return and its risk profile. Asset prices adjust until all assets yield the same risk-adjusted return. This is an implication of the assumption of no arbitrage opportunities. Translating these ideas into the language of project valuation, there are no financial investments with positive net present value (NPV) in frictionless assets markets.

Contrast this situation with the task of valuing corporate investment in nonfinancial projects. The main challenge in capital budgeting is the identification of positive NPV opportunities. In other words, the whole idea of corporate investment is based on the notion that the law of one price does not hold for investment in real assets. That is, a company may have an opportunity to invest in a project that, once fully adjusted for risk, yields a return that is significantly higher than that of (virtually) riskless financial assets (such as U.S. government bonds).

When making capital budgeting decisions, the assumption of zero-NPV investments in financial assets allows simplifying the potentially very complicated task of comparing project cash flows in different periods and under different scenarios. Analysts only need to understand the risk properties of these cash flows and then look at financial markets to figure out the appropriate discount rate associated with each type of risk. As the market does not explicitly give a "price for each type of risk," models such as the CAPM are needed, as they enable extraction of the relevant discount rates from observed data. Although in practice different models and different data give different answers, the main benefit of the assumption of no arbitrage in frictionless financial markets is to allow the use of simplified models and formulas to get estimates of discount rates.

As the law of one price does not hold for real investments, simplified models such as those available for financial assets cannot be easily developed for real investments. In particular, no benchmark model exists for estimating cash flows. Instead, a long list of formal and informal theories have been developed to understand why there exist positive NPV opportunities in real investments. This chapter refers to these theories collectively as *strategy*.

Strategy is usually viewed as being outside the realm of financial economics. Thus, strategy is only briefly, if at all, discussed in corporate finance and valuation textbooks. In practice, however, an interrelation occurs among strategic, financial, and investment decisions. In academic finance, many empirical studies focus on interactions between strategic considerations and corporate investment.

The key practical idea in strategic management is simple: Understanding the reasons some projects have positive NPVs can help a firm find those positive-NPV projects. Thus, most of the academic writings on strategy focus on identifying the sources of positive NPV opportunities, also called the sources of value.

Understanding strategy is important not only for selecting the set of projects worth being considered in capital budgeting analyses but also for the difficult task of estimating cash flows in DCF analyses. The material covered in this chapter is not detailed enough to offer practical advice as to how to estimate cash flows. Rather, the chapter discusses general principles in business strategy that are useful for many valuation exercises. However, Chapter 10 provides a detailed discussion of estimating cash flows.

KEY CONCEPTS AND IDEAS IN STRATEGY

An example provides a useful starting point. General Electric (GE) is a *conglomerate*, that is, a company that operates in many different industries, such as jet engines, power generation, and financial services, among others. Jack Welch, GE's legendary chief executive officer (CEO), ran the company from 1981 to 2001. As part of the strategy intended for GE, he set the goal of "being number one or number two in every industry GE operates in." In fact, GE managers were told that if a division was not number one or number two, they should fix it, sell it, or shut it down. This simple strategy description is useful because it tells managers what to do and helps corporate headquarters allocate resources across divisions. According to such a strategy, GE would hardly fund even positive NPV projects if divisions are laggards in their industries, unless the investment is aimed at "fixing" the division so that it becomes a leader.

Although such a strategy is useful as a guide for the allocation of funds across unrelated businesses, it does not explain why being number one or number two is the best way of creating value for shareholders. A strategy must always explain its underlying logic: why the stated goals will deliver shareholder value. Although many believe that GE's overall strategy under Welch was responsible for delivering huge gains for shareholders, much controversy still exists about why it did so. In fact, some statistical evidence indicates that conglomerates such as GE normally do not outperform a comparable portfolio of stand-alone (i.e., single industry) companies (see Lang and Stulz, 1994; Berger and Ofek, 1995). But before reviewing the literature on investment and performance in diversified corporations, the basic theoretical ideas that aim to explain the sources of superior performance—the *sources of value*—for companies and businesses more generally should be examined.

Competitive Advantage

One of the best known concepts in strategy is that of *competitive advantage* (Porter, 1980). Competitive advantage is a firm's attribute that may allow the firm to generate *economic profits*. The term "may" generate profits is used because the logic of the strategy must first be tested. If misused, a potential competitive advantage may not deliver superior performance.

In this definition, economic profit refers to the (risk-adjusted) present value of revenue minus all costs, including the opportunity cost of capital. For simplicity, this discussion abstracts from capital market imperfections and other frictions and considers shareholder value as being equivalent to economic profit. In practice, there are situations in which such imperfections and other frictions should be treated differently.

The attribute that gives the firm a competitive advantage in a specific market can be a number of things. It could be an asset that the firm owns, including tangible assets (e.g., plants, machines, land, mines, and oil reserves), proprietary intangible assets (e.g., patents, intellectual property, and trademarks), or nontradable intangible assets (e.g., reputation, know-how, culture, and management practices). A competitive advantage could also arise from the company's position in the industry, which generates *barriers to entry* due to government protection, first-mover advantages (e.g., brand name and reputation), control of distribution channels, market size, or technology (e.g., network effects, platforms, and standards compatibility).

Regardless of its origins, a sustainable competitive advantage must be built upon something unique. A *unique asset or position* is something that is very difficult for others to imitate or reproduce. It may be prohibitively costly for most, but a few could buy or create such assets or positions. Because these assets or positions need not be literally unique, perhaps a better term would be *scarce resources*. As long as this qualification is understood, no harm is done by sticking to the traditional terminology.

Consider the example of Apple Inc., which is a company that has successfully delivered shareholder gains over extended periods of time (although not necessarily at every moment in its history). Some believe that one of Apple's main competitive advantages is its excellence in product design. By producing computers and other consumer electronic products with innovative designs, Apple can target a niche of consumers who value design. But excellence per se is not enough. What prevents other competitors from imitating Apple? Apple must be better at producing well-designed gadgets than other firms. In other words, Apple needs to have a unique capability in design.

The importance of asset uniqueness is easily understood by analogy to hypothetical markets in which assets are not unique. In the frictionless financial markets found in finance textbooks, financial assets are never unique; they can be easily replicated and traded with no direct costs. In such markets, no trader has a competitive advantage; all buy and sell zero-NPV securities. In the aggregate, financial markets create economic value by allowing investors to diversify optimally and by allocating capital efficiently. But the production of financial securities by itself does not generate extra rents.

Added Value

Having a unique resource, capability, or position is a necessary condition for maintaining a sustainable competitive advantage, but it is not sufficient. Continuing with the example of Apple, according to Kahney (2009), Steve Jobs (Apple's CEO) once insisted on changing the design of the original Mac's motherboard because it "looked ugly." Engineers and other managers replied that consumers did not care about how their motherboards look; motherboards are located inside computers and thus cannot be seen. But that argument did not convince Jobs. Eventually, for technical reasons, he was forced to drop the idea.

Despite the fact that Job is a brilliant strategist, his insistence on exploiting Apple's excellence in design for improving the appearance of motherboards seems difficult to justify. There is no point in using one's unique capabilities to produce something for which consumers are not willing to pay. A unique capability must be able to create value in order to be called a competitive advantage.

Brandenburger and Stuart (1996) develop a rigorous framework for the analysis of value-based strategies. They start from the fact that value creation must imply a wedge between what customers are willing to pay for a product and the supplier's opportunity cost of producing it. This wedge is the *total value* created by a (buying and selling) transaction. Brandenburger and Stuart develop the concept of a company's *added value* to a specific transaction, which is the total value created by the transaction in which the company participates minus the value of this transaction without the company.

Added value is a very simple idea. If a company is really unique and valuable, some value would be permanently lost if the company ceased to exist. Such unique and valuable companies have positive added values. Thus, a positive added value is a necessary condition for a sustainable competitive advantage.

The concept of positive added value is related but not identical to positive NPV in capital budgeting analysis. Having positive added value is a necessary condition for a project to have positive NPV. However, the NPV concept measures the total value that is captured by shareholders, which is in general just a fraction of the project's added value.

Industry Analysis

In perfectly competitive product markets with free entry, such as those found in microeconomics textbooks, producers do not own unique assets. Their added value is zero. Consequently, they all enjoy zero economic profit. In monopolistic markets, in contrast, an assumption is that competition is somehow restricted, and economic profits are positive.

Porter (1980) realized that competitive advantage is intimately linked to monopoly power, or, in other words, to the strength of competitive forces in the industry. He thus saw a firm's position within its industry as one of the key sources of competitive advantage.

The key to identifying positional advantages is to understand the industry in which a firm operates. In the strategy literature, this is called *industry analysis*. The goal of industry analysis is to facilitate the design of strategies by describing the competitive environment in which the firm operates. Firms may find themselves in a unique position in the industry, and such a position may or may not give them a competitive advantage.

Industry analysis is usually identified with Porter's (1980) five forces framework. Porter argues that the attractiveness of an industry can be assessed by carefully analyzing the relative strengths of five competitive forces: (1) the intensity of rivalry among industry incumbents, (2) the bargaining power of suppliers, (3) the bargaining power of buyers, (4) the threat of entry of new firms, and (5) the availability of substitute products.

The Industry Life Cycle

A natural complement to the static industry analysis framework is a set of empirical regularities that are jointly known as the *industry (or product) life cycle* (e.g., Keppler, 1996). The industry life-cycle view recognizes that industries evolve over time, but also that they often change in predictable ways. As the strength of each of the competitive forces varies over the different stages of the life cycle, successful firm strategies must also evolve over time and adapt themselves to the new challenges.

In its simplest form, the industry life-cycle view postulates that the life of an industry has three different stages: emergence, growth, and maturity. Some also add a fourth one, which is the stage of decline. In the emergence stage, many small firms experiment with different varieties of a product. Many firms enter the industry and sales levels and growth rates are low. The growth stage begins when a dominant product format or business model arises. When consolidation in the industry occurs, the number of firms falls and entry in the industry becomes rare. Industry sales grow at high rates. In this stage, most incumbent firms direct their innovation efforts toward improving processes rather than products. Finally, in the maturity stage, dominant firms have stable market shares and generate high profits. However, they experience low rates of sales growth and have few investment opportunities.

Applications

Industry analysis including the industry life cycle is widely used, although mostly informally, in valuation exercises. The following list provides some examples of how industry analysis can offer insights that are valuable for investment decisions:

- Understanding the nature of competition in the industry can be useful for forecasting revenues (sales) and some of the costs such as advertising and research and development (R&D) expenditures.
- A typical approach to estimating future sales is using the average sales growth rate in the industry. This assumption may be reasonable if the sources of value from a project are cost efficiency improvements rather than gains in market share.
- In industries in which suppliers are powerful, efficiency improvements at the firm level could be partly appropriated by suppliers via contract renegotiation. Thus, one must be careful not to overestimate the cash flows generated by such efficiency improvements. For example, in an industry with a unionized workforce, not only may efficiency improvements be more difficult to achieve, but also the gains from such improvements may end up being shared with employees.
- Analysts implicitly use the industry life-cycle view in project valuation. For example, many pro forma estimates assume some higher rates of industry growth for the first few years and then a much slower growth rate implicit in the project's terminal value.

Challenges to Traditional Industry Analysis

Industry analysis, while extremely useful as a normative tool for strategic decision making, has been criticized on two fronts. First, the typical approach to industry analysis puts too much emphasis on value capture while paying little attention to value creation. In the most straightforward applications of Porter's (1980) principles, the firm's goal is to capture the largest possible share of potential industry profits. The five competitive forces, if strong, limit the ability of an incumbent firm to capture a large share of the value created in the industry. In contrast to this emphasis on value capture, Nalebuff and Brandenburger (1996) emphasize the importance of what they call "co-opetition," which is the exertion of joint efforts by competitors to increase potential profits for the industry as a whole.

The second objection to industry analysis concerns its excessive focus on differences among industries rather than on differences among companies in the same industry. The key empirical challenge to the conventional view comes from an influential paper by Rumelt (1991), who shows that most of the variation in profitability across firms comes from intra-industry heterogeneity rather than from differences among industries. Such an interpretation has been challenged empirically by McGahan and Porter (1997).

Although Porter's (1980) approach can easily accommodate such criticisms, these challenges are important because they underscore the usefulness of complementary frameworks for the analysis of strategy. Of particular importance are the analyses that place the firm, rather than the industry, at the center stage.

Theories of the Firm

To understand firm heterogeneity within industries and its relations to competitive advantage, reviewing some of the most influential theories of the firm is important.

Starting with Coase (1937), academic research in economics and management has nurtured a long tradition of trying to unveil the "essence of the firm." Some scholars believe that discovering the true nature of the firm permits understanding real-world firms.

Whether things or concepts have "essences" is questionable. From a practical standpoint, finding this essence is not essential, but having a practical definition of the firm may be needed. A good "theory of the firm" is one that helps managers identify and choose the best projects among all feasible ones. It must also provide a definition of "best."

A brief review of three theories of the firm follows. The first theory views the firm as a nexus of contracts. Most valuation and project selection frameworks implicitly assume this view. The second one views the firm as an efficient solution to the problem of economizing on transaction costs. Such a view is particularly useful for understanding acquisitions and divestitures, especially in those cases involving vertical integration or outsourcing decisions. The third theory views the firm as the locus of crucial resources. This view is particularly helpful for understanding corporate strategy and value creation.

The Firm as a Nexus of Contracts

Some argue that the firm is nothing more than a *nexus of contracts*. Under this view, most stakeholders such as employees, bondholders, and suppliers are thought to be protected by bilateral contracts with the firms' equity holders. Equity holders own the firm in the sense that they have residual cash flow rights: After all stakeholders are paid according to their contracts, equity holders are entitled to the residual profits (Alchian and Demsetz, 1972; Jensen and Meckling, 1976).

Inspired by the nexus-of-contracts view of the firm, leading strategy consulting firms teach their staff and clients to focus on value creation for equity holders. Similarly, textbooks on valuation and corporate finance usually assume that managers should aim at maximizing the market value of shareholders' equity. The reason for focusing on shareholder value alone is the presumption that other stakeholders are well protected by contracts. For example, debt holders have financial claims with priority, employees are protected by labor contracts, and regulation and taxes protect and compensate society. Shareholders are the residual claimants; they get whatever is left after the firm pays taxes, wages, and interest.

Such a view is only partially correct, considering the fact that, in the real world, contracts are incomplete. Contractual incompleteness and other market imperfections can explain why other stakeholders may also be residual claimants. However, in practice most of these subtleties are ignored and firms are assumed to be fully owned by shareholders. This view is also the dominant one in the strategy literature.

Firm Scope and the Transaction-Cost View of the Firm

Coase (1937) initiated the tradition of viewing firms and markets as substitutes. To understand what that means, consider a specific transaction such as the supply of an input that is used in the production of a final good. The classic example in this literature is the case of Fisher Body, a supplier of car bodies to General Motors (GM) in the 1920s. The key issue here is the "make or buy" decision or the vertical integration problem: Should GM produce its own car bodies in-house or should it outsource production, buying bodies from an independent supplier (such as Fisher)?

If a transaction is conducted through the market, contracts will regulate the conditions of the deal (e.g., price, product characteristics, delivery dates, and guarantees). If a transaction is conducted within a single firm, the conditions of the deal will be regulated through management. The market can thus be seen as a system of coordination by prices (or contracts), while the firm can be seen as a system of coordination by management.

The transaction-cost view assumes that the most efficient mode of coordinating a transaction will usually be chosen. Thus, firms are chosen over markets when the former implies lower transaction costs than the latter (and vice versa). More generally, the transaction-cost view is a theory of firm scope (or firm boundaries): It aims to determine what the firm should and should not do. The determination of firm scope is an important strategic consideration. In practice, companies are continuously redefining their boundaries, mainly through mergers, acquisitions, divestitures, and spin-offs.

A key concept in the transaction-cost view of the firm is that of *asset specificity* (e.g., Williamson, 1985). When two parties meet each other and decide to write an incomplete long-term contract, the nature of their relationship changes in fundamental ways. Both parties may undertake investments that are specific to their relationship. For example, GM could design its cars to fit car bodies built by Fisher, while Fisher could modify its machines to create car bodies that fit GM's demands. Thus, after relationship-specific investments are made, the value of GM and Fisher's assets is higher inside the relationship than it is outside. That is, asset specificity creates a surplus, which is the difference between the value of assets inside and outside the relationship between the contracting parties.

If the two parties are not integrated in a single firm, they will have to bargain with each other over the division of the surplus after relationship-specific investments are made. This bargaining can be very costly. Furthermore, the possibility exists that no agreement is reached, which implies that the surplus might go to waste. To avoid such transaction costs, the theory predicts that the parties should be integrated in a single firm in those cases in which relationship-specific assets are important.

The Resource-Based View of the Firm

What is collectively known as the resource-based view of the firm is a set of different ideas that have been developed by various scholars. Wernerfelt (1984) is normally credited with introducing what is currently known as the resource-based view; the main idea, however, dates back to Penrose (1959). Wernerfelt distinguishes between the traditional product-based view of the firm, which looks at the firm from the perspective of the portfolio of products it sells, and the resource-based view, which looks at the firm from the perspective of the set of resources it owns. Resources are unique assets that can be strengths or weaknesses.

This view is particularly useful for understanding corporate strategy, as it provides a potential rationale for product-market diversification. A firm that operates in multiple, seemingly distinct product markets may be exploiting synergies created by the unique resources that it owns. These resources may create competitive advantages in different product markets. Thus, to look for synergies by analyzing the degree of similarity among products can be misleading if the main source of economic value created by conglomerates is their ownership of unique resources. Some resources can be leveraged across different markets and thus create a competitive advantage in more than one product market.

Commitment versus Adaptation

Two important issues in the resource-based tradition are the nature of unique resources and the relative importance of commitment versus adaptation. The first issue concerns the question of whether human or nonhuman resources are the most important sources of sustainable competitive advantage. In principle, valuable unique resources can be tangible and tradable, such as physical assets; intangible and tradable, such as intellectual property; or intangible and nontradable, such as corporate culture. Because theory offers little guidance, the question about the relative importance of each type of resource must be settled empirically.

The second issue, the tension between commitment and adaptation, is more open to theoretical analysis. The strategy literature that emphasizes first-mover advantages holds a rather positive view of the commitment effect associated with irreversible investment decisions (e.g., Ghemawat, 1991). Firm-specific resources are investments that are difficult to reverse and may provide a source of competitive advantage. Irreversible investments create credible barriers to entry and are thus valuable. Thus, viewed under this light, the commitment provided by investing in firm-specific resources seems to be a more reliable source of competitive advantage than the flexibility associated with less specialized resources.

As a simple example of the value of commitment, consider the adoption of most-favored-customer contractual clauses (which here can be understood as a form of irreversible investment). Such clauses, which offer a buyer the best possible price that is given to any of a firm's customers, may a priori seem to increase buyer power and thus reduce profits. However, understanding such clauses involves taking the value of commitment into account. By binding itself to such a contractual clause, the supplier firm commits to be a tough negotiator with all customers, as any discount to one buyer must also be offered to all other buyers. By increasing the cost of making price concessions, a seller may actually improve her bargaining position and capture a larger share of industry profits.

Without totally discrediting the importance of commitment and strategic continuity, some scholars believe that strategic flexibility and the ability to adapt are at the core of strategy. For example, Montgomery (2008) argues against a static view of strategy. According to her, a firm's strategy is in constant motion, evolving not only in big steps but also in mostly smaller ones. A static view of strategy is dangerous as it may lead corporate leaders to try to defend their perceived competitive advantages long after they stopped being profitable. Montgomery sees the main goal of strategy as the search for a corporate identity, or what the company "wants to be." More concretely, she uses Brandenburger and Stuart's (1996) notion of added value to give a more precise meaning to this corporate soul-searching exercise. The company must be something distinctive in the sense that someone would miss it if the company disappeared.

In Montgomery's (2008) view, leadership is one of the crucial resources that a company has. The author sees the CEO as the steward of the company, responsible for continuously adapting to change and redefining the company's strategy. She argues that leadership requires a continuous reassessment of strategy as well as frequent changes and reformulation.

The relative importance of commitment versus flexibility in corporate strategy is still an unsettled issue, just as are many other questions reviewed in this chapter. Ultimately, empirical evidence is necessary to provide further insights on the practical aspects of corporate strategy.

CORPORATE STRATEGY, INVESTMENT, AND PERFORMANCE: SOME EVIDENCE

With few exceptions, the empirical literature on corporate investment and performance has evolved independently from most of the theoretical work in corporate strategy. Thus, the link between theory and evidence is still tenuous. This section provides a selective review of some studies that focus on questions related to corporate strategy, investment, and performance.

As strategy influences all corporate decisions, virtually all studies of businesses are somehow related to strategy. The few examples discussed here highlight the importance of strategic considerations for corporate investment decisions.

The Evolution of Firms

Recent work by Kaplan, Sensoy, and Stromberg (2009) provides evidence that is related to many of the topics discussed in this chapter. They analyze the evolution of 50 (mostly high technology) firms from their birth to almost maturity. Their sample consists of entrepreneurial firms that were initially backed by venture capitalists and eventually became publicly traded companies. The authors of this study follow their sample firms through three different stages: (1) the business plan stage (not long after the firm is founded—on average 23 months old); (2) the initial public offering (IPO) stage (on average 34 months after the business plan); and (3) the public company stage (for which they take data from annual reports on average 34 months after the IPO).

Kaplan et al. (2009) report the following findings:

- *Firm scope is important*: Almost all firms keep the same core businesses or business ideas throughout these three stages. Firms tend to grow around these initial ideas, rather than by replacing them with new ones.
- *Resource uniqueness is key*: Almost all managers in their sample believe that the importance of a unique resource remains high during all three stages.
- *The relative importance of expertise declines over time*: Firms claim that the importance of the expertise of their managers and workers is high during the business plan stage, but it becomes less so after the company goes public.
- *Human capital changes rapidly*: Only 72 percent of the CEOs at the IPO were CEOs at the business plan; this number falls to only 42 percent at the public company stage. Founders leave the firm frequently, often relinquishing control at the IPO stage or soon afterward.
- *Nonhuman assets are key*: Proprietary intellectual property, patents, and physical assets remain important throughout the firm's life.

Kaplan et al. (2009) conclude that, more often than not, firms distinguish themselves by their critical nonhuman resources, rather than by the entrepreneurial talent of few individuals. Thus, investments in those critical nonhuman assets are the main sources of value. Their evidence provides broad support for the resource-based view of the firm. The evidence is also relevant for the debate on the relative merits of commitment versus adaptation. At least in their sample, leadership and ability to adapt seem less important than commitment to a business model.

Guedj and Scharfstein (2004) study the investment behavior of biopharmaceutical firms in drug development projects. They find that small, early-stage companies are reluctant to drop the development of unsuccessful new drugs. Large and mature companies in the industry are more efficient in their project termination decisions and thus enjoy better performance. Their evidence shows that firms' investment behavior varies over the stages of their own life cycle. Their results suggest that, unlike mature firms, new firms are more willing to take risks and to hold on to losers.

Investment in Conglomerates and the Diversification Discount

Financial economists first became interested in corporate strategy when they (implicitly) applied the added value principle to a large sample of diversified companies. Lang and Stulz (1994) and Berger and Ofek (1995) conduct the following experiment involving a conglomerate, which is a corporation that operates in many different industries. They construct a portfolio of stand-alone companies closely resembling industries in the conglomerate. That is, the stand-alone portfolio is a comparable for the conglomerate. Now, if the conglomerate did not exist, shareholders who currently invest in it could obtain similar risk exposures by investing in the stand-alone portfolio instead. Thus, would any value be lost if the conglomerate did not exist? That is the added value question. The authors compare the market value of diversified companies (scaled by their book values) to a portfolio of stand-alone companies. Perhaps surprisingly, they find that, on average, conglomerates display negative added values. This finding is known as the *diversification discount* in the corporate finance literature.

The diversification discount is the most controversial finding in the academic literature linking corporate strategy and investment decisions. There are many explanations for this finding, ranging from data issues to misclassifications, statistical problems, spurious correlations, and reverse causality. Maksimovic and Phillips (2007) provide a summary of the literature. Regardless of whether most conglomerates have negative added values, considering that possibility is important. What does it mean? A negative added value means that a conglomerate is pursuing a corporate strategy that destroys value. The optimal strategy in such a case would be to either shut down or spin off all divisions but one.

Why would conglomeration destroy value? The most widely suggested explanation is that conglomerates have inefficient internal capital markets (Scharfstein and Stein, 2000). Due to corporate politics, funds for investments are allocated across divisions for reasons that are not fully related to the quality of their investment opportunities. According to this view, the diversification discount is a symptom of bad investment decisions in conglomerates. Motivated by this idea, various papers try to test empirically for the efficiency of investment decisions in conglomerates. The evidence is mixed (Maksimovic and Phillips, 2002; Dittmar and Shivdasani, 2003; Ahn and Denis, 2004). Although corporate politics is certainly a problem in many large and diversified companies, there is insufficient convincing, large-sample evidence that such a problem can explain the diversification discount.

The conglomerate investment literature contains other relevant findings. Perhaps the most important one concerns the mode of investment. Maksimovic and Phillips (2008) find that conglomerate divisions invest more via acquisitions relative to capital expenditures than similar stand-alone companies. This evidence has important implications for investment decisions in large corporations. For example, one of the most important tasks of division managers is to identify and value suitable targets. In contrast, managers in stand-alone companies need to worry more about organic growth and must possess skills in valuing and implementing greenfield investments, which are investment in a manufacturing, office, or other physical company-related structure or group of structures in an area where no previous facilities exist.

Growth through Acquisitions

A key question in corporate strategy is: How can firms create value by redefining firm boundaries? Any reasonable answer must mention the creation of a unique resource. In M&As, the value created by such unique resources is loosely referred to as *synergy*.

Business people are often believed to be overly optimistic about the prospect of synergies. Porter (2008, p. 154) offers a skeptical view: "If you believe the text of the countless corporate annual reports, just about anything is related to just about anything else! But imagined synergy is much more common than real synergy." However, the academic research on the stock return effects of deal announcements shows that M&A deals create shareholder value on average, although there is considerable variation (Andrade, Mitchell, and Stafford, 2001).

The key puzzle raised by the M&A literature is not related to value creation but to value capture: Acquirer returns are on average negative, while target returns are positive and large. Acquirers appear to overpay for their targets. Thus, even if acquirers competently identify and value potential synergies, the evidence suggests that they do not do as well when dividing the gains.

Notwithstanding the problem of the division of gains, the task of identifying synergies is still very important. This task requires much strategic knowledge. Consider, for example, the case of Cisco's acquisition strategy. Cisco's Internet Operating System (IOS) is a platform that became dominant in the 1990s. Dominant platforms are unique in that they are more valuable to customers exactly because they are dominant. This is the essence of network effects; ownership of a platform is a competitive advantage only insofar as a large number of customers choose to adopt the platform. Thus, Cisco's success relies on its platform being dominant. By understanding the source of its competitive advantage, Cisco's investment policy is centered at acquiring new companies developing systems that may threaten IOS's dominance. An example was its acquisition of StrataCom in 1996, a small start-up that was the developer of a cheap and efficient transmission system, the ATM (asynchronous transmission mode). Because ATM and IOS were not initially compatible, the spread of ATM in the market was a threat to the dominance of IOS.

After a few attempts to coordinate the two companies without integration, Cisco chose to acquire StrataCom. The stock market viewed that decision favorably, as evidenced by Cisco's share price increasing by 10 percent on the day of the announcement. This description follows Hart and Holmstrom (2010).

This example illustrates the importance of a broad understanding of corporate strategy for making sense of a company's investment policy. Understanding why the company creates value for shareholders helps in assessing the types of investment that it needs to undertake. Cisco knew that preserving IOS was its most important goal. An aggressive acquisition policy toward potential competitors and producers of complementary systems was then paramount. Ignoring the importance of network effects and coordination among systems would have led Cisco to undervalue such acquisitions and thus fail to create value for shareholders.

Interactions between Financing and Investment Decisions

Because firms are usually financially constrained, they must coordinate their investment strategies with their financing policies. The synchronization of investment opportunities and access to funds for investment is the key goal of modern corporate risk management (Froot, Scharfstein, and Stein, 1993). This fact implies that corporate liquidity has strategic value. Consequently, investment decisions must take into account a project's potential for generating cash flows in those states in which liquidity is most needed. Even when firms are not currently financially constrained, they may prefer to invest in projects that generate cash flows exactly when firms are likely to be financially constrained (Almeida, Campello, and Weisbach, 2010).

Financing decisions may also have direct effects on investments due to contractual arrangements. Evidence suggests that as creditors gain more control rights after debt covenant violations, corporate investment falls (Chava and Roberts, 2008). Thus, the financing mix between debt and equity may also have direct consequences for investment decisions. Campello (2006) finds that moderate levels of debt lead to superior sales growth; this growth occurs by gaining market share at the expense of industry rivals. However, he also finds that excessive debt leads to underperformance.

Fresard (2010) finds that cash-rich companies gain market share at the expense of their rivals. He argues that the evidence is consistent with the "deep pocket" effect: Financially strong firms overinvest in capacity and adopt aggressive competitive strategies to drive financially weak companies out of the market (Telser, 1966; Bolton and Scharfstein, 1990).

Zingales (1998) analyzes the interactions between industry competition and financial slack by studying the effects of deregulation in the trucking industry on the survival of firms. He finds that the increase in competition caused by deregulation forced highly levered firms to exit the industry. Zingales shows that both the most efficient firms (the "fittest") and the ones with more financial slack (the "fattest") were more likely to survive in the long run. The author also finds that, after deregulation, highly levered firms invest less than their competitors, suggesting that high leverage hinders the ability of firms to invest when competition is tough. Further, his evidence shows that the underinvestment problem associated with high levels of debt is partially responsible for these firms exiting the market.

The evidence discussed in this section shows that a firm's competitive strategy cannot be dissociated from its financial decisions, and its financial and investment decisions are embedded in the competitive landscape. When rivalry among competitors is weak and barriers to entry are high, firms may choose to invest heavily via debt financing. However, when competition is fierce and barriers to entry are low, financial slack is important, so investment decisions that require debt financing and deliver cash flows only in the distant future leave the company exposed to predatory strategies by rivals.

SUMMARY AND CONCLUSIONS

Understanding the environment in which a firm competes and the source of its competitive strength is crucial for making investment decisions. Many investments have direct strategic consequences such as investments in capacity, R&D, and acquisitions. Even the more mundane projects can be more easily valued if their relation with the strategy of the company is explicitly spelled out.

The arguments and examples discussed in this chapter underscore the complexity of the issues related to corporate strategy and investment decisions. There is "no rule for riches," i.e., there are no general rules in strategy that are guaranteed to create value (Rumelt, Schendel, and Teece, 1991). The goal of this chapter is to highlight the importance of a careful analysis of the internal and external context in which the firm operates for making decisions that deliver superior returns.

DISCUSSION QUESTIONS

1. The industry life cycle is not a given; it is affected by the strategic decisions made by the firms in the industry. Give one or more examples of strategic decisions that can affect the dynamics of an industry. Explain how those strategic issues can be taken into account when valuing new investments.

2. The efficient internal capital markets theory such as that of Stein (1997) holds that conglomerate headquarters may add value by allocating funds for investment across divisions more efficiently than would the market in case all divisions were stand-alone units. Explain the logic of this argument.

3. Explain the differences between the "resource-based view of the firm" and the view of the firm as a "nexus of contracts." What are the practical implications of these views? Are the two views compatible?

4. How does competition among different standards or platforms affect corporate decisions?

REFERENCES

Ahn, Seoungpil, and David J. Denis. 2004. "Internal Capital Markets and Investment Policy." *Journal of Financial Economics* 71:3, 489–516.

Alchian, Armen A., and Harold Demsetz. 1972. "Production, Information Costs, and Economic Organization." *American Economic Review* 62:5, 777–795.

Almeida, Heitor, Murillo Campello, and Michael S. Weisbach. 2010. "Corporate Financial and Investment Policies When Future Financing Is Not Frictionless." *Journal of Corporate Finance*, forthcoming.

Andrade, Gregor, Mark Mitchell, and Erik Stafford. 2001. "New Evidence and Perspectives on Mergers." *Journal of Economic Perspectives* 15:2, 103–120.

Berger, Philip G., and Eli Ofek. 1995. "Diversification's Effect on Firm Value." *Journal of Financial Economics* 37:1, 39–66.

Bolton, Patrick, and David Scharfstein, 1990. "A Theory of Predation Based on Agency Problems in Financial Contracting." *American Economic Review* 80:1, 93–106.

Branderburger, Adam M., and Harborne W. Stuart, Jr. 1996. "Value-based Business Strategy." *Journal of Economics and Management Strategy* 5:1, 5–24.

Campello, Murillo. 2006. "Debt Financing: Does It Hurt or Boost Firm Performance in Product Markets?" *Journal of Financial Economics* 82:1, 135–172.

Chava, Sudheer, and Michael R. Roberts. 2008. "How Does Financing Impact Investment? The Role of Debt Covenants." *Journal of Finance* 63:5, 2085–2121.

Coase, Ronald. 1937. "The Nature of the Firm." *Economica* 4:16, 386–405.

Dittmar, Amy, and Anil Shivdasani. 2003. "Divestitures and Divisional Investment Policies." *Journal of Finance* 58:6, 2711–2744.

Fresard, Laurent. 2010. "Financial Strength and Product Market Behavior: The Real Effects of Corporate Cash Holdings." *Journal of Finance* 65:3, 1097–1122.

Froot, Kenneth A., David S. Scharfstein, and Jeremy C. Stein. 1993. "Risk Management: Coordinating Corporate Investment and Financing Policies." *Journal of Finance* 48:5, 1629–1658.

Ghemawat, Pankaj. 1991. *Commitment: The Dynamics of Strategy*. New York: Free Press.

Guedj, Ilan, and David Scharfstein. 2004. "Organizational Scope and Investment: Evidence from the Drug Development Strategies and Performance of Biopharmaceutical Firms." NBER Working Paper 10933.

Hart, Oliver, and Bengt Holmstrom. 2010. "A Theory of Firm Scope." *Quarterly Journal of Economics* 125:2, 483–513.

Jensen, Michael C., and William H. Meckling. 1976. "Theory of the Firm: Managerial Behavior, Agency Costs and Ownership Structure." *Journal of Financial Economics* 3:4, 305–360.

Kahney, Leander. 2009. *Inside Steve's Brain*. London: Atlantic Books.

Kaplan, Steven, Berk Sensoy, and Per Stromberg. 2009. "Should Investors Bet on the Jockey or the Horse? Evidence from the Evolution of Firms from Early Business Plans to Public Companies." *Journal of Finance* 64:1, 75–115.

Keppler, Steven. 1996. "Entry, Exit, Growth, and Innovation over the Product Life Cycle." *American Economic Review* 86:3, 562–583.

Lang, Larry H. P., and René M. Stulz. 1994. "Tobin's q, Corporate Diversification, and Firm Performance." *Journal of Political Economy* 102:6, 1248–1280.

Maksimovic, Vojislav, and Gordon Phillips. 2002. "Do Conglomerate Firms Allocate Resources Inefficiently Across Industries? Theory and Evidence." *Journal of Finance* 57:2, 721–767.

Maksimovic, Vojislav, and Gordon Phillips. 2007. " Conglomerate Firms and Internal Capital Markets." In B. Espen Eckbo, ed. *Handbook of Corporate Finance: Empirical Corporate Finance*, 423–475. Amsterdam: Elsevier/North-Holland.

Maksimovic, Vojislav, and Gordon Phillips. 2008. "The Industry Life-Cycle, Acquisitions and Investment: Does Firm Organization Matter?" *Journal of Finance* 63:2, 629–64.

McGahan, Anita, and Michael E. Porter. 1997. "How Much Does Industry Matter, Really?" *Strategic Management Journal* 18 (Special Issue), 15–30.

Montgomery, Cynthia A. 2008. "Putting Leadership Back into Strategy." *Harvard Business Review* 86:1, 54–60.

Nalebuff, Barry J., and Adam M. Brandenburger. 1996. *Co-opetition*. London: Harper Collins Business.

Penrose, Edith G. 1959. *The Theory of the Growth of the Firm*. New York: Wiley.

Porter, Michael E. 1980. *Competitive Strategy: Techniques for Analyzing Industries and Competitors*. New York: Free Press.

Porter, Michael E. 2008. *On Competition*. Boston: Harvard Business Press.

Rumelt, Richard P. 1991. "How Much Does Industry Matter?" *Strategic Management Journal* 12:3, 167–185.

Rumelt, Richard P., Dan Schendel, and David J. Teece. 1991. "Strategic Management and Economics." *Strategic Management Journal* 12 (Special Issue), 5–29.

Scharfstein, David S., and Jeremy C. Stein. 2000. "The Dark Side of Internal Capital Markets: Divisional Rent-Seeking and Inefficient Investment." *Journal of Finance* 55:6, 2537–2564.

Stein, Jeremy C. 1997. "Internal Capital Markets and the Competition for Corporate Resources." *Journal of Finance* 52:1, 111–133.

Telser, Lester G. 1966. "Cutthroat Competition and the Long Purse." *Journal of Law and Economics* 9:1, 259–277.

Wernerfelt, Birger. 1984. "A Resource-Based View of the Firm." *Strategic Management Journal* 5:2, 171–180.

Williamson, Oliver E. 1985. *The Economic Institutions of Capitalism*. New York: Free Press.

Zingales, Luigi. 1998. "Survival of the Fittest or the Fattest? Exit and Financing in the Trucking Industry." *Journal of Finance* 53:3, 905–938.

ABOUT THE AUTHOR

Daniel Ferreira joined the London School of Economics in 2006 after previous appointments as assistant professor in Portugal, Sweden, and Brazil. He became Reader (i.e., associate professor with tenure) in 2008. Professor Ferreira teaches courses in both management and finance. He has published widely in leading academic journals in finance, accounting, and economics. He is also the director of the Corporate Finance and Governance program at the Financial Markets Group and a research associate at the Center for Economic Policy Research and the European Corporate Governance Institute. Professor Ferreira received a Ph.D. in economics from the University of Chicago in 2002.

CHAPTER 3

Corporate Governance and Investment Decisions

FODIL ADJAOUD
Professor, Telfer School of Management, University of Ottawa

DORRA CHARFI
Assistant Professor, Tunis School of Business

LAMIA CHOUROU
Ph.D. student, Queen's University

INTRODUCTION

In theory, managers of modern organizations should undertake all investment projects with a positive net present value (NPV) or an internal rate of return (IRR) higher than the prescribed hurdle rate, which for normal-risk projects should be the weighted average cost of capital (WACC). In so doing, managers should enhance firm market value and consequently increase owners' wealth.

Within the asymmetric information framework, however, investment distortions such as underinvestment (when managers pass up profitable projects), over-investment (when managers undertake unprofitable projects), or suboptimal risk taking may occur. The purpose of this chapter is to provide an overview of the literature dealing with the causes of investment distortions as well as the effectiveness of corporate governance mechanisms in alleviating these distortions.

Several financial studies focus on asymmetric information between managers and external investors (new shareholders and lenders) (e.g., Myers and Majluf, 1984; Greenwald, Stiglitz, and Weiss, 1984). These studies show that in the presence of information asymmetry, external funds are more expensive than internal funds because external suppliers of funds require a premium when financing new projects. Consequently, rather than looking for new investors, managers may prefer to underinvest.

Other studies emphasize the consequences of asymmetric information between managers and existing shareholders of the firm. According to agency theory, asymmetric information is one of the main causes of conflict between the interests of the managers and those of the owners. Indeed, as a result of asymmetric information, managers could undertake decisions that maximize their own private benefits. This would create agency costs that could destroy firm value, especially when managers have a minimal shareholding in the firm. For instance, managers may waste corporate free cash flows to build empires (e.g., Jensen, 1986; Chirinko and Schaller, 2004), secure their careers (e.g., Narayanan, 1985; Hirshleifer and Thakor, 1992), and maximize their compensation (e.g., Dechow and Sloan, 1991). In some instances, managers may simply be lazy (e.g., Bertrand and Mullainathan, 2003).

Building on the social psychology literature, several recent papers try to explain overinvestment by a factor unrelated to asymmetric information or agency considerations (e.g., Roll, 1986; Heaton, 2002; Malmendier and Tate, 2005, 2008). According to these authors, overconfident chief executives officers (CEOs) overinvest if they have sufficient internal funds because they overestimate the returns associated with the investment projects of their firms.

In recent decades, corporate governance has emerged as a potential tool to alleviate the negative effects of asymmetric information, align managerial interests with those of the owners, monitor managers, and motivate them to make efficient investment decisions. Corporate governance mechanisms include the choice of capital structure, managerial compensation contracts, board structure, and ownership structure.

The remainder of the chapter is organized as follows. The first section presents theoretical and empirical studies dealing with the causes of investment distortions. The second section is concerned with the role of corporate governance mechanisms in reducing investment inefficiencies. The last section summarizes and concludes the chapter.

THE CAUSES OF INVESTMENT DISTORTIONS

The finance literature identifies three main causes of investment distortions. First, information asymmetry between managers and external financiers may give rise to the underinvestment problem. Second, agency conflicts between managers and owners may lead managers to overinvest or underinvest and/or to undertake a suboptimal risk level. Finally, overconfident managers may overinvest the firm's free cash flows.

Asymmetric Information between Corporate Managers and Capital Markets

In perfect capital markets without asymmetric information or financial constraints, firm value and investment decisions are independent of financing decisions (Modigliani and Miller, 1958). Consequently, no difference exists between internal and external financing, and optimal investment decisions are determined by the firm's investment opportunities (Tobin, 1969). In real markets, however, frictions arise due to asymmetric information, among other things, between managers and suppliers of external capital. This asymmetric information makes the cost of external funds more expensive than the cost of internal funds and in some cases leads to underinvestment.

Informed Managers and Equity Markets
Drawing on Akerlof's (1970) model of the "lemons" market, Myers and Majluf (1984) build an adverse selection model in which managers (assumed to act in

the interest of existing shareholders) are better informed than potential future shareholders about the firm's prospects. Due to information asymmetry, suppliers of external finance cannot assess the quality of investment projects and expect managers (or current owners) to issue overvalued shares to finance new projects. Hence, these external financiers will require a premium creating higher costs of external finance. If this premium is too high, firms should turn down some positive NPV projects rather than raise equity capital.

In a similar spirit, Greenwald et al. (1984) refer to Ross (1977) and use signalling effects to explain underinvestment decisions. The authors show that uninformed external suppliers of funds interpret equity issues as bad news (a signal that equity is overvalued) compared to debt issues and demand a large premium. Firms are, therefore, reluctant to issue new equity and may prefer to pass up some profitable projects rather than look for new shareholders.

Informed Managers and Debt Markets
The problems of adverse selection and moral hazard may also exist in debt markets. Indeed, borrowers have private information about their projects, meaning lenders cannot distinguish "good borrowers" from "bad borrowers." Myers and Majluf (1984), adapting their model to debt markets, argue that when firms issue default-risk-free debt, there is no underinvestment. However, when firms can only issue risky debt, the cost of debt can be so high that managers may pass up positive NPV investments.

Several authors focus on the impact of asymmetric information on credit rationing. They predict that lenders set an interest rate that allows them to maximize their profits in equilibrium. In this case, riskier borrowers cannot obtain debt financing because of credit rationing (Jaffee and Russell, 1976; Stiglitz and Weiss, 1981, 1983; Bencivenga and Smith, 1993). Thus, the borrowers will be unable to undertake the selected projects, leading them to underinvest.

The Pecking Order Theory
Extending Myers and Majluf's (1984) results, Myers (1984) builds a theory demonstrating that in the presence of information asymmetry, firms tend to follow a certain hierarchy for alternative financing sources called "the pecking order theory." According to this theory, companies prefer using securities that are less sensitive to managers' private information. This implies that firms prefer to finance their new projects with internally generated funds. When externally generated funds are required, firms issue debt followed by various kinds of hybrid debt such as convertible bonds and finally issue equity.

Investment Cash Flow Sensitivity
Because both asymmetric information and pecking order theory suggest that managers prefer internal funds to finance new investments, a reasonable expectation is to find a positive relationship between cash flow availability and investment. Such a relationship is consequently a symptom of underinvestment.

Fazzari, Hubbard, and Petersen (1988) show that investment is more sensitive to cash flow for firms that are more financially constrained (i.e., firms with restricted access to external finance and limited internal funds) than those that are not. The authors divide firms according to their dividend payout policies, assuming that firms retaining more of their earnings are more likely to be liquidity constrained.

They find that these firms exhibit higher investment cash flow sensitivity than firms paying higher dividends.

In the same way, Hoshi, Kashyap, and Scharfstein (1991) examine two sets of Japanese firms: independent firms and firms belonging to a *keiretsu* (i.e., a Japanese company group formed by interlocking shareholdings). Independent firms are thought to face more information problems and to be more financially constrained than *keiretsu* members. The authors' results show that for the independent set of firms, investment is more sensitive to liquidity. These results are consistent with the asymmetric information hypothesis suggesting that financial slack can mitigate the underinvestment problem arising from asymmetric information.

Several other studies reach the same conclusion, including Schaller (1993) for Canadian firms as well as Whited (1992), Lamont (1997), and Ascioglu, Hegde, and McDermott (2008) for U.S. firms. Other empirical work, including Aggarwal and Zong (2006) and Islam and Mozumdar (2007), uses international data to examine the investment cash flow relationship. These studies also corroborate the asymmetric information hypothesis.

Kaplan and Zingales (1997), however, provide evidence that investment cash flow sensitivity is not a good indicator of financial constraints. They consider the group of constrained firms examined by Fazzari et al. (1988) and show that the sensitivity is higher for the most unconstrained firms of this group. Cleary (1999) and Kaplan and Zingales (2000) confirm these findings. Allayannis and Mozumdar (2004) show that the existence of negative cash flow observations, which strongly affect investment cash flow sensitivities, can explain the findings of Kaplan and Zingales (1997). After excluding these negative observations, the results reaffirm the positive relation between investment cash flow sensitivity and financial constraints. Moreover, Lyandres (2007) points out that the mixed results found in the literature are due to a nonmonotonic relation between investment cash flow sensitivity and financial constraints. His theoretical and empirical models predict a negative (positive) relationship between the sensitivity of investment to cash flow and the cost of external funds for low (high) cost levels. Similarly, Cleary, Povel, and Raith (2007) and Almeida and Campello (2007) find a nonmonotonic U-shaped relationship between the availability of internal funds and investment.

Manager-Shareholder Conflict

Asymmetric information between managers and shareholders leads to a moral hazard problem. In fact, managers have the incentive to engage in unobservable actions not in the interests of the shareholders (Jensen and Meckling, 1976). For instance, managers have the incentive to build empires and entrench themselves, or conversely to work less, imitate the decisions of other managers, and take unjustifiable risks.

Increasing Managerial Power
Self-interested managers seeking to increase their power will maximize their utility when running larger firms (Stein, 2003). Hence, managers have incentives to undertake the highest level of investment so that they can derive private benefits.

Such behavior is commonly referred to as "empire-building" and has been primarily emphasized by Baumol (1959), Marris (1964), and Donaldson (1984).

Jensen (1986) argues that managers derive private benefits when investing a firm's free cash flow in unprofitable (i.e., negative NPV) projects rather than paying dividends to shareholders. Kanniainen (2000) builds a model integrating the neoclassical theory of investment and agency theory. Consistent with Jensen's argument, the model predicts that corporate managers use internal funds to invest in projects with a lower marginal value to shareholders than marginal cost. Wu and Wang (2005) consider a model similar to the one of Myers and Majluf (1984) but assume that managers derive private benefits of control from overinvestment. They find that private benefits amplify overinvestment but alleviate underinvestment. However, insider ownership has the opposite effect. When private benefits are small, an increase in insider ownership attenuates overinvestment but exacerbates underinvestment.

Most empirical studies support the free cash flow hypothesis. For instance, Berger and Ofek (1995) show that the decrease in firm value stemming from diversification is partly explained by overinvestment in segments from industries with limited investment opportunities. Chirinko and Schaller (2004) provide direct evidence of overinvestment in Canadian firms. Using a "revealed preference" approach, they measure the effective discount rates used by executives to make investment decisions. Their results show that in firms suffering from agency costs of free cash flow, managers choose their investment projects using risk-adjusted discount rates lower than the market rate by 350–400 basis points. Moreover, the capital stock of these firms is approximately 7 to 22 percent higher than if executives were to maximize firm value. Richardson (2006) studies the overinvestment of free cash flow in a large sample of U.S. firms. Using accounting-based measures of free cash flow and overinvestment, he documents that overinvestment is concentrated in firms with the highest level of free cash flow. Specifically, he finds that for firms with positive free cash flow, the average firm overinvests 20 percent of its free cash flow.

Another set of empirical work considers acquisition activity of firms as a means used by managers to increase their power. This evidence documents a negative market reaction to the announcement of acquisitions and shows that the negative announcement effect is stronger when the acquirer holds more cash (Lang, Stulz, and Walking, 1991; Harford, 1999). Schlingeman (2004) reports a negative and significant relationship between internally generated free cash flow and bidder gains. This relationship is particularly pronounced for firms with poor investment opportunities.

Jensen's (1986) free cash flow hypothesis implies a positive relationship between cash flow and investment. Many empirical studies try to assess whether investment cash flow sensitivity is due to asymmetric information or to managerial discretion. Unlike Hadlock (1998), whose findings are consistent with the asymmetric information hypothesis, Degryse and de Jong (2006) and Wei and Zhang (2008) document strong support for the overinvestment hypothesis caused by the agency costs of free cash flow. In their sample of Dutch firms, Degryse and de Jong distinguish between low Tobin's q firms (which supposedly face more managerial discretion problems) and high Tobin's q firms (which supposedly face more asymmetric information problems). The authors find that investment cash flow sensitivity is higher for low-q firms, suggesting that the managerial discretion problem is more relevant than the asymmetric information problem. Wei and Zhang use data from eight Asian emerging markets before the financial crisis (during the period 1993 to 1996) to show that investment cash flow sensitivity is higher when a divergence exists between the control rights and cash flow rights of the firm's largest shareholders.

While these studies consider the asymmetric information and managerial discretion arguments as mutually exclusive interpretations of the sensitivity of investment to cash flow, other empirical works suggest that both arguments may be potential explanations for the investment cash flow relationship. Vogt (1994) shows that large, low-dividend firms investing in tangible assets tend to overinvest because of managerial selfishness. By contrast, smaller, low-dividend firms and those making less tangible investments underinvest due to pecking order behavior.

Franzoni (2009) tests stock price reactions to a reduction in financial slack coming from the payment of mandatory pension contributions to a firm's defined benefit pension plan. Consistent with the asymmetric information hypothesis, he finds that a drop in cash is followed by a decrease in price that is more pronounced for financially constrained firms. This negative price reaction is attenuated if managers overinvest due to their selfishness. Furthermore, Franzoni's findings show that overinvestment seems to be more important in larger and more mature firms, whereas underinvestment is more relevant in the entire sample of listed firms.

Compensation and Career Concerns

Managerial compensation might be an incentive behind investment distortions. Indeed, since managers' compensation is often a function of firm size, managers are incited to undertake projects that increase firm size but do not necessarily increase profitability. Also, a nontrivial part of executive compensation, such as a bonus, is based on short-term accounting performance. When a manager is short-term oriented, basing compensation on current accounting measures of performance will not provide adequate investment incentives. In fact, managers might be too focused on reporting good short-term accounting profits and hence be reluctant to undertake projects that generate profits only in the long run.

At the empirical level, the results are inconclusive. While Dechow and Sloan (1991) show that CEOs approaching the end of their careers spend less on research and development (R&D) in order to increase their immediate accounting performance-based compensation, the results derived by Gibbons and Murphy (1992) suggest that managers approaching retirement do not necessarily decline to undertake long-term profitable investment projects. Bizjak, Brickley, and Coles (1993) find that when information asymmetry is high, a compensation contract with extreme emphasis on the current stock price may lead to overinvestment or underinvestment. In a similar vein, Bebchuk and Stole (1993) show that when information is imperfect and managers have short-term objectives, they may overinvest or underinvest in long-run projects. Finally, to avoid greater variation in their compensation, risk-averse managers may prefer not to reveal information about their ability to the labor market and, hence, do not undertake new investment projects (Holmstrom and Ricart i Costa, 1986).

Career concerns may lead to inefficient investment decisions. Indeed, career concerns may also encourage managers to be too focused on reporting short-term accounting profits and to take a suboptimal level of risk. Narayanan (1985) shows that managers concerned with their careers prefer short-term, lower-valued projects to long-term, higher-valued projects. Hirshleifer and Thakor (1992) find that managers prefer to invest in relatively safe projects for reputational concerns. Further, career concerns may induce managers to herd (e.g., Scharfstein and Stein, 1990; Stein, 2003). In fact, if a bad performance is attributed to a common negative shock, managers are less likely to be fired. As a result, they may prefer to follow the investment decisions of others, leading to suboptimal risk taking. Finally, risk-averse managers strive to diversify their employment risk. For instance, they may engage their firms in conglomerate mergers, even if these mergers are not beneficial to investors (Amihud and Lev, 1981).

Managerial Laziness
Managers who face private costs in selecting and implementing new investment projects and managers who prefer to avoid the private costly effort needed to acquire firm-specific information may forgo some positive NPV projects leading to underinvestment. Knyazeva, Knyazeva, Morck, and Yeung (2008) find empirical evidence supporting the hypothesis of managerial shirking in information acquisition. Their results show that managers base their investments on industry-level information that is publicly available as well as on the observable actions of other firms.

The "quiet life" hypothesis formulated in Bertrand and Mullainathan (2003) implies that managers are reluctant to shut down old plants and to open new plants in order to exert less effort. At the empirical level, the authors conclude that less monitoring by owners makes managers invest less rather than more to enjoy the "quiet life."

Overconfidence Bias

Investment distortions may also stem from another factor not related to asymmetric information or managers' selfishness, but related to the personal characteristics of the CEOs. In fact, managers may be overconfident and, as a result, overestimate the returns to their firm's investment projects. Consequently, overconfident CEOs may overinvest if they have sufficient internal resources.

Roll (1986), who proposes the "hubris hypothesis" of corporate takeovers, first introduced to corporate finance this overconfidence or optimism approach, which was established in the social psychology literature (Weinstein, 1980). Roll argues that managers of acquiring firms overbid their targets because they are overly optimistic and overestimate the potential synergies of takeovers. Hayward and Hambrick (1997) provide empirical evidence that strongly supports Roll's hubris hypothesis. Using a sample of 106 large acquisitions in the United States, they find that CEO hubris is highly associated with the amount of the premium paid. Using Australian data for the period 1994 to 2003, Brown and Sarma (2007) show that overconfident CEOs are more likely to make diversifying acquisitions than nonoverconfident CEOs. Malmendier and Tate (2008) reach the same conclusion using a sample of 394 large U.S. firms from 1990 to 1994. They show that overconfident CEOs (those who fail to diversify their personal portfolios) are more likely to complete mergers. Their results also indicate that the market reacts more negatively to merger announcements of optimistic CEOs than those of rational CEOs.

Heaton (2002) and Malmendier and Tate (2005) build theoretical models explaining the relation between corporate investment distortions and overconfidence. They document that overconfident CEOs overvalue their investment projects and believe that the market undervalues their firms, thereby making external financing too expensive. As a result, if such CEOs have sufficient internal funds, they overinvest relative to the optimal investment level. However, if they do not have sufficient internal funds, the CEOs underinvest.

Malmendier and Tate (2005) provide empirical evidence of managers' overconfidence using panel data on CEOs' personal portfolios for a sample of U.S. companies. They conclude that investment cash flow sensitivity can be explained by overconfidence rather than asymmetric information or misalignment of managerial and shareholder interests. Malmendier and Tate (2005) document that overconfident managers may make suboptimal investment decisions even if they do not face any informational asymmetries and their interests are aligned with those of shareholders. Lin, Hu, and Chen (2005) confirm this result for Taiwanese firms. When measuring managerial optimism with earnings forecasts, the authors find that investment cash flow sensitivity is higher for optimistic managers, especially in financially constrained firms. Glaser, Schäfers, and Weber (2008) corroborate these findings for German firms.

IMPACT OF CORPORATE GOVERNANCE ON INVESTMENT DISTORTIONS

Different corporate governance mechanisms help to alleviate investment distortions. These mechanisms include the choice of an appropriate capital structure, the provision of incentives to managers through compensation contracts, the monitoring of managers by the board members, and the choice of a suitable ownership structure.

Leverage

Jensen (1986) shows that overinvestment can be mitigated by issuing debt because managers will be forced to use free cash flows to pay the debt service instead of investing in wasteful projects. Following the same argument, Stulz (1990) derives a model assuming that managers are likely to waste firm assets by investing in bad projects. He documents that shareholders, anticipating this behavior, choose to increase the level of firm debt outstanding. In fact, debt payments force managers to disgorge future cash flows and hence reduce the overinvestment problem. However, excess debt may also lead to underinvestment decisions. Indeed, when internal cash flows are low, managers cannot credibly convince shareholders that they need additional funds to finance positive NPV projects. Hence, the optimal level of leverage is determined by trading off the positive and negative effects of debt financing.

Harris and Raviv (1990) and Fairchild (2003) show that a threat of bankruptcy provides an incentive for managers to increase efforts and enhance firm value.

Zwiebel (1996) considers that managers, not shareholders, make capital structure decisions and that constant pressure on managers exists from a discipliner such as a creditor, the market, or a potential raider. Managers choose the optimal capital structure by trading off their desire to overinvest with the need to ensure sufficient dynamic efficiency to prevent a discipliner's actions.

Using a sample of large U.S. industrial firms, Lang, Ofek, and Stulz (1996) find a negative relationship between leverage and firm growth, especially for firms with a low Tobin's q ratio. This finding supports the hypothesis that leverage has a disciplinary role for firms with poor growth opportunities.

More recently, D'Mello and Miranda (2010) present direct evidence of the role of debt in attenuating overinvestment. They examine the pattern of abnormal investments around a debt issue by unlevered firms. Using a sample of 366 debt offers by unlevered firms, they show that firms' cash ratios decrease dramatically after introducing debt and that this decrease is more pronounced in firms with poor investment opportunities. Moreover, D'Mello and Miranda argue that firms overinvesting in real assets experience a dramatic decline in abnormal capital expenditures after introducing debt. This decrease in overinvestment is due to the debt service payment obligation that reduces the free cash flow at the manager's disposal. Finally, the authors' results indicate a positive relation between the decline in overinvestment and equity value, especially in firms facing greater agency costs of free cash flow.

Other studies conducted in countries with low shareholders' rights protection find no evidence that debt serves as a disciplinary device. Referring to Zwiebel (1996), these studies show that when governance mechanisms are inefficient, entrenched managers manipulate the level of debt in order to avoid its disciplining role (Poincelot, 1999; De Jong and Veld, 2001; De Jong, 2002).

Managerial Compensation

Numerous studies examine the effect of managerial compensation on management behavior. For example, Heckerman (1975) argues that if the owners know the manager's employment opportunities, investment alternatives, and risk preferences, as well as some of the characteristics of the investment opportunities, a managerial compensation contract can be structured to induce the manager to act in the shareholders' best interests. Bizjak et al. (1993) argue that in the presence of asymmetric information, optimal investment decisions might be induced by offering a compensation contract that balances current and future stock price. Their empirical results show that when designing managerial compensation plans, high-growth firms (i.e., those with considerable information asymmetry) place less emphasis on current performance relative to future performance than do low-growth firms.

On the other hand, Bernardo, Cai, and Luo (2001) find that the optimal compensation contract depends on the characteristics of the firm's investment opportunities as well as the determinants of managerial preference for capital. For instance, managers will receive greater performance-based pay when the firm has high R&D expenditures and/or requires the manager to have highly firm-specific human capital. Hutchinson and Gul (2004) hypothesize that the negative relation between firms' investment opportunities and performance is weaker for firms with a higher level of managerial remuneration.

Aggarwal and Samwick (2006) develop a principal-agent model in which the provision of incentives to managers through compensation may alleviate problems of overinvestment (private benefits of investment) as well as underinvestment (private costs of investment). They argue that if private benefits or costs increase (decrease), the manager should receive larger (lower) incentives. The authors empirically estimate the joint relationships between incentives and firm performance and between incentives and investment. The results are consistent with the attenuation of underinvestment problems through the use of optimal incentive contracts.

As stock options represent a nontrivial part of executive compensation, many studies focus on this particular component as a means to help reduce investment distortions. Indeed, stock options might help mitigate the risk aversion problem as well as the short horizon problem. By introducing convexity into the manager's compensation function, stock options offer incentives to risk-averse managers to invest in high-risk, high-return projects that maximize the value of their stock options. Stock options might also mitigate the short horizon problem because managers are forced to focus on profitability in order to increase their own compensation package.

Agrawal and Mandelker (1987), Hirshleifer and Suh (1992), and Hemmer, Kim, and Verrecchia (1999) show empirically that stock options give managers incentives to adopt risky projects. The results derived by Rajgopal and Shevlin (2002) in a sample of oil and gas firms also corroborate that the use of stock options increases firm risk. Datta, Datta, and Raman (2001) illustrate the importance of providing stock option incentives to top executives in corporate acquisitions. They document a strong positive relationship between equity-based compensation received by acquiring managers and stock price response around corporate acquisition announcements. Comparing managers who receive low versus high equity-based compensation, the authors conclude that the latter pay significantly lower acquisition premiums, acquire targets with higher growth opportunities, and engage in acquisitions engendering larger increases in leverage-adjusted firm risk. Furthermore, firms offering high equity-based compensation to their managers do not underperform in the postacquisition period, while those with low equity-based compensation do.

The Board of Directors

The role of the board of directors may be crucial in monitoring managers and screening the project ideas the CEO proposes (Song and Thakor, 2006). As a result, a common assumption in the literature is that an effective board helps mitigate investment distortions. While many studies investigate the relationship between the characteristics of the board and firm performance (e.g., Adjaoud, Zeghal, and Andaleeb, 2007), only a few papers examine the direct relationship between the characteristics of boards of directors and firm investment.

The most investigated characteristic of board effectiveness is board composition. Heaton (2002) argues that the presence of outside directors on the board might help mitigate managerial optimism problems and hence reduce the investment distortions inherent to managerial overconfidence. Brown and Sarma's (2007) findings provide empirical support for Heaton's argument.

Chung, Wright, and Kedia (2003) examine board composition and find a significant and positive correlation between firm value and investment, as measured by both capital and R&D expenditures for firms with a high proportion of outside directors. Hutchinson and Gul (2004) conclude that firms with a higher proportion of nonexecutive directors on the board experience a weaker negative relationship between growth opportunities and performance. Malmendier and Tate (2005) find that the number of outside directors who are currently CEOs in other companies has a weak negative effect on investment cash flow sensitivity.

Knyazeva et al. (2008) test the hypothesis that managers shirk with regard to information acquisition. The hypothesis suggests that managers rely on public information rather than on firm-specific private information about investment opportunities when making investment decisions, leading to comovement in investment. The authors find that board independence decreases this comovement. They also find that levels of R&D activity are higher when the boards are more independent and that board independence increases the dispersion of R&D spending across firms in the industry. More recently, Knyazeva and John (2009) show that during negative industry cash flow shocks, an increase in board independence is associated with a higher change in capital expenditure and R&D as a fraction of total assets. Their evidence shows no such association effects from board independence during good times (i.e., during positive industry cash flow shocks). Accordingly, they conclude that board independence mitigates investment conservatism during bad times.

Faleye (2007) examines another aspect of the board of directors. He studies the effect of classified boards (a structure for a board of directors in which a portion of the directors serve for different term lengths, depending on their particular classification) on R&D and long-term physical assets. He concludes that classified boards are associated with a decrease in R&D spending as well as a decrease in capital expenditures on new property, plant, and equipment. Faleye also finds that classified boards are associated with firm value reduction, thus excluding the potential explanation that firms with classified boards reduce capital spending and R&D whenever doing so is optimal.

The governance role played by the board of directors in reducing investment distortions is limited. First, the CEO may control the information received by the board, which affects the board's judgment. Second, as Song and Thakor (2006) suggest, career concerns may lead even an independent board to be ineffective. They argue that career concerns induce the board to distort its investment recommendation pro-cyclically. In particular, career concerns tempt the board to overinvest during economic upturns and to underinvest during economic downturns.

Ownership Structure

Ownership structure is one of the main corporate governance mechanisms serving to mitigate the manager-shareholder conflict. The financial literature focuses on the influence of insider ownership and ownership concentration.

Insider Ownership

Since the seminal work by Berle and Means (1932) on the consequences of the separation of ownership from control, numerous studies have tried to identify the effect of insider ownership on corporate value (e.g., Jensen and Meckling, 1976; Demsetz and Lehn, 1985). Morck, Shleifer, and Vishny (1988) document a nonmonotonic relation between directors' ownership and firm performance: Tobin's q increases up to an ownership level of 5 percent, then decreases in the 5 percent to 25 percent range, and increases again beyond 25 percent. The authors argue that there are two conflicting effects: an alignment effect (when ownership is less than 5 percent or over 25 percent) and an entrenchment effect (when ownership is between 5 percent and 25 percent).

Building on these results, Hadlock (1998) and Pawlina and Renneboog (2005) point out that investment cash flow sensitivity depends on insider ownership in a nonmonotonic way. The results of Hadlock, using U.S. data, show that the investment to cash flow relation results from asymmetric information. However, evidence by Pawlina and Renneboog, using U.K. data, tends to support the free cash flow hypothesis. The authors contend that overinvestment is attenuated when managers' and shareholders' interests are aligned.

Pindado and de la Torre (2009) follow a similar approach for Spanish firms. In order to distinguish the role of ownership structure in the two alternative cases (asymmetric information and managerial discretion), they differentiate firms according to their propensity to suffer from underinvestment or overinvestment. To do so, they use a free cash flow index and a criterion for financial constraints. Consistent with Pawlina and Renneboog (2005), Pindado and de la Torre document that the convergence of interests between owners and managers reduces overinvestment problems.

Ownership Concentration and the Presence of Large Shareholders

Ownership concentration, particularly the presence of large shareholders, plays a prominent role in promoting good corporate governance (Shleifer and Vishny, 1997). Many empirical studies show that the presence of large outside shareholders can reduce investment distortions. On the one hand, enhanced monitoring by large shareholders decreases the overinvestment of free cash flows by management (Chirinko and Schaller, 2004; Richardson, 2006). On the other hand, these activist shareholders can spend time and effort to gather information about investment projects. Consequently, they help reduce information asymmetries and hence underinvestment problems (Goergen and Renneboog, 2001; Pawlina and Renneboog, 2005).

Garvey (1992) finds, however, that concentrated share ownership is unrelated to the magnitude of free cash flow, suggesting that large shareholders are not particularly effective in resolving the free cash flow problem. These results may be attributed to the negative entrenchment effects associated with large shareholders (Shleifer and Vishny, 1997). Pindado and de la Torre (2009) show that ownership concentration reduces the sensitivity of investment to cash flow in both underinvestor and overinvestor firms. By contrast, in the presence of controlling owners, as when ownership concentration is above 87 percent, underinvestment and overinvestment problems are exacerbated. Wei and Zhang (2008) and Chen, Xu, and Yu (2009) study the effect of the separation of ownership and control of the largest shareholders on investment. They provide evidence that cash flow rights have a positive enhancement effect and control rights have a negative entrenchment effect on investment.

Governance Scores

Hasan, Kadapakkam, and Kumar (2008) examine the effect of corporate governance quality on investment decisions. They try to identify whether financing constraints are attenuated in the presence of higher quality corporate governance rules. They develop three aggregate indices of corporate governance for seven Pacific Rim emerging economies measuring business environment, legal environment, and investor rights. The authors also develop an overall index of corporate governance. Their empirical results show that better quality corporate governance reduces the reliance of firms on internal resources and facilitates access to capital markets. These results imply that improvements in corporate governance rules serve to mitigate the underinvestment problem stemming from asymmetric information between managers and investors.

In order to address the opportunistic behavior of managers, Bøhren, Cooper, and Priestley (2007) use the corporate governance index defined by Gompers, Ishii, and Metrick (2003) to test the influence of corporate governance mechanisms on the efficiency of real investment decisions in a sample of U.S. manufacturing firms. The authors show that investment decisions are more sensitive to investment opportunities for well-governed firms than for poorly governed firms. Furthermore, their results suggest that better corporate governance induces managers to invest more and to manage their investments more efficiently. Still, in poorly governed firms, managers invest less, implying that they underinvest. Bøhren et al. conclude that good governance improves the efficiency of capital allocation within firms by mitigating the underinvestment problem caused by managers' laziness. Harford, Mansi, and Maxwell (2008) find that firms with weaker governance dissipate their cash reserves more quickly than well-governed firms. The results show that poorly governed managers prefer spending their cash on acquisitions rather than internal investment such as capital expenditures and R&D, and that these acquisitions often reduce future profitability.

SUMMARY AND CONCLUSIONS

Managers do not usually choose efficient or suitable investment decisions. Further, investment distortions may occur especially when information is not equally well known to management and investors. Three main factors may explain the origin of inefficient investment decisions. First, the asymmetric information between managers and external suppliers of funds increases the cost of external financing, inducing the managers to reject some positive NPV projects. Second, according to agency theory, managers' discretion and their desire to maximize their own wealth gives rise to different kinds of investment distortions. Indeed, managers could prefer to build empires, maximize their compensation, secure their career, or shirk their responsibilities. Such behavior may lead them to underinvest or overinvest or to choose projects that are more or less risky than is optimal. Finally, overconfident managers may overvalue their investment projects and therefore overinvest the internal resources of their firms.

Several corporate governance tools are designed to resolve asymmetric information and agency problems. These mechanisms help to ensure better investment decisions and attenuate investment distortions. This chapter covers the use of leverage as a disciplining mechanism; the role of structured managerial compensation, which provides shareholder alignment incentives to managers; the monitoring role of the board of directors; and the ownership structure, which can serve as a tool to attenuate asymmetric information. Empirically, the extant literature fails to establish without ambiguity the real impact of the quality of corporate governance in reducing investment distortions.

DISCUSSION QUESTIONS

1. Why do some authors view investment cash flow sensitivity as a symptom of underinvestment while others see it as a symptom of overinvestment?
2. Why do some managers prefer to invest in projects with short-term performance?
3. Why do some managers follow other managers in their investment decisions, a behavior known as herding?
4. Are boards of directors typically effective in reducing investment distortions? Why or why not?
5. Does the presence of large shareholders attenuate investment inefficiencies?

REFERENCES

Adjaoud, Fodil, Daniel Zeghal, and Syed Andaleeb. 2007. "The Effect of Board's Quality on Performance: A Study of Canadian Firms." *Corporate Governance: An International Review* 15:4, 623–635.
Aggarwal, Raj, and Sijing Zong. 2006. "The Cash Flow-Investment Relationship: International Evidence of Limited Access to External Finance." *Journal of Multinational Financial Management* 16:1, 89–104.
Aggarwal, Rajesh K., and Andrew A. Samwick. 2006. "Empire-Builders and Shirkers: Investment, Firm Performance, and Managerial Incentives." *Journal of Corporate Finance* 12:3, 489–515.
Agrawal, Anup, and Gershom N. Mandelker. 1987. "Managerial Incentives and Corporate Investment and Financing Decisions." *Journal of Finance* 42:4, 823–837.
Akerlof, George A. 1970. "The Market for 'Lemons': Quality and the Market Mechanism." *Quarterly Journal of Economics* 84:3, 488–500.
Allayannis, George, and Abon Mozumdar. 2004. "The Impact of Negative Cash Flow and Influential Observations on Investment-Cash Flow Sensitivity Estimates." *Journal of Banking and Finance* 28:5, 901–930.
Almeida, Heitor, and Murillo Campello. 2007. "Financial Constraints, Asset Tangibility and Corporate Investment." *Review of Financial Studies* 20:5, 1429–1460.
Amihud, Yakov, and Baruch Lev. 1981. "Risk Reduction as a Managerial Motive for Conglomerate Mergers." *Bell Journal of Economics* 12:2, 605–617.
Ascioglu, Asli., Shantaram P. Hegde, and John B. McDermott. 2008. "Information Asymmetry and Investment-Cash Flow Sensitivity." *Journal of Banking and Finance* 32:6, 1036–1048.

Baumol, William J. 1959. *Business Behavior, Value, and Growth*. New York: Macmillan.

Bebchuk, Lucian Arye, and Lars A. Stole. 1993. "Do Short-Term Objectives Lead to Under-or Overinvestment in Long-Term Projects?" *Journal of Finance* 48:2, 719–729.

Bencivenga, Valerie R., and Bruce D. Smith. 1993. "Some Consequences of Credit Rationing in an Endogenous Growth Model." *Journal of Economic Dynamics and Control* 17:1–2, 97–122.

Berger, Philip G., and Eli Ofek. 1995. "Diversification's Effect on Firm Value." *Journal of Financial Economics* 37:1, 39–65.

Berle, Adolf A., and Gardiner C. Means. 1932. *The Modern Corporation and Private Property*. New York: Macmillan.

Bernardo, Antonio E., Hongbin Cai, and Jiang Luo. 2001. "Capital Budgeting and Compensation with Asymmetric Information and Moral Hazard." *Journal of Financial Economics* 61:3, 311–344.

Bertrand, Marianne, and Sendhil Mullainathan. 2003. "Enjoying the Quiet Life? Corporate Governance and Managerial Preferences." *Journal of Political Economy* 111:5, 1043–1075.

Bizjak, John M, James A. Brickley, and Jeffrey L. Coles. 1993. "Stock-Based Incentive Compensation, Asymmetric Information and Investment Behavior." *Journal of Accounting and Economics* 16:1–3, 349–372.

Bøhren, Øyvind, Ilan Cooper, and Richard Priestley. 2007. "Corporate Governance and Real Investment Decisions." Paper, 2007 European Finance Association Meeting. Available at SSRN: http://papers.ssrn.com/sol3/papers.cfm?abstract_id=891060.

Brown, Rayna, and Neal Sarma. 2007. "CEO Overconfidence, CEO Dominance and Corporate Acquisitions." *Journal of Economics and Business* 59:5, 358–379.

Chen, Baizhu, Longbing Xu, and Honghai Yu. 2009. "Overinvestment when Control Separates from Ownership." Available at SSRN: http://papers.ssrn.com/sol3/papers.cfm?abstract_id=1376829.

Chirinko, Robert S., and Huntley Schaller. 2004. "A Revealed Preference Approach to Understanding Corporate Governance Problems: Evidence from Canada." *Journal of Financial Economics* 74:1, 181–206.

Chung, Kee H., Peter Wright, and Ben Kedia. 2003. "Corporate Governance and Market Valuation of Capital and R&D Investments." *Review of Financial Economics* 12:2, 161–172.

Cleary, Sean. 1999. "The Relationship between Firm Investment and Financial Status." *Journal of Finance* 54:2, 673–692.

Cleary, Sean, Paul Povel, and Michael Raith. 2007. "The U-Shaped Investment Curve: Theory and Evidence." *Journal of Financial and Quantitative Analysis* 42:1, 1–39.

D'Mello, Ranjan, and Mercedes Miranda. 2010. "Long-term Debt and Overinvestment Agency Problem." *Journal of Banking and Finance* 34:2, 324–335.

Datta, Sudip, Mai Iskandar Datta, and Kartik Raman. 2001. "Executive Compensation and Corporate Acquisition Decisions." *Journal of Finance* 56:6, 2299–2336.

De Jong, Abe. 2002. "The Disciplining Role of Leverage in Dutch Firms." *European Finance Review* 6:1, 31–62.

De Jong, Abe, and Chris Veld. 2001. "An Empirical Analysis of Incremental Capital Structure Decisions under Managerial Entrenchment." *Journal of Banking and Finance* 25:10, 1857–1895.

Dechow, Patricia M., and Richard G. Sloan. 1991. "Executive Incentives and the Horizon Problem." *Journal of Accounting and Economics* 14:1, 51–89.

Degryse, Hans, and Abe de Jong. 2006. "Investment and Internal Finance: Asymmetric Information or Managerial Discretion?" *International Journal of Industrial Organization* 24:1, 125–147.

Demsetz, Harold, and Kenneth Lehn. 1985. "The Structure of Corporate Ownership: Causes and Consequences." *Journal of Political Economy* 93:6, 1155–1177.

Donaldson, Gordon. 1984. *Managing Corporate Wealth*. New York: Praeger.

Fairchild, Richard. 2003. "Conflicts between Managers and Investors over the Optimal Financial Contract." *International Journal of Business and Economics* 3:2, 197–212.

Faleye, Olubunmi. 2007. "Classified Boards, Firm Value, and Managerial Entrenchment." *Journal of Financial Economics* 83:2, 501–529.

Fazzari, Steven M., R. Glenn Hubbard, and Bruce C. Petersen. 1988. "Financing Constraints and Corporate Investment." *Brookings Papers on Economic Activity* 1988:1, 141–206.

Franzoni, Francesco. 2009. "Underinvestment vs. Overinvestment: Evidence from Price Reactions to Pension Contributions." *Journal of Financial Economics* 92:3, 491–518.

Garvey, Gerald. 1992. "Do Concentrated Shareholdings Mitigate the Agency Problem of Free Cash flow? Some Evidence." *International Review of Economic and Finance* 1:4, 347–369.

Gibbons, Robert, and Kevin J. Murphy. 1992. "Optimal Incentive Contracts in the Presence of Career Concerns: Theory and Evidence." *Journal of Political Economy* 100:3, 468–505.

Glaser, Markus, Philipp Schäfers, and Martin Weber. 2008. "Managerial Optimism and Corporate Investment: Is the CEO Alone Responsible for the Relation?" Paper, 2009 American Finance Association Annual Meeting.

Goergen, Marc, and Luc Renneboog. 2001. "Investment Policy, Internal Financing and Ownership Concentration in the UK." *Journal of Corporate Finance* 7:3, 257–284.

Gompers Paul A., Joy L. Ishii, and Andrew Metrick. 2003. "Corporate Governance and Equity Prices." *Quarterly Journal of Economics* 118:1, 107–155.

Greenwald, Bruce, Joseph E. Stiglitz, and Andrew Weiss. 1984. "Informational Imperfections in the Capital Market and Macroeconomic Fluctuations." *American Economic Review* 74:2, 194–199.

Hadlock, Charles J. 1998. "Ownership, Liquidity, and Investment." *RAND Journal of Economics* 29:3, 487–508.

Harford, Jarrad. 1999. "Corporate Cash Reserves and Acquisitions." *Journal of Finance* 54:6, 1969–1997.

Harford, Jarrad, Sattar A. Mansi, and William F. Maxwell. 2008. "Corporate Governance and Firm Cash Holdings in the US." *Journal of Financial Economics* 87:3, 535–555.

Harris, Milton, and Artur Raviv. 1990. "Capital Structure and the Informational Role of Debt." *Journal of Finance* 45:2, 321–349.

Hasan, Tanweer, Palani-Rajan Kadapakkam, and P.C. Kumar. 2008. "Firm Investments and Corporate Governance in Asian Emerging Markets." *Multinational Finance Journal* 12:1–2, 21–44.

Hayward, Mathew, and Donald C. Hambrick. 1997. "Explaining the Premiums Paid for Large Acquisitions: Evidence of CEO Hubris." *Administrative Science Quarterly* 42:1, 103–127.

Heaton, J. B. 2002. "Managerial Optimism and Corporate Finance." *Financial Management* 31:2, 33–45.

Heckerman, Donald G. 1975. "Motivating Managers to Make Investment Decisions." *Journal of Financial Economics* 2:3, 273–292.

Hemmer, Thomas, Oliver Kim, and Robert E. Verrechia. 1999. "Introducing Convexity into Optimal Compensation Contracts." *Journal of Accounting and Economics* 28:3, 307–327.

Hirshleifer, David, and Yoon Suh. 1992. "Risk, Managerial Effort, and Project Choice." *Journal of Financial Intermediation* 2:3, 308–345.

Hirshleifer, David, and Anjan Thakor. 1992. "Managerial Conservatism, Project Choice, and Debt." *Review of Financial Studies* 5:3, 437–470.

Holmstrom, Bengt, and Joan Ricart i Costa. 1986. "Managerial Incentives and Capital Management." *Quarterly Journal of Economics* 101:4, 835–860.

Hoshi, Takeo, Anil Kashyap, and David Scharfstein. 1991. "Corporate Structure, Liquidity and Investment: Evidence from Japanese Industrial Groups." *Quarterly Journal of Economics* 106:1, 33–60.

Hutchinson, Marion, and Ferdinand A. Gul. 2004. "Investment Opportunity Set, Corporate Governance Practices, and Firm Performance." *Journal of Corporate Finance* 10:4, 595–614.

Islam, Saiyid S., and Abon Mozumdar. 2007. "Financial Market Development and the Importance of Internal Cash: Evidence from International Data." *Journal of Banking and Finance* 31:3, 641–658.

Jaffee, Dwight M., and Thomas Russell. 1976. "Imperfect Information, Uncertainty, and Credit Rationing." *Quarterly Journal of Economics* 90:4, 651–666.

Jensen, Michael C. 1986. "Agency Costs of Free Cash Flow, Corporate Finance, and Takeovers." *American Economic Review* 76:2, 323–329.

Jensen, Michael C., and William H. Meckling. 1976. "Theory of the Firm: Managerial Behavior, Agency Costs and Ownership Structure." *Journal of Financial Economics* 3:4, 305–360.

Kanniainen, Vesa. 2000. "Empire Building by Corporate Managers: The Corporation as a Savings Instrument." *Journal of Economic Dynamics and Control* 24:1, 127–142.

Kaplan, Steven N., and Luigi Zingales. 1997. "Do Investment-Cash-Flow Sensitivities Provide Useful Measures of Financing Constraints?" *Quarterly Journal of Economics* 112:1, 169–215.

Kaplan, Steven N., and Luigi Zingales. 2000. "Investment-Cash-Flow Sensitivities Are Not Valid Measures of Financing Constraints." *Quarterly Journal of Economics* 115:2, 707–712.

Knyazeva, Anzhela, Diana Knyazeva, Randall Morck, and Bernard Yin Yeung. 2008. "Comovement in Investment." Working Paper, Simon School, University of Rochester. Available at SSRN: http://papers.ssrn.com/ sol3/papers.cfm?abstract_id=1017323.

Knyazeva, Diana, and Kose John. 2009. "Corporate Governance and Investment Conservatism: Evidence from Industry Shocks." Available at SSRN: http://papers.ssrn.com/sol3/papers.cfm?abstract_id=891674.

Lamont, Owen. 1997. "Cash Flow and Investment: Evidence from Internal Capital Markets." *Journal of Finance* 52:1, 83–109.

Lang, Larry H. P., René M. Stulz, and Ralph A. Walkling. 1991. "A Test of Free Cash-Flow Hypothesis: The Case of Bidder Returns." *Journal of Financial Economics* 29:2, 315–335.

Lang, Larry, Eli Ofek, and René M. Stulz. 1996. "Leverage, Investment, and Firm Growth." *Journal of Financial Economics* 40:1, 3–30.

Lin, Yueh-hsiang, Shing-yang Hu, and Ming-shen Chen. 2005. "Managerial Optimism and Corporate Investment: Some Empirical Evidence from Taiwan." *Pacific-Basin Finance Journal* 13:5, 523–546.

Lyandres, Evgeny. 2007. "Costly External Financing, Investment Timing and Investment-Cash Flow Sensitivity." *Journal of Corporate Finance* 13:5, 959–980.

Malmendier, Ulrike, and Geoffrey Tate. 2005. "CEO Overconfidence and Corporate Investment." *Journal of Finance* 60:6, 2661–2700.

Malmendier, Ulrike, and Geoffrey Tate. 2008. "Who Makes Acquisitions? CEO Overconfidence and the Market's Reaction." *Journal of Financial Economics* 89:1, 20–43.

Marris, Robbin. 1964. *The Economic Theory of Managerial Capitalism.* Glencoe, IL: Free Press.

Modigliani, Franco, and Merton H. Miller. 1958. "The Cost of Capital, Corporation Finance, and the Theory of Investment." *American Economic Review* 48:3, 261–297.

Morck, Randall, Andrei Shleifer, and Robert W. Vishny. 1988. "Management Ownership and Market Valuation." *Journal of Financial Economics* 20:1–2, 293–315.

Myers, Stewart C. 1984. "The Capital Structure Puzzle." *Journal of Finance* 39:3, 575–592.

Myers, Stewart C., and Nicholas S. Majluf. 1984. "Corporate Financing and Investment Decisions When Firms Have Information That Investors Do Not Have." *Journal of Financial Economics* 13:2, 187–222.

Narayanan, M. P. 1985. "Observability and the Payback Criterion." *Journal of Business* 58:3, 309–323.

Pawlina, Grzegorz, and Luc Renneboog. 2005. "Is Investment-Cash Flow Sensitivity Caused by Agency Costs or Asymmetric Information? Evidence from the UK." *European Financial Management* 11:4, 483–513.

Pindado, Julio, and Chabela de la Torre. 2009. "Effect of Ownership Structure on Underinvestment and Overinvestment: Empirical Evidence from Spain." *Accounting and Finance* 49:2, 363–383.

Poincelot, Evelyne. 1999. "Le Rôle de l'Endettement dans le Contrôle du Comportement Managérial: Le Cas des Firmes Dégageant du Free Cash-flow." *Finance Contrôle Stratégie* 2:1, 75–89.

Rajgopal, Shivaram, and Terry Shevlin. 2002. "Empirical Evidence on the Relation between Stock Option Compensation and Risk Taking." *Journal of Accounting and Economics* 33:2, 145–171.

Richardson, Scott. 2006. "Over-investment of Free Cash-Flow." *Review of Accounting Studies* 11:2–3, 159–189.

Roll, Richard. 1986. "The Hubris Hypothesis of Corporate Takeovers." *Journal of Business* 59:2, 197–216.

Ross, Stephen A. 1977. "The Determination of Financial Structure: The Incentive-Signalling Approach." *Bell Journal of Economics* 8:1, 23–40.

Schaller, Huntley. 1993. "Asymmetric Information, Liquidity Constraints, and Canadian Investment." *Canadian Journal of Economics* 26:3, 552–574.

Scharfstein, David S., and Jeremy C. Stein. 1990. "Herd Behavior and Investment." *American Economic Review* 80:3, 465–479.

Schlingemann, Frederik P. 2004. "Financing Decisions and Bidder Gains." *Journal of Corporate Finance* 10:5, 683–701.

Shleifer, Andrei, and Robert W. Vishny. 1997. "A Survey of Corporate Governance." *Journal of Finance* 52:2, 737–783.

Song, Fenghua, and Anjan V. Thakor. 2006. "Information Control, Career Concerns, and Corporate Governance." *Journal of Finance* 61:4, 1845–1896.

Stein, Jeremy C. 2003. "Agency, Information and Corporate Investment." In George Constantinides, Milt Harris, and René Stulz (eds.), *Handbook of the Economics of Finance*, 111–165. Amsterdam: North-Holland.

Stiglitz, Joseph E., and Andrew Weiss. 1981. "Credit Rationing and Markets with Imperfect Information." *American Economic Review* 71:3, 393–410.

Stiglitz, Joseph E., and Andrew Weiss. 1983. "Incentive Effects of Terminations: Applications to the Credit and Labor Markets." *American Economic Review* 73:3, 912–927.

Stulz, René M. 1990. "Managerial Discretion and Optimal Financing Policies." *Journal of Financial Economics* 26:1, 3–27.

Tobin, James. 1969. "A General Equilibrium Approach to Monetary Theory." *Journal of Money, Credit and Banking* 1:1, 15–29.

Vogt, Stephen C. 1994. "The Cash-Flow/Investment Relationship: Evidence from U.S. Manufacturing Firms." *Financial Management* 23:2, 3–20.

Wei, K. C. John, and Yi Zhang. 2008. "Ownership Structure, Cash Flow, and Capital Investment: Evidence from East Asian Economies before the Financial Crisis." *Journal of Corporate Finance* 14:2, 118–132.

Weinstein, Neil D. 1980. "Unrealistic Optimism about Future Life Events." *Journal of Personality and Social Psychology* 39:5, 806–820.

Whited, Toni M. 1992. "Debt, Liquidity Constraints, and Corporate Investment: Evidence from Panel Data." *Journal of Finance* 47:4, 1425–1460.

Wu, Xueping, and Zheng Wang. 2005. "Equity Financing in a Myers-Majluf Framework with Private Benefits of Control." *Journal of Corporate Finance* 11:5, 915–945.

Zwiebel, Jeffrey. 1996. "Dynamic Capital Structure under Management Entrenchment." *American Economic Review* 86:5, 1197–1215.

ABOUT THE AUTHORS

Fodil Adjaoud, Ph.D., FCGA, CMA, teaches undergraduate and graduate (MBA) courses in accounting and finance at the Telfer School of Management of the University of Ottawa (Canada), especially financial management, financial and managerial accounting, activity-based management, and activity-based costing. Professor Adjaoud conducts research in wealth-creation strategies, performance indicators, dividend policy, and corporate governance. His work has been published in major academic and professional journals such as the *Canadian Journal of Administrative Sciences, Journal of Banking and Finance, Corporate Governance: An International Review*, and *Journal of Business Finance and Accounting*. Professor Adjaoud has participated in many conferences in Canada and abroad including those of the Administrative Sciences Association of Canada, the Canadian Academic Accounting Association, the European Accounting Association, and the American Accounting Association.

Dorra Charfi is Assistant Professor at Tunis School of Business of the University of Manouba, Tunisia. Her teaching interests are in corporate finance and accounting. She holds a Ph.D. in finance from the Faculty of Economics and Management Sciences, University of El Manar, Tunisia. Her main research interests include corporate governance and financing decisions.

Lamia Chourou holds a Ph.D. in finance and is currently a Ph.D. student in financial accounting at Queen's University. Her research interests include executive compensation and corporate governance. Dr. Chourou has participated in many finance conferences such as those of the Financial Management Association, European Finance Association, Southern Finance Association, and European Financial Management Association. She has published in refereed journals such as the *Journal of Multinational Financial Management, Canadian Investment Review,* and *Canadian Journal of Administrative Sciences*.

PART II

Capital Investment Choice

CHAPTER 4

Measuring Investment Value

Free Cash Flow, Net Present Value, and Economic Value Added

TOM ARNOLD
F. Carlyle Tiller Chair in Business, University of Richmond

TERRY NIXON
Associate Professor of Finance, Miami University

INTRODUCTION

Project evaluation is critical to the success of almost any firm. Conceptually, two economic forces are set against each other, risk or cost versus reward or benefit. In the case of a project, an investment is expected to generate cash flows that not only recover the investment but also generate additional cash flows to compensate for the investment's risk. The best possible scenario is a project that generates cash flows that overcompensate for the project's risk. Consequently, firms should actively seek any project that compensates (or overcompensates) for the risky investment.

Although this process is not conceptually difficult to understand, the process is much more complex in practice. A firm can generate the source of funds for an investment using new debt, the capital created from the firm's existing operations (i.e., internal equity), or an issue of new equity. Because these sources of capital have differential risk and tax burdens, the choice of the capital mix is of strategic importance and the offsetting compensation by the project may need to account for the differential risk within the capital mix.

Further, the cash flow needed to compensate for the investment is not clearly defined. Net income is not the same as cash flow because net income includes noncash expenses such as depreciation and also includes expenses that provide tax savings (or tax breaks) such as interest on debt. Some definitions of cash flow include a portion of the interest on debt (i.e., the tax savings generated from the interest on debt) and do not subtract it out as is the case when calculating net income. Other definitions of cash flow eliminate the tax benefit of debt completely.

Given an acceptable definition of cash flow, how much compensation for risk should a project provide? Overcompensation is certainly desirable, but the deeper issue is really about how much risk is associated with the project. Is the risk commensurate with the cost of raising the funds for the project measured as the return desired by the providers of the sources of the funds, issuers of debt, and shareholders? Or is the risk a completely unique attribute of the project separate from the choice of funding? Although these two issues may seem separate, the issues are related because even if one prefers to see risk as unique to the project, the risk-adjusted return for the project must be higher than the return associated with raising funds or no value is created. In other words, if a credit card is the sole source of funding at a rate of 14 percent annually, projects that produce less than a 14 percent annual return should not be considered even when the project's return is appropriate for the project's level of risk.

Each of these issues directly or indirectly begins in the finance literature with the work of Modigliani and Miller (1958) (hereafter MM). MM developed a theory for the value of a firm that is funded with a combination of debt and equity. With the removal of many frictions, debt and equity are viewed to be equivalent as sources of funding. Once frictions are introduced in later papers, the strategic nature of using debt or equity begins to emerge. Although MM focuses on firm valuation, it becomes the starting point in the literature for project valuation, particularly regarding the mix of debt and equity used for funding a project and the calculation of cash flows. In this chapter, the methods discussed for evaluating a project are net present value (NPV), internal rate of return (IRR), and economic value added (EVA). NPV and EVA both allow comparing the project's benefit through cash flow generation versus the investment/cost to generate cash flow. NPV and EVA are measured in units of monetary value with the monetary value being the additional value created for the firm from investing in the project. IRR is a special case of NPV and is the actual percentage return generated by a project. To determine if the project's IRR is sufficient to justify its risk/cost, the project's return needs a benchmark return (sometimes called a "hurdle rate" or "cutoff rate") for comparison.

In the United States, NPV and IRR are the most popular means for performing a project evaluation (Graham and Harvey, 2001; Ryan and Ryan, 2002). EVA is a more recent metric that has generated great interest and shares some attributes with NPV. However, the same valuation issues mentioned previously need to be addressed within each method: an appropriate definition of cash flow, the effect of the capital mix for funding the project, and the level of compensation that is sufficient relative to the risk/cost of the project.

The chapter begins with a discussion of NPV and how IRR relates to NPV to set a basis for the rest of the chapter. The chapter continues by introducing two definitions of cash flow followed by intertwined issues concerning tax shields, risk, and the appropriate discount rate for the cash flows. Putting some of these issues aside, a dynamic version of NPV is introduced to demonstrate the limitations of the textbook version of NPV. The final part of the chapter focuses on EVA, which is compared and contrasted with NPV with a further discussion of the managerial benefits that emerge from EVA.

NPV AND IRR

The NPV of a project is the sum of the discounted cash flows (inflows) less the sum of the discounted costs (outflows). If the NPV is zero, the project returns a rate equal to its discount rate. If the project's NPV is greater than zero, its return exceeds its discount rate and the value of the NPV calculation is the additional value created from executing the project. Related to the NPV calculation is the IRR, which is the discount rate that sets the NPV to zero and can be viewed as the "true" return of the project. Logically, a project with an NPV greater than zero should generate an IRR that is greater than the discount rate, but that may not be the case because the IRR depends on when inflows and outflows occur through time.

If a project has a textbook structure in which an initial cost (cash outflow) is followed by future cash inflows, the initial logic of NPV being greater than zero reflecting an IRR greater than the discount rate is correct. However, suppose a project's cash flows are the receipt of $100 today (i.e., an inflow of $100) for a service to be provided one year from today at a cost of $112. The IRR is 12 percent annually because discounting the cost at 12 percent annually is exactly equal to the $100 received today. If the discount rate is lower than the IRR of 12 percent, the project loses money even though the IRR is greater than the discount rate. Consequently, unless the project cash flows follow the textbook structure, the relationship between IRR and NPV is not directly transparent.

Although IRR is the subject of another chapter, this issue of how IRR and NPV are related is important here. In practice, an appropriate discount rate is not always available to assess the NPV of a project. In this case, an NPV profile is generated (i.e., the NPV is calculated for multiple discount rates), and IRRs (there can be multiple IRRs for a project depending on when cash inflows and outflows are received through time) are assessed against a hurdle or cutoff rate (i.e., the IRR must exceed the hurdle or cutoff rate). Most often, the hurdle or cutoff rate is the return necessary for raising funds for the project. Further, even when a discount rate is readily available, if the discount rate is less than the return necessary for raising funds for the project, the project may still be acceptable if the IRR exceeds the return necessary for raising funds for the project.

Returning to the discussion of NPV, other aspects about the presentation of NPV within textbooks and business curricula need to be addressed. The discount rate for the NPV calculation is generally considered to be constant similar to the yield to maturity on a bond even though future cash flows are more uncertain and generally higher rates are assessed when cash flow is withheld for a greater period of time. Although a constant discount rate can be generated to produce a correct NPV, the finance literature tends to simplify the evaluation process by using a constant rather than a dynamic discount rate. Given the complexity of actually executing a project, oversimplifying an evaluation mechanism for a project may seem disingenuous. Thus, another section of the chapter addresses the dynamic aspect of NPV.

The chapter next addresses the cash flows generated by a project. These expected cash flows are uncertain because they occur in the future. Yet, the typical textbook version of NPV tends to disregard this aspect of the project by assuming a constant discount rate despite the fact that more distant cash flows are generally more uncertain than closer cash flows. The discussion of a dynamic NPV later in the chapter addresses this issue. In theory, both discount rates and cash flows should be viewed as dynamic. However, the more immediate concern is calculating a project's cash flows, which is the subject of the next section.

CASH FLOWS

Profit (revenue less expenses) serves as a starting point for calculating cash flow However, cash flow is more complicated than profit because some expenses are operational (e.g., cost of goods sold) and some expenses are more long-term investment oriented (e.g., the purchase of equipment). These two types of expenses must be disentangled from tax-driven expenses, such as depreciation in which no physical money is actually spent. Tax is also an expense, but the treatment differs somewhat from other expenses in that it is not a matter of merely paying tax, but also expensing so as to avoid additional tax. When a firm avoids paying additional taxes, the savings may or may not be viewed as a part of the cash flow.

Operating expenses (e.g., cost of goods sold and selling, general, and administrative expenses) are included in calculating net income (also known as earnings after tax [EAT] or profit after tax [PAT]). The investment-oriented expenses are separate from net income and are changes in accounts on the balance sheet: a change in fixed assets to reflect new fixed asset purchases and a change in net working capital, where net working capital is current assets less current liabilities (assuming no accruals in current liabilities). Other expenses (depreciation and interest expense) within net income have to be removed, but a question remains regarding the tax consequences associated with removing these expenses. Net income less depreciation less interest expense is equivalent to:

$$\text{(Revenues} - \text{Operating Expenses) (1} - \text{Tax Rate)} \atop +\text{Depreciation (Tax Rate)} + \text{Interest Expense (Tax Rate)} \qquad (4.1)$$

Essentially, this adjustment to net income (often called an operating cash flow) focuses on operating expenses and the tax savings created by depreciation and the interest expense. Other variations of this calculation include:

$$\text{EBIT (1} - \text{Tax Rate)} + \text{Depreciation} + \text{Interest Expense (Tax Rate)} \qquad (4.2)$$

EBIT is the earnings before interest and taxes and is calculated as revenue less operating expenses less depreciation. EBIT(1 − Tax Rate) is often called NOPAT (net operating profit after taxes) or EBIAT (earnings before interest after taxes). Although Equation 4.2 is equally valid, the preference in this chapter is to use the calculation in Equation 4.1 because of the direct calculation of the tax savings from depreciation and interest expense.

To produce the appropriate cash flow for project assessment, Equation 4.1 is reduced by the change in net working capital and the change in fixed assets (i.e., the investment expenses from the balance sheet). This cash flow is called the capital cash flow (CCF) from Ruback (2002) or the cash flow from assets (CFA) as shown in Ross, Westerfield, and Jordan (2009):

$$\text{CFA} = \text{(Revenues} - \text{Operating Expenses)(1} - \text{Tax Rate)} + \text{Depreciation (Tax Rate)}$$

$$+ \text{Interest Expense (Tax Rate)} \qquad (4.3)$$

$$- \text{Change in Net Working Capital} - \text{Change in Fixed Assets}$$

Generally, the initial investment for the project is a particular case of CFA that only has the cash outflow of both a fixed asset purchase (i.e., change in fixed assets) and an increase in net working capital (i.e., change in net working capital). Other investments in fixed assets and net working capital may occur throughout a project's life, but the expectation is that inflows generated from operations will more than compensate for these expenses. Should this not occur and expenses/losses occur during the project, a case of multiple IRRs can emerge, making an NPV profile necessary to evaluate the project.

However, an alternate definition called free cash flow (FCF) is consistent with texts such as Damodaran (1994), Brigham and Ehrhardt (2011), and Graham, Smart, and Megginson (2010). FCF is similar to CFA except that the tax savings from the interest expense is not included in the calculation.

$$\text{FCF} = (\text{Revenues} - \text{Operating Expenses})(1 - \text{Tax Rate}) + \text{Depreciation}\,(\text{Tax Rate})$$

$$-\text{Change in Net Working Capital} - \text{Change in Fixed Assets} \qquad (4.4)$$

Petty and Rose (2009) note the difference in the definition of cash flow is an inconsistency within finance textbooks, but conclude that the difference is a minor issue while emphasizing the need to have the cash flow reflect back to the accounting statement of cash flow. The CFA definition is more consistent with the accounting statement of cash flow because it defines the cash flow to creditors (CFC) as the interest expense less the change in long-term debt. The cash flow to shareholders (CFS) is defined as dividends less the change in the stock account. The following reconciliation of the balance sheet emerges:

$$\text{CFA} - \text{CFC} - \text{CFS} = 0 \qquad (4.5)$$

By extracting the change in the cash account from the change in net working capital (i.e., adding back the change in cash to CFA) in Equation 4.5, the adjusted reconciliation mirrors the accounting statement of cash flow when all accounts are separated within the calculation of CFA, CFC, and CFS.

$$\text{CFA} + \text{Change in Cash} - \text{CFC} - \text{CFS} = \text{Change in Cash} \qquad (4.6)$$

However, mirroring the accounting statement of cash flow is insufficient justification to promote using CFA over FCF. One possible resolution to using FCF over CFA is to view FCF as the all-equity equivalent (i.e., if a firm/project has no debt funding) of CFA and consequently, when discounted, FCF should be discounted at a lower rate relative to CFA. Using "k" as the discount rate for FCF and "α" as the additional discounting needed for CFA (define CFA as FCF + interest expense(tax rate)), the following identity emerges:

$$\text{FCF}/(1+k)^N = [\text{FCF} + (\text{Interest Expense})(\text{Tax Rate})]/[(1+k)^N(1+\alpha)^N] \quad (4.7)$$

Solving for α:

$$\alpha = [1 + (\text{Interest Expense})(\text{Tax Rate})/\text{FCF}]^{1/N} - 1 \qquad (4.8)$$

Notice that the effect of α dissipates as N increases, making the discount rate for CFA converge in time to the discount rate for FCF. In one sense, the difference between the two cash flow definitions from a risk-adjusted basis matters little at some point in the future.

Although the difference between the two cash flow calculations may conveniently dissipate through time, there are still some pragmatic issues to address. Is the scale of a project really unaffected by the level of debt? In a sense, stating FCF as the all-equity equivalent of CFA implicitly grants a firm ownership of all of the assets necessary for the project (i.e., eliminating debt from the balance sheet does not offset an equal elimination of assets because the equity is simply scaled up to offset the debt). If the firm does not use debt, it would most likely invest in smaller scale projects that generate less cash flows. In other words, the all-equity equivalent of CFA would most likely be a cash flow that differs by more than just the tax savings from interest because the scale of the project would most likely be smaller as well. To illustrate this point, consider the scale of an individual's assets without the ability to have a mortgage to buy a house. The individual's assets will most likely be smaller and having this property as an investment vehicle (i.e., a project) would not exist.

No convenient solution is available for this conundrum because one can only conclude that debt used prudently makes a project more valuable by increasing the scale of the project and its associated operations beyond simply the value of the tax savings from interest. Perhaps the additional value compensates for the default risk that is present with debt but not with equity. Or the added value as suggested by Jensen (1986) is the curbing of agency issues with management. Management becomes more efficient in order to avoid the default risk from issuing debt. The main conclusion becomes that when considering value that debt may add to a firm or project, the value generated by debt is not fully captured as the difference between FCF and CFA. Putting this issue aside, much of the finance literature in the area focuses on the effect of the tax savings from interest. The main question is: How should this tax savings be discounted or valued, if at all? Further, although risk-adjusted discount rates have yet to be fully addressed, this aspect of project evaluation along with the capital mix for funding projects are part of this debate and are discussed in the next section.

TAX SAVINGS, DISCOUNT RATES, AND THE FUNDING MIX OF CAPITAL

In the previous section, the notion of the appropriate cash flow became a choice between FCF and CFA where the two calculations differed by the tax savings from interest. Using Modigliani and Miller (1958) as a basis, Myers (1974) suggests separating the tax savings from interest in the cash flow within the valuation process. Myers names the technique the adjusted present value (APV), which is a combination of the NPV applied to FCF and a separate valuation of the tax savings from interest. An individual discounted cash flow becomes:

$$FCF/(1 + k)^N + [(Interest)(Tax\ Rate)]/(1 + q)^N \qquad (4.9)$$

"k" is a discount rate associated with equity as the sole source of financing (i.e., an all-equity discount rate with the appropriate level of risk) and "q" is a lower rate because interest payments are not as volatile as earnings. Appealing to MM, "q" would be set to the risk-free rate. Myers does not necessarily advocate setting "q" to the risk-free rate, but makes the conclusion in order to fit the analysis back into the context of MM.

Summing the discounted FCFs with "k" and then subtracting the amount of investment is equivalent to the NPV using FCF. The second portion of Equation 4.9 equates to summing the discounted tax savings from interest over time and is the additional value generated from using debt financing for the project. Extensive debate concerns the choice of the discount rates "k" and "q" within an APV analysis. Before discussing the debate, note that if "k" and "q" are both equal, then Equation 4.9 is equivalent to discounting CFA with "k" (remember, k = q) as the discount rate.

$$FCF/(1+k)^N + [(Interest)(Tax\ Rate)]/(1+k)^N = CFA/(1+k)^N \qquad (4.10)$$

In assessing APV, Luehrman (1997) suggests, similar to Myers (1974), using a discount rate from an equivalently risky firm that has no debt for "k," but proposes using a slightly higher rate than the interest rate on debt for "q" to account for the possibility of financial distress. Ruback (2002), based on Ruback (1986) and Arditti and Levy (1977), states that the appropriate cash flow is CFA (Ruback calls it a capital cash flow or CCF) and should be discounted using a pretax weighted average cost of capital (P-TWACC):

$$P\text{-}TWACC = k_D(D/V) + k_E(E/V) \qquad (4.11)$$

"k_D" and "k_E" are the returns demanded on debt and equity, respectively. "D" and "E" are the debt and equity levels of the firm, respectively, and when summed equal "V." This is equivalent to setting "k" and "q" both equal to the P-TWACC in Equation (4.9) or using P-TWACC for "k" in Equation (4.10). In essence, Ruback as well as Arditti and Levy do not agree that the tax savings from interest should have a different discount rate than the FCF portion of the cash flow. This is an implicit assumption that the tax savings from interest and FCF have equivalent risk. Further, the cost of capital calculation is taken on a pretax basis so as not to double count the tax benefit of the interest on debt within the cash flow and within the discount rate.

Before Ruback (2002) echoed the analysis of Arditti and Levy (1977), the Arditti and Levy paper sparked some debate. Ben-Horim (1979), Bourdreaux and Long (1979), Ezzell and Porter (1979), and Shapiro (1979) either question the use of CFA and P-TWACC instead of FCF and the after-tax weighted average cost of capital (A-TWACC) or demonstrate under what conditions both are equal.

$$A\text{-}TWACC = k_D(1 - Tax\ Rate)(D/V) + k_E(E/V) \qquad (4.12)$$

One other portion of the debate was whether A-TWACC was a better cutoff rate than the higher P-TWACC. In other words, the debate concerned the appropriate rate to use to compare to a project's IRR for making a judgment about the acceptability of the project. Another portion of the debate was whether CFA is inconsistent with any cost of capital calculation that assumed a constant proportion of debt relative to equity.

This is an important issue because if the tax savings from interest changes through time (i.e., during the life of the project), then the debt level and/or the proportion of debt within the funding could change as well. Alternatively, the tax savings from debt may not change through time, but equity could increase or decrease proportionately, making the cost of capital change through time independent of the tax benefit of debt. In essence, there may be an implicit assumption that the debt and equity proportions of funding are constant and that the tax benefit of the interest is also constant. In reality, both interest payments and debt proportion within funding are unlikely to be constant at the same time unless the economy is also in a constant state.

Chambers, Harris, and Pringle (1982) also discuss this issue. In order to maintain a constant proportion of debt and equity, the firm needs to increase debt as equity increases in value during good economic times and sell debt when equity decreases in value during poor economic times. However, funding is really a function of the firm (i.e., the creditworthiness of the firm as a borrower, not the project, attracts debt financing; Harris and Pringle, 1985) and is not assigned to specific projects. As a result, the change in the tax benefit of debt upon the project is not of consequence even though the level of debt and the level of interest on the debt may be changing. However, this implies that firms consciously and continuously monitor the debt and equity mix, which may or may not be true. If true, is the monitoring for strategic advantages rather than for project evaluation metrics? Consequently, the reason for monitoring debt and equity levels may be correlated with project evaluation metrics, but the correlation is unlikely to be perfect.

Continuing with reconciling between CFA, FCF, A-TWACC, and P-TWACC, Ruback (2002) demonstrates that if the cash flows are taken into perpetuity and if market prices reflect book value, FCF discounted by A-TWACC is equivalent to CFA discounted by P-TWACC. Notice that A-TWACC can be adjusted to contain P-TWACC:

$$\text{A-TWACC} = \text{P-TWACC} - k_D(\text{Tax Rate})(D/V) \tag{4.13}$$

Taking a discounted value of FCFs into perpetuity using A-TWACC as the discount rate, it can be shown that it is equal to the associated discounted CFAs (= FCF + k_D(D)(Tax Rate)) in perpetuity using P-TWACC as the discount rate. The value of the perpetuity "V" is assumed to be equal to the book values of E and D added together.

$$
\begin{aligned}
V &= \text{FCF/A-TWACC} = \text{FCF}/[\text{P-TWACC} - k_D(\text{Tax Rate})(D/V)] \\
V[&\text{P} - \text{TWACC} - k_D(\text{Tax Rate})(D/V)] = \text{FCF} \\
V(&\text{P} - \text{TWACC}) - k_D(D)(\text{Tax Rate}) = \text{FCF} \\
V &= [\text{FCF} + k_D(D)(\text{Tax Rate})]/\text{P-TWACC} = \text{CFA/P-TWACC}
\end{aligned}
\tag{4.14}
$$

A similar proof can also be performed when valuing a single FCF using A-TWACC as the discount rate that occurs one period in the future. However, when there are a limited number of multiple cash flows in the future, the equivalence between FCF with A-TWACC and CFA with P-TWACC disappears, creating a relationship/difference similar to that displayed in Equation 4.8.

One issue ultimately disappears from the debate and remains unresolved: Should the tax savings from interest be discounted at a rate lower than FCF? The closest resolution appears to be either CFA discounted with the P-TWACC, meaning that FCF and the tax savings from interest are discounted at an equivalent rate, or the tax savings from interest is encompassed in the A-TWACC calculation used to discount FCF.

Most of this literature focuses on firm valuation and is adapted to project valuation within this chapter. Without much debate, the firm's cost of capital, whether pretax or after-tax (usually after-tax is the accepted norm), is universally viewed as the correct discount rate for finding the value of the firm. However, a project is different in the same sense as an individual security within a portfolio. The portfolio may generate a specific return, but that specific return is not the return produced by all of the securities within the portfolio. Consequently, the weighted average cost of capital (WACC) may provide a hurdle or cutoff rate for projects (i.e., new projects that cannot generate enough return to compensate for risk and be higher than the cost of capital are unacceptable). Yet, WACC is not necessarily the correct risk-adjusted rate for evaluating the project. For example, assuming a credit card that charges annual interest of 16 percent is the sole means of funding available (i.e., the cost of capital), purchasing a AAA-rated bond does not also make the bond's discount rate 16 percent. Further, the bond is a project/purchase that cannot be considered because the appropriate risk-adjusted return will most likely not be higher than 16 percent to compensate for the cost of funding even though the risk has been appropriately compensated.

Harris and Pringle (1985) state that the WACC works as a project discount rate only when the project has the same average risk as the firm or as the firm's operations. Such projects are generally extensions of existing operations. Even when such conditions exist, a dynamic version of the cost of capital (for reasons stated previously) is likely to be appropriate as debt levels or proportion relative to equity change through time. Miles and Ezzell (1985) and Inselbag and Kaufold (1997) suggest schemes for making the cost of capital dynamic through time. What if the project is something new and innovative or has a different risk profile than the firm that warrants a discount rate different from the firm's cost of capital?

Risk-adjusted discount rates can be implied from publicly traded firms that have the same risk profile as the project. Appealing to the capital asset pricing model (CAPM) (Sharpe, 1964), a CAPM beta can be extracted from the comparable firm's discount rate and adjusted for the debt level pertaining to the project (Hamada, 1972). However, a market-implied beta does not necessary correspond to a real asset beta (Ang and Lewellen, 1982; Gahlon and Gentry, 1982). Further, the added complexity of CAPM can trigger more opportunities for mistakes (Fernandez, 2007) even when assuming the CAPM is correctly specified. This does not suggest that trying to find an appropriate risk-adjusted rate for a project is an unimportant or impractical task. However, the task adds more complexity to correctly specifying a project's NPV particularly when compared to finding a WACC coming from data that are a matter of record.

Ultimately, decision makers face a dilemma when they cannot determine a risk-adjusted rate. For example, this difficulty can occur when a project has non-normal cash flows (i.e., the cash flows have more than one change in sign from negative to positive), which implies the possibility of having multiple IRRs. If a project has multiple IRRs, the NPV will fluctuate more than once between positive and negative values as the discount rate changes. Making an investment decision in this setting can be difficult and the fact that a project's risk outweighs its benefits could be completely obscured. Firms can use strategies such as launching the project on a smaller scale to learn more about the project, which is in the realm of analysis called "real options." However, such strategies and their analysis are the subject of other chapters. The next section addresses dismantling NPV to make the process more dynamic in viewing cash flows and discount rates for these cash flows.

DYNAMIC NPV

Although the issue of FCF versus CFA is not technically resolved, the following numerical examples consider FCF as the appropriate cash flow for the project. Exhibit 4.1 displays the FCFs for a project over a five-year period. Also, the project's initial investment occurs in period zero, which is consistent with textbook treatments of NPV. This is done for clarity purposes and is not a limitation of the dynamic NPV process.

The FCFs in Exhibit 4.1 appear to be projected into the future with perfect certainty, which is an oversimplification and does not reflect reality. The cash flows are "expected" in the probabilistic sense meaning the actual cash flow that occurs can vary substantially from the values reported in the exhibit, particularly values that are more distant into the future. Given this growing degree of uncertainty or risk that emerges in the future, higher discount rates should be used to discount positive cash flows that are farther into the future. As mentioned earlier in the chapter, despite logical arguments for having a discount rate that changes relative to the risk of the cash flow, textbook treatments of NPV generally use a constant discount

Exhibit 4.1 Calculation of FCFs for a Five-Year Project

	Year 1	Year 2	Year 3	Year 4	Year 5
Revenue (Rev)	$70,000	$70,000	$69,000	$66,000	$65,000
Operating expenses (OE)	53,000	55,000	56,000	53,000	51,000
Rev – OE	17,000	16,000	13,000	13,000	14,000
(Rev – OE)(1 – 0.40)	10,200	9,600	7,800	7,800	8,400
Tax savings on depreciation (40 percent)	2,800	2,800	2,800	2,800	2,800
Change in net working capital	1,000	1,650	400	1,130	835
Change in fixed assets	0	0	0	0	0
Free cash flow (FCF)	$12,000	$10,750	$10,200	$9,470	$10,365

This exhibit shows the calculation of the free cash flow for a five-year project. The depreciable basis of the initial investment is $35,000. Because the firm uses straight-line depreciation with no salvage value, the annual depreciation expense is $7,000. The tax rate is assumed to be 40 percent.

rate similar to how a yield to maturity is applied to a bond's cash flows, even though a yield curve generally demonstrates that interest rates vary by maturity.

Hayes and Garvin (1982) as well as Hodder and Riggs (1985) address issues with cash flows becoming more variable the farther into the future the cash flow occurs and using a different discount rate for cash flows with different risk profiles. Although these issues have an intuitive appeal, resolving them within a textbook presentation of NPV is difficult. However, once analysts view NPV in a more dynamic form, other analyses such as sensitivity analysis and Monte Carlo simulation can be viewed as other means of capturing this dynamic aspect of NPV. Exhibit 4.2 reintroduces the FCFs from Exhibit 4.1 with probability distributions and appropriate discount rates that grow when more risk is evident within the given cash flow.

The next step is to find the annual expected cash inflow for each year. The expected cash inflow is calculated by multiplying each possible observation by its associated probability and then summing the result (e.g., in Year 1, the expected cash flow is $12,000 = 0.50(\$15,000) + 0.50(\$9,000)$). Next, each expected cash flow

Exhibit 4.2   Project Cash Flows and Discount Rates

Initial Cash Outflow	$35,000 Cash Inflow	Probability	Discount Rate (%)
Year 1	$15,000	0.50	8.0
	9,000	0.50	
Year 2	20,000	0.25	8.7
	9,000	0.50	
	5,000	0.25	
Year 3	30,000	0.10	9.3
	11,000	0.15	
	9,000	0.50	
	5,000	0.15	
	3,000	0.10	
Year 4	50,000	0.03	10.2
	14,000	0.07	
	10,000	0.15	
	9,000	0.50	
	5,000	0.15	
	3,000	0.07	
	1,000	0.03	
Year 5	80,000	0.03	12.9
	17,000	0.05	
	12,000	0.07	
	10,000	0.10	
	9,000	0.50	
	5,000	0.10	
	3,000	0.07	
	1,000	0.05	
	500	0.03	

This exhibit shows the probability distributions underlying the FCFs presented in Exhibit 4.1 and appropriate discount rates. The discount rate increases as the uncertainty about the cash flow increases.

Exhibit 4.3 Discounted Cash Flows and NPV

Initial Cash Outflows	$35,000 Expected Cash Inflow	Discount Rate (%)	Discounted Expected Cash Inflow
Year 1	$12,000	8.0	$11,111.11
Year 2	10,750	8.7	9,098.07
Year 3	10,200	9.3	7,811.59
Year 4	9,470	10.2	6,421.31
Year 5	10,365	12.9	5,650.67
		Total cash inflows	40,092.75
		Initial cash outflows	35,000.00
		NPV	$ 5,092.75

This exhibit demonstrates the discounting of expected cash flows to arrive at NPV. The differing discount rate for each cash flow reflects its relative uncertainty.

is discounted by the associated discount rate. Finally, the NPV is calculated as the sum of the discounted cash inflows less the initial investment of $35,000 as shown in Exhibit 4.3.

Now that the dynamic element of NPV is displayed, how does it become hidden from view when NPV is presented in texts? Notice that the expected annual cash inflow is the annual FCF from Exhibit 4.1. Consequently, even though the cash flows are dynamic, only the expected FCF is provided without any discussion of the probability distribution from which the expected FCF is calculated. As stated earlier, this gives the impression that the FCF values are more precise than the cash flows actually are. Further, a single static discount rate is used to perform all of the discounting in the NPV calculation. Using a discount rate of 10.27 percent (or 10.270192 percent to be precise) produces the same NPV even though earlier calculations are overdiscounted and later calculations are underdiscounted as shown in Exhibit 4.4.

The simplistic model shown in Exhibit 4.4 uses only a single static discount rate suggesting that risk is constant over all the cash flows. This single static discount rate is actually a summary value of the different discount rates shown in Exhibit 4.3.

Exhibit 4.4 Discounted Cash Flows and NPV Using a Single Discount Rate

Initial Cash Outflows	$35,000 Expected Cash Inflow	Discount Rate (%)	Discounted Expected Cash Inflow
Year 1	$12,000	10.27	$10,882.36
Year 2	10,750	10.27	8,840.81
Year 3	10,200	10.27	7,607.22
Year 4	9,470	10.27	6,404.98
Year 5	10,365	10.27	6,357.39
		Total cash inflows	40,092.75*
		Initial cash outflows	35,000.00
		NPV	$5,092.75

Similar to Exhibit 4.3, this exhibit demonstrates the discounting of expected cash flows to arrive at NPV. However, the discounting is accomplished at a static discount rate.
*Rounding error of one cent and the actual discount rate used is 10.270192 percent.

The single discount rate simplifies the calculation, but leads many to miss the fact that it is actually a summary figure for a more complex process. The main point of this section is to not to suggest changing the way various finance textbooks present NPV, but to encourage the presentation and understanding of the true level of complexity embodied by NPV analysis. By understanding this element of NPV, other analyses such as real option and scenario analysis become much more transparent and more beneficial as a result.

NPV analysis including the more dynamic version presented here assumes that the firm executes the project for its entire lifespan. Basically, the assumption implies that once accepted, the execution of the project cannot be stopped or reevaluated. Such an assumption is counter to what actually happens within a well-run firm. Projects and personnel should be constantly evaluated and reevaluated through time based on performance. Projects that looked exceptional initially may begin to fail or risky projects may need to be expanded to capture more return. In other words, the decision to start a project is not the last decision made on a project. Management is generally very active regarding future and existing projects.

NPV can be enhanced by using scenario analysis and simulation analysis to demonstrate what can potentially happen with a project through time and possibly provide probabilities of the likelihood of certain events occurring in the future. Most scenario and simulation analyses still have the project executed for its full lifetime without any management interaction. However, these analyses are still valuable because management can start to see where managerial intervention may be critical within the execution of the project. Given that management can know where intervention is valuable via scenario and simulation analysis, the question remains as to how management intervention can enhance the value of the project.

Real option analysis brings in the manager during the lifespan of the project to make critical decisions that may extend or halt the project. By introducing active decisions by management through time, the firm can avoid potentially bad economic situations and exploit potentially good economic situations within the project valuation process. In theory, NPV can be made to recognize these attributes of real option analysis, but making discount rate adjustments to the NPV analysis outside of the real option analysis framework is difficult (Feinstein and Lander, 2002; Arnold and Crack, 2004).

Although NPV has its shortcomings as a means of analyzing capital budgeting projects, all of these other possible analyses are rooted within NPV. Further, without understanding NPV in its more dynamic form, comprehending or using scenario, simulation, and real option analyses will be very difficult. While project valuation starts with the fundamental understanding of NPV, project valuation does not end here.

In the next section, a newer variant of NPV analysis is introduced that assesses economic gains relative to cost in a different manner. This metric, called economic value added (EVA), uses a structure for the project's relevant cash flow that differs from FCF and CFA.

ECONOMIC VALUE ADDED

In the 1990s, a new variant of cash flow emerged called EVA (O'Hanlon and Peasnell, 1998). Although EVA has some similarities with NPV, EVA is a decidedly different form of analysis that can be used for project valuation (like NPV) and as a performance measurement for managerial goals and pay bonuses (unlike NPV). EVA, created by Stern Steward & Company, is calculated as:

$$EVA = NOPAT - cK \qquad (4.15)$$

where NOPAT = Net operating profit after taxes = (Revenues – Operating expenses – Depreciation)(1 – Tax rate); c = the cost of capital; and K = operating capital employed. EVA shares some FCF characteristics in that operating profits are compared to investment, but it is a decidedly different calculation. FCF components, such as a change in net working capital and a change in fixed assets, become part of the operating capital employed and are adjusted by the cost of capital, which would also account for the financing employed.

For example, let the cost of capital be 10 percent and calculate the EVA for Year 1 in Exhibit 4.1. The capital employed is $36,000 ($35,000 initial cost plus the additional net working capital of $1,000), and NOPAT is $6,000 [($70,000 – $53,000 – $7,000)(1 – 0.40)]. The EVA is $2,400 ($6,000 – 0.10($36,000)) compared to an FCF of $12,000.

Continuing this example, the capital employed would increase by the change in net working capital and decrease by the previous period's depreciation (i.e., the value of the fixed assets employed is measured net of accumulated depreciation) with the difference between EVA and the FCF calculations still being relatively far apart.

Related to EVA, market value added (MVA) is found by summing discounted EVA (discounted by the cost of capital, "c," usually A-TWACC from Equation 4.12) through time. Some analysts believe that MVA is reflected in stock price as the total value added from economically profitable operations. Mathematically, MVA could be considered an NPV calculation using the cost of capital as the discount rate and EVA as the project cash flow calculation. However, as stated earlier in the chapter, NPV does not necessarily require the cost of capital to be a project's discount rate unless the project has risk that is similar to the average risk of the firm. When the project's risk profile deviates from the risk profile of the firm, a risk-adjusted discount rate other than the cost of capital is appropriate. However, within the EVA/MVA metric, the only discount rate available is the cost of capital, creating a possible limitation to using EVA/MVA as a project valuation method.

Leaving the discount rate issue aside, EVA and MVA generally require some alterations from traditional accounting methods to focus on value creating assets. This requirement may make EVA even more distinct from FCF and CFA. Following Young and O'Byrne (2001), Exhibit 4.5 displays some of the common accounting alterations that are necessary.

Although the authors state that not all of these adjustments are necessary, making the adjustments is no small task. The overall philosophy is to focus the EVA calculation on the contribution of value creating assets relative to the capital employed. Many of the adjustments above have to do with determining the correct capital charge (cK in Equation 4.15) and undoing many practices that result in tax savings given that tax is not part of the EVA metric.

Again, following Young and O'Byrne (2001), these adjustments can become very difficult when the capital employed has to be divided among divisions that use the same resources (i.e., the case when each division is responsible for its own

Exhibit 4.5 Accounting Adjusted for Implementing EVA/MVA

- Use "successful efforts accounting" (i.e., expense any assets that do not contribute to value such as expensing research and development costs).
- Use straight-line methods instead of amortization methods to depreciate value.
- Discount future cash costs (e.g., deferred tax expense) to current value.
- Eliminate pooling of interest accounting and incorporate off–balance sheet debt and stock options as expenses.
- Eliminate accruals for bad debt and warranties.
- Eliminate noncash charges such as goodwill and deferred tax expenses.
- Capitalize restructuring and other special charges excluding nonoperating income and assets.

This exhibit lists items that require modification from standard accounting entries to arrive at data necessary for calculating EVA and MVA.

individual EVA management within a value-based management system). Possible solutions exist where each division or unit is allotted a percentage of a given resource as part of the capital employed. However, such distinctions are difficult to make and an under- (over)-assessment of capital employed biases the divisional EVA measure upward (downward). Although the task is possible, it is certainly difficult finding an equitable solution.

Because EVA can be employed in a value-based management system where managerial goals and bonuses are assessed through the EVA metric, the valuation component through MVA can become difficult to assess. In theory, EVA can be split among managers and divisions within the firm and reconstituted for the overall firm or project to eventually generate the MVA for the overall firm or project. Agency issues exist because managers have an incentive to manipulate EVA to their advantage, which can lead to problems in the overall assessment of the firm or project. Because the adjustments needed to assess the capital employed are partially open to interpretation, the agency problem is of genuine concern.

Although this chapter focuses on valuation, when dealing with EVA, disentangling the value-based management component is impossible. In fact, much of the debate surrounding EVA can be viewed as a trade-off between the benefits of a value-based management system versus the benefit of finding a true valuation for a firm or project.

Baker, Deo, and Mukherjee (2009) review the extensive EVA literature based on three issues: computational, measurement, and effectiveness. Exhibit 4.6 displays these issues. When considering the computational issues, the consensus view is that the book value issue can be mitigated within a large capital base. However, the issue with differing depreciation schedules distorting EVA (because depreciation is part of the operating income generated and part of the capital employed) is important but may be mitigated by using MVA. The third issue concerning the complexity of the adjustments is an issue that will not go away. Ultimately, decision makers will have to consider the trade-off between EVA's complexity in computation and the potential gains from using EVA.

When considering the measurement issues, the consensus view is that EVA is a short-term measure. However, using MVA may alleviate this problem. Although

Exhibit 4.6   EVA Issues: Computational, Measurement, and Effectiveness

Computational Issues

- The use of book values.
- The effect of depreciation schedules not using straight-line.
- Complexity of adjustments.

Measurement Issues

- EVA is not different from cash flow.
- EVA is not different from residual income.
- EVA is only a short-term measure.
- EVA is only a financial measure.

Effectiveness Issues

- EVA is unsuitable for some firms.
- EVA is an absolute dollar measure and not a relative measure.
- Residual cash flow performs better than EVA.
- EVA does not explain the stock price.

This exhibit lists issues found in the literature about the calculation and interpretation of EVA.

the other issues also appear to be true, they do not represent major obstacles relative to EVA's benefits.

When considering effectiveness, the issues that EVA is an absolute measure and is not correlated with stock price appear to be valid. For the latter issue, MVA may offer a solution. However, currently no evidence shows that MVA is correlated with stock price or that MVA is correlated with EVA.

Taken as a whole, EVA's proponents tend to emphasize the managerial benefits of the measure. However, there is a lack of substantive evidence that EVA or MVA is an effective project or firm valuation metric. Although the theory that value is created when operating income exceeds the cost of capital employed is appealing, NPV with its risk-adjusted discount rate appears to have more substance in the realm of project valuation.

SUMMARY AND CONCLUSIONS

Discounted cash flow methods for project evaluation tend to perform the best relative to other methods (Kaplan and Ruback, 1996), of which NPV and IRR are the most popular, especially in the United States. This chapter explores the components of NPV—cash flows and the discount rate—in two different ways. First, the calculation of cash flow generated two possible versions that differ by the tax savings from interest on debt, FCF and CFA. Given a particular version of cash flow, the associated discount rate also differs when the project risk profile is similar to the average risk of the firm, P-TWACC versus A-TWACC. Similarly, when analysts need to find a risk-adjusted rate for projects that differ in risk when compared to the firm's risk profile, an all-equity version of a risk-adjusted rate or a levered version of a risk-adjusted rate can be used dependent on the cash flow calculation. Although the issues are not completely resolved, FCF with a tax-adjusted discount rate (or tax-adjusted levered version of a risk-adjusted rate) tend to be used in practice.

The second exploration of NPV expands a project's expected cash flows into probability distributions with different risk-adjusted discount rates for each cash flow through time. This dynamic version of NPV allows the riskiness of the cash flows to be more evident than what is available in the traditional textbook version of NPV. By recombining the cash flow distributions into expected cash flows and solving for a constant discount rate, the textbook version of NPV is re-assembled. However, by working through the dynamic NPV, the basis for other analyses such as scenario, sensitivity, and real option analyses becomes apparent.

The final section of the chapter evaluates a variant of NPV called EVA. EVA uses a definition of cash flow that is different from FCF and CFA. The cost portion of the cash flow relies on the cost of capital for assets that generate NOPAT. These assets are not directly available from accounting statements making various accounting adjustments necessary for calculating EVA. Empirically, EVA and MVA do not appear to perform well as a project valuation method. However, EVA has a benefit as a short-term metric for evaluating managers in a value-based management system. NPV analysis cannot provide a similar metric.

DISCUSSION QUESTIONS

1. Assuming that the book value of equity and debt are the same as their market values ($V = E + D$) in Equations 4.11 through 4.14, demonstrate that FCF / (1 + A-TWACC) equals CFA / (1 + P-TWACC).

2. Why is using CFA with A-TWACC considered double counting the tax benefit of debt?

3. Why is the constant discount rate used in the textbook version of NPV similar to the yield to maturity measure for a bond?

4. Discuss the issue of an FCF being an all-equity version of CFA regarding the scale of the project when debt is unavailable for funding a project.

5. If debt funding is unavailable for a project, is there a difference between CFA and FCF and between P-TWACC and A-TWACC?

6. How do different depreciation schedules (accelerated versus straight-line) affect EVA?

REFERENCES

Ang, James S., and Wilbur G. Lewellen, 1982. "Risk Adjustment in Capital Investment Project Evaluations." *Financial Management* 11:2, 5–14.

Arditti, Fred D., and Haim Levy. 1977. "The Weighted Average Cost of Capital as a Cutoff Rate: A Critical Analysis of the Classical Textbook Weighted Average." *Financial Management* 6:3, 24–34.

Arnold, Tom, and Timothy F. Crack. 2004. "Real Option Valuation Using NPV." Available at http://ssrn.com/abstarct=644081.

Baker, H. Kent, Prakash Deo, and Tarun Mukherjee. 2009. "EVA Revisited." *Journal of Financial Education* 35:Fall, 1–22.

Ben-Horam, Moshe. 1979. "The Weighted Average Cost of Capital as a Cutoff Rate." *Financial Management* 8:2, 18–21.

Boudreaux, Kenneth J., and Hugh W. Long. 1979. "The Weighted Average Cost of Capital as a Cutoff Rate: A Further Analysis." *Financial Management* 8:2, 7-14.

Brigham, Eugene F., and Michael C. Ehrhardt. 2011. *Financial Management: Theory and Practice*. Mason, OH: South-Western Cengage Learning.

Chambers, Donald R., Robert S. Harris, and John J. Pringle. 1982. "Treatment of Financing Mix in Analyzing Investment Opportunities." *Financial Management* 11:2, 24–41.

Damodaran, Aswath. 1994. *Damodaran on Valuation, Security Analysis for Investment and Corporate Finance*. New York: John Wiley & Sons.

Ezzell, John R., and R. Burr Porter. 1979. "Correct Specification of the Cost of Capital and Net Present Value." *Financial Management* 8:2, 15–17.

Feinstein, Stephen P., and Diane M. Lander. 2002. "A Better Understanding of Why NPV Undervalues Managerial Flexibility." *Engineering Economist* 47:4, 418–435.

Fernandez, Pablo. 2007. "Company Valuation Methods: The Most Common Errors in Valuations." Available at http://ssrn.com/abstract=274973.

Gahlon, James M., and James M. Gentry. 1982. "On the Relationship between Systematic Risk and the Degrees of Operating and Financial Leverage." *Financial Management* 11:2, 15–23.

Graham, John R., and Campbell R. Harvey. 2001. "The Theory and Practice of Corporate Finance: Evidence from the Field." *Journal of Financial Economics* 60:2–3, 187–243.

Graham, John R., Scott Smart, and William Megginson. 2010. *Corporate Finance*. Mason, OH: South-Western Cengage Learning.

Hamada, Robert S. 1972. "The Effect of the Firm's Capital Structure on the Systematic Risk of Common Stocks." *Journal of Finance* 27:2, 435–452.

Harris, Robert S., and John J. Pringle. 1985. "Risk-Adjusted Discount Rates—Extensions from the Average Risk Case." *Journal of Financial Research* 8:3, 237–244.

Hayes, Robert H., and David A. Garvin. 1982. "Managing as If Tomorrow Mattered." *Harvard Business Review* 60:3, 71–79.

Hodder, James E., and Henry E. Riggs. 1985. "Pitfalls in Evaluating Risky Projects." *Harvard Business Review* 63:1, 128–135.

Inselbag, Isik, and Howard Kaufold. 1997. "Two DCF Approaches for Valuing Companies under Alternative Financing Strategies (and How to Choose between Them)." *Journal of Applied Corporate Finance* 10:1, 114–122.

Jensen, Michael C. 1986. "Agency Cost of Free Cash Flow, Corporate Finance, and Takeovers." *American Economic Review* 76:2, 323–329.

Kaplan, Steven N., and Richard S. Ruback. 1996. "The Market of Cash Flow Forecasts: Discounted Cash Flow vs. the Method of 'Comparables'." *Journal of Applied Finance* 8:4, 45–60.

Luehrman, Timothy A. 1997. "Using APV: A Better Tool for Valuing Operations." *Harvard Business Review* 75:3, 145–154.

Miles, James A., and John R. Ezzell. 1985. "Reformulating Tax Shield Valuation: A Note." *Journal of Finance* 40:5, 1485–1492.

Modigliani, Franco, and Merton H. Miller. 1958. "The Cost of Capital, Corporate Finance and the Theory of Investment." *American Economic Review* 48:3, 261–297.

Myers, Stewart C. 1974. "Interactions of Corporate Financing and Investment Decisions— Implications for Capital Budgeting." *Journal of Finance* 29:1, 1–25.

O'Hanlon, John, and Ken Peasnell. 1998. "Wall Street's Contribution to Management Accounting: The Stern Stewart EVA Financial Management System." *Management Accounting Research* 9:4, 421–444.

Petty, J. William, and John T. Rose. 2009. "Free Cash Flow, the Cash Flow Identity, and the Accounting Statement of Cash Flows." Journal of Financial Education 35:Fall, 41–55.

Ross, Stephen, Randolph Westerfield, and Bradford Jordan. 2009. *Fundamentals of Corporate Finance*. Boston: McGraw-Hill Irwin.

Ruback, Richard S. 1986. "Calculating the Market Value of Riskless Cash Flows." *Journal of Financial Economics* 15:3, 323–339.

Ruback, Richard S. 2002. "Capital Cash Flows: A Simple Approach to Valuing Risky Cash Flows." *Financial Management* 31:2, 85–103.

Ryan, Patricia, and Glenn Ryan. 2002. "Capital Budgeting Practices of the Fortune 1000: How Have Things Changed?" *Journal of Business and Management* 8:4, 355–364.

Shapiro, Alan C. 1979. "In Defense of the Traditional Weighted Average Cost of Capital as a Cutoff Rate." *Financial Management* 8:2, 22–23.

Sharpe, William F. 1964. "Capital Asset Prices: A Theory of Market Equilibrium Under Conditions of Risk." *Journal of Finance* 19:3, 452–442.

Young, S. David, and Stephen F. O'Byrne. 2001. *EVA and Value-Based Management—A Practical Guide to Implementation*. New York: McGraw-Hill.

ABOUT THE AUTHORS

Tom Arnold, CFA, is an Associate Professor of Finance and the F. Carlyle Tiller Chair in Business at the Robins School of Business, University of Richmond. Professor Arnold has more than 40 publications appearing in such journals as the *Journal of Finance, Journal of Business, Financial Analysts Journal, Journal of Futures Markets, Journal of Applied Finance*, and *Journal of Financial Education*. His work has been cited in the *Economist, Wall Street Journal, New York Times*, and other non-U.S. news outlets. Professor Arnold's specialties include derivative securities, real option valuation, market microstructure, corporate valuation, and finance pedagogy. He received a Ph.D. from the Terry College of Business at the University of Georgia.

Terry Nixon is an Associate Professor of Finance at the Farmer School of Business at Miami University. During his career, Professor Nixon has been recognized many times for his teaching, which focuses on corporate finance. Professor Nixon has published articles in such journals as the *Financial Review, Research in International Business and Finance, Journal of Applied Finance, Journal of Financial Education, Applied Financial Economics, Journal of Real Estate Finance and Economics*, and the *Review of Quantitative Finance and Accounting*. His research interests include corporate restructuring and agency theory. Professor Nixon received a Ph.D. from the University of South Carolina.

CHAPTER 5

Alternative Methods of Evaluating Capital Investments

TOM ARNOLD
F. Carlyle Tiller Chair in Business, University of Richmond

TERRY NIXON
Associate Professor of Finance, Miami University

INTRODUCTION

The previous chapter examined net present value (NPV) and economic value added (EVA) in detail, but these are not the only two forms of project evaluation. Although internal rate of return (IRR) is a special case of NPV in which IRR is the discount rate that sets the NPV to zero, this chapter presents a more thorough discussion of IRR. In particular, cases where the IRR and NPV provide divergent project recommendations receive attention due to an extensive literature on this topic.

This chapter also examines another metric called the payback period (PB). PB is relatively easy to calculate because it is simply the amount of time needed to recover a project's initial investment. This is similar to media advertising when the savings generated by a product "pays for itself" within a set period of time. Two other variants of PB—the discounted payback period (DPB) and the project balance method (PBL)—are also analyzed, but neither metric captures the simplicity of PB. Despite having no discounting element in the calculation of PB, the lack of sophistication does not appear to detract from its usage.

The chapter has the following organization. It begins with a discussion of an agency problem between shareholders and managers. Although many different types of agency are present in this context, this particular version of the agency problem focuses on management's desire to perform well in the short-term while possibly sacrificing longer-term performance. Based on this agency issue, PB is then introduced as a possible by-product of the issue. To complete the discourse on PB, two other variants, the DPB and PBL, are examined, as well.

The chapter then centers on discussing the IRR followed by the profitability index (PI). First, the effects of cash flow timing and scale on IRR are presented to provide some context in which NPV and IRR can disagree between two mutually exclusive projects. The proposed solutions in the literature for when IRR and NPV disagree are discussed. Next, the issue of multiple IRRs being present within a project's cash flows is examined fully with some of the solutions provided by the literature on the subject. The chapter concludes after a discussion of PI and how it relates to NPV and IRR.

AN AGENCY PROBLEM BETWEEN MANAGERS AND SHAREHOLDERS

Shareholders (the principal) hire management (the agent) to operate a firm in a manner that accrues, as much as possible, all of the benefits to the shareholders. However, management can choose to operate the firm in a manner that benefits management at the expense of its shareholders. This is the crux of a typical principal-agent conflict between the owner/shareholder and the manager. For this chapter, the principal-agent conflict revolves around managers being short-term–result oriented (Narayanan, 1985). Statman (1982) attributes this issue to shareholders being risk-neutral and managers being risk-averse. In essence, managers are more focused on meeting short-term liquidity goals than on considering longer-term projects that may add more value to the firm. Consequently, managers are motivated to meet near-term performance goals in order to maintain their jobs. Because managers are risk-averse, they have no incentive to sacrifice short-term success for longer-term, more profitable projects.

The PB calculation tends to be short-term oriented because a project is only acceptable if the cash inflows recover a project's initial cost (cash outflows) within a set period of time. Following the logic of the principal-agent conflict just described, managers have an incentive to follow project decision criteria that favor short-term performance goals such as expedient cost recovery. Empirically, Statman and Sepe (1984) find no connection between management incentive plans and using PB. Later studies by Pike (1985) and Chen and Clark (1994) find a connection between manager compensation and the use of PB.

However, the principal-agent conflict may not be the lone reason for using PB over more sophisticated techniques. Myers (1977) discusses how the use of more debt creates short-term liquidity needs that are important to both shareholders and managers. He also notes that managers may dismiss better projects that cannot produce the needed liquidity for this reason. Further, capital budgeting procedures can vary widely depending on industry (Block, 2005).

The extant literature stresses that PB has appeal because it focuses on liquidity (Weingartner, 1969), is easily understood both inside and outside of the firm (Longmore, 1989; Lefley, 1996), and is less costly to use than discounted methods (Binder and Chaput, 1996). Consequently, reasons other than a principal-agent conflict are plausible. Following Weingartner, PB is stable and managers initially use it to create a cycle in which projects that return cash flow quickly generate momentum that eventually leads to longer-term bigger risk types of projects being accepted in the future. This sort of logic is consistent with the findings of Block (1997) that smaller firms tend to use PB for project evaluation because cash is very limited at this developmental stage of the firm.

According to Binder and Chaput (1996), firms recognize that some projects require sophisticated analysis whereas others do not. Because data can be difficult or expensive to obtain (Brigham, 1975) and near-term projections are the most certain of projected cash flows, firms perform a cost-benefit analysis regarding how much effort evaluating a project requires. Particularly with low-risk or low-cost projects, PB is a good metric that exploits near-term cash flows. Thus, managers use PB for this reason.

Other variants of the PB measure exist and are discussed in the next section along with a more expansive description of how PB is calculated. PB has a firm place within the capital budgeting process and many firms use PB because of the desire for liquidity and ease of communication or because more sophisticated techniques are unwarranted. However, other firms often use PB to supplement more sophisticated discounted cash flow (DCF) techniques (Lefley, 1996).

THE PAYBACK PERIOD AND ITS VARIATIONS

PB is the amount of time needed for a project's cash inflows to equal its cash outflows on a nondiscounted basis. Cash flows are not all assumed to occur at year end as in methods such as NPV and IRR, but are instead assumed to be received proportionately over the course of the year. Excess cash outflows are not considered within the metric and generally no single convenient formula is available for calculating PB. Although PB is not conceptually difficult, many do become frustrated with any metric that lacks a set formula. Putting such issues aside, PB is generally easy to calculate, but will often require linear interpolation. A simple example illustrates this point.

Suppose a project requires $1,000,000 in initial cost and then produces four annual cash inflows of $300,000 over the next four years. After three years, the firm has recovered $900,000 ($300,000 x 3) of the initial cost as a result of the accumulated cash inflows. Only $100,000 of additional inflows is necessary to completely recover the initial cost. However, more than $100,000 of cash inflows is available in the fourth year. Here is where linear interpolation is necessary due to the assumption of proportionate cash flows. Only $100,000 of the $300,000 in cash inflow is needed from year four. Assume that the cash flow is evenly distributed throughout the fourth year making only one-third (i.e., $100,000 / $300,000) of the fourth year cash flow necessary to completely recover the initial cost of the project. Consequently, the payback period is 3.33 years.

When taking a critical look at the PB method, three particular issues emerge. First, the remaining $200,000 in cash inflow from the fourth year is still important in considering the viability of the project, but is ignored when using the PB method. To emphasize this point using an extreme example, consider whether the PB changes if a $5 million cash inflow became available in the fifth year of the project. PB still remains 3.33 years as cash flows occurring after the recovery of cost are of no consequence in the PB calculation and do not affect the acceptability of the project when using this criterion even though it represents an amount of money substantially exceeding the money invested in the project. Second, the calculation of PB does not consider the time value of money. This may not matter very much with short-term, less risky projects, but not discounting cash flows is counter-intuitive relative to techniques such as NPV and IRR. Third, the decision rule for PB is subjective. A positive NPV (assuming certainty) indicates an acceptable project. In the example, the payback period is shown to be 3.33 years, but does this indicate an acceptable project? The answer is "it depends." Each firm must set a cutoff period for project acceptability (i.e., a maximum payback). This cutoff is a choice on the part of decision makers who may arrive at this cutoff period as a result of experience rather than any economic or financial underpinning. A cutoff of 3 years makes this project unacceptable, whereas a 4-year cutoff makes this an acceptable project. Methods to augment PB to make it more like an NPV criterion exist. Some evidence is available showing that the selection of the cutoff period is not necessarily arbitrary (Yard, 2000).

Leaving the cutoff period and extraneous cash flow issues aside, two variant methods of PB have emerged over time: the discounted payback period (DPB) and the project balance method (PBL). The DPB method, which is credited to Rappaport (1965), is similar to PB only because the calculations consider cost recovery through time. Unlike PB, DPB discounts all cash flows. Just as in PB, DPB uses the same method to determine the time needed to recover costs. In other words, DPB is the PB methodology applied to DCFs.

Suppose a project has an initial cost of $800,000 and three annual cash inflows are received beginning next year: $330,000, $363,000, and $399,300, respectively. Assuming a 10 percent annual discount rate, discount each cash inflow as follows:

$$\text{Year 1: } \$330,000/(1.10)^1 = \$300,000$$
$$\text{Year 2: } \$363,000/(1.10)^2 = \$300,000$$
$$\text{Year 3: } \$399,300/(1.10)^3 = \$300,000$$

The cost is recovered based on these DCFs at some point in time between the second and third year. The first two years of discounted cash inflows recover $600,000 of the $800,000 cost. Consequently, only $200,000 of the $300,000 (or $0.67 = \$200,000/\$300,000$) in discounted cash inflow in the third year is necessary to completely recover the cost. Applying linear interpolation, DPB is 2.67 years.

Although an adjustment to PB, DPB still does not consider all of the cash flows because the calculation only considers cost recovery. Notice, just as with PB, an additional $5 million cash inflow following the third year does not change DPB from being equal to 2.67 years.

Placing DPB within the context of NPV and IRR is straightforward. One can define DPB as the amount of time needed for a project to have an NPV of zero. Further, if the DPB is equal to the length of the project, the project has an NPV of zero and the discount rate is equal to the IRR.

Given that the DPB is more rigorous than PB but similar in complexity to calculating the NPV, seeing the benefit in calculating DPB is difficult when an NPV calculation includes all cash flows and provides a better analysis. Relative to the PB calculation, DPB accounts for the time value of money (a slight improvement) but the metric still does not account for all cash flows and has a subjective decision rule. Although DPB tends to be infrequently used in practice (Graham and Harvey, 2001; Ryan and Ryan, 2002), this metric provides a logical connection to NPV and IRR that has some pedagogic value.

Like DPB, PBL also has a PB element in that PBL measures the length of time for cost recovery in a cash budgeting manner (Remer and Nieto, 1995b; Jacobs, 2007). Using the cash flows from the DPB example: initial cost of $800,000 followed by annual cash inflows of $330,000, $363,000, and $399,300, respectively, allow the initial cost to be carried with interest (usually the discount rate associated with the project, 10 percent annually in this example) until the cost is repaid by future cash inflows. After one year, the cost is now $ 880,000 (=$800,000(1.10)) and $330,000 of cash inflow reduces the cost to $550,000 (=$880,000 − $330,000). One year later, the cost with interest is $605,000 (=$550,000(1.10)) and $363,000 of cash inflow reduces the cost to $242,000 (=$605,000 − $363,000). In the third year, the cost with interest is $266,200 (=$242,000(1.10)) and is completely recovered by the $399,300 cash inflow for that year. Using interpolation, the cost recovery takes 2.67 years (exactly equal to DPB). However, an inconsistency exists in that the cost accrues a full year of interest while potentially being paid off before the end of the year. Consequently, the interpolated value is biased upward and given the equivalence to DPB, potentially, DPB is also biased for a similar reason (i.e., the DCF is discounted on an annual basis, while the interpolated value assumes cost recovery earlier in the given year making the discounted cash flow too small).

Given the added complexity of DPB and PBL relative to PB, seeing why firms use PB solely or use PB to supplement an NPV/IRR analysis is not difficult. In the next section, the IRR is developed more fully than in Chapter 4. The IRR is connected to DPB and PBL by being the discount rate that sets both of these measures equal to the project's life and is considered a rate of return measure (Remer and Nieto, 1995a) rather than a duration measure such as PB, DPB, and PBL or a measure of added value such as NPV and EVA.

IRR: SCALE AND TIMING EFFECTS

Chapter 4 described IRR as the actual return generated by the project because IRR is the discount rate that sets NPV to zero. For example, if a 10 percent discount rate is applied to a project with an initial cost followed by a series of cash inflows to produce an NPV > 0, IRR will be some value greater than 10 percent, say, 15 percent. However, this does not mean the project produces a return that is five percentage points greater than the appropriate risk-adjusted discount rate (McDaniel, McCarty, and Jessell, 1988). Although the working definition used in Chapter 4 is imprecise, many analysts and managers use this definition for IRR.

The 15 percent IRR is a compounded rate that implicitly assumes $100 today can become $115 one year into the future because the cash flow can be invested at 15 percent (i.e., earn the IRR), which is generally not the case. Phalippou (2008) encounters this issue when considering the returns on a private equity investment. In the private equity case, the actual profit generates a return much different from IRR because of this inability to have intermediate cash flows appreciate at the IRR until the end of the project or investment.

The fault of IRR not being the actual return on the project is a problem in interpreting IRR and not a fault in calculating IRR. However, because of the inability to reinvest intermediate cash flows at the IRR, the issue is known as the "reinvestment rate problem." Keane (1979) and Keef and Roush (2001) are adamant about the issue of IRR not specifying a reinvestment rate in its calculation and that the reinvestment rate problem is an issue of interpretation, not calculation. Consequently, the appropriate interpretation of the reinvestment rate problem is that the attempts to resolve the issue are meant to make IRR a better metric rather than considering IRR to be incorrect. Before approaching the reinvestment rate issue, understanding a different issue about IRR regarding the timing of cash flows within a project and about the scale of the project is important.

Suppose a project has an initial cost of $10,000 and then produces four annual cash inflows of $3,500 beginning next year for four years. The project's IRR is 14.963 percent annually. Change the annual cash inflows for the project to $3,000, $3,000, $3,000, and $5,000, and IRR decreases to 13.664 percent as the cash flows become larger toward the end of the project (relative to the initial case). In a similar manner, change the annual cash inflows to $5,000, $3,000, $3,000, and $3,000, and IRR increases to 16.657 percent as the cash flows become larger toward the beginning of the project (relative to the initial case). Notice that the "timing" of the cash inflows influences IRR even though, nominally, the total cash inflow has not changed. When NPV and IRR disagree on the selection of the better of two projects (note: IRR selects based on the higher IRR and NPV selects based on the higher NPV > 0), the "timing" issue is considered one of the reasons this occurs.

Suppose another project has an initial cost of $5,000 and then produces annual cash inflows of $1,800 beginning next year for four years. The project's IRR is 16.367 percent, which is higher than the IRR of 14.963 percent from the initial project just discussed. However, using a 10 percent discount rate to calculate NPV, the smaller project has an NPV of $705.76 while the larger project has an NPV of $1,094.53, implying that the larger project is better because it adds more value to the firm. The reason for the confounding result is because the two projects differ in scale. Generally, a firm cannot accept two versions of the smaller project to create a combined project that is better than the larger project. How the firm resolves its selection of projects is not the subject of this chapter, but this simple example illustrates that one should not ignore NPV when considering IRR.

In fact, the "timing and scale" issues of IRR are only issues because of situations when IRR is inconsistent with NPV. Ironically, survey-based studies such as Graham and Harvey (2001) and Ryan and Ryan (2002) find practitioners responding to their surveys generally prefer IRR because it is a rate of return measure. By contrast, academics tend to prefer NPV. In fact, a large portion of the literature deals with schemes for resolving this inconsistency between IRR and NPV including the reinvestment rate problem. Setting the stage for where NPV and IRR clash routinely involves considering two mutually exclusive projects.

NPV AND IRR: MUTUALLY EXCLUSIVE PROJECTS

Projects are mutually exclusive when one project "precludes" the selection of the other project. In other words, both projects cannot exist at once for various reasons (e.g. both products appeal to the same market and are not complementary). Suppose Project A has an initial cost of $10,000 and produces annual cash inflows of $3,500 beginning next year for the next four years. From the previous section, Project A's IRR is known to be 14.963 percent. A second project, Project B, also has an initial cost of $10,000 with four annual cash inflows beginning next year: $4,000, $1,000, $2,000, and $7,500, respectively. Project B's IRR is 14.660 percent and is below Project A's IRR, making Project A the dominant project. However, if the discount rate for the two projects is 9 percent (note: the discount rates do not necessarily need to be the same), Project A's NPV is $1,339.02 and Project B's NPV is $1,368.96, making Project B the superior project, contrary to the IRR metric by which Project A is the dominant project.

Because selecting a project's discount rate involves various issues as discussed in Chapter 4, sensitivity analysis may be in order. Changing the discount rate to 10 percent, Project A's NPV becomes $1,094.53 while Project B's NPV becomes $1,088.04. Now, Project A is the dominant project based on IRR and NPV. Somehow, between the 9 percent and 10 percent discount rate, NPV switched to favor Project A. In fact, at a discount rate of 9.817 percent, both projects have the same NPV. This rate is known as Fisher's rate of return (FROR) (Alchian, 1955; Hirshleifer, 1958; Dudley, 1972; Hajdasinski, 1997a), named after Irving Fisher (1930).

Assuming the FROR is below the IRRs of the two projects, whenever the discount rate is above the FROR, IRR and NPV agree as to which project is the dominant project. If the FROR is above the IRRs of the two projects (i.e., a rate when the two projects have equal NPVs < 0), IRR and NPV agree as to which project is the dominant project. The key to this insight is finding the FROR.

Also attributed to Fisher (1930) is a procedure for finding the FROR by taking the difference between the two sets of cash flows, say Project A's cash flows less Project B's cash flows, and then finding the IRR for the differences between the cash flows:

Year 0: (−$10,000 less − $10,000) = $0
Year 1: ($3,500 less $4,000) = −$500
Year 2: ($3,500 less $1,000) = $2,500
Year 3: ($3,500 less $2,000) = $1,500
Year 4: ($3,500 less $7,500) = −$4,000

IRR for these "differenced" cash flows is 9.817 percent, that is, the FROR.

Although finding the FROR is an exercise that allows identifying a conflict between IRR and NPV, it does not necessarily provide a policy or metric for resolving the conflict other than the insight that choosing the discount rate is critical in making a decision. However, if the FROR value is a relatively low value and a discount rate is elusive, choosing the project with the higher IRR appears to be a pragmatic solution that is consistent with NPV. Further, if the FROR results in a negative NPV for both projects (i.e., the FROR is greater than both project IRRs), choosing the project with the higher IRR is again the pragmatic and correct solution. Ultimately, the benefit of the IRR metric in the case of a project with an initial cash outflow followed by cash inflows is that an IRR can always be calculated while an NPV is dependent upon an appropriate risk-adjusted discount rate (RADR). In this vein of logic, the FROR becomes beneficial to the decision maker as a means of following the selection criteria of NPV while not actually calculating NPV. This discussion depends upon the two projects' IRRs being sufficiently high to consider them as viable projects.

What still needs to be addressed is the reinvestment rate problem and the potential possibility of multiple IRRs, because cash flows switch from being inflows to outflows more than once through time instead of an initial outflow (costs) followed only by inflows (benefits). Both of these issues are the subject of the next section.

REINVESTMENT RATES AND MULTIPLE IRRs

The reinvestment rate problem, as described before, arises from the inability to invest intermediate cash flows at the IRR until the end of the project. Although NPV also suffers from this problem, the resolution of the reinvestment issue within an NPV analysis is that the company can reinvest intermediate cash flows in future projects of similar risk. In other words, within an NPV analysis assuming future projects of similar risk, the possibility exists of reinvesting intermediate cash flows at the same risk-adjusted rate throughout a given project's life (Hartley, 1990).

Whether companies actually follow or maintain such a policy is questionable. Further, using a single rate for all cash flows no matter when the cash flows occur in the future is an issue within an NPV analysis as discussed in Chapter 4. Leaving such issues aside, a similar claim of the firm maintaining a constant reinvestment rate cannot be made with an IRR analysis. Future projects having the same IRR as current projects is an unlikely scenario. Such a scenario cannot be the by-product of company policy to maintain a particular debt and equity mix yielding a stable NPV discount rate. A particular debt and equity mix could maintain a specific weighted average cost of capital (WACC), which analysts could use as the RADR within an NPV analysis.

As stated earlier, IRR is the discount rate that sets NPV to zero, but it cannot be precisely interpreted as the actual return generated by the project. To illustrate the issue, use one of the projects from the previous section: initial cost of $10,000 followed by four annual cash inflows of $3,500 beginning next year. The project's IRR is 14.963 percent, but assuming the firm can reinvest intermediate cash flows at 10 percent annually, what is the actual return on the project? The four cash inflows at the end of the project are worth $16,243.50 (=$3,500.00((1.10)^4 − 1)/0.10), making the annual return on the project 12.894 percent (=(($16,243.50/$10,000.00)^{0.25} − 1). Notice that the project's actual return is lower than the IRR. If the reinvestment rate were 14.963 percent (i.e., equal to the IRR) instead of 10 percent, the actual return would be equal to the IRR.

Assuming the above discussion convinces a decision maker to consider reinvestment rates (Solomon, 1956; Renshaw, 1957; Teichroew, Robichek, and Montalbano, 1965a, 1965b; Dudley, 1972; Dorfman, 1981), Marglin (1963) offers the following question: What reinvestment rate should be used? Solomon suggests an opportunity cost expressed as a rate for the reinvestment rate and concludes that the reinvestment rate should be the firm's cost of capital. The only cost to be considered is the initial cost and all the following cash flows accrue interest at the cost of capital until the project ends. The terminal value of all the cash flows with interest is then compared to the initial cost to find a holding period return that is compared to a hurdle rate. This process is exactly what is performed previously, assuming that 10 percent is the cost of capital (reinvestment rate) to find the project return of 12.894 percent and is a variant of what Lin (1976) calls the modified internal rate of return (MIRR).

MIRR discounts all costs to the present (no assumption of only using the initial cost), appreciates all inflows to the end of the project, and then finds a holding period return. However, Lin (1976) does not specify which rates should apply for discounting and compounding. Combining the work of McDaniel et al. (1988), Shull (1992, 1994), and Hajdasinski (1997b), the appreciation rate and discount rate become the cost of capital. To illustrate the difference from Solomon's (1956) procedure, change the cash flows in the project to an initial cost of $10,000 and a second cost of $500 in the first year of the project. The four annual cash inflows become $4,000, $3,500, $3,500, and $3,500, respectively. Assuming a cost of capital of 10 percent, the discounted costs or investment base becomes $10,454.55.

$$\$10,454.55 = \$10,000.00 + \$500.00/(1.10)^1$$

The appreciated cash inflows become $16,909 as shown below:
$16,909.00 = \$4,000.00/(1.10)^3 + \$3,500/(1.10)^2 + \$3,500/(1.10)^1 + \$3,500$. MIRR, or holding period return, is 12.772 percent $(=(\$16,909/\$10,454.55)^{0.25} - 1)$. In Solomon's (1956) procedure, the cash flow in the first year would have been netted to $3,500 (i.e., $4,000 − $500), leading to a holding period value of 12.894 percent. However, because the project cash flows have not been changed, the Solomon procedure and the MIRR would produce the same answer. Although a subtle difference exists between Solomon's procedure and the MIRR, the true benefit of the MIRR over Solomon's procedure is seen when multiple IRRs become present within the project cash flows (Lorie and Savage, 1955; Teichroew et al., 1965a, 1965b; Oehmke, 2000; Saak and Hennessy, 2001). This issue will be addressed later in this section.

Returning to the MIRR calculation, what is the criterion for determining whether a project is acceptable? The project is acceptable assuming MIRR is higher than a particular hurdle rate. The current convention appears to set the hurdle rate at the cost of capital, 10 percent in this example. Further, MIRR is consistent with NPV decisions, that is, higher MIRRs are better than lower MIRRs, and equates to a similar project ranking based on NPV (i.e., a higher NPV corresponds to a higher MIRR). How MIRR reflects NPV can be shown in the following example.

A project has an initial cost of $5,000 and generates two annual cash flows of $2,750.00 and $2,970.25 over the next two years, respectively. Assuming a cost of capital of 9 percent annually, the investment base is $5,000, which is the sum of all of the discounted costs, and the terminal value is $5,940.50 (=$2,750.00(1.09) + $2,970.25), which is the sum of all of the cash inflows appreciated at the cost of capital until the end of the project. MIRR is 9 percent $(=(\$5,940.50/\$5,000.00)^{0.5} - 1)$ and is equal to the cost of capital. This situation is equivalent to NPV equaling zero when the project returns exactly the risk-adjusted rate. Assuming this project is of equivalent risk as other projects within the firm, 9 percent becomes the appropriate discount rate for an NPV calculation and the NPV calculation is equal to zero.

$$NPV = 0 = (\$2,750.00/(1.09) + \$2,970.25/(1.09)^2) - \$5,000.00$$

Change the project cash inflows to $3,000 annually beginning next year. The investment base does not change from $5,000, but the terminal value increases to $6,270.00 (=$3,000.00(1.09) + $3,000.00), making MIRR equal to 11.982 percent $(=(\$6,270.50/\$5,000.00)^{0.5} - 1)$. MIRR is greater than the hurdle rate of 9 percent and an NPV greater than zero also emerges.

$$NPV = \$277.33 = (\$3,000/(1.09) + \$3,000/(1.09)^2) - \$5,000.00$$

Thus, an MIRR above the hurdle rate reflects an NPV > 0.

Change the project cash inflows to $2,000 annually beginning next year. Again, the investment base does not change from $5,000, but, the terminal value decreases to $4,180 (=$2,000(1.09) + $2,000), making MIRR equal to −8.567 percent (=($4,180/$5,000)$^{0.5}$ − 1). MIRR is less than the hurdle rate of 9 percent and an NPV less than zero also emerges.

$$NPV = -\$1,481.78 = (\$2,000/(1.09) + \$2,000/(1.09)^2) - \$5,000$$

Thus, an MIRR below the hurdle rate reflects an NPV < 0. Having demonstrated how MIRR and NPV are consistent with each other in a simple framework, the issue of multiple IRRs and the application of MIRR can now be addressed.

Multiple IRRs can occur when cash flows alternate from being inflows to outflows more than once. All of the previous project examples except for one example have had an initial cost followed by inflows. In practice, costs emerge throughout a project and costs can be higher than the cash inflow generated within a given operating period. Thus, having only an initial cost appears to be an oversimplification that should be addressed.

The NPV calculation is unaffected by having alternating cash inflows and outflows through time, but the specification of the discount rate matters greatly because there may be multiple regions in which the NPV is greater than zero instead of just a single region. IRR is affected because mathematically each time the cash flows alternate from inflow to outflow a new discount rate that sets NPV to zero may emerge. This is equivalent to finding zero roots for a polynomial where the degree of the polynomial is determined by number of times the cash flows change from inflow to outflow through time. That is, a project with unconventional cash flows (i.e., more than one change in the sign of the cash flows) may potentially have as many IRRs as the number of changes in sign of the cash flows. A numerical illustration is helpful for demonstrating this issue.

A project has the following cash flows: −$757.58 initially, $1,742.42 one year from today, and −$1,000.00 two years from today. Assume the project has a discount rate of 15 percent, which is also the project's cost of capital. Calculating NPV, the project adds value to the firm because of the positive NPV.

$$NPV = \$1.43 = (\$1,742.42/(1.15) - \$1,000.00/(1.15)^2) - \$757.58$$

Change the discount rate to 8 percent and NPV becomes negative.

$$NPV = -\$1.56 = (\$1,742.42/(1.08) - \$1,000.00/(1.08)^2) - \$757.58$$

Change the discount rate to 22 percent and NPV is also negative.

$$NPV = -\$1.22 = (\$1,742.42/(1.22) - \$1,000.00/(1.22)^2) - \$757.58$$

Given what is happening to the NPV calculation at the different discount rates, there appear to be two rates that set NPV to zero between 8 percent and 22 percent. In fact, the two rates are 10 percent and 20 percent and both are considered to be an IRR for the project.

Applying the MIRR technique, the investment base becomes $1,513.72 (=$757.58 + $1,000.00/(1.15)^2) and the terminal value is $2,003.78 (=$1,742.42 (1.15)). MIRR is 15.054 percent (=($2,003.78/$1,513.72)$^{0.5}$ − 1), which is above the hurdle rate of 15 percent and indicates an acceptable project similar to that found using the NPV calculation.

If the cost of capital becomes 22 percent, is MIRR still consistent with NPV (negative in this case)? The answer is MIRR is consistent with NPV. The investment base becomes $1,429.44 (=$757.58 + $1,000.00/(1.22)^2) and the terminal value is $2,125.75 (=$1,742.42(1.22)). MIRR is 21.95 percent (=($2,125.75/$1,429.44)$^{0.5}$ − 1), which is below the hurdle rate of 22 percent. As noted above, having the correct RADR for the NPV calculation is critical to this analysis. Given the values of IRRs, imprecision in evaluating the discount rate near the values of 10 percent and 20 percent could lead to accepting a project that has a negative NPV or rejecting a project that has a zero or positive NPV.

Can a conflict exist when a project's RADR differs from the cost of capital? A strict adherence to MIRR being calculated with the cost of capital can lead to some issues depending on the RADR rate being higher or lower than the cost of capital. However, appealing to the work of Solomon (1956) and Lin (1976), the appropriate rate is supposed to be the opportunity cost, which is the cost of capital. Thus, the argument is that the opportunity cost in this case is the RADR for the project despite the rate being different from the cost of capital (most likely higher than the cost of capital).

Other techniques also exist to evaluate capital investments having multiple IRRs. In each method, finding all of the possible IRRs is important (Hajdasinski, 1993). In some cases, however, IRRs with imaginary components ("imaginary" in the mathematical sense) are the conclusion of such a search. Hazen (2003), Hartman and Shafrick (2004), Zhang (2005), and Osborne (2010) propose such techniques. These newer techniques are highly sophisticated. The next section introduces the profitability index (PI), which shares some similarities to the development of MIRR and NPV.

PROFITABILITY INDEX

PI is the discounted sum of the cash inflows divided by the discounted sum of the cash outflows. PI can be considered a ratio version of NPV. As Ross, Westerfield, and Jordan (2009) note, PI measures the "bang for the buck" provided by a project. Although, consistent with NPV, a PI > 1 is equivalent to an NPV > 0, a PI = 1 is equivalent to an NPV = 0, and a PI < 1 is equivalent to an NPV < 0, PI is not as useful as NPV. When considering mutually exclusive projects, due to scale issues similar to what happens with IRR, PI can disagree with NPV. A simple example demonstrates this point.

Project A has an initial cost of $10,000 and has an NPV of $2,000 (implying the sum of the discounted cash inflows is $12,000), generating a PI of 1.20 (=$12,000/$10,000). Project B has a cost of $5,000 and has an NPV of $1,200 (implying the sum of the discounted cash inflows to be $6,200), generating a PI of 1.24. Due to the scale of the projects, the PI measure considers Project B to be superior while Project A adds more value to the firm as measured by NPV.

Consequently, when considering mutually exclusive projects, PI should not be used as a decision metric.

However, PI does have value as a metric when there are more NPV > 0 projects available than the firm can fund at a given time. In this case, PI can be used successfully as a ranking metric. For example, a consumer arrives at a store and finds two desirable items, but cannot afford both items. The consumer decides to buy the item that generates more benefit relative to the cost (i.e., the item with the higher PI). This is different from a mutually exclusive decision where the other item will not be considered again because the other item is available for purchase at a later date. Consequently, when a capital constraint limits what desirable projects can be accepted, PI can become a useful metric.

Relative to MIRR, PI has a common link in that both metrics require calculating a ratio of benefits over costs. The benefit/cost ratios differ in that the benefits are discounted in the PI rather than appreciated as in the MIRR. To see the linkage more clearly between the two measures, allow the cost of capital to be 11 percent, which is also the discount rate for a project with the following cash flows: −$1,000 initially, $700 one year from today, and $800 two years from today. Following the MIRR technique, the investment base is $1,000 and the terminal value is $1,577.00 (=$700.00(1.11) + $800.00). MIRR is 25.579 percent.

$$\text{MIRR} = 25.579\,\text{percent} = (\$1{,}577/\$1{,}000)^{0.5} - 1 = (1.577)^{0.5} - 1$$

Compared to previous MIRR calculations, the solution equation has been extended to demonstrate how PI is contained within the MIRR calculation.

Following the PI calculation, the sum of the discounted cash outflows is $1,000 and the sum of the discounted cash inflows is $1,279.93 (=($700.00/(1.11) + ($800/(1.11)^2) generating a PI of 1.280 (=$1,279.93/$1,000.00). To demonstrate how the PI is within the MIRR calculation, let PI appreciate by the discount rate for the full life of the project:

$$1.577 = 1.280(1.11)^2$$

In fact, the MIRR calculation can be put in terms of the PI ("k" is the cost of capital and hurdle rate) as shown in Equation 5.1.

$$\text{MIRR} = (PI(1+k)^N)^{1/N} - 1 \qquad (5.1)$$

The previous section demonstrated numerically how MIRR is consistent with NPV. Given Equation (5.1), this fact can be shown to be true. To make the proof clearer, adjust Equation (5.1) in the following manner.

$$(1 + \text{MIRR})^N/(1+k)^N = PI \qquad (5.2)$$

If PI > 1, meaning that NPV > 0, then MIRR > k. If PI = 1, meaning that NPV = 0, then MIRR = k. If PI < 1, meaning that NPV < 0, then MIRR < k. Because the NPV, through the PI, is integrated into the MIRR, MIRR must always agree with the associated NPV analysis.

SUMMARY AND CONCLUSIONS

The dominance of NPV as a project evaluation method among academics does not appear to be shared by practitioners who often prefer to use IRR and the seemingly inferior PB measure. The use of PB appears to be a combination of focus on short-term liquidity needs (with or without an agency issue) and a cost-benefit analysis relative to project evaluation. In other words, safe or lesser valued projects do not warrant extensive analysis and are not good candidates for a NPV analysis.

The popularity of IRR is more puzzling in that it is an imprecise rate of return metric. For instance, having an IRR of 13 percent versus an appropriate risk-adjusted return of 10 percent does not imply a gain of three percentage points. Consequently, the interpretation that people often assign to the IRR is incorrect because the percentage point gain can only be obtained if intermediate cash flows can appreciate at the IRR throughout the project's life. This "problem" became known as the "reinvestment problem," which led to much research to better define the issue and to potentially mitigate the problem by calculating MIRR.

MIRR is consistent with NPV because the NPV calculation is actually within the MIRR calculation. This equivalence can be seen by evaluating the MIRR calculation in terms of the PI, which is an NPV calculation in a ratio format. PI is generally not as useful as the NPV calculation, but PI does have some benefits when evaluating acceptable projects under a capital constraint.

In general, all of these metrics are related in some fashion. IRR is the discount rate that sets NPV to zero, PI to one, and DPB and PBL to the duration of the project. An NPV > 0 implies that the project life is greater than PB, DPB, and PBL, PI > 1, and MIRR > cost of capital (or a hurdle rate). An NPV < 0 implies that the project life is less than DPB and PBL, PI < 1, and MIRR < cost of capital (or a hurdle rate). Being able to see these relationships allows the decision maker to use more than one metric, convert a given metric into another, and understand the biases of each metric. Ultimately, the decision maker should realize that these project evaluation techniques are simply tools to help in the decision-making process. All of the considerations necessary for making the decision are not contained within any one of these metrics alone or combined.

DISCUSSION QUESTIONS

1. Why may smaller firms use PB initially to evaluate projects and then use more sophisticated evaluation techniques as the firm grows in size?

2. What is Myers's (1977) contention that makes firms short-term focused?

3. When considering two projects, what is Fisher's rate of return?

4. What causes a project to have multiple IRRs?

5. Consider a mining project in which there are costs to open the mine and to seal the mine at the end of the project. Consider the following cash flows for the project: −$3,787,879 initially, $8,712,121 one year from today, and −$5,000,000 two years from today. How many potential IRRs exist for the project?

6. Why must the MIRR agree with an associated NPV analysis?

REFERENCES

Alchian, Armen A. 1955. "The Rate of Interest, Fisher's Rate of Return over Costs and Keynes' Internal Rate of Return." *American Economic Review* 45:5, 938–943.

Binder, John J., and J. Scott Chaput. 1996. "A Positive Analysis of Corporate Capital Budgeting Practices." *Review of Quantitative Finance and Accounting* 6:3, 245–257.

Block, Stanley. 1997. "Capital Budgeting Techniques Used by Small Business Firms in the 1990s." *The Engineering Economist* 42:4, 289–302.

Block, Stanley. 2005. "Are There Differences in Capital Budgeting Procedures Between Industries? An Empirical Study." *The Engineering Economist* 50:1, 55–67.

Brigham, Eugene F. 1975. "Hurdle Rates for Screening Capital Expenditure Proposals." *Financial Management* 4:3, 17–26.

Chen, Shimin, and Ronald L. Clark. 1994. "Management Compensation and Payback Method in Capital Budgeting: A Path Analysis." *Accounting and Business Research* 24:94, 121–132.

Dorfman, Robert. 1981. "The Meaning of Internal Rates of Return." *Journal of Finance* 36:5, 1011–1021.

Dudley, Carlton L. 1972. "A Note on Reinvestment Assumptions in Choosing Between Net Present Value and Internal Rate of Return." *Journal of Finance* 27:4, 907–915.

Fisher, Irving. 1930. *The Theory of Interest*. New York, Kelley and Millman.

Graham, John R., and Campbell R. Harvey. 2001. "The Theory and Practice of Corporate Finance: Evidence from the Field." *Journal of Financial Economics* 60:2–3, 187–243.

Hajdasinski, Miroslaw M. 1993. "The Suitability of the Perpetuity Rate of Return as a Project Evaluation Criterion." *The Engineering Economist* 38:4, 309–320.

Hajdasinski, Miroslaw M. 1997a. "Comments on 'Using Heuristics to Evaluate Projects: The Case of Ranking Projects by IRR'." *The Engineering Economist* 42:2, 163–166.

Hajdasinski, Miroslaw M. 1997b. "NPV-Compatibility, Project Ranking, and Related Issues." *The Engineering Economist* 42:4, 325–339.

Hartley, Ronald V. 1990. "Teaching Capital Budgeting with Variable Reinvestment Rates." *Issues in Accounting Education* 5:2, 268–280.

Hartman, Joseph C., and Ingrid C. Shafrick. 2004. "The Relevant Internal Rate of Return." *The Engineering Economist* 49:2, 139–158.

Hazen, Gordon B. 2003. "A New Perspective on Multiple Internal Rates of Return." *The Engineering Economist* 48:1, 31–51.

Hirshleifer, Jack. 1958. "On the Theory of Optimal Investment Decision." *Journal of Political Economy* 66:4, 329–352.

Jacobs, Jan F. 2007. "Capital Budgeting: NPV v. IRR Controversy, Unmaking Common Assertions." Available at http://ssrn.com/abstract=981382.

Keane, Simon M. 1979. "The Internal Rate of Return and the Reinvestment Fallacy." *Abacus* 15:1, 48–55.

Keef, Stephen P., and Melvin L. Roush. 2001. "Discounted Cash Flow Methods and the Fallacious Reinvestment Assumptions: A Review of Recent Texts." *Accounting Education* 10:1, 105–116.

Lefley, Frank. 1996. "The Payback Method of Investment Appraisal: A Review and Synthesis." *International Journal of Production Economics* 44:3, 207–224.

Lin, Steven A. 1976. "The Modified Internal Rate of Return and Investment Criterion." *The Engineering Economist* 21:4, 237–247.

Longmore, Dean R. 1989. "The Persistence of the Payback Method: A Time-Adjusted Decision Rule Perspective." *The Engineering Economist* 34:3, 185–194.

Lorie, James H., and Leonard J. Savage. 1955. "Three Problems in Rationing Capital." *Journal of Business* 28:4, 229–239.

Marglin, Stephen A. 1963. "The Social Rate of Discount and the Optimal Rate of Investment." *Quarterly Journal of Economics* 77:1, 95–111.

McDaniel, William R., Daniel E. McCarty, and Kenneth Jessell. 1988. "Discounted Cash Flow with Explicit Reinvestment Rates: Tutorial and Extension." *Financial Review* 23:3, 369–385.

Myers, Stewart C. 1977. "Determinants of Corporate Borrowing." *Journal of Financial Economics* 5:2, 147–175.

Narayanan, M. P. 1985. "Managerial Incentives for Short-Term Results." *Journal of Finance* 40:5, 1469–1484.

Oehmke, James F. 2000. "Anomalies in Net Present Value Calculations." *Economic Letters* 67:3, 349–351.

Osborne, Michael. 2010. "A Resolution to the NPV-IRR Debate?" *Quarterly Review of Economics and Finance* 50:2, 234–239.

Phalippou, Ludovic. 2008. "The Hazards of Using IRR to Measure Performance: The Case of Private Equity." Available at http://ssrn.com/abstract=1111796.

Pike, Richard H. 1985. "Owner-Manager Conflict and the Role of the Payback Method." *Accounting and Business Research* 16:61, 47–51.

Rappaport, Alfred. 1965. "The Discounted Payback Period." *Management Services* (July–August), 30–36.

Remer, Donald S., and Armando P. Nieto. 1995a. "A Compendium and Comparison of 25 Project Evaluation Techniques. Part 1: Net Present Value and Rate of Return Methods." *International Journal of Production Economics* 42:1, 79–96.

Remer, Donald S., and Armando P. Nieto. 1995b. "A Compendium and Comparison of 25 Project Evaluation Techniques. Part 2: Ratio, Payback, and Accounting Methods." *International Journal of Production Economics* 42:2, 101–129.

Renshaw, Ed. 1957. "A Note on the Arithmetic of Capital Budgeting Decisions." *Journal of Business* 30:3, 193–201.

Ross, Stephen, Randolph Westerfield, and Bradford Jordan. 2009. *Fundamentals of Corporate Finance*. Boston: McGraw-Hill Irwin.

Ryan, Patricia, and Glenn Ryan. 2002. "Capital Budgeting Practices of the Fortune 1000: How Have Things Changed?" *Journal of Business and Management* 8:4, 355–364.

Saak, Alexander, and David A. Hennessy. 2001. "Well-behaved Cash Flows." *Economic Letters* 73:1, 81–88.

Shull, David M. 1992. "Efficient Capital Project Selection Through a Yield-Based Capital Budgeting Technique." *The Engineering Economist* 38:1, 1–17.

Shull, David M. 1994. "Overall Rates of Return: Investment Bases, Reinvestment Rates and Time Horizons." *The Engineering Economist* 39:2, 139–163.

Solomon, Ezra. 1956. "The Arithmetic of Capital-Budgeting Decisions." *Journal of Business* 29:2, 124–129.

Statman, Meir. 1982. "The Persistence of the Payback Method: A Principal-Agent Perspective." *The Engineering Economist* 27:2, 95–100.

Statman, Meir, and James F. Sepe. 1984. "Managerial Incentive Plans and the Use of the Payback Method." *Journal of Business, Finance, and Accounting* 11:1, 61–65.

Teichroew, Daniel, Alexander A. Robichek, and Michael Montalbano. 1965a. "Mathematical Analysis of Rates of Return under Uncertainty." *Management Science* 11:3, 395–403.

Teichroew, Daniel, Alexander A. Robichek, and Michael Montalbano. 1965b. "An Analysis of Criteria for Investment and Financing Decisions under Uncertainty." *Management Science* 12:3, 151–179.

Weingartner, H. Martin. 1969. "Some Views on the Payback Period and Capital Budgeting Decisions." *Management Science* 15:12, B594–B607.

Yard, Stefan. 2000. "Developments of the Payback Method." *International Journal of Production Economics* 67:2, 155–167.
Zhang, Dou. 2005. "A Different Perspective on Using Multiple Internal Rates of Return: The IRR Parity Technique." *The Engineering Economist* 50:4, 327–335.

ABOUT THE AUTHORS

Tom Arnold, CFA, is an Associate Professor of Finance and the F. Carlyle Tiller Chair in Business at the Robins School of Business, University of Richmond. Professor Arnold has more than 40 publications appearing in such journals as the *Journal of Finance, Journal of Business, Financial Analysts Journal, Journal of Futures Markets, Journal of Applied Finance,* and *Journal of Financial Education.* His work has been cited in the *Economist, Wall Street Journal, New York Times,* and other non-U.S. news outlets. Professor Arnold's specialties include derivative securities, real option valuation, market microstructure, corporate valuation, and finance pedagogy. He received a Ph.D. from the Terry College of Business at the University of Georgia.

Terry Nixon is an Associate Professor of Finance at the Farmer School of Business at Miami University. During his career, Professor Nixon has been recognized many times for his teaching excellence, which focuses on corporate finance. Professor Nixon has published articles in such journals as the *Financial Review, Research in International Business and Finance, Journal of Applied Finance, Journal of Financial Education, Applied Financial Economics, Journal of Real Estate Finance and Economics,* and *Review of Quantitative Finance and Accounting.* His research interests include corporate restructuring and agency theory. Professor Nixon received a Ph.D. from the University of South Carolina.

CHAPTER 6

Capital Rationing for Capital Budgeting

ALEXANDER BRÜGGEN
Associate Professor, Maastricht University

INTRODUCTION

Decisions on capital budgeting are among the most important decisions of management, especially in terms of the financial consequences. Typically, capital budgeting involves relatively large amounts of money. Many techniques and mechanisms are available that help to improve capital budgeting decisions.

Organizations with abundant capital rarely have capital budgeting problems because sufficient capital is available to fund all desirable projects. There is, hence, no allocation problem where some projects are funded and some are not, or some projects are funded at the expense of others. Scarcity or the abundance of capital has an important influence on decision making for two reasons: (1) With scarce or rationed capital management needs to make much more difficult choices, and (2) scarcity of capital means that the firm must reject some investments.

The purpose of this chapter is to introduce capital rationing as a mechanism to improve capital budget decisions. The chapter begins by defining capital rationing and describing the mechanism and the different parties involved in such a process. Next, the chapter describes the purpose of capital rationing as well as the advantages of this mechanism for organizations. Following the advantages, capital rationing can have several disadvantages that could render this capital budgeting mechanism useless. These are described in the next section. After that, the chapter provides an outlook on the future and describes questions that remain unanswered on capital rationing. The final section of this chapter summarizes and concludes.

DEFINITION OF CAPITAL RATIONING FOR CAPITAL BUDGETING

The literature provides various definitions of capital rationing. *Capital rationing* is a limit of funds available in a market for investment projects. This, however, does not provide any insights into the mechanism of capital rationing for capital budgeting. In general, to maximize value, investment projects increase value for the investor if the projects have a positive net present value (NPV). According to this simple rule and under the assumption that capital markets are efficient, all projects with a

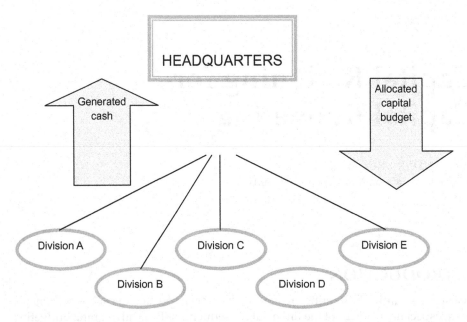

Exhibit 6.1   An Internal Capital Market

Note: This exhibit describes the flow of capital in a firm with different divisions. Divisions generate cash that is transferred to headquarters and then reallocated to divisions based on the perceived capital needs in the next period.

positive NPV should be accepted and receive funding. According to theory, capital rationing can only exist in the presence of severe market imperfections where a firm cannot raise enough capital to fund all its projects.

Despite the theoretical prediction that capital rationing only exists in the presence of market imperfections, capital rationing can be actively introduced in capital markets. Such capital markets are not necessarily external capital markets that are difficult to discipline and steer by authorities, but capital markets within organizations, the so-called internal capital markets. In such internal capital markets different parts of an organization, such as business divisions, generate cash that is transferred to a central position that redistributes cash to different areas of the organization in order to fund investment projects. Exhibit 6.1 provides an example of an internal capital market where divisions generate cash that is transferred to headquarters, and in turn, headquarters decides on the allocation of the funds back to the divisions with regard to the investment decisions. The management of organizations can limit the available capital for such capital budgeting decisions particularly at the individual division level. As a consequence, some investment projects will be rejected and will not be funded. Management thus has to make choices about which investment projects to fund. Further, different investment projects compete with each other for capital. The mechanism of capital rationing induces competition and, based on certain criteria, only some of the competing investment projects will "win" funding.

Capital rationing seems to be a widely used mechanism in firms (Mukherjee and Hingorani, 1999). In organizational practice, there are primarily two ways of applying capital rationing. First, the firm can set a hurdle rate higher than the cost of capital. This ensures that only projects that are expected to generate returns higher than the hurdle rate are accepted and funded. Setting the hurdle rate is at the discretion of management and can lead to higher or lower levels of capital rationing. Second, the firm can set a fixed investment budget. With a fixed investment budget, different projects compete for funding and projects to be funded are ranked based on certain selection criteria.

The main difference between a fixed investment budget and a hurdle rate is that theoretically, the firm could fund an unlimited number of projects if they fulfill the hurdle rate criterion. In contrast, with a fixed investment budget, the number of projects is limited to the total amount of funds available for investment. Once the selected projects meet the total amount of the fixed budget, all other projects must be rejected.

Capital rationing as a mechanism to improve investment decisions is a voluntarily installed mechanism. Capital might be rationed for other reasons such as inefficient markets. The intention is then different, but the actual process of capital rationing and the resulting competition remains similar. This chapter focuses on capital rationing imposed voluntarily by firms rather than capital rationing imposed by external capital markets due to market imperfections.

HOW DOES CAPITAL RATIONING WORK TO IMPROVE CAPITAL BUDGETING?

As previously mentioned, the main purpose of capital rationing in a capital budgeting context is to improve decision making in order to enhance the value of the organization that funds investments. Besides other mechanisms for capital budgeting, such as NPV analysis, an early survey shows that about two-thirds of Fortune 1000 firms use capital rationing in the process of capital budgeting (Gitman and Mercurio, 1982). A later survey conducted by Mukherjee and Hingorani (1999) indicates that the majority of Fortune 500 firms ration capital in the capital budgeting process.

Setting hurdle rates or fixed investment budgets induces competition for capital. Improving decision making in a capital budgeting context means both a reduction of agency costs and control over agency costs. The next section provides an explanation of these agency costs.

Reduction and Control of Agency Costs

Much of the literature on capital rationing takes capital rationing as a given. Many studies investigate how to optimize capital rationing and capital budgeting decisions. Fewer studies, however, examine the question of why firms use capital rationing. Hirshleifer (1970) and Weingartner (1970) argue that capital rationing is a response to organizational problems such as agency problems. Eisenhardt (1989, p. 58) makes the following observation about agency theory:

> Agency theory is concerned with resolving two problems that can occur in agency relationships. The first is the agency problem that arises when (a) the desires or goals of the principal and agent conflict and (b) it is difficult or expensive for the

principal to verify what the agent is actually doing. The problem here is that the principal cannot verify that the agent has behaved appropriately. The second is the problem of risk sharing that arises when the principal and agent have different attitudes toward risk. The problem here is that the principal and the agent may prefer different actions because of the different risk preferences.

In capital budgeting, agency problems occur when information asymmetry exists in the capital budgeting process regarding the expected returns of investment projects. For example, the divisional managers in Exhibit 6.1 have more and better information on divisional investment prospects than do managers at headquarters because divisional managers are closer to the products and markets.

In addition to information asymmetry, moral hazard is another condition that can induce agency costs. Managers engage in moral hazard (i.e., act in their own interest rather than the interest of the firm) possibly by acting myopically (i.e., have a short-term orientation) so that the organization does not have the best information about investment opportunities. Information asymmetry and moral hazard are the most important conditions for agency problems to exist. A result of agency problems can be agency costs. According to the literature, agency costs in a capital budgeting context result from two sources: (1) overinvestment in low-return projects that occurs when managers have private information and incentives for controlling more assets (Antle and Eppen, 1985; Zhang, 1997; Inderst and Laux, 2005), and (2) managerial understatement of current performance in order to lower their future performance targets (Fisher, Maines, Peffer, and Sprinkle, 2002). The next section explains these two sources in more detail.

Overinvestment

Much empirical evidence shows that managers prefer to control more assets rather than fewer assets (Stein, 1997). Schumpeter (1934) already recognized that managers have a tendency to build empires and that such empires are not necessarily the result of efficient capital allocation but can harm investor value. Controlling more assets, however, does not mean that the firm uses these assets economically. A consequence of this empire-building behavior is that managers tend to overinvest in projects to increase the "empire" that they control. Agency costs due to overinvestment are actually opportunity costs. Instead of increasing the empire of a particular manager, the firm could have invested funds in projects with a higher return elsewhere or could have paid out dividends to shareholders or repurchased shares if no economically beneficial projects were available. With competition for capital, different investment projects compete for capital and the firm will not fund projects with relatively low expected returns. This mechanism is a form of "winner-picking," where the firm funds only a fraction of projects based on a relative ranking. Capital rationing is thus a response to the problem of overinvestment (Holmström and Ricart i Costa, 1986).

Understating Future Performance

Understating expected returns is a way of reducing future performance targets for managers. Setting performance targets below what is actually possible, however, could lead to severe misallocations of resources in firms, which result in agency costs. Competitive capital rationing is an effective mechanism to address this problem because a firm funds only the highest ranked projects. Competitive capital rationing can be a helpful mechanism in capital budgeting because it provides incentives for agents to predict higher returns for their projects. Managers are less inclined to understate expected returns for reasons of lower future performance targets. Capital rationing thus provides a countervailing force against this tendency (Zhang, 1997; Fisher et al., 2002). Also, to the extent that control mechanisms limit the divergence between managers' predictions and reality, pressure to predict higher returns provides an incentive to discover new business opportunities with genuinely higher expected returns (Inderst and Laux, 2005). For example, divisions of the company in Exhibit 6.1 compete for capital. If divisions A, B, and C have good investment opportunities, competition forces divisions D and E to search for investment opportunities that are at least comparable in terms of quality so that divisions D and E do not lose any chance of funding upfront. Capital rationing is thus a mechanism that induces a constant search for investment opportunities.

CONDITIONS FOR SUCCESSFUL CAPITAL RATIONING

In the process of capital budgeting, different players are involved who contribute to the complexity of capital budgeting and capital rationing. In essence, the players are those who have authority to provide capital and those who apply for funding. With agency theory as the major theory describing this relationship, those players with budget authority are principals and those who apply for funding and actually work with the budget are agents. Successful capital rationing means that agency costs, that is, costs that occur due to information asymmetry and moral hazard in the relationship between principals and agents, are reduced to a minimum and capital budgeting decisions are successful for a firm.

One condition for agency costs to exist is that agents have superior information about investment projects than the principals. In a capital budgeting setting, this could be divisional managers (agents) knowing more about a project in their relevant division than headquarters (principal) does. According to the Fortune 500 survey by Mukherjee and Hingorani (1999), more than 40 percent of the responding firms have divisions submitting project information to headquarters. Moreover, headquarters decides on the capital allocation (capital budget), as illustrated in the example used earlier in this chapter. Information asymmetry provides agents with the opportunity to misrepresent investment information that is relevant for investment decisions.

According to a survey by Gitman and Forrester (1977) on capital budgeting practices of major U.S. firms, more than 64 percent of the respondents indicate that the most difficult stage in the capital budgeting process is cash flow estimation and project definition. Based on a theoretical model of capital budgeting, Zhang (1997) predicts that capital rationing as a control mechanism for managers is more effective with increasing levels of information asymmetry, because in high levels of information asymmetry capital rationing can be used to apply forms of winner-picking and ranking projects based on the predicted performance that has the highest benefit. In contrast, if information asymmetry is low, capital rationing is simply not necessary because headquarters has good ideas about each divisional investment project. So, the more information asymmetry between, for example, divisional managers and headquarters, the more of a disciplinary effect capital rationing actually has. By extending this argument of information asymmetry, one can expect more information asymmetry in larger firms where less detailed information is available at the headquarters level than at the division level. Firm characteristics thus seem to have an important influence on the role of capital rationing. Headquarters engaging in winner-picking (i.e., selecting projects for funding that are ranked highest relative to each other) will provide divisions with relatively better investment opportunities with more funds and at the same time penalize those divisions with unfavorable investment opportunities.

Capital rationing thus provides incentives to generate good investment opportunities and is especially important in settings with high information asymmetry. This is confirmed by the survey conducted by Mukherjee and Hingorani (1999). Internal capital rationing is most important in situations when senior management cannot trust project forecasts and the downside risk of a project is large. Another important reason for the use of internal capital rationing is to discourage biased cash flow forecasts.

Capital rationing can have negative incentive effects in settings where divisions are highly heterogeneous. Divisions that are very different from each other are difficult to compare and the same is true of their investment opportunities. Under competitive capital rationing, headquarters selects the "best" investment projects. A problem with highly heterogeneous divisions is that investment projects are dissimilar. Thus, managers of two divisions could both work equally hard, but one division could generate much greater expected profits than another division due to the nature of the business, the stage in the business cycle, or other reasons.

For example, assume that the company in Exhibit 6.1 is heterogeneous. Division A is a bank; Division B is an insurance company; Division C is a manufacturer of motorcycles; Division D is a supplier for Division C; and Division E is a selling division. The divisions could be somewhat related, but they are all active in different markets and industries. Performance indicators could differ in terms of their benchmarks and interpretation. Comparison is difficult and without further (costly) investigation, it may be impossible.

A high level of comparability of divisions is important for capital rationing to work and to function as an incentive and control mechanism. Otherwise, capital rationing serves as a disincentive for managers and could even lead to lower firm value due to a misallocation of funds (Inderst and Laux, 2005).

NEGATIVE SIDE EFFECTS OF COMPETITIVE CAPITAL RATIONING

The success of capital rationing is the result of competition between different investment projects and a capital budget that is allocated to the projects that appear to be the most promising projects. Capital rationing thus creates relative performance evaluation based on a selection of different criteria. An important challenge for all parties involved in the capital budgeting process is the prediction of the future economic benefit of an investment project. Given the fact that firms typically allocate capital based on predicted values, room exists for misrepresentation of the future. Whereas competition can have beneficial effects for capital budgeting, competition can also have negative effects on the budgeting process, especially on the reported information for budgeting purposes. A problem not only for capital budgeting decisions but also for other budgeting decisions is that with increasing levels of information asymmetry, principals need to rely increasingly on the input of their agents for decision making. With high information asymmetry and a strong reliance on information reported by agents, principals have fewer opportunities to verify the information that is provided to them by agents. As a consequence, agents could use this dependency for their own purposes and report information that is not necessarily correct but serves their own private benefits such as personal empire building. Stronger competition could increase the pressure to report information that shows future investment projects in a better light simply to warrant chances of funding.

As mentioned earlier, when divisions are heterogeneous ex ante in terms of resources and investment opportunities, competitive rationing is likely to provide less incentives than noncompetitive rationing for the least advantaged divisions to make the effort of developing profitable new projects (Inderst and Laux, 2005). More heterogeneity can cause the effort of disadvantaged divisions to be useless, given the difficulties in comparing performance predictions of investment projects. Moreover, insofar as competition increases incentives for managers, this is not unambiguously beneficial: Some actions that increase the probability of receiving funding are detrimental to the organization (e.g., sabotage and dishonesty), and competition is likely to increase these actions as well (Harbring and Irlenbusch, 2008). But exactly how competition due to capital rationing affects misrepresentation in budget proposals depends on whether and how individuals' utility for honesty provides a counterweight against the incentive to misrepresent. In particular, it depends on how individuals trade off honesty and the benefits of misrepresentation. The next section provides an overview on the effects of competition on managerial reporting behavior; for example, investment projects competing for funding under capital rationing.

RESEARCH RESULTS ON THE EFFECTS OF COMPETITION ON THE RELIABILITY OF MANAGERIAL REPORTING

Although surveys indicate that capital rationing is complex and difficult, especially in terms of cash flow projection and project selection (Gitman and Forrester, 1977), the mechanism of capital rationing and how it should be applied is relatively straightforward. Capital rationing and the capital allocation decision are vulnerable to the quality of the criteria used for project selection and misreporting by subordinates. Whereas the criteria for capital budgeting decisions are mostly internal rate of return (IRR) or net present value (NPV) (Mukherjee and Hingorani, 1999), the input for these measures is based on information developed by the subordinate managers, the agents. The use of the allocation measures is only as good as the information used to calculate those measures. Here, the process of capital rationing has its weakest part. In the context of competition, there are conflicting results on the influence of competition on behavior of agents. The following section provides an overview on research findings relating to competition and reporting behavior.

HONESTY IN MANAGEMENT REPORTING AND BUDGET PROPOSALS

People usually prefer to think of themselves as being honest (Alicke, Klotz, Breitenbacher, and Yurak, 1995) and to avoid actions that clearly conflict with this self-image (Mazar and Ariely, 2006; Mazar, Amir, and Ariely, 2008). Past research shows that people are willing to incur costs in order to avoid dishonesty (e.g., Goldstone and Chin, 1993; Evans, Hannan, Krishnan, and Moser, 2001; Greenberg, 2002). The participative budgeting literature offers several examples of this behavior. In studies by Hannan, Rankin, and Towry (2006) as well as in Rankin, Schwartz, and Young (2008), individuals give up a considerable amount of welfare by reporting information more honestly to a superior. Despite evidence that misrepresentation frequently occurs in organizations, the magnitude of the misrepresentation is often well below the amount that apparently would maximize the subordinates' utility from wealth, and the magnitude varies with factors other than the monetary payoffs for misrepresentation (Luft, 1997).

Experimental research on budgeting finds that the performance of budgeting mechanisms depends in complex ways on managers' preferences for honesty (Evans et al., 2001, Hannan et al., 2006). Antle and Eppen (1985) suggest that a hurdle rate well above the cost of capital can be an efficient mechanism to improve capital allocation efficiency. With a hurdle rate above the cost of capital, not all projects in an organization are likely to be funded and capital is rationed. However, Evans et al. provide evidence that the higher-hurdle capital rationing mechanism proposed by Antle and Eppen does not perform very well. Rather, mechanisms that rely on the honesty of agents seem to be relatively effective.

Evans et al. (2001) also provide evidence that agents will sacrifice more cash payoffs to be honest when the compensation system does not award a disproportional share of the common surplus to the principal. So, when agents feel that a principal receives a fair share of the surplus, honest behavior increases. Hannan et al. (2006) find that individuals sacrifice cash payoffs not only to be honest but also to appear honest in a face-to-face interaction with a superior, even though this is a one-time interaction that can generate no future economic gains from reputation building.

The effects of honesty and related social preferences, such as accepting moral standards and group norms, in motivating "organizational citizenship behavior" have been identified as significant economic forces in firms (Williamson, 1985). These effects generate organizational capital and reduce transaction costs via "consummate cooperation," that is, cooperation beyond what can be cost effectively induced through purely economic incentives in contracts (Deckop, Mangel, and Cirka, 1999; Fehr and Falk, 1999; Podsakoff, MacKenzie, Paine, and Bachrach, 2000). The question is, however, how robust are social preferences and preferences for honesty in the context of competition for resources within one firm?

The following sections provide an overview of the literature on competition and misrepresentation in budget proposals. For reasons of clarity, the sections are divided into three relevant effects on misrepresentation: (1) maximum misrepresentation as soon as there is some form of competition, (2) highest level of misrepresentation in medium competition, and (3) increasing levels of misrepresentation with increasing levels of competition (Brüggen and Luft, 2011).

Maximum Misrepresentation in the Presence of Competition

Economically, preferences for honesty can be modeled as a disutility from lying. People making choices in their daily work can trade off welfare as a result of their choices, and a disutility from lying can play a role here. However, in most formal agency models, honesty is virtually nonexistent or it is assumed to be too small to play a role. In an experiment where participants need to report their skill level to potential future employers, Baiman and Lewis (1989) find that participants communicate very opportunistically for very low monetary incentives. This suggests that the disutility from lying is rather low, providing support for many formal agency models.

If the disutility of lying is too small to affect reporting decisions (as in most formal agency models), and if under capital rationing the firm funds only projects with the highest forecasted performance characteristics, then agents do not have any reason to forecast anything but the highest credible performance prediction. Any lower prediction reduces their chances of funding and thereby reduces their control over firm assets, an important driver for managerial misreporting. If common knowledge suggests that the disutility of lying is zero (i.e., there are no significantly honest "types" among agents), then agents cannot gain by imitating an honest type and reporting less than maximum revenues in order to increase the likelihood of receiving funding from the principal. As a result, all subordinates report the highest possible performance prediction in order to gain funding. This tendency to strongly misreport exists as soon as some level of competition exists, because disutility from lying is almost zero and the chances of getting a project funded decrease without lying. So, in order to warrant chances for funding, agents misstate their project performance predictions as soon as competition for capital (or stricter capital rationing) exists. In this setting, with almost no disutility of lying, there is theoretically no major difference between lower or higher levels of competition. As soon as competition exists, agents will misrepresent to the maximum what is credibly possible. Consequently, headquarters (the principal) cannot separate good from bad investment projects and capital allocation becomes very difficult and distorted.

Nonmonotonic Relationship between Competition and the Reporting Behavior

Besides views that the disutility of lying is almost zero, other studies suggest that this is not the case. Rather, people have a preference for honesty that has a strong weight in individuals' economic decisions.

If the psychological cost (disutility) of misrepresentation is a nontrivial amount, then it can be modeled in a manner similar to how effort is modeled in economics, with effort that is personally costly to agents. Agents are willing to deliver effort if the expected monetary payoff is high enough (Brickley, Smith, and Zimmerman, 2004). Just as individuals vary in ability, and therefore have different costs of effort to reach a given level of performance, so individuals also vary in their utility for honesty, resulting in different psychological costs for a given level of misrepresentation.

Moldovanu and Sela (2001) model tournaments with contestants of differing ability and show that when effort-cost functions are convex, multiple-prize tournaments or medium levels of competition result in higher expected effort than single-prize (high competition) tournaments. The reason for this is that chances of winning appear better to contestants because with a single prize only those with the highest skills are likely to win the tournament, which reduces effort for all others. With multiple-prize tournaments, however, not only those with absolute top skills but also others have chances to win a prize. Accordingly, medium competition should also result in higher misrepresentation than high competition if misrepresentation can be modeled as effort, and if large misrepresentations are disproportionally more costly than small ones. Goldstone and Chin (1993) find evidence for this in a university setting where individuals report the number of copies made. Results show that intermediate levels of dishonesty are quite common, but that extreme levels of misreporting are very rare. Large misrepresentations seem to be disproportionally more costly than small or intermediate ones. This is also supported in a study by Mazar et al. (2008). They examine the tension between dishonesty that results in monetary benefits and honesty for the sake of one's own self-image. Results of the experiments show that people are likely to act dishonestly in order to gain some advantage or profit, but to act honestly enough so that their own integrity is not deluded.

Freeman and Gelber (2006) use the Moldovanu and Sela (2001) model to explain (unanticipated) experimental evidence of an inverted-U-shaped function relating the level of competition to the amount of cheating in tournaments: Cheating (like productive effort) was highest at a medium level of competition. Capital budget settings, however, differ from standard tournaments in that an agent who wins with an honest proposal earns more money than an agent who wins with a dishonest proposal because in many organizations, the agents' welfare depends on the actual success of the project. This difference tends to make large misrepresentations less attractive in capital budget settings than in a standard tournament and is one of the important disciplining mechanisms of capital rationing. After all, agents in real life work for multiple periods and need to live with the consequences of their actions. Excessive misrepresentation is therefore unlikely.

However, instead of massive misrepresentation agents need to consider the credibility of their reported information. According to this reasoning, with high levels of competition and limits to misrepresentation, agents would rather report honestly than misrepresent excessively. As a result, misrepresentation is highest under medium levels of competition when misrepresentation does not have to be excessive in order to warrant chances of funding. Under low levels of competition, misrepresentation is unnecessary because funding is very likely; under high levels of competition, misrepresentation is "not worth it" because the disutility from (massive) lying is higher than the expected gain from getting a project funded. Following this argument, discovering misrepresentation is very difficult for strategic reasons because misrepresentation is never extreme. Therefore, "stretching the truth" and biasing information are the problems here. This might appear less of a problem than severe misrepresentation. However, no clear borderline exists between stretching the truth and misrepresentation so that stretching the truth and biasing information can be considered to be harmful for a firm.

Increasing Levels of Misrepresentation with Increasing Levels of Competition

Various psychological considerations could motivate individuals to misrepresent more in high competition. If these forces are strong enough, they could motivate individuals to misrepresent more when competition is high. First, the prediction that misrepresentation will peak at medium competition and then decline is driven by the expectation that agents with strong utilities for honesty are disadvantaged competitors and will drop out of the competition when it becomes particularly difficult (high competition). This may not happen. For example, experimental research provides evidence that disadvantaged competitors often do not drop out as readily as equilibrium models predict, but increase their efforts to levels that are very costly for them in an attempt to win (Bull, Schotter, and Weigelt, 1987; Schotter and Weigelt, 1992; Orrison, Schotter, and Weigelt, 2004). The presence of competition often seems to drive extremely costly actions: excess market entry (Camerer and Lovallo, 1999; Fischbacher and Thöni, 2008) and excess investment to deter competitors (Krishnan, Luft, and Shields, 2002; Lankton and Luft, 2008). Excess market entry increases as the intensity of competition increases (i.e., with larger winner-take-all markets in Fischbacher and Thöni) and "excess misrepresentation" may do so as well.

Second, Messick (1999) argues that when individuals interpret a situation as more competitive, they regard it as socially appropriate for self-interest to dominate their decision making. Interestingly, the same individuals would consider self-interest dominating their decision making as being inappropriate in noncompetitive situations. Managers can believe that part of their job is to gain funding for projects, and succeeding in this task is a quasi-normative obligation that justifies some misrepresentation. If agents in a budget setting think this way and expect others to have the same view, misrepresentation will increase with competition because the cost of misrepresentation—the uncomfortable sense that it is wrong—decreases when competition is high.

Third, misrepresentation could be highest in high competition for the same reason that competition eliminates fairness behavior. The more competitive the setting, the higher is the total (monetary and psychological) cost of off-equilibrium choices such as fairness or honesty (Roth, Prasnikar, Okuno-Fujiwara, and Zamir, 1991).

This can be similar in a capital budget setting with capital rationing. For example, if one agent in a firm is willing to make large misrepresentations, there is still a possibility in medium competition that another agent with a good project can win funding with little or no misrepresentation and achieve the goal of not only earning money but also assisting the principal to earn. Gneezy (2005) and Rankin et al. (2008) provide evidence of concern for the other party's welfare as a driver of honesty. But in a setting with high competition, if one agent makes a large misrepresentation and the principal chooses this agent's project, then other agents' honesty benefits neither themselves nor the principal, and honesty may therefore seem less worthwhile.

The previous sections have provided an overview of the literature on reporting behavior of agents under different levels of competition. Some arguments and empirical findings provide very mixed evidence. Whereas some studies suggest that a competitive setting can improve the capital budgeting procedure by ensuring that only the best projects are funded; other studies imply that competition does not come without a cost. The cost of competition could be dysfunctional behavior that nullifies the benefits of a competitive setting. Future research can help to clarify the mixed results. Further, combinations of different capital budgeting mechanisms can be a successful way to go for companies that are confronted with capital allocation decisions. A combination of different capital budgeting mechanisms, such as capital rationing and NPV analysis, could help to reduce gaming effects based on one mechanism and reduce dysfunctional behavior.

SUMMARY AND CONCLUSIONS

Capital rationing for capital budgeting is a mechanism to reduce and control agency costs in capital budgeting. By limiting funds that are available for divisional investment opportunities, firms can create a competitive environment where divisions, for example, compete for funding. Firms can select divisions based on a relative ranking (winner-picking) or based on a hurdle rate (projects with performance predictions beyond a threshold level receive funding). Competitive capital rationing helps to reduce and to control agency costs. In particular, it helps to avoid problems of overinvestment, which can occur when firms fund projects without stricter selection and in the absence of comparable and competing projects. Competition for capital also means that managers are less inclined to understate future performance, which is typically done to decrease performance targets. A negative side effect of capital rationing is, however, that managers are pressured to present successful projects or projects that "beat" other projects in terms of future performance. As a result of this pressure managers have a tendency to overstate future performance of their projects so that truthful reporting in a firm is seriously harmed.

Research on the role and effect of capital rationing shows mixed results in terms of improvements in investment decisions. The main question in the context of capital rationing is how the level of competition influences the reporting behavior of managers. One stream of research argues that there is overstatement to the maximum possible extent as soon as "some" level of competition exists in order to warrant chances of funding. Here, individuals bear no private costs or disutility of lying or acting unethically. Another stream of literature suggests that individuals tend to trade off the potential benefits of overstating predicted performance of their investment projects and the disutility from misreporting. This trade-off leads to more misreporting under medium levels of competition, but less misreporting under high levels of competition, because here individuals need to overstate too much to warrant chances of funding so that the disutility from lying is too high relative to the potential benefits from receiving funding. A third stream of literature argues that a linear relationship exists between the level of competition and the level of misreporting because individuals feel that the level of competition justifies the level of misreporting.

Capital rationing is thus a mechanism that helps to improve capital budgeting. While this mechanism has some potential disadvantages, overall practice and research findings indicate that capital rationing is an efficient way to control and limit agency costs in the process of capital budgeting. Further, some of the negative effects, such as overstating predicted performance of investment projects, are much less of a problem when managers are concerned with their reputation. Managers try to avoid a reputation of constantly overstating investment outlooks because this could harm their success in getting funding in other future projects. Long-term considerations can help to mitigate the negative effects of capital rationing mentioned in this chapter.

DISCUSSION QUESTIONS

1. A main purpose of capital rationing is to control and reduce agency costs in the process of capital budgeting. Explain agency costs in the context of capital budgeting and how capital rationing can help to reduce and control these costs.

2. Discuss the trade-off between more competition among parts of an organization as a consequence of capital rationing and the perceived benefits of capital rationing.

3. What are possible reasons to apply capital rationing in highly heterogeneous organizations and highly homogeneous organizations?

4. Research on the effects of capital rationing is relatively scarce. Different streams of literature provide different results about the effects of competition on reporting behavior of managers. Explain the different streams of the literature.

5. Explain the assumptions of human behavior regarding the three different arguments in the literature on the possible effects of competition on the level of misreporting of divisional managers toward headquarters. Why may some of the assumptions not hold in a setting with multiple periods and investment "rounds"?

REFERENCES

Alicke, Mark D., M. L. Klotz, David Breitenbacher, and Tricia J. Yurak. 1995. "Personal Contact, Individuation, and the Better-than-Average Effect." *Journal of Personality and Social Psychology* 68:5, 804–825.

Antle, Rick, and Gary D. Eppen. 1985. "Capital Rationing and Organizational Slack in Capital Budgets." *Management Science* 31:2, 163–174.

Baiman, Stanley, and Barry L. Lewis. 1989. "An Experiment Testing the Behavioral Equivalence of Strategically Equivalent Employment Contracts." *Journal of Accounting Research* 27:1, 1–20.

Brickley, James A., Clifford W. Smith, and Jerold L. Zimmerman. 2004. *Managerial Economics and Organizational Architecture*. Boston: McGraw-Hill-Irwin.

Brüggen, Alexander, and Joan Luft. 2011. "Capital Rationing, Competition, and Misrepresentation in Budget Forecasts." Working paper, Maastricht University.

Bull, Clive, Andrew Schotter, and Keith Weigelt. 1987. "Tournaments and Piece Rates: An Experimental Study." *Journal of Political Economy* 95:1, 1–33.

Camerer, Colin, and Dan Lovallo. 1999. "Overconfidence and Excess Entry: An Experimental Approach." *American Economic Review* 89:1, 306–318.

Deckop, John R., Robert Mangel, and Carol C. Cirka. 1999. "Getting More Than You Pay For: Organizational Citizenship Behavior and Pay-for-Performance Plans." *Academy of Management Journal* 42:4, 420–428.

Eisenhardt, Kathleen M. 1989. "Agency Theory: An Assessment and Review." *Academy of Management Review* 14:1, 57–74.

Evans III, John, Lynn Hannan, Ranjani Krishnan, and Donald Moser. 2001. "Honesty in Managerial Reporting." *Accounting Review* 76:1, 537–559.

Fehr, Ernst, and Armin Falk. 1999. "Wage Rigidity in a Competitive Incomplete Contract Market." *Journal of Political Economy* 107:1, 106–134.

Fischbacher, Urs, and Christian Thöni. 2008. "Excess Entry in an Experimental Winner-Take-All Market." *Journal of Economic Behavior and Organization* 67:1, 150–163.

Fisher, Joseph G., Laureen A. Maines, Sean A. Peffer, and Geoffrey B. Sprinkle. 2002. "Using Budgets for Performance Evaluation: Effects of Resource Allocation and Horizontal Information Asymmetry on Budget Proposals, Budget Slack, and Performance." *Accounting Review* 77:4, 847–865.

Freeman, Richard G., and Alexander M. Gelber. 2006. "Optimal Inequality/Optimal Incentives: Evidence from a Tournament." Working Paper, National Bureau of Economic Research.

Gitman, Lawrence J., and John R. Forrester, Jr. 1977. "A Survey of Capital Budgeting Techniques Used by Major U.S. Firms." *Financial Management* 6:3, 66–71.

Gitman, Lawrence J., and Vincent A. Mercurio. 1982. "Cost of Capital Techniques Used by Major U.S. Firms: Survey and Analysis of Fortune's 1000." *Financial Management* 11:4, 21–29.

Gneezy, Uri. 2005. "Deception: The Role of Consequences." *American Economic Review* 95:1, 384–394.

Goldstone, Robert L., and Calvin Chin. 1993. "Dishonesty in Self-report of Copies Made: Moral Relativity and the Copy Machine." *Basic and Applied Psychology* 14:1, 19–32.

Greenberg, Jerald. 2002. "Who Stole the Money, and When? Individual and Situational Determinants of Employee Theft." *Organizational Behavior and Human Decision Processes* 89:1, 985–1003.

Hannan, Lynn R., Frederick W. Rankin, and Kristy L. Towry. 2006. "The Effect of Information Systems on Honesty in Managerial Reporting: A Behavioral Perspective." *Contemporary Accounting Research* 23:4, 885–918.

Harbring, Christine, and Bernd Irlenbusch. 2008. "How Many Winners Are Good to Have? On Tournaments with Sabotage." *Journal of Economic Behavior and Organization* 65:3–4, 682–702.

Hirshleifer, Jack 1970. *Investment, Interest and Capital.* Englewood Cliffs, NJ: Prentice Hall.

Holmstrom, Bengt, and Joan Ricart i Costa. 1986. "Managerial Incentives and Capital Management." *Quarterly Journal of Economics* 101:4, 835–860.

Inderst, Roman, and Christian Laux. 2005. "Incentives in Internal Capital Markets: Capital Constraints, Competition, and Investment Opportunities." *The RAND Journal of Economics* 36:1, 215–228.

Krishnan, Ranjani, Joan Luft, and Michael D. Shields. 2002. "Competition and Cost Accounting: Adapting to Changing Markets." *Contemporary Accounting Research* 19:2, 271–302.

Lankton, Nancy, and Joan Luft. 2008. "Uncertainty and Industry Structure Effects on Managerial Intuition about Information Technology Real Options." *Journal of Management Information Systems* 25:2, 203–240.

Luft, Joan. 1997. "Fairness, Ethics and the Effect of Management Accounting on Transaction Costs." *Journal of Management Accounting Research* 9, 199–216.

Mazar, Nina, On Amir, and Dan Ariely 2008. "The Dishonesty of Honest People: A Theory of Self-concept Maintenance." *Journal of Marketing Research* 45:6, 633–644.

Mazar, Nina, and Dan Ariely. 2006. "Dishonesty in Everyday Life and Its Policy Implications." *Journal of Public Policy and Marketing* 25:1, 117–126.

Messick, David M. 1999. "Alternative Logics for Decision Making in Social Settings." *Journal of Economic Behavior and Organization* 38:1, 11–28.

Moldovanu, Benny, and Aner Sela. 2001. "The Optimal Allocation of Prizes in Contests." *American Economic Review* 91:3, 542–558.

Mukherjee, Tarun K., and Vineeta L. Hingorani. 1999. "Capital-rationing Decisions of Fortune 500 Firms: A Survey." *Financial Practice and Education* 9:1, 7–15.

Orrison, Alannah, Andrew Schotter, and Keith Weigelt. 2004. "Multiperson Tournaments: An Experimental Examination." *Management Science* 50:2, 268–279.

Podsakoff, Philip M., Scott B MacKenzie, Julie B. Paine, and Daniel G. Bachrach. 2000. "Organizational Citizenship Behaviours: A Critical Review of the Theoretical and Empirical Literature and Suggestions for Future Research." *Journal of Management* 26:3, 513–563.

Rankin, Frederick W., Steven T. Schwartz, and Richard A. Young. 2008. "The Effect of Honesty and Superior Authority on Budget Proposals." *Accounting Review* 83:4, 1083–1099.

Roth, Alvin E., Vesna Prasnikar, Masahiro Okuno-Fujiwara, and Shmuel Zamir. 1991. "Bargaining and Market Behaviors in Jerusalem, Lubljana, Pittsburgh, and Tokyo: An Experimental Study." *American Economic Review* 81:4, 1068–1095.

Schotter, Andrew, and Keith Weigelt. 1992. "Asymmetric Tournaments, Equal Opportunity Laws, and Affirmative Action: Some Experimental Results." *Quarterly Journal of Economics* 107:2, 511–539.

Schumpeter, Joseph A. 1934. *The Theory of Economic Development.* Cambridge, MA: Harvard University Press.

Stein, Jeremy C. 1997. "Internal Capital Markets and the Competition for Corporate Resources." *Journal of Finance* 52:1, 111–133.

Weingartner, H. Martin. 1977. "Capital Rationing: Authors in Search of a Plot." *Journal of Finance* 32:5, 1403–1431.

Williamson, Oliver E. 1985. *The Economic Institutions of Capitalism: Firms, Markets, Relational Contracting.* New York: Free Press.

Zhang, Guochang. 1997. "Moral Hazard in Corporate Investment and the Disciplinary Role of Voluntary Capital Rationing." *Management Science* 43:6, 737–750.

ABOUT THE AUTHOR

Alexander Brüggen is an Associate Professor at Maastricht University, where he received his master's and Ph.D. In 2006, his dissertation *Incentives in Multi-Task Settings* received the runner-up title of the "Outstanding Doctoral Dissertation Award" of the American Accounting Association, Section Management Accounting. In 2007, Professor Brüggen was a visiting researcher at Michigan State University for one semester. His research focuses on the role of performance measures and incentive schemes on managerial behavior, the role of internal capital markets, and trade-offs between explicit and implicit incentives. Besides academic research, Professor Brüggen is involved in several projects with organizations, including Lufthansa Cityline GmbH, Medrad, Federation des Experts Comptables Européens (FEE), and the Authoriteit Financiële Markten (AFM). In 2008, he received the JMAR best paper award for his paper, "The Role of Financial Incentives and Social Incentives in Multi-task Settings," co-authored with Frank Moers.

CHAPTER 7

Analyzing Foreign Investments

WIM WESTERMAN
Assistant Professor, University of Groningen

JOHN HENRY HALL
Associate Professor, University of Pretoria

INTRODUCTION

Investing at home and investing abroad may seem similar, but many differences exist. Building up a presence in another country poses several challenges. First, the investment process is more complicated with foreign investments than with domestic investments. Strategic and organizational issues make a difference, even at the level of the financial valuation processes. Second, the financial modeling of international investments presents particular difficulties, especially regarding risk, financing, and taxes. Third, the financial selection of cross-border investments abroad involves much the same techniques as within-border investments, but the perspective of the parent in the home country differs from that of the subsidiary in the host country.

In this chapter, the term *investments* refers to investments in assets ("capital") under the (direct) control of a nonfinancial firm. These may be related to greenfields ("startups"), expansions, replacements, and acquisitions (takeovers). *Foreign investments* are made in a country other than the home country of a firm, which is a *multinational enterprise* (MNE) in that it has subsidiaries in more than one country. These subsidiaries are not just local legal entities, but are involved in substantial operations, which may include procurement, production, logistics, sales, marketing, and/or other activities. MNEs try to optimize their company-wide operations to increase their economic value.

The chapter has the following organization. The analysis of foreign investments starts with an overview of the financial valuation process followed by financial modeling basics. Next, modeling complications relating to foreign investments are discussed and supplemented by a comprehensive example. The final section provides a summary and conclusions.

FINANCIAL VALUATION PROCESS

Before looking at financial calculations for foreign investments, the financial valuation process for such investments—as financial modeling and financial investment selection do not occur in a vacuum—is discussed. Financials do not rely only on the financial habits of (often) experienced investors, but they also occur in a context where strategic and organizational considerations matter. Moreover, firms often make investments in stages or phases. Therefore, this chapter takes a broad view, starting with financially oriented literature on foreign investment phases and moving on to how the valuation process typically occurs, illustrating the process with a case example.

Phasing Investments

Academics often strongly emphasize the final decision making on investments. However, economic value is actually created in the phases before and after the ultimate decision. Aharoni (1966), a pioneer on foreign investment processes, studied U.S. investments in Israel and identified perception, analysis, and choice (decision making) as crucial components of the process. King (1975) was among the first to disentangle the phases in a capital budgeting process preceding the decision. Later authors added a realization phase. Haspeslagh and Jemison (1991) break up the takeover process into seven phases: (1) strategic objectives, (2) search and screening, (3) strategic evaluation, (4) financial evaluation, (5) negotiation, (6) agreement, and (7) integration. Westerman (2004) distinguishes between five phases in the financial valuation process of foreign greenfields and acquisitions and shows that organizational, strategic, and financial issues all interact. Titman and Martin (2008) describe three investment evaluation phases, separated by documents: (1) investment (idea) origination and analysis, (2) managerial review and recommendation, and (3) managerial decision and approval.

Hall and Westerman (2008) expand the above ideas and look at the financial valuation process for foreign investments in MNEs. Three views on the planning and control of the process appear to prevail. The *project control approach* stresses the organization of investments with loose planning but tight control procedures along the way. The *financial planning approach* focuses on financial valuations before making investments and treats control as a minor issue. The *strategic planning approach* highlights centralized strategy formation with only limited control of the results of the strategic course taken. In practice, the three approaches are often combined. Additionally, there are four foreign investment phases: (1) setting the scene, (2) information management, (3) risk management, and (4) decision making. Financial managers assess the givens of the firm, assemble and process data, deal with the risks involved, and contribute to the final decision. Exhibit 7.1 combines the three views on the foreign investment process with the four phases into the framework stated below.

Typical Valuation Process

The idea for a foreign investment may originate with just one sales or production officer, but it may also be the result of a screening process by business developers or a proposal from external parties. If the investment seems attractive at first glance, management forms a project team, which includes the financial function, assigns specific tasks and responsibilities to individual project team members, and confirms hierarchical authorization lines. The team looks at the strategic fit of the

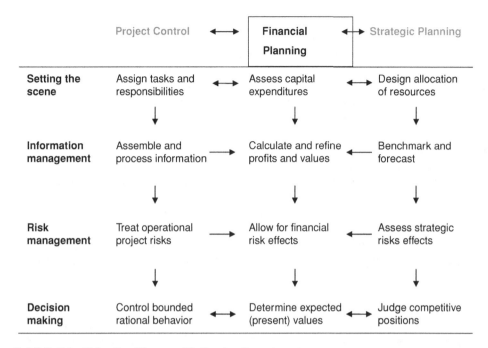

Exhibit 7.1 Valuation Phases with Foreign Investments
Note: The subsequent foreign investment phases are put in four rows. Three views on the foreign investment process are discerned in the columns. The cells show the activities undertaken.

investment with the firm's resources. If the investment requires resources that are unavailable, such as management capacity or production lines, it is turned down. Specific commercial, production, and other investment motives must comply with the strategy. Also, a project team estimates the total amount of capital needed and examines the available financial funds. Calculations must show positive outcomes in terms of basic yardsticks such as margins.

If the investment looks promising after a preliminary review, the investment team starts to gather the data it needs from sources such as market forecasts, accommodation locations, and accounting regulations. The data assembly is restricted by time and money but is intensive. Benchmarking with other firms and internal operations helps to specify the strategic alternatives, which vary from up or downscaling operations to selling off parts of businesses. The competitiveness of the operations must be guaranteed as much as possible. However, synergy effects may strengthen the case for the investment. Analysts conduct the financial modeling using a spreadsheet model adapted to the case at hand. Volumes and prices, margins, profits and returns, as well as liquidity and solvency can be calculated in this way. The management does not give much weight to paybacks and present values at this stage, as the financial risks still have to be assessed.

Next, the remaining information gaps are filled. The project team looks especially at the risks of the investment and tries to limit them. Major risks can include local market regulation, product responsibility, customer creditworthiness, supply chain reliability, machine and equipment quality, the availability of bank funds, local shareholder requirements, and local tax regulations including transfer pricing requirements. Strategic risk ranges ("limits") are specified by the management. Where they are not met, management can take diverse measures including the intensification of controls, insurance and hedging, and operational changes. Cash flows and discount rate estimations are reassessed and possible forecast errors are taken into account. Analysts incorporate the risks into the financial model. Profits, returns, and present values indicate the economic feasibility of the project. Sensitivity analysis with one important variable at a time and scenario analyses with more or less optimistic general conditions show the strength of the investment case. The project team can also assess strategic ("real options") values.

When the final decision is reached, the project team specifies how the investment should be shaped. The underlying document usually consists of a management summary, a brief introduction of the investment, a strategic analysis, a financial historical analysis (with acquisitions), a financial forecast, a suggested price range (with acquisitions), and organizational recommendations. The strategic analysis may take the form of a strengths, weaknesses, opportunities and threats (SWOT) analysis or a Porterian analysis that positions the investment vis-à-vis market forces (Porter, 1980). Next, the investment proposal goes to the decision-making stage. Depending on the size of the project, the board of directors and (if applicable) the board of supervisors may have final say and specify the limits for the implementation of the investment, especially the performance levels. These limits are more or less formally monitored (postcompletion audit). Whereas the relative competitive positions created are normative, foreign investments are usually selected on the basis of economic values.

Example: Euro Sport Hotels in Surinam

Euro Sport Hotels (ESH) (names and identifying details have been altered for the sake of confidentiality) operates hotels and restaurants in Europe. ESH is a market leader in the Netherlands and a major player in Germany and Belgium. The British leisure chain United Leisure (UL) owns ESH, but ESH operates on a stand-alone basis. A manager of a Dutch ESH hotel originally came from Surinam and he still visits the country regularly. He believes that Surinam has the potential for a small hotel that targets enthusiasts of water sports, as the weather in Surinam is pleasant all year. Tourism to the former Dutch colony has grown since the end of political upheaval in the late 1990s. Business will initially rely mainly on Dutch and U.S. guests, but the venture may soon receive guests from neighboring South American countries. Following up the suggestion by the initiator, the board of directors has appointed a multi-focus group to study the feasibility of the first ESH hotel in Surinam from January 2011 onward. The process evolves in the standard way that was described in the former section.

FINANCIAL MODELING BASICS

Financial modeling refers to framing investments in financial calculation schemes. The following discusses how these calculation schemes are framed in a general investment valuation setting. The schemes are oriented toward calculating results, book values, and cash flows. A realistic numerical example is introduced to demonstrate the basic issues with MNEs that should be emphasized.

Financial Modeling Design

Computer advances in the last 50 years and advanced programming techniques have made complex financial modeling feasible. Analysts can now use large data sets with multiple mutual links to make financial forecasts. Thus, the depth (in terms of assumptions) and width (in terms of aspects addressed) of the models have improved. Bromiley (1986) developed a capital investment model that is closely linked to the corporate planning and control process. It uses sales and production forecasts to improve corporate planning. The model is accounting-oriented. Rappaport (1986) developed a shareholder value approach (SVA) that focused on modeling cash flows to forecast business performance, especially with acquisitions. The economic value added (EVA) approach of Stewart (1991) is useful to measure past performance in economic terms. Schlosser (1992) applies value creation models to investments of multiple kinds. Buckley (1996) was among the first to build complicated models of foreign investments.

One advantage of computerized financial modeling is that sensitivity analyses became possible because analysts can easily test the rigor of the outcomes of key variables, called *value drivers*. Rappaport (1986) identifies seven value drivers: (1) value growth duration, (2) sales growth rate, (3) operating margin, (4) income tax rate, (5) working capital investment, (6) fixed capital investment, and (7) cost of capital. In addition to sensitivity analysis, analysts can perform simulations, which are experiments with models. When optimistic and pessimistic values are added to expected values of sets of variables, the potential advantages and disadvantages of the base model become clear. Sensitivity and scenario analyses are especially useful with foreign investments, which bring about additional uncertainties compared to their domestic counterparts. (Part IV of this book provides more detailed information about these techniques.)

An MNE may already have an investment valuation spreadsheet, but changes may be needed on a case-by-case basis, necessitating a (re-)design of the spreadsheet model (Schlosser, 1992; Westerman, 2004; Koller, Goedhart, and Wessels, 2010). The model framework is built up gradually, keeping additions and modifications under control. The main model sets the scene and uses data from various submodels. The model frameworks can be developed privately, but may also be bought from software or financial analysis firms. If the actual modeling is left to consultants, accountants, and banks, the MNE will have to stay in charge. Model analyses may seem basic, but skillful users can employ advanced views. The financial forecast period reflects the MNE's vision in planning future foreign investments. The actual terms, which may vary from only a few years to as many as 20 years, can be adapted by users. After the forecast period, a terminal value has to be assumed.

Regarding the focus of a financial valuation model, knowing the starting point of view of the MNE is essential. Accounting methods and economic methods can be discerned (Schlosser, 1992; Koller et al., 2010). Accounting methods are based on standard financial reporting formats, such as the profit and loss account, the balance sheet, and the cash flow statement. If economic cash flows prevail in the analysis, the focus is on the difference between receipts and disbursements. Requirements around the alignment of internal and external reporting can complicate matters here; so cash flow calculations always need a profit analysis and balance sheets. If financial statements are normalized, they refer to an average and stable situation. Otherwise, growth plans can be modeled. The terminal book or cash flow value may determine a large part of the value of an investment. Last, MNEs may distinguish explicitly between the stand-alone and synergy effects of a foreign investment.

Profits and cash flows can be discounted to account for time value and risk. The analyst can use multiple hurdles to evaluate foreign investments (Buckley, 1996; Westerman, 2004). Accounting and economic approaches look at book interest rates or the cost of debt, the return on equity or the cost of equity, and the return on investment (ROI) or the weighted average cost of capital (WACC). Analysts can set hurdle rates more or less arbitrarily by benchmarking against the figures of comparable firms or by applying the capital asset pricing model (CAPM). Analysts may also take into account specific conditions such as the sector or country in which the investment occurs when finalizing the financial modeling heuristics. Various charges may be added to the base rates. The design of the valuation model (including the determination of profits, balance sheet items and cash flows, and the hurdle rates used) sets the scene for the financial investment selection methods to be applied with foreign investments.

ESH in Surinam—Continued

The financial director of UL wonders whether ESH should be allowed to set up the new business and makes sure that ESH collects the financial data needed to assess the venture. Key value drivers in the hotel business relate to the time that elapses between overhauls, growth of the target group(s), occupancy rate of the rooms, restaurant and bar utilization, operational efficiency, fixed investment level, and cost of capital. The occupancy rate in particular is subject to much scrutiny, as many of the costs are fixed. In the industry, contracts are closed with major customers, often at a sizeable bargain. Unfortunately, as ESH's proposed hotel does not yet exist, the company cannot take advantage of this opportunity. Nevertheless, the project group sketches the market outlook, identifies other key success factors, and develops the financial data shown below. It assumes exchange rates of the British pound (£) versus euro (€) and Surinam dollar (SRD) of £1 = €1.20 = SRD 6.

The sales revenues of the new business are assumed to start at SRD 20 million in 2011 and will grow by 10 percent per year. The variable costs start at 80 percent of the sales revenues, but will drop by 4 percentage points per year until 2016 (they will be 76 percent of the sales revenues in 2012, 72 percent thereof in 2013, and so forth). The yearly fixed outlay costs are SRD 5 million. The fixed investment in the venture is SRD 6 million, to be written off straight-line in six years. The working capital investment is SRD 2 million. All investments are made at the end of 2010. Assume that the corporate tax rate is 35 percent and losses can be compensated. The business may be wrapped up on strategic grounds by the end of 2016. If so, the closure budget for the hotel will have to be SRD 20 million because of contract buy-offs and staff layoffs. ESH assumes 50 percent likelihood that it will continue the local business after 2016. The residual value in 2016 is estimated at SRD

Exhibit 7.2 Financial Forecast ESH Surinam (Before Disposal): Tentative Model

	2010	2011	2012	2013	2014	2015	2016
Sales revenues		20.0	22.0	24.2	26.6	29.3	32.2
Variable costs		16.0	16.7	17.4	18.1	18.7	19.3
Fixed outlays		5.0	5.0	5.0	5.0	5.0	5.0
Depreciation		1.0	1.0	1.0	1.0	1.0	1.0
EBIT		−2.0	−0.7	0.8	2.5	4.5	6.9
Taxes		−0.7	−0.3	0.3	0.9	1.6	2.4
Earnings (net profit)		−1.3	−0.5	0.5	1.6	3.0	4.5
Depreciation		1	1	1	1	1	1
Operating cash flow		−0.3	0.5	1.5	2.6	4.0	5.5
Investment cash flow	−8	0	0	0	0	0	0
Free cash flow	−8	−0.3	0.5	1.5	2.6	4.0	5.5
PV factor	1	0.8929	0.7972	0.7118	0.6355	0.5674	0.5066
Present value	−8.0	−0.3	0.4	1.1	1.7	2.2	2.8

This is the first model of ESH's proposed investment. All amounts are x SRD million.

40 million. According to ESH's control department, the relevant cost of capital is 12 percent. ESH Surinam is to be financed entirely with equity.

Exhibit 7.2 shows the forecasted financial results of operating the new venture. It indicates that the earnings and the cash flows are negative in the first year, but that the results will improve afterwards. Cumulative earnings, operating cash flows, and free cash flows are SRD 7.8 million, SRD 13.8 million, and SRD 5.8 million, respectively. The payback period is six years. The ROI can be calculated as SRD (7.8 million/6)/SRD 4 million = 0.33 = 33 percent. The net present value (NPV) without considering the disposal of the business is SRD –0.1 million. A highly insecure 0.50 × SRD – 20 million + 0.50 × SRD 40 million = SRD 10 million is to be expected with the disposal of the business. For safety's sake, one may want to exclude this value from the calculations, but if taking this terminal value amount into account, the free cash flow in 2016 becomes SRD 15.8 million. The NPV is SRD 5.0 million. In terms of euros and pounds, this is 1.0 million and 0.8 million, respectively.

FINANCIAL MODELING COMPLICATIONS

This section discusses how to deal with specific problems involving foreign investments. These problems may include asset (and liability) valuation differences, intracompany transfer pricing, differing tax systems, noncomplete transferal of results, exchange rate changes over time, political risks abroad, and foreign financing conditions. The discussion also distinguishes between parent firm and subsidiary views on results and hurdle rates. Each of the topics is treated separately. (For more background, see Buckley, 1996 on international capital budgeting, Koller et al., 2010 on corporate valuation, Levi, 2009 on international finance, and Westerman, Van der Meer-Kooistra, and Langfield-Smith, 2010 on international management accounting and control.) The treatment of these issues is illustrated by continuing the ESH example.

Asset Valuation

Analysts around the world do not value revenues, costs, assets, and liabilities identically. The International Accounting Standards Board (IASB) has issued International Financial Reporting Standards (IFRSs) (www.iasb.org/IFRSs/IFRs.htm). IFRS standards are not accepted worldwide. The standards used in the United States (U.S. GAAP) remain particularly important. Interpretations of accepted international standards may differ in each country. For example, profits in German-type countries are generally calculated more conservatively than profits in Anglo-Saxon–type countries. Countries often allow various standards to be used. Local standards remain in force alongside international ones. Smaller and non-listed firms often apply local standards, which may be poorly documented. Last, depending on local customs, firms use fiscal, economic, or accounting standards.

Locally accepted accounting principles differ from country to country with regard to the realization of profits (the timing of realization in particular), the valuation of work in progress, inflation corrections on assets, the treatment of goodwill (value not directly attributable to specific balance sheet items), the valuation of leases (which may be recognized as assets or are directly expensed), the terms and timing of the various kinds of depreciations, and the valuation base of loans (book value or market value). As long as the corrections are only book matters, there are no material influences (other than accounting fees). However, loan covenants may be broken and tax obligations influenced. In the case of ESH's investment in Surinam, a country where accounting practices are lax and which has a Dutch regulatory heritage, the influence of valuation issues is negligible.

Intracompany Transfer Pricing

Foreign investment involves deliveries from the parent firm to the subsidiary, from the subsidiary to the parent firm, and between the subsidiaries. The resulting transactions may refer to goods including machines, equipment, semi-finished products, and final products. They may also refer to services including packaging, product licenses, technical assistance, management services, and general services (holding cost allocations). The intracompany prices charged are called *transfer prices*. Transfer pricing guidelines for MNEs are set by the Organization for Economic Cooperation and Development (OECD) (subscribers can access these via the OECD portal, http://titania.sourceoecd.org). Local tax authorities and accounting regulators may use private interpretations of the guidelines. They may also allow standards not approved by the OECD. Approval procedures may be quite challenging at times and for certain countries. Double taxation cannot always be avoided.

The OECD encourages using market prices for internal transactions, but market prices are not always easily observed. Often, "cost plus" (a profit charge) pricing is used, and local customs may be long-lived. In the example case, the Dutch and Surinam regulators leave some room for the actual approach. Advance pricing arrangements (APAs) may even be made. ESH aims to charge license costs and general ("overhead") costs to its Surinam venture. The project group originally planned a charge set at 20 percent of the sales revenues, which is considered reasonable from a management accounting perspective. However, ESH may lower

Exhibit 7.3 Financial Forecast ESH Surinam (Before Disposal): Transfer Pricing Issues

	2010	2011	2012	2013	2014	2015	2016
Sales revenues		20.0	22.0	24.2	26.6	29.3	32.2
Direct variable costs		12.0	12.3	12.6	12.8	12.9	12.9
Indirect variable costs		2.0	2.2	2.4	2.7	2.9	3.2
Fixed outlays		5.0	5.0	5.0	5.0	5.0	5.0
Depreciation		1.0	1.0	1.0	1.0	1.0	1.0
EBIT		0.0	1.5	3.2	5.2	7.5	10.1
Taxes		0.0	0.5	1.1	1.8	2.6	3.5
Earnings		0.0	1.0	2.1	3.4	4.9	6.6
Depreciation		1	1	1	1	1	1
Operating cash flow		1.0	2.0	3.1	4.4	5.9	7.6
Investment cash flow	−8	0	0	0	0	0	0
Free cash flow	−8	1.0	2.0	3.1	4.4	5.9	7.6
PV factor	1	0.8929	0.7972	0.7118	0.6355	0.5674	0.5066
Present value	−8.0	0.9	1.6	2.2	2.8	3.3	3.8

The second model of ESH's proposed investment takes into account transfer price change consequences. All amounts are x SRD million.

this amount to just 10 percent of the sales revenues, taking into account probable requirements set by the Dutch and Surinam tax authorities.

The direct variable costs in Exhibit 7.3 refer to all variable local expenditure, whereas the indirect variable costs refer to the intracompany costs charged. With a transfer price of 20 percent of the revenues, there is no change, compared to that shown in Exhibit 7.2. However, a transfer price of 10 percent leads to higher profits and cash flows in Surinam. The startup losses disappear and the total of the profits becomes €18 million. The ROI rises to (SRD 18 million/6)/SRD 4 million = 0.75 = 75 percent per year. By adding the sum of the present values shown in Exhibit 7.3 and the present value of the terminal value of SRD 5.066 million, the NPV of the business increases to SRD 11.6 million. There is one drawback: Total profits in the Netherlands fall by the same SRD 18 million – SRD 7.8 million = SRD 10.2 million as the profit increases in Surinam. However, the Dutch corporate tax rate is 25 percent. So, a loss of (35 percent – 25 percent) x SRD 10.2 million = SRD 1.0 million (= €0.2 million) must be cashed in for the MNE as a whole. Clearly, the transfer price should not be lowered. Nevertheless, ESH may be urged to do so.

Differing Tax Systems

In an international setting, several kinds of tax are in place, such as *indirect taxes* (sales taxes in North America, value added taxes in Europe, and excise duties and import duties), and *direct taxes* (income taxes and corporate taxes). According to a KPMG (2009) survey, indirect taxes have become more important globally as direct taxes have become less important, resulting in tax competition between countries. Corporate taxes levied on profits vary from 0 percent to 70 percent or more, depending on the size of the firm, its legal incorporation, and the tax status of its owners. A specific issue relates to *withholding taxes* (local charges on

Exhibit 7.4 Financial Forecast ESH Surinam (Before Disposal): Tax System Differences

	2010	2011	2012	2013	2014	2015	2016
Earnings		0.0	1.0	2.1	3.4	4.9	6.6
Dividends		0.0	0.7	1.6	2.5	3.6	4.9
Depreciation		1	1	1	1	1	1
Operating cash flow		1.0	1.7	2.6	3.5	4.6	5.9
Investment cash flow	−8		0	0	0	0	0
Free cash flow	−8	1.0	1.7	2.6	3.5	4.6	5.9
PV factor	1	0.8929	0.7972	0.7118	0.6355	0.5674	0.5066
Present value	−8.0	0.9	1.4	1.8	2.2	2.6	3.0

The third model of ESH's proposed investment takes into account the influence of tax system specifics. For lines not shown, refer to Exhibit 7.3. All amounts are x SRD million.

royalty payments, interest payments, and dividend payments to an MNE parent firm), which typically vary between 0 percent and 30 percent of the distribution. Last, *subsidies*, which are effectively negative taxes granted on investments and operations, may also apply.

In the Surinam case, there is no separate corporate tax—firms are taxed just like individuals. In the example provided, the corporate tax rate used is derived from the actual one for small and medium enterprises. Surinam levies a withholding tax of 25 percent on dividends, but this can be waived when there is a tax treaty with the MNE's home country, as with the Netherlands. If Surinam did not exempt Dutch firms from withholding taxes and if all profits would be distributed immediately, with a transfer price of 10 percent of sales revenues, the surcharge would be 25 percent of the total profits of SRD 18 million (SRD 4.5 million). The net dividend payout is lowered by this amount, such as Exhibit 7.4 shows. The local NPV becomes SRD 9.0 million and therefore the loss would be SRD 11.6 million − SRD 9.0 million = SRD 2.6 million (= €0.5 million). Although this not a high figure, ESH might want to consider relocating profits in this case.

Blocking Funds

Although host countries generally welcome foreign investments, they may also worry about MNE disinvestment later. One way to discourage disinvestment is to partially or wholly stop cash outflows to the home country. Another reason for so-called exchange controls is foreign exchange shortages. The *blocked funds* may include dividends, interest payments, royalties, and even management fees. Blocking has to be temporary or else an MNE would not invest at all since eternal blocking would in fact be expropriation. ESH's Surinam investment may become an issue when the free cash flow is positive and even more with the planned disposal. But even then, the Surinam government is not expected to stop the remittance of sales proceeds, although it may influence the sale in such a way that losses occur, for example, with sale hold-ups and forced investments to local investors. Shapiro (1978) provides general formulae for calculating the NPV with blocked funds.

Exhibit 7.5 uses figures already included in Exhibit 7.3 but assumes that ESH's Surinam profits cannot be distributed to the Netherlands until the disposal of

Exhibit 7.5   Financial Forecast ESH Surinam (Before Disposal): Blocking Funds

	2011	2012	2013	2014	2015	2016
Earnings	0.0	1.0	2.1	3.4	4.9	6.6
PV factor loss	0.8219	0.8548	0.889	0.9246	0.9615	1
Present value	0.0	0.8	1.8	3.1	4.7	6.6
Present value loss	0.0	0.1	0.2	0.3	0.2	0.0

The fourth model of ESH's proposed investment examines the consequences of blocking of funds. For lines not shown, refer to Exhibit 7.3. All amounts are x SRD million.

the venture. The funds must be placed in the bank in Surinam and earn a risky 8 percent. Moreover, another assumption is that the sale will realize a 20 percent lower price than previously expected. The effect on the NPV of the business is an opportunity loss of (12 percent − 8 percent) = 4 percent over the profits in the first five years. Its NPV is SRD 0.81 million (€0.16 million). An opportunity loss of SRD 2 million × 0.50 = SRD 1 million (€0.20 million) also exists because the terminal value of the hotel is reduced.

Exchange Rate Changes

A major problem with the analysis of foreign investments (outside currency zones such as the Eurozone) is the volatility of exchange rates between currencies. Interest rate differences induce money flows that are corrected by exchange rate changes. Purchasing power and trade balance differences also play a role, but in a rather indirect way. MNEs ask banks for advice when forecasting the future *spot rates* (cash rates) and may also look at spot *futures rates* that are arranged now and settled later. Two approaches for calculating NPVs cashed in by the ultimate owners prevail (Ross, Westerfield, Jaffe, and Jordan, 2011). One approach involves judging the results against the hurdle rate applicable at home (*home currency approach*). Another method involves converting the (net present) value of the investment in the foreign currency against the spot rate, if the local hurdle rate is known (*foreign currency approach*).

ESH does not distinguish explicitly between a home country discount rate and a host country discount rate, but ESH actually uses a home country rate. Hence, it has to produce exchange rate forecasts. There are no usable SRD futures rates, especially not in the long run. The spot rate for the SRD is SRD 6 = EUR 1.20 = GBP 1. (Because the British firm UL owns ESH, the British pound exchange rate is also relevant). ESH assumes a depreciation of the SRD versus the euro of 5 percent per year and versus the pound of 7.5 percent per year. Thus it effectively forecasts a depreciation of the euro versus the pound.

Exhibit 7.6a uses the same assumptions as Exhibit 7.3. With a stable exchange rate, the NPV of the venture excluding the disposal effect is €1.3 million and £1.1 million, respectively, and with this effect the NPV amounts to €3.3 million and £2.8 million, respectively.

Exhibit 7.6b uses the data in Exhibit 7.3. Here, the depreciation factors are cumulative. The depreciation factor in euro terms is equal to $0.95 \times 0.95 = 0.9025$

Exhibit 7.6a   Financial Forecast ESH Surinam (Before Disposal): Exchange Rate Changes

	2010	2011	2012	2013	2014	2015	2016
Free cash flow (SRD)	−8	1.0	2.0	3.1	4.4	5.9	7.6
Free cash flow (€)	−1.6	0.2	0.4	0.6	0.9	1.2	1.5
Free cash flow (£)	−1.3	0.2	0.3	0.5	0.7	1.0	1.3
PV factor	1	0.8929	0.7972	0.7118	0.6355	0.5674	0.5066
Present value (SRD)	−1.3	0.9	1.6	2.2	2.8	3.3	3.8
Present value (€)	−1.6	0.2	0.3	0.4	0.6	0.7	0.8
Present value (£)	−1.3	0.1	0.3	0.4	0.5	0.6	0.6

Panel A of the fifth model of ESH's proposed investment assumes stable exchange rates. For lines not shown, refer to Exhibit 7.3. All amounts are x SRD million.

in 2013. If the exchange rate decreases as predicted, the NPV of the Surinam venture without the probable disposal drops to €0.8 million and £0.3 million, respectively. Including this effect, the NPV becomes €2.2 million and £1.3 million, respectively. The NPV decreases the most in pound terms because of the appreciation of the pound versus the euro. Nevertheless, the investment remains financially feasible.

Political Risks

Political risks include, among others, the consequences of armed conflict, governmental turmoil, and strikes and slowdowns (for a full discussion, see Chapter 13). If such events affect a local economy as a whole, hurdle rate adjustments may be in place. Analysts can incorporate specific risks in the profit and cash flow forecasts. An MNE may also arbitrarily adjust either hurdle rates or cash flows for all the political risks. For example, ESH may have to lower the sales revenue forecasts for its Surinam venture by 15 percent because of local political circumstances in the host country. The sales revenues are decreasing slowly at present, because the growth factor is $1.1 \times 0.85 = 0.94$. The yearly earnings will become barely positive in the very last (sixth) year of the planned period. The NPV of the venture, assuming the

Exhibit 7.6b   Financial Forecast ESH Surinam (Before Disposal): Exchange Rate Changes

	2010	2011	2012	2013	2014	2015	2016
Free cash flow	−8	1.0	2.0	3.1	4.4	5.9	7.6
Depreciation factor (€)	1.0	1.0	0.9	0.9	0.8	0.8	0.7
Free cash flow (€)	−1.6	0.2	0.4	0.5	0.7	0.9	1.1
Depreciation factor (£)	1.0	0.9	0.8	0.7	0.7	0.6	0.6
Free cash flow (£)	−1.3	0.1	0.3	0.4	0.5	0.6	0.7
PV factor	1	0.8929	0.7972	0.7118	0.6355	0.5674	0.5066
Present value	−8.0	0.9	1.6	2.2	2.8	3.3	3.8
Present value (€)	−1.6	0.2	0.3	0.4	0.5	0.5	0.6
Present value (£)	−1.3	0.1	0.2	0.3	0.3	0.3	0.4

Panel B of the fifth model of ESH's proposed investment assumes specific exchange rate changes. For lines not shown, refer to Exhibit 7.3. All amounts are x SRD million.

Exhibit 7.7a Financial Forecast ESH Surinam (Before Disposal): Political Risks

	2010	2011	2012	2013	2014	2015	2016
Sales revenues		17.0	15.9	14.9	13.9	13.0	12.1
Direct variable costs		10.2	8.9	7.7	6.7	5.7	4.9
Indirect variable costs		1.7	1.6	1.5	1.4	1.3	1.2
Fixed outlays		5.0	5.0	5.0	5.0	5.0	5.0
Depreciation		1.0	1.0	1.0	1.0	1.0	1.0
EBIT		−0.9	−0.6	−0.4	−0.2	0.0	0.1
Taxes		−0.3	−0.2	−0.1	−0.1	0.0	0.0
Earnings		−0.6	−0.4	−0.2	−0.1	0.0	0.0
Depreciation		1	1	1	1	1	1
Operating cash flow		0.4	0.6	0.8	0.9	1.0	1.0
Investment cash flow	−8	0	0	0	0	0	0
Free cash flow	−8	0.4	0.6	0.8	0.9	1.0	1.0
PV factor	1	0.8929	0.7972	0.7118	0.6355	0.5674	0.5066
Present value	−8.0	0.4	0.5	0.5	0.6	0.6	0.5

Panel A of the sixth model of ESH's proposed investment assumes politically induced sales drops. All amounts are x SRD million.

base case used in Exhibit 7.3, drops to SRD −4.9 million without disposal effects and SRD 0.1 million including these effects (see Exhibit 7.7a).

For political risks against which a company can take out insurance, an (opportunity) cost charge can be included in the profit and cash flow calculations (Stonehill and Nathanson, 1968). However, insurance is not possible for all political risks, if any. If, instead of the former alternatives, ESH raises the discount rate to 30 percent, the NPV is lowered to SRD 0.0(05) million, if excluding the terminal value NPV of SRD 2.1 million (see Exhibit 7.7b).

Financing Conditions

The foreign operations of an MNE are financed by equity, debt, and/or hybrids. The cost of equity can be assessed with various concepts. Besides the book return on equity, the CAPM and the dividend discount model (DDM) are used. The cost of debt can be drawn from book interest rates and market interest rates. In addition to internally generated cash flows, an array of financial instruments is used including various types of shares and loans. The funds to be used can come from the home country, the host country, or elsewhere, causing various costs levels. If funds cannot

Exhibit 7.7b Financial Forecast ESH Surinam (Before Disposal): Political Risks

	2010	2011	2012	2013	2014	2015	2016
Free cash flow	−8.0	1.0	2.0	3.1	4.4	5.9	7.6
PV factor	1	0.7692	0.5917	0.4552	0.3501	0.2693	0.2073
Present value	−8.0	0.8	1.2	1.4	1.5	1.6	1.6

Panel B of the sixth model of ESH's proposed investment assumes a politically induced discount rate rise. For lines not shown, refer to exhibit 7.7a. All amounts are x SRD million.

be obtained from the cheapest sources, financial market segmentation applies. Prohibitive local regulations and good citizenship considerations may provoke this. All in all, with foreign investments, financing and investment may easily become intertwined. Lessard (1985) shows that the adjusted present value (APV) method can effectively single out financing effects.

Calculating the cost of equity and the cost of debt with foreign investments is not easy because many methods are available. With regard to the cost of equity, Stulz (1995) suggests using a global CAPM for integrated markets. The CAPM is as follows:

$$R_s = R_f + \beta(R_m - R_f) \tag{7.1}$$

where R_s is the risk-free rate of return, R_m is the market rate of return, and β is the beta coefficient that measures the systematic risk of a security. All variables used should have global reference bases. Now that global indices and databases are increasingly in place, applying the global CAPM has become relatively easy. Even basic benchmarking with other firms may already be helpful. Aside from the cost of equity, the cost of debt can also be derived from the global CAPM, and benchmarks derived from various sources may suffice (in integrated markets only). If markets are not wholly integrated, local CAPM and local benchmarks also become important.

In the case of ESH in Surinam, only equity is in place for reasons of convenience. The local equity market is very thin, whereas ESH and UL have funds available. Therefore, the cost of equity used at the parent firm(s) is applicable. This rate has been set at the 12 percent used above. Alternatively, local book rates, UL benchmarks with similar countries, and private hunches may lead ESH to set the rate of locally acquired equity at 16 percent. A notable effect of local equity would be that the venture gets local owners but the use of preferred shares, for example, may limit their control rights. The relevant local interest rate is set at 8 percent, in accordance with long-term bank lending rates. With a mix of 50 percent equity and 50 percent debt, the cost of capital becomes $0.16 \times 0.50 + 0.09 \times (1 - 0.35) \times 0.50 = 0.10925 \approx 11$ percent. The NPV of the venture then rises to SRD 5.7 million without the disposal effect and SRD 11.0 million with this effect. All in all, the net effect of local financing would be negligible (as indicated by comparing Exhibits 7.3 and 7.8).

Parent Firm Viewpoint

So far, the discussion mainly applies the subsidiary's point of view on the values likely to be obtained with foreign investments. However, subsidiary and parent firm perspectives must be clearly distinguished (Ahkam and Baker, 1993). Issues that may matter to MNE parent firms include operational cash transfers, termination values, foreign exchange risks, and political risks. The following discussion shows the joint effects of these items for ESH by building an expected case for its Surinam business. The case uses a transfer price of 10 percent of the sales revenues (this includes a 2 percent license fee and 8 percent overhead charge), a terminal value of SRD 8 million (= discount of $0.20 \times$ SRD 10 million), as well as operational payout and SRD conversion schemes as follows: All excess operational cash flows

Exhibit 7.8 Financial Forecast ESH Surinam (Before Disposal): Financing Conditions

	2010	2011	2012	2013	2014	2015	2016
EBIT		0.0	1.5	3.2	5.2	7.5	10.1
Interest		0.4	0.4	0.4	0.4	0.4	0.4
EBT		−0.4	1.1	2.8	4.8	7.1	9.7
Taxes		0.0	0.5	1.1	1.8	2.6	3.5
Earnings		−0.4	0.6	1.7	3.0	4.5	6.2
Depreciation		1	1	1	1	1	1
Operating cash flow		0.6	1.6	2.7	4.0	5.5	7.2
Investment cash flow	−8	0	0	0	0	0	0
Free cash flow	−8	0.6	1.6	2.7	4.0	5.5	7.2
PV factor	1	0.9174	0.9174	0.9174	0.9174	0.9174	0.9174
Present value	−8.0	0.6	1.5	2.5	3.7	5.0	6.6

The seventh model of ESH's proposed investment takes into account specific financing conditions. For lines not shown, refer to Exhibit 7.3. All amounts are x SRD million.

are put in a bank account and earn 8 percent, until they are released by the end of Year 6. The spot exchange rate is SRD 1 = EUR 5 = GBP 6, and the SRD depreciates after 2011 versus the euro by 5 percent per year and versus the pound by 7.5 percent per year. The Dutch corporate tax rate is 25 percent and the dividend payments to the United Kingdom are tax-free.

Exhibit 7.9 first calculates the earnings directly made by the Dutch parent company. The Surinam operating cash flow, expected to be transferable in 2016, is the sum of the operating cash flows and the interest earned. The resulting ESH free cash flow is calculated in terms of SRD first and then converted into euros and pounds. The parent firm's earnings are SRD 11.6 million + 27.0 million = SRD

Exhibit 7.9 Financial Forecast ESH Surinam Business; Parent Firm Viewpoint

	2010	2011	2012	2013	2014	2015	2016
License fee		0.4	0.4	0.5	0.5	0.6	0.6
Overhead charge		1.6	1.8	1.9	2.1	2.3	2.6
EBIT		2.0	2.2	2.4	2.7	2.9	3.2
Taxes		0.5	0.6	0.6	0.7	0.7	0.8
Earnings		1.5	1.7	1.8	2.0	2.2	2.4
Operating cash flow		0	0	0	0	0	27.0
Investment cash flow	−8	0	0	0	0	0	8
Free cash flow (SRD)	−8	1.5	1.7	1.8	2.0	2.2	37.4
Depreciation factor (€)	1.0	1.0	0.9	0.9	0.8	0.8	0.7
Free cash flow (€)	−1.3	0.3	0.3	0.3	0.3	0.3	5.5
Depreciation factor (£)	1.0	0.9	0.8	0.7	0.7	0.6	0.6
Free cash flow (£)	−1.3	0.2	0.2	0.2	0.2	0.2	3.6
PV factor	1	0.8929	0.7972	0.7118	0.6355	0.5674	0.5066
Present value (SRD)	−8.0	1.3	1.3	1.3	1.3	1.2	19.0
Present value (€)	−1.3	0.3	0.2	0.2	0.2	0.2	2.8
Present value (£)	−1.3	0.2	0.2	0.2	0.1	0.1	1.8

The eighth model of ESH's proposed investment assumes Dutch and British parent viewpoints. All amounts are x million.

Exhibit 7.10   Financial Forecast ESH Surinam Business (Parent Firm Viewpoint Revisited)

	2010	2011	2012	2013	2014	2015	2016
License fee		0.3	0.3	0.3	0.3	0.3	0.2
Overhead charge		1.4	1.3	1.2	1.1	1.0	1.0
EBIT		1.7	1.6	1.5	1.4	1.3	1.2
Taxes		0.4	0.4	0.4	0.3	0.3	0.3
Earnings		1.3	1.2	1.1	1.0	1.0	0.9
Operating cash flow		0	0	0	0	0	22.1
Investment cash flow	−8	0	0	0	0	0	8
Free cash flow	−8	1.3	1.2	1.1	1.0	1.0	31.0
Depreciation factor (€)	1.0	1.0	0.9	0.9	0.8	0.8	0.7
Free cash flow (€)	−1.3	0.3	0.2	0.2	0.2	0.2	4.6
Depreciation factor (£)	1.0	0.9	0.8	0.7	0.7	0.6	0.6
Free cash flow (£)	−1.3	0.2	0.2	0.1	0.1	0.1	3.0
PV factor	1	0.8929	0.7972	0.7118	0.6355	0.5674	0.5066
Present value	−8.0	1.1	1.0	0.8	0.7	0.6	15.7
Present value (€)	−1.3	0.2	0.2	0.1	0.1	0.1	2.3
Present value (£)	−1.3	0.2	0.1	0.1	0.1	0.1	1.5

Note: The ninth model of ESH's proposed investment examines a negative scenario from both Dutch and British parent viewpoints. All amounts are x million.

38.6 million, which is €1.9 million + €4.0 million = €5.9 million. The payback period of the parent firm's investment of €8 million, taking into account the depreciation of the SRD, is a little over five years in euro terms. The parent firm's investments are wholly depreciated in six years. This promises a healthy ROI of 74 percent per year, even excluding the disposal gains. The expected NPV of the business for the parent firm is a sound €2.6 million or £1.3 million.

In the end, the NPV of the parent firm is what matters. Thus, the expectation is that those involved would greet the investment proposal with enthusiasm and that nothing would prevent ESH from happily investing in Surinam. However, there are some caveats. Assume, for instance, that Surinam sales lag 15 percent behind the original forecast. Recall that with a similar assumption, the local NPV becomes almost zero. The parent firm's ROI then falls to 48 percent, excluding the disposal. If the hurdle is 40 percent, this is still acceptable. Also, the NPV is still positive, with €1.7 million or £0.7 million (see Exhibit 7.10). Thus, the revised scenario remains acceptable. But suppose that the local sales become 75 percent of the original forecast. Then, the parent firm's ROI, excluding the disposal, drops to 10 percent and the parent firm's NPV becomes negative at €−0.4 million and £−0.5 million, respectively. Such scenarios raise doubt about the venture.

Concluding the Story

How does the ESH story end? The analysis has combined and adapted two similar cases. In the first case, the hotel was never established. Analysts studied the prospects of the business in depth and the financial outlook seemed positive, but uncertainties about the competitiveness of the location overshadowed the decision making. The project ended the way that it had started—gradually. The other hotel had already been in business for a long time but needed a major over-haul and upgrade to serve the target group. The strategic and financial prospects were exciting, but the owners and managers perceived the local risk to be very high. Thus, they postponed the investment. However, as new windows of opportunity opened later, "real options came in the money" and resulted in realizing much of the original investment plan despite the foreign investment process taking several years.

SUMMARY AND CONCLUSIONS

In a foreign setting, financial valuation basics are much the same as those in a domestic setting. They are about managing processes, profits or cash flows, hurdles or discount rates, and returns or present values. However, there are some differences. First, the investment valuation process is less straightforward for activities abroad than for activities back home, as shown in the phase framework of the activities undertaken. Second, foreign outcomes do not resemble domestic ones. This is due especially to asset and liability valuation differences, intracompany transfer pricing, different tax systems, incomplete transfer of results, exchange rate changes over time, political risks abroad, foreign financing conditions, and the parent versus daughter perspective. Third, investment valuation techniques work in environments abroad differently than in those at home. Whereas this is largely an outcome of the above, it may influence the mutual priority of the techniques.

In this chapter, the treatment of the analysis of foreign investments started with a process view. This treatment dealt with the setting of the investment (emphasizing information management), took into account risk management, and discussed the final decision making. The chapter focused on modeling profits and cash flows and largely left hurdling and discounting issues to other chapters. Although sensitivity analyses and scenario analyses play a large role in the actual financial modeling, they are not discussed here in depth. The chapter dealt with common financial investment selection techniques such as payback, ROI, and NPV largely as outcomes of a financial modeling process. (Part V of this book discusses the relevance of real option techniques in financial investment selection).

DISCUSSION QUESTIONS

1. A business development manager of a financial institution that was enthusiastically capturing Eastern European markets commented as follows: "Yes, we do make some basic calculations. But no, we do not discuss our ideas with the financial department beforehand. However, now that you mention it, the final investment proposal must indeed be sent to the financial staff. This is just a matter of rubber stamping." Comment.

2. "The financial modeling of foreign investments is a matter of sensitivity analysis and scenario analysis. This is not necessarily the case for domestic investments." Is this statement true? Why or why not?

3. U.S. firms are typically less interested in the payback periods of foreign investments than, for example, German firms. Relate this to U.S. domestic depreciation practices.

4. "Since I want to behave as a good local citizen, I am not really interested in foreign exchange rates," the financial director of ESH said in regards to a foreign investment. Others in the firm disagree with this statement. Comment on this attitude.

5. An Australian firm, National Boomerang Beer (NBB), is preparing to enter the Litoromian market, which it considers a greenfield investment (startup). The Litoromian beer market is fragmented. Only a few firms have substantial market shares, none of which exceed 5 percent. In fact, the market is regionally divided, except for some special beers and three firms competing for a country-wide presence. Market share gains can only be acquired by accepting large price cuts.

   - As of today, the Litos is pegged to the dollar and the beer prices are dollar related. As Litoromia will adopt the euro eventually, it will give up the peg. NBB expects a gradual changeover and depreciation. The exchange rate of the Litos vis-à-vis the Australian dollar will be AUD 1 = LTO 2.0 on January 1, 2011 and will gradually drop to AUD 1 = LTO 3.0 by December 31, 2020.
   - NBB must invest LTO 10 million by January 1, 2011, to be straight-line depreciated in 10 years. The yearly revenues will be LTO 7.5 million. Royalties and fees paid to the mother firm are 8 percent of the revenues. The yearly outlay costs for sales/marketing, production and general purposes are LTO 2.2 million, LTO 1.6 million and LTO 0.9 million, respectively. The European Union will subsidize half of the investment outlay. The Litoromian government offers NBB tax exemption during the planning period of 10 years, unless any dividend is paid before year-end 2020.
   - All cash flows after the investment are expected to occur at the year-end. NBB plans to reinvest depreciation funds in the business immediately. No terminal values are to be included. The cost of capital employed is 12 percent, although NBB uses a hurdle rate of 8 percent in Australia. NBB's corporate tax rate is 30 percent. Items not provided (e.g., working capital changes) are neglected.
     A. Is the investment attractive from a subsidiary point of view? Provide both an ROI and an NPV calculation.
     B. Is the investment attractive from a parent firm's point of view? Include an NPV calculation. Assume that NBB can earn 8 percent per year with its local excess cash flows.

REFERENCES

Aharoni, Yair. 1966. *The Foreign Investment Decision Process.* Boston: Division of Research, Graduate School of Business Administration, Harvard University.

Ahkam, Sarif N., and James C. Baker. 1993. "Cash Flow Estimation and Cost of Capital for Overseas Projects." *Accounting and Business Research* 23:4, 90, 99–109.

Bromiley, Philip. 1986. *Corporate Capital Investment: A Behavioral Approach.* Cambridge: Cambridge University Press.

Buckley, Adrian. 1996. *Multinational Capital Budgeting.* London: Prentice Hall.

Hall, John, and Wim Westerman. 2008. "Capital Expenditures with a Multinational Enterprise." *Journal of Corporate Treasury Management* 2:2, 139–147.

Haspeslagh, Philippe C., and David B. Jemison. 1991. *Managing Acquisitions: Creating Value through Corporate Renewal.* New York: Free Press.

King, Paul. 1975. "Is the Emphasis of Capital Budgeting Theory Misplaced?" *Journal of Business Finance and Accounting* 2:1, 69–81.

Koller, Tim, Marc Goedhart, and David Wessels. 2010. *Valuation: Measuring and Managing the Value of Companies*, 5th ed. New York: McKinsey/Wiley.

KPMG. 2009. *KPMG's Corporate and Indirect Tax Rate Survey 2009.* Amsterdam: KPMG International.

Lessard, Donald R. 1985. " Evaluating International Projects: An Adjusted Present Value Approach." In Donald R. Lessard, ed. *International Financial Management, Theory and Application*, 2nd ed., 570–584. New York: Wiley.

Levi, Maurice. 2009. *International Finance*, 5th ed. New York: Routledge.

Porter, Michael E. 1980. *Competitive Strategy: Techniques for Analyzing Industries and Competitors.* New York: Free Press.

Rappaport, Alfred. 1986. *Creating Shareholder Value: The New Standard for Business Performance.* New York: Free Press.

Ross, Stephen A., Randolph W. Westerfield, Jeffrey F. Jaffe, and Bradford Jordan. 2011. *Corporate Finance*, 9th ed. Homewood, IL: McGraw-Hill.

Schlosser, Michel. 1992. *Corporate Finance: A Model-building Approach*, 2nd ed. Hemel Hempstead: Prentice Hall.

Shapiro, Alan C. 1978. "Capital Budgeting for the Multinational Corporation." *Financial Management* 7:1, 7–16.

Stewart, G. Bennett, III. 1991. *The Quest for Value: The EVA Management Guide.* New York: HarperBusiness.

Stonehill, Arthur, and Leonard Nathanson. 1968. "Capital Budgeting and the Multinational Corporation." *California Management Review* 10:4, 39–54.

Stulz, René M. 1995. "The Cost of Capital in Internationally Integrated Markets: The Case of Nestlé." *European Financial Management* 1:1, 1–22.

Titman, Sheridan, and John D. Martin. 2008. *Valuation: The Art and Science of Corporate Investment Decisions.* Boston: Pearson/Addison Wesley.

Westerman, Wim. 2004. "From Nutricia to Numico: Valuing a Pan-European Acquisition." *Investment Management and Financial Innovations* 3:2, 90–97.

Westerman, Wim, Jeltje Van Der Meer-Kooistra, and Kim Langfield-Smith, eds. 2010. *International Management Accounting and Control.* London: McGraw-Hill.

ABOUT THE AUTHORS

Wim Westerman is an Assistant Professor of Financial Management at the Faculty of Economics and Business with the University of Groningen (UoG), where he was awarded his PhD. He coordinates the International Financial Management program and also supervises master's theses. Professor Westerman has taught courses in international financial management and financial management and has contributed to various research courses. His research focuses on financial management, specifically in capital budgeting, corporate valuation, treasury management, and management control. He is an editor of the *Journal of Corporate Treasury Management* (JCTM) and a fellow of the UoG Centre for International Banking, Insurance and Finance (CIBIF) and its Energy and Sustainability Centre (ESC). He initiated the Global Center for Energy and Value Issues (CEVI) in 2006.

John Henry Hall is an Associate Professor at the University of Pretoria, where he received both an MBA and DBA. Before joining the University of Pretoria, he worked at the South African Revenue Service's Head office and in regional offices as a tax inspector and also as the financial manager of a civil engineering and manufacturing firm. Professor Hall has published numerous articles in scholarly journals including the *Investment Analysts Journal* and the *Journal of Corporate Treasury Management* and received several best paper awards. He has also has presented research papers at conferences both locally and internationally. Professor Hall presents courses on financial management and consults on a wide range of issues in the private sector.

CHAPTER 8

Postcompletion Auditing of Capital Investments[*]

JARI HUIKKU
Assistant Professor, Aalto University School of Economics

INTRODUCTION

Success in capital investment greatly affects the extent to which a company can achieve its strategic objectives. Academic researchers posit that postcompletion auditing (PCA) of capital investments can provide valuable feedback for current and future investments, and consequently make capital investment more effective (Neale, 1991a; Pierce and Tsay, 1992). Other synonymous terms for PCA are *postaudit, postcompletion review*, and *postappraisal* (of capital investments). *Postcompletion audit* and *postaudit* seem to be the two most often presented terms in recent studies. PCA is a formal process that checks the outcomes of individual investment projects after the initial investment is completed and when the project is operational (Chenhall and Morris, 1993; Huikku, 2007). It can be regarded as one formal control system within a company's management control system (MCS) package, which consists of various formal and informal controls (Otley, 1999; Malmi and Brown, 2008). According to Merchant and Otley (2007, p. 785), MCS is a system that is "designed to help an organization adapt to the environment in which it is set and to deliver the key results desired by stakeholder groups."

Researchers particularly emphasize that PCA information can facilitate organizational learning (OL) with regard to planning future investment projects (e.g., Huikku, 2009). In other words, PCA information has the potential to help a company avoid previous mistakes and to systematically identify successful processes that can be repeated (Shapiro, 2005; Northcott and Alkaraan, 2007). Additionally, scholars suggest that PCA can be used to measure the performance of an investment, to provide feedback to aid control of current investments, to enhance the integrity of investment appraisals, and to evaluate management (e.g., Huikku, 2008). Researchers examining PCA emphasize the fact that the appropriate design of PCA systems, particularly regarding PCA reports and aspects of their communication, is a prerequisite for effective knowledge transfer and sharing, and hence for

---

[*]The author appreciates the helpful comments provided by Seppo Ikäheimo, H. Kent Baker, and Philip English.

organizational learning (Mills and Kennedy, 1993; Azzone and Maccarrone, 2001; Huikku, 2010). Commonly referred-to aspects of PCA design are related to the selection of projects for PCA, the timing of PCA, the location of responsibility for a PCA system, the persons conducting PCA, and the format and communication of a PCA report (e.g., Neale and Holmes, 1991; Pierce and Tsay, 1992; Kennedy and Mills, 1993). The use of PCA is very common among large companies in the United States and the United Kingdom, and many companies in other countries have also adopted the approach (Neale, 1994; Arnold and Hatzopoulos, 2000).

The recent empirical PCA research is not voluminous (for a literature review, see Haka, 2007). This chapter provides a synthesis of academic empirical research on PCA. First, it discusses the definition of PCA and adoption rates. The chapter continues by addressing managerial uses of PCA, its perceived problems, reasons for adoption/nonadoption, and the design of PCA systems. The final section provides a summary and conclusions including suggestions for future studies.

Definition of PCA

Capital budgeting can be understood as a process consisting of distinct stages. There are many different capital budgeting process models (e.g., Mukherjee and Henderson, 1987; Northcott, 1992; Pike and Neale, 2003). Their common feature is that the control phase (i.e., PCA) is always presented as the final and concluding phase. Northcott proposes that the capital budgeting process comprises the following stages: (1) project identification, (2) project definition and screening, (3) analysis and acceptance, (4) implementation, and (5) monitoring and postaudit. Such a presentation suggests dividing the concluding phase into two stages. Monitoring refers to the control that takes place during the implementation of a capital investment project (i.e., the phase before completion of a project). In this phase, a typical approach is to follow up on the cost budget, scheduling, and technical specifications to see that they are progressing according to plan.

PCA can be described as a formal review of a completed investment project fulfilling the following criteria: (1) PCA takes place after an investment has been completed (commissioned) and has begun to generate cash flows (or savings); (2) PCA reporting is at least partly focused on a comparison between the pre-investment estimates of an investment project and the actual figures and achievements after completion; and (3) PCA is a systematic, regular, and formalized process with instructions that provide guidance. This description is congruent with that suggested by Gadella (1986), Pierce and Tsay (1992), Chenhall and Morris (1993), and CIMA (2005), but is more explicit with regard to criterion (3). In practice, monitoring of the implementation phase and PCA are overlapping concepts because monitoring is, to some extent, a prerequisite for PCA. Nevertheless, monitoring alone cannot be considered as fulfilling the criteria for PCA. In a monitoring phase, estimating whether an investment project will achieve its targets typically occurs too early. Besides monitoring, this PCA description rules out routine reporting as well as informal ways of controlling capital investments. Internal and external routine reporting such as monthly, quarterly, and annually do not usually fulfil all the criteria required for PCA. For example, routine reporting is typically (1) profit-center or cost-center focused, not investment project-focused; and (2) does not compare the preinvestment objectives of an investment project with the actual achievements. Neale and Holmes (1991), Azzone and Maccarrone (2001), and Huikku (2007) provide discussions about the distinction between PCA and other control mechanisms.

PCA ADOPTION RATES

The adoption rates of PCA have been much studied in the United States and the United Kingdom. According to the latest studies, most large companies within these countries use PCA. In the United Kingdom the following adoption rates have been reported: 98 percent (Arnold and Hatzopoulos, 2000) and 79 percent (Neale, 1991b). Correspondingly, in the United States reported adoption rates are 88 percent (Farragher, Kleiman, and Sahu, 1999), 76 percent (Gordon and Myers, 1991), and 90 percent (Klammer and Walker, 1984). Neale (1994) provides a list of older PCA adoption studies. In other countries, adoption rate studies have been rare. Examples of such studies include Neale (1994) in Norway and Azzone and Maccarone (2001) in Italy. Neale finds that 41 percent of large Norwegian companies use PCA. The corresponding figure in large Italian companies is 71 percent. Furthermore, Huikku (2007) reports that 20 out of the 30 largest Finnish manufacturing companies (i.e., 67 percent) conduct PCA at least to some extent. The remaining 10 companies do not formally compare preinvestment estimates of investment projects with the actual outcomes after the projects have been commissioned and have started to generate cash flows. Interestingly, a "grey area" appears within PCA adopters; namely, companies that conduct formal PCA but do so only irregularly and unsystematically. Consequently, Huikku suggests that the inclusion of ad hoc adopters tends to drive adoption rates upward.

Besides the inclusion of ad hoc adopters, other issues may challenge the comparison of different adoption studies. The concept of PCA and the criteria for adopters is not necessarily the same in all studies. The potential "grey areas" include, at a minimum: monitoring vs. PCA; routine reporting vs. PCA; and informal control vs. PCA. Also, companies with less sophisticated capital investment procedures may not be eager to respond to surveys. Consequently, these findings may challenge the reliability of mail surveys. Furthermore, due to different types of population and different sized companies, comparing these adoption rate figures is problematic. Some studies concentrate on the largest companies, others use only industrial companies, while still others selectively include firms from manufacturing and nonmanufacturing sectors.

MANAGERIAL USES OF PCA

Prior studies have examined both the objectives of PCA (Neale and Holmes, 1991; Neale, 1994; Azzone and Maccarrone, 2001; Huikku, 2010) and the benefits accruing from applying PCA (Neale and Holmes, 1991; Neale, 1994; Pierce and Tsay, 1992; Mills and Kennedy, 1993; Huikku, 2008). These studies suggest that enhancing organizational learning (OL) is the major reason for conducting PCA. Also, the major perceived benefits of PCA for the adopters are related to organizational learning. Nevertheless, further objectives/benefits have also been proposed.

Based on evidence from the empirical literature, the next section reviews the relevance of PCA to various managerial uses. The review covers PCA's role in measuring performance, assisting correction/abandonment decisions, enhancing the integrity of investment appraisals, evaluating and rewarding personnel, and enhancing organizational learning. Besides these managerial uses of PCA, Neale (1989) has studied whether companies use the approach to reduce management autonomy at a local level. The findings indicate, however, that the companies studied consider this kind of usage to be trivial. Furthermore, Neale (1991a) examines whether companies perceive PCA to be beneficial for improving corporate performance, but this is ruled out as an ultimate, catch-all use in this chapter.

Measuring Performance

Performance measurement (evaluating the success of a completed investment) is a core function of PCA. In practice, companies measure performance by comparing and analyzing the ex-post outcomes of an investment project with its ex-ante objectives (Neale and Holmes, 1991). Huikku (2007, 2008) maintains that performance measurement is not perceived to be beneficial per se, but rather it is a prerequisite function supporting other PCA uses. According to Huikku (2008), technical difficulties such as the separation of incremental cash flows, changes in the business environment, and estimation of future cash flows do not dramatically challenge the appropriateness of PCA for measuring investment project performance.

Assisting Correction/Abandonment Decisions

PCA has the potential to be of value with regard to current underperforming investment projects by providing early warning or helping companies to analyze different correction/abandonment alternatives. Busby and Pitts (1997) and Shapiro (2005) provide discussions about the various choices for companies dealing with underperforming projects. The beneficial role that PCA plays in providing feedback to assist in decision making for corrections is perceived within companies to be of minor, but not negligible, importance (Neale, 1989; Pierce and Tsay, 1992; Huikku, 2008). Neale (1991a) proposes that the earlier the first PCA, the greater the ability of a company to successfully modify an investment project.

Another suggestion is that benefits regarding modifications might primarily come from regular monitoring of projects before commissioning rather than from PCA (Neale and Buckley, 1992). Huikku (2008) posits that the potential for PCA to contribute to decisions concerning the course of an investment can be marginal for two reasons. First, making any changes after commissioning an investment project can be too late. Second, triggers for change are likely to come from alternative mechanisms such as routine reporting.

Howe and McCabe (1983) suggest that a company should abandon a commissioned investment if the abandonment value exceeds the net present value for the remaining lifetime of the investment. Smith (1993) finds a positive association between abandonment decisions and firm performance in companies with a PCA system. That is, the existence of a PCA system in a company increases the probability of timely abandonment decisions and of avoiding unjustified ones. Nevertheless, consistent with Corr (1983) and Neale (1991a), who report the limited importance of PCA for assisting abandonment decisions, Huikku's (2008) findings indicate that the approach can be perceived as insignificant in this context. One reason for the low importance may be that the main focus in cases of an under-performing investment is on improving its performance and not on terminating it (Neale, 1989). Likewise, as with corrections, triggers for change are likely to come from other sources (Huikku, 2008).

Enhancing the Integrity of Investment Appraisals

Investment project appraisals can include intentional upward biases (and less often downward) because managers may exaggerate project cash flows in order to gain approval for their proposals (e.g., Pruitt and Gitman, 1987; Pohlman, Santiago, and Markel, 1988). Pierce and Tsay (1992) suggest that companies consider PCA beneficial for enhancing the integrity of investment project appraisals. Similarly, Neale (1989, 1991a), and Mills and Kennedy (1993) propose that PCA encourages greater realism in project appraisals. In a similar vein, Lumijärvi (1990) argues that PCA is the only factor diminishing harmful game-playing behavior in capital investment processes. Because of asymmetric information distribution, managers may be in a position to play games in the capital investing process. They may use their information advantage to enhance their self-interest, for example, by focusing only on certain aspects of information, by filtering information, or by manipulating information.

In addition to intentional biases related to game playing, project appraisals may include unintentional biases by managers who believe that they are acting in the best interest of shareholders (Roll, 1986). Managers may be overconfident and/or overoptimistic about investment decisions and therefore overestimate the returns of their investment projects. According to Huikku (2008), the perceived status of the integrity of investment appraisals seems to affect whether companies consider PCA to be relevant. That is, if the status is good, the approach is not considered relevant for enhancing integrity of appraisals. Furthermore, Huikku suggests that the existing alternative methods for evaluating the success of an investment and preapproval reviews seem to diminish the relevance of PCA for these purposes.

Evaluating and Rewarding Personnel

Some propose that facilitating evaluation and rewarding of the personnel involved in the capital investment process is one of the purposes for carrying out PCA (Neale, 1989; 1994). Nevertheless, according to research, few companies use PCA in formal evaluation of managers (Smith, 1994; Huikku, 2008) or consider it beneficial to evaluation (Neale, 1994). Huikku (2008) suggests that some basic challenges may discourage companies from integrating PCA into their formal evaluation systems such as incentive systems.

One problem in trying to connect PCA and personnel evaluation can be the lengthy time interval between investment appraisal and PCA. This may mean that the people involved in the appraisal phase may already be in other positions. Another difficulty is that formal evaluation systems are often related to the financial year, and this frequency is not necessarily optimal for the aims of PCA. Moreover, the interim character of PCA reports may discourage companies from relying on these in formal evaluation. That is, PCA is typically conducted at the beginning of the life cycle of an investment and may consist of uncertain forecasts. In practice, an informal evaluation of personnel occurs through the process of PCA when management compares the investment plan and the actual outcome and attempts to explain the reasons for the deviations from that plan (Huikku, 2008).

Enhancing Organizational Learning

Research suggests that the major objective for companies to implement PCA is the enhancement of organizational learning for future capital investments (Neale, 1989, 1994; Azzone and Maccarrone, 2001; Huikku, 2009). Similarly, the major perceived benefits from PCA within companies are related to its enhancement of organizational learning (Corr, 1983; Neale, 1991a, 1994: Pierce and Tsay, 1992; Huikku, 2008). Organizational learning is a process whereby an organization responds to changes in its environment by detecting errors and correcting them in order to maintain the central features of the organization (Argyris, 1977, 1990). OL is not merely the sum of individual learning in an organization. It is a process involving the sharing of knowledge, beliefs, or assumptions among individuals, influenced by a broader set of social, political, or structural elements (Marquardt and Reynolds, 1994).

Argyris (1977, 1990) distinguishes between two types of OL: single-loop and double-loop learning. Single-loop learning focuses on problem solving but does not address the causes of the problems. In double-loop learning, organizations not only detect and correct errors but also question underlying policies and goals. In its ultimate form, double-loop learning may lead to resolving incompatible organizational norms by setting new priorities or restructuring norms, and to creating a new operational paradigm (Senge, 1990).

Huber (1991) proposes that OL processes include four constructs: (1) knowledge acquisition, (2) information distribution, (3) information interpretation, and (4) organizational memory. Knowledge is first obtained in a knowledge acquisition process. Thereafter, information from various sources is shared and new information (or understanding) is created in an information distribution process. In the next step—the information interpretation phase—commonly understood interpretations are attached to information. Finally, in the organizational memory phase, knowledge is stored for later use.

The effective reuse of knowledge assets that exist within a firm is essential to the realization of a competitive advantage (Teece, Pisano, and Shuen, 1997; Jensen and Szulanski, 2007). Communication plays a major role by enabling knowledge transfer and knowledge sharing (Ghoshal and Bartlett, 1988; Ghoshal, Korine, and Szulanski, 1994; Tucker, Meyer, and Westerman, 1996). Similarly, Garvin (1993) emphasizes the importance of the quick and efficient transfer of learning experiences as a prerequisite for OL. Kolb (1984) emphasizes the vital role of concrete experiences in the learning process.

Management control systems can play a pivotal role in facilitating or hindering OL (Kloot, 1997; Carmona and Grönlund, 1998). More specifically, some suggest that the information resulting from PCA has the potential to aid a company in avoiding previous mistakes and in systematically identifying successful processes that can be repeated in future investment projects (Neale, 1989; Northcott and Alkaraan, 2007). According to Huikku (2008), companies perceive PCA to be relevant to the double-loop type of learning because it helps them address why problems arise in the first place. Specifically, PCA can help companies improve the accuracy of underlying assumptions and goals in their planning material.

In a similar vein, Chenhall and Morris (1993) maintain that PCA feedback can enhance managerial learning at the project definition stage, particularly in relatively certain operating situations, whereas environmental uncertainty can moderate learning. At the project definition stage, PCA feedback can potentially enhance the development of proposals for new projects, improve the understanding of key factors affecting investment projects, and develop knowledge related to strategy formulation. Furthermore, Mills and Kennedy (1993) maintain that PCA can be conducive to learning for capital investment processes in general—not merely for project-specific investment activities. PCA information may, for example, trigger improvements in capital investment procedures and instructions.

PROBLEMS ASSOCIATED WITH PCA

The difficulties and drawbacks associated with PCA may diminish its power as a management tool and in extreme cases discourage firms from adopting the approach or even encourage its abandonment. Pierce and Tsay (1992) classify problems further into three groups: (1) technical, (2) organizational, and (3) economic problems. Studies by Neale (1989), Mills and Kennedy (1993), and Huikku (2001) also report problems associated with PCA. The technical problems can, for example, be related to the separation of incremental cash flows of an investment project, changes in business environment, estimation of future cash flows, and difficulties in planning material. Organizational problems include reluctance of people to conduct PCA, the lack of top management interest, the lack of personnel resources, and increased risk aversion. Economic problems are related to the costs of implementing and conducting PCA.

According to Neale and Holmes (1991), managers consider changes in the business environment and the presence of qualitative factors to be principal difficulties for PCA. As Azzone and Maccarrone (2001) note, however, companies consider the incompleteness or inadequacy of data and insufficient resources to be the most relevant difficulties likely to be encountered in PCA. In a study of Norwegian companies, Neale (1994) mentions the difficulty of separating incremental cash flows of investment projects as the primary problem of PCA. Similarly, Linder (2005) finds, in his review of empirical PCA studies, that this is the most often mentioned and first-ranked problem. Based on the empirical evidence, however, companies do not necessarily perceive that technical difficulties jeopardize PCA's measurement ability to a great extent (Huikku, 2008). For example, companies seem to be able to reduce the difficulties related to separating incremental cash flows by using sophisticated cost accounting systems and by regarding integrated investments as an investment bundle, that is, a package of investments (Miller and O'Leary, 1997).

EXPLAINING ADOPTION AND NONADOPTION OF PCA

Empirical studies maintain that the likelihood of PCA adoption is associated with the size of the company. A larger company is more likely to adopt the approach

(Scapens, Sale, and Tikkas, 1982; Neale, 1989, 1994; Huikku, 2007). Furthermore, Huikku suggests that companies having a critical mass of absolute tangible assets combined with a high tangible assets/turnover ratio have a tendency to adopt PCA more often than other companies. This is plausible because implementing and running a PCA system is not without cost, and from a cost-benefit viewpoint, capital-intensive companies are more likely to find PCA useful.

Studies examining PCA adoption rates report, however, that despite the apparent benefits, some large companies still do not consider PCA adoption appropriate to their organization. Little empirical research on PCA nonadoption exists per se. A few comprehensive surveys (Ghobadian and Smyth, 1989; Neale and Holmes, 1991; Pierce and Tsay, 1992; Azzone and Maccarrone, 2001) provide a discussion of nonadoption, but it has not been the primary interest of any study. Taken together, these studies report three overlapping groups of reasons for PCA nonadoption: (1) scarcity of investments; (2) difficulties of PCA; and (3) alternative ways to achieve the benefits expected from PCA. Scarcity of investments can be considered an obvious reason for nonadoption.

With regard to difficulties, Pierce and Tsay (1992) and Azzone and Maccarrone (2001) report changes in the technologies/business environment and the uniqueness of projects as among the main reasons for PCA nonadoption. The utility of PCA can be diminished if feedback is irrelevant to future investments. Other major difficulties that have been reported to influence nonadoption are the separation of project-specific profit (Neale and Holmes, 1991; Pierce and Tsay, 1992) and the difficulty of employing PCA to modify ongoing projects (Neale and Holmes, 1991; Azzone and Maccarrone, 2001). Furthermore, all four studies mentioned above note a lack of resources required to carry out PCA as a reason for nonadoption.

The third main explanation for PCA nonadoption relates to alternative ways to achieve the benefits thought to accrue from the use of PCA. Neale and Holmes (1991) and Azzone and Maccarrone (2001) suggest that personal contacts between corporate and divisional managers (or operating managers and controllers) are one reason for nonadoption.

Huikku (2007) explicitly addresses the types of alternative capital investment controls in a field study, and examines if and how companies can evaluate their completed investments and enhance organizational learning by using them. The investigation results in the discovery and mapping of controls that discretely or as a package enable companies to achieve PCA benefits. Regarding the evaluation of success, Huikku finds that companies use many different means to help them understand whether or not the targets of an investment are being met. These means include formal systems for routinely following up key production figures, sales, and profit centers. Also, visiting investing sites, presentations, and discussions can be formally arranged for investment control purposes, but typically the practices seem to be more informal. Huikku also discovers that companies acquire relevant capital investment knowledge for organizational learning purposes in many ways. In particular, the utilization of central expertise and experienced internal resources seems to be crucial. The author suggests that smaller companies without major strategic, complex, and repetitive investments in particular perceive that the package of different simultaneous alternative control mechanisms yields a performance that is equal, or close to equal, to formal PCA. Consequently, these companies do not adopt PCA.

DESIGN OF A PCA SYSTEM

This section presents commonly referred aspects of PCA design and discusses how these aspects could be taken into consideration in designing a PCA system for organizational learning.

Aspects of PCA Design

Common aspects of the design of PCA concern the selection of projects undergoing PCA, timing of PCA, location of responsibility for the PCA system, persons conducting PCA, and content and communication of a PCA report (e.g., Neale and Holmes, 1991; Pierce and Tsay, 1992; Kennedy and Mills, 1993; Huikku, 2010). Gordon and Smith (1992) suggest that using sophisticated PCA procedures is positively correlated with firm performance.

Regarding the selection of projects undergoing PCA, Mills and Kennedy (1990) propose that the greatest benefit can be achieved by focusing on major investment projects, making such projects worthy of inclusion. This is especially true for projects that provide the company with substantial potential for learning, such as pilot projects and repetitive investments. Project size is by far the primary selection criterion for PCA (e.g., Gordon and Myers, 1991; Pierce and Tsay, 1992, Huikku, 2010), and few if any companies conduct PCA for all their investments (e.g., Ghobadian and Smyth, 1989; Neale, 1994). According to Kennedy and Mills (1993), size can be the only selection criterion, or it can be combined with unexpected outcomes or degrees of investment risk.

The appropriate timing of a PCA depends upon the objectives set for it (Gadella, 1986). Neale (1991a) suggests that timing has an important bearing on the benefits related to the control of ongoing investments, whereas timing is not so critical for obtaining learning-related benefits for future projects. Accordingly, if a company uses PCA to assist in detecting underperforming investment projects and in analyzing the appropriate actions required (correction/abandonment), a sufficiently early PCA after commissioning the investments is essential. Nevertheless, with regard to enhancing learning for future projects, the prerequisite for obtaining reliable PCA data is that it will be conducted in a suitably timely period after commissioning such investments when stable working patterns are discernible. In other words, firms conduct PCA after they resolve any teething troubles identified at the start of the project and after the investment is operational (Neale, 1995).

The decision regarding the timing of PCA is a trade-off between PCA's role in providing well-timed assistance for planning subsequent investment projects and the accuracy of PCA data. Consequently, PCAs that are conducted earlier may be appropriate for providing valuable learning experiences for projects under consideration, whereas later PCAs can provide more comprehensive and accurate feedback about the success factors of an investment. On the other hand, late timing may cause PCA reports to be irrelevant due to radical changes in premises of capital investments such as changes in technology and the business environment (Huikku, 2010). Neale and Holmes (1991) report that two-thirds of the companies studied conducted their first PCA at around one year after project completion, and only a minority of the firms undertook more than one PCA per investment project (see also Mills and Kennedy, 1993; Neale, 1994; Gordon and Myers, 1991; Huikku, 2010).

The location of responsibility for the PCA system can reside centrally at the corporate level or locally in divisions or in their subsets (e.g., business units). The unit responsible for the PCA system has ownership of PCA activities and is in charge of tasks such as the development of the system and the general functioning of PCA activities including providing policies, giving instructions, and ensuring that the company adheres to them (Huikku, 2010). Furthermore, such tasks may include selecting investment projects to be included in PCA, choosing PCA auditors, and checking draft PCA reports. Azzone and Maccarrone (2001) report that in more than 80 percent of the large Italian companies they studied, the responsibility for the PCA system resides at the corporate level, and that the responsibility was more centralized in companies stressing OL as their PCA objective. These authors suggest that aspects of communication such as the need for generalization and dissemination of PCA results can explain this phenomenon. Huikku (2010) finds that managers in highly diversified companies delegate responsibility for the PCA system to a divisional level. This may indicate that there is no immediate need to disseminate investment experiences across the whole corporation. In other words, capital investment can vary considerably between the divisions and transferring division-specific investment knowledge to the other divisions may be inappropriate.

Researchers have different opinions about who would be the most suitable person or team to conduct PCA. According to one approach, objectivity can be achieved by using outsiders or a team that has not been involved in the investment project (Gulliver, 1987). Other researchers such as Dillon and Caldwell (1981) contend that the compilation of a PCA report requires the contribution of people with detailed knowledge. Yet obtaining objectivity could be difficult if the investment project group members are allowed to review their own investments. The members may present the situation subjectively or even be tempted to use their information advantage to manipulate figures or exaggerate performance estimations, thereby downgrading the potential for PCA reports to contribute to OL.

In practice, the persons and teams conducting PCA appear to vary widely among firms, although studies report controllers in business units making the investments to be the key resource (Kennedy and Mills, 1993; Azzone and Maccarrone, 2001; Huikku, 2010). According to Azzone and Maccarrone, using "hybrid" PCA review teams including both fully external persons and those with prior involvement with the project is common. In larger companies, Scapens et al. (1982) and Corr (1983) find that responsibility for conducting PCA is more likely to be delegated to divisional management, whereas in the smaller companies corporate staff is more involved. Additionally, Farragher et al. (1999) report that few companies use individuals or teams with no prior involvement in the project to conduct PCA. Nevertheless, the companies allowing an investing unit itself to conduct PCA do not necessarily consider it problematic from the objectivity point of view if divisional or head office staff is checking draft PCA reports and "objective" controllers are involved in carrying out PCA (Huikku, 2010). Furthermore, Huikku suggests that connecting people from the business unit making the investment with outside persons can enhance the quality of PCA reports in terms of objectivity.

A company can consider the following aspects of the content of a PCA report (e.g., Mills and Kennedy, 1990; 1993; Azzone and Maccarrone, 2001; Huikku, 2001, 2010): (1) the language used; (2) a standard versus nonstandard format for reporting; (3) an analysis for both monetary and nonmonetary targets; (4) ex-post calculations, including or excluding future estimates; (5) the inclusion of detailed ex-post calculations; and (6) proposals for action such as suggestions, helpful hints, and lessons learned. Although proposals are likely to be conducive to learning, few PCA reports include proposals (Azzone and Maccarrone, 2001; Huikku, 2010). Even when they do include a proposal, few companies have a formal mechanism for following up. The prerequisite for ex-post performance evaluation is the existence of documented investment appraisal material and the availability of such material to those conducting the PCA. Moreover, using the same ex-ante and ex-post capital budgeting calculation methods enables the required comparisons to be made. Farragher et al. (1999) report, however, that companies do not always use the same methods.

PCA scholars emphasize the fact that an appropriate communication of PCA reports is a prerequisite for effective knowledge transfer and sharing, and hence for organizational learning (Mills and Kennedy, 1993; Azzone and Maccarrone, 2001). The communication aspects of PCA reports can be described in terms of their forum of presentation, dissemination, and storage. According to Azzone and Maccarrone, companies typically have common meetings of PCA auditors and other staff involved in the investment process in which they discuss PCA results and implement potential actions.

A common forum can be valuable for three principal reasons: (1) disseminating knowledge among the attendees, (2) facilitating the interpretation of the results, and (3) generating shared understanding (Huikku, 2010). Such a forum can also help to confirm that the results and proposals in a final PCA report represent shared understanding in an organization. Without a forum, the readers of the reports may become suspicious about the reliability and general acceptability of the reports; for example, relevant proposals may be omitted. Huikku finds that although almost all the companies he studied have a formal forum, this forum is usually not intended for interactive discussion and interpretation. The dominating noninteractive forums in these companies are executive group meetings, which characteristically feature one-way reporting of performance measurement issues to decision makers rather than an interactive discussion of issues for the purposes of organizational learning.

Mills and Kennedy (1993) emphasize the importance of effective dissemination of PCA reports to ensure enhanced organizational learning. Huikku (2010) reports that a common practice is to disseminate PCA reports to those responsible for initiating, planning, and implementing the project, whereas less than half of the companies studied automatically communicate PCA results back to the ultimate approvers of investments—the executive group and board of directors. According to Kennedy and Mills (1993), the distribution of final PCA reports tends to be relatively limited, and routine distribution to other divisions is rare. In a similar vein, Azzone and Maccarrone (2001) report that companies pay little attention to the dissemination of PCA results.

According to Walsh and Ungson (1991), companies should appropriately store information from the organization's history so that it can be brought to bear on present decisions. Studies pinpoint turnover of personnel (Levitt and March, 1988; Huber, 1990) and organizational forgetting (Carmona and Grönlund, 1998) as major threats leading to a loss of the information itself and what that information conveyed. Studies also identify formal control systems and their documents (i.e., information repositories within a company including codified explicit knowledge) to be essential for developing organizational memory (Levitt and March, 1988; Huber, 1991). Little empirical research focuses on storing and retrieving aspects of PCA reports. According to Huikku (2010), few companies have comprehensive databases or archives for PCA data that permit conveniently retrieving valuable learning experiences. Consequently, companies may repeat past mistakes or, even in the best case, may search for the same data again (Huber, 1991; Walsh and Ungson, 1991).

Designing a PCA System for Organizational Learning

The design of a PCA system can play a major role in enabling effective reuse of learning experiences relating to capital investment. Azzone and Maccarrone (2001) suggest that the design of a PCA system is associated with the main objectives set for it—OL vs. decision-making support for current investments. They find, for example, that responsibility for the PCA system appears to be more centralized to the headquarters in firms in which organizational learning is cited as the most important PCA objective. Additionally, Neale (1991a) examines the association between the objectives and design of PCA on the one hand and the perceived benefits of PCA on the other. He states that benefits are associated with the degree of emphasis placed on the objectives (e.g., companies stressing OL-related objectives are more likely to reap the benefits of OL). Furthermore, he finds that the companies selecting only major investment projects for PCA are more likely to generate OL benefits than those investigating all the projects.

In his study, Huikku (2010) focuses on examining the relationship between PCA design and organizational learning. Based on a synthesis of the OL and PCA literature, he proposes an OL-conducive PCA design as shown in Exhibit 8.1. Drawing on Huber's (1991) subphases of organizational learning, the properties of PCA design are presented under the following headings: knowledge acquisition, information distribution/interpretation, and organizational memory. Furthermore, Huikku suggests that problems in conveying capital investment experiences can be related to PCA design. In particular, issues relating to organizational memory such as inappropriate filing and difficult access to PCA reports appear to hinder the effective conveyance of investment experiences to new projects. Other aspects related to the communication of PCA reports may also hinder OL such as the lack of improvement proposals and their systematic follow-up, a lack of interactive forums for interpretation of results, and restricted dissemination. Additionally, these findings provide support for the contention that sophisticated PCA designs help companies to transfer and share learning experiences more effectively. Furthermore, in line with the management control system literature such as Chenhall (2003), evidence suggests that the smaller the size of a company, the lower is the likelihood of a sophisticated PCA system (and vice versa). Other means of managing capital investment knowledge such as the use of central expertise and experienced internal resources also seem to affect the degree of sophistication. Thus, in smaller companies, some may perceive that a sufficient OL outcome can be achieved by relying on the combination of less sophisticated PCA systems and alternative means for controlling investments.

Exhibit 8.1   The Proposed Organizational Learning Conducive PCA Design

Organizational Learning Subphases/Design Properties	Proposed Criteria for PCA Design
Panel A. Knowledge Acquisition	
Selection of projects for PCA	All major capital investment projects selected
Timing of PCA	After an investment has reached a relatively settled state, but not too late to ensure that lessons learned are still useful
Location of responsibility for PCA system	Centralized; corporate level, or alternatively in highly diversified corporations also division level (not business unit level)
PCA auditor	Can be from business unit making the investment or outside (both expected to be involved in making PCA reports)
Panel B. Information Distribution and Interpretation	
Content of PCA report	The same capital budgeting calculation methods used ex ante and ex post
	Detailed comparisons of ex-ante and ex-post calculations
	Comments on the achievement of objectives
	Common PCA reporting language
	Standard format
	Proposals for future investing
Presentation forums for PCA reports	At least one formal forum for interactive discussion and presentation of the reports
	Executive group meeting (if investment approved by it)
	Board of directors (if investment approved by them)
Dissemination of final PCA reports	Extensive dissemination at least to all people involved in the project (planning, approval, implementation, and PCA)
Panel C. Organizational Memory	
Archiving and filing of PCA reports	Database or archive of PCA reports exists and its existence and content is known to relevant persons
	Relevant persons can conveniently find and retrieve appropriate reports from the database/archive

SUMMARY AND CONCLUSIONS

The empirical findings lend support to the notion that enhancing organizational learning is the major reason for conducting PCA and that the major perceived benefits of PCA relate to OL. Specifically, PCA appears to help companies enhance the accuracy of assumptions and goals in planning future capital investments.

PCA can also be marginally beneficial to problem detection and solving for current investments (Huikku, 2008). Although studies show that the evaluation and reward of personnel is a fundamental element of functioning control systems (Otley, 1999), coupling PCA with formal evaluation and reward appears to be rare due to timing-related difficulties.

Studies report difficulties in separating the incremental cash flows of differing investment projects as the primary problem of PCA. Nevertheless, companies do not necessarily perceive that technical difficulties jeopardize the measurement ability of PCA to a great extent (Huikku, 2008). Although the use of PCA is very common among large companies, many such companies have not adopted the approach. Scarcity of investment is an obvious reason for this, but existing alternative control mechanisms may also discourage companies from adopting PCA (Huikku, 2007). Specifically, smaller companies that do not have major strategic, complex, and repetitive capital investments can perceive that alternative controls are sufficient for their purposes and do not adopt PCA. An appropriate design of a PCA system appears important for organizational learning. In particular, improved methods of communication, such as appropriate filing and convenient access to PCA reports, improvement proposals and their systematic follow-up, and interactive forums for interpretation of results may enhance the effective conveyance of investment experiences to new projects (Huikku, 2010).

Despite the widespread diffusion of PCA and its suggested usefulness for enhancing OL, empirical research focusing on PCA is not voluminous. Many research gaps still need to be addressed. With regard to issues of PCA adoption/nonadoption, research addressing the reasons for adoption could also cast more light on nonadoption. A worthwhile study would be to investigate the role of human factors such as key decision makers or teams in connection with adoption (Miller, 1987). Researchers could further investigate the circumstances (e.g., capital-intensity, the characteristics of investments, size, technology, strategy, and organization structure) in which companies perceive alternative control mechanisms to be insufficient and adoption of PCA to be appropriate.

Adoption studies could also be based on approaches from theories of institutional sociology (e.g., Meyer and Rowan, 1977; Powell and DiMaggio, 1991) and management fashions (Abrahamson, 1991, 1996). Researchers could use the lens of institutional sociology to examine how companies attempt to legitimize their PCA (non)adoption decisions and whether coercive, normative, and mimetic pressures (or lack of them) can explain their behavior. Furthermore, by applying the notions of management fashion theory, researchers could examine to what extent the motives relate to managerial fads/fashions or efficient-choice affects PCA (non)adoption decision.

Prior studies indicate that companies having a more sophisticated PCA design, specifically one related to aspects of communicating PCA results, are more successful at achieving OL benefits. Nevertheless, more research is needed to deepen knowledge of the design-benefit relationship. Additionally, with regard to PCA design, there is still no consensus about who would be the most suitable person or team to conduct PCA. From an accountability or organizational learning point of view, is this lack of consensus relevant? As Northcott and Alkaraan (2007) suggest, more studies could address the issue of what managers actually learn from PCA. In a similar vein, following Neale's (1991b) call, investigating the concrete effects of

PCA would be a worthwhile endeavor. For example, researchers could analyze in more detail how tacit investment knowledge is acquired and transferred to future capital investment and the role that PCA plays in this process. These research gaps provide examples of research questions that might benefit from using case-study methods.

Evidence suggests that alternative methods of managing capital investment knowledge discourage the development of PCA systems. By drawing on notions in the management control package literature (e.g., Otley, 1999), further examination could address the complementarity issues of formal PCA and alternative control mechanisms (Fisher, 1995). Furthermore, inspired by the results of alternative controls in the PCA context, future management control research could explicitly investigate the role of alternative controls in the (non)adoption of management accounting innovations (e.g., activity-based costing, balanced scorecard, and value-based management). Clearly, important avenues exist for further research in this field.

DISCUSSION QUESTIONS

1. What kinds of organizational learning can PCA facilitate?
2. For what reason might PCA have only a minor role in assisting correction/abandonment decision making of ongoing investment projects?
3. Who would be the most suitable person or team to conduct PCA? What are the pros and cons of the different alternatives?
4. Discuss how alternative formal and informal control mechanisms can affect the adoption of PCA and the sophistication of PCA systems.

REFERENCES

Abrahamson, Eric. 1991. "Managerial Fads and Fashions: The Diffusion and Rejection of Innovations." *Academy of Management Review* 16:3, 586–612.

Abrahamson, Eric. 1996. "Management Fashion." *Academy of Management Review* 21:1, 254–285.

Argyris, Chris. 1977. "Organizational Learning and Management Information Systems." *Accounting, Organizations and Society* 2:2, 113–123.

Argyris, Chris. 1990. "The Dilemma of Implementing Controls: The Case of Managerial Accounting." *Accounting, Organizations and Society* 15:6, 503–511.

Arnold, Glen C., and Panos D. Hatzopoulos. 2000. "The Theory-Practice Gap in Capital Budgeting: Evidence from the United Kingdom." *Journal of Business Finance & Accounting* 27:5/6, 603–626.

Azzone, Giovanni, and Paolo Maccarrone. 2001. "The Design of the Investment Post-audit Process in Large Organizations: Evidence from a Survey." *European Journal of Innovation Management* 4:2, 73–87.

Busby, Jerry, and C. G. C. Pitts. 1997. "Real Options in Practice: An Exploratory Survey of How Finance Officers Deal with Flexibility in Capital Appraisal." *Management Accounting Research* 8:2, 169–186.

Carmona, Salvador, and Anders Grönlund. 1998. "Learning from Forgetting, an Experiential Study of Two European Car Manufacturers." *Management Learning* 29:1, 21–38.

Chenhall, Robert H. 2003. "Management Control Systems Design within Its Organizational Context: Findings from Contingency-based Research and Directions for the Future." *Accounting, Organizations and Society* 28:2–3, 127–168.

Chenhall, Robert H., and Deigan Morris. 1993. "The Role of Post Completion Audits, Managerial Learning, Environmental Uncertainty and Performance." *Behavioral Research in Accounting* 5, 171–186.

CIMA. 2005. *Management Accounting Official Terminology.* London: CIMA.

Corr, Arthur V. 1983. *The Capital Expenditure Decision.* Hamilton, Canada: National Association of Accountants and the Society of Management Accountants of Canada.

Dillon, Ray, and James C. Caldwell. 1981. "A System for Postauditing Capital Projects." *Managerial Planning.* January/February, 18–30.

Farragher, Edward J., Robert T. Kleiman, and Anandi P. Sahu. 1999. "Current Capital Investments Practices." *Engineering Economist* 44:2, 137–150.

Fisher, Joseph. 1995. "Contingency-based Research on Management Control Systems: Categorization by Level of Complexity." *Journal of Accounting Literature* 14, 24–53.

Gadella, Jan W. 1986. "Post Auditing the Capital-investment Decision." *Management Accounting* (United Kingdom). November, 36–37.

Garvin, David. 1993. "Building a Learning Organization." *Harvard Business Review* 71:4, 78–91.

Ghobadian, Abby, and David A. Smyth. 1989. "The Role of the Post-audit Procedure in Effective Control of Capital Projects." In Douglas K. Macbeth and Geoff Southern, eds. *Proceedings of the Operations Management Association UK Annual International Conference,* January 5–6. Dunblane, Scotland. Bedford, United Kingdom: IFS Publications/Springer-Verlag.

Ghoshal, Sumantra, and Christopher A. Bartlett. 1988. "Creation, Adoption, and Diffusion of Innovations by Subsidiaries of Multinational Corporations." *Journal of International Business Studies* 19:3, 365–388.

Ghoshal, Sumantra, Harry Korine, and Gabriel Szulanski. 1994. "Interunit Communication in Multinational Corporations." *Management Science* 40:1, 90–110.

Gordon, Lawrence A., and Mary D. Myers. 1991. "Postauditing Capital Projects; Are You in Step with the Competition?" *Management Accounting* (United States). January, 39–42.

Gordon, Lawrence A, and Kimberly J. Smith. 1992. "Postauditing Capital Expenditures and Firm Performance: The Role of Asymmetric Information." *Accounting, Organizations and Society* 17:8, 741–757.

Gulliver, Frank R. 1987. "Post-Project Appraisals Pay." *Harvard Business Review* 65:2, 128–132.

Haka, Susan F. 2007. "A Review of the Literature on Capital Budgeting and Investment Appraisal: The Past, Present, and Future Musings." In C. Chris Chapman, Anthony Hopwood, and Michael Shields, eds. *Handbook of Management Accounting Research*, Volume 2, 697–728. Oxford: Elsevier.

Howe, Keith, and George M. McCabe. 1983. "On Optimal Asset Abandonment and Replacement." *Journal of Financial and Quantitative Analysis* 18:3, 295–305.

Huber, George P. 1990. "A Theory of the Effects of Advanced Information Technologies on Organizational Design, Intelligence, and Decision Making." *Academy of Management Review* 15:1, 47–71.

Huber, George P. 1991. "Organizational Learning: The Contributing Processes and the Literatures." *Organization Science* 2:1, 88–115.

Huikku, Jari. 2001. "*Investointien Tarkkailun Motiivien ja Toteutustavan Välinen Yhteys—Case-Tutkimus.*" ["Interdependence of Motives and Design of Post-completion Auditing of Capital Investments—Case Study]. Licentiate thesis. Helsinki, Finland: HSE Print.

Huikku, Jari. 2007. "Explaining the Non-Adoption of Post-Completion Auditing." *European Accounting Review* 16:2, 363–398.

Huikku, Jari. 2008. "Managerial Uses of Post-completion Auditing of Capital Investments." *Finnish Journal of Business Economics* 57:2, 139–164.

Huikku, Jari. 2009. "*Post-Completion Auditing of Capital Investments and Organizational Learning.*" Doctoral Dissertation, Helsinki School of Economics, Series A-347. Helsinki, Finland: HSE Print.

Huikku, Jari. 2010. "Design of a Post-Completion Auditing System for Organizational Learning." Available at http://ssrn.com/abstract=1542660.

Jensen, Robert J., and Gabriel Szulanski. 2007. "Template Use and the Effectiveness of Knowledge Transfer." *Management Science* 53:11, 1716–1730.

Kennedy, Alison J., and Roger W. Mills. 1993. "Post-completion Auditing in Practice." *Management Accounting* (United Kingdom). October, 22–25.

Klammer, Thomas P., and Walker, Michael C. 1984. "The Continuing Increase in the Use of Sophisticated Capital Budgeting Techniques." *California Management Review* 27:1, 137–148.

Kloot, Louise. 1997. "Organizational Learning and Management Control Systems: Responding to Environmental Change." *Management Accounting Research* 8:1, 47–73.

Kolb, David A. 1984. *Experiential Learning*. Englewood Cliffs, NJ: Prentice Hall.

Levitt, Barbara, and James G. March. 1988. "Organizational Learning." *Annual Review of Sociology* 14, 319–340.

Linder, Stefan. 2005. "Problems Associated with Conducting Post-completion Audits: A Review of the Research." *Corporate Finance Review* 10:1, 10–20.

Lumijärvi, Olli-Pekka. 1990. *Gameplaying in Capital Budgeting*. Doctoral Dissertation, Turku School of Economics and Business Administration, Series A-7:1990. Turku, Finland: TSEBA.

Malmi, Teemu, and David A. Brown. 2008. "Management Control Systems as a Package—Opportunities, Challenges and Research Directions." *Management Accounting Research* 19:4, 287–300.

Marquardt, Michael, and Angus Reynolds. 1994. *The Global Learning Organization*. Burr Ridge, Illinois: Irwin.

Merchant, Kenneth A., and David T. Otley. 2007. "A Review of the Literature on Control and Accountability." In Chris Chapman, Anthony Hopwood, and Michael Shields, eds. *Handbook of Management Accounting Research*, Volume 2. Oxford: Elsevier.

Meyer, John, and Brian Rowan. 1977. "Institutionalized Organizations: Formal Structure as a Myth and Ceremony." *American Journal of Sociology* 83:2, 340–363.

Miller, Danny. 1987. "The Genesis of Configuration." *Academy of Management Review* 12:1, 686–701.

Miller, Peter, and Ted O'Leary. 1997. "Capital Budgeting Practices and Complementarity Relations in the Transition to Modern Manufacture: A Field-Based Analysis." *Journal of Accounting Research* 35:2, 257–271.

Mills, Roger W., and Alison J. Kennedy. 1990. *Post-Completion Audit of Capital Expenditure Projects*. Management Guide No. 9. London: CIMA.

Mills, Roger W., and Alison J. Kennedy. 1993. "Experiences in Operating a Post-audit System." *Management Accounting* (United Kingdom). November, 26–28.

Mukherjee, Tarun K., and Glenn V. Henderson. 1987. "The Capital Budgeting Process: Theory and Practice." *Interfaces* 17:2, 78-90.

Neale, Charles W. 1989. "Post Auditing Practices by UK Firms: Aims, Benefits and Shortcomings." *British Accounting Review* 21:4, 309–328.

Neale, Charles W. 1991a. "The Benefits Derived from Post-auditing Investment Projects." *OMEGA International Journal of Management Science* 19:2/3, 113–120.

Neale, Charles W. 1991b. "A Revolution in Post-Completion Audit Adoption." *Management Accounting* (United Kingdom). November, 44–46.

Neale, Charles W. 1994. "Investment Post-auditing Practices among British and Norwegian Companies: A Comparative Study." *International Business Review* 3:1, 31–46.

Neale, Charles W. 1995. "Post-completion Audits: Avoiding the Pitfalls." *Managerial Auditing Journal* 10:1, 17–24.

Neale, Charles W., and Peter J. Buckley. 1992. "Differential British and U.S. Adoption Rates of Investment Project Post-completion Auditing." *Journal of International Business Studies* 23:3, 443–459.

Neale, Charles W., and David E. A. Holmes. 1991. *Post-Completion Auditing.* London: Pitman.

Northcott, Deryl. 1992. *Capital Investment Decision-Making.* London: CIMA, Academic Press.

Northcott, Deryl, and Fadi Alkaraan. 2007. Strategic Investment Appraisal. In Trevor Hopper, Deryl Northcott, and Robert Scapens, eds. *Issues in Management Accounting*, 3rd ed., 199–221. Harlow, United Kingdom: Prentice Hall.

Otley, David. 1999. "Performance Management: A Framework for Management Control Systems Research." *Management Accounting Research* 10:4, 363–382.

Pierce, Bethane J., and Jeffrey J. Tsay. 1992. "A Study of the Post-Completion Audit Practices of Large American Corporations: Experience from 1978 and 1988." *Journal of Management Accounting Research* 4, 131–155.

Pike, Richard, and Bill Neale. 2003. *Corporate Finance and Investment: Decisions and Strategies.* Harlow, United Kingdom: Pearson.

Pohlman, Randolph A., Emmanuel S. Santiago, and F. Lynn Markel. 1988. "Cash Flow Estimation Practices of Large Firms." *Financial Management* 17:2, 71–79.

Powell, Walter W., and Paul J. DiMaggio, eds. 1991. *The New Institutionalism in Organizational Analysis.* Chicago: University of Chicago Press.

Pruitt, Stephen, and Lawrence J. Gitman. 1987. "Capital Budgeting Forecast Biases: Evidence from the Fortune 500." *Financial Management* 16:1, 46–51.

Roll, Richard. 1986. "The Hubris Hypothesis of Corporate Takeovers." Journal of Business 59:2, 197–216.

Scapens, Robert W., J. Timothy Sale, and Pantelis A. Tikkas. 1982. Financial Control of Divisional Capital Investment. London: CIMA.

Senge, Peter. 1990. *The Fifth Discipline.* New York: Currency Doubleday.

Shapiro, Alan C. 2005. *Capital Budgeting and Investment Analysis.* Upper Saddle River, NJ: Pearson Prentice Hall.

Smith, Kimberly J. 1993. "Investment Monitoring Systems, Abandonment of Capital Assets, and Firm Performance." *Journal of Management Accounting Research* 5, 281–299.

Smith, Kimberly J. 1994. "Post-auditing Capital Investments." *Journal of Financial Practice & Education* 4:1, 129–137.

Teece, David J., Gary Pisano, and Amy Shuen. 1997. "Dynamic Capabilities and Strategic Management." *Strategic Management Journal* 18:7, 509–533.

Tucker, Mary L., G. Dale Meyer, and James W. Westerman. 1996. "Organizational Communication: Development of Internal Strategic Competitive Advantage." *Journal of Business Communication* 33:1, 51–69.

Walsh, James P., and Gerardo R. Ungson. 1991. "Organizational Memory." *Academy of Management Review* 16:1, 57–91.

ABOUT THE AUTHOR

Jari Huikku received his licentiate's and doctoral degree in economics and business administration from Helsinki School of Economics, Finland (now Aalto University School of Economics). He also holds a master's degree in finance from Turku School of Economics and Business Administration. He currently is an assistant professor at Aalto University School of Economics. Before entering his Ph.D. studies and joining the academic community, he worked for 15 years in several multinational companies such as Partek, Wärtsilä, Sanitec, and Evac and held various control and general management positions. His principal research and teaching interests include capital budgeting, capital investments, and management control. He has published in academic journals such as *European Accounting Review* and *Finnish Journal of Business Economics*.

CHAPTER 9

Capital Budgeting Techniques in Practice: U.S. Survey Evidence

TARUN K. MUKHERJEE
Moffett Chair in Financial Economics, University of New Orleans

NASEEM M. AL RAHAHLEH
Assistant Professor, Park University

INTRODUCTION

Capital budgeting may best be understood when viewed as a process that requires several tasks to be performed at different stages of development. This process progresses in four stages: (1) identification, (2) development, (3) selection and implementation, and (4) postcompletion auditing (PCA). First, ideas for possible investment of company assets are identified. Ideas are then screened and those with greater potential are developed into investment plans. In the selection stage, investment opportunities are compared and those that appear to be in the best interests of the company are selected. Finally, investments are monitored for variations from expectations to gain insights for future improvement of the budgeting process.

Many studies investigate the question of how the capital budgeting process is actually translated into practice by firms. Several studies analyze the results of surveys to discern patterns in capital budgeting practices. In the mid-1980s, Scott and Petty (1984), Mukherjee (1987), and Mukherjee and Henderson (1987) synthesized the results of surveys regarding capital budgeting practices of large U.S. firms performed up until that point. Later, Kim and Ulferts (1996) provided a summary of survey results focusing primarily on the selection techniques employed by multinational firms. Recently, Burns and Walker (2009) updated previous work to examine the progress made toward understanding the entire capital budgeting process since the mid-1980s.

This chapter reexamines the results of many important surveys involving U.S. firms beginning with Istvan (1961). The major purpose is to analyze and synthesize their results in order to achieve three goals: (1) understand how large firms in the United States make their decisions involving the entire capital budgeting process; (2) detect and possibly reconcile any gap that might remain between the relevant theories and actual practices; and (3) identify areas requiring new survey evidence.

The remainder of the chapter has the following organization. First, the chapter briefly discusses the four stages of the capital budgeting process and relevant issues pertaining to each stage. Second, it presents a discussion of the surveys that are reviewed in this chapter. Third, the chapter examines survey results to understand actual capital budgeting practices in each stage of the capital budgeting process. The final section presents a summary and conclusions.

CAPITAL BUDGETING PROCESS

As previously mentioned, the capital budgeting process involves four stages: (1) identification, (2) development, (3) selection and implementation, and (4) postcompletion auditing. Many questions need to be answered to better understand the firm's decision-making process relevant to capital budgeting. Below is a sample of these questions.

Identification

In the first stage of the capital budgeting process, companies attempt to identify possible uses of capital. Suggested questions for this stage include:

- How do companies initiate project proposals? Do they continually solicit ideas for capital projects or do they identify projects only when needed?
- At what level within the firms are projects generally generated?
- Do companies have a formal process for submitting ideas? If so, how does that process work?
- Does an incentive system exist for suggesting good project ideas?

Development

The suggested questions at the development stage consist of two categories: those pertaining to screening ideas and those relating to developing an idea into a full proposal (i.e., estimating the cost-benefit data needed to justify a proposal).

Screening

Questions relating to the screening process include:

- Do all ideas develop into specific projects proposals or are the ideas screened before further development?
- At what level within the firm are these ideas reviewed or screened?
- What criteria do firms use to screen ideas? What role does the project size or organizational structure play in this regard?

Estimating Cash Flows

Questions relating to estimating project data include:

- Who is responsible for the data estimation?
- What type of cost-benefit data (for example, net income versus cash flows) is used?

- How are the data estimated? Do common guidelines exist about what data to exclude and include?

Selection and Implementation

Questions at this stage include the following:

- Who (or which department) analyzes capital expenditures?
- What techniques do firms use to evaluate competing projects? Has the use of discounted cash flow (DCF) techniques increased over time? Do firms continue to use both DCF and non-DCF techniques? If so, why?
- How is the discount rate determined? Is the discount rate company-wide, division-wide, or project specific?
- How is the risk defined in the context of capital budgeting? How is risk incorporated into decision making?
- How prevalent is capital rationing? How are projects selected in the presence of capital rationing?
- Do firms consider real options? How do they make decisions regarding research and development (R&D)?
- Who makes the final decision on an investment?

Postcompletion Auditing

Suggested questions for this stage are as follows:

- Is project performance evaluated? How often? Who performs such evaluation? How is the evaluation done?
- What action does the company take when it finds that actual performance is below the projected performance?
- Is there an expenditure control procedure?
- Is management penalized or rewarded depending on the relationship between the estimated and actual outcomes? How?

SURVEYS ON U.S. FIRMS

Exhibit 9.1 provides a partial list of some notable surveys focusing on U.S. companies from the mainstream academic literature in finance and accounting. Exhibit 9.1 shows that about 90 percent of these surveys are questionnaire based. Only three surveys (Mao, 1970; Rosenblatt, 1979; Ross, 1986) are based solely on interviews to gather information and only one (Mukherjee, 1988) presents analyses based on capital budgeting manuals obtained from large firms. Scapens and Sale (1981) combine questionnaires and interviews (before and after the survey). Because each method has limitations, a combination of these methods may be desirable to draw reliable conclusions.

Scott and Petty (1984), Gordon and Pinches (1984), and Mukherjee (1987) call for academia to understand the entire capital budgeting process instead of primarily focusing on the question of the extent to which practitioners use DCF tools such as net present value (NPV) and internal rate of return (IRR). Almost all surveys

Exhibit 9.1 Capital Budgeting Surveys of Large U.S. Firms

Survey Years	Survey Author(s)	Method	Number of Usable Responses	Sample
1959	Istvan (1961)	Interview	48	67 percent from large industrials
1960	Miller (1960)	Questionnaire	127	Fortune 500
1964	Christy (1966)	Questionnaire	108	S&P Stock Guide
1969	Mao (1970)	Interview	8	Medium and large firms in five industries
1969	Williams (1970)	Questionnaire	100	Fortune 500 and 29 small manufacturing firms
1959, 1964, and 1970	Klammer (1972)	Questionnaire	184	Compustat large industrial firms
Early 1970s	Petty, Scott, and Bird (1975)	Questionnaire	109	Fortune 500
1971	Fremgen (1973)	Questionnaire	177	Dun & Bradstreet Reference Book
1972	Brigham and Pettway (1973)	Questionnaire	53	Compustat public utilities
1972	Osteryoung (1973)	Questionnaire	94	Fortune 500
1975	Kim (1978)	Questionnaire	114	Dun & Bradstreet Million Dollar Directory
1976	Gitman and Forrester (1977)	Questionnaire	103	74 percent from large industrial firms
1978	Schall, Sundem, and Geijsbeek (1978)	Questionnaire	189	Compustat large industrial firms
1975 and 1979	Kim and Farragher (1981)	Questionnaire	200	Fortune 1000
1979	Oblak and Helm (1980)	Questionnaire	58	Fortune 500
1979	Rosenblatt (1979)	Interview	21	67 percent from Fortune 500
1980	Scapens and Sale (1981)	Pre- and Postquestionnaire and Interviews	205	Fortune 500

Year	Study	Method	N	Sample
1980	Moore and Reichert (1983)	Questionnaire	298	Fortune 500
1965, 1970, 1975, and 1980	Klammer and Walker (1984)	Questionnaire	188	Compustat large industrials
1982	Stanley and Block (1984)	Questionnaire	121	Fortune 1000 multinationals
1983	Farragher (1986)	Questionnaire	149	Fortune Service 500 Directory
1981 and 1982	Ross (1986)	Interview	12	Large firms
1985	Kim, Crick, and Kim (1986)	Questionnaire	367	Fortune 1000
1985	Mukherjee (1988)	Capital budgeting Manuals	60	Fortune 500
1991	Gilbert and Reichert (1995)	Questionnaire	151	Fortune Magazine Directory CFOs
1992	Bierman (1993)	Questionnaire	74	100 largest of Fortune 500
1992	Trahan and Gitman (1995)	Questionnaire	84	Fortune 500 CFOs plus Forbes 200 CFOs
1992	Burns and Walker (1997)	Questionnaire	180	Fortune 500
1994	Payne, Heath, and Gale (1999)	Questionnaire	155	U.S.- and Canadian-based firms from S&P Compustat database
1999	Graham and Harvey (2001)	Questionnaire	392	CFOs from Financial Executives Institute corporations
2008	Chen (2008)	Questionnaire	115	Publicly traded manufacturing firms identified from the Disclosure Database

This exhibit provides a partial list of the surveys of capital budgeting practices of U.S. firms from the early 1960s to the present. In most cases, the survey year differs from the publication year of the survey results. When the year of the survey is unknown, the year of publication is shown. Graham and Harvey's (2001) survey contains both large and smaller firms including some Canadian firms.

listed in Exhibit 9.1 focus on the selection stage of the process, with their primary emphasis being the tools employed to evaluate projects. Istvan (1961), Farragher (1986), and Mukherjee (1988) are notable exceptions in that they consider the entire process.

As Exhibit 9.1 shows, the number of capital budgeting surveys appears to have decreased in recent years. Identifying the reasons for this decline is speculative. First, Baker and Mukherjee (2007) point out that the editors of main-stream finance journals might be unwilling to publish survey-based articles if they do not add substantially to existing knowledge about the topic. Second, managers and executives appear less willing to respond to academic surveys than in the past. Third, financial economists often point out drawbacks to using DCF tools when making capital budgeting decisions (e.g., Trigeorgis, 1993; Triantis and Borison, 2001; Copeland, 2002). These researchers suggest using real options to supplement existing evaluation methods.

Several surveys focus on a specific aspect of the capital budgeting process such as hurdle rate, capital rationing, real options, R&D, and postcompletion auditing. Exhibit 9.2 provides a partial list of such surveys.

Survey-based studies often have shortcomings that temper making definitive conclusions. Potential shortcomings may include the following: nonresponse bias; lack of knowledge on the part of the respondents about the questions being asked; difficulties in framing questions so as not to be leading or subject to misinterpretation; potential that academic jargon differs from that used or understood by practitioners; and the possibility that choices given to the same (or similar) question might vary among surveys.

ANALYSIS OF PAST SURVEYS

This section analyzes and synthesizes actual capital budgeting practices of firms regarding each of the four stages of the capital budgeting process. In so doing, it evaluates results of surveys listed in Exhibits 9.1 and 9.2.

Stage One: Identification

Because only a few surveys examine the identification stage of the process, knowledge about this stage is incomplete. Evidence shows that the number of firms seeking or encouraging ideas from their employees has increased over the years. While Istvan (1961) finds that less than 2 percent of firms in his sample make special efforts to stimulate ideas for capital expenditures, Klammer (1972) puts this percentage at 82 percent in 1959 and 94 percent in 1972. According to Farragher (1986), 58 percent of firms, on average, seek ideas for capital budgeting projects from their employees with retail firms being the highest at 94 percent.

Surveys are unanimous in suggesting that ideas originate from the bottom up rather than from the top down (Istvan, 1961; Mao, 1970; Petty, Scott, and Bird, 1975; Stanley and Block, 1984). Surveys also suggest that directly rewarding the employee for suggesting a good idea is uncommon among large firms. Although the evidence is about 25 years old, Farragher (1986) reports that only 5 percent of the firms in his sample use a formal reward system for valuable ideas, with diversified services group being the highest at 15 percent.

Exhibit 9.2 Capital Budgeting Surveys on Specific Issues

Survey Years	Survey Author(s)	Method	Number of Usable Responses	Sample
Panel A. Forecast Bias				
1986	Pruitt and Gitman (1987)	Questionnaire	121	Vice president finance or treasurer of the largest industrials in the Fortune 500
Panel B. Hurdle Rate				
1974	Brigham (1975)	Questionnaire	33	Large firms in different activities
1990	Poterba and Summers (1995)	Questionnaire	160–228	Fortune 1000 CEOs
Panel C. Cost of Capital				
1980	Gitman and Mercurio (1982)	Questionnaire	177	Fortune 1000
1996–1997	Bruner, Eades, Harris, and Higgins (1998)	Telephone survey	7, 27, 10	7 best-selling texts, 27 prestigious CFOs, and 10 leading financial advisors
1997	Gitman and Vandenberg (2000)	Questionnaire	111	Fortune 1000 CFOs
Panel D. Cash Flow Estimation				
1986	Pohlman, Santiago, and Markel (1988)	Questionnaire	232	Fortune 500 CFOs

(continued)

157

Exhibit 9.2 (*Continued*)

Survey Years	Survey Author(s)	Method	Number of Usable Responses	Sample
Panel E. Postauditing Stage				
1988	Gordon and Myers (1991)	Questionnaire	282	Executives and capital budgeting directors of large U.S. industrials except utilities and transportation
1988	Myers, Gordon, and Hamer (1991)	Questionnaire	282	Large public firms from the FASB Data Bank
Panel F. Research and Development				
1984	Cook and Rizzuto (1989)	Questionnaire	117	BusinessWeek's annual scoreboard of major R&D firms
Panel G. Capital Rationing				
1992–1993	Mukherjee and Hingorani (1999)	Questionnaire	102	Fortune 500 CFOs
1992–1993	Mukherjee, Baker, and D'Mello (2000)	Questionnaire	102	Fortune 500 CFOs
Panel H. Real Options				
1999	Triantis and Borison (2001)	Interview	39	Executives of large companies
2005	Block (2007)	Questionnaire	40	Top-ranking officers of Fortune 1000
Panel I. Risk Analysis				
1992	Shao and Shao (1996)	Questionnaire	188	Managers of foreign manufacturing subsidiaries of U.S. industrials

This exhibit provides a partial list of surveys that focus only on a specific issue pertaining to capital budgeting decisions. In most cases, the survey year differs from the publication year of the survey results. When the year of the survey is unknown, the year of publication is shown.

Stage Two: Development

The second stage in the capital budgeting process includes eliminating infeasible ideas, implementing the mandatory projects (i.e., projects that do not require economic justification), and developing the remaining economic ideas into project proposals. Firms consider this stage more difficult yet more critical than project selection or project auditing (Fremgen, 1973; Gitman and Mercurio, 1982).

Screening Ideas

Survey evidence suggests that firms screen ideas before developing them into in-depth proposals. Istvan (1961) finds that 55 percent of his sample requires that the proposals be reviewed by a nonspecialist before being forwarded to decision makers. Also, the screening is more likely to take place at the divisional or plant level rather than at the central level (Petty et al., 1975). Scapens and Sale (1981) note, however, that divisional and senior managers interact when developing an expenditure plan. However, U.S. surveys have not explored how the screening process works. Thus, several questions remain: Are ideas screened based on their excellence, or are only the projects preferred by divisional managers put forward? Are the ideas favored by the top managers the only ones likely to be further developed by divisional managers? Do some good proposals fail to reach top management?

Cost-Benefit Data

Due to the complicated nature of the cost-benefit data, the finance department should be deeply involved in developing proposals. However, evidence suggests that the finance department's role in this endeavor has been less than desirable. Williams (1970) finds that the engineering (39 percent) and accounting (33 percent) departments primarily share this responsibility, with the finance or budget committee being the next closest group (17 percent). In a later study, Pohlman, Santiago, and Markel (1988) report that 85 percent of the firms in their sample have specific individuals with a wide variety of backgrounds (e.g., accountant, financial analyst, treasurer, vice president, department manager, controller, division director, assistant controller, or assistant treasurer) oversee the process of preparing the firm's cost-benefit data for project evaluation. According to Farragher (1986), this responsibility belongs primarily to the finance department (55 percent).

Data requirements for proposals vary with the project size and classification. Mukherjee (1988), who reviews capital budgeting manuals collected from large U.S. firms, provides a typical description of supporting data requirements depending on the project's size and classification.

Most firms estimate cash flows rather than just net income in determining a project's worth. Pohlman et al. (1988) report that 85 percent of their sample firms have a company-wide procedure for estimating cash flows, with 78 percent of firms having standard forms and worksheets for this purpose. Schall, Sundem, and Geijsbeek (1978) find that a majority of firms (62 percent) consider theoretically correct cash flows as the appropriate cost-benefit stream. They also report that the most common method for estimating cash flows is to forecast net income and then adjust it for noncash items such as depreciation. Meier and Tarhan (2007) find that about 78 percent of firms in their sample compute cash flows by using the following model or a slight variation of this model: earnings before interest and after taxes (EBIAT) + depreciation – capital expenditures – net change in working capital.

Cash flow estimates must incorporate opportunity costs such as cannibalization (i.e., when a proposed project takes away sales from an existing product). Meier and Tarhan (2007) find that about 81 percent of the firms in their sample take into account the effect of cannibalization in estimating a project's cash flows.

Inflation introduces a downward bias in determining a project's worth because the discount rate (cost of capital) is stated in nominal terms and thus reflects the expected inflation rate while the cash flows are stated in real terms and therefore are unadjusted for inflation. A practical and theoretically correct solution to this problem is to adjust cash flows for inflation. Surveys show that many firms follow this procedure. The following are the percentages of firms in specific surveys that make such adjustment: 50 percent in Hendricks (1983), 31.4 percent in Ryan and Ryan (2002), and 68.2 percent in Meier and Tarhan (2007). Hendricks also finds that firms using DCF as a primary tool utilizing a computer in the capital budgeting process or having a large capital budgeting project are more likely to adjust for inflation.

Stage Three: Selection

Conventional capital budgeting theory dictates that firms select only those projects that add value. To this end, there are several theoretical prescriptions. For example, firms should use DCF methods to select the highest NPV project among mutually exclusive projects and the projects with positive NPVs among independent projects. Also, firms should select the project favored by NPV when confronted with a ranking conflict between NPV and IRR. Theory also suggests that in an efficient market, capital rationing should not exist. Further, a project's hurdle rate should be based on the risk inherent in the project's future cash flows. Thus, a firm's weighted average cost of capital (WACC) may serve as a hurdle rate for average-risk projects only.

Personnel
As in the case of proposal development, the finance department should also be heavily involved in analyzing proposals. The survey evidence in this regard, however, is mixed. Williams (1970) indicates that companies rely more on engineering departments for developing proposals, but accounting departments play a greater role in analyzing the proposals. He also notes that 56 percent of corporations assign at least one full-time person to analyze capital projects, with 80 percent of them assigning three or more people to this job. Yet, Gitman and Forrester (1977) report that the finance department is primarily responsible for project analysis in 60 percent of their sample and 24.2 percent of the cases, respectively. Comparing the results of Williams to those of Gitman and Forrester (1977) is impractical because these authors provide a different set of choices to similar questions in their questionnaires.

Selection Techniques
Over the past five decades, the most extensively researched area in capital budgeting surveys is the way in which firms assess and compare projects. Here, survey

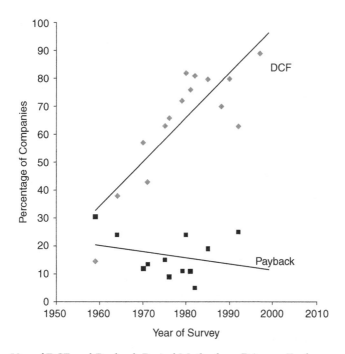

Exhibit 9.3   Use of DCF and Payback Period Methods as Primary Tools
Note: This exhibit shows the trend in percentages of firms using DCF methods versus the payback period as a primary tool in evaluating capital budgeting projects. When two surveys are conducted during the same year, the exhibit reflects the midpoint of the percentage usage reported in the two surveys. This exhibit demonstrates an upward trend in using DCF methods and a downward trend in using the payback period. Sources: Istvan (1961), Klammer (1972), Petty, Scott, and Bird (1975), Gitman and Forrester (1977), Oblak and Helm (1980), Kim and Farragher (1981), Moore and Reichert (1983), Hendricks (1983), Gilbert and Reichert (1995), Klammer and Walker (1984), Stanley and Block (1984), Kim, Crick, and Kim (1986), Shao and Shao (1993), and Bruner, Eades, Harris, and Higgins (1998).

questions focus on whether firms, especially large firms, have adopted DCF techniques. The survey results show that the use of DCF techniques has increased substantially over time. Further, the use of DCF methods as primary selection criteria has steadily increased, while the use of the payback period as a primary tool has steadily declined. Exhibit 9.3 captures the upward trend of DCF tools and the downward trend of the payback period.

Theory suggests that NPV is superior to IRR but surveys consistently show that firms typically prefer IRR to NPV. Based on their survey results, Burns and Walker (1997) seem to imply that firms prefer IRR because it is easier to understand and compute than NPV. IRR is easier to understand than NPV as it can be more readily compared with returns from other investment opportunities. However, the claim that IRR is easier to compute than NPV is questionable.

Despite the greater popularity of IRR compared to NPV, firms apparently favor NPV when conflict occurs. Apap and Masson (2004–2005) find that 56 percent of firms rely on NPV to resolve conflicts, compared to 19 percent and 4 percent of firms who favor IRR and the modified internal rate of return (MIRR), respectively. Ryan and Ryan (2002) report a similar finding.

Payback remains a popular secondary tool for project evaluation despite its declining popularity as a primary tool. The percentage of firms that use the payback period method as a secondary selection tool ranges from 39 percent in Kim and Farragher (1981) to 72 percent in Trahan and Gitman (1995). Burns and Walker (1997) report that payback's continued popularity results from its ease of computation and its usefulness in conjunction with DCF techniques as a measure of both liquidity and risk.

Surveys indicate that firms often use more than one selection technique. Moreover, many firms combine pure financial techniques (DCF or non-DCF) with nonfinancial measures such as strategic consideration. At least two surveys attempt to find reasons for using multiple methods. Based on responses to their survey, Apap and Masson (2004–2005) report that some methods give more information than others (72 percent); different management executives want different methods (31 percent); and managers lack confidence in using only one method (16 percent). Chen (2008) concludes that firms with high product standardization tend to emphasize DCF analysis, while firms with low standardization tend to focus on using nonfinancial measures such as firm strategy, growth potential, and competition. Thus, firms with projects that require complex manufacturing processes or high R&D expenses (uncertain outcome) rely more on nonfinancial measures.

Choice of Hurdle Rate

Several questions involving the choice of an appropriate hurdle rate are relevant. First, to what extent do firms use a hurdle rate to make project selections? Second, do firms use the same hurdle rate to evaluate all projects? Third, how do firms define a hurdle rate? Finally, how do firms select a project's hurdle rate?

Survey evidence shows that at least three-quarters of the firms surveyed employ at least one hurdle rate in capital budgeting (Petty et al., 1975; Schall et al., 1978; Gitman and Mercurio, 1982). Poterba and Summers (1995) report that most firms have more than one hurdle rate based on a specific project being selected or considered. Early surveys indicate that less than 30 percent of the firms report using WACC as a hurdle rate (Christy, 1966; Williams, 1970; Petty et al. 1975). Later studies show a substantial increase in the WACC usage, from 46 percent in Schall et al. (1978) to 93 percent in Bruner, Eades, Harris, and Higgins (1998). More recent studies by Ryan and Ryan (2002) and Meier and Tarhan (2007) report a similar trend.

Bruner et al. (1998) examine how firms compute WACC. Their findings show that firms generally base WACC weights on market values rather than book values and base the after-tax cost of debt on the marginal tax rate. Survey evidence also shows that the use of the CAPM to estimate the cost of equity has increased substantially since 1980 when, as reported by Gitman and Mercurio (1982), less than 22 percent of firms employed the CAPM. In more recent years, the use of the CAPM is reported to be 85 percent in Bruner et al. (1998), 93 percent in Gitman and Vandenberg (2000), and 74 percent in Graham and Harvey (2001).

Risk Analysis

Several questions for this area are relevant: How do firms assess risk? How do they incorporate risk in making capital budgeting decisions? Is the risk assessment process purely ad hoc? Do firms use one hurdle rate for all projects?

Evidence suggests that firms use sensitivity analysis as the primary risk-assessment tool. Most, if not all, surveys that ask this question indicate it as such (for example, Brigham and Pettway, 1973; Kim and Farragher, 1981; Kim, Crick, and Kim, 1986; Ferreira and Brooks, 1988; Shao and Shao, 1996; Payne, Heath, and Gale, 1999; Ryan and Ryan, 2002). Regarding risk adjustment, the three primary methods used by firms for this purpose are changing the required rate of return, adjusting cash flows, and modifying the payback period. Except for results reported by Petty et al. (1975), shortening the payback period is less popular than the other risk adjustment methods. Stanley and Block (1984) and Shao and Shao (1996) find that firms use risk-adjusted cash flows more frequently than risk-adjusted discounted rates.

The process of incorporating risk by adjusting discount rates or cash flows is not formal but ad hoc. Trahan and Gitman (1995) ask why firms shun formal techniques. The respondents answer that formal models are impractical, based on unrealistic assumptions, hard to explain to top management, and difficult to apply. According to Mukherjee (1987), other reasons for avoiding sophisticated models are their inability to reflect risk from the firm's perspective, their need for massive amounts of data, and their requirement for high data processing efficiency.

Finally, firms typically do not adjust for investment risks in foreign countries. Graham and Harvey (2001) find that 58.8 percent of the firms surveyed use a company-wide discount rate when evaluating cross-border projects.

Capital Rationing

Theoretically, there should be no limit to the amount that firms can invest in projects as long as the return is equal to or greater than the required rate of return. In other words, in efficient capital markets, capital rationing in which firms limit the size of their capital budgeting consequently rejecting positive NPV projects should not exist. However, evidence shows that a substantial percentage of firms surveyed (between 40 and 70 percent) operate under a capital constraint or fixed budget (Brigham and Pettway, 1973; Fremgen, 1973; Petty et al., 1975; Gitman and Forrester, 1977; Ferreira and Brooks, 1988; Mukherjee and Hingorani, 1999).

Survey evidence suggests that capital constraints are imposed internally by senior managers rather than externally by the suppliers of funds. According to Scapens and Sale (1981), 93 percent of firms in their sample impose a ceiling on capital expenditures as a tool for central control. Although Fremgen (1973), Gitman and Forrester (1977), and Gitman and Mercurio (1982) report that limits on borrowing are the primary reason for capital rationing, the borrowing limit is more likely set by senior managers based on the firm's debt ratio relative to its target than on the lenders' unwillingness to provide money to the firm. In fact, Gitman and Vandenberg (2000) report that capital rationing is due to the debt restrictions imposed by top-level management. Mukherjee and Hingorani (1999) find that of the 64 percent of firms operating under a capital rationing environment, 82 percent consider the limit to be internally imposed.

The literature offers three major explanations for the prevalence of internal capital rationing: (1) the presence of forecast bias among the firm's middle managers; (2) the firm's reluctance to issue external financing; and (3) senior managers' aversion to downside risk. Proponents of the biased forecast rationale (e.g., Antle and Eppen, 1985; Hirshleifer, 1993; Holmstrom and Ricart i Costa, 1986) argue that senior managers use capital rationing as a tool to discourage biased cash flow projections by junior managers. Based on their survey, Pruitt and Gitman (1987) note that senior managers are aware of this potential bias in junior manager' estimates (overstating revenues and understating costs). Myers and Majluf (1984) support managerial reluctance to issue external financing as a reason for capital rationing. This explanation is rooted in the information asymmetry problem between the firm and external capital markets, which makes external financing more costly than internal financing. Consequently, senior managers limit the amount to be invested in a given year to the capital that the firm can raise internally. Myers (1984) further suggests that firms may forego a marginally acceptable project, especially if it needs external financing, in order to maintain a reserve borrowing capacity to fund a potentially high NPV project in the future. Bierman and Smidt (1993) are the main proponents of the argument that senior managers might reject a positive NPV project if they perceive its downside risk as too high. Based on the survey response, Mukherjee and Hingorani (1999) report that the three most common explanations for capital rationing are aversion to downside risk first, followed by maintaining reserve borrowing power and reducing the impact of optimistic forecasts.

Mukherjee, Baker, and D'Mello (2000) further compare the biased-forecast and costly external financing explanations to determine which of the two motivations better explains the prevalence of capital rationing among U.S. firms. The authors attempt analysis to explain the frequency of capital rationing experienced by Fortune 500 firms during 1981 to 1991 by using proxies for these two explanations. The authors obtain the frequency data from the Mukherjee and Hingorani (1999) survey with 0 to 3 years of capital rationing defined as low frequency and 7 to 10 years as high frequency. They hypothesize that, if avoiding costly external financing is the primary motive, then firms with low profitability (lower level of internal capital), higher debt ratios (relative to the industry), and lower institutional ownership would experience a higher frequency of capital rationing. On the other hand, if reducing forecast bias is the primary motive, then the higher the job mobility (in the affiliated industry) and the number of business segments, the higher is the frequency of capital rationing facing a firm. Based on univariate analyses, Mukherjee et al. report that high-frequency firms have significantly lower profitability and lower debt capacity than the low-frequency firms do. Logit analysis yields similar results. They conclude that avoiding external financing is the primary motive behind capital rationing.

Despite the prevalence of capital rationing, only a small percentage of firms report using management optimization tools to deal with this issue. Klammer (1972) shows an increase in the use of linear programming from 4 percent to 17 percent between 1959 and 1970. Fremgen (1973) and Kim and Farragher (1981) report that 19 percent of firms use linear programming, while Ryan and Ryan (2002) indicate that only 5.4 percent of their respondents frequently employ linear programming in a capital constraint situation. Mukherjee and Hingorani (1999) report that none of the firms in their sample use linear programming for project selection under capital rationing. Additionally, they note that the failure to use this management tool does not result from unfamiliarity but from a lack of sufficiently accurate data.

Although the use of linear or integer programming is rare under capital rationing, firms do select projects following theoretical prescriptions. Mukherjee and

Hingorani (1999) find that firms rank projects in terms of the IRR or the profitability index and select the bundle that maximizes NPV. According to Graham, Harvey, and Puri (2010), NPV ranks highest as the most popular vehicle for allocating capital to projects under capital rationing.

Project Approval

Including a capital project in the annual capital budget does not constitute approval to commit funds for that project. Therefore, a system must outline the level of authorization as well as the steps needed to get the budget approved. Upon analyzing 60 manuals on capital budgeting, Mukherjee (1988) notes that almost 75 percent of most manuals focus on this specific aspect of the capital budgeting process. He reports that the level of approval depends primarily on two factors: (1) budget status (budgeted or nonbudgeted) of the project, and (2) project size. The level of the approval authority also rises with the project size, consistent with the data requirements reported in Exhibit 9.3 above. However, a nonbudgeted project, irrespective of its size, requires approval from a higher authority than a budgeted project.

Stage Four: Postcompletion Auditing

The final step of the capital budgeting process involves conducting postcompletion auditing (PCA). PCA analysis has three primary objectives: (1) to take necessary action (such as expenditure control) on the projects being reviewed; (2) to use the information learned from the postaudit review to improve future proposals; and (3) to implement a reward/punishment system for responsible personnel based on the performance of the projects being reviewed. Chapter 8 provides an in-depth discussion of PCAs.

Survey evidence suggests that PCAs appear to be growing in importance. The percentage of firms performing PCAs ranges from 50 percent (Istvan, 1961) to 90 percent (Gitman and Mercurio, 1982). Many firms conduct PCAs but typically not on a regular basis, as indicated by Gordon and Myers (1991), who report that the postauditing stage is not a standard part of a firm's capital budgeting process.

The issue of who performs the postaudit (e.g., corporate headquarters or the originating division) and the circumstances under which PCA is conducted are important issues. If the division is responsible for project development, corporate headquarters might conduct PCA as a control measure. On the other hand, if project development is mostly an interaction between the divisional and senior managers within the overall strategic framework of the firm, PCA might be routine and therefore delegated to the division. Scapens and Sale (1981) report that 53 percent of firms in their sample perform this function at the division level and 44 percent conduct PCAs at the corporate headquarters. Little evidence is available, however, concerning when headquarters takes on this responsibility and when it delegates PCAs to a division.

Does the intensity of PCA vary depending on the type of project? Brigham and Pettway (1973) find that utility firms in general do not re-review operating costs and operating revenues because these investments are mandatory. Gordon and Myers (1991) find that the intensity of performance evaluation is tied to the asset base. Thus, the level of intensity is highest for strategic assets (e.g., expansion projects), followed by administrative assets (e.g., replacement projects), and then operating assets (e.g., minor office equipment).

As stated above, a major objective of the postaudit system is to reward or reprimand project sponsor(s) based on the review of project performance. Early surveys show that many firms reward (Rosenblatt, 1979) or reprimand (Istvan, 1961) managers based on how the project has performed.

A project's performance is best measured by its DCF that focuses on long-term profitability. Myers, Gordon, and Hamer (1991) compare the overall performance of a group of firms that employ DCF technique in the postaudit stage with a control group that does not employ such techniques. They attribute superior performance to the former group. Measuring performance using short-term returns (e.g., return on investment [ROI]) leads to a distorted reward system that encourages managers to forego good long-term projects in favor of projects that look good in the short run but might turn out to be poor investments in the long haul. Despite the shortcomings of short-term measures, surveys show firms commonly use ROI to measure performance of a project or a division (Miller, 1960; Williams, 1970; Scapens and Sale, 1981). A possible explanation of this behavior might be that investors react more strongly to short-term news about the firm than to its long-term potential. Also, due to many external factors beyond a manager's control, isolating the level of contribution a manager might make to the long-term performance of a project is often difficult.

SUMMARY AND CONCLUSIONS

Over the past five decades, numerous surveys have examined the capital budgeting practices of large U.S. firms. This chapter reviews a broad cross-section of these surveys to learn about investment practices pertaining to the four stages of the capital budgeting process. The analysis suggests that the gap between traditional capital budgeting theory and actual practices has narrowed over the last few decades. In the development stage, most firms agree that cash flows are the appropriate cost-benefit data. For example, most firms estimate cash flows in a manner consistent with theory including consideration of opportunity costs associated with the project. In the selection stage, the use of DCF analysis as the primary selection tool has steadily increased while the use of the payback period as the main evaluation method has steadily declined. The use of WACC has also increased over the years. Cost computation of individual components of a firm's target capital structure appears to be consistent with theory. Managers recognize risk differences in projects and adjust the hurdle rate, albeit on an ad-hoc basis, accordingly.

On first glance, certain practices seem to be inconsistent with the traditional theory. These practices include: (1) continued preference of IRR to NPV; (2) continued use of the payback method; and (3) prevalence of capital rationing. On further analyses, however, these practices might not necessarily violate theory. Firms might prefer IRR because of its comparability with returns from other investment opportunities, which are almost always expressed in percentage terms. Further, reliance on IRR does not necessarily imply that managers overlook NPV. Upon reviewing 60 capital budgeting manuals obtained from large U.S. firms, Mukherjee (1988) notes that all firms require project sponsors to compute both NPV and IRR. When NPV and IRR give conflicting ranking of mutually exclusive projects, emphasis on IRR might lead to incorrect decisions. However, according to Apap and Masson (2004–2005) and Ryan and Ryan (2002), firms prefer NPV when a conflict occurs between NPV and IRR. Also, in the presence of capital rationing, most firms rank the projects by their IRRs but select the bundle that maximizes a firm's overall NPV (Mukherjee and Hingorani, 1999).

Continued use of the payback method may not be inconsistent with theory for several potential reasons. First, for most firms, the payback method plays a secondary role to DCF methods. Nothing is inherently wrong with choosing from two competing projects the one with the lower payback as long as no large difference exists in the projects' NPVs. Second, continued use of payback period might be justified as a secondary selection tool based on its simplicity of calculation, emphasis on liquidity, and ability to serve as a quick risk-screening device.

The ubiquitous presence of capital rationing might not necessarily contradict theory for several reasons. For example, Mukherjee and Hingorani (1999) find that capital rationing is mostly soft in kind in that firms do not strictly adhere to the ceiling and raise it when complying with the ceiling amounts to giving up high NPV projects. Also, according to Thakor (1990), capital rationing is consistent with theory because managers might intentionally decide to forego current projects in favor of future higher NPV projects.

The gap between conventional theory and practice is not entirely bridged. For instance, firms seem to continue to employ a company-wide hurdle rate to evaluate almost all projects including cross-border projects. Additionally, firms appear to evaluate employees based on the short-term performance of their sponsored projects. Overall, however, practitioners appear to have generally adopted traditional capital budgeting theory.

Before celebrating the successful applications of traditional models, a word of caution is in order. Many researchers question whether DCF models are appropriate when decisions depend on many factors beyond simply calculating a project's NPV. Traditional capital budgeting theory assumes that once a firm accepts the project using DCF models, it can no longer influence the project's final outcome. In practice, however, the firm can influence a project's final outcome by exploiting options such as abandoning the project before its economic life expires or postponing implementation of an accepted project. According to Brigham and Ehrhardt (2008), the assumption underlying traditional capital budgeting theory (DCF models) is akin to a roulette wheel in which a gambler cannot change the outcome once the wheel is in motion. Yet, the assumption underlying real options is more like draw poker, which allows the gambler to change the ultimate outcome of the game and possibly win by drawing additional cards.

Myers (1984) is perhaps the first to point out the inadequacy of DCF analysis in evaluating a firm's strategic options including investments in R&D. Some researchers, such as Trigeorgis (1993), Triantis and Borison (2001), and Copeland (2002), opine that NPV analysis systematically undervalues investment opportunities relative to real options analysis, which incorporates uncertainty and flexibility.

The use of real options analysis lags behind DCF analysis but is increasing, especially among large firms. For example, Block (2007) reports that, although the use of real options is limited to only 14 percent of Fortune 1000 firms sampled, this percentage is substantially higher than what previous surveys report. McDonald (2006) argues that DCF analysis is not dead but can coexist peacefully with real option analysis, and the two types of analysis can play a complementary role to each other.

DISCUSSION QUESTIONS

1. What are several inherent shortcomings with survey-based research?
2. Of the four major stages of the capital budgeting process, which stage is the most difficult but most crucial for making correct capital budgeting decisions? Which stage is the most extensively researched in surveys?
3. Survey findings about capital budgeting selection techniques used by firms imply several apparent departures from theory. Explain two of these deviations.
4. Why, in theory, might capital rationing run counter to the goal of shareholder wealth maximization?
5. Capital rationing might be internally or externally imposed. Briefly discuss two major information-asymmetry–based explanations for the existence of internal capital rationing.
6. Based on survey findings, identify several areas in which the gap between theory and practice has narrowed over the years and other areas in which a gap continues to exist.

REFERENCES

Antle, Rick, and Gary D. Eppen. 1985. "Capital Rationing and Organizational Slack in Capital Budgeting." *Management Science* 31:2, 163–174.
Apap, Antonio, and Dubos J. Masson. 2004–2005. "A Survey of Capital Budgeting in Publicly Traded Utility Companies." *Southwest Business and Economics Journal* 13, 45–52.
Baker, H. Kent, and Tarun K. Mukherjee. 2007. "Survey Research in Finance: Views from Journal Editors." *International Journal of Managerial Finance* 3:1, 11–25.
Bierman, Harold, Jr. 1993. "Capital Budgeting in 1992: A Survey." *Financial Management Letters* 22:3, 1–24.
Bierman, Harold, Jr., and Seymour Smidt. 1993. *The Capital Budgeting Decision: Economic Analysis of Investment Projects.* New York: Macmillan.
Block, Stanley B. 2007. "Are 'Real Options' Actually Used in the Real World?" *Engineering Economist* 52:3, 255–268.
Brigham, Eugene F. 1975. "Hurdle Rates for Screening Capital Expenditure Proposals." *Financial Management* 4:3, 17–26.
Brigham, Eugene F., and Michael C. Ehrhardt. 2008. *Financial Management: Theory and Practice.* Mason, OH: Thomson South-Western.
Brigham, Eugene F., and Richard H. Pettway. 1973. "Capital Budgeting by Utilities." *Financial Management* 2:3, 11–22.
Bruner, Robert F., Kenneth M. Eades, Robert S. Harris, and Robert C. Higgins. 1998. "Best Practices in Estimating the Cost of Capital: Survey and Synthesis." *Financial Practice and Education* 8:1, 13–28.
Burns, Richard M., and Joe Walker. 1997. "Capital Budgeting Techniques among the Fortune 500: A Rationale Approach." *Managerial Finance* 23:9, 3–15.

Burns, Richard M., and Joe Walker. 2009. "Capital Budgeting Surveys: The Future Is Now." *Journal of Applied Finance* 19:1/2, 78–90.

Chen, Shimin. 2008. "DCF Techniques and Nonfinancial Measures in Capital Budgeting: A Contingency Approach Analysis." *Behavioral Research in Accounting* 20:1, 13–29.

Christy, George. A. 1966. *Capital Budgeting: Current Practices and Their Efficiency.* Eugene, OR: Bureau of Business and Economic Research, University of Oregon.

Cook, Thomas J., and Ronald J. Rizzuto. 1989. "Capital Budgeting Practices for R&D: A Survey and Analysis of Business Week's R&D Scoreboard." *Engineering Economist* 34:4, 291–303.

Copeland, Thomas E. 2002. "What Do Practitioners Want?" *Journal of Applied Finance* 12:1, 5–12.

Farragher, Edward J. 1986. "Capital Budgeting Practices of Non-industrial Firms." *Engineering Economist* 31:4, 293–302.

Ferreira, Eurico J., and LeRoy Brooks. 1988. "Capital Budgeting: A Key Management Challenge." *Business* 38:4, 22–29.

Fremgen, James M. 1973. "Capital Budgeting Practices: A Survey." *Management Accounting* 54:11, 19–25.

Gilbert, Erika, and Alan Reichart. 1995. "The Practice of Financial Management among Large US Corporations." *Financial Practice and Education* 5:1, 16–23.

Gitman, Lawrence J., and John R. Forrester, Jr. 1977. "A Survey of Capital Budgeting Techniques Used by Major U.S. Firms." *Financial Management* 6:3, 66–71.

Gitman, Lawrence J., and Vincent A. Mercurio. 1982. "Cost of Capital Techniques Used by Major U.S. Firms: Survey and Analysis of Fortune's 1000." *Financial Management* 11:4, 21–29.

Gitman, Lawrence J., and Pieter A. Vandenberg. 2000. "Cost of Capital Techniques Used by Major U.S. Firms: 1997 vs. 1980." *Financial Practice and Education* 10:2, 53–68.

Gordon, Lawrence A., and Mary D. Myers. 1991. "Post-Auditing Capital Projects: Are You in Step with the Competition?" *Management Accounting* 72:7, 39–42.

Gordon, Lawrence A., and George E. Pinches. 1984. *Improving Capital Budgeting: A Decision Support System Approach.* Reading, MA: Addison-Wesley.

Graham, John R., and Campbell R. Harvey. 2001. "The Theory and Practice of Corporate Finance: Evidence from the Field." *Journal of Financial Economics* 60:2–3, 187–243.

Graham, John R., Campbell R. Harvey, and Manju Puri. 2010. "Capital Allocation and Delegation of Decision-making Authority within Firms." Available at http://ssrn.com/abstract=1527098.

Hendricks, John A. 1983. "Capital Budgeting Practices Including Inflation Adjustments: A Survey." *Managerial Planning* 31:4, 22–28.

Hirshleifer, David. 1993. "Managerial Reputation and Corporate Investment Decisions." *Financial Management* 22:2, 145–160.

Holmstrom, Bengt, and Joan Ricart i Costa. 1986. "Managerial Incentives and Capital Management." *Quarterly Journal of Economics* 101:4, 835–860.

Istvan, Donald F. 1961. "Capital-expenditure Decisions: How They Are Made in Large Corporations." *Indiana Business Reports 33. Bureau of Business Research*, Bloomington, IN: Indiana University.

Kim, Suk H. 1978. "Capital-Budgeting Practices in Large Corporations and Their Impact on Overall Profitability." *Baylor Business Studies* 9:4, 49–66.

Kim, Suk H., and Edward J. Farragher. 1981. "Current Capital Budgeting Practices." *Management Accounting* 62:12, 26–30.

Kim, Suk H., Trevor Crick, and Seung H. Kim. 1986. "Do Executives Practice What Academics Preach?" *Management Accounting* 68:5, 49–52.

Kim, Suk H., and Gregory Ulferts. 1996. "A Summary of Multinational Capital Budgeting Studies." *Managerial Finance* 22:1, 75-85.

Klammer, Thomas P. 1972. "Empirical Evidence of the Adoption of Sophisticated Capital Budgeting Techniques." *Journal of Business* 45:3, 387–397.

Klammer, Thomas P., and Michael C. Walker. 1984. "The Continuing Increase in the Use of Sophisticated Capital Budgeting Techniques." *California Management Review* 27:1, 137–148.

Mao, James C. T. 1970. "Survey of Capital Budgeting: Theory and Practice." *Journal of Finance* 25:2, 349–360.

McDonald, Robert L. 2006. "The Role of Real Options in Capital Budgeting: Theory and Practice." *Journal of Applied Corporate Finance* 18:2, 28–39.

Meier, Iwan, and Vefa Tarhan. 2007. "Corporate Investment Decision Practices and the Hurdle Rate Premium Puzzle." Working Paper, Loyola University of Chicago.

Miller, James H. 1960. "A Glimpse at Practice in Calculating and Using Return on Investment." *N.A.A. Bulletin* (now *Management Accounting*) 41: June, 65–76.

Moore, James S., and Alan K. Reichert. 1983. "An Analysis of the Financial Management Techniques Currently Employed by Large US Corporations." *Journal of Business Finance & Accounting* 10:4, 623–645.

Mukherjee, Tarun K. 1987. "Capital Budgeting Surveys: The Past and the Future." *Review of Business and Economic Research* 22:2, 37–56.

Mukherjee, Tarun K. 1988. "The Capital Budgeting Process of Large U.S. Firms: An Analysis of Capital Budgeting Manuals." *Managerial Finance* 14:2/3, 28–34.

Mukherjee, Tarun K., H. Kent Baker, and Ranjan D'Mello. 2000. "Capital Rationing Decisions—Part II." *Financial Practice and Education* 10:1, 69–77.

Mukherjee, Tarun K., and Glenn V. Henderson. 1987. "The Capital Budgeting Process: Theory and Practice." *Interfaces* 17:2, 78-90.

Mukherjee, Tarun K., and Vineeta L. Hingorani. 1999. "Capital-Rationing Decisions of Fortune 500 Firms: A Survey." *Financial Practice and Education* 9:1, 7–15.

Myers, Stewart, and Nicholas Majluf. 1984. "Corporate Financing and Investment Decisions When Firms Have Information That Investors Do Not Have." *Journal of Financial Economics* 13:2, 187–221.

Myers, Mary D., Lawrence A. Gordon, and Michelle M. Hamer. 1991. "Post-Auditing Capital Assets and Firm Performance: An Empirical Investigation." *Managerial and Decision Economics* 12:4, 317–327.

Myers, Stewart C. 1984. "Finance Theory and Financial Strategy." *Interfaces* 14:1, 126–137.

Oblak, David J., and Roy J. Helm, Jr. 1980. "Survey and Analysis of Capital Budgeting Methods Used by Multinationals." *Financial Management* 9:4, 37–41.

Osteryoung, Jerome S. 1973. "A Survey into the Goals Used by Fortune's 500 Companies in Capital Budgeting Decisions." *Akron Business and Economic Review* 4:3, 34–35.

Payne, Janet D., Will C. Heath and Lewis R. Gale. 1999. "Comparative Financial Practice in the US and Canada: Capital Budgeting and Risk Assessment Techniques." *Financial Practice and Education* 9:1, 16–24.

Petty, William J., David F. Scott, and Monroe M. Bird. 1975. "The Capital Expenditure Decision-Making Process of Large Corporations." *Engineering Economist* 20:3, 159–172.

Pohlman, Randolph A., Emmanuel S. Santiago, and F. Lynn Markel. 1988. "Cash Flow Estimation Practices of Large Firms." *Financial Management* 17:2, 71–79.

Poterba, James M., and Lawrence H. Summers. 1995. "A CEO Survey of U.S. Companies' Time Horizon and Hurdle Rates." *Sloan Management Review* 37:1, 43–53.

Pruitt, Stephen W. and Lawrence J. Gitman. 1987. "Capital Budgeting Forecast Biases: Evidence from the Fortune 500." *Financial Management* 16:1, 46–51.

Rosenblatt, Meir J., 1979. "A Survey and Analysis of Capital Budgeting Decision Process in Multi-Division Firms." *Engineering Economist* 25:4, 259–273.

Ross, Marc. 1986. "Capital Budgeting Practices of Twelve Large Manufacturers." *Financial Management* 15:4, 1–22.

Ryan, Patricia A., and Glenn P. Ryan. 2002. "Capital Budgeting Practices of the Fortune 1000: How Have Things Changed?" *Journal of Business and Management* 8:4, 355–364.

Scapens, Robert W., and J. Timothy Sale. 1981. "Performance Measurement and Formal Capital Expenditure Controls in Divisionalized Companies." *Journal of Business Finance & Accounting* 8:3, 389–420.

Schall, Lawrence D., Gary L. Sundem, and William R. Geijsbeek, Jr. 1978. "Survey and Analysis of Capital Budgeting Methods." *Journal of Finance* 33:1, 281–287.

Scott, David F., and William Petty. 1984. "Capital Budgeting Practices in Large American Firms: A Retrospective Analysis and Synthesis." *Financial Review* 19:1, 111–123.

Shao, Lawrence P., and Alan T. Shao. 1993. "Capital Budgeting Practices Employed by European Affiliates of U.S. Transnational Companies." *Journal of Multinational Financial Management* 3:1/2, 95–109.

Shao, Lawrence P., and Alan T. Shao. 1996. "Risk Analysis and Capital Budgeting Techniques of US Multinational Enterprises." *Managerial Finance* 22:1, 41–57.

Stanley, Marjorie T., and Stanley B. Block. 1984. "A Survey of Multinational Capital Budgeting." *Financial Review* 19:1, 36–54.

Thakor, Anjan. 1990. "Investment Myopia and the Internal Organization of Capital Allocation Decisions." *Journal of Law, Economics and Organization* 6:1, 129–154.

Trahan, Emery A., and Lawrence J. Gitman. 1995. "Bridging the Theory-practice Gap in Corporate Finance: A Survey of Chief Financial Officers." *Quarterly Review of Economics and Finance* 35:1, 73–87.

Triantis, Alex, and Adam Borison. 2001. "Real Options: State of the Practice." *Journal of Applied Corporate Finance* 14:2, 8–24.

Trigeorgis, Lenos. 1993. "Real Options and Interactions with Financial Flexibility." *Financial Management* 22:3, 202–224.

Williams, Ronald B., Jr. 1970. "Industry Practice in Allocating Capital Resources." *Managerial Planning* 18:6, 15–22.

ABOUT THE AUTHORS

Tarun K. Mukherjee is the Moffett Chair in Financial Economics at the University of New Orleans. He is also co-editor of the *Review of Financial Economics*. He has published in many refereed journals including *Financial Management*, *Financial Review*, and *Journal of Financial Research*. Three of his articles have been reprinted in books of readings. His 1990 paper on leasing is ranked among the top 25 articles published in *Financial Management* that are referenced in corporate finance textbooks. Professor Mukherjee has also received multiple best professor awards from the Executive MBA programs offered in the United States, Jamaica, and Puerto Rico by the University of New Orleans.

Naseem M. Al Rahahleh is an Assistant Professor of Finance at Park University. He worked for seven years in a USAID-funded project in the Jordanian Ministry of Planning. His research during this period was published in a book titled *The Jordan's Competitiveness Book: Confronting the Competitiveness Challenge*. Professor Al Rahahleh received a B.S. and an M.S. in Economics from Yarmouk University, Jordan. He received a Master of Science in Financial Economics and a Ph.D. in Financial Economics from the University of New Orleans. His research interests include mergers and acquisitions, capital budgeting, futures markets, and market integration and efficiency.

Project Cash Flows and Inflation

CHAPTER 10

Estimating Project Cash Flows

KYLE MEYER
Executive-in-Residence, Rollins College

HALIL KIYMAZ
Bank of America Chair and Professor of Finance, Rollins College

INTRODUCTION

On June 18, 2010, the Universal Orlando Resort held the grand opening of the Wizarding World of Harry Potter attraction. The grand opening was the culmination of more than five years of planning and the investment of more than $200 million of the entertainment giant's capital (Garcia, 2010). Before making the decision to invest firm resources into the Harry Potter attraction, Universal evaluated this investment opportunity. The process of evaluating investment opportunities and making investment decisions is called *capital budgeting*.

From inception through maturity, firms make capital budgeting decisions on a recurring basis. Often capital budgeting decisions are limited to evaluating whether existing productive capacity needs to be replaced or repaired. In many cases, firms must weigh the costs and benefits of capital investments intended to increase productive capacity or to expand into new product lines or markets (Danielson and Scott, 2006).

Capital budgeting has a long-term focus that provides a link to an organization's *strategic plan*, which is a road map for accomplishing the organization's long-term strategic goals. Capital budgeting decisions generally commit substantial amounts of corporate resources, and capital investments are difficult to convert to more liquid assets (Migliore and McCracken, 2001). Therefore, decisions made in the capital budgeting process should be consistent with the goals set forth in the organization's long-term strategic plan and provide inputs for the organization's short-term budgeting process. As a road map for the achievement of organizational goals, capital budgeting seeks to maximize future net cash inflows realized from the investment of the organization's limited resources (Casolari and Womack, 2010).

THEORETICAL DISCUSSION

Capital budgeting decisions generally fall into three broad categories: replacements of existing assets, investments to expand existing product lines, and investments

175

to expand into new product lines. Danielson and Scott (2006) report the results of a survey conducted by the National Federation of Independent Business (NFIB) related to capital budgeting decisions made by 792 small businesses, defined in the NFIB survey as those with fewer than 250 employees. The NFIB survey addressed capital budgeting decisions made during the period from May 2002 to April 2003. Respondents indicate that, on average, 46 percent of capital investment decisions made during the survey period were for the replacement of existing equipment, 21 percent related to the expansion of existing product lines, and 23 percent related to expansion into a new product line.

Casolari and Womack (2010) classify capital investment decisions as replacement or maintenance projects, mandatory projects (that is, those pursuant to legislative or regulatory initiatives), core mission investments (related to existing product lines), and new business and market expansion projects. They discuss these classifications in the context of prioritizing capital projects when companies are constrained by limited capital resources.

Finance theory suggests that companies make decisions intended to maximize firm value. However, Danielson and Scott (2006) suggest that owners/managers of small firms may not seek to maximize firm value. They suggest that owners/managers may focus more on sustaining the viability of the firm, or may seek to provide "an alternative to unemployment" for the owners/managers rather than maximizing firm value. As Danielson and Scott (2006) note, more sophisticated capital budgeting models may not be deemed appropriate or necessary by such firms. More sophisticated models are more likely to result in decisions that maximize firm value.

Replacement decisions do not necessarily fit well into the typical capital budgeting models. As a result, replacement decisions tend to be based more on "gut feel" than theoretically sound models. For example, the decision to replace a vehicle used by a maintenance worker may ultimately be based on the manager's perception of the best vehicle for the money, rather than on a comparison of operating and maintenance costs of competing vehicles. Replacement decisions are not discretionary in nature. Evaluating investments intended to expand existing product lines or to expand into new product lines, on the other hand, would generally be more likely to benefit from using more sophisticated decision models.

RELEVANT CASH FLOWS

Companies typically have two alternatives when making capital budgeting decisions: The investment opportunity can be either accepted or rejected. *Relevant information* related to capital budgeting decisions is defined as any cash flows that differ between alternatives. *Relevant cash flows* are incremental cash flows (inflows and outflows) that would not occur if not for the investment being evaluated. After identifying investment opportunities, the first steps in the capital budgeting process are to identify the relevant cash flows for each investment opportunity and then map out cash flows for each year of the investment's expected term. Relevant cash flows typically fall into three categories: (1) the initial investment, (2) the expected incremental future annual cash inflows and outflows resulting from the investment, and (3) the expected terminal value of the investment.

Since incremental future cash flows result from investing large amounts of firm resources and affect a firm's long-term future, capital budgeting decisions should be consistent with its long-term strategic plan. Migliore and McCracken (2001) suggest that the advent of capital budgeting models has reduced capital budgeting decisions to selecting the investment opportunity with "the best set of numbers." They discuss the importance of tying the capital budget to the firm's strategic plan, and identify three stages in the asset management process: acquisition, maintenance, and disposition. Capital budgeting describes the investment analyses leading up to the acquisition of productive assets. However, capital budgeting addresses the other two stages as well. Properly prepared capital budgets include estimates not only of the initial acquisition cost of an asset but also estimates of the costs of operating and maintaining the asset and estimates of the asset's salvage value at the end of the project period. Relevant cash flows used in the capital budgeting process address all three stages. Estimates of the initial investment impound acquisition costs, future annual cash flows include estimated maintenance costs, and the terminal value addresses the disposition of the asset at the end of its useful life.

Initial Investment

Cash outflows associated with the initial investment include all costs the company expects to incur to ready the asset for its intended use. In many ways, this parallels the treatment in financial accounting. That is, the initial investment includes acquisition costs plus other costs that would typically be capitalized for financial accounting purposes. However, for capital budgeting, the initial investment may also include costs that would be expensed or listed in other parts of the balance sheet for financial accounting purposes. Costs incurred to prepare the asset for its intended use vary based on the type of investment. For example, if an organization is evaluating the purchase of production equipment, the initial investment includes delivery, installation, testing, and training costs in addition to the acquisition cost of the asset.

The initial investment may also include the estimated change in the organization's working capital as a direct result of the investment. Investments in productive assets generally result in increases in current assets, such as inventory and accounts receivable, that the organization carries on its balance sheet, but can also result in decreases in net working capital. This expected increase in current assets is generally offset by expected increases in current liabilities directly related to the asset's operation, such as accounts payable and accrued liabilities. For Universal, the initial investment in the Harry Potter attraction would include resources tied up in merchandise inventories in addition to construction and development costs.

Often, evaluating the investment opportunity involves purchasing new productive assets to replace old assets. In these cases, any proceeds from the sale of the old assets reduce the initial investment in the asset. This treatment differs from the treatment of a sale for financial accounting purposes. Under generally accepted accounting principles (GAAP), the sale of an existing asset would result in a gain or loss being recognized on the company's income statement and the removal of the asset that is sold from the company's balance sheet. Investments in smaller productive assets are usually accomplished within a relatively short period, generally under a year. Initial investments in larger, longer-term investments, such as the construction of a manufacturing facility or the development of income-producing property, can occur over several years. In the case of the Wizarding World of Harry Potter, Universal reported that it began incurring costs five years before it realized the first investment related cash inflow. Such costs likely included, among others, the acquisition of the right to use the Harry Potter name and likeness, legal fees associated with the acquisition of such rights, preliminary market studies, and preliminary engineering and cost studies. Since Universal already owned the property where the attraction is located, the acquisition costs of the land would not be included in the initial investment. However, Universal likely included the fair value of the land (as an opportunity cost) in its assessment of the investment and its expected returns.

A company evaluating the acquisition of land with the intention of constructing and equipping a manufacturing facility may begin incurring costs well in advance of the actual acquisition of the land and construction of the facility. Preacquisition costs include fees for property appraisals, various types of engineering services, traffic studies, and legal fees to prepare and negotiate purchase contracts. Once the company acquires the land, it may incur additional costs for zoning changes, permits, and other issues related to land use regulations. The production facility must be designed. Therefore, the company will incur architectural and engineering fees. The company may also procure the services of consultants to assist with the layout of the production areas and the specification of the equipment needed to operate the facility.

Once the building design is complete, the company typically solicits bids from several contractors to construct the facility. After the construction contract has been awarded, the company incurs construction costs along with architect fees to oversee the project's construction. All of these costs, from preacquisition through construction management, are included in the initial investment for capital budgeting purposes. These costs could be incurred over two or more years for a large project. Accordingly, larger capital projects may incur several years of cash outflows before realizing cash inflows from the investment. Many costs of this nature would likely be part of the $200 million investment made by Universal in its Harry Potter attraction.

Assume that Acme Company, a hypothetical U.S. company, is evaluating the purchase of a new machine for its production process. The list price of the equipment is $525,000, but Acme expects to negotiate the price down to $500,000. Acme expects to pay a common carrier $25,000 to transport the equipment from the manufacturer's plant to Acme's plant. The common carrier will not insure the equipment during delivery, so Acme must provide insurance while the equipment is in transit. Acme's insurance agent has provided a premium quote of $1,000 for this coverage. Once the equipment arrives at Acme's manufacturing plant, the manufacturer will send a team to install, test, and calibrate the equipment before its integration into the production process. The manufacturer typically charges its customers $2,500 for this service. Acme expects the manufacturer's installation team to use $1,250 of raw materials in connection with testing and calibrating the equipment. Acme's controller has estimated that the accounts receivable and inventories associated with this investment will be, on average, $10,000 greater than the current liabilities associated with this investment during the project life. The initial investment in

Exhibit 10.1   Acme Company's Initial Investment in Equipment

Description	Expected Costs
Acquisition cost	$500,000
Delivery	25,000
Insurance during delivery	1,000
Installation, testing, and calibration	2,500
Materials used during installation, testing, and calibration	1,250
Working capital	10,000
Total initial investment	$539,750

This exhibit lists the cash expenditures that comprise the initial cash outflow for the investment contemplated by Acme Company.

this equipment is expected to be $539,750. Exhibit 10.1 provides a summary of Acme's initial investment.

Estimated Future Annual Cash Flows

Estimated future annual cash flows are the cash inflows and outflows that are expected to occur as a result of the company making the proposed investment. Expected future cash inflows are increases in cash receipts from the sale of goods and/or services to customers, decreases in costs incurred to provide goods and/or services to customers, or a combination of the two. Expected future cash outflows are increases in costs incurred as a result of the operation of the acquired assets.

The Harry Potter attraction provides a useful example of factors to consider when forecasting future cash flows that arise as a result of the investment. An admission ticket to the Universal theme park provides visitor access to all attractions within the park. Therefore, identifying ticket sales directly resulting from opening the particular attraction is difficult. Instead, Universal analysts likely forecast increased sales of admission tickets that could be attributed to the new attraction. Universal's analysts probably included increases in food and beverage sales within the park, sales of Harry Potter merchandise, increased hotel occupancy rates, and other peripheral sales expected to be realized as a result of this attraction. Cash outflows associated with the attraction are somewhat easier to identify. Clearly, costs associated with the operation of the attraction, such as payroll, utilities, taxes, and cost of merchandise sales can be easily traced directly to the attraction. Other costs, such as additional staffing in park areas and adjacent hotels, are more difficult to trace directly to the investment. However, management must make every effort to identify cash flows that would differ between alternatives.

In many organizations, someone from the accounting or finance departments assembles estimated future annual cash flows. Regardless of who actually assembles these data, input should be solicited from representatives of various disciplines within the organization when preparing the capital budget. Ideally, representatives from marketing, operations (production), finance, accounting, human resources, and corporate counsel should provide input when forecasting initial investments and future cash flows.

Marketing Input
Capital investments should support the firm's long-term strategic plan. The strategic plan should focus on the needs and expectations of the firm's customers (current or projected). Once these are adequately identified and documented, the assets required to meet customer needs and expectations can be more easily identified. Experienced operations personnel can develop estimates of initial acquisition costs and related operation and maintenance costs with a relatively high degree of certainty. Product volumes, market sizes, and price points are more difficult to forecast. The expertise provided by marketing personnel can reduce the level of uncertainty inherent in such forecasts.

The customer-centric focus of the firm's marketing personnel makes their input into the capital budgeting process vital. Marketing personnel should have a thorough understanding of current and potential markets for the firm's goods and services, and should be in the best position to identify and document opportunities to expand current product lines and enter new markets. Marketing costs are frequently overlooked in capital budgeting (IOMA, 2003). Marketing personnel are the best source of cost estimates related to the promotion, distribution, and market research associated with a proposed product. Marketing personnel should have their fingers on the pulse of the firm's existing and potential competition.

Marketing personnel provide data about the estimated market size for the goods or services related to the investment, market shares the company expects to command, and expected price points for the goods or services offered to customers. These types of data may be obtained from market studies, focus groups, or industry publications.

Operations Input
Representatives from operations (production) provide insight into production capacity, expected cost behaviors, and other potential constraints. The practical knowledge provided by operations personnel may need to be supplemented with cost information and other studies performed by independent consultants. Costs incurred in the operation of capital assets acquired may be the largest portion of future cash outflows related to a proposed investment. Thus, the importance of objective input from operations personnel cannot be overstated if management is to optimize the organization's return on the investment of limited resources in capital projects.

Input from Other Departments
Finance personnel can provide guidance regarding required rates of return for investment opportunities. Additionally, finance personnel can determine whether the organization has sufficient liquidity to make the proposed investment from available cash. Larger capital investments may require the organization to issue debt and/or equity in public or private markets to finance the project. Accounting personnel provide historical cost data that can be used to estimate future product costs. Human resources personnel can determine whether the firm's current staff possesses the skills necessary for the production process. If no employees with the appropriate skill set are available, human resources personnel can provide estimates about the cost and time requirements for production staff to develop the necessary skills. Corporate counsel can identify any potential legal issues relating to

the product or service such as patent infringements, product liabilities, or potential problems with any unions representing company employees.

Many firms rely on management judgment to estimate relevant cash flows for evaluating investment opportunities. Estimates of future cash flows resulting from investments involving either the replacement of existing productive assets or the expansion of a firm's productive capacity typically involve less uncertainty than cash flows associated with investment decisions involving new lines of business. Expected cash flows derived from the firm's entry into new markets are more difficult for managers to project. Thus, firms considering entering new lines of business, either through acquiring productive capacity or an operating entity, may find engaging outside consultants useful. Such consultants may have the expertise necessary to provide insights about market size and competition, estimated price points, and estimated fixed and variable operating costs for proposed new lines of business.

Example of Expected Future Cash Inflows and Outflows

Acme is contemplating the acquisition of equipment (as described above) for use in its production process. Assume that Acme intends to use this equipment to introduce the next generation of a product that complements an existing product line. Acme's vice president of marketing believes that the product life cycle, from inception through growth and maturity to product decline, will be five years. The vice president expects to achieve a 10 percent market share by the end of the second year after the product is introduced. That market share is expected to hold until the last year of the product life, when Acme expects to command half of the remaining market share. The current market for this type of product is about 100,000 units per year, but the vice president believes the market will be 1,000,000 units per year at product maturity in Year 4. Based on expected technological innovations, the vice president expects the next generation of products to be introduced in Year 4, which will cause the market for this product to cease by the end of Year 5. Exhibit 10.2 provides expected sales volumes in units and market shares for the new product's five-year life.

Based on prices charged for the prior generation of similar products, Acme believes that the appropriate selling price for this product is $15.00 per unit. Acme's vice president expects this price to hold for the first two years of the product life

Exhibit 10.2   Acme Company Expected Sales Volumes

Year	Sales (Units)	Expected Market Share (%)
1	5,000	5
2	55,000	10
3	90,000	10
4	100,000	10
5	10,000	50
Total	260,000	

cycle, with an increase in the selling price to $15.50 per unit for the last three years of the product life.

Acme's vice president of marketing expects to incur about $7,500 per year of fixed costs on marketing campaigns during the first four years that the product is on the market. Since this new product will be in the decline stage of its life cycle during Year 5, Acme does not plan to engage in marketing campaigns in the last year. Acme expects to provide its sales force with its customary commissions equal to 1.5 percent of the selling price of this new product.

Personnel from Acme's operations department have reviewed the sales forecasts submitted by marketing and believe that the equipment has the capacity to handle expected volumes. Further, the operations manager estimates variable manufacturing costs for this product as $11.00 per unit for the first two years, increasing to $11.25 per unit for the last three years of the product's life. Variable manufacturing costs include direct materials and direct labor, as well as costs for repairs and maintenance, tools and supplies, and utilities. Acme's operations manager expects to incur $15,000 per year of fixed manufacturing overhead. Fixed manufacturing overhead includes additional costs such as property taxes, property insurance, and the salaries and benefits of production support staff that would need to be hired if this project is accepted. Acme's operations manager believes that performing a minor overhaul of the equipment will be necessary at the end of Year 3 at a cost of $50,000.

Acme's vice president of finance indicates that Acme will not need to seek external financing for this equipment purchase because the firm can buy it using Acme's available cash. Based on prior experience, the controller determines that the cost estimates provided by the operations manager and the vice president of marketing are reasonable. Acme's human resources manager, after meeting with the operations manager, has determined that Acme has personnel with the training necessary to properly operate the equipment. Corporate counsel has verified that the new product will not infringe on any existing patent rights and that the potential for product liability claims is remote. Acme's controller has also determined that Acme has adequate insurance to cover any product liability claims that may arise.

Once the necessary input has been received from all appropriate disciplines, future annual cash inflows and outflows related to this investment can be forecast. Exhibit 10.3 provides the forecast of Acme's expected annual cash inflows from operating activities for each year of the project's expected life. Cash inflows are based on the expected sales volumes and price points provided by Acme's vice president of marketing.

Exhibit 10.4 provides the forecast of Acme's cash outflows from operating and marketing activities related to the new product based on the cost behaviors provided by the operations manager and the vice president of marketing.

Terminal Value

Part of any cash flow forecast includes an estimate of the value of the asset at the end of the forecast period. This value is generally referred to as the *terminal*

Exhibit 10.3   Acme Company Forecast of Cash Inflows from Operating Activities

	Year 1	Year 2	Year 3	Year 4	Year 5	Total
Estimated unit sales	5,000	55,000	90,000	100,000	10,000	260,000
Selling price per unit	$15.00	$15.00	$15.50	$15.50	$15.50	
Estimated cash inflows	$75,000	$825,000	$1,395,000	$1,550,000	$155,000	$4,000,000

This exhibit provides a summary of the estimated annual cash inflows to Acme Company as a result of expected sales volumes and price points for the units that will be produced by the equipment if Acme accepts the investment opportunity.

value. The terminal value represents a cash inflow at the end of the last year of the forecast period, and can be expressed as a specific amount or as a percentage of the original cost. Either approach is acceptable. Depending on the type of investment, the terminal value could be nominal (i.e., small relative to the initial investment) or substantial. Terminal values for investments in productive equipment tend to be nominal while terminal values for investments in real estate developments tend to be more substantial. Investments in real properties are generally expected to have large terminal values by virtue of positive cash flows expected to be generated by the property at the end of the project term and general upward trends in real estate values.

The estimated terminal value for an asset used in the production process generally comes from someone in the operations area, as this may be the person most familiar with the market for used equipment in the company's specific industry. However, the firm may also use independent sources, such as used equipment brokers, trade publications, or "blue book" type reference materials, to estimate the terminal value. Productive assets may be expected to decline in value over the project life, resulting in little or no terminal value. Land and buildings, on the other hand, may appreciate in value over the project life. Assume in the Acme example that the operations manager has estimated that the equipment originally purchased for $539,750 will have a terminal value of $25,000 at the end of Year 5.

Exhibit 10.4   Acme Company Forecast of Cash Outflows from Operating and Marketing Activities

	Year 1	Year 2	Year 3	Year 4	Year 5	Total
Estimated unit sales	5,000	55,000	90,000	100,000	10,000	260,000
Manufacturing costs						
Variable cost per unit	$11.00	$11.00	$11.25	$11.25	$11.25	
Total variable cost	$55,000	$605,000	$1,012,500	$1,125,000	$112,500	$2,910,000
Total fixed costs	$15,000	$15,000	$15,000	$15,000	$15,000	$75,000
Marketing costs						
Total variable costs	$1,125	$12,375	$20,925	$23,250	$2,325	$60,000
Total fixed costs	$7,500	$7,500	$7,500	$7,500	$0	$30,000

FORECAST OF NET CASH FLOWS

The next step in the capital budgeting process is to combine forecasts of cash inflows and outflows and estimate the net cash flow for each year in the forecast period. The net cash flow in any given year may be a net inflow or a net outflow, depending on the expected timing of cash receipts and disbursements.

Panel A of Exhibit 10.5 provides a summary of the cash flows for each year of the project life for the Acme investment opportunity, using the data provided in Exhibits 10.3 and 10.4 and the terminal value described above. Note that the initial investment is presented as a cash outflow in the Year 0 column of Exhibit 10.5. This indicates the cash outflow for the initial investment is made during the current period (i.e., today) while other cash inflows and outflows are expected to occur in future periods. The cash inflow for the terminal value of the asset is included in the Year 5 column of Panel A of Exhibit 10.5, as this cash inflow is expected to occur at the end of the five-year project life.

During the capital budgeting process, the assumptions underlying future cash inflows and outflows should be adequately documented. In general, documenting as many assumptions as possible related to the initial investment and subsequent annual cash inflows and outflows is desirable. The availability of detailed capital budget data allows for an audit of the initial investment, expected annual cash inflows and outflows, and terminal value of the project at various stages during the project life.

Net Present Value

Panel A of Exhibit 10.5 presents expected current and future cash flows related to the investment opportunity. The data in Panel A implicitly assume that the cash flows all have the same purchasing power. That is, Panel A does not incorporate the effects of the time value of money. The time value of money is predicated upon the assumption that a dollar today is worth more than a dollar at some point in the future. Accordingly, dollars collected or spent in future years do not have the same purchasing power as dollars invested today. The computation of present values for each year adjusts for this mismatch in the value of cash flows over the project life by restating future cash flows in today's dollars. This is accomplished by discounting future cash flows at an appropriate discount rate. The appropriate discount rate, often referred to as the *hurdle rate*, is generally based on the company's weighted average cost of capital (WACC), adjusted for perceived project risk.

The *net present value* (NPV) of the project is the sum of cash outflows for the initial investment plus the present values of future cash flows discounted at the hurdle rate. A positive NPV indicates that the project is expected to generate a return that is higher than the company's hurdle rate, and a negative NPV indicates that the project is expected to generate a return that is lower than the company's hurdle rate. The firm should reject negative NPV projects and should consider accepting positive NPV projects. The firm may not accept all positive NPV projects due to capital rationing (e.g., limitations on capital available for investment). Because companies generally have limited resources available for investment, they may be able to accept only those positive NPV projects that generate the highest combined NPV.

Exhibit 10.5 Acme Company Cash Flow Projections

	Year 0	Year 1	Year 2	Year 3	Year 4	Year 5	Total
Panel A. Undiscounted Cash Flows							
Initial investment	$(539,750)						$(539,750)
Cash flows from operating activities							
Cash inflows from sales		$75,000	$825,000	$1,395,000	$1,550,000	$155,000	$4,000,000
Cash outflows							
Manufacturing costs							
Variable		(55,000)	(605,000)	(1,012,500)	(1,125,000)	(112,500)	(2,910,000)
Fixed		(15,000)	(15,000)	(15,000)	(15,000)	(15,000)	(75,000)
Marketing costs							
Variable		(1,125)	(12,375)	(20,925)	(23,250)	(2,325)	(60,000)
Fixed		(7,500)	(7,500)	(7,500)	(7,500)	0	(30,000)
Overhaul year 3				(50,000)			(50,000)
Terminal value						25,000	25,000
Net cash flows	$(539,750)	$(3,625)	$185,125	$289,075	$379,250	$50,125	$360,250
Panel B. Discounted Cash Flows							
Net cash flows	$(539,750)	$(3,625)	$185,125	$289,075	$379,250	$50,125	$360,250
Present value factor	1.000	0.893	0.797	0.712	0.636	0.567	
Present value	$(539,750)	(3,237)	147,581	205,758	241,020	28,471	
Net present value	$79,843						
Internal rate of return	16.9%						

Research provides evidence that, for U.S.-based firms, the use of discounted cash flow (DCF) methods for evaluating investment opportunities is positively correlated with firm size and the education of the chief executive officer (CEO) but negatively correlated with the age of the firm and the age of the owner (Bailes, Nielsen, and Lawton, 1998; Graham and Harvey, 2002; Danielson and Scott, 2006). Canadian firms favor the use of DCF models when evaluating investment opportunities (Bennouna, Meredith, and Merchant, 2010). However, survey evidence suggests that firms in other countries are less likely to use DCF methods, preferring instead to use the payback period and accounting rate of return to evaluate investment opportunities (Verma, Gupta, and Batra, 2009; Haddad, Sterk, and Wu, 2010).

NPV Example

Acme's vice president of finance has reviewed the project and believes that the appropriate hurdle rate for this investment is 12 percent, based on the project's perceived risk. Panel A of Exhibit 10.5 shows that Acme's net cash inflows for the forecast period are expected to be $360,250 greater than the $539,750 initial investment. Panel B of Exhibit 10.5 provides the present value computations for Acme's expected cash flows for each year in the expected life of the investment. The present value factors decrease each year, reflecting the concept that cash flows occurring farther in the future have lower values in today's dollars. The initial investment, a cash outflow of $539,750, is not discounted because the initial outlay is already stated in today's dollars.

Panel B of Exhibit 10.5 shows that Acme's proposed investment has a positive NPV of $79,843, indicating that the investment will generate a return that exceeds the 12 percent hurdle rate for this type of investment. Knowing that the investment exceeds the hurdle rate only provides a portion of the story. Determining by how much the project's return exceeds the hurdle rate is just as relevant. The last line of Panel B of Exhibit 10.5 provides the internal rate of return (IRR) for this investment opportunity. The IRR is the discount rate at which the present value of future cash flows is exactly equal to the initial investment. That is, the IRR is the discount rate at which the project's NPV is equal to zero. Acme's proposed investment is expected to generate an IRR of 16.9 percent, which exceeds Acme's hurdle rate of 12 percent.

NPV vs. IRR

When companies are evaluating several potentially positive NPV investment opportunities, they should rank the opportunities in order to identify which opportunities should be accepted and rejected. The magnitude of positive NPVs may not provide an appropriate basis for making such decisions. That is, larger investments may be associated with higher NPVs, biasing the decision in favor of larger investment opportunities. The IRR serves as one means for resolving this problem. A positive NPV indicates that the investment is expected to generate a return that exceeds the company's hurdle rate. The IRR provides a measure of how much the investment's return exceeds the hurdle rate. Managers often rank positive NPV investment opportunities based on their expected IRRs. Companies should then accept only those investment opportunities that are expected to generate the highest IRRs.

Graham and Harvey (2002) conducted a survey of the chief financial officers (CFOs) of 392 Fortune 500 companies concerning which capital budgeting methods they are most likely to use. The survey data indicate that 76 percent of the CFOs always or almost always use IRR when making capital budgeting decisions, compared with 75 percent that always or almost always use NPV. The authors find that almost 57 percent of the CFOs use the payback period method to evaluate investment opportunities. Their evidence also shows that the use of the payback period is positively correlated with the age and educational background of CFOs, and smaller firms with fewer resources are more likely to use the payback period. This latter finding is consistent with results from Danielson and Scott (2006), who report that smaller firms tend to rely more on the payback period and management's "gut feel" when making investment decisions. In fact, Danielson and Scott report that more than half of investment decisions made by small firms in their sample involve the replacement of existing productive capacity rather than expansions into new markets or product lines. Thus, using the payback period and "gut feel" may not be as inappropriate as it would seem for these firms. Jackson (2010) finds that many firms use the payback period as an initial screening method. That is, firms reject projects with payback periods that exceed an established maximum without preparing DCF analyses. The frequency of payback period as a capital budgeting method reported for U.S. firms is consistent with surveys conducted in Cyprus (Lazaridis, 2002), India (Verma et al., 2009), Canada (Bennouna et al., 2010), and Taiwan (Haddad et al., 2010).

Effects of Income Taxes

Panel A of Exhibit 10.5 indicates that Acme expects to generate cumulative net cash inflows of $900,000 from Year 1 to Year 5. Cash flows, whether inflows or outflows, generally have tax consequences. Ignoring the tax effects of cash inflows and outflows projected during the five-year project period omits substantial cash flows from the analysis. Exhibit 10.6 includes the income tax effects of the projected cash flows for Acme's investment opportunity. The amounts included as a tax effect in Exhibit 10.6 are based on the assumption that Acme has adequate income to use any net operating losses generated (e.g., Year 1). Another assumption is that Acme is taxed at 35 percent for ordinary income and 15 percent on long-term capital gains (LTCG).

The initial investment of $539,750 is presented in the Year 0 column of Panel A of Exhibit 10.5. However, under current tax laws, there is no immediate tax effect from the initial investment. Tax effects associated with the initial investment are realized through the depreciation deduction taken in future years. Had Acme planned to sell an old asset and replace it with a new asset, the sale of the old asset would have generated a tax liability associated with a gain for tax purposes or would have provided tax benefits associated with a loss for tax purposes. Since Acme is not planning to sell an asset in connection with this investment opportunity, the firm does not realize any tax consequences in Year 0.

Panel A of Exhibit 10.6 shows the tax effects of expected cash inflows and outflows for Year 1 through Year 5. By showing the tax effects of each major activity, this format isolates the effect that each type of cash flow has on Acme's income tax payments. The major categories in Panel A are cash flows associated

Exhibit 10.6   Acme Company Cash Flow Projects including Income Tax Effects

Panel A. Cash Flows Including Income Tax Effects

	Year 0	Year 1	Year 2	Year 3	Year 4	Year 5	Total
Initial investment	$(539,750)						$(529,750)
Cash flows from operating activities							
Cash inflows from sales		$75,000	$825,000	$1,395,000	$1,550,000	$155,000	$4,000,000
Cash outflows:							
Product costs							
Variable		(55,000)	(605,000)	(1,012,500)	(1,125,000)	(112,500)	(2,910,000)
Fixed		(15,000)	(15,000)	(15,000)	(15,000)	(15,000)	(75,000)
Marketing costs							
Variable		(1,125)	(12,375)	(20,925)	(23,250)	(2,325)	(60,000)
Fixed		(7,500)	(7,500)	(7,500)	(7,500)	0	(30,000)
Annual cash flows		(3,625)	185,125	339,075	379,250	25,175	925,000
Tax effect of annual cash flows		1,269	(64,794)	(118,676)	(132,738)	(8,811)	(323,750)
Overhaul year 3				(50,000)			(50,000)
Tax benefit from overhaul at 35 percent ordinary income rate				17,500			17,500
Tax benefit from depreciation at 35 percent ordinary income rate		62,965	83,972	27,978	13,998	0	188,913
Terminal value						25,000	25,000
Tax on gain on sale at termination at 15 percent LTCG rate						(3,750)	(3,750)
Net cash flows	$(539,750)	$60,608	$204,303	$215,877	$260,511	$37,614	$239,163
Present value factor	1.000	0.893	0.797	0.712	0.636	0.567	
Present value	$(539,750)	54,115	162,869	153,657	165,559	21,343	
Net present value	17,793						
Internal rate of return	13.3%						

Panel B. Tax Depreciation

MACRS depreciation rate	33.33%	44.45%	14.81%	7.41%	0%
MACRS depreciation	(179,899)	(239,919)	(79,937)	(39,995)	(539,750)
Tax benefit at 35 percent ordinary income rate	62,965	83,972	27,978	13,998	188,913

Panel C. Tax on Gain on Sale at Termination

Terminal value	$25,000
Original cost	$539,750
Accumulated tax depreciation	(539,750)
Tax basis	0
Gain (loss) on sale at termination	25,000
Tax on gain (loss) on sale at termination at 15 percent LTCG rate	$(3,750)

This exhibit summarizes the cash flows including tax effects that Acme anticipates as a result of accepting the investment opportunity.

with operating the asset, costs of the minor overhaul expected to occur in Year 3, tax benefits expected to be derived from tax depreciation, and the sale of the asset at the end of the project life (the terminal value) along with related tax effects.

Expected cash flows in Panel A associated with operating the asset include cash inflows from sales and cash outflows from production and marketing activities. The tax effects of net cash flows for each year are calculated by multiplying the projected net cash flows for each year by Acme's 35 percent effective tax rate. Projected cash flows for Year 1 are a net outflow of $3,625, which generates an expected tax benefit of $1,269. That is, Acme expects to reduce its payments for income taxes as a result of tax losses generated by the investment in Year 1. Accordingly, Panel A of Exhibit 10.6 shows the tax effect for Year 1 as a cash inflow. Cash inflows related to income taxes can only be assumed if Acme expects to generate taxable income in other operating areas in Year 1. Otherwise, tax losses in Year 1 would be carried forward and cash outflows for tax payments in future years would be reduced accordingly. In Years 2 through 5, the investment is expected to generate cash inflows, which would result in taxable income. Therefore, Acme expects cash outflows in the form of income tax payments in each of those years. Cumulative cash flows from operating activities from Year 1 through Year 5 are expected to be $925,000, which, in turn, are expected to generate net tax payments of $323,750 (35 percent of $925,000).

Shown separately in Panel A is the tax effect of the minor overhaul that is expected to occur at the end of Year 3. The assumption is that this expenditure is tax deductible. If this is not the case, then the overhaul costs would not have a tax effect in Year 3. Instead, the tax effect of the minor overhaul would be realized as tax benefits associated with tax depreciation in future periods. The minor overhaul at the end of Year 3 is expected to result in a cash outflow of $50,000, which is expected to reduce income tax payments for Year 3 by $17,500 (35 percent of $50,000).

Panel A of Exhibit 10.6 shows the benefits derived from the depreciation of the assets. Panel B of Exhibit 10.6 provides the computation of tax depreciation and related tax benefits. Depreciation is a noncash expense that companies are allowed to deduct from taxable income before computing their income tax liabilities. Panel A of Exhibit 10.6 excludes depreciation but includes the reduction of income taxes associated with the depreciation deduction. Tax depreciation in Panel B of Exhibit 10.6 is computed using the Modified Asset Cost Recovery System (MACRS). MACRS is a depreciation method dictated by federal taxing authorities in the United States for taxpayers that use depreciable assets in their businesses. Exhibit 10.7 provides the annual depreciation rates for the various depreciable lives assigned under MACRS. Other tax depreciation methods are allowed in limited circumstances. Since most U.S. taxpayers use some version of MACRS, this example uses depreciation rates published in the MACRS tables. Assets are assigned depreciable lives under MACRS regardless of the expected useful lives used to calculate book depreciation. The data in Panel B of Exhibit 10.6 are based on the assumption that the equipment is MACRS 3-year property and that Acme uses the mid-year convention (that is, all assets are assumed to be put into service halfway through the year for tax purposes).

The sale of the equipment at the end of its useful life (at its expected terminal value) also has tax consequences. Panel C of Exhibit 10.6 provides a computation of the expected taxable gain on the sale of the asset and the computation of income

Exhibit 10.7 Modified Accelerated Cost Recovery System (MACRS) 3-, 5-, 7-, 10-, 15-, and 20-Year Property Half-year Convention

Year	3-Year Property	5-Year Property	7-Year Property	10-Year Property	15-Year Property	20-Year Property
1	33.33%	20.00%	14.29%	10.00%	5.00%	3.750%
2	44.45	32.00	24.49	18.00	9.50	7.219
3	14.81	19.20	17.49	14.40	8.55	6.677
4	7.41	11.52	12.49	11.52	7.70	6.177
5		11.52	8.93	9.22	6.93	5.713
6		5.76	8.92	7.37	6.23	5.285
7			8.93	6.55	5.90	4.888
8			4.46	6.55	5.90	4.522
9				6.56	5.91	4.462
10				6.55	5.90	4.461
11				3.28	5.91	4.462
12					5.90	4.461
13					5.91	4.462
14					5.90	4.461
15					5.91	4.462
16					2.95	4.461
17						4.462
18						4.461
19						4.462
20						4.461
21						2.231

This exhibit provides the percentages used to depreciate assets for tax purposes.

taxes associated with this gain. This example assumes that the firm will sell the equipment for its terminal value of $25,000 and that long-term capital gains will be taxed at 15 percent.

Acme's tax basis in the equipment must be computed to determine the taxable gain or loss on the sale. An asset's tax basis is similar in concept to its net book value for financial reporting purposes. While net book value for financial reporting is the original cost minus accumulated book depreciation, tax basis is original cost minus accumulated tax depreciation. The description of tax basis provided here is the general rule. Exceptions to this general rule in computing tax basis abound and are beyond the scope of this chapter. Since the asset is fully depreciated for tax purposes (that is, it has a tax basis of zero) when it is sold, Acme will realize a gain for tax purposes that is equal to the expected proceeds from the sale of the asset at the end of the project's life. Cash flows associated with the equipment's terminal value include the expected proceeds from the sale in Year 5 ($25,000 inflow) and a cash outflow of $3,750 (15 percent of $25,000), which is the tax effect of the sale at LTCG rates The expected book value of the asset at the end of the project life is ignored in capital budgeting, as it does not directly affect cash flows in Year 5.

In Panel A of Exhibit 10.6, the project's NPV is reduced from $79,843 to $17,793 when including the respective tax consequences of cash inflows and cash outflows in the analysis. Additionally, the IRR for this investment opportunity decreases from 16.9 percent to 13.3 percent when including the cash outflows for income taxes.

As Danielson and Scott (2006) report, 74 percent of responding firms surveyed by the National Federation of Independent Businesses consider the tax implications of investment decisions. Traditional corporations (referred to as C Corporations in the U.S. tax code) must pay taxes based on corporate earnings. Other types of legal entities, such as partnerships (limited and general), limited liability corporations (LLCs), and S Corporations, do not pay taxes at the entity level. Instead, income for these entities flows through to the owners (partners, members, or shareholders), and taxes are paid at the owner level. The proliferation of these types of entities likely explains why only 74 percent of respondents consider taxes in their capital budgeting analyses.

Risk Assessment

Based on their nature, expected future cash flows are inherently uncertain. Management makes its best estimate of the future based on the assumptions and market intelligence available today. However, actual project cash flows are unlikely to exactly equal estimated cash flows used to evaluate the investment. Thus, the risk exists that actual project returns will be lower than projected returns. *Risk* in capital budgeting is often defined as the likelihood of the investment not achieving a positive NPV. Firms consider investments that expand operations into markets (geographic and/or product lines) in which the firm has little or no experience to be of higher risk than investments involving the replacement of existing productive capacity (Hogaboam and Shook, 2004). Firms adjust for this type of risk in several ways. Commonly cited methods include increasing the appropriate discount rate used in DCF models to reflect higher risk, adjusting the project life downward, and using sensitivity analysis.

Sensitivity analysis is accomplished by adjusting the underlying assumptions used to prepare DCF models. That is, analysts adjust assumptions related to each of the three types of cash flows to assess the impact on the project's expected NPV and IRR. As part of a sensitivity analysis, cash flow estimates typically include contingencies that increase the initial investment, decrease annual cash inflows, or decrease expected terminal values. Using sensitivity analysis helps to quantify the investment's *margin for error*, which is the amount by which the initial investment could increase, future cash inflows could decrease, or the expected terminal value could decrease and still have the project produce a positive NPV.

Finance theory supports more statistical approaches to risk assessment. Among the statistical methods frequently cited are expected outcome analysis, simulation, and decision tree analysis (Bierman, 1978; Hogaboam and Shook, 2004). Graham and Harvey (2002) report that almost three-quarters of survey respondents use the capital asset pricing model (CAPM) to estimate the cost of capital used in DCF models. However, most surveys find that smaller, less sophisticated firms generally use sensitivity analysis and judgmental adjustments to the firm's cost of capital to adjust for project risk (Bailes et al., 1998; Lazaridis, 2002; Hogaboam and Shook, 2004).

SUMMARY AND CONCLUSIONS

Each year organizations are confronted with various investment opportunities. However, capital constraints limit their ability to accept every opportunity. Organizations address these constraints using methods that have been developed to assist in evaluating and ranking investment opportunities. These methods are based on cash flow forecasts for each project. This chapter discusses factors that firms should consider when preparing cash flow forecasts.

Capital budgeting describes the process of evaluating investment opportunities. Such decisions should be consistent with the long-range strategic goals of the organization. Capital budgeting decisions depend on the quality of the assumptions used to evaluate investment opportunities. Relevant assumptions include forecasts of cash inflows and outflows. Relevant cash outflows include the initial investment and future operation and maintenance costs. Relevant cash inflows include expected future cash flows generated by the asset and the expected value of the asset at the end of the project life (the terminal value). The accuracy and reliability of future cash flows is dependent upon the extent that input is solicited from the various disciplines within an organization. Input should be obtained from operations, marketing, sales, finance, accounting, legal, and human resources personnel throughout the capital budgeting process.

Once cash flow forecasts are compiled, organizations must evaluate and rank investment opportunities so that limited capital can be optimally allocated and firm value maximized. Methods commonly employed to evaluate and rank investment opportunities include DCF models and the payback period. Larger, more sophisticated organizations generally rely on DCF models while smaller, less sophisticated organizations tend to rely both on the payback period and judgment ("gut feel") when making capital budgeting decisions. Managers often base capital budgeting decisions involving the replacement of existing productive capacity on the payback period and judgment, while decisions involving expansion of existing product lines or entering new product lines are more reliant on DCF models.

DISCUSSION QUESTIONS

1. A proposed project has a negative NPV. Does this mean that the project has a negative IRR? Why or why not?

2. Does including the tax consequences of estimated future cash flows in DCF models likely increase, decrease, or have no effect on a project's NPV? Explain.

3. List three methods commonly used to adjust for project risk in the capital budgeting process and discuss why these methods might be appropriate.

4. What are some reasons that may explain the pervasive use of the payback period method to evaluate investment opportunities?

REFERENCES

Bailes, Jack, James Nielsen, and Stephen Lawton. 1998. "How Forest Product Companies Analyze Capital Budgets." *Management Accounting* 80:4, 24–30.

Bennouna, Karim, Geoffrey Meredith, and Teresa Merchant. 2010. "Improved Capital Budgeting Decision Making: Evidence from Canada." *Management Decision* 48:2, 225–226.

Bierman, Harold. 1978. "Investment Decisions with Sampling." *Financial Management* 7:3, 19–24.

Casolari, Cara, and Steve Womack. 2010. "Prioritizing Capital Projects When Cash Is Scarce." *Healthcare Financial Management* 64:3, 114–116.

Danielson, Morris, and Jonathan Scott. 2006. "The Capital Budgeting Decisions of Small Businesses." *Journal of Applied Finance* 16:2, 45–56.

Garcia, Jason. 2010. "Can New Harry Potter Attraction Put Universal on Par with Disney as a Vacation Destination?" Available at http://blogs.orlandosentinel.com/business_tourism_aviation/?p=2646.

Graham, John, and Campbell Harvey. 2002. "How Do CFOs Make Capital Budgeting and Capital Structure Decisions?" *Journal of Applied Corporate Finance* 15:1, 8–23.

Haddad, Kamal, William Sterk, and Anne Wu. 2010. "Capital Budgeting Practices of Taiwanese Firms." *Journal of International Management Studies* 5:1, 178–182.

Hogaboam, Liliya, and Steven Shook. 2004. "Capital Budgeting Practices in the US Forest Products Industry: A Reappraisal." *Forest Products Journal* 54:12, 149–158.

IOMA. 2003. "Analyzing New Products: Choice of Hurdle Rate & Cash-Flow Assumptions Key to Decision Making." *IOMA's Report on Financial Analysis, Planning & Reporting* 3:10, 4–7.

Jackson, Jerry. 2010. "Promoting Energy Efficient Investments with Risk Management Decision Tools." *Energy Policy* 38:8, 3865–3873.

Lazaridis, Ioannis. 2002. "Cash Flow Estimating and Forecasting Practices of Large Firms in Cyprus: Survey Findings." *Journal of Financial Management and Analysis* 15:2, 62–68.

Migliore, R. Henry, and Douglas McCracken. 2001. "Tie Your Capital Budget to Your Strategic Plan." *Strategic Finance* 82:12, 38–43.

Verma, Satish, Sanjeev Gupta, and Roopali Batra. 2009. "A Survey of Capital Budgeting Practices in Corporate India." *VISION—The Journal of Business Perspective* 13:3, 1–17.

ABOUT THE AUTHORS

Kyle Meyer is an Executive-in-Residence who teaches Managerial Accounting and Contemporary Financial Accounting at the Crummer Graduate School of Business, Rollins College. Professor Meyer brings extensive business experience to the classroom, having spent five years on the audit staff of Arthur Andersen & Co. and many years in private industry, working mostly with real estate development and construction companies. He received his undergraduate degree in accounting from Florida State University, his MBA from the Crummer Graduate School of Business, and his Ph.D. from Florida State University.

Halil Kiymaz is Bank of America Chair and Professor of Finance at the Crummer Graduate School of Business, Rollins College. Before joining the Crummer School, Professor Kiymaz taught at the University of Houston–Clear Lake, Bilkent University, and the University of New Orleans. He holds the Chartered Financial Analyst (CFA) designation and has served as a grader for the CFA Institute. Professor Kiymaz maintains an extensive research agenda focusing on international mergers and acquisitions, emerging capital markets, linkages among capital markets of developing economies, IPOs, and financial management of multinationals. He has published more than 50 articles in scholarly and practitioner journals. Professor Kiymaz received his BS in Business Administration from the Uludag University and an MBA, MA in Economics, and Ph.D. in Financial Economics from the University of New Orleans. Professor Kiymaz also holds visiting professor positions at the IMADEC University, School of International Business in Vienna, Austria, East Chinese University of Science and Technology in Shanghai, China, and the Copenhagen Business School in Denmark.

CHAPTER 11

Capital Budgeting and Inflation

IGNACIO VÉLEZ-PAREJA
Associate Professor, Universidad Tecnológica de Bolívar

JOSEPH THAM
Visiting Assistant Professor, Duke Center for International Development
and Sanford Institute of Public Policy, Duke University

INTRODUCTION

Adjusting for inflation is an important aspect of capital investment analysis because inflation can dramatically affect the attractiveness of specific capital investments. For example, Walter (1972, p. 46) says that "There is little doubt that the explicit recognition of anticipated rates of price change can contribute to improved investment planning." Hodder and Riggs (1985, p. 131) stress that "the error that arises from the failure to include inflation in cash flow estimates compounds with time as long as inflation is positive." Properly dealing with inflation requires recognizing expected inflation in the projection of cash flows and using a discount rate that appropriately reflects investors' expectations of future inflation. Unfortunately, no simple relationship exists between inflation and cash flows for specific investments. Also, determining an appropriate discount rate that incorporates investors' expectations of future inflation is not a simple matter. The extant literature sets forth several approaches for dealing with inflation when analyzing a capital budgeting project. One approach involves using nominal cash flows and nominal interest rates while the other involves using real cash flows and real interest rates.

Analysts often consider the following methods when evaluating capital budgeting projects.

1. *Nominal prices that include inflation and real price increases.* When using this method, the forecasting takes the actual prices that are expected to occur into consideration. That is, the analyst must forecast inflation rates and real increases in prices.
2. *Real prices that include only real price increases.* Although using the real prices method is similar to the previous method, the analyst does not consider inflation in the forecast.
3. *Constant prices that exclude inflation and real price increases.* This means that the price used in the forecast is the price valid in the initial year or year zero.

This chapter discusses that conducting capital budgeting and investment appraisal based on financial statements with real prices is potentially misleading. Under certain circumstances, the adverse effects of inflation could result in selecting "bad" projects. The chapter also shows that modeling with nominal prices is not only feasible but also relatively simple using a spreadsheet program on a personal computer.

The remainder of the chapter consists of four major sections. The first section presents the literature review on the subject. The next section discusses reasons that the real prices approach persists in investment appraisal. For example, using real prices continues in the development agencies such as the International Bank for Reconstruction and Development at the World Bank (Belli, Anderson, Barnum, Dixon, and Tan, 2001; Vélez-Pareja, 2006). The third section provides a review of some main impacts of inflation and uses a simple numerical example to illustrate the ideas. The final section offers a summary and conclusions.

LITERATURE REVIEW

Inflation refers to an increase in average prices. In an early paper, Cooley, Roenfeldt, and Chew (1975, p. 18) discuss how to introduce inflation adjustments into the capital budgeting process and note that "failure to consider the impact of inflation tends to produce suboptimal decisions." They mention the effect of inflation on depreciation tax shields and consequently on value. Bailey and Jensen (1977), who analyze how price level adjustments might change the ranking of projects, comment that the presence of general price level changes affects the evaluation of investment proposals. Chen (1984, p. 335) notes that "a serious error in capital budgeting decision may [result] if the impact of uncertain inflation is ignored in the valuation process."

Nelson (1976) demonstrates the theoretical impact of inflation on capital budgeting and shows how inflation would shift the entire net present value (NPV) schedule of a capital budget downward for a set of projects. According to Nelson (p. 923), "after-tax present values are not neutral with respect to different rates of inflation, because depreciation charges are based on historical costs." He says that inflation affects the optimal level of capital investment and influences the firm's choice of technologies of production. The NPV ranking of mutually exclusive investment projects depends on the rate of inflation. Typically, rankings are biased toward projects with lower duration when inflation is high. Nelson indicates that replacement policy generally depends on the rate of inflation and defers the replacement decision.

The literature offers numerous warnings about consistency between cash flows and the corresponding discount rates (e.g., Van Horne, 1971; Watts and Helmers, 1979; Hill and Gough, 1981; Hodder and Riggs, 1985; Delson, 1992; Harvey, 1995; Levy and Sarnat, 1995; Brealey, Myers, and Marcus, 1995; Canada and White, 1996; Damodaran, 1996; Benninga and Sarig, 1997; Luenberger, 1998; Day, 2001; Brealey and Myers, 2003; Ross, Westerfield, and Jaffe, 2004; Benninga, 2006). When conducting a capital budgeting analysis, analysts should treat inflation the same in both the discount rate and the cash flow. That is, they should not mix real rates and nominal free cash flows and vice versa.

According to Rappaport and Taggart (1982, p. 5), "If corporate income tax effects are ignored, and if one assumes that inflation affects all prices and costs simultaneously and at the same rate, then all ... approaches [for dealing with inflation: real or nominal prices] yield identical results." Copeland, Koller, and Murrin (2000) note that using real free cash flows, discounted with the real discount rate is equivalent to using nominal free cash flows discounted with the nominal discount rate. Van Horne (2001) recognizes that inflation destroys value and advocates consistency in the analysis: using real cash flows with a real discount rate and nominal cash flows with a nominal discount rate. Brealey and Myers (2003) echo this sentiment.

Although some including Hodder and Riggs (1985) prefer the real prices approach, others including Berk and Demarzo (2009) prefer using nominal or current prices to estimate future free cash flows and discount these flows at the nominal rate of return. Findlay, Chapman, Frankle, Cooley, Roenfeldt, and Chew (1976) find no theoretical justification to conduct analysis at the firm level in real terms. Further, Rappaport and Taggart (1982, p. 6) point out that "of the two theoretically superior approaches, the nominal cash flow approach is probably easier to understand and marginally easier to calculate than the real cash flow approach." Ezzell and Kelly (1984, p. 53) say, "The analysis also implies that when inflation is present, it is not generally appropriate to calculate NPV, the project's NPV under inflation, by discounting the project's real cash payoff." In short, decision makers might reject a project under the nominal prices scenario but accept it under the real price one and vice versa. Mehta, Curley, and Fung (1984) view the nominal method as more expedient than the real method for implementation purposes and consider following the real discount rate technique as inconsistent.

As Schall (1984, p. 104) notes, "A shareholder's ranking of alternative firm policies can change as a result of a purely neutral inflation, in which case a policy which does not maximize share price will be preferred under some inflation rates." Failing to include inflation in the analysis could shift the decision from one alternative to other. Dixon and Hufschmidt (1986), who recognize that neutral inflation cannot be assumed when working with constant prices, use the increase in relative price or real prices. They think that the results are identical once including the increases in relative prices.

Howe (1992, p. 31) states that "Inflation and taxes, through their interaction, change both the discount rate and cash flows used in capital investment analysis. Prior studies show that estimation of cash flows under inflation, though more difficult, poses no intractable problem." Using a detailed example, Weston and Copeland (1992) show that when there is no or neutral inflation, the results are the same. When inflation is not neutral, the results differ. However, assuming that the same decision results would be incorrect, Levy and Sarnat (1995) illustrate that when taxes exist, depreciation introduces an upward bias when working with the constant approach, which assumes that prices are fixed and equal to the prices at time or instant zero. Although the current practice is to name that instant as year or period zero, there is no such period zero. It is an instant in time from where the time is counted forward or backward. Mills (1996, p. 86) concludes that a good project at constant or real prices can be a bad project at nominal prices and "that the capital budgeting process is not neutral with respect to inflation, even if output prices rise at the same rate as costs." Moyer, McGuigan, and Kretlow (1998) recognize that inflation reduces the NPV for a project because inflation is included in the discount rate. That is, the higher inflation, the higher will be the discount rate. As discussed below, some conditions, such as cash in hand, accounts receivables, and payables, negatively affect the NPV of a project.

English (2001) includes inflation in the forecasting for model building. Lord (2002, p. 2) suggests "that in many cases we are projecting real sales and cost-of-goods-sold figures, and are then using nominal required returns to discount them. To use the old economics adage, this is mixing apples and oranges." He shows the bias when not including inflation in the valuation.

Various international organizations including the Independent Evaluation Group of the International Finance Corporation (2008) support constant prices despite long lasting evidence to the contrary. Some practitioners appear to support the notion that the right procedure is the constant or the real price approach. For example, Vélez-Pareja (2006), using a case from the International Bank for Reconstruction and Development—The World Bank (2002), which supports the constant dollar or constant price approach, shows how the constant price approach might lead to overvaluation of a project.

Although many capital budgeting surveys exist, few mention the problem of inflation. However, Ross (1986) and Summers (1987) analyze the effect of inflation on the current corporate capital budgeting practices. Ross has only one reference to inflation, which reflects a response from one of the interviewed executives about the possible overestimation of the internal rate of return (IRR) in some projects. On the other hand, Summers (p. 27) states "In both corporate investment decisions and economists' evaluations of tax policies, the present value of the depreciation deductions associated with specific investments plays a key role. . . . For example, the adverse effect of inflation in conjunction with historic cost depreciation on investment results from the increased discount rate that must be applied to future nominal depreciation allowances."

In summary, financial economists generally agree that ignoring inflation may affect the outcome of capital investment analysis. Although consensus exists that having consistency between cash flows and the corresponding discount rates is important, views differ on whether to use real cash flows with real discount rates or nominal cash flows with nominal discount rates. Some consider that either approach gives the same results while others contend that the two approaches give different results. One way to illustrate differences between these two approaches is to use simple examples. The evidence and arguments shown in the following section suggest that the nominal approach is preferable to the real approach.

REASONS TO JUSTIFY A REAL OR CONSTANT PRICES APPROACH

The "real prices" method is appealing for various reasons. First, many analysts believe that using the nominal and real prices gives the same results. Second, analysts think that even if the results are not identical, the error in using the real prices method is sufficiently small and acceptable. Third, some analysts contend that the "simplicity" of real prices outweighs any marginal benefits of using the nominal prices approach. Fourth, some analysts believe that "forecasting" future inflation rates is too difficult and consequently prefer to do the analysis in real terms.

Equivalence

As previously stated, a widely held belief is that using the real prices approach and the nominal prices approach give the same answers. The false logic of the argument favoring this equivalence goes as follows. With nominal prices, the procedure is to inflate the values by the expected inflation rates and then discount with the nominal discount rate. With real prices, the procedure is to discount the real cash flows with the real discount rate. Therefore, the answers from both methods must be the same. The argument fails to realize that other factors such as credit transactions and taxes create wedges between the results derived from the two methods. Under certain stringent but unrealistic conditions, the equivalence between the two methods is true (Vélez-Pareja, 2000, 2006). However, in general, if the necessary conditions are not satisfied, the results from the two methods differ and a high probability exists that a project could be incorrectly selected and approved because of improper modeling of the inflation effects. Later, the details of some of the conditions are discussed.

In some cases, special conditions may hold for specific projects in the public sector. For example, the use of the real prices approach may be suitable in an environmental project where the financial analysis is less relevant and the benefits and costs are mostly economic in nature. That is, the project pays no taxes and involves no credit transactions. However, with the continued involvement of the private sector in areas that have traditionally been in the public domain, the conditions under which these two methods are equivalent become less likely.

The main conditions that must be satisfied for the equivalence between the two methods to hold are no taxes and no credit sales or purchases. Vélez-Pareja (2000, 2006) discusses additional conditions. In some public sector projects, there may be no tax payments. However, with the increased emphasis on the privatization of public companies, the presence of taxes will be more relevant in the financial analysis that precedes evaluating capital budgeting projects. Even traditional public sectors such as water and power have accounts receivable. Moreover, the present value of the cash revenues is eroded because the water and power tariffs rarely keep pace with inflation and high rates of inflation. Thus, modeling the tariffs as constant in real terms would be a heroic assumption. In some cases, tariffs are constant in nominal terms. Therefore, with increases in inflation, the present value of the tariffs decreases in real terms. Moreover, lags occur in the inflation adjustments of the water and power tariffs. By constructing the financial statement in nominal rather than real terms, the impact of inflation is modeled explicitly with less likelihood of making errors in the analysis.

A "Good Enough" Approximation

In the past without the easy availability of computing power, using nominal prices in capital budgeting was difficult because conducting sensitivity and scenarios analyses would have been extremely time consuming. Thus, justification existed for using the real prices method with suitable approximations. Currently, using real prices is inappropriate because conducting the analysis in nominal prices and performing the relevant sensitivity and scenario analyses is relatively easy. Vélez-Pareja (2006) shows that overvaluation due to using the constant prices approach might exceed 10 percent.

Misleading Simplicity

Another supposed argument favoring the real prices approach in capital budgeting is its simplicity. Before the common use of spreadsheets, the simplicity argument had merit. Today, the simplicity argument is a poor excuse for avoiding the use of nominal terms.

Forecasting Inflation

A final argument against the nominal prices approach is the belief that forecasting inflation is impossible. Consequently, the analysis must be done in real terms. Although forecasting inflation is a notoriously difficult activity, this does not imply that the analysis must be conducted in real terms. Forecasting the future demand for outputs and inputs in real terms is no easier than forecasting the inflation rates. Nevertheless, the appropriate modeling and analysis with nominal prices can and should be done. Without the availability of computing power, this argument against nominal prices might have some merit. With the availability of inexpensive and widespread computing power and the means to conduct extensive sensitivity and scenario analyses without too much difficulty, the insistence on using real prices seems anachronistic and betrays a lack of knowledge about the new techniques that are available in computing and modeling. Perhaps this view reflects the typical slowness in adopting new techniques.

The preference for "real" or "constant" prices is difficult to understand. Moreover, investors are unfamiliar with transactions in real prices. All the cash flows and returns in commercial transactions are in nominal terms. The term "real prices" is misleading and a misnomer. The financial statements constructed with real prices are make-believe because the "real" values stated are not the actual values that the investor will face in the future years. For example, in year N, the investor will receive $X in nominal terms. The investor will not receive some real amount $Y that has been adjusted in terms of a base year. Similarly, in year N, the investor may have to make tax payments based on the nominal income in year N. The actual tax payments are not based on the "real" income that has been calculated with respect to a base year. The tax payments for year t are based on the nominal income for that particular year t.

The same logic applies to constructing a loan schedule. The interest payments are calculated with the nominal interest rate and have to be paid in nominal terms. Constructing a loan schedule with the real interest rate is a fiction. The real interest rates are unobserved and the loan repayments are not in real terms; the real interest rates and the real payments are artificial constructs.

In the constant price method, the only items that are kept constant are prices. This does not affect items such as depreciation and interest rates. This means that the forecasted cash flows are a strange mix of constant (real) items and interest payments that are calculated with an interest rate that has implicitly an inflationary component. Most importantly, using the real prices approach could lead to incorrect project selection. Typically, inflation has a negative impact on a project's NPV. The expected inflation rate is an uncertain parameter in the analysis and the impact of fluctuations in the expected inflation rate should be part of the analysis. For example, suppose the analysis is based on an expected inflation rate of 8 percent and the NPV is positive. The NPV would be negative if the expected inflation rate were 10 percent. Without explicitly modeling the impacts of inflation in nominal terms, incorrect project selection could occur. All this would invalidate a proper capital budgeting process. With scenario analyses, analysts can easily specify the likely profiles for the expected inflation rates and examine the impacts of the different inflation profiles on the NPV of the project.

IMPACTS OF INFLATION ON THE FINANCIALS: AN EXAMPLE

This section reviews some of the main impacts of inflation and uses a simple numerical example to illustrate the ideas. Inflation has both direct and indirect effects upon the analysis of a project. The direct effects of inflation occur due to credit sales, credit purchases, and changes in the minimum cash requirements for running the business or project. Essentially, the direct effects involve the "time value of money." The indirect effects of inflation occur through increases or decreases in the taxes due to the depreciation allowance, cost of goods sold (COGS), and the interest deduction from debt financing. Other effects include loss carry forwards (LCF), investment and reinvestment of excess cash, price elasticity of demand effects, and salvage values.

Necessary Conditions for Equivalence

The equivalence between the real prices and nominal prices approach would hold if all of the above effects do not occur. To be specific, if there are no taxes, no credit sales or purchases, and no minimum cash requirements, the two approaches would be equivalent. However, proponents of the real prices approach do not mention or insist on the necessary conditions for equivalence. Vélez-Pareja (2000, 2006) provides a more complete discussion of some of the necessary assumptions for the equivalence between the two methods to hold.

Direct Impacts

A detailed exposition of the direct impacts of inflation that occur through accounts receivable, accounts payable, and minimum cash requirement (MCR) is presented below. If the project allows credit sales and the expected rate of inflation is positive, the present value of the cash receipts decreases. The higher the inflation rate, the lower is the present value of cash receipts. The rationale is simple. With credit sales, the customers have postponed the payment and with an increase in the expected inflation rate, the postponed payments by the customers have lower value for the project.

ACCOUNTS RECEIVABLE

Let R_t be the revenues at the end of year t (or the beginning of year $t + 1$) and assume that beginning in year 1 the expected nominal increase in the revenues is δ_{Rev}. Let α be the accounts receivable in year t as a percentage of the revenues in year t. For simplicity, assume that both δ_{Rev} and α are constant. Also assume that the firm has no bad debts and collects all accounts receivable in the year following their creation.

The cash receipts in year t are equal to the revenues in year t less the accounts receivable (AR) in year t plus the accounts receivable in the previous year $t - 1$. In year t, the accounts receivable for the current year t is subtracted because α percent of the sales are on credit and will be received in the following year. In year t, the accounts receivables from the previous year $t - 1$ are added because the customers pay for the credit sales from the previous year.

$$\text{Cash receipts}_t = R_t - AR_t + AR_{t-1} \qquad (11.1)$$

Let the change in the accounts receivable be the difference between the accounts receivable in year t and the year $t - 1$.

$$\Delta AR_t = AR_t - AR_{t-1} \qquad (11.2)$$

Then the cash receipts can be written as the annual revenues less the change in the accounts receivable.

$$\text{Cash receipts}_t = R_t - \Delta AR_t \qquad (11.3)$$

Let R_0 be the revenues in the beginning of year 1 (or the end of year 0). Then the cash receipts in year t can be rewritten in terms of the revenues in year 1, the expected annual increase in revenues and the change in the accounts receivable.

$$\text{Cash receipts}_t = R_0(1 + \delta_{Rev})^t - \Delta AR_t \qquad (11.4a)$$

$$= R_0(1 + \delta_{Rev})^t - \alpha[R_t - R_{t-1}] \qquad (11.4b)$$

Similarly, if the project has credit purchases and the expected inflation rate increases, the present value of the cash expenditures is lower. With credit purchases, the project has postponed the payments for the purchases; with an increase in the expected inflation rate, the project gains from the postponement of the payments for the purchases.

ACCOUNTS PAYABLE

Let Z_t be the purchases at the end of year t and assume that beginning in year 1 the expected nominal increase in the purchases is δ_{Pur}. Let β be the accounts payable in year t as a percent of the purchases in year t. For simplicity, assume that both δ_{Pur} and β are constant. Assume that the firm will pay accounts payable in full.

The cash expenditures in year t are equal to the purchases in year t less the accounts payable (AP) in year t plus the accounts payable in the previous year t − 1. In year t, the accounts payable for the current year t are subtracted because β percent of the purchases are on credit and will be paid in the following year. In year t, the accounts payable from the previous year t − 1 are added because the credit purchases from the previous year have been paid.

$$\text{Cash expenditures} = Z_t - AP_t + AP_{t-1} \tag{11.5}$$

Let the change in the accounts payable be the difference between the accounts payable in year t and the year t − 1.

$$\Delta AP_t = AP_t - AP_{t-1} \tag{11.6}$$

Then, the cash expenditures can be written as the annual purchases less the change in the accounts payable.

$$\text{Cash expenditures}_t = Z_t - \Delta AP_t \tag{11.7}$$

Let Z_0 be the purchases in the beginning of year 1 (or the end of year 0). Then cash expenditures in year t can be written in terms of the purchases in year 1, the expected annual increase in purchases and the change in the accounts payable.

$$\text{Cash expenditures}_t = Z_0(1 + \delta_{Pur})^t - \Delta AP_t \tag{11.8a}$$

$$= Z_0(1 + \delta_{Pur})^t - \beta(Z_t - Z_{t-1}) \tag{11.8b}$$

A third effect of inflation occurs through the change in the cash balance or the minimum cash requirement (MCR) for the project. To operate a business, a minimum amount of cash is required to pay for various expenses. Assume that the cash does not receive any interest. Here the impact of changes in the expected inflation rate on the MCR is examined.

An increase in the MCR is a cash outflow because additional cash is required for running the business. With an increase in the inflation rate, the present value of the increases in the MCR is higher, and this represents a real increase in the cash outflow for the project.

Indirect Tax Effects of Inflation

The indirect effects of inflation occur through the impact on the tax payments. There are three main channels for the indirect impacts of inflation: the depreciation allowance, COGS, and the interest deduction.

The previous section presents the direct effects of increases in the expected inflation rate on the change in accounts receivable, the change in accounts payable, and the change in the MCR. This section provides a discussion of the indirect effects of inflation through the impact on the tax payments.

Depreciation Allowance

Typically, the depreciation allowance is not adjusted for inflation. Thus, even though the depreciation allowance is unchanged in nominal terms, the present value of the depreciation allowance has decreased in real terms. If the expected inflation rate increases, the annual nominal revenue and the annual taxable income also increase. Since the tax payments are based on the nominal values of the taxable income, the present value of the tax payments is higher with an increase in the inflation rate.

Assume that at the end of year 0, the cost of a machine for a project is spread during an economic life of N years. The direct impact of inflation via the depreciation allowance affects the tax payments. The effect of depreciation has to be seen as the PV of a depreciation allowance that decreases with inflation and by the resulting tax payment that increases with inflation. Given a constant nominal depreciation allowance, taxes are higher and the present value of taxes is also higher.

A negative relationship exists between the present value of the depreciation allowance and the expected inflation rate, holding constant the expected growth rate for revenues. The annual depreciation allowances are constant in nominal terms. With increases in the expected inflation rates, the present value of the depreciation allowance decreases in real terms.

With the decrease in the present value of the depreciation allowance, tax payments increase. What is the explanation for the increase in the tax payments? The reason is as follows. The depreciation allowance is unadjusted for inflation. Thus, with a given expected inflation rate, the nominal taxable income increases and consequently the tax payments have also increased. The increase in the tax payments is equal to the change in the present value of the depreciation allowance times the tax rate.

$$\text{Change in tax payments} = (\text{tax rate})(\text{change in PV of depreciation}) \qquad (11.9)$$

With higher inflation rates, the present value of the depreciation allowance would be lower and the increase in the present value of the tax payments would be higher. In the presence of expected rates of inflation that are high and uncertain, the effect on the present value of the tax payments would be higher for capital intensive projects.

The present value of the depreciation allowance is lower with a higher expected inflation rate. Thus, there is a negative impact on the overall value of the cash flow profile due to the impact of the expected inflation rate through the tax payments.

Cost of Goods Sold

A similar effect occurs with the COGS. With the first-in, first-out (FIFO) method, COGS is understated with an increase in the inflation rate. Again, as taxable income increases, the present value of the tax payments is higher. Bernstein and Wild (1998, p. 168) provide further details on FIFO and last-in, first-out (LIFO).

Interest Deduction

The nominal cost of debt incorporates the expected inflation rate. With a higher expected inflation rate, the cost of debt is correspondingly higher. With a higher inflation rate, the present value of the principal repayments on a loan has a lower value. To compensate for the decrease in the value of the principal repayments, the higher nominal discount rate increases the present value of the interest payments by the corresponding amount. The higher present value of the interest deductions means that the tax shield is higher and consequently the tax payments are lower. Recall that the present value of the project is assumed to be independent of the debt financing, and the effect of debt financing only occurs through the tax savings from the interest deductions. Thus, even if the nominal interest rate fully incorporates the expected inflation rate and the present value of the loan remains unchanged under both expected inflation rates, the present value of the tax shield is higher with the higher expected inflation rate. If the expected inflation rate is lower than expected, the present value of the loan may differ and the project may lose or gain.

Numerical Example

The following numerical example illustrates the previous ideas. Exhibit 11.1 shows the input data. In this example, the project is 100 percent equity financed.

- *Revenues*. The nominal increase for the revenues is 9 percent [(1 + 0.0800) (1+ 0.0093) – 1 = 9 percent]. Appendix 11.1 provides an explanation of this rule, which is also known as the Fisher equation. Relative to the expected inflation rate, the nominal increase for the revenues is one percentage point higher. For example, if the expected inflation rate is 10 percent and the real increase in revenues is 0.91 percent, then the expected increase in the revenues is 11 percent. Accounts receivable are 10 percent of the annual revenues as shown in Exhibit 11.1. Due to the Fisher relationship between real and nominal prices, the real increase in revenues, purchases, and expenses

Exhibit 11.1 Project's Input Data

Inputs		Year				
	0	1	2	3	4	5
Inflation rate		8.00%	8.00%	8.00%	8.00%	8.00%
Real return rate		6.00	6.00	6.00	6.00	6.00
Real increase in revenues		0.93	0.93	0.93	0.93	0.93
Real increase in purchases		1.85	1.85	1.85	1.85	1.85
Real increase in expenses		0.46	0.46	0.46	0.46	0.46
Accounts payable policy	7%					
Accounts receivables policy	10%					
MCR as a % of expenses	20%					
Tax rate	34%					
Annual revenues	$700					
Annual purchases	$200					
Annual expenses	$300					
Assets	$800					
Depreciation life	8 years					

This exhibit shows the input data for a simple example with the purpose to show how inflation affects value.

is slightly less than the additional nominal increase above inflation. For example, with revenues, the real increase is 0.93 percent, which is less than the extra nominal increase of 1 percent.

- *Purchases.* The nominal increase for the purchases is 10 percent. Relative to the expected inflation rate, the nominal increase for the purchases is two percentage points higher.
- *Expenses.* The values for the annual expenses are shown in Exhibit 11.5. Relative to the expected inflation rate, the nominal increase for the expenses is one-half percentage point higher.
- *Minimum cash requirement.* The minimum cash requirement is 20 percent of the annual expenses. Assume that there are no inventory requirements.
- *Machine.* The machine is purchased at instant 0 for $800 with an economic life of 8 years.

Based on the above parameters, the income statement, the balance sheet, and the free cash flows (FCF) are constructed and shown below.

INCOME STATEMENT AND BALANCE SHEET

Exhibit 11.2 shows the project's income statement. Every year, the taxable income is positive. There is no interest deduction because here the assumption is no debt financing. Note that the depreciation allowance remains constant and is independent of the expected inflation rate. Exhibit 11.3 shows the project's balance sheet.

Free Cash Flow

Chapter 10 discuses the derivation of cash flows for capital budgeting, especially free cash flow. Exhibit 11.4 shows the FCFs, their present value, and NPV. Because the NPV is positive, the project should be accepted. Here the assumption is that the correct value for the expected inflation rate is 8 percent. However, because the expected inflation rate is uncertain, the impact of changes in the expected inflation rates on the project's NPV must be examined.

Exhibit 11.2 Project's Income Statement

	Year				
	1	2	3	4	5
Annual revenues	$763.00	$831.67	$906.52	$988.11	$1,077.04
COGS	220.00	241.99	266.19	292.80	322.07
Gross profit	543.00	589.68	640.33	695.31	754.96
Expenses	325.49	353.15	383.15	415.71	451.03
Depreciation	100.00	100.00	100.00	100.00	100.00
Taxable income	117.51	136.53	157.18	179.60	203.93
Taxes	39.95	46.42	53.44	61.06	69.34
Net income	77.56	90.11	103.74	118.54	134.60

This exhibit shows the resulting income statement when the input data from Exhibit 11.1 are used in a simple model that has the financial statements as outputs.

Exhibit 11.3 Project's Balance Sheet

	0	1	2	3	4	5
				Year		
Assets						
Cash	$ 65.10	$ 70.63	$ 76.63	$ 83.14	$ 90.21	
Accounts receivable		76.30	83.17	90.65	98.81	
Current assets	800.00	800.00	800.00	800.00	800.00	$800.00
Accumulated depreciation		100.00	200.00	300.00	400.00	500.00
Net assets	800.00	700.00	600.00	500.00	400.00	300.00
Total assets	865.10	846.93	759.80	673.79	589.02	300.00
Liabilities and equity						
Accounts payable		15.40	16.94	18.63	20.50	
Debt	0.00	0.00	0.00	0.00	0.00	0.00
Equity	865.10					
New equity		−33.57	-88.67	−87.70	−86.64	−268.52
Total equity	865.10	831.53	742.86	655.16	568.52	300.00
Total equity and liabilities	865.10	846.93	759.80	673.79	589.02	300.00

This exhibit shows the balance sheet, which is consistent with the income statement from Exhibit 11.2. The depreciation charge from the income statement is accumulated under the line of accumulated depreciation.

Sensitivity Analysis of the Project's NPV

Exhibit 11.5 shows the effects of the expected inflation rate and real increase in revenues on NPV. If the expected inflation rate is 10 percent and the real increase is 0.5 percent, the NPV of the project is negative and should be rejected.

Why does the NPV decline with the increase in the expected inflation rate from 8 percent to 10 percent? To find the answer requires calculating the PV of each line item in the FCF statement and identifying the specific effects of inflation. Observe that even for one-digit inflation (7 percent to 9 percent), the project should be rejected when the real increase in revenues is 0 percent. Notice that for inflation at 0 percent the NPV is highest, which corresponds to the real price approach. The constant prices approach is equivalent to having inflation at 0 percent and real increase of sales revenues at 0 percent. This means that constant and real prices overvalue the NPV for the project in the presence of inflation.

Exhibit 11.4 Project's Free Cash Flow

	0	1	2	3	4	5
				Year		
Free cash flow	−$865.10	$111.13	$178.78	$191.44	$205.18	$823.88
PV of FCF	899.54	918.67	872.91	807.87	719.67	
NPV(FCF)	34.44					

This exhibit shows the resulting free cash flow (FCF) derived from the income statement and balance sheet from previous exhibits. This FCF is discounted at the discount rate of 14.48 percent that is derived from an inflation rate of 8 percent and a real interest rate of 6 percent and using the Fisher equation (see Appendix 11A).

Exhibit 11.5 Sensitivity of NPV to Inflation Rates and Real Increases in Prices

	NPV		ΔReal Sales		
Inflation rate	$34.44	0.0%	0.5%	0.93%	1.5%	2.0%
	0.0%	$145.94	$174.01	$198.21	$231.25	$260.43
	7.0%	0.00	27.89	51.94	84.76	113.75
	8.0%	−17.45	10.42	34.44	67.24	96.21
	9.0%	−34.20	−6.35	17.65	50.42	79.36
	10.0%	−50.29	−22.47	1.52	34.26	63.17

This exhibit combines two variables: Δreal sales and inflation, and shows the resulting NPV for different combinations of these two variables. For some combinations NPV is negative. Overall, the exhibit shows that inflation and real increase in prices change the NPV. The maximum NPV for each increase in price is obtained when inflation is zero.

Exhibit 11.6 Sensitivity of NPV to Inflation Rates and Accounts Receivables Policy

	NPV		Accounts Receivables Policy		
Inflation rate	**$34.44**	0.0%	5.0%	10.00%	15.0%	20.0%
	0.0%	$212.25	$205.23	$198.21	$191.19	$184.17
	7.0%	81.29	66.61	51.94	37.26	22.59
	8.0%	65.82	50.13	**34.44**	18.76	3.07
	9.0%	51.01	34.33	17.65	0.97	−15.71
	10.0%	36.83	19.17	1.52	−16.14	−33.80

This exhibit shows the same sensitivity of NPV to the inflation rate and accounts receivables policy. The greater the accounts receivable, the lower the NPV, and the larger the inflation rate, the lower the NPV. The highest NPV is reached when inflation is zero.

Exhibit 11.6 shows the interaction between accounts receivables policy and NPV and their effects on the NPV. As Exhibit 11.6 shows, the NPV for the project becomes negative and the project is now unacceptable due to relatively high AR policies and one-digit inflation. Increasing the AR policy decreases the NPV. Also, the maximum NPV occurs when the inflation rate is 0 percent.

Exhibit 11.7 shows the interaction of accounts payable policy and inflation and their effects on the NPV. As Exhibit 11.7 shows, for a given inflation rate, the NPV

Exhibit 11.7 Sensitivity of NPV to Inflation Rates and Accounts Payables Policy

	NPV		Accounts Payable Policy		
Inflation rate	**$34.44**	0.0%	7.00%	10.0%	15.0%	20.0%
	0.0%	$195.34	$198.21	$199.44	$201.49	$203.54
	7.0%	45.93	51.94	54.51	58.80	63.08
	8.0%	28.03	**34.44**	37.19	41.78	46.36
	9.0%	10.83	17.65	20.57	25.45	30.32
	10.0%	−5.71	1.52	4.61	9.77	14.93

This exhibit shows the same effect on NPV but this time it considers the accounts payable (AP) policy and inflation. The results regarding the AP policy are contrary to the AR policy. The greater the AP policy, the greater is the NPV. Again, inflation negatively affects the NPV. Given a level of AP, the highest NPV is found when inflation is zero.

of the FCFs increases due to the reasons mentioned in this section. Once more, when inflation is 0 percent, NPV is highest.

SUMMARY AND CONCLUSIONS

The example presented supports the evidence and arguments announced in the literature. Inflation alters the capital budgeting analysis and may lead to selecting inappropriate projects. As the simple example shows, a project might appear to be optimal when analyzed at real or constant prices. When considering inflation and hence nominal prices, the project might become unacceptable. Reality is based on nominal or current prices, not real or constant prices. The simple numerical examples with sensitivity analysis show that changes in the expected inflation rates have direct and indirect impacts on the project's NPV. The failure to properly model the impacts of inflation in nominal prices may lead to mistakes in capital budgeting and result in incorrect project selection. This chapter has shown the inconvenience of working with real or constant prices when analyzing alternatives. This is an invitation to adopt the practice of appraising projects with nominal prices.

DISCUSSION QUESTIONS

1. The constant prices approach assumes that the expected real increase in prices is zero. Briefly discuss an example where this assumption is invalid.

2. Assume that the annual revenues increase at the expected inflation rate of 5 percent and that accounts receivable are 10 percent of the annual revenues. What is the impact of the expected positive inflation rate on the present value of the cash receipts, relative to an expected inflation rate of 0 percent? Is the impact positive, negative, or unchanged?

3. Assume that the cost of debt is fully indexed to the expected positive inflation rate so that the NPV of the loan and loan repayment, discounted by the cost of debt, is zero. What is the present value of the interest payments in the presence of inflation, relative to the case where the expected inflation rate is zero? Is it higher, lower or unchanged? What is the impact of inflation on the tax savings from the interest deduction?

4. Typically, annual depreciation allowances are not indexed to inflation. What is the impact of inflation on the tax savings from the annual depreciation allowances?

5. Many authors insist that by using real discount rates and real cash flows they obtain the same results as if using nominal rates and flows. However, an ambiguity exists in the definition of the "real" WACC. First, real WACC can be defined in terms of real parameters. Second, real WACC can be obtained from the nominal WACC using the Fisher relationship to get the deflated WACC. Using the formula for WACC, $K_d \times D\%(1-T) + K_e E\%$, where K_d = the nominal cost of debt; $D\%$ = leverage; T = the tax rate; K_e = the cost of equity, and $E\%$ = the weight of equity in the cost of capital and the following parameters, show that a difference exists between the real and deflated WACC. Assume that $D\%$ = 40 percent, $E\%$ = 60 percent, T = 20 percent; expected inflation rate, g = 5 percent, real cost of debt, K_d = 6 percent, and real cost of equity, K_e = 10 percent.

REFERENCES

Bailey, Andrew D., Jr., and Daniel L. Jensen, 1977. "General Price Level Adjustments in the Capital Budgeting Decision." *Financial Management* 6:1, 26–31.

Belli, Pedro, Jock R. Anderson, Howard N. Barnum, John A. Dixon, and Jee-Peng Tan. 2001. *Economic Analysis of Investment Operations. Analytical Tools and Practical Applications.* Washington, DC: World Bank.

Benninga, Simon. 2006. *Principles of Finance with Excel.* New York: Oxford University Press.

Benninga, Simon, and Oded Sarig. 1997. *Corporate Finance: A Valuation Approach.* New York: McGraw-Hill.

Berk, Jonathan B., and Peter Demarzo. 2009. *Corporate Finance: The Core.* Boston: Pearson.

Bernstein, Leopold A., and John J. Wild. 1998. *Financial Statement Analysis.* New York: McGraw-Hill.

Brealey, Richard A., and Stewart C. Myers. 2003. *Principles of Corporate Finance.* New York: McGraw-Hill.

Brealey, Richard A., Stewart C. Myers, and Alan J. Marcus. 1995. *Fundamentals of Corporate Finance.* New York: McGraw-Hill.

Canada, John R., and John A. White, Jr. 1996. *Capital Investment Decision Analysis for Engineering and Management.* Englewood Cliffs: Prentice Hall.

Chen, Son Nan. 1984. "Capital Budgeting and Uncertain Inflation." *Journal of Economics and Business* 36:3, 335–344.

Cooley, Philip L., Rodney L. Roenfeldt, and It-Keong Chew. 1975. "Capital Budgeting Procedures under Inflation." *Financial Management* 4:4, 18–27.

Copeland, Tom, Tim Koller, and Jack Murrin. 2000. *Valuation. Measuring and Managing the Value of Companies.* New York: John Wiley & Sons.

Damodaran, Aswath. 1996. *Investment Valuation. Tools and Techniques for Determining the Value of Any Asset.* New York: John Wiley & Sons.

Day, Alastair. 2001. *Mastering Financial Modelling: A Practitioner's Guide to Applied Corporate Finance.* London: Pearson.

Delson, Jerome. K. 1992. "Engineering Economics on Inflation." *IEEE Transactions on Power Systems* 7:1, 73–80.

Dixon, John A., and Maynard M. Hufschmidt, eds. 1986. *Economic Valuation Techniques for the Environment. A Case Study Workbook.* Baltimore: Johns Hopkins University Press.

English, James. 2001. *Applied Equity Analysis, Stock Valuation Techniques for Wall Street Professionals.* New York: McGraw-Hill.

Ezzell, John R., and William A. Kelly, Jr. 1984. "An APV Analysis of Capital Budgeting under Inflation." *Financial Management* 13:3, 49–54.

Findlay, M. Chapman, III, Alan W. Frankle, Philip L. Cooley, Rodney L. Roenfeldt, and It-Keong Chew. 1976. "Capital Budgeting Procedures under Inflation: Cooley, Roenfeldt and Chew vs. Findlay and Frankle." *Financial Management* 5:3, 83–95.

Harvey, Campbell R. 1995. *WWWFinance Project Evaluation.* Available at http://www.duke.edu/~charvey/Classes/ba350/project/project.htm.

Hill, Stephen, and Julian Gough. 1981. "Discounting Inflation: A Note." *Managerial and Decision Economics* 2:2, 121–123.

Hodder, James E., and Henry E. Riggs. 1985. "Pitfalls in Evaluating Risky Projects." *Harvard Business Review* 63:1, 127–135.

Howe, Keith M. 1992. "Capital Budgeting Discount Rates under Inflation: A Caveat." *Financial Practice and Education* 2:1, 31–36.

Independent Evaluation Group. International Finance Corporation. 2008. *Preparing Expanded Project Supervision Report Instructions for Non-Financial Markets Projects.* Washington, DC: World Bank Group.

International Bank for Reconstruction and Development—The World Bank. 2002. *Financial Modeling of Regulatory Policy*, two CD set. Washington, DC: World Bank.

Levy, Haim, and Marshall Sarnat. 1995. *Capital Investment and Financial Decisions*. Englewood Cliffs: Prentice Hall.

Lord, Richard. 2002. *FINC 490-03 Seminar in Finance, Fall 2002, Lecture #3, Inflation and Capital Budgeting*. Available at http://frontpage.montclair.edu/lordr/courses/490_04/lecture3/InflationCB.PDF.

Luenberger, David G. 1998. *Investment Science*. New York: Oxford University Press.

Mehta, Dileep R, Michael D Curley, and Hung-Gay Fung. 1984. "Inflation, Cost of Capital, and Capital Budgeting Procedures." *Financial Management* 13:4, 48–54.

Mills, Geofrey T. 1996. "The Impact of Inflation on Capital Budgeting and Working Capital." *Journal of Financial and Strategic Decisions* 9:1, 79–87.

Moyer, R. Charles, James R. McGuigan, and William J. Kretlow. 1998. *Contemporary Financial Management*. New York: Thomson.

Nelson, Charles R. 1976. "Inflation and Capital Budgeting." *Journal of Finance* 31:3, 923–931.

Rappaport, Alfred, and Robert A. Taggart, Jr. 1982. "Evaluation of Capital Expenditure Proposals under Inflation." *Financial Management* 11:1, 5–13.

Ross, Marc. 1986. "Capital Budgeting Practices of Twelve Large Manufacturers." *Financial Management* 15:4, 15–22.

Ross, Stephen A., Randolph Westerfield, and Jeffrey Jaffe. 2004. *Corporate Finance*. New York: McGraw-Hill.

Schall, Lawrence D. 1984. "Taxes, Inflation and Corporate Financial Policy." *Journal of Finance* 39:1, 105–126.

Summers, Lawrence H. 1987. "Corporate Capital Budgeting Practices and the Effects of Tax Policies on Investment." In Martin Feldstein, ed. *Taxes and Capital Formation*, 27–36. Chicago: University of Chicago Press.

Van Horne, James C. 1971. "A Note on Biases in Capital Budgeting Introduced by Inflation." *Journal of Financial and Quantitative Analysis* 6:1, 653–658.

Van Horne, James C. 2001. *Financial Management and Policy*. Englewood Cliffs: Prentice Hall.

Vélez-Pareja, Ignacio. 2000. "Project Evaluation in an Inflationary Environment." Working Paper, Universidad Javeriana, Bogotá. Available at www.ssrn.com. http://papers.ssrn.com/sol3/Delivery.cfm/99020216.pdf?abstractid=148410.

Vélez-Pareja, Ignacio. 2006. "Valuating Cash Flows in an Inflationary Environment: The Case of World Bank." In Barbara T. Credan, ed. *Trends in Inflation Research*, 87–141. New York: Nova Publishers.

Walter, James E. 1972. "Investment Planning Under Variable Price Change." *Financial Management* 1:3, 36–50.

Watts, Myles J., and Glenn A. Helmers. 1979. "Inflation and Machinery Cost Budgeting." *Southern Journal of Agricultural Economics* 11:2, 83–88.

Weston, J. Fred, and Thomas E. Copeland. 1992. *Managerial Finance*. Fort Worth: Dryden Press.

ABOUT THE AUTHORS

Ignacio Vélez-Pareja is an Associate Professor at the School of Economics and Business Administration, Universidad Tecnológica de Bolívar. He received an M.Sc. in Industrial Engineering at the University of Missouri. Professor Vélez-Pareja has worked in the different functional areas of manufacturing and service at private firms including top management. He has taught at top universities in Argentina, Colombia, Panama, Portugal, Spain, and the United States. His articles on various management and finance topics appear in domestic and international peer-reviewed journals. One of his three books, *Principles of Cash Flow Valuation: An Integrated Market-based Approach* (Academic Press, 2004), is co-authored with Joseph Tham.

Joseph Tham is a Visiting Assistant Professor at the Sanford School of Public Policy, Duke University and the Duke Center for International Development (DCID). At Duke University and developing countries around the world, Professor Tham teaches courses and workshops on project appraisal and empirical analysis for economic development. In the fall of 2005, he taught a course on Cash Flow Valuation. In collaboration with Ignacio Vélez-Pareja, Professor Tham published *Principles of Cash Flow Valuation: An Integrated Market-based Approach*. His numerous papers on cash flow valuation, project evaluation, cost of capital, and risk analysis are available on the website of the Social Science Research Network (SSRN).

APPENDIX 11.1 NOMINAL RATES VERSUS REAL RATES: FISHER EQUATION

Before examining the impacts of inflation, discussing the relationship between the expected inflation rate (π), the nominal rate (i), and the real rate r is useful. One plus the nominal return i divided by one plus the expected inflation rate π is equal to one plus the real rate r.

$$(1 + i)/(1 + \pi) = 1 + r \tag{A11.1a}$$

Solving for the nominal return in line A11.1a,

$$1 + i = (1 + r)(1 + \pi) \tag{A11.1b}$$

$$i = (1 + r)(1 + \pi) - 1 \tag{A11.1c}$$

$$i = r(1 + \pi) + \pi = r + \pi + r \times \pi \tag{A11.1d}$$

The real rate fluctuates in the short term but the real rate is reasonably stable in the long term. For simplicity, assume that the real rate is constant. In other words, assume that the nominal rate incorporates both the real rate and the expected inflation rate. For example, suppose the real rate is 6 percent and the expected inflation rate is 8 percent. Then the required nominal rate is 14.48 percent.

$$i = 6\% + 8\% + 6\%(8\%) = 14.48\%$$

This Fisher relationship applies for interest rates and price increases. Sensitivity and scenario analyses can be used to examine the impact of changes in the real rates on the project's NPV.

PART IV

Risk and Investment Choice

CHAPTER 12

Basic Risk Adjustment Techniques in Capital Budgeting

JOHN H. HALL
Associate Professor, University of Pretoria

WIM WESTERMAN
Assistant Professor, University of Groningen

INTRODUCTION

Investment decisions are usually based on long-term future predictions or estimates of financial, technological, or other variables. Management must inevitably consider risk and uncertainty when dealing with these long-term estimates, especially regarding their influence on a capital budgeting project, the project's accept/reject decision, and the influence of these decisions on the overall risk profile and value of the firm. Ignoring or failing to incorporate risk into the capital budgeting process can lead to destroying shareholder value.

Long before the evolution of modern capital budgeting theories, prudent financial managers incorporated risk in the capital budgeting process. Just as some actions or decisions are more or less risky than others, so are some investment projects. These projects should be adjusted to compensate for the level of risk. This adjusting is usually accomplished by requiring a higher return for more risky projects and a lower return for less risky projects than normal. Over the years, the difficulties of incorporating risk in the capital budgeting process have grown, due mainly to increasing uncertainty in the underlying economic environment, instability in the inflation and exchange rates, and the general concern for shareholder value creation.

This chapter addresses basic risk analysis methods. The first methods discussed are judgment and shortening the payback, followed by the certainty equivalent (CE) method of adjusting cash flows. The bulk of the chapter focuses on the risk-adjusted discount rate method (RADR), which cannot be explained without including a brief discussion of the capital asset pricing model (CAPM). None of these methods can eliminate risk, but they may provide a rational and fundamentally prudent way of incorporating risk in the capital budgeting process. Each of these methods has strengths and shortcomings, and each requires various assumptions to deal with the difficult concept of predicting the future.

DECISION-MAKING TECHNIQUES FOR RISKY CAPITAL BUDGETING PROJECTS

There are various ways to categorize the differing techniques used to incorporate risk in the capital budgeting process. For example, Baker and Powell (2005) use the size of the capital budgeting project as a classification criterion. Relatively small projects often require only good judgment to adjust for risk, while major projects require more time and effort from management and employ more sophisticated techniques. Stand-alone or single-project risk can be evaluated by using sensitivity and scenario analysis, but these methods do not provide any guidelines for accepting or rejecting a project. More sophisticated techniques for assessing single-project risk include simulation and decision-tree analysis. One way to overcome the shortcomings of accept/reject guidelines is to use the CAPM, which, despite its inherent problems, provides a wealth of information and some solutions. One advantage of the CAPM is that it allows analysts to incorporate risk into the capital budgeting process and represents a fairly sophisticated technique that provides accept/reject guidelines. The chapter discusses CAPM later in more detail.

Ho and Pike (1991) contend that risk-handling techniques fall broadly into two categories. One category involves using intuitive methods based on adjusting the cash flows or the capital budgeting technique itself. An example of such an approach is shortening the payback period. Another category involves a more comprehensive analysis of a project's risk-return trade-off by applying techniques such as basic probability analysis, sensitivity analysis, decision-tree analysis, Monte Carlo simulation, and incorporating the CAPM to allow for risk adjustment by changing the discount rate and cash flows of a particular project. The more rigorous the analysis, the more prudent is the firm's accept/reject decision on a given capital budgeting project.

Vishwanath (2007) argues that two main approaches exist to incorporate risk in the capital budgeting process, which in turn determines the techniques chosen to appraise a capital budgeting project. First, an estimation of alterations in the net present value (NPV) and internal rate of return (IRR) results in changes in the actual determinants of the project, such as sales growth, market share, and various cost factors. Techniques used to make adjustments to these relevant input variables (sales and cost factors) include best case–worst case analysis, simulation, scenario analysis, and sensitivity analysis. Second, the cash flow or discount rate can be adjusted to allow for the riskiness of the project. This entails applying the CAPM to culminate in the CE or RADR approach.

Hill (1998) identifies six techniques that can be applied to address the problem of incorporating risk in the capital budgeting process. These methods are: (1) a judgmental adjustment and modification of a project's acceptance criteria, based on the perceived risk of the project; (2) sensitivity analysis; (3) a three-point estimation of the project; (4) a probability estimation of all the inputs in the project; (5) the calculation of the standard deviation of the outcomes; and (6) the application of the project's certainty cash equivalent in order to adjust the cash flows.

This chapter deals with basic risk adjustment techniques—basic in the sense that they are fundamental to the incorporation of risk into the capital budgeting process. Therefore, as a precursor to the more popular techniques, the chapter addresses judgment considerations followed by adjusting the payback period. The chapter emphasizes the CE approach of adjusting the cash flows and the RADR approach where various aspects of the CAPM apply. Subsequent chapters deal with methods such as sensitivity analysis, break-even analysis, decision trees, and simulation.

THE JUDGMENT APPROACH

When management considers the risk-return relationship of a project and makes a decision based on its perceived judgment of the outcome, it is not using any scientific procedures or techniques. This approach may be justified if the project is sufficiently small in monetary terms or if decisions are made by vote of a capital budgeting committee, executive committee, or board of directors. Management may be aware of future events containing risk factors that cannot be sufficiently incorporated into another technique for a numerical analysis of the project. The main use of the judgment approach is to supplement and support other more scientific and prudent techniques for incorporating risk into the capital budgeting process. As Seitz and Ellison (2005) note, judgment decision making may seem haphazard, but people often make important decisions without a predefined selection formula and then select a project (alternative) that appears (feels) to be the best. That is, people collect information and apply judgment instead.

ADJUSTING THE PAYBACK PERIOD

Many academics regard adjusting the payback period as an unsophisticated capital budgeting technique because it ignores risk and the time value of money (e.g., Blatt, 1979; Herbst, 1982; Seitz and Ellison, 2005; Moyer, McGuigan, and Rao, 2005). Yet, Bierman and Smidt (2007, p. 164) note that "the payback calculation is an effective way of communicating how rapidly the investment recovers its initial outlay." As discussed in Chapter 9, numerous empirical studies indicate that the NPV and IRR are more popular with advanced practitioners than adjusting the payback period (Kee and Bublitz, 1988; Graham and Harvey, 2001).

The payback period can play a substantial role in incorporating risk into the evaluation of a capital investment project. The well-known relationship between risk and time can lead management to apply a technique that can indicate the recovery period (i.e., the time required before the firm and its investors are restored to the position they were in before undertaking the investment). The longer the estimated life of a project, the more uncertain are its cash flows and discount rate. Also, there is the increasing probability that some unfavorable event may occur as the project's length increases. All these arguments favor using the payback period, but in a modified version.

One of the main disadvantages of the payback period is that it does not take the time value of money into account. This disadvantage can be overcome by discounting the cash flows at the required rate of return and then calculating a discounted payback period. Management then has to set a payback period that reflects the risk of the project under review, resulting in a payback requirement that is shorter than the firm's normal payback benchmark.

When management uses other profitability measures such as the NPV or IRR, the payback period can serve as a control measure. Boyle and Guthrie (2006, p. 7) indicate that the "payback period should be used in conjunction with the NPV or some other discounted cash flow method rather than in isolation." Kee and Bublitz (1988) also support this view. An established firm with a large, profitable portfolio of projects can use the payback period as an additional measure to lower risk because the initial investment is recovered within an acceptable length of time. Furthermore, the use of a payback criterion can become a greater priority, even a compulsory requirement, for a firm's project evaluation process during uncertain economic periods. The payback period can also serve as an indicator of a project's liquidity. Further, firms often apply this approach when investing in politically unstable regions in order to account for their fear of nationalization and possible loss of the firm's investment through expropriation (Seitz and Ellison, 2005). Finally, firms use the payback period to evaluate relatively small projects without having to go through a rigorous analysis process.

In summary, firms should probably not use the payback period as the sole or main technique to evaluate and account for risk in an investment project. Instead, they should use this approach in conjunction with other techniques to arrive at a more informed accept/reject decision.

THE CERTAINTY EQUIVALENT METHOD

A capital budgeting project that is ready for evaluation typically consists of cash flows that have been carefully compiled, estimated, and projected on the basis of a large amount of information. An appropriate discount rate is applied to the cash flows and, depending on the techniques used and the benchmark set by the firm, a simple answer can result in a guideline or decision about whether to accept/reject the project. Therefore, if the firm changes its estimates of the cash flows or discount rate, the answer and perhaps the accept/reject decision will change.

The CE method of Robichek and Myers (1965) is a technique to establish a cash flow that can be accepted with certainty, in contrast to the original uncertain cash flows resulting from the estimator's forecasts and possible ignorance of future risk regarding the project's cash flows. The further into the future that one needs to forecast or estimate, the more difficult obtaining correct amounts or values becomes. Hence, the probability that the original forecasted cash flow will differ from the actual cash flow is greater for longer-lived projects. As Sick (1986) notes, the certainty equivalent cash flow is a risky cash flow that has been converted so that analysts are willing to accept it with certainty. These certain, risk-free cash flows are then discounted at the risk-free rate, normally the return on government bonds or the Treasury bill rate. The initial investment is then deducted and the result is a risk-adjusted NPV. The risk-adjusted cash flows are not discounted at the firm's cost of capital because the risk component already included in the cost of capital would mean that provision for risk has been made twice.

Determining the Certainty Equivalent Factors

Calculating the certain cash flows requires adjusting the normal cash flows with a risk factor—the certainty equivalent factor (CEF). The most difficult aspect of the CE method is to determine the CEFs, therefore, to calculate or assign a risk profile to each future cash flow. Seitz and Ellison (2005, p. 400) note that "a problem with certainty equivalents is the question of perception of managers or decision makers regarding the degree of risk associated with the forecasted cash flow distribution and their degree of aversion to perceived risk."

One method of determining CEFs involves first categorizing the different types of project a firm can undertake (Clark, Hindelang, and Pritchard, 1984). For example, a firm can distinguish between replacement projects, new investments (expansion), and research and development (R&D) projects. Next, for each category for each year, the appropriate measures of risk and return are determined and a probability distribution of the annual cash flows is computed based on historical information and the performance of past projects. From these data, the coefficient of variation (CV) for the annual cash flow is calculated. The CEF is then assigned, for example, in line with the manager's preference in terms of risk aversion to each project category, based on the size of the coefficient of variation. This method uses the economic concept of utility theory, which formalizes individual preferences.

Lee and Finnerty (1990) claim that the obstacles to measure utility have so far proved insurmountable because an appropriate unit of measurement for utility has not yet been found and because of the problem of keeping external factors constant. The CEF can vary between 0 and 1. Baker, Mukherjee, and Van Belle (2003) offer a procedure to generate the necessary CEFs needed to use certainty equivalents to evaluate risky projects.

Cash inflows can then be adjusted with this factor. Exhibit 12.1 shows a hypothetical example of the CEFs based on the utility preferences for a firm at a given time. An uncertain cash flow in Year 3 of $250,000 for a replacement project

Exhibit 12.1 Certainty Equivalent Factors for Different Project Categories for a Hypothetical Company

Type of Project	Coefficient of Variation (CV)	Certainty Equivalent Factor (CEF)			
		Year 1	Year 2	Year 3	Year 4
Replacement	CV ≤ 0.1	0.95	0.92	0.89	0.85
Replacement	0.1 < CV ≤ 0.25	0.90	0.86	0.82	0.77
Replacement	CV > 0.25	0.84	0.79	0.74	0.68
Expansion	CV ≤ 0.25	0.85	0.82	0.78	0.73
Expansion	CV > 0.25	0.80	0.75	0.70	0.63
R&D	Irrespective	0.70	0.60	0.50	0.10

This exhibit contains the coefficient of variations (CVs) for different categories of projects and the corresponding certainty equivalent factor (CEF) based on the utility preferences for one firm at a given time.

with a coefficient of variation of 0.30 will become a certain cash flow of $185,000 ($250,000 × 0.74). The opposite relationship exists for risky cash outflows, whether it is the initial investment or an operating cash outflow in a future year. Assume that the CEF for a cash outflow is 1.1. The certainty equivalent value of an amount of $1,000,000 would then be $1,100,000. That is, the decision maker would be indifferent between a certain outflow of $1,100,000 and a risky outflow of $1,000,000. The CEFs should be reviewed at least annually because any change in the risk-free rate, cost of capital, or management's utility preferences alters the CEF. For this firm, R&D projects are so risky that, irrespective of the coefficient of variation, management uses only one set of CEFs. This assumption includes a good measure of judgment.

Another method to determine the CEFs is to derive them by relating the certain return (in monetary value or percentage return) to the risky return (in monetary value or percentage return). For example, if the risk-free rate is 8 percent and the RADR 17 percent, the CEF is calculated as follows:

$$CEF = \frac{1 + 0.08}{1 + 0.17} = 0.92$$

Steps in Calculating the Certainty Equivalent Net Present Value [CE(NPV)]

The CE method results in the CE(NPV) and involves the following steps:

1. Forecast the cash flows for the project.
2. Assign the appropriate CEF to its corresponding yearly cash flow.
3. Multiply the cash flow by its CEF to determine the certain cash flow.
4. Discount the cash flows at the risk-free rate, deduct the initial investment, and obtain the CE(NPV).

The CE(NPV) is therefore calculated as follows:

$$CE(NPV) = \sum_{t=1}^{n} \frac{CEC_t \times CF_t}{(1 + R_f)^t} - (I_0 \times CEC_0) \qquad (12.1)$$

where I_0 = initial investment; CEC_0 = certainty equivalent coefficient of the initial investment amount; CEC_t = certainty equivalent coefficient of the cash flow in period t; CF_t = net cash flow in period t; R_f = risk-free discount rate; and n = expected life of the project (periods 1, 2, 3 . . . n).

The decision rule for the CE(NPV) is the same as that for the NPV. For independent projects, accept the project if the CE(NPV) is positive or zero, and reject the project if the CE(NPV) is negative. For mutually exclusive projects, the decision rule is to accept the project with the highest positive CE(NPV).

Examples of Calculating the CE(NPV)

The following are two examples involving calculating the CE(NPV).

Example 1

The hypothetical company that developed the CEFs in Exhibit 12.1 is contemplating investing in an expansion project with an estimated initial investment of $500,000. The after-tax cash flows with their risk characteristics are the following:

Year	Cash Flow	Standard Deviation	Coefficient of Variation (CV)
1	$100,000	$15,000	0.15
2	200,000	50,000	0.25
3	300,000	100,000	0.33
4	200,000	120,000	0.60

The analyst calculates the initial investment's CEF as 1.05; the firm's weighted average cost of capital (WACC) is 17 percent and the risk-free rate is 7 percent. What are the project's NPV and its CE(NPV)?

Suggested Solution   NPV @ 17% = $25,614

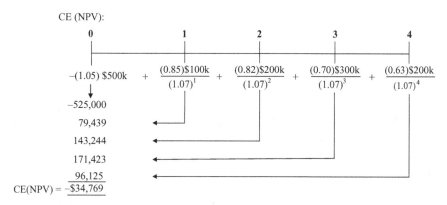

Using the normal NPV as a guideline, the project should be accepted with a positive value of $25,614. However, the CE(NPV) gives an answer of –$34,769, indicating that, if the project is adjusted for risk, it will destroy value if the firm accepts the project. Therefore, the final decision must be to reject the project.

Example 2 A Changing Risk-Free Rate

The hypothetical company is considering replacing one of its existing machines. The replacement investment is $200,000 and the following additional information applies:

Year	Cash Flow	Coefficient of Variation (CV)	Risk-free Rate (%)
1	$50,000	0.05	7
2	100,000	0.10	6
3	100,000	0.20	5
4	200,000	0.27	6

What is the CE(NPV) of the project?

Suggested Solution

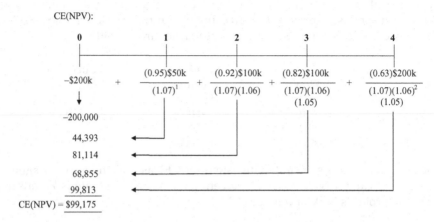

CE(NPV):

$$-\$200k + \frac{(0.95)\$50k}{(1.07)^1} + \frac{(0.92)\$100k}{(1.07)(1.06)} + \frac{(0.82)\$100k}{(1.07)(1.06)(1.05)} + \frac{(0.63)\$200k}{(1.07)(1.06)^2(1.05)}$$

```
-200,000
  44,393
  81,114
  68,855
  99,813
CE(NPV) = $99,175
```

The project should be accepted because the CE(NPV) is positive (i.e., $99,175).

Strengths and Weaknesses of the CE Method

According to Shapiro (2005), many financial theorists consider the CE method superior to the RADR method for several reasons. When valuing future cash flows, the CE method accounts for the time value of money and risk separately. That is, the CE method uses the discount rate to account for the time value of money and the CEF to account for the riskiness of each individual cash flow. Also, Seitz and Ellison (2005) note that the CE method allows decision makers to incorporate their own risk preferences directly into the analysis.

The major weakness of the CE method lies in the difficulty of determining the correct CEFs. Determining whose certainty equivalents to consider is unclear. Should those of the shareholder be used or should the total project risk be taken into account? The utility theory to determine the CEFs formalizes individuals' preferences, but it is difficult to measure because no appropriate units of measurement exist and external factors can play a role. The risk preferences of individual decision makers differ, are highly subjective, and may change over time. These preferences may even influence the accept/reject decision regarding the project. Further, the CE method suffers from the same limitations as NPV, especially regarding the reinvestment rate assumptions (Hill, 1998). That is, an underlying assumption of the NPV method is that the firm can reinvest any positive cash flows at the rate used to discount the project.

Although the CE method is conceptually superior to the RADR method, practitioners rarely use the CE approach. For example, Kim, Crick, and Kim (1986) offer survey data indicating that only 7 percent of their survey respondents use the CE method, versus 29 percent for the RADR method. Their evidence shows that the most common method is to make risk adjustments subjectively (49 percent). Only 7 percent of their respondents report shortening the payback period to adjust for risk.

THE RISK-ADJUSTED DISCOUNT RATE METHOD

When incorporating risk in the capital budgeting process, the cash flows or the discount rate must be adjusted (see also Chapter 7). Adjusting the discount rate is arguably the method best understood by management, as the principle of increasing a discount rate to reflect higher risk is intuitively appealing. The principle is that a high-risk project is penalized by a higher discount rate. This in turn lowers the NPV of the project and thereby sets a higher benchmark for the project to be accepted or rejected.

The implication of using a higher than normal discount rate to evaluate a risky project is that the overall cost of capital or WACC also increases. When a firm adds a project with more than normal risk to its current portfolio, the overall risk increases and the required rate for shareholders and debt holders also increases, leading to an increase in the WACC. This has several implications for the overall value of the firm, which fall beyond the scope of this discussion.

Calculating the Risk-Adjusted Net Present Value

The risk-adjusted net present value [RADR(NPV)] is calculated in a similar way to the normal NPV, except that WACC is not used as a discount rate for the cash flows. The risk-adjusted discount rate, r, is used instead.

Calculating the RADR(NPV) involves the following steps:

1. Forecast the cash flows for the project.
2. Determine the RADR.
3. Discount the cash flows at the RADR, deduct the initial investment, and obtain the RADR(NPV).

The RADR(NPV) is calculated using the following formula:

$$RADR(NPV) = \sum_{t=1}^{n} \frac{CF_t}{(1+r)} - I_0 \qquad (12.2)$$

where I_0 = initial investment; CF_t = net cash flow in period t; r = risk-adjusted discount rate; and n = expected life of the project (periods 1, 2, 3 ... n).

The decision rule for the RADR(NPV) is the same as that for the NPV. For independent projects, accept the project if the RADR(NPV) is positive or zero, and reject the project if the RADR(NPV) is negative. For mutually exclusive projects, the decision rule is to accept the project with the highest positive RADR(NPV). Accepting a project with a positive RADR(NPV) compensates the firm for risk and adds value. The opposite is true of a project with a negative RADR(NPV). According to Ariel (1998), in capital budgeting, discount rates for risky cash flows are independent of whether the flow is a cost or revenue. That is, risky cash outflows (costs) need not to be discounted at a lower rate, but must be discounted at the same rate than the cash inflows. This chapter adheres to this principle but makes an adjustment to accommodate for a risky initial investment.

Determining the Risk-Adjusted Discount Rate

The firm's WACC is the appropriate discount rate for projects of average or normal risk. According to Clark et al. (1984) the RADR consists of the following three parts:

1. The risk free rate, R_f;
2. An adjustment for the normal business risk of the firm, R_b; and
3. An adjustment for the risk of a specific project, R_p, which can be positive or negative depending on the risk profile of the project in relation to the firm's existing project portfolio.

The RADR can therefore be stated as follows:

$$r = R_f + R_b + R_p \quad \text{and} \quad \text{WACC} = (R_f + R_b) \tag{12.3}$$

The WACC is the rate at which projects of average risk, or risk similar to that of the firm, should be discounted. In such cases, R_p is zero. Where the risk of a project differs from that of the firm, R_p has a positive value (for a higher risk project) or a negative value (for a lower risk project).

The success of the RADR(NPV) method is a function of how accurately management can determine or estimate the RADR, and more specifically, the applicable risk factor, R_p. Unfortunately, there is no easy way to do this. Scenario analysis or computer simulation can give some indication of the riskiness of past projects, but no specific risk adjustment factor flows from this. Management must use its judgment and experience to quantify the risk factor for a specific project. Three major ways are available for doing this: (1) project classification, (2) project-specific discount rates, and (3) the CAPM.

Project Classification

Companies can classify projects according to type and then assign a risk factor to each project type. Projects are classified in a similar way to the CE method. Projects can be classified as replacement, expansion, or R&D projects. Replacement projects pose a lower risk than R&D projects. Assigning a risk factor to each project class is subjective and both management's judgment ability and risk aversion play a role. Exhibit 12.2 lists the types of projects for a hypothetical company with their respective risk adjustment factors.

Replacement projects carry the lowest risk because their performance is known and trusted. Expansion projects usually have a risk premium well above the firm's WACC. Expansion projects in existing product lines have a lower risk premium than that of expansion into new markets where the cash flows are more difficult to predict. R&D has the highest risk factor due to the high level of uncertainty of the cash flows.

Project-Specific Discount Rates

Instead of classifying the various projects into risk categories, management could analyze each project and determine its risk characteristics. The firm analyzes past projects on the basis of the variability of their cash flows and NPV and calculates a coefficient of variation (CV) for each project. The firm can now rank these projects

Exhibit 12.2   Risk Premiums for Different Project Categories for a Hypothetical Company

Risk Category	Type of Project	Risk Adjusted Discount Rate, RADR
RP1	Replacement	WACC
RP2	Replacement	WACC + 2%
RP3	Replacement	WACC + 5%
EP1	Expansion	WACC + 4%
EP2	Expansion	WACC + 8%
RD1	R&D	WACC + 12%

This exhibit lists the various types of projects for a firm. Using a firm's WACC as the appropriate discount rate for projects of average or normal risk, the exhibit also shows the respective risk adjustment factor for each type of project.

according to the CV of their NPVs. Based on this CV, the analyst can decide upon a risk premium. For example, projects with a CV lower than 0.5 represent the lowest risk and can be discounted with the firm's WACC minus, say, 2 percent. Projects with a CV between 0.5 and 1 represent average risk and can be discounted at the WACC. If a project has a CV toward the upper end of the ranking, a risk premium can be added to the WACC to arrive at a risk-adjusted discount rate of WACC plus, say, 8 percent. This discussion shows that all calculations must be executed correctly. This method of project classification is not only firm specific but also industry specific. It arrives at a unique RADR for each situation, mainly because the risk premium to be added or subtracted is based on the analyst's judgment and differs between situations and firms.

The Capital Asset Pricing Model

Analysts and others use the CAPM to calculate the expected return of a well-diversified portfolio of assets at a certain level of risk. The model deals with systematic or market risk only, as it assumes that firm specific risk can be diversified away. Analysts use the CAPM at the firm level, but the model can also be applied at the project level. The model, adapted to determine the expected return of a capital investment project, is calculated as follows:

$$r_p = R_f + \beta_p(R_m - R_f) \tag{12.4}$$

where r_p = return of the capital budgeting project; R_f = risk-free rate of return; β_p = beta coefficient of the project; and R_m = expected return on the market.

The CAPM states that the required rate of return of a specific capital budgeting project is the risk-free rate, plus a risk premium consisting of the market risk premium $(R_m - R_f)$ multiplied by the project specific risk factor, that is, the beta of the project (β_p). The CAPM implies that only the market risk (beta) of the project explains the risk-return relation, but Baker and Powell (2005) cite studies showing that factors such as firm size and the book-to-market equity also affect the risk of a project. An alternative to the CAPM, the multivariable arbitrage pricing theory (APT), includes a number of risk factors to find the required rate of return of an investment project (Ross, 1976). The CAPM is a simplification of a very complex real-world situation. Because the CAPM is easy to use, it is implemented widely in practice despite its disadvantages and assumptions. Numerous empirical studies both support and condemn the CAPM such as Fama and French (2004) and Giaccotto (2007). In spite of any condemnation, analysts use the CAPM to determine the required return for a company, a portfolio of assets, and a single investment project.

This section uses the CAPM as part of the RADR(NPV) to determine the RADR of a single capital budgeting project. Therefore, showing how best to calculate or estimate the three inputs in the model, namely R_f, β_p, and R_m, is important.

The risk-free rate of return is usually regarded as the return on government bonds (Northcott, 1992; Baker and Powell, 2005). However, financial analysts must make sure that the project life of the capital investment project is the same as the time to maturity of the government bond that they use. For example, if the project has a 7-year time period, the yield on the 7-year U.S. Treasury bonds should be used as R_f.

The next input in the CAPM formula is the estimated market return, R_m. The historical market return can be measured by looking at the movement in the total market capitalization (market value) of a stock exchange or index (such as the S&P 500) over a given period. Usually, the longer the period (e.g., the past 10, 20, or 30 years), the more accurately a yearly return can be presented. The problem arises when using historical returns to estimate an expected future return, r_p. Studies that take a forward-looking perspective show that the actual historic average return on equities substantially overstates the market equity premium used by analysts using the CAPM. Jagannathan and Meier (2002) cite various studies in this regard. Brigham and Ehrhardt (2002, p. 429) state that "we use typically a risk premium of 5 percent." Also, measuring and using the total market return when the market consists of hundreds of companies in various sectors is a gross generalization. Remember that the objective is to estimate the required return of a unique project of a single firm. Nevertheless, studies such as Jagannathan and Meier show a historical average market return of between 4.5 percent and 6 percent.

The beta is probably the most difficult CAPM input variable to determine. Unlike the beta of stocks, a project's beta cannot be observed. Further, a project's beta shifts over time (Brealey and Myers, 2003). A project's beta, β_p, measures the sensitivity of the project's return to that of the market. Project betas are usually between 0.5 and 2, where 2 reflects a project with a return twice as volatile and risky as that of the market. Several ways are available for estimating a project's beta. For example, one method is to compare the historical return of similar projects to that of the total market return. This method has the disadvantage of comparing two variables that have little in common. A slightly more sophisticated version of the first method is to calculate the historical return on equity of a whole division of a firm and compare that to the market return such as the S&P 500. Reliable records must exist and the firm must be large enough to have a division within which the project under review can be identified. Lasher (2011) calls this the *accounting beta method*. Lee and Finnerty (1990) and Keown, Martin, and Petty (2008) discuss this method.

Probably the best method to estimate a project specific beta is to examine the risk characteristics of projects undertaken by similar companies. These companies must be publicly traded and in the same line of business as the proposed project. This is called the *pure-play method* (Fuller and Kerr, 1981; Keown et al., 2008). Although finding companies in a similar line of business, especially in a country or industry with limited participants, may be difficult, the betas of those companies are readily available from services such as Bloomberg, Standard & Poor's (S&P), or Value Line. Once the companies have been identified, they can be ranked according to their similarity to the project under consideration, eliminating some and averaging the betas of those most closely resembling the company to determine a project beta. If financial managers can identify pure-play companies very close to the project under review, they can even assign weights to the betas to obtain a weighted average pure-play beta.

Example to Calculate a Project's Required Rate of Return with CAPM

Assume that a company manufactures writing materials and wants to invest in two projects. Project X is a new investment that differs from the current line of business and involves manufacturing ballpoint pens. Project Z involves replacing existing manufacturing equipment to continue the manufacture of pencil erasers. Project Z's risk is similar to the overall company risk and can be evaluated at the company beta of 1.3. Finding pure-play companies that manufacture ballpoint pens proves a challenge, but after an extensive search, the financial manager finds two companies, one with a beta of 1.8 and the other with a beta of 2. The risk-free rate amounts to 5 percent and the company's policy is to use a market risk premium of 6 percent. Based on this information, Project X carries a higher risk than replacement Project Z. Project X has an average pure-play beta of 1.9. The two projects' required rates of return using the CAPM are calculated as follows:

$$\text{Project X}: \quad r_X = 5\% + 1.9(6\%) = 16.4\%$$

$$\text{Project Z}: \quad r_Z = 5\% + 1.3(6\%) = 12.8\%$$

Analysts at the firm should evaluate Project X at a discount rate of 16.4 percent and Project Z at 12.8 percent.

Unlever Beta

In this example, the pure-play companies may be in the same industries and conduct the same type of projects that the analyst wants to evaluate, but they may have different financing structures and therefore different levels of risk. Total risk for a firm consists of a risk-free portion, a risk premium for business risk, and a risk premium for financial risk. In Exhibit 12.3, risk is measured by the total debt ratio. Business risk comes from the normal operation of the firm and its projects. Financial risk refers to the way the firm is financed, essentially the total debt ratio. Financial risk does not influence the firm's business risk.

Both business and financial risk influence a firm's beta. If an analyst wants to use the beta to evaluate a project using the CAPM, the analysis should exclude financial risk and the required rate of return of the project should reflect only business or operational risk. If the pure-play company uses debt in its financing structure, the beta must be adjusted downward (unlevered) to reflect business risk

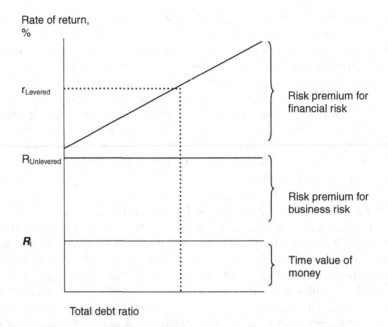

Exhibit 12.3   Relationship between the Required Rate of Return and Financial Leverage
Note: This exhibit indicates the components of the required rate of return for a firm: the time value of money plus the business and the financial (leverage) risk premiums.
Source: Adapted from Baker and Powell (2005, p. 298).

only. If this is done, the required rate of return for the project also decreases. Baker and Powell (2005) propose the following formula to unlever a company's beta:

$$\beta_u = \frac{\beta_{pp}}{1 + (1 - T_{pp})\frac{D_{pp}}{A_{pp}}} \qquad (12.5)$$

where β_u = the unlevered beta of the project; β_{pp} = the levered beta of the pure-play company; T_{pp} = the marginal tax rate of the pure-play company; D_{pp} = the market value of debt of the pure-play company; and A_{pp} = the market value of equity of the pure-play company. This estimate of beta serves as an improved measure of risk for evaluating the project because of removing the financial risk influence.

Example of Unlevering a Beta
The hypothetical company has obtained additional information from the pure-play company that it used to calculate the project's required rate of return in the example. Recall that the betas are 1.8 and 2.0, respectively. The betas are averaged to obtain a beta of 1.9. The financial manager has now established that the two companies have a debt ratio of 35 percent and 45 percent respectively, their tax rate is 30 percent, and the first company's operations are closest to the proposed project.

Therefore, the analyst decides to give the first company an 80 percent weight. The two betas must be unlevered using Formula 12.5 above:

$$\beta_u = \frac{1.8}{1 + (1 - 0.30)(0.35)} = \frac{1.8}{1.25} = 1.44$$

$$\beta_u = \frac{2}{1 + (1 - 0.30)(0.45)} = \frac{2}{1.14} = 1.75$$

$$\beta_{Weighted} = 1.44(0.8) + 1.75(0.20) = 1.50$$

Because the betas have been unlevered and properly weighted, the project beta (β_p) has decreased from 1.9 to 1.5. If the risk-free rate is 5 percent and the market risk premium is 6 percent, the required rate of return for Project X can be calculated as follows:

$$\text{Project X}: \quad r_X = 5\% + 1.5(6\%) = 14\%.$$

This is lower than the original required rate of return of 16.4 percent for this project.

Using the Security Market Line in Capital Budgeting

The security market line (SML) is the graphic presentation of the CAPM. The positive slope of the SML indicates that projects with a higher risk have a higher required rate of return, in contrast to applying a constant WACC to all projects. Presenting the SML graphically permits determining which projects to accept or reject, based on a changing required rate of return (Baker and Powell, 2005). The changing risk level is represented by a corresponding changing required rate of return. Projects that plot above the SML have an expected rate of return higher than the required rate of return. These projects should yield a positive NPV and should be accepted. The opposite is also true. Projects with a required rate of return (risk) higher than the expected rate of return should yield a negative NPV and should be rejected. Thus, the firm should make accept/reject decisions irrespective of the firm's WACC. In fact, the firm can accept a project with an expected rate of return less than its WACC if the (risk-adjusted) required rate of return is less than the expected rate of return. An example follows.

Example Using the SML in Capital Budgeting Decision Making

The hypothetical company is still considering Projects X and Z, but is now also considering Project Y. Exhibit 12.4 summarizes specifics about these projects. As Exhibit 12.5 shows, plotting the three projects provides a means of determining the accept/reject decision for each project.

Project X falls in the acceptance region above the SML and Project Z in the rejection region below the SML. Project X has an expected rate of return of 18 percent, while its required rate of return is only 14 percent. Project Z has a required rate of return of 12.8 percent. This required rate of return of Project Z lies on the intersection of the SML and r, which is the WACC of the firm based on the fact that the company beta is 1.3. However, the expected rate of return of Project Z is only 11 percent and the project should therefore be rejected.

Exhibit 12.4   Required and Expected Rates of Return for a Hypothetical Company

Project	Beta, β	Required Rate of Return, r (%)	Expected Rate of Return, IRR (%)	Decision
X	1.5	14.0	18.0	Accept
Z	1.3	12.8	11.0	Reject
Y	0.7	9.2	10.0	Accept

This exhibit sets out the expected and required rates of return for three projects, the beta and the accept/reject decision for each project.

Now consider Project Y. The CAPM can be used to calculate the required rate of return as 9.2 percent ($r_Y = 5\% + 0.7(6\%) = 9.2\%$). This required rate of return is less than the firm's WACC of 12.8 percent, but the expected rate of return of Project Y is 10 percent, so the firm should accept the project.

The project acceptance region is not above the firm's WACC of 12.8 percent but it is above the SML. This illustrates the value of the CAPM and the SML. Its application adjusts the required rates of return for risk; it modifies the accept/reject decision so that it is improved from just using the WACC for all projects. Using WACC as a hurdle rate in the evaluation of the three projects would have incorrectly caused Project Z to be accepted and Project Y to be rejected. Shareholder value would have been destroyed. Instead, using RADRs facilitates the process of making correct accept/reject decisions. The riskiness of projects differs and is also different from the WACC of the firm. If a project with a lower relative risk is accepted, the

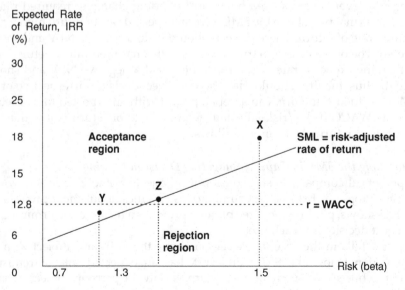

Exhibit 12.5   The SML and WACC

Note: The SML is the graphical exposition of CAPM and is used here to place three projects in the accept/reject region, based on their expected rates of return, using a firm's WACC as the appropriate discount rate for projects of average or normal risk.

WACC or hurdle rate should decrease. Using the CAPM to determine the correct RADR for each project and the SML to determine the accept/reject criteria enhances shareholder value.

Strengths and Weaknesses of the CAPM
Although the CAPM's appeal largely stems from its ease of use, this method has been challenged in the academic literature (Roll, 1977; Myers and Turnbull, 1977; Ang and Lewellen, 1982; Lee and Finnerty, 1990; Lasher, 2011) Jagannathan and Meier (2002) cite numerous studies in this regard, especially one by Fama and French (1992). The implicit assumptions of the CAPM (in the model itself and in its application) are as follows: The market is efficient; the betas derived are stable; the RADR derived from the CAPM can be used for a multi-period project; the beta can be unlevered with relative ease (that is, the risk of debt can simply be adjusted with the debt ratio and the corporate tax rate); and capital markets are perfect.

The main problem seems to be with finding a correct beta for the project, which means identifying an applicable pure-play company. Furthermore, assuming that a project's beta will not change over time is unrealistic because the risk-free rate and the market return change according to Brealey and Myers (2003) as well as Baker and Powell (2005). As previously mentioned, the market risk premium is controversial and depends on the subjective judgment of analysts. Some projects can become less risky over time while the risk level of others increases. A more basic problem is that beta considers only systematic risk. Disregarding unsystematic risk may be inappropriate. Total risk, as measured by a project's standard deviation of returns, is higher than systematic risk because it consists of both systematic and unsystematic risk (Lasher, 2011). Lewellen (1977), Jagannathan and Meier (2002), and Giaccotto (2007) discuss the problems with the CAPM, especially its use in capital budgeting.

Despite its imperfections and practical difficulties, the CAPM approach is probably the most correct way to determine a RADR, especially when it is extended with the SML to incorporate accept/reject decisions. Part of the strength of the CAPM method is that decision makers are forced to at least consider the risk issue rather than mechanically applying a single discount rate to all capital investments. In a survey of financial practice, Graham and Harvey (2001) find that almost 74 percent of the responding firms in their sample always or almost always use the CAPM to estimate the cost of capital.

Example in Calculating the RADR(NPV)
Assume that a company wants to evaluate an investment project involving the production of a new product. The initial investment is $300,000. Analysts estimate that the project will generate after tax cash flows of $50,000 in Year 1, $100,000 in each of Years 2 and 3, and $200,000 in Year 4. The firm's WACC is 11 percent, but the board of directors believes that, due to the uncertain nature of this investment, the project should be adjusted for risk. Specifically, the board thinks that the discount rate should be adjusted to compensate for the risk. The financial manager proposes using the CAPM to determine the RADR. After careful research, analysts provide the following additional information: the return on the government bonds is 6 percent, the total market return is 13 percent, and the project's beta is estimated

to be 2.0 based on using an average of comparable companies. What are the NPV and RADR(NPV) for the firm?

Suggested Solution
Discounting the firm's cash flows at the firm's WACC of 11 percent results in an NPV of \$31,073. The RADR is calculated using the CAPM as follows: $r_p = 6\% + 2(13\% - 6\%) = 20\%$.

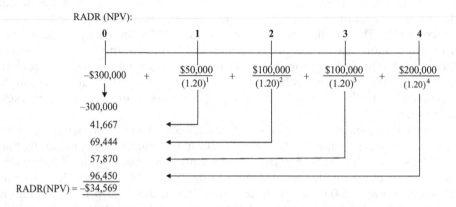

RADR (NPV):

According to the normal NPV, the project should be accepted given a positive NPV of \$31,073. Yet, the RADR(NPV) is –\$34,569, indicating that the project on risk-adjusted basis will destroy value if it is accepted. Thus, the firm should reject the project. However, the IRR of a project can be an indication to management what the RADR should be to accept or reject the project. The IRR of this project is 14.9 percent. Therefore, if the project should have a RADR of less than 14.9 percent, it will have a positive RADR(NPV) and should then be accepted.

Strengths and Weaknesses of the RADR(NPV)
The main advantage of the RADR method is its apparent simplicity—the principle that a relatively high-risk project's cash flows must be discounted at a higher rate is both appealing and relatively simple to apply. The opposite applies for a relatively low-risk project and its cash flows—discount the project at a lower rate. This method leads to an adjusted NPV, which provides the basis for making an accept/reject decision.

The RADR method has several drawbacks. More than four decades ago, Robichek and Myers (1966) started to highlight conceptual problems with the RADR. The greatest obstacle seems to be determining the RADR and more specifically the inputs in the CAPM. The same shortcomings and problems already discussed concerning the CAPM apply here. Other problems include the difficulty of obtaining a project beta (Northcott, 1992) and using judgment to get a market risk premium (Lumby, 1991). Butler and Schachter (1989) discuss the problem of estimation risk and its influence on the RADR. A high probably exists that given the same set of circumstances, different financial managers will each have a different RADR. Also, the same RADR is used over the entire project life. This amplifies the risk adjustment over time, penalizing the project based on a lower NPV, and can lead to unnecessary rejections. No adjustment is made to a changing riskiness due to the time factor (Haley, 1984; Giaccotto, 2007). Over time, some projects might become more risky while others might become more certain. Categorizing projects into risk classes is also subjective. In practice, firms deal with projects on an individualized or single-project basis (Clark et al., 1984). Ouederni and Sullivan (1991) contend that traditional approaches to capital budgeting have only been partially success-ful in explicitly accounting for risk and offers a utilitarian semivariance model for risk treatment in the evaluation of a capital budgeting project.

COMPARING THE CE AND RADR METHODS

One of the criticisms of the RADR method is the fact that analysts often categorize projects into risk groups and use a constant discount rate over time. Further, the application of the relatively high RADR increases the discount factor over time. CEs address this problem in the sense that analysts adjust cash flows for each project for each period, generally on a yearly basis. Analysts further adjust cash flows with the relatively low risk-free rate, which reduces the compounding discount rate effect over time. Thus, the CE method seemingly has a more refined risk-adjusting process than the RADR approach. Similar to the RADR method, the CE method suffers because it is based on personal judgments involving the inputs. Analysts may choose the method (CE or RADR) having in their opinion the most dependable set of inputs or estimates.

Herbst (1982) argues that, if the CEF relates the cash flow to its expected value and if R_f is the risk-free rate and r_p is the risk-adjusted discount rate, the relationship between these variables can be stated as follows:

$$\overset{\text{CE}}{\frac{\text{CEF} \times \text{CF}_t}{(1 + R_f)^t}} = \overset{\text{RADR}}{\frac{\text{CF}_t}{(1 + r_p)^t}} \tag{12.6}$$

which, after rearranging terms, yields:

$$r_p = \frac{(1 + R_f)}{\text{CEF}^{1/t}} - 1 \tag{12.7}$$

Analysts who are perfectly consistent in applying the CE and the RADR meth-ods should obtain identical NPVs, therefore the CE(NPV) should be equal to the RADR(NPV). However, the question is whether decision makers use only one or both methods. Vishwanath (2007) reports on a survey of Fortune 1000 companies reporting that of those respondents incorporating risk into their capital budgeting decisions, 39 percent of respondents risk-adjust the cash flows of a project (CE method), 32 percent risk-adjust the cost of capital applied to each project (RADR method), 20 percent adjust both cash flows and discount rate, while the rest use some other method. The study reports that almost one-third of respondents do not adjust for risk. Ho and Pike (1991) find that firms prefer relatively simple risk adjustments and sensitivity analysis, while advanced risk analysis techniques such as CAPM are still in an experimental stage in practice. Relative simple approaches tend not to be replaced by more advanced ones, but are used to supplement the analysis.

SUMMARY AND CONCLUSIONS

Analysts should incorporate risk into the capital budgeting process because projects may have different levels of risk. Some projects have a risk level similar to that of the firm; other carry a risk level less than that of the firm; and still others have a markedly higher level of risk. The level of difficulty in estimating future cash flows and returns varies for each project. Because both projects and firms can have markedly different levels of risk, the level of return required to compensate for the risk also varies.

This chapter examines several methods used to incorporate risk in the capital budgeting process. The adjusted payback period method is helpful because it indicates the liquidity of the project and supplements other methods. The CE method focuses on adjusting the cash flows of the project to compensate for risk. Although this method suffers because of judgments and personal utility preferences, it customizes the incorporation of risk for each project. That is, the analyst adjusts the periodic cash flows and discounts these adjusted cash flows by the risk-free rate.

The RADR method of incorporating risk is by far the most appealing method and the most popular in practice. Several methods are available to obtain the discount rate such as using project risk classification. To mitigate personal judgment from the process of determining the discount rate, analysts often use the CAPM. Because the CAPM incorporates several restrictive assumptions, finance researchers have scrutinized this approach for decades. Capital investment projects with higher than normal risk require using a higher discount rate than a firm's WACC. Because analysts do not change this rate over the project's life, the continuous use of a high discount rate in contrast to a lower rate aggravates the compounding effect over time (Haley, 1984). Both the CE and RADR methods produce a NPV upon which the firm can base an accept/reject decision. If the firm consistently applies the inputs of these methods, the same NPV should result.

Ultimately, many decisions regarding which method to use, which inputs to apply, and where to set crucial benchmarks for the accept/reject decision rest with individual analysts. These analysts face the important task of incorporating risk into the capital budgeting process so that every accept/reject decision, with the possible exception of mandatory projects, adds value to the firm.

DISCUSSION QUESTIONS

1. List the basic steps involved in using the CE method to incorporate risk in the capital budgeting process.
2. List the basic steps involved in using risk-adjusted discount rates to obtain an adjusted NPV. How does this process relate to the CAPM?
3. A company wants to replace a machine with a modern, more efficient model with a longer life expectancy. The equipment requires an initial investment of

$600,000 in Year 0. The expected cash flows and standard deviations are as follows:

Year	Cash Flow	Standard Deviation
1	$140,000	$15,000
2	160,000	50,000
3	300,000	100,000
4	400,000	120,000

The firm's WACC is 16 percent and the risk-free rate is 6 percent. The analyst develops the following CEFs.

	Certainty Equivalent Factor (CEF)			
Coefficient of Variation (CV)	Year 1	Year 2	Year 3	Year 4
CV ≤ 0.30	0.95	0.92	0.89	0.85
CV > 0.30	0.85	0.82	0.78	0.73

What are the project's NPV and its CE(NPV)?

4. Millennium Catering Company is considering two mutually exclusive investments. The company wants to use the RADR method in its analysis. Millennium's WACC is 15 percent, which is similar to the total market return using the CAPM. The risk-free rate of return is 7 percent. Analysts provide the following additional information about the investments:

	Project X	Project Y
Initial investment	$400,000	$500,000
Year	Cash Flow	Cash flow
1	$100,000	$150,000
2	$200,000	$200,000
3	$300,000	$300,000
4	$300,000	$400,000
Project beta	1.5	2.0

What is the RADR(NPV) for each project? Which project should be preferred? Why?

5. Compare and contrast the CE and RADR methods. Can these two methods provide the same adjusted NPV? Why or why not?

REFERENCES

Ang, James S., and Wilbur G. Lewellen. 1982. "Risk Adjustment in Capital Investment Project Evaluations." *Financial Management* 11:2, 5–14.

Ariel, Robert. 1998. "Risk-adjusted Discount Rates and the Present Value of Risky Costs." *Financial Review* 33:1, 17–30.

Baker, H. Kent, and Gary E. Powell. 2005. *Understanding Financial Management—A Practical Guide*. Malden, MA: Blackwell.

Baker, H. Kent, Tarun K. Mukherjee, and Magli Van Belle. 2003. "Using Certainty Equivalents to Evaluate Risky Projects." *Corporate Finance Review*, January/February, 20–24.

Bierman, Jr. Harold, and Seymour Smidt. 2007. *Advanced Capital Budgeting—Refinements in the Economic Analysis of Investment Projects.* New York: Routledge.

Blatt, John M. 1979. "Investment Evaluation under Uncertainty." *Financial Management* 8:2, 66–81.

Boyle, Glenn, and Graeme Guthrie. 2006. "Payback without Apology." *Accounting and Finance* 46:1, 1–10.

Brealey, Richard A., and Stewart C. Myers, 2003. *Principles of Corporate Finance,* 7th ed. New York: McGraw-Hill.

Brigham, Eugene F. and Michael C. Ehrhardt. 2002. *Financial Management: Theory and Practice,* 10th ed. Orlando, FL: Harcourt College Publishers.

Butler, J. S., and Barry Schachter. 1989. "The Investment Decision: Estimation Risk and Risk-Adjusted Discount Rates." *Financial Management* 18:4, 13–21.

Clark, John J., Thomas J. Hindelang, and Robert E. Pritchard. 1984. *Capital Budgeting. Planning and Control of Capital Expenditures,* 2nd ed. New Jersey: Prentice-Hall.

Fama, Eugene F., and Kenneth R. French. 1992. "The Cross-Section of Expected Stock Returns," *Journal of Finance* 47:2, 427–465.

Fama, Eugene F., and Kenneth R. French. 2004. "The Capital Asset Pricing Model: Theory and Evidence." *Journal of Economic Perspectives* 18:3, 25-46.

Fuller, Russell J., and Halbert S. Kerr. 1981. "Estimating the Divisional Cost of Capital: An Analysis of the Pure-Play Technique." *Journal of Finance* 36:5, 997–1009.

Giaccotto, Carmelo. 2007. "Discounting Mean Reverting Cash Flows with the Capital Asset Pricing Model." *Financial Review* 42:2, 247–265.

Graham, John R., and Campbell R. Harvey. 2001. "The Theory and Practice of Corporate Finance: Evidence from the Field." *Journal of Financial Economics* 60:2–3, 187–244.

Haley, Charles W. 1984. "Valuation and Risk-Adjusted Discount Rates." *Journal of Business Finance and Accounting* 11:3, 349–353.

Herbst, Anthony F. 1982. *Capital Budgeting: Theory, Quantitative Methods and Applications.* New York: Harper & Row.

Hill, Allan. 1998. *Corporate Finance.* London: Pitman.

Ho, Simon S. M., and Richard H. Pike. 1991. "Risk Analysis in Capital Budgeting Contexts: Simple or Sophisticated?" *Accounting and Business Research* 21:83, 227–238.

Jagannathan, Ravi, and Iwan Meier. 2002. "Do We Need CAPM for Capital Budgeting?" *Financial Management* 31:4, 55–77.

Kee, Robert, and Bruce Bublitz. 1988. "The Role of Payback in the Investment Process." *Accounting and Business Research* 18:70, 149–155.

Keown, Arthur J., John D. Martin, and J. William Petty. 2008. *Foundations of Finance: The Logic and Practice of Financial Management,* 6th ed. Upper Saddle River, NJ: Pearson Education.

Kim, Suk H., Trevor Crick, and Seung H. Kim. 1986. "Do Executives Practice What Academics Preach?" *Management Accounting* 68:5, 49–52.

Lasher, William R. 2011. *Practical Financial Management,* 6th ed. Mason, OH: South-Western, Cengage Learning.

Lee, Cheng F., and Joseph E. Finnerty. 1990. *Corporate Finance—Theory, Method, and Applications.* Orlando, FL: Harcourt Brace Jovanovich.

Lewellen, Wilbur G. 1977. "Some Observations on Risk-Adjusted Discount Rates." *Journal of Finance* 32:4, 1331–1337.

Lumby, Stephen. 1991. *Investment Appraisal and Financing Decisions,* 4th ed. London: Chapman & Hall.

Moyer, R. Charles, James R. McGuigan, and Ramesh P. Rao. 2005. *Contemporary Financial Management Fundamentals.* Willard, OH: Thomson South-Western.

Myers, Stewart C., and Stuart M. Turnbull. 1977. "Capital Budgeting and the Capital Asset Pricing Model: Good News and Bad News." *Journal of Finance* 32:2, 321–332.

Northcott, Deryl. 1992. *Capital Investment Decision-Making.* London: Academic Press.

Ouederni, Bechir N., and William G. Sullivan. 1991. "A Semi-Variance Model for Incorporating Risk into Capital Investment Analysis." *Engineering Economist* 36:2, 83–106.
Robichek, Alexander A., and Stewart C. Myers. 1965. *Optimal Financing Decisions.* Englewood Cliffs, NJ: Prentice Hall.
Robichek, Alexander A., and Stewart C. Myers. 1966. "Conceptual Problems in the Use of Risk-Adjusted Discount Rates." *Journal of Finance* 21:4, 727–730.
Roll, Richard. 1977. "A Critique of the Asset Pricing Theory's Tests; Part 1: On Past and Potential Testability of the Theory." *Journal of Financial Economics* 4:2, 129–176.
Ross, Stephen A. 1976. "The Arbitrage Theory of Capital Asset Pricing." *Journal of Economic Theory* 13:3, 341–360.
Seitz, Neil, and Mitch Ellison. 2005. *Capital Budgeting and Long-Term Financial Decisions*, 4th ed. Mason, OH: Thomson South-Western.
Shapiro, Alan C. 2005. *Capital Budgeting and Investment Analysis.* Upper Saddle River, NJ: Pearson Education.
Sick, Gordon. 1986. "A Certainty-Equivalent Approach to Capital Budgeting." *Financial Management* 15:4, 23–32.
Vishwanath, S. R. 2007. *Corporate Finance Theory and Practice.* New Delhi: Sage.

ABOUT THE AUTHORS

John H. Hall was awarded a BCom and BCom (Hons) (Economics) by the University of Port Elizabeth, South Africa, after which he worked with the South African Revenue Service as a tax inspector. He completed his MBA at the University of Pretoria, South Africa, in 1989, and then worked as the financial manager of a civil engineering and manufacturing firm. He joined the University of Pretoria as a lecturer in financial and investment management in 1994. He completed his DBA at the University of Pretoria in 1998 and currently is an Associate Professor. He has published numerous articles in scholarly journals, received best paper awards, and presented research papers at conferences both locally and internationally. Professor Hall also presents short courses in financial management and consults in a wide range of issues in the private sector.

Wim Westerman is an Assistant Professor at the Faculty of Economics and Business at the University of Groningen, where he received his Ph.D. in 2003. Besides teaching courses in financial management, Professor Westerman contributes research courses, supervises master theses, and coordinates the International Financial Management program. His research interests focus on capital budgeting, corporate valuation, treasury management, and management control. He is an editor of the *Journal of Corporate Treasury Management* and a fellow of the University of Groningen Center for International Banking, Insurance and Finance and its Energy and Sustainability Center. Professor Westerman initiated the global Center for Energy and Value Issues.

CHAPTER 13

Capital Budgeting with Political/Country Risk

YACINE BELGHITAR
Senior Lecturer in Finance, Middlesex University

EPHRAIM CLARK
Professor of Finance, Middlesex University and Univ. Lille Nord de
France-SKEMA Research Center

INTRODUCTION

The notion of political risk emerged in the literature of the 1960s with such authors as Usher (1965), Zenoff (1967), and Root (1968) in response to the opportunities and risks of doing business in the newly formed countries created from postwar decolonization. From the outset, authors treated political risk in the vague, general terms of investment climate. As noted by many authors such as Kobrin (1979), Brewer (1981), Merrill (1982), Simon (1982), Fitzpatrick (1983), Desta (1985), Howell and Chaddick (1994), and Rivoli and Brewer (1997), there is no consensus on a comprehensive definition of political risk.

Various terminologies that are used to deal with similar and/or overlapping issues compound the difficulty of reaching a comprehensive definition of political risk and agreeing on its meaning. When dealing with the risk of doing business abroad, the two terms most frequently encountered are political risk and country risk. Yet, others refer to cross-border risk and sovereign risk. Political risk is the oldest terminology. Country risk became popular in the banking industry in the 1970s and 1980s in the aftermath of the international debt crises of those two decades. The term country risk as opposed to political risk has been gaining ascendency because it has a broader meaning in that it can include any risk specific to a given country, whereas political risk restricts the risks to those that are exclusively political in nature.

In the financial literature, risk is often defined as the variance or standard deviation of a performance measure. In this context, political risk can result in gains as well as losses and refers to the probability of occurrence of political events that will change the prospects for the profitability of a given investment. Another approach adopts a more practical stance and analyzes risk as a negative outcome. In this context, political risk involves only a loss and refers to the probability that a loss-causing event will occur (i.e., downside risk).

For risk assessment, some authors such as Robock (1971), Haendel, West, and Meadow (1975), Kobrin (1979), and Feils and Sabac (2000) focus on political risk as it affects the volatility of an investment's overall profitability both negatively and positively. Other authors, such as Root (1968), Simon (1982), Howell and Chaddick (1994), Roy and Roy (1994), and Meldrum (2000), adopt a more practical stance and analyze risk as an explicit negative event that causes an actual loss or a reduction of the investment's expected return. Tests of political risk on investment outcomes reflect these two approaches. Cutler, Poterba, and Summers (1989), Chan and Wei (1996), Bittlingmayer (1998), and Kim and Mei (2001) consider political risk with respect to stock market volatility. Other papers, such as Bekaert (1995), Cosset and Suret (1995), and Bekaert and Harvey (1997) focus on losses and test for the impact of political risk regarding stock market performance. Other studies, such as Aggarwal, Rao, and Hiraki (1989), and Bekaert, Erb, Harvey, and Viskanta (1998), establish the skewness of the return distribution at the international level, thus offering a further case for limiting analysis to downside risk versus the increasingly challenged choice of variance.

A review of the literature over the last 40 years shows that the political/country risk field always refers to doing business abroad and includes a wide range of different situations. Bouchet, Clark, and Groslambert (2003) provide a review of the literature. The particular features of each investment or transaction type must be taken into account. Adopting an overall perspective is also necessary because the sources of risk all interact and possibly impact several if not all sectors of an economy. For example, Meldrum (2000) says that all business transactions involve some degree of risk. When business transactions occur across international borders, they carry additional risks not present in domestic transactions. These additional risks, called country risks, typically include risks arising from various national differences in economic structures, policies, sociopolitical institutions, geography, and currencies. Country risk analysis attempts to identify the potential for these risks to decrease the expected return of a cross-border investment. This definition rejoins the early work of Gabriel (1966) and Stobaugh (1969a, 1969b) on how the investment climate in a foreign country and at home may differ. These works also highlight the specific risks encountered when doing business abroad (i.e., outside the national borders of a firm's country of origin). Of particular note is that country risk exists irrespective of the level of a country's economic development. Even the most economically advanced countries can generate a substantial degree of country risk.

Until now, no comprehensive theory of political/country risk has yet been formulated because of the multiplicity of the sources of risk, the complexity of their interactions, and the variety of social sciences involved. The literature has simply built on the implicit assumption that, for a given country, imbalances in the economic, social, and political fields are likely to increase the risk of investing there. However, a comprehensive theory would greatly help to identify the variables at stake and make testing the respective relevance of the various approaches possible. So far, most of the research merely consists of classifying and describing various potential sources of risk and assessing methods that turn these elements into numerical variables without any scientific justification.

Kobrin (1979) and Desta (1985) identify two main sources of political risk. The first focuses on government or sovereign interference with business operations.

This focus refers to political risks that arise from the actions of national governments who interfere with or prevent business transactions, change the terms of agreements, or cause the confiscation of wholly or partially foreign owned business property (e.g., Zenoff, 1967; Aliber, 1975; Baglini, 1976; Feils and Sabac, 2000). The second source of political risk, represented by Root (1968), Robock (1971), and Haendel et al. (1975), refers to environmental instability and its impact on business conditions. This line provides a broader perspective and includes, besides governmental sources of risk, any other causes that may impede the functioning of any foreign organization abroad.

Over the last four decades, a series of crises has mainly driven research in the field of country risk: the political crises of the 1960s and 1970s, the debt crises of the 1970s and 1980s, and the financial crises of the 1990s. Each type of crisis induced a plethora of papers that tried to explain ex post the causes of the foregoing events. The period ranging from the 1960s to the end of the 1970s featured studies on multinational corporations (MNCs) and their exposure to political risk. At that time, many countries had just recovered their sovereignty from colonial powers and gradually had started to question the benefits of having extremely powerful foreign firms nesting in their backyard. The research over this period primarily concerned the influence of governments on firms doing business abroad. The second series of crises took place in the 1970s and 1980s with the oil price shock and the advent of the international debt crisis. A large part of the literature examined creditworthiness assessment. Finally, the third series of crises emerged in the 1990s with the Mexican peso crisis in 1994, the Asian meltdown in 1997, the Russian default, and a series of other currency crises in the late 1990s. Although currency and banking crises have occurred regularly over the last decades, the crises of the 1990s generated a particularly rich literature on banking and currency crises.

The remainder of the chapter consists of the following sections. The next section discusses the different methods used to analyze political/country risk. In particular, this section compares and contrasts the following methods: comparative techniques, analytical techniques, econometric techniques, and Monte Carlo simulation. Following that is a section on how to implement political/country risk in the capital budgeting decision. The section shows how to account for political/country risk in the net present value (NPV) framework. The final section summarizes and concludes.

METHODS AND TECHNIQUES OF POLITICAL/COUNTRY RISK ANALYSIS

As discussed above, the sources of political/country risk are many and varied. They include all aspects of a country's economic, financial, social, and political organization as well as its geographic location and strategic importance. As an example, comprehensive checklists of political/country risk sources include almost every situation that could conceivably occur in any given country. Such sources include war, occupation by a foreign power, civil war, revolution, riots, disorders, takeover by an extremist government, state takeover of the enterprise, and indigenization (forced relinquishment of control by foreign owners of enterprises). Other sources of political/country risk are politically motivated debt default, renegotiation or rescheduling, unilateral change in debt service terms, and overextension in external borrowing. Still other sources relate to the economy including depression or severe recession, mismanagement of the economy, credit squeeze, long-term slowdown in real GNP growth, strikes, rapid rise in production costs, fall in export earnings, sudden increase in food and/or energy imports, and devaluation or depreciation of the currency. Finally, natural calamities can lead to political/country risk.

Potential entries in a list like this are virtually limitless and the heterogeneous nature of the information suggests that risk identification is a major problem. Furthermore, a problem also exists in how to digest this menu of diverse information. Even if the analytical assessment is entirely accurate, determining how to translate the assessment into a comprehensible statement of the consequences for a foreign direct investment (FDI) is unclear.

An analysis of the effects of political risk often divides the events affecting foreign operations into three general categories: hard political risk, administrative or soft political risk, and social risk. The first group includes expropriation, confiscation, nationalization, forced local shareholding. The second group covers decisions such as control of prices, foreign exchange, and remittances. Finally, social risk encompasses such areas as strikes, lack of an experienced labor force, war, and ethnic strife. The methods for analyzing political risk can be grouped into three categories: comparative, analytical, and econometric.

Comparative Techniques: Rating Systems

The aim of rating systems in political risk analysis is to compare all countries or some subset of them, such as the less developed countries, according to an analytical grid based on a set of relevant parameters. Because of the nature and scope of political risk, the set of what is deemed to be the relevant parameters is wide ranging and often includes elements that are difficult to measure with any precision.

The rating approach generally proceeds in two stages. First, each country is graded on the parameters selected as judgmental criteria. Second, the resulting data are weighted into a global rating, which makes comparing all the countries on the same scale possible. The quality of the rating depends on the accuracy of the analysis as well as on the relevance of the judgmental parameters and the weights assigned to each.

Many types of rating systems are available. For instance, Business Environment Risk Intelligence (BERI) S.A. covers about 50 countries and has been available since the mid-1970s. BERI provides four types of ratings: (1) the Political Risk Index (PRI), (2) the Operations Risk Index (ORI), (3) the Remittance and Repatriation Factor (R Factor), and (4) the Composite Score, which represents a combination of the other three. For each type of rating, an assessment of the present situation as well as a one-year and a five-year forecast is published.

Political Risk Services (PRS) publishes Political Risk Services (PRS) as well as the International Country Risk Guide (ICRG). The PRS method is a kind of "modified Delphi technique" that treats and systematically processes several experts' opinion for each country under review. It produces 18-month and five-year forecasts. The International Country Risk Guide (ICRG) covers about 140 countries.

It produces three distinct risk categories on a monthly basis: political, economic, and financial, as well as a composite risk rating derived from the previous three indexes. ICRG assesses the current situation and makes forecasts over one-year and five-year time horizons.

The Economist Intelligence Unit (EIU) produces country risk ratings for 100 developing countries on a quarterly basis. The EIU method flows from experts' answers to a series of 77 predetermined qualitative and quantitative questions. It results in a 100-point index (the higher the score, the riskier is the country), which is divided into five bands from A (lowest risk) to E (highest risk). Four general risk categories are analyzed (political risk, economic policy risk, economic structure risk, and liquidity risk) and are combined into an overall risk index. Besides this broad macro measure of risk, EIU produces other more investment-specific micro risk ratings (currency risk, sovereign debt risk, and banking sector risk) that address the particular needs and concerns of certain groups of investors.

The weaknesses of comparative systems are obvious. First, no objective theoretical basis exists for including or excluding the numerous parameters employed in the different rating systems. Second, the process for attributing the respective weights given to the various parameters has no indisputable foundation. Different weights might give different results. Third, the same grid is applied to all countries, whatever their regional location or specific characteristics. Moreover, "extreme" situations (e.g., the Iranian revolution or the Gulf War) cannot be anticipated from comparative approaches. Nevertheless, comparative methods can be useful as a screening process designed to eliminate the countries that are completely unacceptable.

Analytical Techniques

In contrast to the rating method, the analytical techniques focus on one country at a time. Among these techniques are (1) the special report approach, (2) the probabilistic approach, (3) the sociological approach based on dynamic segmentation, (4) the multicriteria methods, and (5) the expert systems approach.

Special Report Approach

The special report approach to political risk analysis focuses on one country, is descriptive, and involves one or several experts who examine the key variables that are supposed to describe a given country's main characteristics and who communicate their findings in the form of a special report. Thus, for each individual country being considered, the report usually contains an analysis of the political, social, and economic outlook that explicitly takes into account the specificities of the local environment. The special reports usually sum up a country's overall strengths and weaknesses and focus on such aspects as the country's political environment, the major characteristics of the current regime, the degree of stability of the domestic currency, the tax system, the regulations pertaining to foreign investment, the social structure and climate, and the country's economic prospects. The advantages of the special report are its ability to focus on the particularities of each country, low cost, and rapidity. The method's main drawbacks are its subjectivity, lack of scientific analysis, and relative partiality. In fact, the quality of any special report basically depends on the capabilities and intuition of the analyst.

Probabilistic Approach
The probabilistic approach uses the decision tree methodology to compute alternative outcomes, each one receiving a certain probability of occurrence associated with specific measures concerning foreign investment. For example, the outcome of a definitive election in a South American country might be depicted by two scenarios: The current government remains in power or the opposition takes over. Each scenario might have a different probability, such as 75 percent for the current regime and 25 percent for the opposition, but the probabilities must sum to 100 percent. Probabilities are then assigned to choices facing each government. For example, if the current government remains in power, its choices might be a subsidy for foreign investment with a 60 percent probability or the status quo with a 40 percent probability. If the opposition wins, its choices might be an increased tax on the foreign operation with a 70 percent probability or expropriation with a 30 percent probability. The effects of each choice are then calculated. The subsidy might make the investment worth $150 million, the status quo $100 million, the increased tax $75 million, and expropriation $10 million. The value of the investment is found by multiplying the joint probability by the value of each outcome and summing up across the products.

The same methodology can be applied to more complicated situations with several steps and numerous possible outcomes. Yet, the obvious difficulty is calculating the different probabilities and estimating the effect that the different measures will have on the outcome of the investment.

Sociological Approach
The sociological approach to political risk analysis seeks to identify a set of variables that can be specific to each country as a means of understanding the country's "degree of stability." The variables can range from state hegemony and political terrorism to such esoteric concepts as a democratic tradition and the capacity to live in peace. Each country requires a specific set of variables and a distinct methodology. The advantage of this approach is its tailor-made nature that makes individualizing the analysis possible. The disadvantages are that it lacks scientific rigor and is difficult to apply in a comparative context.

One of the oldest and most respected techniques of the sociological approach is the "dynamic segmentation" methodology, known as the ALLY method. The ALLY method seeks to analyze the fundamental trends of a country that are likely to influence the relationship between the investing company and the political powers. Dynamic segmentation divides a society into various behavior-homogenous groups, called segments. A segment can be socioeconomic or ethnic. The incumbent power in the society is based on the coalition of a group of these segments. The segments outside the coalition form the opposition. As time passes, new segments may appear and others disappear, but many of them continue to exist no matter what coalitions come to power. The technique considers the fact that demographic, economic, and social developments in a given country can, in the space of a few years, substantially modify the relative importance of the individual segments. However, certain segments occupy a pivotal position, thereby guaranteeing them a place in all possible power coalitions. Therefore, focusing information gathering on the medium-term developments and short-term fluctuations of these pivotal segments is essential.

Some segments have natural or historic ties, which make possible identifying the coalitions of segments that are likely to wield power. From these, the coalition of maximum homogeneity and importance is selected and its future evolution is assessed by analyzing whether the coalition will stay in power or when it will be replaced by another coalition. Based on these forecasts, the investing foreign corporation will attempt to take advantage of the situation by modifying its policy.

Multicriteria Method

The multicriteria method aims at supporting decision makers, experts, or analysts in their judgmental assessment. It has been applied to country choice in global index funds (Khoury, Martel, and Yougourou, 1994), portfolio management (Zopounidis, Godefroid, and Hurson, 1995) and country risk (Cosset, Siskos, and Zopounidis, 1992; Clark, Cusin, and Lesourd, 1998). The multicriteria method starts with a decision-support tool that serves as an analytical guideline, which makes the final decision easier and quicker to achieve. The final decision, however, is still subjective in that it is based entirely on the analyst's judgment. The multicriteria method tackles a decision problem rather than a modeling problem. The decision could be described in terms of preference theory. An aggregation function or a partial aggregation function, which, in effect, is a utility function, is determined. The possible decisions are then classed in terms of the values of this function. Typically, these methods employ a stepwise process in which the departures from the initial goal are introduced into the problem while taking into account the relative importance of each criterion.

Expert Systems Approach

The expert systems approach requires a database and an inference paradigm. The database includes quantitative information such as population, economic growth, and current account balance, as well as symbolic information that ranges from management definitions and rules to the description of international institutions (e.g., the International Monetary Fund and World Bank), national institutions (e.g., the government, central bank, and armed forces), and private agents (e.g., multinational and domestic firms). The inference paradigm replicates the thinking of an expert through chains of causality such as event x causes effect y that causes effect z.

Econometric Techniques

Econometric techniques for political risk estimation, in contrast to the techniques discussed above, are completely objective. Econometric analysis starts from the assumption that certain economic indicators such as growth rates, debt ratios, current account balance, and other economic measures have predictive value. During the late 1970s and early 1980s, many banks began to develop their own econometric models. The World Bank and several central banks including the Bank of England also experimented with such models. Although the shortcomings of econometric forecasting are well known, econometric analysis can be a powerful complement to the comparative and analytical techniques described above. The two most popular econometric techniques are discriminant analysis and logit/probit models.

Other techniques include regression analysis and model building as well as Monte Carlo simulation.

Discriminant Analysis
Discriminant analysis is a statistical technique that enables classification of an observation into one of several *a priori* groupings. In the case of political risk analysis, the idea is to classify countries according to whether or not they are likely to expropriate (default). Basically, this technique involves three steps:

1. Establish mutually exclusive group classifications. Each group is distinguished by a probability distribution of the characteristics.
2. Collect data for each of the groups.
3. Derive the linear combinations of the characteristics that best discriminate among the groups. "Best" in this sense means that the discriminations minimize the probability of misclassification.

Logit and Probit Models
Logit and probit models enable the modeling of dichotomous variables, that is, variables that take a value of 1 or 0. These types of models are adapted to many types of political risk, which often have either/or outcomes: for example, either the country defaults or it does not; either the country expropriates or it does not.

Let xi be a k × 1 vector of independent variables and a k × 1 vector of coefficients. The logit model assumes that the probability that y_i equals 1 is $\frac{e^{\alpha' x_i}}{(1+e^{-\alpha' x_i})}$, which can be written as

$$\text{Prob}(y = 1) = \frac{e^{\alpha' x_i}}{(1 + e^{\alpha' x_i})} \qquad (13.1)$$

$$y_i = \begin{cases} 1 & \text{if default occurs} \\ 0 & \text{if it does not occur} \end{cases}$$

The probit model is similar to the logit model except that it uses the normal distribution

$$\text{Prob}(y = 1) = \int_{-\infty}^{\alpha' x_i} \phi(t) dt \qquad (13.2)$$

where $\Phi(t)$ represents the density function for the normal distribution.

One way of using logit (probit) analysis in cross-border lending decisions is to assign a maximum default probability above which no loans are granted. As previously mentioned, however, using the data from logit analysis as a complement to other analytical techniques is more common.

Regression Analysis and Model Building
As applied to political/country risk, the logit/probit models developed above generally lack a strong theoretical underpinning. Their methodology involves drawing up a list of variables that theory or practice suggests might influence the phenomenon in question and testing whether they enter the model as significant

explanatory variables. An alternative procedure to this ad hoc, empirical approach is to develop a theoretical model and then test its ability to explain the phenomenon in question. Recent studies have started to adopt this approach. For example, Clark and Kassimatis (2004, 2009) employ this methodology to estimate the country financial risk premiums that they test against equity returns and FDI flows. Merrick (1999) reports tests of bond pricing models for Argentine and Russian bonds, Pagès (2000) and Keswani (2005) for Latin American Brady bonds, and Dullmann and Windfuhr (2000) for European government credit spreads. Clark and Zenaidi (1999) develop an optimal stopping model for sovereign willingness to pay and test its relevance for 21 countries in four geographic regions.

Most risk models that drive economic and financial analysis are linear in their structure. Consequently, most tests are designed to detect a linear structure in the data. The risk models are also parametric in that they specify a particular distribution for the variables in question. The techniques are many and varied and include straightforward regressions using least squares, maximum likelihood or generalized method of moments (GMM), as well as event studies, cointegration, and error correction models, to mention only a few.

However, many aspects of economic and financial behavior are nonlinear and in many cases the parametric form of the variables is unknown. For variables such as these, nonparametric estimation is a growing area of econometrics. Parametric models that capture nonlinearities in economic phenomena, such as the family of ARCH/GARCH models, are also a growing area of econometrics.

Monte Carlo Simulation

Monte Carlo simulation is a well-known technique that is used in many economic and financial applications. Basically, Monte Carlo simulation is a sampling procedure that uses a table of random numbers to generate the probability distributions and risk estimates. The process involves three steps.

1. Identify the relevant variables and their interdependencies across time. The complete model should include a set of equations for each variable describing its evolution over time. The more complete the model, the more complex is the system of equations.
2. Determine for each variable the probabilities for forecast errors.
3. Use a computer to sample from the distribution of forecast errors to calculate the resulting cash flows for each period and to record them. After a large number of simulations, accurate estimates of the probability distributions of the project's cash flows are obtained.

In a Monte Carlo simulation, the effects of political risk are estimated directly and the role of the political risk analyst is to identify the relevant variables and the probabilities for forecast errors.

Although statistical approaches are considerably more objective and usually more rigorous than the politico-judgmental systems, they are not necessarily more reliable. Such approaches suffer from conceptual and statistical shortcomings and are based on the dubious premise that historical data have substantial value for predicting future outcomes. Furthermore, none of the foregoing methodologies is adapted to building efficient portfolios.

INCORPORATING POLITICAL RISK IN THE CAPITAL BUDGETING DECISION

For the foregoing techniques to have any practical value, the political risk assessments must be integrated into the capital budgeting process. The orthodox theory of capital budgeting and investment under uncertainty taught in most business schools and economics departments revolves around the NPV rule. The theoretical superiority of the NPV rule to the other approaches such as the payback period, the accounting rate of return, or the internal rate of return (IRR) explain its widespread acceptance in theory and practice. As discussed in the foregoing chapters, to calculate the NPV, expected cash flows of income and expenditure are estimated for each period and discounted at the appropriate rate. The present values for expenditure are then subtracted from the present values of income to find the NPV. A positive NPV indicates that the investment should be accepted, and a negative NPV indicates that it should be rejected. Three major methods are available for including political/country risk in the NPV analysis: (1) adjust the required rate of return, (2) adjust the expected cash flows, and (3) evaluate the project's NPV as if there were no political risk, quantify the political risk separately, and then subtract the quantified political risk from the project's NPV.

Adjusting the Discount Rate

One way to include political risk in NPV analysis is to adjust the discount rate to reflect the incremental political risk. Let κ represent the premium required to compensate the investor for the political risk, which depends exclusively on the country in which the investment is being considered, and CF_t the net cash flow for period t. The project's required rate of return per period in the absence of the country specific political risk is represented by r.

Thus, in the absence of country-specific political risk, the risk-adjusted discount factor is equal to $1 + r$. With country specific political risk, the discount factor is adjusted to $1 + r + \kappa$. The project's NPV, adjusted for political risk, can then be expressed as

$$NPV = \sum_{t=0}^{n} CF_t(1 + r + \kappa)^{-t} \tag{13.3}$$

The NPV will be smaller because the discount factor is larger. The drawback to this procedure is that there is no theory for determining κ, which makes the choice of κ arbitrary. Some rating agencies assign ad hoc values to κ depending on the ranking. However, some methods are available for determining the total required rate of return that includes political risk.

Determining the Required Rate of Return Using the CAPM
One method for estimating the risk-adjusted required rate of return on an international investment is to use the capital asset pricing model (CAPM) with an international market index denominated in a convertible currency, usually the USD. Let $r_{j,w}$ represent the required rate of return adjusted for systematic political

risk for project j, r_F the risk-free rate of interest, r_w the return on the world market portfolio, and $\beta_{j,w} = Cov(r_j, r_w)/Var(r_w)$. Using the CAPM to estimate $\beta_{j,w}$ gives the required rate of return as

$$r_{j,w} = r_F + \beta_{j,w}(r_w - r_F). \qquad (13.4)$$

This procedure is attractive because the CAPM is a centerpiece of economic evaluation, the formula is simple, and, if implemented correctly, only systematic political risk would be captured. The disadvantages relate to the shortcomings of mean-variance analysis in general and of the CAPM in particular. Furthermore, for this equation to be valid, all capital markets would have to be fully integrated. Although recent events have shown a surprising degree of market integration, most analysts doubt that perfect market integration has been achieved.

Bekaert and Harvey (1995) develop a modified version of the CAPM that accounts for the possibility that markets are not fully integrated and that risk measures change over time. This time-varying, segmented/integrated solution to the problem proposes using the time-varying form of the CAPM if the country under consideration is fully integrated. If the country is only partially integrated, the required rate of return should be modified to account for the degree of integration. Besides the problems with the CAPM in general, the problem with this model is that implementation is difficult in practice, and it only works for countries with equity markets.

Ibbotson Associates uses an ad hoc adjustment to the world CAPM to estimate the required rate of return adjusted for political risk. Their methodology is to estimate the required rate of return using the world CAPM and then to add a risk premium estimated from the past performance of the country's market. The problem with this approach is that it is also ad hoc. Other models, such as the Goldman-Integrated or the Credit Suisse First Boston (CSFB) methodology, use variations of the CAPM along with other variables such as bond spreads. Apart from the CAPM components, these models have no economic intuition or theoretical underpinning.

The macro CAPM uses the Clark (1991, 2002) methodology to estimate the country, risk-adjusted required rate of return that is not constrained by the existence of certain markets or an estimation of their integration or degree of segmentation. The methodology starts with the construction of the world macroeconomic index. It then uses this index to estimate the country beta and calculates the project beta with respect to the country index. The overall beta is the product of the country beta multiplied by the project beta. The advantage of this methodology is that all calculations are carried out in international relative prices, and the index includes all cash flows accruing to all capital (physical, commercial, and human). Thus, it is the most general market index. The disadvantage is the difficulty of calculating the individual country market values (V). The methodology has shown itself to be effective in forecasting high performing, international portfolios of money market assets, long-term government bonds, and market indices as well forecasting sovereign debt defaults and reschedulings (Clark, 2002).

Adjusting the Expected Cash Flows

Another method of accounting for political risk involves adjusting the cash flows to reflect the country-specific political risk. Let k_t represent the probability for year t that something bad will not happen, which depends exclusively on the country where the investment is to be located with $0 < k_t < 1$. Suppose that in the absence of country-specific political risk, the expected net cash flow for year t is CF_t. When political risk is included, the expected cash flow is reduced by $(1 - k_t)CF_t$ and the expected cash flow will be k_tCF_t. The project's NPV adjusted for political risk can thus be expressed as

$$NPV = \sum k_t CF (1 + r)^{-t}. \tag{13.5}$$

The theoretical difficulty with this method is that it assumes political risk has no effect on the project's cost of capital. The practical difficulty with the method is determining the k_t coefficients. However, its advantage lies in associating a specific coefficient to each period. This enables the analysis to reflect the specific time profile of the country's political, social, and economic cycles. For example, the k_t's in election years or renegotiation years for union contracts might be adjusted downward while years when international agreements take effect might be adjusted upward.

Measuring Political Risk as an Insurance Premium

Clark (1997, 1998) develops a third approach for incorporating political/country risk in the NPV. It involves measuring the effects of political risk on the outcome of an FDI as the value of an insurance policy that reimburses all losses resulting from the political event or events in question. Explicit loss-causing events are distinguished from ongoing change. Explicit events include such things as changes in legislation or decrees such as expropriations, nationalizations, and devaluations, or to direct actions such as strikes, boycotts, and terrorist acts. The nature of explicit events is that they arrive intermittently at discrete intervals and generate an actual loss. A Poisson jump process can be used to model explicit events.

Ongoing change refers to continuous activity resulting from macroeconomic management and monetary policy, legislation, or social and political evolution that affects some or all aspects of the FDI's overall environment. Ongoing change affects the level of loss if an explicit event occurs and can be represented by geometric Brownian motion.

To see how this works using Clark (1997), let x represent the exposure to loss in the case of an explicit political event. Its evolution through time follows a geometric Brownian motion:

$$dx(t) = (\alpha + \beta) x(t) dt + \sigma x(t) dz(t) \tag{13.6}$$

where α represents the rate of growth of the intensity of political risk. The term α can be greater than, equal to, or less than zero. It measures the intensity of the political environment surrounding the particular risk in question. The interpretation of

α is that as the intensity of the political risk increases, the severity or cost of the measures undertaken increases when an explicit event does occur. If α is less than zero, the intensity of the political risk in question is expected to decline on average; if α is greater than zero, it is expected to increase on average; if α is equal to zero, it is expected to remain the same. The term β represents the rate of growth of the investment and depends on the investment's IRR and the rate of reinvestment out of profits. The term $dz(t)$ is a Wiener process with zero mean and variance equal to dt. The term σ^2 is the variance of $dx(t)/x(t)$ due to political risk and can be interpreted as the level of the political risk.

Suppose that political events occur at random times according to an independent Poisson arrival process where q is a random variable that increases by steps of u every time a Poisson event occurs and λ is a constant intensity parameter such that:

$$dq\,(t) = \begin{cases} 1 & \text{with probability} \quad \lambda dt \\ 0 & \text{with probability} \quad 1 - \lambda dt \end{cases}$$

This means that losses arrive at a rate of λdt and that λ is the political risk probability parameter, that is, the probability that a loss-causing political event actually occurs over the interval dt. If $x(t)$ represents the potential loss when a Poisson event occurs, the expected loss per interval dt is equal to $\lambda x(t)dt$. In the more advanced forms of the model, λ itself can be a random variable or even a dependent stochastic process.

To measure the cost of political/country risk, let W represent the value of a hypothetical insurance policy covering the investment against losses arising from the political risk so that when losses occur, they are reimbursed by the insurer. The expected total return on the insurance policy is equal to $E(dW)$ plus the expected cash flow generated by the explicit event, $\lambda x(t)dt$. Assume risk neutrality and a constant risk-free interest rate r, apply Ito's lemma, and take expectations. This gives the following differential equation:

$$\frac{1}{2}\sigma^2 x(t)^2 W''(x(t)) + W'(x(t))(\alpha + \beta)x(t) - r\,W(x(t)) + \lambda x(t) = 0 \qquad (13.7)$$

where the primes denote first and second derivatives.

The solution to this equation depends on the values of the various parameters and the boundary conditions associated with each investment. For example, assuming that speculative bubbles are ruled out and that the policy has no value when there is nothing at risk, the value of the policy covering a series of losses is:

$$W = \frac{\lambda x(t)}{r - (\alpha + \beta)} \qquad (13.8)$$

The value of a policy covering only one loss, such as expropriation, is:

$$W = \frac{\lambda x(t)}{r + \lambda - (\alpha + \beta)} \qquad (13.9)$$

Once political risk quantified as the value of the insurance policy has been estimated, it can be integrated into the capital budgeting process in a two-step methodology:

1. Estimate the NPV of the project in the absence of political risk.
2. Subtract the value of the insurance policy from the project's NPV in the absence of political risk. This gives $NPV - W$, the NPV of the investment adjusted for political risk.

This methodology has the advantage of being theoretically consistent with modern portfolio theory. It also avoids the difficulty of estimating risk-adjusted required rates of return or forecasting risk parameters far into the future. In its more advanced forms, the policy can be valued to reflect various options available to managers, such as the option to abandon the project if things go badly. It can also be valued to reflect the change from one level of political risk to another. For example, Clark (1998) uses this approach to model the political risk associated with the transition of Hong Kong from British to Chinese rule. The political risk parameter, λ, can also be modeled to reflect uncertainty about the risk parameter itself and to be reestimated in an endogenous Bayesian updating process as in Clark and Tunaru (2003, 2008). The difficulty lies in estimating the relevant parameters.

For example, assume that the amount of the investment is $100 million and its risk-neutral growth rate is zero: $\beta = 0$. The risk-free rate can be observed: $r = 5$ percent, the interest rate on a 30-year U.S. government separately traded registered interest and principal security (STRIPS). The country risk analysts estimate that the probability of an expropriation is 0.02: $\lambda = 0.02$. In case of an expropriation, they estimate the recovery rate at 20 percent: $x = (1 - 0.20) \times \$100 = \$80$. They also estimate the risk-neutral change in the political climate as equal to zero: $\alpha = 0$. Using this information in equation 13.9 gives

$$W = \frac{0.02 \times \$80}{0.05 + 0.02 - (0 + 0)} = \$22.86$$

Suppose that the NPV of the investment in the absence of expropriation risk is $20 million. The NPV adjusted for political risk is $20.00 - \$22.86 = -\$2.86$ and the project should not be undertaken.

SUMMARY AND CONCLUSIONS

The notion of political risk has been around at least since the 1960s. Besides referring to doing business abroad and including a wide range of different situations, no consensus exists on a comprehensive definition. The wide range of assessment techniques and the difficulty of integrating political risk into the capital budgeting decision reflect this lack of consensus. Evidence suggests, however, that political risk analysis is evolving to incorporate the modern techniques of asset evaluation and portfolio analysis.

DISCUSSION QUESTIONS

1. Why has the concept of political risk been so difficult to define?
2. Compare the advantages and disadvantages of the comparative, analytical, and econometric techniques for assessing political risk.
3. How can analysts incorporate political risk into the capital budgeting process?
4. How has the CAPM been modified to account for political risk?
5. How can the concept of an insurance premium be used to estimate political risk?

REFERENCES

Aggarwal, Raj, Ramesh P. Rao, and Takato Hiraki. 1989. "Skewness and Kurtosis in Japanese Equity Returns: Empirical Evidence." *Journal of Financial Research* 12:3, 253–260.

Aliber, Robert Z. 1975. "Exchange Risk, Political Risk, and Investor Demand for External Currency Deposits." *Journal of Money, Credit & Banking* 7:2, 161–179.

Baglini, Norman A. 1976. *Risk Management in International Corporations*. New York: Risk Studies Foundations.

Bekaert, Geert, Claude B. Erb, Campbell R. Harvey, and Tadas E. Viskanta. 1998. "Distributional Characteristics of Emerging Market Returns and Asset Allocation." *Journal of Portfolio Management* 24:2, 102–116.

Bekaert, Geert. 1995. "Market Integration and Investment Barriers in Emerging Equity Markets." *The World Bank Economic Review* 9:1, 75–107.

Bekaert, Geert, and Campbell R. Harvey. 1995. "Time-Varying World Market Integration." *Journal of Finance* 50:2, 403–444.

Bekaert, Geert, and Campbell R. Harvey. 1997. "Emerging Equity Market Volatility." *Journal of Financial Economics* 43:1, 29–77.

Bittlingmayer, George. 1998. "Output, Stock Volatility, and Political Uncertainty in a Natural Experiment: Germany, 1880–1940." *Journal of Finance* 53:6, 2243–2257.

Bouchet, Michel H., Ephraim Clark, and Bertrand Groslambert. 2003. *Country Risk Assessment: A Guide to Global Investment Strategy*. London: John Wiley & Sons.

Brewer, Thomas L. 1981. "Political Risk Assessment for Foreign Direct Investment Decisions: Better Methods for Better Results." *Columbia Journal of World Business* 16:1, 5–12.

Chan, Yue-cheong, and K. C. John Wei. 1996. "Political Risk and Stock Price Volatility: The Case of Hong Kong." *Pacific-Basin Finance Journal* 4:2–3, 259–275.

Clark, Ephraim. 1991. *Cross Border Investment Risk*. London: Euromoney Publications.

Clark, Ephraim. 1997. "Valuing Political Risk." *Journal of International Money and Finance* 16:3, 477–490.

Clark, Ephraim. 1998. "Political Risk in Hong Kong and Taiwan: Pricing the China Factor." *Journal of Economic Integration* 13:2, 278–293.

Clark, Ephraim. 2002. *International Finance*. London: Thomson.

Clark, Ephraim, Roger Cusin, and Jean-Baptiste Lesourd. 1998. "Risk Assessment and Sovereign Debt Instruments: A Multicriteria Approach." Presented at the International Conference on Forecasting Financial Markets, London.

Clark, Ephraim, and Konstantinos Kassimatis. 2004. "Country Financial Risk and Stock Market Performance: The Case of Latin America." *Journal of Economics and Business* 56:1, 21–41.

Clark, Ephraim, and Konstantinos Kassimatis. 2009. "The Effect of Country Default Risk on Foreign Direct Investment." *Economia Internazionale* 62:3, 342–361.

Clark, Ephraim, and Radu Tunaru. 2003. "Quantification of Political Risk with Multiple Dependent Sources." *Journal of Economics and Finance* 27:2, 125–135.

Clark, Ephraim, and Radu Tunaru. 2008. "Modelling Stochastic Political Risk for Capital Budgeting: Currency Crises." *Banque et Marchés* 95:July–August:, 45–56.

Clark, Ephraim, and Amel Zenaidi. 1999. "Sovereign Debt Discounts and the Unwillingness to Pay." *Finance* 20:2, 185–199.

Cosset, Jean-Claude, Yannis Siskos, and Constantin Zopounidis. 1992. "Evaluating Country Risk: A Decision Support Approach." *Global Finance Journal* 3:1, 79–95.

Cosset, Jean-Claude, and Jean-Marc Suret. 1995. "Political Risk and the Benefits of International Portfolio Diversification." *Journal of International Business Studies* 26:2, 301–318.

Cutler, David M., James M. Poterba, and Lawrence H. Summers. 1989. "What Moves Stock Prices?" *Journal of Portfolio Management* 15:3, 4–12.

Desta, Asayehgn. 1985. "Assessing Political Risk in Less Developed Countries." *Journal of Business Strategy* 5:4, 40–53.

Dullmann, Klaus, and Marc Windfuhr. 2000. "Credit Spreads Between German and Italian Sovereign Bonds: Do One-Factor Affine Models Work?" *Canadian Journal of Administrative Sciences* 17:2, 166–179.

Feils, Dorothee J., and Florin M. Sabac. 2000. "The Impact of Political Risk on the Foreign Direct Investment Decision: A Capital Budgeting Analysis." *Engineering Economist* 45:2, 129–143.

Fitzpatrick, Mark. 1983. "The Definition and Assessment of Political Risk in International Business: A Review of the Literature." *Academy of Management Review* 8:2, 249–254.

Gabriel, Peter P. 1966. "The Investment in the LDC: Asset with a Fixed Maturity." *Columbia Journal of World Business* 1:3, 109–119.

Haendel, Dan, Gerald T. West, and Robert G. Meadow. 1975. *Overseas Investment and Political Risk.* Lexington, Kentucky: Lexington Books.

Howell, Llewellyn D., and Brad Chaddick. 1994. "Models of Political Risk for Foreign Investment and Trade." *Columbia Journal of World Business* 29:3, 70–91.

Keswani, Aneel. 2005. "Estimating a Risky Term Structure of Brady Bonds." *The Manchester School* 73:s1, 99–127.

Khoury, Nabil, Jean-Marc Martel, and Pierre Yougourou. 1994. "A Multicriterion Approach to Country Selection for Global Index Funds." *Global Finance Journal* 5:1, 17–35.

Kim, Harold Y., and Jianping P. Mei. 2001. "What Makes the Stock Market Jump? An Analysis of Political Risk on Hong Kong Stock Returns." *Journal of International Money and Finance* 20:7, 1003–1016.

Kobrin, Stephen J. 1979. "Political Risk: A Review and Reconsideration." *Journal of International Business Studies* 10:1, 67–80.

Meldrum, Duncan H. 2000. "Country Risk and Foreign Direct Investment." *Business Economics* 35:1, 33–40.

Merrick, John J. 1999. *Crisis Dynamics of Implied Default Recovery Ratios: Evidence from Russia and Argentina.* New York: New York University, Leonard N. Stern School of Business.

Merrill, James. 1982. "Country Risk Analysis." *Columbia Journal of World Business* 17:1, 88–91.

Pagès, Henri. 2000. *Estimating Brazilian Sovereign Risk from Brady Bond Prices.* Working Paper, Banque de France.

Rivoli, Pietra, and Thomas L. Brewer. 1997. "Political Instability and Country Risk." *Global Finance Journal* 8:2, 309–321.

Robock, Steely H. 1971. "Political Risk: Identification and Assessment." *Columbia Journal of World Business* 6:4, 6–20.

Root, Franklin R. 1968. "The Expropriation Experience of American Companies: What Happened to 38 Companies." *Business Horizons* 11:2, 69–74.

Roy, A., and P. G. Roy. 1994. "Despite Past Debacles, Predicting Sovereign Risk Still Presents Problems." *Commercial Lending Review* 9:3, 92–95.

Simon, Jeffrey D. 1982. "Political Risk Assessment: Past Trends and Future Prospects." *Columbia Journal of World Business* 17:3, 62–70.

Stobaugh, Robert B. 1969a. "Where in the World Should We Put That Plant?" *Harvard Business Review* 47:1, 129–136.

Stobaugh, Robert B. 1969b. "How to Analyze Foreign Investment Climates." *Harvard Business Review* 47:5, 100–108.

Usher, Dan. 1965. "Political Risk." *Economic Development & Cultural Change* 13:4, 453–462.

Zenoff, David. 1967. "Profitable, Fast Growing, But Still the Stepchild." *Columbia Journal of World Business* 2:4, 51–56.

Zopounidis, Constantin, M. Godefroid, and Christian Hurson. 1995. "Designing a Multi-criteria Decision Support System for Portfolio Selection and Management." In Jacques Jansen, Christos H. Skiadas, and Constantin Zopounidis, eds. *Advances in Stochastic Modelling and Data Analysis*, 261–292. Dordrecht: Kluwer Academic Publishers.

ABOUT THE AUTHORS

Yacine Belghitar is Senior Lecturer in Finance, Program Leader and School Research Coordinator at Middlesex University. He is an expert on corporate strategy, corporate risk management, small and medium business finance, and performance measurement. He teaches modules on investment, corporate finance, financial modeling, and research methods. Before his role at Middlesex University, Professor Belghitar was at the Barclays Centre for Entrepreneurship at Durham University where he worked on an ESRC-funded project researching the risk behavior of nascent entrepreneurs and self-employed people. He published the findings of this research in the *Economic Journal* and *Small Business Economics*, among others. He has an undergraduate degree in statistics from the Algiers School of Statistics and Applied Economics, and postgraduate degrees in financial economics from Cardiff University and Durham University.

Ephraim Clark is Professor of Finance at Middlesex University and SKEMA Research Center. His published work includes eight books and more than 70 articles in a wide range of academic and professional journals such as *Management Science, Journal of International Money and Finance, European Journal of Operational Research, European Financial Management, Review of International Economics, Garp Risk Review,* and *Euromoney.* Honors and awards include numerous research grants and best paper awards. He serves on the editorial boards of various scholarly journals and is the founding editor of the *European Journal of Finance.* Professor Clark has been elected president of the Multinational Finance Society, president of the International Society for the Intercommunication of New Ideas, and vice president of the International Association of Finance and Banking. He has undergraduate and graduate degrees from the University of Madrid and the University of Paris, respectively.

CHAPTER 14

Risk Management in Project Finance

STEFANO GATTI
Associate Professor of Banking and Finance, Bocconi University, Milan

STEFANO CASELLI
Professor of Banking and Finance, Bocconi University, Milan

INTRODUCTION

Project finance can be defined as the financing of a specific economic entity, the special-purpose vehicle (SPV), also known as the project company. The vehicle is created by already operating firms (known as sponsors) that provide equity or mezzanine debt and by external lenders (banks or investors in the bond market). Lenders consider cash flows the primary source of loan reimbursement and the SPV assets as additional collateral (Yescombe, 2002; Finnerty, 2007; Gatti, 2007).

Project finance is extensively used in both developing and industrialized countries in many different sectors. From a long-term perspective four geographic areas—Western Europe, North America, Eastern Europe, and Southeast Asia—account for the largest share of project finance loans (Megginson and Kleimeier, 2000; Gatti, Kleimeier, Megginson, and Steffanoni, 2008; Kleimeier and Versteeg, 2010). In developing countries, the use of project finance is concentrated in basic infrastructure projects such as power, mining, oil and gas, and telecom. Given the more advanced stage of economic development, industrialized countries have started to apply the technique in the field of public works, such as hospitals, prisons, and social housing, under public-private partnership (PPP) programs (HM Treasury, 2003; European Commission, 2003; Eurostat, 2004; Archer, 2005; Hodge and Greve, 2005; Hammami, Ruhashyankiko, and Yehoue, 2006).

The SPV carries out only one single investment with a finite economic life, in contrast to what happens in standard corporate finance settings where capital investment is a repeated process. All the cash flows generated by the project are not reinvested in the business but are used to repay the creditors and to pay dividends to the project sponsors. In this sense, the SPV does not manage a portfolio of real assets on a continuous basis. Instead, the SPV is created with the sole purpose of managing one project and is liquidated once the project has come to the end of its economic life.

This basic difference between corporate borrowers and SPVs has important consequences from the point of view of capital budgeting. Probably the crucial difference is that deal sustainability relies on a careful allocation of risks among the parties involved in the transaction with the objective of assigning risks to the contractual counterparties best able to control and manage them. The allocation of risks should limit cash flow volatility and the spread paid on external debt. Furthermore, it can also allow sponsors to exploit higher leverage ratios (Corielli, Gatti, and Steffanoni, 2010).

Another consequence is that the borrower is a vehicle that is financially and legally independent from the sponsors. Lenders have only limited recourse (or in some cases, no recourse at all) to the sponsors throughout the life of the project. A third consequence is that cash flows generated by the SPV are the only source available for the payment of operating costs, debt service for principal and interest, as well as dividends to project sponsors. Although lenders can take security on the SPV assets, their high specificity and low redeployable value makes them of marginal benefit as collateral (Habib and Johnsen, 1999).

The purpose of this chapter is to present the most important characteristics of project finance and their effect on capital budgeting. By analyzing the nexus of contracts underpinning the deal and its role as a risk management tool, the chapter clarifies how effective risk management affects the definition of the optimal capital structure and how it influences the level of financial covenants that lenders impose on the borrower. The chapter has the following organization. The next section introduces the nature of project finance as a "nexus of financial and nonfinancial contracts." The following section is dedicated to the risk management process in project finance deals in terms of both risk analysis and risk allocation. The next to last section covers the capital budgeting issues of project finance and highlights the distinctive features a financial analyst must take into consideration when approaching this type of deal. The final section offers a summary and conclusions.

PROJECT FINANCE AS A NEXUS OF CONTRACTS

In a standard project finance deal, the SPV is the center of a complex network of contracts (Dailami and Hauswald, 2007; Bonetti, Caselli, and Gatti, 2010). The reason this network is set up is that in most cases the SPV is a "fictitious" company, created with the sole purpose of capturing the cash flows generated by a new venture. For this reason, third parties must buy everything that is needed to design, build, manage, and finance the project.

Exhibit 14.1 shows the contractual structure of a project finance deal. The upper part of the exhibit shows the relations among the SPV, host government, and parties providing funds (banks and sponsor firms) or insurance coverage against risks. The host government is the entity that can authorize the SPV to carry out the project with authorizations and permits. Sometimes, the private sector is authorized to operate the business based on a long-term concession agreement. This occurs in the case of a build, operate, and transfer (BOT) or a build, own, operate, and transfer (BOOT) project (Välilä, 2005).

Banks provide funds on a limited or no-recourse basis and take security on all the project assets. Banks often provide additional tranches of funding for the project, similar to what happens in other structured finance transactions such

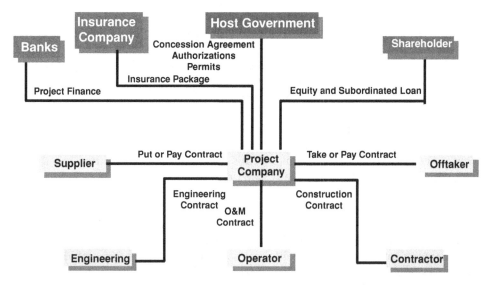

Exhibit 14.1 The Contractual Structure of a Project Finance Deal

Note: This exhibit shows the typical contractual structure of project finance deals. The upper part of the exhibit shows the most relevant financial contracts (project finance loans, insurance contracts, and equity contribution from project sponsors) together with the contracts signed with the host government. The lower part of the exhibit shows the four key nonfinancial contracts (Construction/Engineering, O&M-Operations and Management, Put or Pay, and Take or Pay Contracts).

as leveraged buyouts (LBOs). The standard combination is the provision of a base facility for the financing of the construction and startup costs (including capitalized interest), a value-added tax facility (VAT) in countries where such a tax is in place, a stand-by facility covering financial needs once the base facility has been exhausted, and finally a working capital facility for the day-by-day needs once completing construction (Finnerty, 2007; Gatti, 2007).

Project sponsors provide equity to the SPV based on an equity contribution agreement. Frequently, the funds are not provided upfront for the whole amount but in proportion to the selected debt-to-equity ratio for the deal on a pro-rata basis. In addition to pure equity, project sponsors also provide subordinated loans to the vehicle with the goal of avoiding a possible "dividend trap"—the situation where net income is lower than the value of free cash flow to equity (FCFE)—particularly in the first years of operation (Yescombe, 2002).

Insurance coverage is an important contractual risk mitigation tool on par with the other key contracts depicted in the lower part of Exhibit 14.1. Banks require the coverage of some risks to the SPV as a condition precedent for the debt financing. The different insurance products available on the market (Gatti, 2007) are coordinated and linked to the project's contractual structure to protect the SPV against the risks that none of the counterparties involved can control and manage.

The lower part of Exhibit 14.1 shows the key nonfinancial contracts (NFCs) underpinning the deal (Corielli et al., 2010). Numerous NFCs can be drafted in a project finance deal (Esty, 2003), but four are particularly important to the soundness of the venture. Construction contracts as well as engineering, procurement, and construction (EPC) contracts are closed on a turnkey basis to make plant and equipment available to the SPV, usually at predefined prices, times of delivery, and standards of performance. These contractual features are useful to shift the construction risk from the SPV to the contractor (Blanc-Brude, Goldsmith, and Välilä, 2006). Purchasing agreements stipulated with raw material suppliers guarantee input to the vehicle at predefined quantities, quality, and prices on a put-or-pay basis, meaning that the supplier unconditionally guarantees the needed input or pays liquidated damages to the vehicle. Selling agreements, often known as take-or-pay or off-taking agreements, enable the SPV to sell part or all of its output to a third party (offtaker) that commits to buy unconditionally, again at predefined prices and for a given period of time. In this way, market risk is shifted to a third party. Operation and maintenance (O&M) agreements are designed to provide the SPV with efficient and effective plant maintenance, compliant with predefined service-level agreements, so as to avoid operational risk to the SPV.

In most project finance transactions, project sponsors are also contractual counterparties of the SPV. This is perfectly natural considering that the primary interest of sponsors is to appropriate the highest share of cash flows generated by the project. The combination of the shareholder role and contractual counterparty role avoids opportunistic behavior of project sponsors and limits agency costs (Brealey, Cooper, and Habib, 1996).

Exhibit 14.1 is also useful from the point of view of capital budgeting. Every relation between the SPV and its counterparties generates cash inflows and outflows that contribute to the overall ability of the venture to repay operational costs, debt service and dividend to sponsors.

Exhibit 14.2 shows the reinterpretation of Exhibit 14.1 from the point of view of the cash flow dynamics. The upper part of the exhibit shows the financial cash flows (debt service, annual premiums to insurance firms, and dividend and

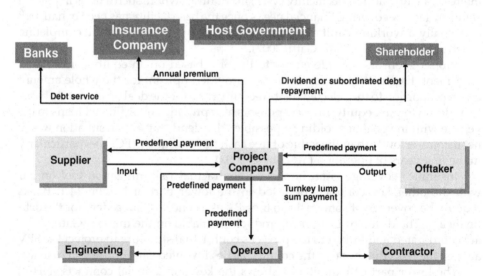

Exhibit 14.2 Cash Flow Dynamics in a Project Finance Deal

Note: This exhibit shows the key counterparties of the SPV and the cash flows generated by every contract illustrated in Exhibit 14.1. The upper part shows the financial cash flows (debt service, annual premiums to insurance firms, and dividend and subordinated loan debt service), the lower part shows the cash flows related to the nonfinancial contracts. Most of the payments related to nonfinancial contracts are predefined in the same contracts to limit cash flow volatility.

subordinated loan debt service), while the lower part shows the cash flows related to the nonfinancial contracts. Most of the payments related to nonfinancial contracts are predefined in the same contracts to limit cash flow volatility.

RISK MANAGEMENT IN PROJECT FINANCE

Although risk management is a relevant responsibility of chief financial officers (CFOs) and contributes to value creation in already existing corporations (Froot, Sharfstein, and Stein, 1993; Minton and Schrand, 1999; Nocco and Stulz, 2006), its importance becomes crucial in project finance. This is because the SPV manages only one single investment. If this investment is excessively risky, creditors could face situations where the cash flows produced by the new initiative are insufficient to repay debt service.

Preliminary to any capital budgeting exercise, sponsors, banks, and respective technical, legal, and financial advisers carry out a careful analysis of all the risks the project will bear during its economic life. The key steps of this process are (1) risk identification, (2) risk analysis, (3) risk transfer and allocation of risks to the actors best suited to ensure coverage against these risks, and (4) residual risk management.

Risk Identification and Risk Analysis

Regarding risk identification and risk analysis, sponsors and lenders try to carefully map all the possible risks that could arise during the life of the project and to evaluate the probability of occurrence and the severity of the risk (Gatti, Rigamonti, and Senati, 2007; Borgonovo, Gatti, and Peccati, 2009). Such risks can arise either during the construction phase when the project is unable to generate cash or during the operating phase. A standard classification of risks (Gatti, 2007) is the following: (1) precompletion risks, (2) postcompletion risks, and (3) risks found in both the pre- and postcompletion phases.

The most common precompletion risks are poor activity planning, technology risk, and construction risk (in the form of delayed completion, cost overruns, or completion with performance deficiency). Postcompletion risks are associated with the supply of inputs, the performance of the plant as compared to project minimum performance standards, and the sale of the product or service. Risks found in both the pre- and postcompletion phases involve financial risks (interest rate risk, currency risk, and inflation risk), regulatory risks particularly related to permits and authorizations, political and country risk (Hainz and Kleimeier, 2003), and legal risk related to contract enforceability and creditor rights protection (Tung, Xue, and Subramanian, 2008).

Risk Allocation and Residual Risk Management

Once the risks are mapped and analyzed, the risk management process defines the strategies the SPV can use to mitigate the impact of risks on project cash flows. Sponsors and lenders can opt for three different strategies: (1) transfer the risk by allocating it to one of the key counterparties, (2) transfer the risk to professional insurers, and (3) retain the risk.

Risk transfer by means of nonfinancial contracts is the most commonly used risk management strategy in project finance and is based on an intuitive principle. Referring to Exhibits 14.1 and 14.2, the key contracts signed by the SPV (EPC, supply, purchase, and O&M agreements) allocate rights and obligations to the SPV itself and its respective counterparties. These contracts can be used as risk mitigation techniques if the counterparty best able to control and manage the risk is considered responsible for the effects of the respective risks on project cash flows. If the risk occurs, some form of indemnification must be paid to the SPV. The relation between the emergence of a loss for the SPV and the indemnification payment due to the SPV incentivizes the counterparty to honor the original agreement to avoid the negative effects created by the outcome of the risk in question. If a risky outcome arises and is allocated (transferred) to a third party, this same party will bear the cost of the risk without affecting the SPV or its lenders.

The second available option for risk management is risk insurance. This alternative must be used for risks that cannot be controlled and managed by any one of the SPV counterparties. Insurers can cover the SPV risks in return for the payment of an insurance premium. These companies can do so because they manage large risk portfolios where the joint probability of emergence of all the risks in the portfolio at the same time is very low.

The final option to control the risk is to retain it and to try to limit its effects on SPV operations by means of well-designed internal risk procedures. Risk retention is a common practice in already existing corporations (Carter, Rogers, and Simkins, 2006). A firm can deliberately retain risks because it considers risk allocation to third parties too expensive or the cost of insurance policies excessive compared to the negative outcomes of that particular risk. Risk retention, as a residual risk management policy, is more effective for existing corporations than for SPVs. This is because in standard corporate finance settings, operational risk can be diversified across the whole portfolio of real assets managed by an existing firm. Instead, operational risk for an SPV is primarily idiosyncratic and confined to a single project. For this reason, the unallocated portion of risk plays a key role in the credit spread and debt-to-equity ratio setting (Corielli et al., 2010).

CAPITAL BUDGETING IN PROJECT FINANCE

Capital budgeting for project finance does not differ from the standard theory of investment valuation. Indeed, the fact that the SPV contains only one single project should, in principle, make project finance valuation easier than in standard corporate finance settings (Gatti, 2007). The peculiar characteristics of the deal require some adaptations to the general capital budgeting framework for already existing firms.

The first difference is due to the fact that project finance involves long-term investments with a clear-cut separation between the construction phase (where no cash is generated) and the operational phase (where cash is produced and no or minimum capital expenditures are made). Exhibit 14.3 shows the standard behavior of project cash flows during the life of a project. The second adaptation that must be made is including a larger set of criteria to evaluate the deal's sustainability. Since the SPV manages only one single project, the project is viable only if the cash flows available for debt service during a certain year of the operational phase

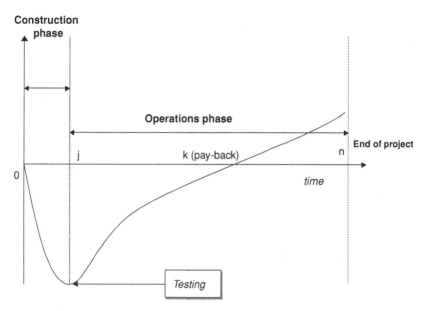

Exhibit 14.3   Cash Flow Behavior during the Project Life
Note: Exhibit 14.3 shows the typical behavior of project cash flows during the life of the SPV. Time is on the horizontal axis and the cumulative value of the unlevered free cash flows is on the vertical axis. Years from 0 to *j* are occupied by the construction phase where the project does not generate positive cash flows. The first period ends with plant testing. Time from *j* to *n* is represented by the operations phase during which the project produces the cash flows necessary to repay bank debt, subordinated debt, and dividends to project sponsors. Year *n* marks the end of the project life (or the end of the concession period in public-private partnership (PPP) programs).

are strictly higher than the payments due for principal and interest to creditors. This condition is an example of the wide set of covenants included in the credit agreement that must be fulfilled by the SPV (Smith and Warner, 1979; Rajan and Winton, 1995).

Capital Budgeting during the Construction Phase

In Exhibit 14.3, the area going from time 0 to time *j* on the horizontal axis represents the period in which the plant is under construction. In this phase, the project absorbs cash in the form of down payments paid to the contractor for work in progress. The SPV profit and loss account is empty, and payments made accrue solely to the SPV's balance sheet.

In terms of capital budgeting, the components of the total capital expenditures incurred by the SPV (and for which sponsors and lenders must provide funding) are the following: (1) cost of construction, (2) cost of purchasing the land where the facility will be built, (3) owners' costs, (4) development costs, (5) cost of insurance policies during construction, (6) capitalized interest during construction, and (7) value-added tax (VAT) when required by country regulations.

The cost of construction is estimated based on the price included in the EPC contract that is typically set on a turnkey basis (fixed price) (Blanc-Brude et al., 2006). The general contractor and the SPV agree on a predefined schedule of down payments that are due for work in progress certified by an independent technical advisor. If the SPV does not hold ownership of the land where the project will be built, this component must be added to the construction budget.

Owners' costs are related to costs linked to project construction (for example, the building of access roads to the plant) while development costs include the cost of consulting fees paid in the initial phase of project feasibility study to the project advisers. The cost of insurance is related to risk coverage during the construction phase by means of insurance policies, as discussed in the previous section.

Capitalized interest must be accounted for in the construction phase of capital budgeting. In fact, since the project cannot produce cash flows, lenders agree to be paid in kind and generally allow the SPV to postpone the interest payments until construction is completed. By doing so, the outstanding amount of loans at the end of the construction period will be the sum of the original outstanding loans plus all the accrued interest during construction.

During the first years of construction, the SPV pays the work in progress to the contractor and these payments will be subject to VAT where applicable pursuant to the existing tax code of the country. Because the project cannot collect payments from customers during this phase of the project, it does not receive cash from VAT on sales to offset the VAT paid to the contractor. For this reason, any VAT payments that the SPV makes to suppliers are a credit toward the VAT authority and the SPV has to finance these expenditures until the VAT office reimburses them or until VAT credits are offset by VAT debts from invoices to SPV customers.

The following example illustrates these concepts. Suppose that a project of $4 billion is financed with a debt-to-equity ratio of 1.0. The interest cost of the senior facility is floating rate but swapped against a fixed interest rate of 5 percent. VAT on agreed down payments during construction is 20 percent. VAT is financed with a specially tailored VAT loan paying a floating rate swapped against a fixed interest rate of 4 percent. The schedule of payments for construction work in progress is 20 percent at the end of years 0 and 1 and 30 percent at the end of years 2 and 3.

Exhibit 14.4 shows the capital budgeting cash flows for the construction phase. Interest on the senior and VAT facilities has been capitalized until the end of the construction phase, so that the outstanding amount subject to amortization during the operational phase will be $2.134 billion and $843 million, respectively.

The capitalization has been done according to the following calculation:

$$CI = \sum_{t=0}^{3} D_t \times (1+i)^{(3-t)} - \sum_{t=0}^{3} D_t \qquad (14.1)$$

where CI = the amount of capitalized interest; D = the facility drawdown during period t; and i = the fixed interest rate.

Because the agreed debt-to-equity ratio is 1.0, the calculation must be iterated until the sum of interest and principal over the amount of equity provided by project sponsors is exactly 1.0 at the end of the construction period. This iteration can be easily done by resorting to macros included in calculation spreadsheets (Yescombe, 2002; Gatti, 2007).

The additional financial fees charged by creditors to the SPV in the form of commitment fees provide a final component to this example. For every period *t*, the undrawn portion of funds at the beginning of the period (that is, the difference

Exhibit 14.4 An Example of Capital Budgeting during Construction

Project value	4000
Equity	50%
Senior debt	50%
VAT	20%
Interest senior	5%
Interest VAT	4%

Schedule of Work in Progress	0	1	2	3	Total Uses
Downpayments	20%	20%	30%	30%	
Amount due	800	800	1200	1200	4000
VAT	160	160	240	240	800
Capitalized interest				176.68	176.68

	0	1	2	3	Total Sources
Equity drawdowns	400	400	600	600	2000
Senior debt drawdowns	400	400	600	600	2134.05
VAT drawdowns	160	160	240	240	842.63
Capitalized interest senior				134.05	
Capitalized interest VAT				42.63	

Note: This exhibit shows an example of capital budgeting during construction. Elements of the capital expenditures during construction are construction cost (project value) plus value-added tax (VAT) and capitalized interest on senior and VAT loans. Interest is capitalized at the end of the construction period and then amortized during the operational phase together with the original loan amounts.

between the total amount of funds and the used portion of the loans) is subject to this fee proportional to the time length of period t. Commitment fees are capitalized until the end of the construction period and will be repaid according to the amortization schedule designed for the senior and VAT facility.

Capital Budgeting during the Operational Phase

In Exhibit 14.3, the area going from time j to n (end of the economic life of the project or end of the concession period in PPPs) represents the operational phase. During this period, the project must be able to generate sufficient cash to repay operating costs, debt service, and dividends to shareholders. The standard waterfall structure of payments (Yescombe, 2002; Finnerty, 2007; Gatti, 2007) is the following (see Exhibit 14.1):

1. Revenues from sales (frequently predefined under take-or-pay agreements).
2. Raw material costs (possibly predefined using put-or-pay agreements).
3. Operation and maintenance costs (preset by resorting to long-term O&M agreements).
4. Costs for insurance policies.
5. Corporate taxes.
6. Changes in working capital.
7. Interest on senior, VAT, stand-by and working capital facilities.
8. Interest on subordinated loans.

9. Principal repayment of senior, VAT, stand-by and working capital facilities.
10. Principal repayment of subordinated loans.
11. Provisions to debt reserve accounts.
12. Dividends to project sponsors.

The sum of items 1 to 6 returns the value of the unlevered free cash flows; the difference between free cash flows and the sum of items 7 to 10 returns the value of free cash flow to equity (FCFE).

Although most of the items do not require explanation, corporate taxes and provisions to debt reserve accounts deserve some additional discussion. Unlike corporate finance settings, in project finance capital budgeting, taxes are not calculated on earnings before interest and taxes (EBIT), and the cost of debt is not reduced by the effect of the tax shield on interest but on earnings before taxes (EBT). As shown later, this is because sponsors are interested in calculating the return on the deal using internal rate of return (IRR) calculated on FCFE. For this reason, the computation of taxes requires using real taxes and not the fictitious taxes calculated on EBIT (Gatti, 2007).

Banks require a provision to debt reserve accounts as one of the many covenants included in the credit arrangement. The SPV must set aside part of the FCFE until this cash reserve reaches a certain predefined amount, for example, four semesters of debt service. After fulfilling this requirement, sponsors can freely sweep out cash from the SPV.

Defining the Optimal Capital Structure

Gatti (2007) and Gatti et al. (2007) propose an iterative process to evaluate the sustainability of a given capital structure in project finance deals and to detect when a project finance deal goes bankrupt. The iteration process is presented in Exhibit 14.5.

Exhibit 14.5 indicates a stepwise approach to defining the optimal capital structure and the criteria that must be met to complete the capital budgeting exercise. Plain lines indicate a feedback iteration on the financial components of the deal (revision of the debt-to-equity ratio) while dotted lines refer to feedback iterations involving the components of the unlevered free cash flow: the construction costs, the level of revenues and operating costs, and the variables influencing the change in working capital items.

A proposed capital structure (in terms of the debt-to-equity ratio and subdivision of debt into the different debt tranches) is used to generate the value of cash flows during construction and during operations. The first criterion that must be met is a satisfactory level of IRR for sponsors (Borgonovo et al., 2009; Esty, 2002).

$$\sum_{t=0}^{M} \frac{C_t}{(1 + IRR_{equity})^t} = \sum_{t=M}^{n} \frac{D_t}{(1 + IRR_{equity})^t} \qquad (14.2)$$

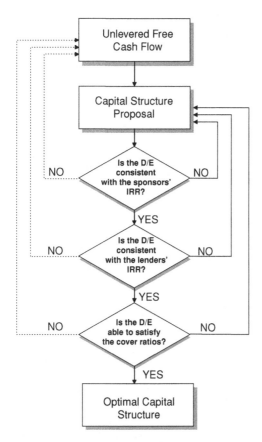

Exhibit 14.5   The Iteration Process for the Definition of the Optimal Capital Structure

Note: This exhibit shows the stepwise approach used in Gatti (2007) to determine the optimal capital structure of a project finance loan. Continuous lines indicate feedback actions aimed at modifying the proposed capital structure. Dotted lines represent feedback actions on the components of the unlevered free cash flows and on the content of nonfinancial contracts.

where C_t = capital contribution in year t; M = last year of equity contribution by sponsors; D_t = dividends received by the sponsors in year t; and IRR_{equity} = internal rate of return for the sponsors.

The term on the left side of the equation represents the discounted value of all equity contributions; the right-hand side shows the present value of all dividends collected by sponsors starting from year M. Naturally, if $M = 0$, there would only be one equity payment at the startup of construction and the left term would be simplified to C_0. IRR_{equity} for a project sponsor is acceptable only when it is higher than its weighted average cost of capital (WACC) or a higher predefined threshold rate (sometimes known as a hurdle rate).

Provided that the selected capital structure meets the expectations of sponsors in terms of a minimum acceptable IRR, the second step of the iteration procedure determines the profitability of the deal for lending banks. Although different measures of profitability can be envisaged for lenders (Gatti, 2007), the most intuitive is again the IRR:

$$\sum_{t=0}^{M} \frac{D_t}{(1 + IRR_{debt})^t} = \sum_{t=M}^{M'} \frac{K_t + I_t}{(1 + IRR_{debt})^t} \qquad (14.3)$$

where D_t = drawdowns on funds in year t; M = last drawdown period on loans; M' = last payback period on funds; K_t = principal repayment in year t; I_t = interest repayment in year t; and IRR_{debt} = IRR for lenders

Banks compare the IRR_{debt} with their weighted marginal cost of funding (WMCF). In terms of interbank loans and equity capital absorption according to the Basel Capital Accord principles:

$$WMCF = IR(1 - RW \times 8\%)(1 - t) + k_e RW(8\%) \qquad (14.4)$$

where IR = interbank rate; RW = risk weight (based on a standardized approach or calculated resorting to internal rating-based (IRB) systems); t = corporate tax rate; k_e = cost of bank equity; and 8% = minimum capital requirement coefficient according to Basel II rules.

Cover Ratios

Standard corporate finance textbooks usually consider a project acceptable if it guarantees an IRR higher than the cost of capital. Following the iterative procedure of Exhibit 14.5, a project finance deal should be acceptable if the first two criteria have been met. In practice, a third criterion must be met to consider a given capital structure optimal for the project. Because banks and the SPV set a predefined amortization schedule for the loans, the value of unlevered free cash flow must be strictly higher than the debt service due to banks in every year of the operational phase where the loans are still outstanding.

Consider the following example. Suppose that banks are granting a loan of $1 billion to an SPV with repayment in five years based on a constant principal repayment. The interest rate has been swapped from floating to fixed (10 percent). Assume that this capital structure is considered optimal and has been used for capital budgeting purposes. Exhibit 14.6 shows the cash flows for lending banks.

Exhibit 14.6 indicates that the IRR for lenders is 10 percent. If the banks have set the interest rate based on their WMCF, the project should be acceptable to the banks. The same IRR of 10 percent can be obtained with several completely different repayment schedules. Exhibit 14.7 illustrates two alternatives: a bullet repayment at the end of year 5 (with only interest payments during the period 1 to 5) and a payment-in-kind reimbursement at the end of year 5.

If banks base their decision to fund the project only on the basis of IRR, the three choices would be equivalent. IRR does not capture the relation between the cash available for debt service and the debt service itself. The problem is that IRR does not consider one important aspect. If banks have agreed to receive a certain debt service in year t, in that year the unlevered free cash flow must be sufficient to cover this obligation of the SPV. Put differently, the IRR cannot capture the

Exhibit 14.6 Amortization Schedule of the Loan

Years	0	1	2	3	4	5
% principal repaid		20%	20%	20%	20%	20%
Principal		200	200	200	200	200
Repaid capital		200	400	600	800	1000
Outstanding	1000	800	600	400	200	0
Interest		100	80	60	40	20
Debt service		300	280	260	240	220
Cash flows for banks	−1000	300	280	260	240	220
IRR	**10%**					

Note: This exhibit shows the amortization schedule of a $1 billion loan and the cash flows used to calculate the IRR for lenders (as reported in the cash flows for banks row).

financial sustainability of a given capital structure and relative payment obligations across time.

This is the reason that the third step of the iterative procedure in Exhibit 14.5 requires calculating cover ratios. Cover ratios are financial covenants that are common in structured finance transactions such as LBOs, acquisition finance, and asset-backed securitization (Fitch Ratings, 2008). The two most used cover ratios are (1) the debt service cover ratio (DSCR) (minimum and average), and (2) the loan life cover ratio (LLCR).

For every year of the operations phase, DSCR indicates the ratio between the unlevered free cash flow and the debt service in a given year t calculated as:

$$DSCR = \frac{UFCF_t}{(K+I)_t} \qquad (14.5)$$

where UFCF = unlevered free cash flow for year t; K = payment on the principal in year t; and I = interest payment in year t.

Banks require the DSCR to be higher than 1 in all years where the loan is not repaid and the desired minimum level depends on the lenders' risk-aversion. The protection that lenders require in setting the minimum level of this cover ratio

Exhibit 14.7 Alternative Repayment Methods for Project Loans

Solution 1. Bullet Repayment						
Years	0	1	2	3	4	5
Cash flows for banks	−1000	100	100	100	100	1100
IRR	**10%**					

Solution 2. Repayment in Kind						
Years	0	1	2	3	4	5
Cash flows for banks	−1000	0	0	0	0	1610.51
IRR	**10%**					

Note: This exhibit shows different repayment alternatives for a $1 billion loan with the same IRR for lenders of 10 percent, which is the same IRR as the loan in Exhibit 14.6.

depends on the degree to which various cash flows are made less volatile (as described in the earlier section on risk management). Projects in the transportation and telecommunications sectors, where long-term off-take contracts cannot be implemented, can generally only be financed with cover ratios in the range 1.5× to 1.7×. By contrast, power projects with financially sound off-takers and long-term take-or-pay agreements can be financed with required minimum DSCR in the range 1.3× to 1.4×.

In addition to the minimum DSCR for every year of the operations phase, lenders also require that the project is compliant with a minimum average DSCR whose value is higher than the minimum DSCR:

$$\text{AVDSCR} = \frac{\sum_{t=1}^{n} \frac{\text{UFCF}_t}{K_t + I_t}}{n} \tag{14.6}$$

where AVDSCR = average debt service cover ratio; and n = length of the loan amortization plan (in number of years). Lenders also require an average DSCR because they prefer to see years where the annual DSCR is higher than the minimum value instead of cases where in all years DSCR are stuck at the minimum level. This occurs as a further consequence of lender risk-aversion.

Together with DSCR, the second financial covenant that must be satisfied to consider a project acceptable is the LLCR. This is the ratio of the sum of the present value of the unlevered free cash flows during the life of the loan plus the existing debt reserve at time t and the outstanding debt (O) at time t or:

$$\text{LLCR} = \frac{\sum_{t=s}^{s+n} \frac{\text{UFCF}_t}{(1+i)^t} + \text{DR}}{O_t} \tag{14.7}$$

where UFCF = unlevered free cash flow; i = cost of debt; DR = debt reserve available at time t; and O = outstanding loan amount at time t. The numerator of the ratio is the present value of all available cash for debt service during the remaining life of the loan. The denominator is the amount still due to banks at time t. When the numerator is higher than the denominator, the SPV can repay the whole outstanding debt with the cash generated during the remaining loan repayment period.

Banks require that the project meets a minimum value of LLCR throughout the life of the loan. Once again, the level required depends on the volatility of cash flows and, consequently, on the effectiveness of the risk management and allocation process carried out during the feasibility study phase (discussed earlier).

Consider the following example. A $200 million project starts up at time $t = 0$. The project is amortized at 20 percent per annum using the straight line method. The project is financed with a senior facility of $100 million at a 5 percent fixed rate, and the loan is amortized in constant principal repayments over five years. The corporate tax rate is 50 percent. Based on sponsors' projections, the project will be able to generate constant earnings before interest, taxes, depreciation, and amortization (EBITDA) of $75 million per year. Exhibit 14.8 shows the data for the calculation of annual DSCR and LLCR at year $t = 0$.

Exhibit 14.8 Calculation of Unlevered Free Cash Flows (UFCFs), Debt Service, and Cover Ratios

PANEL A. Senior Facility Repayment Schedule

		1	2	3	4	5	6	7
% repaid		20%	20%	20%	20%	20%	0%	0%
Principal repaid		20	20	20	20	20	0	0
Outstanding	100	80	60	40	20	0	0	0
Interest		5	4	3	2	1	0	0
Debt service		25	24	23	22	21	0	0

PANEL B. P&L of the SPV

	1	2	3	4	5	6	7
EBITDA margin	75	75	75	75	75	75	75
Depreciation	20	20	20	20	20	0	0
(=) EBIT	55	55	55	55	55	75	75
(−) interests	5	4	3	2	1	0	0
(=) EBT	50	51	52	53	54	75	75
(−) taxes	25	25.5	26	26.5	27	0	0
(=) Net income	25	25.5	26	26.5	27	75	75

PANEL C. Statement of Cash Flows

	1	2	3	4	5	6	7
EBITDA margin	75	75	75	75	75	75	75
(−) taxes	25	25.5	26	26.5	27	0	0
Change in working capital	0	0	0	0	0	0	0
Capex	0	0	0	0	0	0	0
Unlevered free cash flow	50	49.5	49	48.5	48	75	75
(−) debt service	25	24	23	22	21	0	0
(=) Free cash flow to sponsors	25	25.5	26	26.5	27	75	75
DSCR	**2.00**	**2.06**	**2.13**	**2.20**	**2.29**		
Discounted UFCF during debt life	47.62	44.90	42.33	39.90	37.61		

LLCR	**2.1236**

Note: This exhibit shows the data needed to calculate annual DSCRs (debt service cover ratios) and the loan life cover ratio (LLCR) in the start-up year ($t = 0$). Panel A shows the amortization schedule of the senior facility and the annual debt service. Panel B includes profit and loss (P&L) data. Panel C summarizes the values of the unlevered free cash flows, debt service, and FCFE. The interest rate on the loan is a fixed rate of 5 percent.

Free Cash Flow to Equity, Dividends, and the Dividend Trap

Referring again to Exhibit 14.5, the exhibit shows that sponsors evaluate the attractiveness of a project finance deal in terms of IRR_{equity}. Earlier, when discussing capital budgeting during the operational phase, the chapter noted that project sponsors can sweep out cash from the SPV only after the repayment of debt service and, when required, provisions to debt reserve accounts.

Suppose now that provisions to debt reserve have already been fulfilled. In this case, IRR_{equity} should be calculated using FCFE in equation (14.2). However, legislation in many countries states that shareholders cannot receive dividends if the firm closes the income statement with a loss and that dividends can be distributed only up to the maximum level represented by the value of the net income. This situation is known as the "dividend trap" and is commonly encountered in project finance deals.

Consider the following example. A $400 million project is amortized 40 percent per year using the straight line method and financed with a senior facility of $250 million (interest rate 10 percent) and $150 million of equity provided by project sponsors. The debt maturity is five years and the loan is amortized in five constant principal repayments. Exhibit 14.9 shows the income statement and cash flows of the project for the first three years of the operations phase.

Exhibit 14.9 Income Statement and Cash Flows Using a Simple Combination of Senior Debt and Equity from Sponsors

Project value	400
Depreciation	20%
Accelerated	2
Debt	250
i	10%
Taxes	40%
Debt maturity (years)	5
Constant repayment	yes

PANEL A: SPV Income Statement

		1	2	3	4	5
EBITDA		80	80	80		
Depreciation		160	160	80		
EBIT		−80	−80	0		
Interests		25	20	15	10	5
Outstanding	250	200	150	100	50	0
EBT		−105	−100	−15		
Taxes		0	0	0		
NI		−105	−100	−15		

PANEL B: SPV Statement of Cash Flows

	1	2	3	4	5
EBIT	−80	−80	0		
Taxes	0	0	0		
D&A	160	160	80		
UFCF	80	80	80		
Interests	25	20	15		
Principal	50	50	50	50	50
FCFE	5	10	15		
Dividend trap	yes	yes	yes		
Payout to sponsors	0	0	0		

Note: This exhibit shows a typical case of the dividend trap. Panel A indicates the value of net income for the first three years of project life. Panel B shows the free cash flows to equity (FCFE) in the same period. The exhibit indicates that, although the project finance deal can generate positive FCFE, project sponsors cannot sweep away cash because net income is negative. This effect, called the "dividend trap," is in action every time the value of depreciation on the profit and loss statement is higher than the value of principal repayment in the statement of cash flows.

Exhibit 14.9 indicates that in the first three years of operations the net income is negative but FCFE is positive. In principle, project sponsors could count on available cash after debt service. However, the net loss hampers the dividend distribution. Hence, shareholders face a dividend trap. Intuitively, this situation occurs every time the value of asset depreciation in the income statement is higher than the value of principal repayment in the cash flow statement.

To maximize their payoff, shareholders tend to provide the SPV with subordinated loans instead of pure equity. As subordinated creditors, they have the right to receive payments before the dividend payment. Returning to the previous example, suppose that shareholders provide funds to the SPV with a combination of $140 million of pure equity and $10 million of subordinated debt (repaid in five years with constant repayments of $2 million per year plus 15 percent interest). Exhibit 14.10 shows the new scenario.

Although the dividend trap is still in action, project sponsors can now benefit from the payment of interest and principal on the subordinated loan. Exhibit 14.10

Exhibit 14.10 Income Statement and Cash Flows Using a Combination of Senior Debt, Subordinated Debt, and Equity from Sponsors

SPV Income Statement

		1	2	3	4	5
EBITDA		80	80	80		
Depreciation		160	160	80		
EBIT		−80	−80	0		
Interests		25	20	15	10	5
Outstanding	250	200	150	100	50	0
Interests on subordinated loan		1.5	1.2	0.9	0.6	0.3
Outstanding subordinated loan	10	8	6	4	2	0
EBT		−106.5	−101.2	−15.9		
Taxes		0	0	0		
NI		−106.5	−101.2	−15.9		

SPV Statement of Cash Flows

	1	2	3	4	5
EBIT	−80	−80	0		
Taxes	0	0	0		
Depreciation	160	160	80		
UFCF	80	80	80		
Interests	25	20	15		
Interests on subordinated loan	1.5	1.2	0.9	0.6	0.3
Principal	50	50	50	50	50
Principal on subordinated loan	2	2	2	2	2
FCFE	1.5	6.8	12.1		
Dividend trap	yes	yes	yes		
Payout sponsors	3.5	3.2	2.9		

Note: This exhibit shows the same case as Exhibit 14.9 but with a different capital structure. Here, shareholders provide a subordinated loan ($10 million) and pure equity ($140 million). The subordinated loan is amortized in five annual constant principal payments. Although the dividend trap is still in action, shareholders can sweep away part of the cash generated by the project in the form of subordinated debt service.

indicates that in the first three years, sponsors can get $3.3, $3.2, and $2.9 million, respectively.

SUMMARY AND CONCLUSIONS

Project finance is the financing of a newly created SPV incorporated with the unique purpose to design, build, manage, and finance a new project. The funding needed for the new venture is provided by the SPV shareholders and by banks in the form of no-recourse or limited recourse financing. Project finance has been and still continues to be used for the financing of large, highly capital-intensive initiatives in both industrialized and development economies.

The success of a project finance transaction depends on a careful mapping of risks and on identifying the best strategies to manage risk. A peculiar characteristic of project finance is that the complex network of contracts revolving around the SPV can be used to allocate risks to the counterparties best able to manage and control them. As a further mitigation of cash flow volatility, insurance policies and derivatives can be used to cover risks that go beyond the capabilities of the available counterparties or more common financial risks like interest rate, exchange rate, or inflation risks.

From the point of view of capital budgeting theory and practice, project finance makes the capital budgeting exercise easier than in standard corporate finance settings due to the perfect coincidence between the SPV and a single initiative with the finite economic life of the SPV. Yet, project finance is more complex because complications arise due to the specific features of the deal. The stepwise approach for the identification of the optimal capital structure and the joint consideration of profitability criteria (IRR_{equity} and IRR_{debt}) and cover ratios are peculiar to structured finance deals.

DISCUSSION QUESTIONS

1. Risk management is crucial in project finance transactions. Discuss how to use the network of contracts set up by the SPV linking it to the different contractual counterparties as an effective risk management tool.

2. From the point of view of project shareholders and lenders, deal sustainability is evaluated with different criteria. Discuss similarities and differences between the two categories of project stakeholders.

3. Cover ratios are financial covenants that creditors require as an element of credit risk mitigation. Discuss if and how an effective risk management program can influence the minimum level of cover ratios required by lenders.

4. When calculating IRR_{equity}, project sponsors may be unable to use FCFE for the calculation. Indicate why this is not always possible and how project shareholders can maximize their payoffs in these cases.

REFERENCES

Archer, Adele. 2005. *Evolution and Innovation in PPP/PFI*. Standard and Poor's Global PPP Credit Survey. London: Standard and Poor's.

Blanc-Brude, Frederic, Hugh Goldsmith, and Timo Valila. 2006. *Ex ante Construction Costs in the European Road Sector: A Comparison of Public-private Partnerships and Traditional Public Procurement.* Economic and Financial Report EIB, 01/2006. Luxembourg: European Investment Bank.

Bonetti, Veronica, Stefano Caselli, and Stefano Gatti. 2010. "Offtaking Agreements and How They Impact the Cost of Funding for Project Finance Deals: A Clinical Case Study of the Quezon Power Ltd Co." *Review of Financial Economics*, 19:2 60–71.

Borgonovo, Emanuele, Stefano Gatti, and Lorenzo Peccati. 2009. "What Drives Value Creation in Investment Projects? An Application of Sensitivity Analysis to Project Finance Transactions." *European Journal of Operational Research* 205:1, 227–236.

Brealey, Richard A., Ian A. Cooper, and Michel A. Habib. 1996. "Using Project Finance to Fund Infrastructure Investments." *Journal of Applied Corporate Finance* 9:3, 25–38.

Carter, David A., Daniel A. Rogers, and Betty Simkins. 2006. "Hedging and Value in the US Airline Industry." *Journal of Applied Corporate Finance* 18:4, 21–33.

Corielli, Francesco, Stefano Gatti, and Alessandro Steffanoni. 2010. "Risk Shifting through Nonfinancial Contracts—Effects on Loan Spreads and Capital Structure of Project Finance Deals." *Journal of Money, Credit and Banking*, 42:7, 1295–1320.

Dailami, Mansoor, and Robert Hauswald. 2007. "Credit Spread Determinants and Interlocking Contracts: A Study of the Ras Gas Project." *Journal of Financial Economics* 86:1, 248–278.

Esty, Benjamin C. 2002. "Returns on Project-financed Investments: Evolution and Managerial Implications." *Journal of Applied Corporate Finance* 15:1, 71–86.

Esty, Benjamin C. 2003. "The Economic Motivation for Using Project Finance." Working Paper, Harvard Business School.

European Commission. 2003. "Guidelines for Successful Public-private Partnerships." Working Paper, European Commission.

Eurostat. 2004. *Treatment of Public-private Partnerships.* Rome: Eurostat.

Finnerty, John D. 2007. *Project Financing: Asset-based Financial Engineering.* Hoboken, NJ, John Wiley & Sons.

Fitch Ratings. 2008. *Global Rating Criteria for Project Finance Collateralized Debt Obligations, CDOs Global Criteria Report.* London, Fitch Ratings.

Froot, Kenneth A., David S. Scharfstein, and Jeremy C. Stein. 1993. "Risk Management: Coordinating Corporate Investment and Financing Policies." *Journal of Finance* 48:5, 1629–1658.

Gatti, Stefano. 2007. *Project Finance in Theory and Practice.* Burlington: Academic Press.

Gatti, Stefano, Stefanie Kleimeier, William L. Megginson, and Alessandro Steffanoni. 2008. "Arranger Certification in Project Finance." Working Paper, University of Oklahoma.

Gatti, Stefano, Alvaro Rigamonti, Francesco Saita, and Massimo Senati. 2007. "Measuring Value-at-Risk in Project Finance Transactions." *European Financial Management* 13:1, 135–158.

Habib, Michel, and D. Bruce Johnsen. 1999. "The Financing and Redeployment of Specific Assets." *Journal of Finance* 54:2, 693–720.

Hainz, Christa, and Stefanie Kleimeier. 2003. "Political Risk in Syndicated Lending: Theory and Empirical Evidence Regarding the Use of Project Finance." LIFE Working Paper 03–014, Maastricht University.

Hammami, Mona, Jean-Francois Ruhashyankiko, and Etienne B. Yehoue. 2006. "Determinants of Public-Private Partnerships in Infrastructure." Working Paper, International Monetary Fund.

HM Treasury. 2003. "PFI: Meeting the Investment Challenge." Working Paper, HM Treasury.

Hodge, Graeme, and Cartsten Greve. 2005. *The Challenge of Public-private Partnerships.* Cheltenham: Edward Elgar.

Kleimeier, Stefanie, and Roald Versteeg. 2010. "Project Finance as a Driver of Economic Growth in Low-Income Countries." *Review of Financial Economics* 19:2, 49–59.

Megginson, William L., and Stefanie Kleimeier. 2000. "Are Project Finance Loans Different from Other Syndicated Credits?" *Journal of Applied Corporate Finance* 13:1, 75–87.

Minton, Bernadette, and Catherine Schrand. 1999. "The Impact of Cash Flow Volatility on Discretionary Investment and the Cost of Debt and Equity Financing." *Journal of Financial Economics* 54:3, 423–460.

Nocco, Brian W., and René Stulz. 2006. "E.R.M., Enterprise Risk Management: Theory and Practice." *Journal of Applied Corporate Finance* 18:4, 8–20.

Rajan, Raghuram, and Andrew Winton. 1995. "Covenants and Collateral as Incentives to Monitor." *Journal of Finance* 50:4, 1113–1146.

Smith, Clifford, and Jeremy B. Warner. 1979. "On Financial Contracting: An Analysis of Bond Covenants." *Journal of Financial Economics* 7:1, 117–161.

Tung, Frederick, Wang Xue, and Krishnamurthy Subramanian. 2008. "Law, Agency Costs and Project Finance." Working Paper, Emory University.

Välilä, Timo. 2005. "How Expensive Are Cost Savings? On the Economics of Public-Private Partnership." *European Investment Bank Papers* 10:1, 95–145.

Yescombe, Ernst R. 2002. *Principles of Project Finance*. Amsterdam: Academic Press.

ABOUT THE AUTHORS

Stefano Gatti is Director of the B.Sc of Economics and Finance at Bocconi University in Milan, where he is also the past Director of the International Teachers' Programme. His main areas of research are corporate finance and investment banking. He has published in these areas in such journals as the *Journal of Money, Credit and Banking*, *European Financial Management*, *Journal of Applied Corporate Finance*, and *European Journal of Operational Research*. Professor Gatti has published texts on banking and has acted as a consultant to several financial and nonfinancial institutions and for the Italian Ministry of the Economy. He has received the prize as the best MBA teacher during the period 2004 to 2009 and the Award for Excellence in Teaching and Research in 2009. He is a financial advisor for the Pension Fund of Health Care Professions and former member of the Board of Directors of BCC Private Equity SGR and Same Deutz Fahr Group.

Stefano Caselli is Professor of Banking and Finance at Bocconi University and Director of Customized Programs for Financial Institutions at SDA Bocconi School of Management. His fields of interest are corporate banking, credit risk management, and private equity. He has extensively published on these topics with recent papers in *European Financial Management* and *Journal of Financial Services Research*. He is a consultant for banks and nonfinancial institutions in Italy and abroad.

CHAPTER 15

Risk Simulation Concepts and Methods

TOM ARNOLD
F. Carlyle Tiller Chair in Business, University of Richmond

DAVID NORTH
David Meade White Distinguished Teaching Fellow, University of Richmond

INTRODUCTION

In one sense, risk can be considered a measure or a concern about the level of certainty of expected future values. For example, if the possible future returns on a security are 10 percent, 20 percent, –4 percent, and –8 percent, the expected value (or mean) is 4.5 percent. However, if the analyst uses 4.5 percent as a prediction of the future return on the security, the prediction is guaranteed to be incorrect because such a return cannot actually occur given the four possibilities that exist. Measures of risk, such as variance and standard deviation, provide a way of determining how accurate the expected value is relative to what is believed to be possible in the future. The larger the standard deviation or variance, the larger the dispersion between what can actually happen in the future and what is predicted using the mean.

Even those who avoid quantitative statistical measures understand that predicting the future involves risk simply because what is predicted may not actually happen. Having this basic insight is what makes simulation analysis beneficial. Risk can be incorporated easily into a financial model and simulation results can frequently be illustrated in a visual manner. Simulation techniques and results can be used to provide a better understanding of risk to those having quantitative or nonquantitative backgrounds.

In finance, simulation is generally used to project cash flow in some manner. The cash flow can be generated by a security or possibly by a firm's operations. Regardless of the source of the cash flow, an initial model needs to exist that identifies pertinent variables that are expected to generate the cash flow. These variables can be assigned specific values to produce one possible cash flow or set of cash flows, sometimes called a *scenario*. Alternatively, the variables can be assigned probability distribution functions to produce a simulation in which values are randomly chosen from the assigned probability distribution for each variable in a given "trial" or "iteration" and then multiple trials/iterations are assessed to produce an overall probability distribution for the resulting cash flow or cash flows.

An understanding of random number generation is not critical for using simulation techniques with the advent of simulation software, such as @RISK and Crystal Ball that link into Excel spreadsheets (see Sugiyama, 2008, for reviews of software packages; Carraway and Jenkins, 2008, provide a tutorial for Crystal Ball). However, a basic understanding of random number generation is helpful, if only to assess current and future Monte Carlo software packages. Basically, the key attribute of any Monte Carlo software package is the ability to randomly select a number between zero and one with all possible outcomes being equally likely. (The appendix provides a demonstration of how such random number generation can be programmed into Excel.) In theory, there are an infinite number of possible outcomes between zero and one. Pragmatically, this requires making some assumption to segment the interval into a finite number of possibilities. The number of possible outcomes is "N" of which each is equally likely, i.e., each outcome has a probability of $1/N$. Next, a means of randomly selecting an outcome is needed. This is the aspect of random number generation for judging Monte Carlo software packages. The analyst should know how "random" the random number generation technique is within the software package. Poor techniques generate trends or biases toward particular outcomes, which in turn bias the simulation.

Assuming a software package has an adequate process to randomly select a number between zero and one, any probability distribution can be simulated. To produce a random number from a particular probability distribution requires knowing the associated cumulative distribution function, which can only have a value between zero and one. By randomly selecting a value between zero and one, the cumulative distribution function can be set to the randomly selected value and then inverted to produce an outcome from the associated probability distribution function. Because the selected value between zero and one is randomly generated, the associated probability distribution outcome (via the inversion of the cumulative distribution function) is also randomly generated.

Arnold and Henry (2003) provide an example of a simulation for a stock price that takes advantage of this inversion technique. More advanced methods are available from Glasserman (2004) and methods for applying the technique for different probability distribution functions are available from Evans, Hastings, and Peacock (2000). Although this chapter sets the application of Monte Carlo simulation in a corporate setting, the connection to what is currently called *financial engineering* is not distant by any means. Thus, the reader is encouraged to take advantage of resources available from the area of financial engineering such as Brigo, Dalessandro, Neugebauer, and Triki (2007).

This chapter focuses on applying Monte Carlo simulation techniques to projects in a corporate setting. The associated cash flows for the project are modeled based on specific inputs that affect the project cash flows. Once modeled, the inputs are assigned probability distribution functions from which outcomes are randomly selected to produce randomly generated project cash flows. The process is more dynamic than evaluating individual scenarios for project cash flows, but is similar to scenario analysis (and sensitivity analysis) in that each trial within the simulation is an example of a scenario. The benefit of Monte Carlo simulation is that many scenarios/trials can be assessed to produce a probability distribution for all of the project cash flows. For this reason, Monte Carlo simulation can be considered a "scaled up" version of scenario analysis.

The chapter introduces a basic pro forma cash flow model and then applies various probability distributions to different variables within the model using a simulation software package called @RISK. A trial version of the software is available for download at www.palisade.com/trials.asp. @RISK is Excel "add-in software" that allows for simulation of pro forma financial statements created in Excel. In the initial simulation, all variables are considered independent. In a second simulation, correlations are introduced between certain variables, meaning that the input variables will exhibit some dependence on each other.

After performing these initial simulations, "compact" pro forma models are introduced that readily accommodate Monte Carlo simulation software because such models have easily integrated inputs that need only be set once. Compact models offer many possibilities for Monte Carlo simulation, but have the disadvantage of not being able to view the individual project cash flows that may be of some importance.

INITIAL STATIC MODEL

Before any simulation can be attempted, an initial static model (a pro forma model in this case) is necessary that is internally consistent and based on the best information possible about future cash flows. In corporate applications, the model is usually a pro forma model based on financial statements and programmed in Excel. From this initial model, decisions are made about how model inputs may follow different probability distributions. After such decisions have been made, simulation can be performed to determine how different future scenarios emerge based on the probability distributions of the different inputs. The different scenarios are then summarized to reflect an overall distribution of future outcomes.

An example helps to visualize the process of Monte Carlo simulation. Suppose a firm is considering a five-year project in which an existing product is introduced into a new market. Because the project involves an existing product, portions of the cost structure are well understood. The initial cost to enter the new market is $3.1 million (this is also the depreciable basis) and will require an initial increase in current assets and liabilities of $500,000 and $340,000, respectively. The market currently has a volume of 1.2 million units, which is expected to grow 3 percent annually over the next five years. Analysts believe that the firm can capture 13.5 percent of the market over the next five years. Exhibit 15.1 displays these assumptions and other assumptions as well.

These inputs produce the following pro forma statement where cash flow is defined as: [net income + depreciation – additional net working capital]. Exhibit 15.2 displays the pro forma analysis.

As noted at the bottom of Exhibit 15.2, the pro forma analysis produces an expected net present value (NPV) of $235,250. This is typical of an NPV analysis in which expected values for the project inputs are used to produce an expected NPV.

However, the analysis does not consider what happens should the expected values not actually occur. In other words, each of these inputs has a certain amount of risk in that expected values are not guaranteed to actually happen in the future.

Exhibit 15.1 Parameters for Initial Pro Forma Analysis of a Five-year Project

	Year 0	Year 1	Year 2
Initial cost	$3,100,000		
Salvage value			
Initial current assets	$500,000		
Initial current liabilities	$340,000		
Current assets per revenues		6.0%	6.0%
Current liabilities per revenues		4.0%	4.0%
Market growth*		3.0%	3.0%
Market share		13.5%	13.5%
Unit selling price		$51	$51
Unit variable cost		$44	$44
Other fixed costs		$200,000	$200,000

	Year 3	Year 4	Year 5
Initial cost			
Salvage value			$80,000
Initial current assets			
Initial current liabilities			
Current assets per revenues	5.0%	5.0%	0.0%
Current liabilities per revenues	3.0%	3.0%	0.0%
Market growth*	3.0%	3.0%	3.0%
Market share	13.5%	13.5%	13.5%
Unit selling price	$51	$51	$51
Unit variable cost	$44	$44	$44
Other fixed costs	$200,000	$200,000	$200,000

This exhibit shows the initial assumptions for the variables used to generate a pro forma analysis to determine the cash flows for calculating NPV.
*In Year 0, the market size is 1,200,000 units.

Monte Carlo simulation allows each input variable to have risk embedded through the selection of a probability distribution function. In the initial simulation, each input variable is assumed to be independent. By performing the simulation, the decision maker receives a much clearer representation of the possible future cash flows of the project.

INITIAL SIMULATION AND ANALYSIS

In practice, after creating a static pro forma analysis such as the analysis shown in Exhibits 15.1 and 15.2, the analyst then identifies and models uncertainty into the model inputs. Generally, the analyst conducts a sensitivity analysis varying individual model inputs to see how sensitive the output is to changes in inputs. This exercise provides a general sense as to how sensitive NPV is to changes in individual model inputs. Additionally, the analyst could conduct a scenario analysis.

  Scenario analysis would involve sets of model inputs that are part of specific scenarios such as the best case, worst case, and most likely case. This allows the

Exhibit 15.2 Initial Pro Forma Analysis of a Five-year Project Based on Inputs from Exhibit 15.1

	Year 0:	Year 1:	Year 2:
Market Units:		1,236,000[a]	1,273,080
Market Share of Market Units:		166,860[b]	171,022
Income Statement:			
Initial Cost:	($3,100,000)		
Salvage Value:			
Revenue:		$8,509,860[c]	$8,765,156
Variable Cost:		$7,341,840[d]	$7,562,095
Depreciation:		$620,000[e]	$620,000
Other Fixed Costs:		$200,000[f]	$200,000
Earnings Before Taxes:		$348,020	$383,061
Tax (35%):		$121,807	$134,071
Net Income:		$226,213	$248,989
Working Capital:			
Current Assets:	$500,000[g]	$510,592[h]	$525,909
Current Liabilities:	$300,000[i]	$340,394[j]	$350,606
Net Working Capital:	$200,000	$170,197	$175,303
Cash Flow:	**($3,260,000)**	**$836,016**	**$863,883**

	Year 3:	Year 4:	Year 5:
Market Units:	1,311,272	1,350,611	1,391,129
Market Share of Market Units:	177,022	182,332	187,802
Income Statement:			
Initial Cost:			
Salvage Value:			$80,000[k]
Revenue:	$9,028,110	$9,298,954	$9,577,922
Variable Cost:	$7,788,958	$8,022,627	$8,263,306
Depreciation:	$620,000	$620,000	$620,000
Other Fixed Costs:	$200,000	$200,000	$200,000
Earnings Before Taxes:	$419,152	$456,327	$574,617
Tax (35%):	$146,703	$159,714	$201,116
Net Income:	$272,449	$296,613	$373,501
Working Capital:			
Current Assets:	$451,406	$464,948	$0
Current Liabilities:	$270,843	$278,969	$0
Net Working Capital:	$180,562	$185,979	$0
Cash Flow:	**$887,190**	**$911,196**	**$1,179,480**

[a]In Year 0, the market size is 1,200,000 units which grows each year at the prescribed rate in Figure 1.
[b]Equals the portion of the market captured by the firm as prescribed in Figure 1.
[c]Equals Unit Selling Price prescribed in Figure 1 multiplied by the Market Share of Market Units.
[d]Equals Unit Variable Cost prescribed in Figure 1 multiplied by the Market Share of Market Units.
[e]Five year straight-line depreciation on a base of $3,100,000.
[f]Other Fixed Costs as prescribed in Figure 1.
[g]Initial Current Assets prescribed in Figure 1.
[h]Equals Current Assets per Revenues prescribed in Figure 1 multiplied by Revenues.
[i]Initial Current Liabilities prescribed in Figure 1.
[k]Equals Current Liabilities per revenues prescribed in Figure 1 multiplied by Revenues.
[k]Salvage Value as prescribed in Figure 1.
Other information: the weighted average cost of capital is 10.0%, which produces a Net Present Value (NPV) of $235,250.

user to see a limited distribution of NPVs in order to assess the uncertainty of the NPV itself. However, the analysis is limited to the number of scenarios performed. To increase the number of scenarios assessed, the next level of analysis is to perform a Monte Carlo simulation.

Assuming the availability of a well-defined model, performing the simulation analysis requires defining the uncertainty within the model inputs with individual probability distribution functions. In this case, the output of interest is the NPV, which is then recalculated thousands of times by randomly drawing model input variables from the respective probability distributions and recalculating NPV. Once complete, the simulation provides a range and probability of all possible outcomes for NPV, that is, a probability distribution for NPV. This probability distribution for NPV provides the decision maker with more information than is available in a simple scenario analysis to make a better decision.

For the model in Exhibits 15.1 and 15.2, the following distributions are defined for specific model inputs:

- *Salvage value* is uniformly distributed with a minimum value of $10,000 and a maximum value of $150,000. This is a single input being allowed to vary. In a uniform distribution, the expected value is equal to (minimum + maximum)/2.
- *Market growth* is a triangular distribution with a minimum value of zero, a "most likely" value of 3.0 percent, and a maximum value of 6.0 percent every year. This allows five inputs to vary. In a triangular distribution, the expected value is equal to (minimum + most likely + maximum)/3.
- *Market share* is uniformly distributed with a minimum value of 12.0 percent and a maximum value of 15.0 percent every year. This allows five inputs to vary.
- *Unit selling price* is a triangular distribution with a minimum value of $47, a "most likely" value of $51, and a maximum value of $55 every year. This allows five inputs to vary.
- *Unit variable cost* is a triangular distribution with a minimum value of $47, a "most likely" value of $51, and a maximum value of $55 every year. This allows five inputs to vary.
- *Other fixed costs* are uniformly distributed with a minimum value of $150,000 and a maximum value of $250,000 every year. This allows five inputs to vary.

Additional model inputs can be allowed to vary (currently, 26 inputs are allowed to vary), at the discretion of the user. The analyst should be careful of the temptation to vary all of the inputs because some inputs may be static due to contracted prices or hedged prices. Ultimately, the analysis is only as good as the care taken in selecting how inputs should or should not vary. Needless complexity only hinders interpretation and generally leads to poor decisions.

As shown in Exhibits 15.3 and 15.4, @RISK produces the following output given the model and the varying inputs defined above. This output corresponds to a simulation of 1,000 iterations. An *iteration* or *trial* is generated by a random draw from each of the defined distributions set into the pro forma analysis.

When viewing the @RISK output, the focus of the simulation is the NPV of the project. After running 1,000 iterations within the simulation, a probability distribution is generated for the NPV of the project. The NPV distribution is influenced by the 26 variables within the pro forma analysis that were designated to follow specific probability distribution functions.

Reading the output allows the user to determine approximately the probability of the NPV being negative. As Panel B of Exhibit 15.3 shows, the probability of negative NPV is between 30 percent and 35 percent. Further, a regression analysis with NPV as the dependent variable and the 26 user-defined random variables as the independent variables determines which of the independent variables most influences the NPV. As Panel C of Exhibit 15.3 shows, selling price and variable cost have the strongest effect on NPV with the impact being more important as the variable is closer in time to the present.

Exhibit 15.4 provides similar information in a visual form displaying the probability distribution, the cumulative probability distribution function, and a *tornado diagram*. The tornado diagram is based on the regression of NPV against the 26 input variable distributions mentioned in the previous paragraph and displays the coefficients of the regression to demonstrate the relative influence of the input variables (Eschenbach, 2006).

Having completed the first simulation, the user must determine if all of the informational needs have been satisfied and if additional structure should be imposed on the simulation making a second simulation necessary. For example, are variable costs dictated by the supplier and cannot be passed on to the consumer in the form of a higher price due to fierce competition? If higher variable costs can be passed on to the consumer, then variable costs should not be permitted to exceed the selling price, which is a possibility in the above simulation. More than likely, some variable costs can be passed on to the consumer, but not all of the cost. Consequently, variable cost and the selling price are most likely positively correlated.

Although attempting to have correlation implemented in the initial simulation is possible, often a more fruitful approach is to produce the simulation without correlation initially. Because correlation is subjective in this venue, debating over such specifications is generally more beneficial when the analyst has a simulation in hand to prevent spurious arguments. For example, if the belief is that correlation emerges later in the model, the tornado diagram in Exhibit 15.4 demonstrates

Exhibit 15.3   @RISK Numerical Output for Five-year Project

Panel A. Simulation Summary

Simulation Summary Information

Workbook name	simulation.xlsx
Number of simulations	1
Number of iterations	10000
Number of inputs	26
Number of outputs	2
Sampling type	Monte Carlo
Simulation start time	2/1/10 10:31:43
Simulation duration	00:00:05
Random # generator	Mersenne Twister
Random seed	2053689167

Exhibit 15.3   *(Continued)*

Panel B. Probability Distribution of NPV

Summary Statistics for NPV

Statistics		Percentile	
Minimum	$(1,365,928)	5	$(521,837)
Maximum	$2,044,706	10	$(352,379)
Mean	$242,204	15	$(242,405)
Std Dev	$463,521	20	$(148,992)
Variance	2.14851E+11	25	$(74,798)
Skewness	0.022898629	30	$(7,223)
Kurtosis	2.907020075	35	$58,336
Median	$244,537	40	$123,266
Mode	$249,598	45	$182,630
Left X	$(521,837)	50	$244,537
Left P	5%	55	$302,327
Right X	$1,002,354	60	$361,737
Right P	95%	65	$418,976
Diff X	$1,524,191	70	$480,372
Diff P	90%	75	$555,434
#Errors	0	80	$634,726
Filter Min	Off	85	$728,931
Filter Max	Off	90	$845,167
#Filtered	0	95	$1,002,354

Panel C. Regression to Determine Most Influential Variables

Regression and Rank Information for NPV

Rank	Name	Regr	Corr
1	Variable cost per unit (Triangular)/1	−0.350	−0.335
2	Selling price per unit (Triangular)/1	0.347	0.324
3	Variable cost per unit (Triangular)/2	−0.325	−0.307
4	Selling price per unit (Triangular)/2	0.324	0.318
5	Variable cost per unit (Triangular)/3	−0.307	−0.295
6	Selling price per unit (Triangular)/3	0.304	0.287
7	Selling price per unit (Triangular)/4	0.285	0.286
8	Variable cost per unit (Triangular)/4	−0.283	−0.271
9	Selling price per unit (Triangular)/5	0.268	0.271
10	Variable cost per unit (Triangular)/5	−0.267	−0.274
11	Market share (Uniform)/1	0.094	0.110
12	Market share (Uniform)/2	0.088	0.083
13	Market share (Uniform)/3	0.081	0.081
14	Market share (Uniform)/4	0.077	0.076

This exhibit shows the numerical output generated for Monte Carlo simulation analysis from @RISK based on the pro forma analysis in Exhibit 15.2

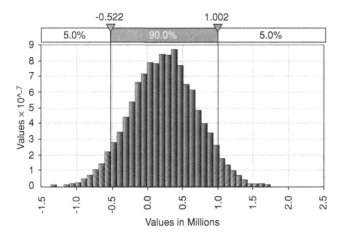

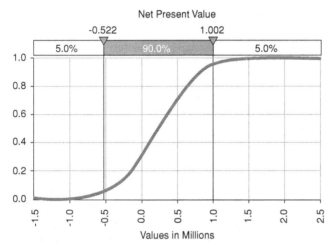

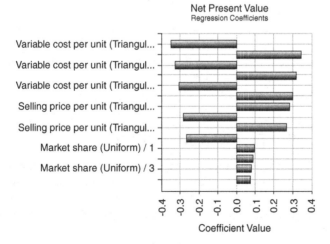

Exhibit 15.4 @RISK Visual Output for Five-year Project. Panel A: Diagram of the NPV Distribution; Panel B: Cumulative NPV Distribution; Panel C: Visual Display of Most Influential Variables

Note: This exhibit provides the visual output generated for a Monte Carlo simulation analysis from @RISK based on the pro forma analysis in Exhibit 15.2.

that variables that occur later in time have much less influence. Consequently, trying to find the best parameterization of correlation in this instance is most likely unnecessary. However, variables that have an effect in the immediate future are worth the effort in trying to have the most appropriate modeling of correlation.

SIMULATION WITH CORRELATED INPUTS

How does correlation affect the distribution of NPV? In a second simulation, the selling price and the variable cost within a given year are set to have a correlation of 0.50. Exhibits 15.5 and 15.6 display the @RISK output.

The selling price and variable costs are set to have a correlation of 0.50. All other variables are independent of each other.

Correlation does have an effect on the NPV distribution. Looking at Panel B of Exhibit 15.5, the probability of the NPV being negative has lowered from between 30 percent and 35 percent to being between 20 percent and 25 percent. The correlation adjustment narrows the distribution (compare the minimum and maximum values in Panel B of Exhibit 15.5 versus Panel B in Exhibit 15.3) and provides a better analysis. However, further review of the model may be necessary. More simulation may be necessary as the user "fine tunes" the analysis to develop a better prediction of what may actually occur in the future.

Fine tuning does not necessarily result in the dispersion of the NPV outcomes becoming narrower. In fact, the dispersion can widen depending on how the model inputs are designed to interact. The goal is to develop a better understanding of the risk of the project by being able to assess the frequency of the multiple possible outcomes. This should not be confused with changing parameter values to narrow the dispersion of NPV outcomes in an attempt to eliminate risk with the false reason of making the forecasted distribution more accurate. Simulation is not about risk mitigation, but about the most accurate realization of what risk exists. Upon accomplishing a realization of the risk inherent in a project, measures for risk mitigation can then be pursued.

The next section introduces "compact" pro forma models that are more parsimonious with Monte Carlo simulation software because the models require fewer input variables. As mentioned earlier in the chapter, these models do not allow the user to view the pro forma statements for the projected time period, but allow for very quick analysis.

COMPACT PRO FORMA MODELS

A *compact pro forma model* is a model using growth annuity and growth perpetuity equations to find the discounted sum of all future cash flows. Arnold and James (2000) introduce the model as a firm value calculator that can be programmed in Excel (also see Arnold, North, and Wiggins, 2005, and Arnold and North, 2009). The pro forma analysis is assumed to be "sales driven" in that a number of the cash flow components are taken as a percentage of the sales figure. Following the Arnold and North version of the compact model, in which cash flows run into perpetuity after a finite period of exceptional growth, assume sales are currently $10,000 and are expected to grow at 49 percent annually for five years and then at ing .

7 percent annually thereafter. The discounted value of all future sales is the sum of a growth annuity and a growth perpetuity. Assuming a discount rate of 20 percent, the discounted sales are worth \$343,181.82:

$$= [\$10,000(1.49)/(0.20 - 0.49)]\,[1 - (1.49)^5/(1.20)^5] +$$
$$[\$10,000(1.49)^5(1.07)]/[(1.20)^5(0.20 - 0.07)]$$
$$= \$100,260.55 + \$242,921.27$$

Exhibit 15.5   @RISK Numerical Output for Five-year Project with Correlation

Panel A. Simulation Summary

Simulation Summary Information

Workbook name	simulation_w_ correlation.xlsx
Number of simulations	1
Number of iterations	10000
Number of inputs	26
Number of outputs	2
Sampling type	Monte Carlo
Simulation start time	3/15/10 15:03:44
Simulation duration	00:00:09
Random # generator	Mersenne Twister
Random seed	1652631541

Panel B. Probability Distribution of NPV

Summary Statistics for NPV

Statistics		Percentile	
Minimum	\$(942,970)	5	\$(313,964)
Maximum	\$1,749,476	10	\$(200,702)
Mean	\$231,051	15	\$(117,573)
Std Dev	\$338,571	20	\$(54,665)
Variance	1.1463E+11	25	\$212
Skewness	0.081753178	30	\$50,658
Kurtosis	3.008766179	35	\$98,962
Median	\$224,013	40	\$140,926
Mode	\$188,915	45	\$185,412
Left X	\$(313,964)	50	\$224,013
Left P	5%	55	\$266,492
Right X	\$798,904	60	\$309,236
Right P	95%	65	\$357,373
Diff X	\$1,112,868	70	\$405,608
Diff P	90%	75	\$458,924
#Errors	0	80	\$515,559
Filter Min	Off	85	\$580,024
Filter Max	Off	90	\$671,313
#Filtered	0	95	\$798,904

Exhibit 15.5   *(Continued)*

Panel C. Regression to Determine Most Influential Variables

Regression and Rank Information for NPV

Rank	Name	Regr	Corr
1	Variable cost per unit (Triangular)/1	−0.474	−0.221
2	Selling price per unit (Triangular)/1	0.473	0.239
3	Selling price per unit (Triangular)/2	0.445	0.227
4	Variable cost per unit (Triangular)/2	−0.445	−0.217
5	Selling price per unit (Triangular)/3	0.420	0.208
6	Variable cost per unit (Triangular)/3	−0.419	−0.213
7	Selling price per unit (Triangular)/4	0.392	0.189
8	Variable cost per unit (Triangular)/4	−0.388	−0.192
9	Variable cost per unit (Triangular)/5	−0.371	−0.206
10	Selling price per unit (Triangular)/5	0.365	0.150
11	Market share (Uniform)/1	0.128	0.124
12	Market share (Uniform)/2	0.121	0.106
13	Market share (Uniform)/3	0.111	0.119
14	Market share (Uniform)/4	0.106	0.111

This exhibit provides the numerical output generated for a Monte Carlo simulation analysis from @RISK based on the pro forma analysis in Exhibit 15.2 with correlation between selling price and variable cost. Selling price and variable cost are set to have a correlation of 0.50. All other variables are independent of each other.

In viewing Equation 15.2, split the sum into two values: sales-annuity (= $100,260.55) and sales-perpetuity (= $242,921.27). Each of the sales values will be adjusted in a different manner to produce the summed discounted cash flows.

Define the cash flow as:

$$(\text{Sales} - \text{Operating Expenses})(1 - \text{Tax rate}) + \text{Depreciation}(\text{Tax rate}) -$$

$$(\text{Change in Current Assets} - \text{Change in Current Liabilities}) -$$

$$\text{Change in Fixed Assets} \tag{15.1}$$

Operating expenses, current assets, current liabilities, and fixed assets will grow proportionately with sales (i.e., these accounts will grow at the same rate as sales). Consequently, the discounted value of accounts are simply taken as a percentage of the discounted value of sales: Operating expenses are 56 percent of sales, current assets are 15 percent of sales, current liabilities are 10 percent of sales, and fixed assets are 135 percent of sales. Applying the appropriate proportion of sales for operating expenses, the sum of all discounted operation expenses is

$$\$192,181.82. = 0.56(\$343,181.82)$$

However, the cash flow calculation requires the change in current assets, fixed assets, and current liabilities. To allow for such an adjustment, the discount

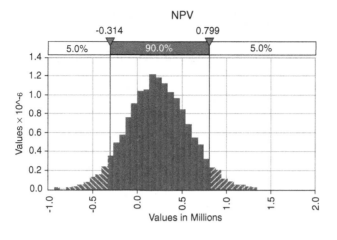

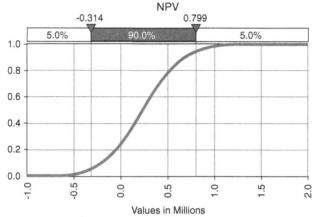

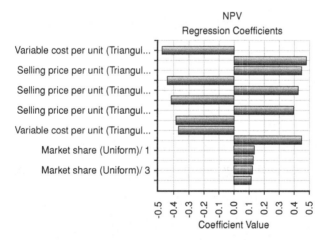

Exhibit 15.6 @RISK Visual Output for Five-year Project with Correlation. Panel A: Diagram of the NPV Distribution (See Exhibit 15.5 Panel B); Panel B: Cumulative NPV Distribution (See Exhibit 15.5 Panel B); Panel C: Visual Display of Most Influential Variables (See Exhibit 15.5 Panel C)

Note: Selling price and variable cost are set to have a correlation of 0.50. All other variables are independent of each other.

Note: This exhibit presents the visual output generated for a Monte Carlo simulation analysis from @RISK based on the pro forma analysis in Exhibit 15.2 with correlation between selling price and variable cost.

value for the sales-annuity portion needs to be multiplied by (1 − 1/(1 + annuity growth rate)) :

$$0.3288591 = 1 - [1/(1.49)]$$

The associated adjustment for the sales-perpetuity portion is (1 − 1/(1 + perpetuity growth rate)):

$$0.0654206 = 1 - [1/(1.20)]$$

Consequently, the sum of the discounted change in current assets is $7,329.55.

$$= 0.3288591(\$100,260.55)0.15 + 0.0654206(\$242,921.27)0.15$$

The sum of the discounted change in fixed assets is $65,965.91. Note: This calculation was computed with greater precision than displayed in the equation below).

$$= 0.3288591(\$100,260.55)1.35 + 0.0654206(\$242,921.27)1.35$$

The sum of the discounted change in current liabilities is $4,886.36.

$$= 0.3288591(\$100,260.55)0.10 + 0.0654206(\$242,921.27)0.10$$

The remaining component of cash flow to be computed is depreciation, which will be straight-line for 33 years and is based on the average of the fixed assets. To adjust the sales-annuity to find the discounted sum of the average sales, the sales-annuity needs to be multiplied by [1 + 1/(1 + annuity growth rate)]/2:

$$0.8355705 = [1 + 1/(1.49)]/2$$

The associated adjustment for the sales-perpetuity is [1 + 1/(1 + perpetuity growth rate)]/2:

$$0.9672897 = [1 + 1/(1.20)]/2$$

Using these adjustments, the discounted sum of the depreciation is $13,039.77.

$$= 0.8355705(\$100,260.55)(1.35)/33 +$$
$$0.9672897(\$242,921.27)(1.35)/33$$

Assuming a tax rate of 52.50 percent, the sum of the discounted cash flows is $10,161.79. Note: This calculation was computed with greater precision than displayed in the equation below.

$$= (\$343,181.82 - \$192,181.82)(1.525) + (\$13,039.77)(0.525)$$
$$-(\$7,329.55 - \$4,886.36) - \$65,965.91$$

Leaving the math aside, the compact pro forma model has eleven inputs: initial sales ($10,000.00), initial sales growth (49 percent), length of initial sales growth (5 years), perpetual sales growth (7 percent), discount rate (20 percent), operating expenses per sales (56 percent), current assets per sales (15 percent), current liabilities per sales (10 percent), fixed assets per sales (135 percent), number of depreciation periods (33), and the tax rate (52.50 percent). The compact pro forma model requires very little, but more complex, programming when compared to the traditional pro forma model. Exhibit 15.7 displays the Excel commands for executing the compact pro forma model.

Exhibit 15.7   Compact Pro Forma Model in Excel

	A	B
1	Initial sales	$10,000.00
2	Initial sales growth	49.00%
3	Length of initial growth	5
4	Perpetual sales growth	7.00%
5	Discount rate	20.00%
6	Operating expenses per sales	56.00%
7	Current assets per sales	15.00%
8	Current liabilities per sales	10.00%
9	Fixed assets per sales	135.00%
10	Straight-line depreciation periods	33
11	Tax rate	52.50%
12		
13	Sales-annuity	$100,260.55
14	Difference adjustment	0.3288591
15	Average adjustment	0.8355705
16	Sales-perpetuity	$242,921.27
17	Difference adjustment	0.0654206
18	Average adjustment	0.9672897
19		
20	(Sales − Operating expenses)∗(1 − Tax rate)	$71,725.00
21	Depreciation(Tax rate)	$6,845.88
22	Change in current assets − Change in current liabilities	$2,443.18
23	Change in fixed assets	$65,695.91
24	Sum of discounted cash flows	$10,161.79

Cell Formulas
B13: = B1 ∗ (1 + B2)/(B5 − B2) ∗ (1 − ((1 + B2)/(1 + B5))^B3)
B14: = 1 − 1/(1 + B2)
B15: = (1 + 1/(1 + B2))/2
B16: = B1 ∗ ((1 + B2)/(1 + B5))^B3 ∗ (1 + B4)/(B5 − B4)
B17: = 1 − 1/(1 + B4)
B18: = (1 + 1/(1 + B4))/2
B20: = (B13 + B16) ∗ (1 − B6) ∗ (1 − B11)
B21: = (B13 ∗ B15 + B16 ∗ B18) ∗ B9 ∗ B11/B10
B22: = (B13 ∗ B14 + B16 ∗ B17) ∗ (B7 − B8)
B23: = (B13 ∗ B14 + B16 ∗ B17) ∗ B9
B24: = B20 + B21 − B22 − B23
This exhibit presents the Excel commands for producing a compact pro forma analysis that continues into perpetuity.

Exhibit 15.8   Compact Pro Forma Model in Excel (Annuity Only Version)

	A	B
1	Initial sales	$10,000.00
2	Sales growth	49.00%
3	Length of project	5
4	Discount rate	20.00%
5	Operating expenses per sales	56.00%
6	Current assets per sales	15.00%
7	Current liabilities per sales	10.00%
8	Fixed assets per sales	135.00%
9	Straight-line depreciation periods	33
10	Tax rate	52.50%
11		
12	Sales-annuity	$100,260.55
13	Difference adjustment	0.3288591
14	Average adjustment	0.8355705
15		
16	(Sales − Operating expenses)(1 − Tax rate)	$20,954.46
17	Depreciation(Tax rate)	$1,799.25
18	Change in current assets − Change in current liabilities	$1,648.58
19	Change in fixed assets	$44,511.65
20	Sum of DCFs	−$23,406.52

Cell Formulas
B12: $= B1 * (1 + B2)/(B4 − B2) * (1 − ((1 + B2)/(1 + B5))^{\wedge}B3)$
B13: $= 1 − 1/(1 + B2)$
B14: $= (1 + 1/(1 + B2))/2$
B16: $= B12 * (1 − B5) * (1 − B10)$
B17: $= B12 * B14 * B8 * B10/B9$
B18: $= B12 * B13 * (B6 − B7)$
B19: $= B12 * B13 * B8$
B20: $= B16 + B17 − B18 − B19$
This exhibit shows the Excel commands for producing a compact pro forma analysis for a finite number of periods.

The benefit of the compact pro forma model is that all of the 11 input cells can be defined by a probability distribution to generate a Monte Carlo simulation. In a traditional pro forma analysis, many of the 11 input variables would have to be set to a probability distribution function for each individual year until reaching a terminal value. The compact pro forma model becomes even smaller if the cash flows belong to a project with a finite life. In this case, all of the perpetuity calculations can be eliminated. In the current example, let the cash flows be for a five-year project with sales growing at 49 percent annually. Exhibit 15.8 shows the resulting sum of discounted cash flows is −$23,406.52 due to the extensive investment in fixed assets.

Applying a Monte Carlo simulation to the compact pro forma model is much easier than the traditional pro forma model because by design the compact pro forma model has one set of input parameters that apply for all cash flows. Technically, the traditional model can be collapsed into one set of inputs, but would still require programming of all of the periodic cash flows associated with the project. What should not be overlooked is the ability of the compact pro forma model to allow the finite length of the first set of cash flows to be modeled with a probability distribution. Such modeling is not pragmatically possible within the traditional pro forma framework and allows for a more robust Monte Carlo analysis because the length of the project is a substantial element of its risk.

Another benefit of the compact pro forma model is the algorithmic manner in which the sum of the discounted cash flows is calculated. Arnold and North (2008) take advantage of this algorithmic scheme to calculate duration measures for project cash flows based not only on the discount rate (such as bond duration measures; also see Barney and Danielson, 2004, and Finch and Payne, 1996) but also based on growth rates from different model inputs. The duration measure provides a sensitivity analysis for the project because higher duration indicates the magnitude of how a change in a particular input affects the overall discounted sum of cash flows (i.e., the value generated by the project). Project inputs with the highest duration measures are the most sensitive input parameters. This analysis is very similar to the analysis provided by the tornado diagram in a Monte Carlo simulation.

Because of the algorithmic nature of the calculation, the compact pro forma model is readily adaptable to other analysis formats. Although the algorithm has been programmed into Excel spreadsheets in Exhibits 15.7 and 15.8, the programming could just as easily be performed in a programming language or within a different software package. This kind of ability eliminates any limits that a particular Monte Carlo software package presents because the user can switch to a different computational format to produce a more robust analysis.

Thus far in the chapter, the focus on Monte Carlo simulation has been with pro forma analysis. However, other simulation-based analyses in the realm of corporate finance also exist and are presented in the next section.

OTHER SIMULATION-BASED APPLICATIONS

Financial engineering for the purpose of pricing securities provides the most examples of the application of Monte Carlo simulation. However, corporate-based applications are also prevalent and not all corporate-based applications are based on pro forma analysis. Gimpelevich (2010) develops a simulation-based excess return model (SERM) for the valuation and risk assessment of a high-rise office project. The benefit of the simulation is that it provides a range of possible values for the project along with sensitivity analysis. Where SERM differs from "traditional" Monte Carlo simulation is that risk premiums are also assessed based on the project's potential outcomes.

Kim, Elsaid, and Kim (1999) use simulation techniques to define intertemporal correlation coefficients between projected cash flows from different time periods within the project. These intertemporal correlations within the cash flow stream, when defined, aid in the calculation of the riskiness, measured as variance, of long-lived projects. Consequently, the ability to capture correlation within project cash flows aids the user in understanding how risk emerges throughout a long-term project and how to take measures to mitigate the risk.

Better and Glover (2006) use simulation to address the situation where a firm has more acceptable projects than it can afford to undertake. The "project portfolio" is not the same as the security portfolio examined in portfolio theory because project cash flows are not solely defined by mean and variance, which is usually the result of assuming normally distributed returns for securities in portfolio theory. Consequently, convenient mathematical models do not exist to produce an optimal selection of projects. However, Monte Carlo simulation can be used to aid in finding the optimal selection of projects.

SUMMARY AND CONCLUSIONS

Monte Carlo simulation has roots in financial engineering, but has emerged as an important tool for corporate financial analysis because of its benefits in visualizing risk and the ever increasing ease of executing the analysis due to more powerful computers and software packages being available. Monte Carlo analysis is a "scaled up" version of scenario analysis in which a whole probability distribution for cash flows can be generated by defining probability distributions for input variables that generate the cash flows. As demonstrated, the output from a Monte Carlo simulation can be either numerical in nature or very visual in the manner in which risk is recognized within the project.

The chapter focused on pro forma applications being simulated using a traditional pro forma model and @RISK software. Such an application tends to be the most used within the corporate setting, but is certainly not the only version of the technique available to the corporate decision maker. A compact pro forma model allows greater degrees of freedom within the Monte Carlo simulation and is readily transferrable to other computing environments. Other applications of Monte Carlo simulation aid in different aspects of corporate decision making, such as the project mix within a portfolio of projects and in determining appropriate discount rates for projects. Going forward, the only limits that appear to exist for Monte Carlo simulation are those imposed by the creativity of the user.

DISCUSSION QUESTIONS

1. Based on the simulation output in Exhibits 15.3 through 15.6, what is the effect of variable costs being correlated with selling price on the range of values for the NPV of the project?

2. If an NPV analysis is based on the mean or expected values for cash flow inputs, how is likelihood of the mean NPV actually occurring affected by an increase in variance in the NPV distribution? Assume a symmetric distribution.

3. When comparing Exhibits 15.3 and 15.5, what is the approximate probability that the NPV is higher than $600,000?

4. Based on Exhibit 15.3, what input variable affects the NPV the most?

5. Based on Exhibit 15.5, what input variable most affects the NPV and has there been any effect due to price and variable cost being correlated?

6. What input variable does the "compact" pro forma model have available for simulation that is unavailable in the traditional pro forma model? Assume a finite number of cash flows.

APPENDIX: GENERATING RANDOM NUMBERS IN EXCEL

The command for generating a random number between zero and one in Excel is: =RAND(). Although a number can be entered into the command between the parentheses that is considered a seed value, such an entry tends to be unnecessary. Once a random number is selected between zero and one, a particular outcome for a probability distribution can be generated based on assigning the random number to the associated cumulative probability distribution and inverting the cumulative probability distribution. The resulting selection from the probability distribution is also random as a result.

Excel has many functions that perform the inversion process. If the desire is to generate a random number from a normal distribution with a mean "X" and a standard deviation of "Y," the function is: =NORMINV(RAND(), X, Y). If the random number is to be generated from a standard normal distribution (i.e., the mean is zero and the standard deviation is one), the command is: = NORMSINV (RAND()) or =NORMINV(RAND(), 0, 1). The ability to generate random numbers from normal distributions is particularly useful for simulating arithmetic Brownian motion and geometric Brownian motion processes (Arnold and Henry, 2003).

Not all cumulative probability distribution functions can be inverted using an Excel function and would consequently require programming in VBA (Visual Basic, which is available within the Excel environment). A list of the cumulative probability distribution functions that can be inverted using Excel functions are the following: beta distribution, chi-square distribution, F-distribution, Fisher distribution, gamma distribution, log-normal distribution, and T-distribution.

REFERENCES

Arnold, Tom, and Stephen Henry. 2003. "Visualizing the Stochastic Calculus of Option Pricing with Excel and VBA." *Journal of Applied Finance* 13:1, 56–65.

Arnold, Tom, and Jerry James. 2000. "Finding Firm Value without a Pro Forma Analysis." *Financial Analysts Journal* 56:2, 77–84.

Arnold, Tom, and David North. 2008. "Duration Measures for Corporate Project Valuation." *The Engineering Economist* 53:2, 103–117.

Arnold, Tom, and David North. 2009. "The Value of Convenience: Programming a Firm Value Calculator on Your PDA." *The Investment Professional* 2:3, 30–31.

Arnold, Tom, David North, and Roy Wiggins. 2005. "Improving Pro Forma Analysis through Better Terminal Value Estimates." *Journal of Financial Education* 31:Fall, 77–95.

Barney, L. Dwayne, and Morris Danielson. 2004. "Ranking Mutually Exclusive Projects: The Role of Duration." *The Engineering Economist* 49:1, 43–61.

Better, Marco, and Fred Glover. 2006. "Selecting Project Portfolios by Optimizing Simulations." *The Engineering Economist* 51:2, 81–97.

Brigo, Damiano, Antonio Dalessandro, Matthias Neugebauer, and Fares Triki. 2007. "A Stochastic Processes Toolkit for Risk Management." Available at http://ssrn.com/abstract=1109160.

Carraway, Robert, and Robert Jenkins. 2008. "Quick-Start Guide for Crystal Ball." Available at http://ssrn.com/abstract=912058.
Eschenbach, Ted. 2006. "Technical Note: Constructing Tornado Diagrams with Spreadsheets." *The Engineering Economist* 51:2, 195–204.
Evans, Merran, Nicholas Hastings, and Brian Peacock. 2000. *Statistical Distributions.* New York: John Wiley & Sons.
Finch, J. Harold, and Thomas Payne. 1996. "Technical Note: Discount Rate Choice and the Application of Duration for Capital Budgeting Decisions." *The Engineering Economist* 41:4, 369–375.
Gimpelevich, David. 2010. "Simulation-Based Excess Return Model for Real Estate Development: A Practical Monte Carlo Simulation-Based Method for Quantitative Risk Management and Project Valuation for Real Estate Development Projects with Case Study." Available at http://ssrn.com/abstract=1627004.
Glasserman, Paul. 2004. *Monte Carlo Methods in Financial Engineering.* New York: Springer-Verlag.
Kim, Sang-Hoon, Hussein Elsaid, and David Kim. 1999. "Derivation of an Intertemporal Correlation Coefficient Model Based on Cash Flow Components and Probabilistic Evaluation of a Project's NPV." *The Engineering Economist* 44:3, 276–294.
Sugiyama, Sam. 2008. "Monte Carlo Simulation/Risk Analysis on a Spreadsheet: Review of Three Software packages." *Foresight* 9:Spring, 36–42.

ABOUT THE AUTHORS

Tom Arnold, CFA, is an Associate Professor of Finance and the F. Carlyle Tiller Chair in Business at the Robins School of Business, University of Richmond. Professor Arnold has more than 40 publications appearing in such journals as the *Journal of Finance, Journal of Business, Financial Analysts Journal, Journal of Futures Markets, Journal of Applied Finance,* and *Journal of Financial Education.* His work has been cited in the *Economist, Wall Street Journal, New York Times,* and other non-U.S. news outlets. Professor Arnold's specialties include derivative securities, real option valuation, market microstructure, corporate valuation, and finance pedagogy. He received a Ph.D. from the Terry College of Business at the University of Georgia.

David North is an Associate Professor of Finance and the David Meade White Distinguished Teaching Fellow at the Robins School of Business at the University of Richmond. He has publications appearing in such journals as the *Financial Analysts Journal, The Engineering Economist, Journal of Corporate Finance,* and *Journal of Financial Education.* Professor North's interests include corporate governance, earnings management, corporate valuation, and finance pedagogy. He received a Ph.D. from the Eli Broad College of Business at Michigan State University.

PART V

Real Options and Project Analysis

CHAPTER 16

Real Options Analysis

An Introduction

TOM ARNOLD
F. Carlyle Tiller Chair in Business, University of Richmond

BONNIE BUCHANAN
Assistant Professor, Seattle University

INTRODUCTION

The main method of valuation taught in most business school courses is discounted cash flow (DCF) analysis. DCF emphasizes expected cash flows discounted at a rate that is appropriate for the risk characteristics of the project and is generally executed within a net present value framework (NPV) (see Chapter 4). In simplified textbook examples of NPV, the firm pays all costs initially and then the project generates positive cash flows into the future. These later cash flows are based on expectations and are not guaranteed. However, to simplify the example, the expected cash flows through time are generally treated the same as actual cash flows. Although these examples are illustrative to introduce NPV, actual projects are reevaluated through time and have expenses that occur throughout the project. Rarely are all costs paid at the start of the project, allowing the decision maker to patiently wait for the project to generate cash flow. In reality, firms initiate and maintain projects in a much more dynamic fashion.

In recent years, corporate decision making has greatly improved through the increased prevalence of real options analysis. Myers (1977) coined the term *real options*. He incorporated three factors into real options analysis: (1) uncertainty about future cash flows; (2) irreversibility of investment (i.e., once a firm initiates a project, it cannot fully recover the investment from sources other than the future project cash flows); and (3) the timing of project initiation. Myers's conditions for a real option extend simplified NPV analysis to consider uncertain cash flows and strategic thought about when and how much to invest in a project. The manager is not a passive observer of the project and its cash flows, but is an active participant in determining the cash flow structure of the project.

Real options analysis helps managers focus on the value of managerial flexibility because such analysis captures the value of being able to make critical decisions at the initiation and throughout the life of a project. By understanding how real options can be created, managers can make certain arrangements that create greater value by allowing more decision points through time during the project. By allowing a manager the ability to abandon, delay, or expand a project through time, losses can be reduced and gains can be increased.

The chapter begins with a numerical example based on the binomial option pricing technique of Cox, Ross, and Rubinstein (CRR) (1979). The example is reasonably generic, but allows for observing how a real option analysis expands beyond an NPV analysis. Another option pricing model by Black and Scholes (1973) is introduced to contrast with the binomial option pricing model. Because the Black and Scholes model can only price options that are executed at the end of the option maturity, the binomial model emerges as the preferred model for real options analysis.

The chapter continues with how the concept of a real option emerged in the finance literature based on dissatisfaction with firms favoring shorter-term projects to satisfy liquidity needs rather than longer-term projects that may allow the firm to grow. Real options analysis emerges in an effort to demonstrate how longer-term projects generate value for the firm. Although categorizing real options is somewhat arbitrary, this chapter presents such a categorization.

The chapter concludes with a discussion of how well practitioners accept real options analysis. Survey data indicate acceptance has increased over time, but also demonstrates that the main reason for not using real options analysis is a lack of management support.

A REAL OPTIONS NUMERICAL EXAMPLE

To illustrate how real options analysis increases the scope of project evaluation, consider a product that can be developed in one year. Similar products sell for $15 currently and are expected to sell for the same price next year. To develop the production facility, the firm invests $3 today and production/administrative costs will be $13. Given that only $2 of profit can be earned one year from today (i.e., $15 − $13 = $2, ignoring taxes), $3 in development costs makes the project undesirable due to having a negative NPV using any reasonable discount rate. However, what if the possibility exists for the price of the product to increase?

Using the binomial option pricing model of Cox et al. (1979) permits introducing volatility into the price of the product (assume 50 percent annually), and a risk-neutral setting (assume a risk-free rate of 2 percent annually) allows for a forecast of future prices with associated (risk-neutral) probabilities. The authors use probability theory to develop a binomial lattice approach with discrete time intervals, which is very similar to decision tree analysis. The value of this model is how the future price path of a security (or cash flow in this case) is illustrated with associated probabilistic information. Beyond being intuitive, the added benefit is that the model can also value highly complex options.

In the Cox et al. (1979) model, a price or cash flow can increase by the multiplicative value "U" or decrease by the multiplicative value "D." The multiplicative values are based on the return volatility σ (or standard deviation) of the underlying security over a specific time period, t. Both measures are generally taken annually; for example, σ can be 25 percent annually and t is 1/52 of a year, indicating it is a length of one week. "U" and "D" are:

$$U = e^{\sigma\sqrt{t}}$$

$$D = e^{-\sigma^*\sqrt{t}} = 1/U \qquad (16.1)$$

where $\sqrt{t}$ is the square root of t.

Why is the square root of t used? Given that variance is an annual measure, σ^2 can be made into a weekly measure by multiplying it by $t = 1/52$. Consequently, the weekly variance is $\sigma^2 t$. To convert the weekly variance into weekly standard deviation (or volatility), take the square root of the weekly variance, which equals $\sigma\sqrt{t}$. Consequently, the square root of t is just a by-product of the relationship between variance and standard deviation and for this reason should not create a distraction by being viewed as a result of complex mathematics.

Recalling that σ is 50 percent annually, each quarter (i.e., $t = 0.25$ years), the price can increase by a factor of 1.284025 ($U = e^{50\%(\sqrt{0.25})} = 1.284025$) or decrease by a factor of 0.778801 ($D = e^{-50\%(\sqrt{0.25})} = 0.778801$). The risk-neutral probability of an increase each quarter is 44.77 percent ($R = 2$ percent annually and is the risk-free rate) as determined by:

$$P(U) = [e^{R(0.25)} - D]/[U - D] = [e^{2\%(0.25)} - 0.778801]/[1.284025 - 0.778801] \qquad (16.2)$$

The risk-neutral probability of a decrease each quarter is 55.23 percent as determined by:

$$P(D) = [U - e^{R(0.25)}]/[U - D] = [1.284025 - e^{2\%(0.25)}]/[1.284025 - 0.778801] \qquad (16.3)$$

Building the binomial tree is a matter of growing the current price of $15 by "U" and "D" over consecutive quarters for one year (see Exhibit 16.1).

Five different possibilities exist for the product's price one year from today. Clearly, the project has a chance of either making money or losing money. Although not shown explicitly in Exhibit 16.1, probabilities of the different prices existing one year from today produce an expected value of $15 (as noted in the initial layout of the project). Because of the volatility of the price, a possibility exists of receiving much more than $2 in profit after one year. The next step is to determine if $3 in development costs is worth taking a chance on higher product prices emerging a year from today.

By looking at the prices that may exist one year from today, the manager may decide to stop production if the price is not above the cost of $13. In essence, the manager has a call option with a strike price of $13. That is, the manager has the right, but not the obligation, to produce the product, just as a call option gives the long position the right, but not the obligation, to buy a security. Production will occur if profitable (i.e., a product selling price above $13) because the manager's call option is "in the money."

To determine if the option to produce or to not produce has more value than the $3 in development costs, evaluate the five different possible prices at the end of the binomial tree. In other words, at what price should the product be produced

Capital Budgeting Valuation

Exhibit 16.1 Construction of the Binomial Tree

Panel A. Forecast for One Quarter

Quarter 0	Quarter 1	
$15.00	$19.26	= $15.00U
	11.68	= $15.00D

Panel B. Forecast for Two Quarters

Quarter 0	Quarter 1	Quarter 2	
$15.00	$19.26	$24.73	= $19.26U
	11.68	15.00	= 11.68U
		9.10	= 11.68D

Panel C. Forecast for Three Quarters

Quarter 0	Quarter 1	Quarter 2	Quarter 3	
$15.00	$19.26	$24.73	$31.76	= $24.73U
	11.68	15.00	19.26	= 15.00U
		9.10	11.68	= 9.10U
			7.09	= 9.10D

Panel D. Forecast for Four Quarters

Quarter 0	Quarter 1	Quarter 2	Quarter 3	Quarter 4	
$15.00	$19.26	$24.73	$31.76	$40.77	= $31.76U
	11.68	15.00	19.26	24.73	= 19.26U
		9.10	11.68	15.00	= 11.68U
			7.09	9.10	= 7.09U
				5.52	= 7.09D

This exhibit constructs a binomial tree by growing the initial cash flow of $15 by "U" and "D" from Equation 16.1 with $\sigma = 50$ percent annually and $t = 0.25$. The initial $15 grows for one year, generating five possible forecasted outcomes.

and how much profit should occur if the firm produces the product? If producing the product is valuable, its profit is zero. By finding the profitability of producing or not producing one year into the future, a new binomial tree is constructed with the year-end profit figures. The year-end figures (five values) are discounted based on expected values to the third quarter (four values remaining). The third quarter figures are discounted based on expected values to the second quarter (three values remaining). The second quarter figures are discounted based on expected values to the first quarter (two values remaining). The first quarter figures are discounted based on expected value to the present and represent the value of the option. Recall that the probability of an upward movement in price is 44.77 percent (P(U)) and the probability of a downward movement in price is 55.23 percent (P(D)).

The value of the ability of the manager to cease production if the product price is below $13 (or the value of the call option is $4.09) and is above the $3 development costs. Consequently, the firm should invest $3 in development to allow for the opportunity of an advantageous product price one year in the future. What appeared to be a negative NPV project based on the future expected product price of $15 has a value because the manager is not a passive participant throughout the project's life.

Real options analysis produces the value of being able to make choices throughout the duration of a project. Further, whenever more opportunities exist to have choices, the possibility of recognizing more value exists. For example, let development costs be spread over three quarters (i.e., the firm invests $1 now and then after each of the first and second quarters). The following section now extends this example.

A REAL OPTIONS NUMERICAL EXAMPLE WITH MULTIPLE DECISION POINTS

By having the development costs spread out over three points in time ($1 now and at the end of each of the next two quarters), a new option exists within the option to not produce the product when the future price is below $13. At each development cost investment point, the manager chooses between saving $1 and investing the $1 to continue developing the product (i.e., the value of the call option less $1). In Exhibit 16.2, at the end of the second quarter, three possible option values exist: $11.86, $3.31, and $0.40. With the values being $11.86 and $3.31, the manager should choose to invest $1 to continue the development (i.e., the call option). The net values for the options become $10.86 ($11.86 − $1.00) and $2.31 ($3.31 − $1.00), respectively. However, when the value of continuing the development is $0.40, the manager should choose to save the $1 in investment. Relative to the binomial tree, the second quarter payoffs become $10.86, $2.31, and $1.00 instead of $11.86, $3.31, and $0.40. Whenever a development cost is to be incurred, the manager can choose not to make the investment because further development may not be worth it. The new cash flows in the second quarter will affect the cash flows in the first quarter, which will, in turn, affect the value of the (dual) option today. Exhibit 16.3 illustrates the value of spreading out the development cost over three time periods.

At first, value appears to have been destroyed: $1.59 versus $4.09. However, this is incorrect because the $4.09 value does not consider the $3.00 development cost making a net value of $1.09. Consequently, having the flexibility in making development payments increases the value of the project because there is an opportunity to stop development in the second or first quarter that would not exist if all investment occurred today. Now, assume that the firm can pay all development costs in the third quarter.

To be consistent with the initial example, the development costs in the third quarter will be $3.05 in order to have a discounted value of $3.00. Unlike the staged development illustrated in Exhibit 16.3, the possibility exists to not invest any development money if the call option value is below $3.05. Going back to Exhibit 16.2, four possible option values are available in the third quarter: $18.82, $6.33, $0.89, and $0.00. The decision rule becomes either to invest in the option or to preserve the $3.05 for a different purpose. Clearly, when the option value is $18.82 or $6.33, the $3.05 is invested, generating net totals of $15.77 (= $18.82 − $3.05) and $3.28 (= $6.33 − $3.05), respectively. When the option value is $0.89 or

Exhibit 16.2   Value of Not Being Obligated to Produce in an Adverse Environment (i.e., the Manager's Call Option)

Panel A. Determine the Profit If Production Occurs (i.e., the value of the call option)

Quarter 4

$27.77 = MAX([$40.77 − $13.00], $0.00)*, production occurs
11.73 = MAX([$24.73 − $13.00], $0.00), production occurs
2.00 = MAX([$15.00 − $13.00], $0.00), production occurs
0.00 = MAX($9.10 − $13.00], $0.00), no production
0.00 = MAX([$5.52 − $13.00], $0.00), no production

Panel B. Iterate the Value of the Call Option Back to the Third Quarter

Quarter 4	Quarter 3	
$27.77	$18.82	$= e^{-2\%*0.25}[P(U)\$27.77 + P(D)\$11.73]$
11.73	6.33	$= e^{-2\%*0.25}[P(U)\$11.73 + P(D)\$2.00]$
2.00	0.89	$= e^{-2\%*0.25}[P(U)\$2.00 + P(D)\$0.00]$
0.00	0.00	$= e^{-2\%*0.25}[P(U)\$0.00 + P(D)\$0.00]$
0.00		

Panel C. Iterate the Value of the Call Option Back to the Second Quarter

Quarter 4	Quarter 3	Quarter 2	
$27.77	$18.82	$11.86	$= e^{-2\%(0.25)}[P(U)\$18.82 + P(D)\$6.33]$
11.73	6.33	3.31	$= e^{-2\%(0.25)}[P(U)\$6.33 + P(D)\$0.89]$
2.00	0.89	0.40	$= e^{-2\%(0.25)}[P(U)\$0.89 + P(D)\$0.00]$
0.00	0.00		
0.00			

Panel D. Iterate the Value of the Call Option to the First Quarter

Quarter 4	Quarter 3	Quarter 2	Quarter 1	
$27.77	$18.82	$11.86	$7.10	$= e^{-2\%(0.25)}[P(U)\$11.86 + P(D)\$3.31]$
11.73	6.33	3.31	1.69	$= e^{-2\%(0.25)}[P(U)\$3.31 + P(D)\$0.40]$
2.00	0.89	0.40		
0.00	0.00			
0.00				

Panel E. Iterate the Values of the Call Option to the Present Time

Quarter 4	Quarter 3	Quarter 2	Quarter 1	Quarter 0	
$27.77	$18.82	$11.86	$7.10	$4.09	$= e^{-2\%(0.25)}[P(U)\$7.10 + P(D)\$1.69]$
11.73	6.33	3.31	1.69		
2.00	0.89	0.40			
0.00	0.00				
0.00					

Exhibit 16.2 (*Continued*)

Panel F. Transpose the Binomial Tree

Quarter 0	Quarter 1	Quarter 2	Quarter 3	Quarter 4
$4.09	$7.10	$11.86	$18.82	$27.77
	1.69	3.31	6.33	11.73
		0.40	0.89	2.00
			0.00	0.00
				0.00

This exhibit uses the year-end figures from Exhibit 16.1 to determine when the investment of $13.00 is profitable and how much profit is available assuming production does or does not occur. In an iterative fashion, the profit is discounted in expectation to produce the value of the option. *MAX(A,B) is the maximization function that equals A if A ≥ B or B if B > A.

Exhibit 16.3   Value of Periodic Development Payments

Panel A. Iterate the Value of the Call Option Back to the First Quarter

Quarter 2	Quarter 1	
$10.86	$5.11	$= e^{-2\%(0.25)}[P(U)\$10.86 + P(D)\$2.31] - \$1.00$ when $e^{-2\%(0.25)}[P(U)\$10.86 + P(D)\$2.31] \geq \$1.00$
		$= \$1.00$ when $e^{-2\%(0.25)}[P(U)\$10.86 + P(D)\$2.31] < \$1.00$
2.31	0.58	$= e^{-2\%(0.25)}[P(U)\$2.31 + P(D)\$1.00] - \$1.00$ when $e^{-2\%(0.25)}[P(U)\$2.31 + P(D)\$1.00] \geq \$1.00$
		$= \$1.00$ when $e^{-2\%(0.25)}[P(U)\$2.31 + P(D)\$1.00] < \$1.00$
1.00		

Panel B. Iterate the Values of the Call Option to the Present Value

Quarter 2	Quarter 1	Quarter 0	
$10.86	$5.11	$1.59	$= e^{-2\%(0.25)}[P(U)\$5.11 + P(D)\$0.58] - \$1.00$ when $e^{-2\%(0.25)}[P(U)\$5.11 + P(D)\$0.58] \geq \$1.00$
			$= \$1.00$ when $e^{-2\%(0.25)}[P(U)\$5.11 + P(D)\$0.58] < \$1.00$
$2.31	$0.58		
$1.00			

Panel C. Transpose the Binomial Tree

Quarter 0	Quarter 1	Quarter 2
$1.59	$5.11	$10.86
	0.58	2.31
		1.00

In this exhibit, the valuation in Exhibit 16.2 is adjusted to account for the development costs being paid over three time periods (now and at the end of the first and second quarters). The iterative process is similar to that in Exhibit 16.2 except a decision point exists everywhere the firm makes an investment because the manager could choose not to invest in the continued development of the project.

Exhibit 16.4   Value of Delaying the Development Payment

Panel A. Iterate the Value of the Call Option Back to the Second Quarter

Quarter 3	Quarter 2	
$15.77	$8.83	$= e^{-2\%(0.25)}[P(U)\$15.77 + P(D)\$3.28]$
3.28	3.13	$= e^{-2\%(0.25)}[P(U)\$3.28 + P(D)\$3.05]$
3.05	3.03	$= e^{-2\%(0.25)}[P(U)\$3.05 + P(D)\$3.05]$
3.05		

Panel B. Iterate the Values of the Call Option to the Present Value

Quarter 3	Quarter 2	Quarter 1	
$15.77	$8.83	$5.66	$= e^{-2\%(0.25)}[P(U)\$8.83 + P(D)\$3.13]$
3.28	3.13	3.06	$= e^{-2\%(0.25)}[P(U)\$3.13 + P(D)\$3.03]$
3.05	3.03		
3.05			

Panel C. Iterate the Values of the Call Option to the Present Value

Quarter 3	Quarter 2	Quarter 1	Quarter 0	
$15.77	$8.83	$5.66	$4.20	$= e^{-2\%(0.25)}[P(U)\$7.97 + P(D)\$3.39]$
3.28	3.13	3.06		
3.05	3.03			
3.05				

Panel D. Transpose the Binomial Tree

Quarter 0	Quarter 1	Quarter 2	Quarter 3
$4.20	$5.66	$8.83	$15.77
	3.06	3.13	3.28
		3.03	3.05
			3.05

In this exhibit, the valuation in Exhibit 16.2 is adjusted to account for the development costs of $3.05 being paid at the end of the third quarter. The iterative process is identical to that in Exhibit 16.2 once the decision to invest is made in the third quarter.

$0.00, preserving the $3.05 investment for other purposes is preferred. Exhibit 16.4 illustrates the value of being able to wait to pay for developing the project and the possibly of making no investment at all.

The value of being able to delay the entire investment for development is $4.20, which is higher than the value of paying the development costs through time (which is more valuable than paying all development costs at the initiation of the project). In essence, whenever a strategically valuable opportunity emerges, real option analysis can be adjusted to demonstrate the value of the new opportunity.

The ability to wait on development (as seen in Exhibit 16.4) or to develop in stages (as seen in Exhibit 16.3) can be rationalized as being strategically important. However, before real options analysis, an ability to quantify the value of this flexibility had proven difficult. If fact, an argument can be made that obtaining the underlying model parameters, such as volatility, is difficult, or that a market for a particular finished product may not exist. However, simply performing the exercise of real option analysis provides information about critical factors to consider through the life of the project or makes clear how to implement additional value by staging development or delaying investment to determine how the economic environment develops in the future. In other words, understanding real options analysis permits thinking more strategically about different aspects of a project. Before discussing the application of real options in the literature, another different and common option pricing model developed by Black and Scholes (1973) is important to note.

THE BLACK-SCHOLES MODEL

Although the Cox et al. (1979) binomial model is illustrative and can be used to value options within options (sometimes called "compound options"), it is not the only option pricing model available. Black and Scholes (1973) developed a closed-form model that will price options based on continuous prices. In other words, if the CRR model was constructed with shorter and shorter time intervals producing many different prices at the end of the tree, the CRR model becomes equivalent to the Black-Scholes model. The drivers/factors used within the Black-Scholes model are similar to those of the CRR model, which are the following: current underlying asset price (S), exercise or strike price (X), time to expiration or the maturity of the option (T), the annual risk-free rate (R), and the return volatility of the underlying asset (σ).

To put these inputs into the context of the previous numerical example: S = $15 (the current product price), X = $13 (production cost), T = 1 year (the amount of time before potential production (note that T is different from t, which equaled 0.25 years), R = 2 percent (annual risk-free rate), and σ = 50 percent (annual return volatility of the product price).

The disadvantage of using the Black-Scholes model is that it can only price options that can be exercised at expiration (i.e., a European-style option). Consequently, the Black-Scholes model can only price the first real option in which the manager decides between investing $3 in development costs for the option to produce a product when the price is above the $13 production cost (recall the CRR model valued this option as being $4.09). The other options are in regard to the different time points in which development costs require extensions to the Black-Scholes framework.

To apply the Black-Scholes model to the option to develop the product, compute d_1 and d_2:

$$d_1 = [\ln(S/X) + (R + 0.5\sigma^2)T]/\sigma\sqrt{T} \qquad (16.4)$$

$$d_2 = d_1 - \sigma^*\sqrt{T} \qquad (16.5)$$

where $\ln(^*)$ is the natural logarithm function.

Using the inputs from the previous example:

$$d_1 = [\ln(\$15/\$13) + (2\% + 0.5(50\%)^2)1]/50\%\sqrt{1}$$

$$d_1 = 0.576202 \tag{16.6}$$

$$d_2 = d_1 - 50\%\sqrt{1} = 0.076202 \tag{16.7}$$

The equation for a call option is:

$$\text{Call} = S^*N(d_1) - X(e^{-R^*T})N(d_2) \tag{16.8}$$

where $N(^*)$ denotes the cumulative standard normal distribution (i.e., a normal distribution with a mean of zero and a standard deviation of one). Applying the relevant values for the real option:

$$\text{Call} = \$4.01 = \$15.00N(0.576202) - \$13.00(e^{-2\%(1)})N(0.076202) \tag{16.9}$$

The real option value is lower than the $4.09 found with the 4-stage (4-quarter) CRR model. However, this is not surprising given that the Black-Scholes model is the continuous time equivalent of the CRR model, making the Black-Scholes model more finely calibrated as a model. As stated earlier, taking smaller intermediate time periods (e. g., a 12-stage tree based on monthly time increments) within the CRR model will allow the CRR model to converge to the Black-Scholes model price.

Unlike the CRR model, implementing more complicated options within the Black-Scholes framework is no small task. Using the compound option framework of Geske (1977) with an approximation by Bensoussan, Crouhy, and Galai (1995) (also see Haug, 2007), the option for the ability to pay development costs of $3.05 after the third quarter can be viewed as a call option on a call option. There is an initial call option on choosing to produce or not to produce based on the product price being greater than $13 one year from today. From Equation 16.9, the value of this option is $4.01. The second call option (or option on the option) is the option to have or not have the initial call option to produce or not produce at the end of the year based on the value of the initial call option being more than $3.05 at the end of the third quarter. An approximate compound option framework emerges in which the option value from Equation 16.9 is needed along with the option's delta. *Delta* is the partial derivative of the option price relative to the underlying security:

$$\text{Delta} = N(d_1) = N(0.576202) = 0.717761 \tag{16.10}$$

The option delta is then used to scale the volatility in the following manner (the scaled volatility will be denoted as "V"):

$$V = \sigma(\text{Delta})S/\text{Call} = [50\%(0.717761)(\$15.00)]/\$4.01 = 134.31\% \tag{16.11}$$

The option on the option is now valued using the Black-Scholes model with $S = \$4.01$ (the value of the initial call option), $X = \$3.05$ (the development cost due at the end of the third quarter), $R = 2\%$, $T = 0.75$ (this option expires at the end of the third quarter, which is different from the expiration of the initial option), and $\sigma = V$.

$$d_1 = [\ln(\$4.01/\$3.05) + (2\% + 0.5(134.31\%)^2)0.75]/134.31\%\sqrt{(0.75)}$$
$$d_1 = 0.796541 \tag{16.12}$$
$$d_2 = d_1 - 134.31\%\sqrt{(0.75)} = 0.369262 \tag{16.13}$$

The value of the call on call option is:

$$\$2.08 = \$4.01(0.796541) - \$3.05(e^{-2\%(0.75)})(0.369262) \tag{16.14}$$

The \$2.08 option price is below the CRR model price of \$4.20 and also below the value of the initial call option of \$4.01. Consequently, according to the compound option, either the real option destroys value or the compound option is incorrectly specified. The latter is correct because the compound option model cannot account for saving the \$3.05 in development costs that is explicitly factored into the CRR model. There is no method for incorporating the development cost savings into the compound option framework, primarily because the compound option framework works better with traded securities.

The purpose for demonstrating the difficulty of using the Black-Scholes framework for complicated options that are easily priced using the CRR framework is to prevent the false sense of security that sometimes emerges when using the Black-Scholes framework. The Black-Scholes model is a capable model that is used extensively in practice, but that should not be the reason for using the Black-Scholes model when considering real options analysis. Any model that cannot be specified appropriately will produce inaccurate valuations. Unless the real option can be viewed as a European-style option, the Black-Scholes model is not the preferred model for valuing the real option. Fortunately, the CRR framework has great flexibility in how it can be specified and is generally the model of choice when performing real options analysis (Block, 2007).

Before leaving this section, a discussion about risk-neutral pricing is necessary. Risk-neutral pricing is the result of changing the probability measure (i.e., the measure is the probability associated with a particular event) of an entire probability distribution to where all risk premiums are zero. This does not mean that market participants are risk-neutral or do not expect to be compensated for risk. Although having risk-neutral participants is a sufficient condition for risk-neutral pricing, it is not a necessary condition for risk-neutral pricing. Consequently, even with risk-averse market participants, the probability space can be transformed into a risk-neutral space. The transformation is particularly simple for a normal probability distribution from which the Black-Scholes model and the CRR model emerge.

Methods are available for valuing options without using risk-neutral pricing. Arnold and Crack (2000, 2004a, and 2004b) demonstrate how a discount rate with a risk premium can be used within a binomial tree and how such a discount rate can value a real option. The authors demonstrate that the value of the option does not change whether the discount rate has a risk premium. Consequently, having a risk premium embedded into an option valuation is a needless complication.

Ultimately, risk-neutral pricing is a mathematical convenience and should not be an issue for accepting the validity of real options analysis. However, should there be skepticism about risk-neutral pricing within a real options analysis, the Arnold and Crack methods should alleviate the skepticism.

Having introduced the standard option pricing models and discussed how a real option emerges by creating decision points, the chapter continues by detailing how real options analysis emerged in the finance literature. Myers (1977) introduced the concept as an underinvestment problem for firms created by having debt in the capital structure. Because the debt level forces firms to address short-term liquidity needs, it favors shorter-term projects that offer liquidity over longer-term projects that offer the potential of future growth.

UNDERINVESTMENT PROBLEM AND EMERGENCE OF REAL OPTIONS ANALYSIS

Although discussing option pricing techniques before introducing how real options developed in the finance literature may seem premature, the numerical examples in the previous sections help to illustrate how real options emerge within a project decision-making framework. Without recognizing the dynamic environment in which a project exists, the benefits of real options analysis and the ability to create real options contractually are lost.

Although Myers (1977) introduced the term *real option*, he does not actually value any real options in the paper. Instead, he discusses what has been called the "underinvestment problem," which emerges in the following manner. Firms that have no debt in their capital structure can accept projects in which future risky growth is present. If the project eventually fails, only equity is lost. However, if the project succeeds, substantial value may accrue to the firm. When debt enters into a firm's capital structure, short-term interest and debt repayment obligations emerge that require cash outflows. To meet these liquidity needs, firms tend to focus on short-term projects that generate liquidity and have little growth prospects. Such projects are likely to be extensions of existing manufacturing or services provided by the given firm. Because of the manner in which firms choose to meet these liquidity needs, firms tend to underinvest in future growth.

Myers (1977) posits that debt levels are determined by the firm's book and/or market values for debt and equity. The underinvestment problem arises because actual debt levels should be inversely related to the proportion of the value of "growth assets" (i.e., the assets associated with projects that provide future risky growth) over the value of the firm. In other words, the inconsistency between how debt and equity are theoretically and actually distributed within the firm leads to the underinvestment problem.

Although Hayes and Garvin (1982) view the underinvestment problem differently from Myers (1977), they come to a similar conclusion: Firms are caught in an environment of underinvestment. Hayes and Garvin first note a decline in investment in research and development (R&D), which Hayes and Abernathy (1980) previously described as the result of seeking "imitation" over "innovation." Hayes and Abernathy demonstrate the problem by noting the trade-off between imitative versus innovative design for an established product line. Market demand is predictable with imitative design, but is unpredictable with the possibility of large gains or losses with innovative design. Market recognition and acceptance are quick with imitative design, but such recognition is likely to be slow with innovative design and less prone to being copied quickly by a competitor. Distribution and sales are readily adaptable with imitative design, but distribution may be highly specialized and may require educating the consumer with innovative design. Imitative design easily integrates into the existing production processes and sales policies, whereas innovative design could cannibalize existing production lines and require new or unfamiliar means of production and sales.

Hayes and Garvin (1982) then look at DCF decision metrics and find the metrics too restrictive in how they are applied. Firms often use *hurdle rates* (i.e., the minimum rate of return that a project must generate to be acceptable) that are abnormally high, favoring imitative over innovative projects. The authors refer to the problem as the "logic of disinvestment" and provide a simple example of two firms considering identical projects that could potentially revolutionize the industry. Because one firm has an abnormally high hurdle rate, it does not pursue the project, but the firm with a reasonable hurdle rate decides to undertake the project. If the project revolutionizes the industry, the firm that did not invest when the opportunity existed will be at a competitive disadvantage and may be unable to recover lost market share or may fail completely.

Hayes and Garvin (1982) suspect that the reason companies apply overly high hurdle rates for DCF metrics is the need for short-term cash flow. The authors do not cite debt specifically as the reason for projects having to provide immediate cash flow, but suspect mergers and acquisitions (M&As), which often require debt, as being a contributing factor. Assuming that Hayes and Garvin would agree that debt causes the need for short-term cash flow, they are in agreement with Myers's contention that firms have too much debt, a condition that causes underinvestment.

Although DCF techniques per se are not necessarily to blame for underinvestment, the way that some firms apply these techniques may promote underinvestment. Hodder and Riggs (1985) address the issue as a need to reevaluate how firms apply DCF techniques, especially NPV. The authors note three "serious pitfalls" in how firms apply NPV: (1) improper treatment of inflation through time; (2) excessive risk adjustments in the discount rate, particularly if the project becomes less risky through time; and (3) failure to see how management interaction can reduce risk through time. Hodder and Riggs then provide a dynamic NPV presentation, similar to that provided in Chapter 4 to demonstrate how a project's discount rate can change as the project becomes more or less successful over time. Following Arnold and Crack's (2004a, 2004b) version of the binomial tree for a real option using risk-adjusted rates provides the same intuition, which is unfortunately lost in a risk-neutral binomial tree.

Hodder and Riggs (1985) do not value an actual real option, but their investigation marks the beginning of evaluating management's ability to change the risk of a project through time by their actions. In essence, the manager stops being passively engaged in the project and starts being able to make decisions that hopefully add value to the project over time. As real options analysis develops in the literature, a classification of particular real options begins to emerge. This is the subject of the next section.

TYPES OF REAL OPTIONS

Separating all real options into a few categories poses difficulties. For example, once having designated the categories, the differentiation between them lacks precision. Further, many real option applications, such as the examples presented earlier, generally combine options, making categorization even more difficult. Despite these complications, Trigeorgis (1993, 1996, 2005) provides what appears to be the most common separation of real option categories.

The "option to defer" is created by a situation in which a firm can have rights to use an asset through a period of time (e. g., a lease on land). By having the right to use the asset and not the obligation, the firm can strategically defer implementing the asset into a particular project. There can be many reasons for deferring, but generally two major reasons emerge in the literature: waiting for the optimal economic climate and learning about a new process before implementing it on a large scale.

The "time to build option" or "staged investment option" emerges when a decision process can be set as a series of decisions rather than a single decision at the outset of a project (e. g., using the example from earlier in the chapter, having three investments of $1 paid through time to develop a product creates more decision points when compared to making one payment of $3 to develop the product). R&D within a firm is a common example of this type of option because research usually occurs in stages based on the scientific method. However, firms can create a staged investment option by taking a large project and implementing it in parts over time. For example, a retailer can experiment with a new store format by retrofitting all of its stores at once or by retrofitting a few stores initially to determine if the new format works. As the firm learns from implementing the new format in a few initial stores, the firm can decide on how quickly to retrofit all the stores or whether to implement the new format at all.

Breaking a project into a series of steps of implementation is an easy way to see the value of thinking in a real options framework without necessarily computing option values. In doing so, the firm commits less capital at the project's outset and learns about the intricacies of the project before committing further capital investment. To make such an option beneficial, the firm has to commit to making crucial decisions at future points in time or when triggered by events or production milestones. Staging the investment without this commitment for review may ultimately delay the project because managers are not making decisions in a timely fashion. In other words, indecision is not a hallmark of real options analysis. Trying to create real option value does not mean putting off decision making to some arbitrary point in the future by not committing to a timeline.

The "option to abandon" is often within a staged investment decision because a firm can choose to end a project during one of the intermediate stages. However, the option to abandon can also be a decision to sell the project during an intermediate stage for profit reasons. For example, suppose an entrepreneur in the retail industry develops a product that is enjoying great local success. The entrepreneur can continue to grow the product's sales or potentially abandon the product by selling its rights to a large retailer who can manufacture and distribute the product over a much wider distribution range. To contractually implement the abandonment option, the entrepreneur can enter into a joint venture with a large retailer to distribute the product with the ability to sell the rights to the product at a future point in time (i.e., abandonment) or to renew the distribution agreement.

The "option to alter operating scale" is the ability to expand operations when it is beneficial to increase production, or to contract (or abandon) production during adverse economic conditions. This kind of production flexibility is desirable and is too often an afterthought by firms. The ability to expand can be created by having some excess capacity, even if it just additional space, to take advantage of sporadic excess demand. The ability to contract can be implemented by contractually having the option to not take delivery from a supplier when demand is low during an economic downturn. Creating these options requires forethought with regard to contracting supply to allow for contraction and building facilities to allow for expansion. A firm often rents excess space in a facility to another manufacturer to defer the cost of creating the option to expand.

The "option to switch" is generally associated with a production process that can use alternative inputs or can be implemented at alternative locations. The value or recognition of this option allows a firm to produce with the lowest cost inputs and to distribute to meet sporadic increases in demand at different locations. To create the option relative to inputs, the firm can design its production process to make use of different forms of energy and can investigate different suppliers of raw materials to keep raw materials competitively priced. Value exists in simply recognizing the option for strategic benefit even if the firm does not place an actual value on this option.

"Growth options" pertain to any investment outside of the sphere of a firm's current production or business practices. Because this is a rather ambiguous designation, it should not be the sole reason for a firm to invest. The idea behind a growth option is that firms should recognize and invest in projects that can potentially promote future growth for the firm. These options emerge through R&D or through actively engaging in joint ventures in markets with potential future benefits. Growth options are the direct antithesis of (or the solution to) the underinvestment problem.

"Multiple interacting options" or "rainbow options" are situations in which multiple options are available within a project. A staged project can be considered a type of rainbow option, but the term is usually used when the firm has simultaneously expiring options to consider. Thus, a rainbow option is more expansive than the usual notion of a staged project. Often in a rainbow option, not all of the options available can be priced. However, managers should at least recognize all of the options and consider them in the decision-making process. The benefit of visualizing a rainbow option is that the project does not exist in a vacuum and the decision maker becomes aware of a project's many aspects. Unfortunately, the enormity of a rainbow option can be intimidating, and issues that delay decisions may arise concerning options that in reality have very little value.

In summary, separating real options into categories can be difficult. However, certain basic options such as to defer, contract, expand, and abandon are frequently used to construct more complicated options. Most agree that visualizing where real options exist is straightforward, but determining the value of these options is complex, even if the CRR model is workable. Consequently, the chapter now turns to seeing whether firms actually use real option analysis and if so, how.

USE OF REAL OPTIONS ANALYSIS IN PRACTICE

Kemna (1993, p. 259) describes how practitioners view using real options analysis:

> Despite this incentive (the ability to value flexibility), the process of adapting OPT (option pricing theory) to the practice of strategic decision-making is far from smooth. In most cases, the introduction of OPT would require practitioners to fundamentally reconsider their standard capital budgeting techniques. And when all this hard work has been done, there is still the question: how do we tell management? That question seems to lead us back to where we started. For practical purposes, we cannot afford to come up with very complicated options techniques that can only be priced with black-box computer programs. The contribution of real options in practice is limited when one cannot explain what the important options are and why DCF (discounted cash flow) analysis cannot be used.

Kemna's (1993) statement strikes at the heart of the issue. If real options analysis cannot be explained to management, then its practical use as a capital budgeting tool is severely limited. Based on 279 responses from Fortune 1000 firms, Block (2007) finds that 14.3 percent of the respondents report using some form of real options analysis. The survey results show that the industries most commonly using real options analysis are technology, energy, and utilities. Respondents report using real options analysis for new product introduction, R&D, and M&As. The main reason firms avoid using real options analysis, reported by 42.7 percent of the survey respondents, is a lack of management support. Why is there a lack of management support? The next two reasons reported by Block (2007) for not using real options analysis may answer the question: DCF is a proven method (25.6 percent of respondents) and real option analysis requires too much sophistication (19.5 percent of respondents). Thus, traditional methods seem to work well. Binder and Chaput (1996) find that managers favor the profitability index over NPV for the pragmatic reason. Because not all projects require extensive study, perhaps many of them do not warrant sophisticated real options analysis. From the perspective of real options advocates, the encouraging news is that the use and acceptance of the method appears to be increasing.

However, firms may be using real options analysis without them actually crediting the method. Moel and Tufano (2002) examine the decisions to both open and close North American gold mines from 1988 through 1997 and find such actions consistent with real options analysis. The impetus for the paper was a study by Brennan and Schwartz (1985) that modeled the decision to open and close a copper mine using real options analysis. The testable implications based on real options analysis from the Brennan and Schwartz paper used by Moel and Tufano are: Mines do not open immediately when commodity spot prices made mining profitable and mines do not close immediately when commodity prices made mining unprofitable. The reason for this behavior is that costs are involved to open or shut a mine, and volatility in commodity prices may mean a profitable or nonprofitable situation can reverse quickly. Consequently, the spot price of copper or gold (the commodity in question from each paper) needs to make operations sufficiently profitable to be more valuable than the cost of opening the mine with the possibility of a price reversal also incorporated. Or, the spot price of copper or gold has to make operations sufficiently nonprofitable to warrant the cost of closing the mine with the possibility of a price reversal incorporated.

The notion that decision makers may actually follow real options behavior without performing real options analysis is plausible. For example, decision tree analysis, which has existed for quite some time, inherently makes a manager acknowledge the real options that are contained in a project. However, making real options analysis a standard formal technique, such as NPV, takes time. Various authors such as Feinstein and Lander (2002), Arnold and Crack (2004b), McDonald (2006), and Favato (2008) extol the virtues of real options analysis and/or demonstrate how traditional DCF techniques encompass real options analysis.

Other authors use traditional DCF techniques to implement real options analysis. Lewis, Eschenbach, and Hartman (2008) use the project's internal rate of return (IRR) to approximate the volatility parameter for a real options analysis. Boyle and Guthrie (1997) demonstrate adjusting the payback period to value the benefit of waiting to invest (the real option to defer). Alessii (2006) uses both the IRR and the payback period to make decisions in a real options context without using option pricing techniques.

Despite the extensive literature on real options analysis, Block (2007) notes that management, as a group, remains unconvinced of the value of real options analysis. Baker, Dutta, and Saadi (2011) conclude that contrary to optimistic predictions, the use of real options appears disproportionate to their potential as a capital budgeting tool.

SUMMARY AND CONCLUSIONS

Real options analysis attempts to capture the benefit of flexibility within a project either by design or due to management discretion. The origins of real options analysis date back to Myers (1977), who was trying to explain why firms tend to accept shorter term projects offering liquidity over longer term projects with growth potential. Myers posits that firms take on debt relative to market-driven debt-to-equity ratios, which is inconsistent with the theoretically correct relationship of less debt when there are proportionately more assets committed to growth options. In essence, a firm can only take on risky growth options if its debt structure does not force it to commit to projects with immediate cash flow to service the debt. Myers refers to this situation as the "under-investment problem."

Potentially consistent with the underinvestment problem caused by debt, researchers during the 1980s noticed an alarming lack of funding within firms for R&D. The catalyst for the trend appeared to be the application of DCF techniques that overpenalized longer-term projects with overly high discount or hurdle rates. Some believed that a misapplication of the DCF methods resulted in such high rates. That is, managers failed to adjust the methods for changes in risk through time and their ability to mitigate losses.

To demonstrate the value of management's ability to act throughout the life of a project, firms began to incorporate option pricing techniques into capital budgeting decisions. By using binomial methods, for example, to demonstrate that certain conditions existed in the forecasted cash flows of the project, management could act to mitigate losses or to increase potential gains. Real options analysis permits valuing the benefit of management discretion and even demonstrating how a negative NPV project could potentially result in a positive NPV because of management discretion.

Beyond valuing options, real options analysis also demonstrates how to create beneficial options by implementing projects in stages or by writing contracts with the ability to increase or decrease raw material supplies. Even when a nominal value for the real option is not easily obtainable, the decision maker still benefits by understanding how to reevaluate past decisions instead of having unwavering commitment to decisions from the past. In a sense, a qualitative real options analysis makes a decision maker more aware of potential choices available in the future.

The most recent survey research on the use of real options by firms indicates that the technique is gaining acceptance, but that the major obstacle appears to be a lack of management support of the technique. Determining whether the problem is with how the technique has been conveyed to practitioners or with the time needed for practitioners to become more familiar with the technique is difficult to say. Perhaps a number of projects simply do not warrant such a sophisticated technique.

As computers and software become more powerful, making managers and analysts more capable, the sophistication argument may eventually dissipate. What makes real options analysis viable and prone to acceptance is that it helps decision makers find and recognize value. If real options techniques fail to aid in adding value to the firm, they are likely to disappear.

DISCUSSION QUESTIONS

1. What is the "underinvestment" problem posed by Myers (1977)?
2. How does management discretion potentially add value to a project?
3. How does the ability to make a series of small investments in a project over time create value when compared to making one large initial investment into a project?
4. When would a firm want to use an option to contract or expand operations?
5. How can real options analysis be valuable to a decision maker without computing a nominal value from an option?
6. What is a rainbow option?

REFERENCES

Alessii, Giuseppe. 2006. "Payback Period and Internal Rate of Return in Real Option Analysis." *Engineering Economist* 51:3, 237–257.

Arnold, Tom, and Timothy Crack. 2000. "Option Pricing in the Real World: A Generalized Binomial Model with Applications to Real Options." Available at http://ssrn.com/abstract =240554.

Arnold, Tom, and Timothy Crack. 2004a. "Using the WACC to Value Real Options." *Financial Analysts Journal* 60:6, 78–82.

Arnold, Tom, and Timothy Crack. 2004b. "Real Option Valuation Using NPV." Available at http://ssrn.com/abstract=644081.

Baker, H. Kent, Shantanu Dutta, and Samir Saadi. 2011. "Management Views on Real Options in Capital Budgeting." *Journal of Applied Finance*. Forthcoming.

Bensoussan, Alain, Michael Crouhy, and Dan Galai. 1995. "Black-Scholes Approximation of Warrant Prices." *Advances in Futures and Options Research* 8, 1–14.

Binder, John J., and J. Scott Chaput. 1996. "A Positive Analysis of Corporate Capital Budgeting Practices." *Review of Quantitative Finance and Accounting* 6:3, 245–257.

Black, Fischer, and Myron Scholes. 1973. "The Pricing of Options and Corporate Liabilities." *Journal of Political Economy* 81:3, 637–654.

Block, Stanley. 2007. "Are 'Real Options' Actually Used in the Real World?" *Engineering Economist* 52:3, 255–267.

Boyle, Glenn, and Graeme Guthrie. 1997. "Payback and the Value of Waiting to Invest." Available at http://ssrn.com/abstract=74.

Brennan, Michael, and Eduardo Schwartz. 1985. "Evaluating Natural Resource Investments." *Journal of Business* 58:2, 135–157.

Cox, Jonathan, Stephen Ross, and Mark Rubinstein. 1979. "Option Pricing: A Simplified Approach." *Journal of Financial Economics* 7:3, 229–263.

Favato, Giampiero. 2008. "Relevance of Real Options to Corporate Investment Decisions." *ICFAI University Journal of Derivatives Markets* 5:3, 91–103.

Feinstein, Steven P., and Diane M. Lander. 2002. "A Better Understanding of Why NPV Undervalues Managerial Flexibility." *Engineering Economist* 47:4, 418–435.

Geske, Robert. 1977. "The Valuation of Corporate Liabilities as Compound Options." *Journal of Financial and Quantitative Analysis* 12:4, 541–552.

Haug, Espen. 2007. *The Complete Guide to Option Pricing Formulas*. New York: McGraw-Hill.

Hayes, Robert H., and William J. Abernathy. 1980. "Managing Our Way to Economic Decline." *Harvard Business Review* 58:4, 67–77.

Hayes, Robert H., and David A. Garvin. 1982. "Managing as If Tomorrow Mattered." *Harvard Business Review* 60:3, 70–79.

Hodder, James E., and Henry E. Riggs. 1985. "Pitfalls in Evaluating Risky Projects." *Harvard Business Review* 63:1, 128–135.

Kemna, Angelian G. Z. 1993. "Case Studies on Real Options." *Financial Management* 22:3, 259–270.

Lewis, Neal A., Ted G. Eschenbach, and Joseph C. Hartman. 2008. "Can We Capture the Value of Option Volatility." *Engineering Economist* 53:3, 230–258.

McDonald, Robert L. 2006. "The Role of Real Options in Capital Budgeting: Theory and Practice." *Journal of Applied Corporate Finance* 18:2, 28–39.

Moel, Alberto, and Peter Tufano. 2002. "When Are Real Options Exercised? An Empirical Study of Mine Closings." *Review of Financial Studies* 15:1, 35–64.

Myers, Stewart C. 1977. "Determinants of Corporate Borrowing." *Journal of Financial Economics* 5:2, 147–175.

Trigeorgis, Lenos. 1993. "Real Options and Interactions with Financial Flexibility." *Financial Management* 22:3, 202–224.

Trigeorgis, Lenos. 1996. *Real Options, Managerial Flexibility and Strategy in Resource Allocation*. Cambridge, MA: MIT Press.

Trigeorgis, Lenos. 2005. "Making Use of Real Options Simple: An Overview and Applications in Flexible/Modular Decision Making." *Engineering Economist* 50:1, 25–53.

ABOUT THE AUTHORS

Tom Arnold, CFA, is an Associate Professor of Finance and the F. Carlyle Tiller Chair in Business at the Robins School of Business, University of Richmond. Professor Arnold has more than 40 publications appearing in such journals as the

Journal of Finance, Journal of Business, Financial Analysts Journal, Journal of Futures Markets, Journal of Applied Finance, and *Journal of Financial Education.* His work has been cited in the *Economist, Wall Street Journal, New York Times,* and other non-U.S. news outlets. Professor Arnold's specialties include derivative securities, real option valuation, market microstructure, corporate valuation, and finance pedagogy. He received a Ph.D. from the Terry College of Business at the University of Georgia.

Bonnie Buchanan is an Assistant Professor of Finance at the Albers School of Business and Economics at Seattle University. Professor Buchanan has published articles in such journals as the *Review of Quantitative Finance and Accounting, Emerging Markets Review, Journal of Structured Finance, Review of International Business and Finance,* and *Journal of Financial Education.* Her work has been cited in the *Financial Times, Global Proxywatch,* and the *National Post* (Canada). Professor Buchanan's research interests include shareholder activism, securitization, law and finance, and real option valuation. Her doctoral degree is from the Terry College of Business at the University of Georgia.

CHAPTER 17

Applications of Real Options Analysis

TOM ARNOLD
F. Carlyle Tiller Chair in Business, University of Richmond

BONNIE BUCHANAN
Assistant Professor, Seattle University

INTRODUCTION

Chapter 16 introduced real options analysis as a means to address the "underinvestment" problem posed by Myers (1977). Myers suggests that firms are overextended in debt, forcing them to prefer short-term projects that are liquid to longer-term projects that have more growth potential. Real options analysis became a means of valuing the growth potential of these longer-term projects, which was not being realized by misapplied discounted cash flow (DCF) models. The term *misapplied* is used here because DCF techniques are consistent with real options analysis (see Arnold and Crack, 2004; McDonald, 2006).

Using a simple example similar to one from McDonald (2006) based on a model by Cox, Ross, and Rubinstein (1979), the equivalence between real options analysis and DCF techniques can be demonstrated. Suppose a project will either have a cash flow one year from today of $35 ($X_U$) with probability 60 percent (p) or $20 ($X_D$) with probability 40 percent (1 − p). The expected cash flow one year from today is $29 = 0.60($35) + 0.40($20). Further, assume the risk-adjusted rate for the project is 10 percent annually, which means that the project NPV is $26.36 = $29.00/(1.10) = [0.60($35) + 0.40($20)]/(1.10).

To produce the equivalent real options analysis in its most simple form requires changing to risk-neutral pricing. First, assume the risk-free rate is 5 percent and then find the futures or forward price (F) for the project: F = $27.68 = $26.36(1.05). Notice that the futures/forward price is "anchored" by the current value of the project. Consequently, the DCF analysis is going to be embedded into the real options analysis.

Using the futures/forward price, new probabilities are calculated to be consistent with risk-neutral pricing. The risk-neutral probability of a price increase to $35 is: q = (F − X_D)/(X_U − X_D) = ($27.68 − $20.00)/($35.00 − $20.00) = 51.21 percent. The corresponding risk-neutral probability of a price decrease to $20.00 is 49.78 percent (i.e., 48.78 percent = 1 − q = 1 − 51.21 percent). The expected risk-neutral price one year from today, which is the same as the forward price, is $27.68 = 0.5121($35) + 0.4878($20). The discounted expected value is $26.36 = $27.68/(1.05), which is equal to the project's value based on the DCF analysis above.

Although the calculations above are circular to some extent, the value of switching to the risk-neutral pricing framework of real options analysis is seen when someone can contract to receive only one or a portion of one of the future cash flows. For example, the project only goes forward if the cash flow is above $25 one year from today. The value of only receiving the $35.00 cash flow if it occurs is $17.07 = 0.5121($35)/(1.05). Correspondingly, the value of only receiving the $20 cash flow if it occurs one year from today is $9.29 = 0.4878($20)/(1.05). Can the same calculation be performed using the actual probabilities for the $35 and $20 cash flows, which are 60 percent and 40 percent, respectively? Under the actual probabilities, the price of only receiving the $35 cash flow if it occurs is $19.09 = 0.60($35)/(1.10). Correspondingly, the price of only receiving the $20 cash flow if it occurs is $7.27 = 0.40($20)/(1.10).

Apparently, techniques sum to the actual project value of $26.36, but the component cash flows do not agree. Which set of component cash flow prices is correct? The results shown above as $17.07 and $9.29 are correct because under risk-neutral pricing the 5 percent risk-free discount rate applies to both of the cash flows individually. The risk differences between the cash flows both warrant the risk-free rate as the discount rate because the probability was adjusted to allow this. The results shown above as $19.09 and $7.27 are priced on a risk-adjusted basis. Both cash flows actually have different individual risk-adjusted discount rates (RADRs) that do not equal to 10 percent because the riskiness of each of the cash flows is different from the other and from the project as a whole. At this point, state-specific individual RADRs can be calculated for the individual cash flows. The appropriate discount rate for receiving the $35 cash flow should it occur is 23.02 percent, where $17.07 = 0.60($35)/(1 + k*) and k* = 23.02 percent = [0.60($35)/17.07] − 1.

Note that this discount rate is well above the 10 percent discount rate for the expected cash flow for the entire project. The discount rate not only adjusts for the cash flow reducing from $19.09 to $17.07, but also for the increased probability (relative to the risk-neutral probability) of the cash flow. One should not be distracted by the fact that the discount rate is much larger than 10 percent because the discount rate for the other cash flow will be much lower than 10 percent for the opposite reasons: the cash flow increases from $7.27 to $9.29 and the probability decreases relative to the risk neutral probability. Both of these factors will actually make the component discount rate so much below 10 percent that the discount rate will become negative. The appropriate discount rate for receiving the $20 cash flow should it occur is 16.13 percent, where −13.89 percent = 0.40($20)/(1 + k**) and k** = −13.89 percent = [0.40($20)/9.29] − 1.

Having found the individual discount rates for the project under a risk-adjusted framework, the connection between real options analysis using risk-neutral pricing and DCF analysis is complete. Consequently, should the two frameworks disagree, one or both of the frameworks has been misapplied. Further, the benefit of risk-neutral pricing is demonstrated in that only one discount rate (i.e., the risk-free rate) needs to be applied to all future possible cash flows, rather than individual discount rates being applied to each possible future cash flow. As stated in Chapter 16, risk-neutral pricing is a mathematical convenience and not an assumption about risk preferences.

In this chapter, the risk-neutral pricing framework serves as the standard tool for valuing the real options presented. The real options valued follow the construct of Trigeorgis (1993a, 1996, 2005) and are examined within seven different but overlapping categories: (1) the option to defer, (2) staged investment options, (3) the option to alter the scale of operations, (4) the option to abandon, (5) the option to switch inputs or outputs, (6) growth options, and (7) rainbow options (or multiple interacting options). For each real option category, an example from the real options literature is used to demonstrate the option and when possible, how to value the option. More exhaustive presentations of these options are available from Trigeorgis (1996), Amram and Kulatilaka (1998), Copeland and Antikarov (2003), and Shockley (2007).

Having an understanding of the state of real options analysis among practitioners is important. Block (2007) shows a greater use of the technique through time, but currently usage is at a relatively low rate (14.3 percent of 279 respondents from Fortune 1000 firms). Baker, Dutta, and Saadi (2011) find similar results when surveying Canadian firms (16.8 percent from 214 respondents). Contrary to these findings, Brounen, de Jong, and Koedijk (2004) find use among various European countries to vary between 29 percent and 53 percent. Triantis (2005) provides an overall assessment of the use of real options analysis by practitioners as not meeting the expected usage rate anticipated in the 1990 s. However, Triantis believes that many aspects of real options analysis are taking hold among practitioners, but pragmatic issues need to be addressed to gain more management acceptance.

Triantis (2005, p. 16) summarizes the situation as follows:

> Corporate acceptance and implementation (of real options) will require senior-level buy-in and strong leadership, careful adoption of simpler versions of the tool, user-friendly software that can handle the modeling complexity, significant investment in training analysts and managers, deliberate alignment of managerial and shareholder incentives, and the creation of appropriate controls in the capital investment process. Despite these challenges, I believe that there will continue to be a gradual and consistent diffusion of real options analysis throughout business organizations over the next few decades, and that real options will eventually become a standard part of corporate investment projects. When this happens, NPV (net present value) will assume its rightful role as a special case of capital investment decision-making, as will other special cases to be used for particular applications—and real options will no longer be considered a "supplementary" capital budgeting tool.

OPTION TO DEFER OR OPTION TO WAIT

In many real options applications, the variability of future cash flows creates the possibility of using an options framework. However, variability in other forms also creates the potential for using real options analysis. Ingersoll and Ross (1992) demonstrate through a simple example how cash flows can be static, but the variability in the discount rate can create an option to wait. Suppose \$100 can be invested today with a discount rate of 9 percent annually for a certain cash flow of \$112 one year from today. The NPV is greater than zero, making the project acceptable: NPV = \$2.75 = (\$112/1.09) − \$100.

Suppose next year the discount rate is expected to be 7 percent annually. Waiting one year to invest in the project, assuming the project can be done once and then never again, increases the NPV: NPV = \$4.67 = (\$112/1.07) − \$100. In fact, discounting 9 percent demonstrates that waiting is more valuable than undertaking the project now: \$4.29 = \$4.67/(1.09) = (\$112/(1.07) − \$100)/(1.09). Notice that the option to wait generates \$1.54 (= \$4.29 − \$2.75) of additional NPV.

This simple example with certain cash flows clearly demonstrates that volatility creates an option to wait even if the volatility is not in the cash flow stream of the project. Ingersoll and Ross (1992) continue their analysis by introducing a model of interest rates applied to a project and find discount rate ranges for considering when to wait and when to execute projects immediately. In this analysis, a project's internal rate of return (IRR) needs to surpass a hurdle rate that is scaled up as the option to wait becomes more valuable. Translated to NPV, the NPV must be sufficiently high and positive to forgo the value of waiting if the project is to be immediately executed. In other words, a positive NPV is not a sufficient condition for executing a project when there is value to waiting.

What creates the value for waiting? Volatility is one component, but the project itself has to have an irreversible investment aspect to it. In other words, once executed, the resources for the project cannot be recovered. This aspect of the project in conjunction with volatility allows Ingersoll and Ross (1992) to state that the project has to "compete with itself." In other words, the execution of the project has to compete with the value of executing the project at a later date under possibly more favorable conditions. McDonald and Siegel (1986, p. 707) state the situation in this manner relative to building a plant:

> The decision to build the plant is irreversible; the plant cannot be used for any other purpose. The decision to defer building, however, is reversible. This asymmetry, when properly taken into account, leads to a rule that says build the plant only if benefits exceed costs by a certain positive amount. The correct calculation involves comparing the value of investing today with the (present) value of investing at all possible times in the future. This is a comparison of mutually exclusive alternatives.

Creating flexibility within the use of a structure may mitigate some of the value of waiting in the McDonald and Siegel (1986) scenario, but it will not mitigate all of the value of waiting given the Ingersoll and Ross (1992) insight that volatility can emerge from sources other than cash flow. Titman (1985) finds such a situation when considering a real options analysis of urban land prices and urban land development. Land can remain vacant even though it is profitable to develop, because uncertainty about future inflation causes the option to wait to become valuable relative to the profit of developing now. Why? The development that is built immediately may not be the best possible use of the land given the future economic conditions that may prevail. Consequently, the best strategy may be to wait. Using data on 2,700 Seattle land transactions, Quigg (1993) empirically tests the implications of Titman's paper and finds support for real estate being modeled within a real options framework. Regarding optimal development, she finds that market prices reflect a mean premium of 6 percent of land value.

The staged investment option, which is highly related to the option to wait or defer, is a series of options through time that may be viewed as a sequential series of options to wait. The next section addresses staged investment options.

STAGED INVESTMENT OPTION

The ability to implement a project through a series of investments rather than all at once is one of the real options insights that Triantis (2005) mentions as being accepted by and beneficial to practitioners. Although staged investment may appear to be a "common sense" approach to addressing volatility, it was not common knowledge that such a strategy actually creates value. Seeing the value of a staged investment is what real options analysis clearly demonstrates. Baldwin (1982) examines sequential investments in a theoretical model and finds that the sequential options to invest, wait, or abandon add substantial value to a project's NPV. Some projects such as research and development (R&D) can be broken into investment stages. Herath and Park (2002) develop a binomial model in which R&D goes through different phases through time where new investment is required at each phase. Unlike the binomial model demonstrated in Chapter 16, each phase of an R&D project has a different associated volatility.

To perform a smaller version of the model, assume a firm can implement an R&D project in two phases with each phase taking one year. After each phase and at the beginning of the project, the firm can either sell the rights to the project or invest additional resources to advance the project. For example, assume that the initial selling price of the rights to the project is $10 million. Based upon performance during the first phase, the value of the rights to the project can increase by a factor of 1.4191 or decrease by a factor of 0.7047 over one year (see Chapter 16 about the structure of the binomial tree; these factors are based on an annual volatility of 35 percent). Consequently, after one year the rights will be worth $14.19 million with a probability of 44.17 percent or $7.05 with a probability of 55.83 percent, assuming a risk-free rate of 2 percent annually.

After the first year, the firm can sell the rights for $14.19 million or $7.05 million or make another investment of two annual payments of $5 million at the end of the first and second years of the project. Assume that after making the initial $5 million investment, the firm invests the second $5 million. This investment will depend on the volatility during the second phase of the project, which is 20 percent annually. The value of the rights can increase by a factor of 1.2214 or decrease by a factor of 0.8187 with probabilities of 50.03 percent and 49.97 percent, respectively. If the value of the rights is $14.19 million at the end of the first year, the rights will be worth either $17.33 million or $11.62 million at the end of the second year. Paying the $5 million investment at the end of the second year reduces each of these values by $5 million, making the values $12.33 million and $6.62 million, respectively. If priced in continuous time, the discounted expected value of these two values at the end of the first year is $9.29 million = [($17.33 − $5.00)0.5003 + ($11.62 − $5.00)0.4997]exp(−2%), where exp(*) is the exponential function.

Because the discounted expected value is above $5 million, the first $5 million investment is made, creating a net gain of $4.29 million. This makes the value of the rights worth $18.48 million = ($14.19 + $4.29). One could view the $14.19 million as the NPV of the rights with the additional value of $4.29 million coming from the option to invest more into the project.

If the rights have a value of $7.05 million after the first year, the value of the rights will increase to $8.61 million or decrease to $5.77 million. After the $5 million investment at the end of the second year, both values decrease by $5 million to $3.61 million and $0.77, respectively. The discounted expected value of $3.61 million and $0.77 million at the end of the first year is $2.15 million = [($8.61 − $5.00) 0.5003 + ($5.77 − $5.00) 0.4997]exp(−2%). Because the $2.15 million discounted expected value is below $5 million, the firm should not undertake the second round of two annual payments of $5 million. However, there is value in the option of $2.15 million, which adds to the $7.05 million rights value, making the total value for the project equal to $9.19 million. Unless the firm can sell the rights for this amount, it should simply wait to move forward until the project becomes more valuable.

Although various mathematical steps are needed to get to this point, the R&D project after one year is worth $18.48 million with a probability of 44.17 percent or $9.19 million with a probability of 55.83 percent. The discounted expected value of the project (i.e., the value of the project today) is $13.03 million = [($18.48)0.4417 + ($9.19)0.5585]exp(−2%). Consequently, the difference between the value of the rights today and the value of the R&D project is $3.03 million ($13.03 − $10.00). If the initial investment in the R&D project is below $3.03 million, the firm should start phase 1 of the project. If the R&D project has an initial cost between $3.04 million and $13.03 million, the firm should wait until the initial costs decrease or the option to start the project becomes more valuable. If the firm receives an offer above $13.03 million for the rights, it should sell the rights. Why would another firm make such an offer? This may occur if a competing firm has better economic prospects for the R&D project that makes the rights more valuable to the competing firm than $13.03 million.

Consistent with Baldwin (1982), the options created by the staged investments increase the project's value. Further, these options can lead to decisions to execute, wait, or abandon depending on the circumstances. Childs and Triantis (1999) are more expansive in the options that become available through staged R&D and add some strategy to approaching R&D. Many projects should go through an initial stage of development and then at the end of each phase (assuming projects can be synchronized), the firm pursues a smaller set of the projects. This sort of contest at the end of each phase develops the best projects to fruition, but also maintains other prospective projects in lower stages of development just in case economic conditions change to favor those projects in the lower stages of development.

The ability to increase or decrease the scale of a project to meet demand needs is related to staged investment. Stages can be implemented to take a large project and break it into smaller intermediate projects or combined to increase and accelerate the size of a project. The ability to change the scale of a project is the subject of the next section.

OPTION TO ALTER THE SCALE OF OPERATIONS

Intuitively, having the ability to increase operations during good economic conditions and the ability to decrease operations during poor economic conditions is valuable. Common examples of allowing for such options to exist include building industrial plants with excess capacity, leasing with an agreement to cancel a lease early, and building structures with foundations that allow for additions. Kemna (1993) examines three different project cases undertaken at Shell International Petroleum Company between 1985 through 1990. In one case, a business unit was in a competitive industry with overcapacity. Consequently, the focus was on when it could reasonably shut down the unit. Because other companies faced the same problem, Shell would become available if other companies shut down units faster. This illustrates the option to alter the scale of operations because an abandonment option is the ultimate reduction in scale. Shell had to consider the value of the abandonment option relative to the value of the option to increase scale while other firms exercised their abandonment options.

Most examples in the literature tend to view the option to alter the scale of operations as the ability to stop and start operations with some cost and then determine when starting or stopping operations is optimal. Brennan and Schwartz (1985) use an example of a copper mine opening and closing when copper prices were sufficiently high or low to illustrate this type of option. They point out that the mine cannot open immediately when it can operate profitably or close immediately when it is not operating profitably. These lags in starting and stopping are consistent with the volatility of the price of copper and the expense of starting or stopping operations. Using real options analysis enables determining the level of profitability necessary for opening the mine and the level of unprofitability necessary for closing the mine.

The next section discusses the option to abandon particularly when considering altering the scale of operations. The options to expand, reduce, abandon, and wait tend to be interrelated. Consequently, real options analysts should be cautious and understand how all of these options emerge in a project and then judiciously consider which are the most important to model and price. Triantis (2005, p. 15) warns of overcomplicating models and then getting lost in the complexity by stating: "If management finds real options analysis to be too complex a tool, or suspects that the tool can be deliberately or unintentionally misused in ways that are difficult to detect, it simply won't be used—and the gains we expect from the better framing and evaluation of projects will not be realized."

OPTION TO ABANDON

The options to abandon or to wait are similar because abandoning frequently requires waiting through difficult economic circumstances until a point where recovery is impossible or highly improbable. Even when project cash flows become negative due to poor economic conditions, the firm may choose not to abandon or "scrap" the project because volatility may allow for better prices in the near future leading to profitable cash flow. This is similar to how a firm may not immediately initiate a project despite having a positive NPV because the possibility of better conditions in the future creates a valuable option to wait.

McDonald and Siegel (1985) provide an intuitive explanation of the option to abandon. They state that if perfect certainty exists about cost and cash flow (or price of the manufactured product), the decision to shut down is at the instant when cost exceeds cash flow (or unit variable cost exceeds selling price). Similar to the example provided by Ingersoll and Ross (1992), the option to abandon has value once volatility exists in any facet of the manufacturing process or in the cash flows (i.e., whenever costs and/or prices become variable). Introducing costs to shutting down a plant generally makes the possibility of waiting to abandon take even longer. Brennan and Schwartz (1985) provide an example about closing a copper mine.

For example, if shutting down a plant requires $2 million, management will not close the plant if losses do not exceed $2 million. Further, in the presence of volatility in the cost of manufacturing or cash flows, management may decide not to close the plant even if losses exceed $2 million. McDonald and Siegel (1985) incorporate stochastic processes to generate the volatility in their real option framework to illustrate this point. However, variability in cash flow and cost can emerge simply by having the price of a raw material increase. If costs are suddenly higher, a firm may be unable to completely reflect these costs in the selling price because of the competitive nature of the industry. Until cost pressure forces the whole industry to increase prices, margins will narrow and the value of the option to abandon will have changed. Following this logic, incorporating a government subsidy, either through granting or removing, will also create volatility.

Although the context for considering abandonment is generally viewed as applicable under poor economic conditions, abandonment can occur when a firm receives an offer for a project that is clearly more than what the project is worth including the options available within the project. A recent trend involves the creation of small research companies by entrepreneurs with the goal of selling the venture or its product rights to a larger company at some point when the research product has become valuable. The entrepreneurial venture may have the means to develop a product, but not the means to widely distribute the product. Consequently, because of the distribution channels available to a larger firm, the product may have more value to the larger firm than to the entrepreneurial venture, giving the entrepreneurial firm a viable option to abandon.

If the goal is to mitigate the abandonment option or to increase the potential waiting time until abandonment, then creating flexibility regarding inputs and outputs is a key decision factor. By creating flexibility, the abandonment option becomes less important and a new set of options emerges in the guise of the option to switch inputs or outputs. These are commonly called switching options. The next section investigates the option to switch inputs and outputs.

OPTION TO SWITCH INPUTS OR OUTPUTS

The more flexibility decision makers have at their discretion, the more valuable the real option paradigm is to management. Although the previous real options introduced have some intuitive aspects, they generally require a different mindset that some managers may not embrace. However, the option to switch inputs or outputs tends to be apparent to decision makers. Consequently, they are likely to implement switching options without much analytical analysis.

Beyond the firm, the option to switch inputs or outputs is becoming relevant as "smart technology" is being developed to allow appliances to use energy when it is least costly and "green technology" is emerging that potentially allows users to sell energy back to utilities. This ability to switch inputs or outputs is valuable and is being incorporated into the pricing of these items. For example, the higher price of hybrid cars is not only to pay for the technology, but also to pay for the value of this option to switch from gasoline to battery power in an efficient manner. From the firm's perspective, developing technology that creates the ability to switch inputs or outputs in the product market means higher profit margins because the option is neither a variable nor fixed cost in the traditional sense.

Although switching options is valuable in the current and evolving product market, initial research in the area mainly focuses on the value of switching fuel sources in the production process or switching output from the production process. Kulatilaka (1993) introduces an example in which a company can switch energy sources. The author demonstrates the valuation of an option to switch between oil and natural gas for fueling an industrial steam boiler. To value the option, input values for oil and gas are determined by the energy units produced by each energy source. Using the energy unit as a basis, the energy unit is priced according to each energy source.

Kulatilaka (1993) demonstrates the possibility of using NPV valuation to compare a natural gas–heated boiler to an oil-heated boiler (ignoring options to wait or to abandon and assuming a low-volatility environment), but cannot capture the value of a boiler that can switch between oil and gas. The inability to value the option is because of the interaction between the natural gas and oil prices, which involves the volatility of each set of prices and not the expected future value of the prices used in a static NPV analysis. Using dynamic programming to find the value of the real option, Kulatilaka demonstrates that a volatile environment practically negates the ability to use NPV in a static form that only considers the future expected values of cash flows. Ingersoll and Ross (1992) also demonstrate this point when considering the option to wait.

Woolley and Cannizzo (2005) point out, however, that because decision makers already understand DCF techniques such as NPV, they should not be totally eliminated from the evaluation process. In using real options analysis at British Petroleum (BP), the authors see the value in real option techniques, but also understand that communication to senior management is critical. Woolley and Cannizzo (p. 94) make the following observation:

> Senior managers want competing projects to be presented to them on a consistent basis so that valuation differences are a function of real factors rather than differences in method, and management can bring its experience into the debate. At BP we refer to this as "the level playing field." The challenge for real options is to gain acceptance while meeting this criteria. Even if the logic of option pricing seems well suited to a given corporate project, how can a senior management team long accustomed to DCF (discounted cash flow) valuation be made comfortable with the results produced by a real-options-based valuation model? The trick, as we will argue, is to make real options a complement rather than a replacement for DCF by showing how real options is consistent with and extends the power of DCF.

The case presented by Woolley and Cannizzo (2005) deals with a gas stabilization plant that takes in pipeline gas and produces stabilized gas and condensate,

which are both sellable outputs. A real option is created with additional investment into the plant and more pipeline gas that allows the plant to also produce
liquefied petroleum gas (LPG) and additional condensate. The goal is to determine
if the additional investment is worth having the option to produce LPG in addition
to stabilized gas. Because of the myriad sources of price volatility—pipeline gas,
stabilized gas, condensate, and LPG—simulation is used to value the option. This
analysis differs from others in that it does not use risk-neutral valuation and NPV
analysis provides the value of the base case in which there is no volatility. In this
manner, management can see the DCF analysis within the real option analysis and
can become comfortable with how volatility affects the option to switch outputs.

Multiple sources of volatility or uncertainty begin to emerge that make simulation analysis or dynamic programming preferred techniques for valuation, particularly when considering the option to switch inputs or outputs. To grasp how such
techniques work, think of each source of volatility having its own binomial tree
to project future values and then think of another binomial tree used to combine
these projected values in order to make decisions. This is still an oversimplification
of simulation and dynamic programming in that the binomial trees act as if they
are independent.

Having the binomial trees become interdependent is difficult. From a visualization perspective, however, the interdependence emerges as a new set of binomial
trees with projected values set in an iterative manner. As one source of volatility
is projected, a second source is projected based on the given value from the first
source. That is, a new binomial tree will be projected for the second source of volatility based on every value change of the initial source of volatility. The number of
binomial trees grows at an exponential rate when using a "small" time step within
the analysis. Simplifying assumptions can relieve the necessity of programming so
many interdependent binomial trees.

The next section examines growth options. These are most likely the least
easily understood options because of the difficulty of precisely defining a growth
option. A benefit of the real options already introduced is that they can provide
an intuitive link to seeing the value of the option despite the difficulty of computing this value. With a growth option, management makes an investment based
on the potential that something valuable may emerge in the future, but the source
of that value is not necessarily evident. For example, Sony introduced laser discs
for movies in the 1970s that were relatively expensive and the equipment did not
permit recording. Although the product did not do well in the marketplace, the
technology allowed for creating the compact disc for music that was highly successful in the 1980s and 1990s. Could Sony in the 1970s see into the future about the potential of this technology for playing music? Such an answer is speculative at best,
but developing the technology created a growth option that paid off handsomely.

GROWTH OPTIONS

Kemna (1993, p. 262) describes a type of growth option called a *pioneer venture*, as
follows:

> [A growth option] ... is typically a project with a high investment outlay and
> relatively low net cash inflows. It is a manufacturing project with substantial

investment costs necessary to prove technology in a period when the project on its own does not appear attractive. But when economic conditions improve, it is important to have the technology proven in order to maintain and enhance market position. Therefore, from the strategic point of view, the pioneer venture may make sense.

Kemna continues with a numerical example using a compound option based on the Black-Scholes framework (1973), but does not provide a specific example. The author demonstrates that volatility is a key component for considering a growth option.

Shockley (2007) provides an example of a growth option in discussing Intel Corp.'s use of a *fab shell*. A fab shell is the first step in developing a manufacturing facility for microchips. In essence, the facility is built except for the manufacturing component. Because the plant is only partially completed, completion can take place when increased chip demand is expected or left as a fab shell for future consideration. In a sense, the growth option is an option to wait, but the waiting is not for the launch of a specific project.

Ultimately, the idea of a growth option goes back to the beginning of the literature on real options emphasizing that firms sacrificed long-term projects for quick payoff, short-term projects. These long-term projects do not necessarily produce immediate cash flows or cash flows that can be immediately attributable to the project. Yet, they have strategic importance because of the amount of uncertainty within a product market (Kester, 1984). Perhaps some of the strategic importance of long-term projects simply comes from the firm not becoming short-sighted or wholly ingrained in a current technology. By having a long-term venture, the firm is forced to investigate and invest in the future.

The next section presents "rainbow" options or multiple interacting options. These options contain multiple options that may include any of the previous six types of real options. For example, growth options often exist in rainbow options. Yet, they usually are not valued and only acknowledged because a specific project with cash flows cannot easily be attributed to the growth option for valuation purposes.

RAINBOW OPTIONS OR MULTIPLE INTERACTING OPTIONS

Rainbow options (Trigeorgis, 1993b) are projects that provide multiple real options that often interact. As demonstrated with the option to switch inputs or outputs, analysts can model each source of volatility, but the interaction of the volatility creates analytical complexities. Assuming that the volatility sources are independent makes the overall calculation simply a matter of valuing separate options and adding the options together. As Trigeorgis notes, the problem with this approach is that due to interaction, the options combined have less value than the independent options summed together. This is similar to how a portfolio reduces risk by combining securities. Because of diversification, the individual risk contribution of each security to the portfolio is generally less than the risk of the individual security.

The first step to approaching a rainbow option is to understand which options are opposite in execution. For example, an option to expand scale is the direct opposite of an option to contract scale or abandon. In these cases, the analyst can value the option most likely to execute (i.e., the option that is "in the money") and then ignore the opposing option because it most likely has little value. The next step is to find where the value of one option complements the value of another option. For example, the option to wait depends on the project having more potential value in the future because of better opportunities. These opportunities could be better future technology that allows for the switching of inputs or outputs such as a different type of real option. However, other options may reduce the option to wait, such as an abandonment option that may exist in the future. Another element to consider is when a particular option emerges because the sequencing of an option also affects its value.

The key to valuing rainbow options is to value a few key options with inter-actions between the options considered and not value other options because the value contribution is minimal. However, the existence of the option may still be considered important. When considering multiple options, the complexity even when tractable can be considerable (Triantis and Hodder, 1990). Consequently, the ability to strategically eliminate the valuation of some "less" important options can reduce much computation. This drawback should not be used an excuse to ignore some options, but as a means to come to a conservative valuation figure that can be communicated easily to decision makers.

Having considered elements involved in valuing a rainbow option, the full gamut of real options analysis becomes apparent. In fact, many begin to see that just about all projects have some real option component to them because of the existence of one or more sources of volatility. Even when analytical solutions are insufficient, there is still strategic benefit to realizing where potential real options exist within a project. Consequently, the rigor associated with rainbow options should not deter management from at least seeking where a real option may exist. However, analysts should be able to communicate their analysis effectively to management so decision makers can recognize real options and incorporate them into the firm's operations.

SUMMARY AND CONCLUSIONS

Real options exist within a project whenever there are one or more sources of volatility. When introduced in the literature, applications of real options were not immediately available, and the concept of a real option was more about investing in projects that made firms consider the future rather than being short-sighted by focusing on immediate cash flows. As the literature progressed, better defined examples of real options analysis emerged: the option to wait or defer, staged in-vestment options, the option to alter the scale of operations, the option to abandon, the option to switch inputs or outputs, growth options, and rainbow options.

The option to wait provides one of the best contexts for considering real option analysis. Ingersoll and Ross (1992) show that a project with certain cash flows and a positive NPV may be better executed in the future due to volatility in the discount rate. This example highlights how volatility creates value from flexibility in the project construct and/or in project decision making. Other options that allow for changing scale or shutting down and starting up optimally demonstrate the value of management discretion. However, the value exists only in the presence of volatility. Woolley and Cannizzo (2005) demonstrate this in valuing the option to change outputs at a gas stabilization plant in which the NPV calculation coincides with zero volatility.

Ultimately, real options analysis differs from DCF techniques in how it considers future cash flows. DCF techniques use expected future cash flows with the discount rate to adjust for risk or to imply a discount rate. Real options analysis considers management behavior in dealing with volatility embedded in the same expected future cash flows. Generally, real options analysis uses risk-neutral pricing rather than adjusting a discount rate for specific cases of future cash flows because a different risk-adjusted rate is often necessary for each possible case in traditional NPV analysis. Unfortunately, the convenience of using risk-neutral pricing tends to hide the fact that risk is being accounted for in the discounting of cash flows. Triantis (2005, p. 10) describes situations for which real options analysis appears to be particularly well suited:

> These main applications (situations where real options analysis has been applied) have some common features that make them particularly well suited to—and often most in need of—real options analysis. They all involve significant up-front investments that often don't lead to immediate cash flows. They also tend to have well-defined stages where the framing of the problem can be logically laid out and where there are major well-defined sources of uncertainty whose resolution is expected to contribute significantly to the outcome and ultimate value of the projects. In addition, in most cases, data are readily available to estimate key parameters of the model.

Although practitioner feedback and use of real options analysis is positive, decision makers still rely on DCF techniques such as NPV and IRR to make capital budgeting decisions. As Triantis (2005) and Woolley and Cannizzo (2005) emphasize, management support is the key to having real options analysis becoming more prevalent in practice. Further, real options analysis should be presented in a manner that encompasses DCF techniques or in a manner that is less complex to be more understandable to gain the confidence of management.

Despite what appears to be management trepidation, management may actually employ real options strategies while not calculating the value of the real options. Triantis (2005, p. 9) lists some examples: dividing projects into a number of stages; investing in information acquisition or production; introducing "modularity" in manufacturing design; developing competing prototypes for new products; and investing in infrastructure that provides a platform for future growth. Thus, management may see the value in creating flexibility but may not explicitly value that flexibility.

Empirically, real options analysis appears to describe the behavior of mine openings and closings (Moel and Tufano, 2002), real estate utilization (Quigg, 1993), and many other aspects of behavior. For example, Schwartz and Moon (2000) value the online bookseller Amazon. The valuation was much lower than the trading price at the time, but was very close to the post–Internet bubble price. Bosse and Arnold (2010) examine the use of trade credit by entrepreneurs as a real option in considering the trade-off between receiving a discount from a supplier or paying full price to the supplier at a later date. Arnold and Buchanan (2010) use a real options approach to demonstrate why a government may decide to keep an industry noncompetitive through trade restrictions. Given the multitude of empirical applications of which only a few are mentioned here, the academic literature has benefitted greatly from real options analysis.

Yet, as Triantis (2005) notes, the goal of real options analysis is to gain acceptance by practitioners. This requires time and a concerted effort to make real options analysis more palatable to management. As Block's (2007) survey results show, the main reason for not using real options is the lack of top management support. Baker et al. (2011) conclude that top managers are unlikely to accept a methodology that they do not understand. Before real options gain widespread acceptance, managers must change their mindset about the appropriate paradigm for evaluating projects.

DISCUSSION QUESTIONS

1. Why is the discount rate for an entire risky project an inappropriate discount rate for individual future cash flows within the project?

2. How does the futures/forward price "anchor" DCF valuation when valuing options using risk-neutral pricing?

3. Suppose a project requires a $10 million initial outlay to produce a guaranteed future cash flow of $12 million one year from today. Assume the appropriate discount rate is 10 percent annually today, which will decrease to 8 percent annually next year. Is there value in waiting to execute the project? If the discount rate remains constant, that is, the rate is always 10 percent annually, is there any value in waiting to execute the project?

4. If management could open and close a mine immediately with an associated cost, explain whether a mine would ever operate at a loss.

5. If an option to expand operations within a project is highly valuable, how valuable is the option to abandon within the project?

6. Is the value of a rainbow option likely to equal the sum of the individual options valued independently of each other?

REFERENCES

Amram, Martha, and Nalin Kulatilaka. 1998. *Real Options: Managing Strategic Investments in an Uncertain World*. Cambridge, MA: HBS Press.

Arnold, Tom, and Bonnie Buchanan. 2010. "A Real Option Approach to Evaluating the Cost of Government Policies within a Foreign Direct Investment." Working Paper. http://papers.ssrn. com/sol3/papers.cfm?abstract_id=987007.

Arnold, Tom, and Timothy Crack. 2004. "Real Option Valuation Using NPV." Available at http://ssrn. com/abstract=644081.

Baker, H. Kent, Shantanu Dutta, and Samir Saadi. 2011. "Management Views on Real Options in Capital Budgeting." *Journal of Applied Finance*, forthcoming.

Baldwin, Carliss. 1982. "Optimal Sequential Investment When Capital Is Not Really Reversible." *Journal of Finance* 37:3 763–782.

Black, Fischer, and Myron Scholes. 1973. "The Pricing of Options and Corporate Liabilities." *Journal of Political Economy* 81:3, 637–654.

Block, Stanley. 2007. "Are 'Real Options' Actually Used in the Real World?" *The Engineering Economist* 52:3, 255–267.

Bosse, Douglas, and Tom Arnold. 2010. "Trade Credit: A Real Option for Bootstrapping Small Firms." *Venture Capital* 12:1, 49–63.

Brennan, Michael, and Eduardo Schwartz. 1985. "Evaluating Natural Resource Investments." *Journal of Business* 58:2, 135–157.

Brounen, Dirk, Abe de Jong, and Kees Koedijk. 2004. "Corporate Finance in Europe: Confronting Theory with Practice." *Financial Management* 33:4, 71–101.

Childs, Paul, and Alexander Triantis. 1999. "Dynamic R&D Investment Policies." *Management Science* 45:10, 1359–1377.

Copeland, Tom, and Vladimir Antikarov. 2003. *Real Options: A Practitioner's Guide.* New York, NY: Thomson-Texere.

Cox, Jonathan, Stephen Ross, and Mark Rubinstein. 1979. "Option Pricing: A Simplified Approach." *Journal of Financial Economics* 7:3, 229–263.

Herath, Hemantha, and Chan Park. 2002. "Multi-Stage Capital Investment Opportunities as Compound Real Options." *The Engineering Economist* 47:1, 1–27.

Ingersoll, Jonathan, and Stephen Ross. 1992. "Waiting to Invest: Investment and Uncertainty." *Journal of Business* 65:1, 1–29.

Kemna, Angelien G. Z. 1993. "Case Studies on Real Options." *Financial Management* 22:3, 259–270.

Kester, W. Carl. 1984. "Today's Options for Tomorrow's Growth." *Harvard Business Review* 62:2, 153–160.

Kulatilaka, Nalin. 1993. "The Value of Flexibility: The Case of a Dual-Fuel Industrial Steam Boiler." *Financial Management* 22:3, 271–280.

McDonald, Robert L. 2006. "The Role of Real Options in Capital Budgeting: Theory and Practice." *Journal of Applied Corporate Finance* 18:2, 28–39.

McDonald, Robert, and Daniel Siegel. 1985. "Investment and the Valuation of Firms When There Is an Option to Shut Down." *International Economic Review* 26:2, 331–349.

McDonald, Robert, and Daniel Siegel. 1986. "The Value of Waiting to Invest." *Quarterly Journal of Economics* 101:4, 707–728.

Moel, Alberto, and Peter Tufano. 2002. "When Are Real Options Exercised? An Empirical Study of Mine Closings." *Review of Financial Studies* 15:1, 35–64.

Myers, Stewart C. 1977. "Determinants of Corporate Borrowing." *Journal of Financial Economics* 5:2, 147–175.

Quigg, Laura. 1993. "Empirical Testing of Real Option-Pricing Models." *Journal of Finance* 48:2, 621–640.

Schwartz, Eduardo, and Mark Moon. 2000. "Rational Pricing of Internet Companies." *Financial Analysts Journal* 56:3, 62–75.

Shockley, Richard. 2007. *An Applied Course in Real Options Valuation.* Mason, OH: Thomson-South-Western.

Titman, Sheridan. 1985. "Urban Land Prices under Uncertainty." *American Economic Review* 75:3, 505–514.

Triantis, Alexander. 2005. "Realizing the Potential of Real Options: Does Theory Meet Practice?" *Journal of Applied Corporate Finance* 17:2, 8–16.

Triantis, Alexander, and James Hodder. 1990. "Valuing Flexibility as a Complex Option." *Journal of Finance* 45:2, 549–565.

Trigeorgis, Lenos. 1993a. "Real Options and Interactions with Financial Flexibility." *Financial Management* 22:3, 202–224.

Trigeorgis, Lenos. 1993b. "The Nature of Option Interactions and the Valuation of Investments with Multiple Real Options." *Journal of Financial and Quantitative Analysis* 28:1, 1–20.

Trigeorgis, Lenos. 1996. *Real Options, Managerial Flexibility and Strategy in Resource Allocation.* Cambridge, MA: MIT Press.

Trigeorgis, Lenos. 2005. "Making Use of Real Options Simple: An Overview and Applications in Flexible/Modular Decision Making." *The Engineering Economist* 50:1, 25–53.

Woolley, Simon, and Fabio Cannizzo. 2005. "Taking Real Options Beyond the Black Box." *Journal of Applied Corporate Finance* 17:2, 94–98.

ABOUT THE AUTHORS

Tom Arnold, CFA, is an Associate Professor of Finance and the F. Carlyle Tiller Chair in Business at the Robins School of Business, University of Richmond. Professor Arnold has more than 40 publications appearing in such journals as the *Journal of Finance, Journal of Business, Financial Analysts Journal, Journal of Futures Markets, Journal of Applied Finance,* and *Journal of Financial Education.* His work has been cited in the *Economist, Wall Street Journal, New York Times,* and other non-U.S. news outlets. Professor Arnold's specialties include derivative securities, real option valuation, market microstructure, corporate valuation, and finance pedagogy. He received a Ph.D. from the Terry College of Business at the University of Georgia.

Bonnie Buchanan is an Assistant Professor of Finance at the Albers School of Business and Economics at Seattle University. Professor Buchanan has published articles in such journals as *Review of Quantitative Finance and Accounting, Emerging Markets Review, Journal of Structured Finance, Review of International Business and Finance,* and *Journal of Financial Education.* Her work has been cited in the *Financial Times, Global Proxywatch,* and the *National Post* (Canada). Professor Buchanan's research interests include shareholder activism, securitization, law and finance, and real option valuation. Her doctoral degree is from the Terry College of Business at the University of Georgia.

PART VI

Estimating the Project Cost of Capital

CHAPTER 18

Cost of Capital

An Introduction

OCTAVIAN IONICI
Executive-in-Residence Professor of Finance and Director, Financial Services Lab,
American University

KENNETH SMALL
Associate Professor and Marshall Butler Chair in Finance, Coastal Carolina
University

FRANK D'SOUZA
Assistant Professor of Finance, Loyola University Maryland

INTRODUCTION

Companies grow and create value by investing in projects that provide sufficient
cash flows to compensate for the risks of investment and foregone opportunities.
When a firm commits capital to an investment, its managers expect a project's
return to exceed the firm's cost of raising funds on a risk-adjusted basis. Making value-enhancing decisions is the lifeblood of a firm's growth, expansion, and
success. Such investments may involve property, plant, and equipment as well as
those relating to operational efficiencies and acquisitions.

Capital budgeting refers to the process of identifying, evaluating, and selecting
long-term investment projects. A major challenge of capital budgeting is correctly
estimating the appropriate rate to use when discounting a project's cash flows to
arrive at a present value. The core of the discount rate is the cost of capital, possibly
with adjustments made for project risk.

The cost of capital, also called the *weighted average cost of capital* (WACC),
refers to a firm's cost of using various funding sources relative to the percentage
usage of each source. Although common sources of capital for large firms are
debt, equity, and preferred stock, many other sources are available. For example,
a small business may first obtain capital from friends or relatives. Such sources
may involve repayment terms that do not fit the classic definition of debt or equity.
Further, large firms may use contracts and funding sources that combine elements
of both debt and equity such as convertible bonds. Estimating the appropriate cost
of capital is important because using incorrect values may lead to capital budgeting
decisions that decrease shareholder wealth.

WACC/IRR

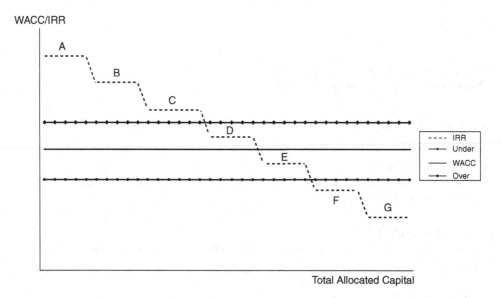

Total Allocated Capital

Exhibit 18.1   WACC Graph Illustrating Over- and Underestimation

Note: This exhibit shows that Projects A through G have identical risk profiles and represent the capital budgeting opportunity set of the firm. The exhibit illustrates that over- or underestimation of the firm's WACC can lead to the acceptance of value-destroying projects or the rejection of value-enhancing projects.

For example, examine the projects in Exhibit 18.1. The distortion effects of an incorrectly estimated WACC are clearly visible when using the rule of accepting projects with an internal rate of return (IRR) greater than the firm's WACC. If the WACC is underestimated, the firm may accept projects that are not value enhancing. In this example, if the firm accepts Project E, this would decrease shareholder value. If the WACC is overestimated, the firm may reject projects that are value enhancing such as Project D. Using an incorrect cost of capital could lead to decisions that are suboptimal. As the error in the cost of capital estimate increases, so does the impact on shareholder value.

This chapter focuses on calculating the cost of capital and adjusting it to compensate for project risk to obtain a risk-adjusted discount rate (RADR). The chapter also examines and discusses how to estimate the cost of equity and debt for projects with risk levels that differ from the firm's overall or normal risk level. For example, some projects represent a substantial risk to the firm such as a new product launch or the expansion of an existing business concept into a new market. In each case, the firm is dealing with unknowns that are difficult to estimate and model. These decisions are much more difficult for senior management to consider than the decision to resurface a staff parking lot or to replace aging manufacturing equipment, where the risks and rewards are more quantifiable and less subject to estimation error.

The chapter concludes with a discussion of how the cost of capital differs for international companies and highlights some challenges of using the global cost of capital. The goal is to shed light on estimating the cost of capital, improving the financial decision-making process for measuring financial performance, assessing the attractiveness of projects, and monitoring project performance. This chapter references a set of relevant papers for providing a summary of the major issues and viewpoints about cost of capital. Given the voluminous literature on this topic, the chapter is not intended to be exhaustive. Those interested in delving into this topic in greater depth can find a wealth of relevant research available in advanced corporate finance textbooks.

COST OF CAPITAL

In general, as discussed in previous chapters, discounted cash flow analysis (DCF) is one of the most widely used methods to evaluate capital expenditure proposals. A study by Graham and Harvey (2001) of capital budgeting techniques in the United States shows that 74.9 percent of chief financial officers (CFOs) always use net present value (NPV) when making capital budgeting decisions. Capital budgeting typically focuses on the concept of present value, which enables the user to compare future expected cash flows (CFs) in current dollar terms. The capital budgeting process encapsulates the time value of money and the risk associated with a particular project. Essentially, the discounting factor used to calculate the present value of the cash flow stream in many capital budgeting problems is based on the core cost of capital with adjustments made for project risk. To select value-enhancing projects, management needs to accurately estimate the cost of capital as well as the expected cash flow. As Equation 18.1 shows, the estimated present value of a series of cash flows is inversely related to the estimated WACC.

$$\text{Present Value} = \frac{CF_1}{(1 + WACC)^1} + \frac{CF_2}{(1 + WACC)^2} + \ldots + \frac{CF_N}{(1 + WACC)^N} \quad (18.1)$$

The cost of capital is the rate of return that suppliers of capital require as compensation for their contribution of capital (Courtois, Lai, and Peterson, 2008). The most common sources of capital are debt, common equity, and preferred stock. Related forms of capital include convertible securities, warrants and options, among others. If estimated using expected rates and target weights, the cost of capital is a forward-looking rate of return that investors require for forgoing the best alternative use of capital at a specific level of risk. When considering the overall financing the company employs, the term WACC or simply the cost of capital is used.

To value a company using DCF techniques involves discounting free cash flows (FCFs) at the weighted average rate of return required by all investors, which represents the minimum acceptable hurdle rate for the providers of capital (Anderson, Byers, and Groth, 2000). As stated previously, firms use the WACC to discount a series of future cash flows with the mix of equity and debt being the target or optimal mix that is expected to prevail in the future.

The general formula for the WACC, where each cost and proportion is considered on a marginal basis, is:

$$\text{WACC} = k_e W_e + k_d W_d (1 - t) + k_p W_p \quad (18.2)$$

where

k_e = Component cost of equity;
k_d = Component cost of debt;
k_p = Component cost of preferred stock;
t = Firm's marginal tax rate;
W_e = Target proportion of equity in the firm's capital structure;
W_d = Target proportion of debt in the firm's capital structure; and
W_p = Target proportion of preferred stock in the firm's capital structure.

COST OF CAPITAL WEIGHT ESTIMATION

This section begins with a discussion of the firm's WACC estimation by first examining how to estimate the component weights. Although managers and analysts can use balance sheet book value figures to calculate the book value weights, a more appropriate approach is to use the target market weights. The manner in which component weights are calculated is as follows:

$$W_D = \frac{\text{Market Value of Debt}}{\text{Total Value of Firm}} \quad W_e = \frac{\text{Market Value of Equity}}{\text{Total Value of Firm}}$$

$$W_P = \frac{\text{Market Value Preferred Stock}}{\text{Total Value of Firm}}$$

The total market value of the firm equals the combined market value of debt, equity, and preferred stock.

$$WACC = R_e^* W_e + E_d^* W_d^* (1 - t) + R_p^* W_p$$

In most real-world situations, firms often use different sources of debt, such as long- and short-term loans, bond issues, and commercial paper. When calculating component cost of capital weights, the target market weights should be employed because securities are typically issued at market value, which may differ from book value. The market weights reflect current conditions and the effects of changing market conditions and, therefore, the cost of capital should measure the market cost of issuing these securities. Also, each firm has a target (or optimal) capital structure defined as the best mix of debt, common equity, and preferred stocks that minimizes the firm's WACC. However, for simplicity, Case 1 involves a firm that uses only one type of debt: a long-term bond with a face value of $1,000,000 and a current market value of $850,000. The yield to maturity on the bond is 9 percent and the coupon rate is 7 percent. Recall that as interest rates increase, the market value of debt declines. This is called *interest rate risk*. Further, assume that the firm's market value of equity is $1,000,000, while its book value of equity is $250,000. This firm uses no preferred stock. The current weight of debt is estimated as:

$$\text{Case 1} \quad W_D = \frac{\text{Market Value of Debt}}{\text{Total Value of the Firm}} = \frac{\$850,000}{\$1,850,000} = 45.95\%$$

If the firm uses short-term loans such as revolving credit lines to acquire fixed assets rather than just to finance working capital needs, then the WACC calculation should include this short-term debt component. In Case 2, the assumption is that the same firm obtains a permanent short-term loan in the amount of $200,000. The firm's W_d would increase to:

$$\text{Case 2} \quad W_D = \frac{\text{Market Value of Debt}}{\text{Total Value of the Firm}} = \frac{\$1,050,000}{\$2,050,000} = 51.22\%$$

The addition of $200,000 in permanent short-term debt increases the percent weight of debt usage in the capital structure of the firm from 45.95 percent to 51.22 percent. The cost of debt is discussed in the next section.

Using the same example as Case 1 above, the weight of equity can be estimated as:

$$\text{Case 1} \quad W_E = \frac{\text{Market Value of Equity}}{\text{Total Value of the Firm}} = \frac{\$1,000,000}{\$1,850,000} = 54.05\%$$

In Case 2, the weight of equity is 48.78 percent. In this situation, as the percentage of debt increases in the firm's capital structure, the percentage of equity declines. These relative percentage usages are called the *capital structure mix*. The general term used to refer to the percentage amounts of the firm's capital source mix is the firm's *capital structure*. In part, firms choose to increase or decrease the use of debt or equity as the cost of debt and equity change.

To this point, the examples of component weight estimation have ignored the use of preferred stock. *Preferred stock* is a financial instrument class of ownership in a corporation that has a higher claim on the assets and earnings than a common stock. The firm must pay its dividend before paying dividends to common shareholders. Typically, preferred stock does not have voting rights. Returning to Case 1, assume that the firm decides to issue $200,000 in market value of preferred stock, $1,000,000 in market value of equity, and $850,000 in market value of debt. Now the firm is using debt, equity, and preferred stock in its capital structure, which becomes Case 3. The W_p can be calculated as:

$$\text{Case 3} \quad W_P = \frac{\text{Market Value of Preferred Stock}}{\text{Total Value of the Firm}} = \frac{\$200,000}{\$2,050,000} = 9.76\%$$

In Case 3, the weight usage of preferred stock is 9.76 percent, the weight of equity is 48.78 percent, and the weight of debt is 41.46 percent. Again, these are the current market weights and are not necessarily the firm's target capital structure. The target weights include the allocation of external financing that the firm believes will produce the optimal results. Corporate finance managers can use the target weights as reflected by the industry averages or those target weights used by comparable firms. For example, as the firm moves from Case 1 to Case 2 or Case 3, the weights change. Any capital budgeting decision should be based on the expected or target market weights of capital sources that the firm expects to use.

As Brigham and Daves (2010) note, managers make several common errors when estimating the weight components. One error is using book values. When estimating the WACC, managers should use the firm's market values. Another common error is using historical weights instead of target weights for each component. To estimate the WACC, managers should use the firm's target capital structure (Daves, Ehrhardt, and Shrives, 2004). Management should avoid falling prey to such errors because they can lead to incorrectly estimated WACCs and project values.

An Example of Estimating Weights for the WACC

Bimini Corporation wants to estimate its current market capital structure.

Sources of Financing	Book Value	Market Value
Stock Issue A	$250,000	$1,000,000
Stock Issue B	300,000	500,000
Bond Issue C	1,000,000	850,000
Bond Issue D	200,000	300,000
Preferred stock Issue A	500,000	500,000
Total	$2,250,000	$3,150,000

The weight of each component is calculated as follows:

Sources of Financing	Market Value	Firm Market Value	Weight (%)
Equity	$1,500,000	$3,150,000	47.62
Debt	1,150,000	3,150,000	36.51
Preferred stock	500,000	3,150,000	15.87
		Total	100.00

The weights sum to 100 percent and represent the firm's current weights.

THE WACC COMPONENT COST ESTIMATION

Managers and financial analysts can use different methods to estimate the component cost of each source of capital. Additionally, they can use several methods for each source. This section provides an overview of commonly used techniques to estimate the cost of equity, debt, and preferred stock.

Component Cost of Equity

The component cost of equity is the required rate of return of the firm's shareholders. Unlike the cost of a bank loan, which a firm could estimate by contacting its lender, most large modern corporations cannot ask their shareholders what they expect in return for buying their common stock. However, both the firm and financial analysts have tools available to gauge the expected return that investors require or expect from the firm. The most commonly used tool to estimate the cost of equity capital is the capital asset pricing model (CAPM), which is expressed as:

$$E(R_i) = R_f + \beta_i[E(R_m) - R_f] \tag{18.3}$$

where

$E(R_i)$ = Expected return on the firm's common equity ignoring flotation costs;
R_f = Risk-free rate;
β_i = Beta coefficient estimate between the stock (i) and a market index; and
$E(R_m)$ = Expected return on the market.

The term in brackets in Equation 18.3 is the *market risk premium* (MRP), which is the expected return on the market minus the risk-free rate. In practice, analysts estimate beta with respect to an equity market index when using the CAPM to estimate the cost of equity. Thus, they are concerned with the *equity risk premium*, which is the expected return on equities minus the risk-free rate (Stowe, Robinson, Pinto, and McLeavey, 2007).

The CAPM's simplicity has led to its widespread usage. For example, Bruner, Eades, Harris, and Higgins (1998), Graham and Harvey (2001), and Bancel and Mittoo (2004) find that corporate managers primarily use the CAPM to estimate the cost of equity capital when considering capital budgeting decisions. For example, survey evidence by Graham and Harvey shows that 74 percent of respondents report using the CAPM while few companies report using the dividend discount model. Ryan and Ryan (2002) surveyed CFOs of Fortune 1000 companies to determine what they consider to be the best discount rate for capital budgeting projects. Their findings show that 83.2 percent of respondents chose the WACC, followed by the rate on debt (7.4 percent), the rate on retained earnings (1.5 percent), and the rate on new equity (1.0 percent). Only 5.4 percent report using the cost of equity for a project financed with equity and the cost of debt for a project financed with debt, while 1.5 percent indicate they have another measure for calculating the base discount rate. In general, survey evidence suggests that respondents strongly prefer the WACC, which is consistent with the approach suggested by finance academics.

Gitman and Vandenberg (2000) replicate an earlier cost of capital survey (Gitman and Mercurio, 1982) of 111 major U.S. companies and report the following key findings:

- 93 percent of companies use the CAPM to estimate their cost of equity.
- Nearly all companies use one cost of capital regardless of the financing needed.
- Companies tend to use target weights instead of book weights.
- A large majority of companies use a type of weighted average of sources of capital for calculating cost of capital.

Other studies find that using the WACC to evaluate capital budgeting projects is also widespread in mainland Europe (Brounen, De Jong, and Koedijk, 2004). Oblak and Helm (1980) examine the cost of capital practices of multinationals and find that 54 percent of respondents use the WACC. Other measures cited in their study include the cost of debt, past experience, expected growth rate, and the CAPM. Stanley and Block (1984) examine various capital budgeting topics involving U.S. companies within a multinational context. They find that 49 percent of respondents use the parent company's cost of capital, 32 percent use the project cost of capital, and some companies use both. To measure the rate on foreign currency–denominated debt, 34 percent of companies report adjusting the cost of capital for changes in foreign exchange rates. Bierman (1993) surveys 74 Fortune 100 companies and finds that all respondents report using some form of discounting in their capital budgeting, and 93 percent use the WACC. Poterba and Summers (1995) survey CFOs of the Fortune 1000 to better understand how they measure and use hurdle rates. Their findings reveal that many companies use more than one hurdle rate and tend to set hurdle rates lower than their cost of capital.

Bruner et al. (1998) survey the cost of capital practices employed by 27 best practice U.S. companies and 10 leading financial advisers, and also examine the seven best-selling textbooks on cost of capital practices. Their evidence shows the WACC is the dominant discount rate with over 85 percent of the 27 best practice firms using CAPM or a modified CAPM version. The authors also find large variations in the choice of the risk-free rate, beta, and the equity market risk premium as well as for the adjustment of costs of capital for specific investment risk.

Given the dominance of the CAPM in estimating the cost of equity capital, how is the CAPM estimated in practice? The CAPM is a single-factor model in which the factor is the market risk premium $[E(R_m) - R_f]$. The coefficient that describes the relationship between the stock's return and the return on the market is known as beta (βi). Beta is estimated using a simple linear regression between the excess return to the market index and the security's excess return. In practice, questions arise as to how many periods to include in the analysis to estimate beta, the periodicity of the data (e.g., weekly versus monthly), the appropriate underlying market index to use, and the best risk-free rate to incorporate into the model.

Regarding the risk-free rate, the primary question is whether the firm should use a short-term government debt rate, such as the Treasury bill (T-bill) rate, or a long-term government bond yield to maturity, such as the rate on a Treasury bond. Should the firm match the length of investment to the length of the corresponding risk-free instrument? Some theorists argue that different risk-free rates and equity risk premiums should be used every year over the life of the investment (Ang and Liu, 2004). Matching the length of the investment to the appropriate risk-free rate length can also be used. For example, a 30-year investment should be matched to the 30-year risk-free rate. Many financial analysts also use long-term government bonds to estimate the cost of equity when evaluating a firm (Fabozzi, 2000; Stowe et al., 2007). The logic is that the duration of the risk-free measure should be matched to the duration of the asset being valued.

With respect to periodicity of the data, there is also no clear answer. Daves, Ehrhardt, and Kunkel (2000) show that for a given estimation period, daily returns provide a smaller standard error of the estimated beta than do weekly, two-weekly, or monthly returns. However, estimates based on monthly observations seem to provide slightly better statistical predictions when judged by R^2 (Bartholdy and Peare, 2001). Regarding the underlying market index, many services use the

S&P 500 index as a market proxy. Theoretically, the S&P 500 is not a good index to proxy the true underlying return of the "market" because it is biased toward large firms and the index includes only a small subset of observable traded equities. However, from a practical standpoint, this index has an understandable appeal. No market index can measure the true underlying return of the "market," but the index employed should be as broad as possible and should include reinvested dividends to capture the total return.

Estimated beta coefficients are readily available online and via many investment data services, such as Standard and Poor's Compustat, Bloomberg, Ibbotson Associates, Thomson Financial, Yahoo Finance, and others. However, each service uses a different length of included data, periodicity of data (e.g., weekly versus monthly), and underlying market index to estimate the firm's beta. When using a beta from an investment data service provider, understanding how it is estimated is important. In practice, the unadjusted beta coefficient derived from regressing the excess stock rate of return on the excess S&P 500 rate of return is then adjusted for regression toward the mean in order to provide a better estimate of the future beta by using Blume's (1971, 1975) adjustment. Both academics and practitioners commonly use these adjustment coefficients, which are derived by regressing the estimated values of beta on the values estimated in the previous period.

$$\text{Adjusted beta} = 0.34 + 0.66(\text{Unadjusted beta}) \qquad (18.4)$$

CAPM Estimation

Recall that Bimini Corporation has two stock issues with a combined market value of $1,500,000. Currently, the price of each share is $25 with 60,000 shares outstanding. The firm's estimated beta is 1.25. The current long-term risk-free rate is 5 percent and the expected return on the stock market is 10 percent. The required rate of return on Bimini's equity is estimated as follows: $E(R_i) = R_f + \beta_i[E(R_m) - R_f] = 0.05 + 1.25(0.10 - 0.05) = 0.1125$ or 11.25 percent.

Risk Premium Estimation

As mentioned previously, the CAPM is composed of two parts: (1) the risk-free rate (R_f), which compensates investors for inflation and the use of their capital in a riskless context; and (2) $[E(R_m) - R_f]$, which is referred to as the *market risk premium*, while $\beta_i[E(R_m) - R_f]$ is the *individual stock's risk premium*. The term *risk premium* refers to the additional return required by investors over the risk-free rate to compensate for the risk associated with investment. As the riskiness of the investment increases, so does the risk premium to entice investors to commit capital. Much debate exists over the correct estimation of the market risk premium, which is used as part of the CAPM as shown in Equation 18.3.

As previously mentioned, when using the CAPM to estimate the cost of equity, analysts estimate beta with respect to an equity market index. Several approaches are available for estimating the equity risk premium. One method is to derive it from the market stock prices using some equity valuation model. For example, the Gordon model determines the price of the stock taking into account the current dividend payment, constant growth rate, and required rate of return. The equity risk premium can be derived by using the current market stock price and solving for the required rate of return. Another method is using a historical equity risk premium, which uses a long series of historical data between the risk-free rate and the stock market to estimate the risk premium. The estimated risk premium could be used as follows:

$$E(R_i) = R_f + \text{Equity risk premium} \qquad (18.5)$$

No agreement exists as to the best way to use historical data to estimate the risk premium. Under the historical approach, the assumption is that history repeats itself. Ibbotson and Chen (2003) find an historical risk premium around 6 percent during the period 1926 to 2000. Questions remain about the appropriate length of the period to use in estimating the risk premium, the use of a short-term or long-term risk-free government bond, the most suitable underlying market index, and the choice of arithmetic versus geometric means. If returns are not correlated over time, the arithmetic mean, which takes into account the uncertainty of period to period returns, can be calculated as the average of the annual historical returns. The geometric mean incorporates the average compound return per year over a period. The greater the standard deviation of returns over time, the greater is the arithmetic mean vis-à-vis the geometric mean. Copeland, Koller, and Murrin (2000) suggest using a downward adjustment of 1.5 percent to 2.0 percent for survivorship bias in the S&P 500 Index when using arithmetic mean estimates. These are the same challenges discussed earlier when considering the CAPM. Furthermore, historic risk premium estimates are generally higher than the prevailing unobserved risk premiums due to *survivorship bias*, which may result when failed or defunct companies are excluded from membership in a group. Survivorship bias tends to inflate historical estimates of the equity risk premium (Stowe et al., 2007). As a rule of thumb, using a longer period and an appropriate risk-free rate leads to a superior estimate (Damodaran, 2001). Most studies of the risk premium focus on high-capitalization (cap) stocks from a market region or country, using a proxy for the market such as the S&P 500 Index for the United States or the FTSE100 for the United Kingdom. Investors often overweight large cap stocks, which are relatively safer than small or medium cap stocks and whose names they recognize and products they use. This large cap focus will, however, introduce a large cap bias. As part of corporate finance analysis, managers and analysts have to be careful and add a premium when dealing with lower cap stocks whose cost of equity is typically higher.

Another approach in estimating the risk premium is the prospective equity premium approach, which is based on expectational data. Under this approach, analysts use an equity valuation model to derive the risk premium that can be regarded as the market's consensus view. Using a version of the dividend discount model, Damodaran (2009) suggests that obtaining or estimating the current level of market value, the expected dividends next period, and the expected dividends and earnings in the long term will lead to the implied required rate of return on stocks. The implied equity risk premium is then derived by subtracting the risk-free rate from the implied required rate of return. Claus and Thomas (2001) and Fama and French (2002) find that the expected risk premium is around 3 percent in the United States. In practice, the prospective equity premium implied by the one-year forward price-earnings (P/E) multiple of the S&P 500 index can be calculated.

Exhibit 18.2 Equity Risk Premium

	Equity Risk Premium			
	Nominal Return		Real Return	
	Arithmetic Average (%)	Geometric Average (%)	Arithmetic Average (%)	Geometric Average (%)
1802 to 2006	4.45	3.09	4.35	3.13
1900 to 2006	6.29	4.47	6.01	4.43
1926 to 2006	5.99	4.18	5.71	4.03
1982 to 2006	1.41	0.92	1.43	0.90

Note: This exhibit shows equity risk premiums estimated over several time periods. It shows that the equity risk premium changes over time and the choice of period of estimation influences the required rate of return calculation. Sources: Adapted from Siegel (2002) and Dimson, Marsh, and Stanton (2002).

Additional required inputs are: (1) a five-year consensus growth rate of earnings; (2) long-term growth rate of earnings; (3) present and long-term payout ratios; (4) annually compounded yield on the 10-year government bond benchmark; and (5) an estimate of a government bond's beta coefficient. The *prospective equity premium* is the difference between the rate required by investors on a market (equity) portfolio minus the riskless long-term government yield.

Graham and Harvey (2006) provide an alternative estimation of the ex-ante equity premium from a global quarterly survey of CFOs who were asked about their expectations for the return on the S&P 500 over the next 10 years. The authors find a spread between expected return on the S&P 500 and the 10-year Treasury bond yield from June 2000 to January 2006 of between 4.35 percent and 2.39 percent. Graham and Harvey also present evidence on the determinants of the long-run risk premium suggesting a positive correlation between the ex-ante risk premium and real interest rates as reflected in Treasury Inflation Indexed Notes. The level of the risk premium also appears to track market volatility as reflected in the VIX index. VIX is the ticker symbol for the Chicago Board Options Exchange Volatility Index, a popular measure of the implied volatility of S&P 500 index options.

Fernandez (2009) highlights at least four definitions of the equity risk premium in 150 textbooks such as a historical risk premium, required risk premium, implied risk premium, and expected risk premium. In his findings, he emphasizes that there is neither a generally accepted equity premium point estimate nor a common method to estimate it, even for the historical risk approach. Exhibit 18.2 contains equity risk premiums estimated over several time periods. The exhibit shows that the equity risk premium changes over time, and the choice of period of estimation influences the required rate of return calculation.

Fernandez and del Campo (2010) survey 436 analysts and 639 companies about the type of books and papers they use as references to justify the market risk premium. The authors find that 127 of them provide more than a reference with a vast majority using internal estimates and studies by Damodaran, Morningstar/Ibbotson, McKinsey, and Copeland. By looking at the difference between professors and analysts in estimating the market risk premium, Fernandez (2010) notices that on average, professors use a higher MRP than analysts for almost every country covered by the study. The dispersion of the MRPs used by professors is also higher than that of analysts.

Component Cost of Debt

Estimating the cost of debt is typically a simpler task than estimating the cost of equity because less debate exists over the validity of the methodologies involved. The component cost of debt is the required rate of return that debt holders require on the firm's debt instruments. A common method of estimating the cost of debt is to use the yield to maturity (YTM) on the firm's debt adjusted for taxes, when applicable.

Consider a noncallable bond with an annual coupon payment. As Equation 18.6 shows, the YTM is the rate that equates the current price of the bond to the present value of the coupon payments and the return of capital. Thus, the YTM represents the before tax cost of debt.

$$\text{Price of Bond} = \frac{CP_1}{(1 + YTM)^1} + \frac{CP_2}{(1 + YTM)^2} + \ldots + \frac{CP_N}{(1 + YTM)^N} + \frac{Par}{(1 + YTM)^N}$$

$$(18.6)$$

where CP = Coupon payment and Par = Face value of the bond.

In the United States, interest paid on corporate debt reduces taxable income. Therefore, when considering the before-tax cost of debt when estimating the firm's WACC, an adjustment should be made for the tax shield. Recall the debt component cost portion of the formula for estimating the firm's WACC is given as $k_d(1 - t)$. Here k_d represents the YTM on the firm's bonds, while t represents the firm's marginal tax rate. For firms with multiple bond issues or with a mix of debt such as loans and commercial paper, the cost of debt is a weighted average of the cost of debt, where the weights are determined by the percentage of each type of debt relative to total debt outstanding.

In practice, the company's treasurer can provide the cost of debt by analyzing the most recent borrowings to get a sense of default spreads. Outside investors can calculate the cost of debt by looking at other companies' yields on debt with similar features, including risk and maturity. If the company has bonds that are traded, the current price of the company's existing bonds can be used to calculate the expected rate of return on bonds. If the bonds are actively traded, information is readily available on individual corporate bond issues, including bond ratings, current yields, and current prices in specialized services such as Thomson Reuters and Bloomberg. Moody's Investor Services, Standard and Poor's Corporation, Fitch Investor Services, Thomson, and Bloomberg provide bond ratings that reflect the default risk on specific bonds. Some banks, bond brokers, and investment boutiques calculate yields on individual bond issues and provide indicative yields for bonds classified in a particular rating and maturity.

After identifying all bond issues for a company, the current traded prices can be found for those bonds and the corresponding risk-free rate that matches the maturity of the bond issues. Next, the rating for that bond or similar bonds with similar size and leverage, if the bonds are not traded, is determined. Finally, the *spread*, which is the difference between the yield on a risky bond and the yield on the risk-free rate for a specific rating and maturity, is calculated. To estimate the cost of issuing new long-term debt requires the following:

$$\text{Cost of new long-term debt} = \text{Risk-free rate} + \text{Spread} \qquad (18.7)$$

Assume that Bimini Corporation wants to estimate its current component cost of debt. Bimini has the following bond issues:

Bond Issue	Book Value	Market Value	Years to Maturity	Coupon (%)	Current YTM (%)
C	$1,000,000	$850,000	10	8.00	10.49
D	200,000	300,000	25	7.00	3.85

First, calculate the percentage weight allocated to each bond issue.

Bond Issue	Market Value	Percent Total
C	$ 850,000	73.91%
D	300,000	26.09
Total	$1,150,000	100.00%

Next, multiply each percentage use by its cost (YTM) and adjust for the tax shield.

Bond Issue	Percent Total	Current YTM
C	73.91%	10.49%
D	26.09	3.85
Before tax cost of debt =		8.76%
Tax rate =		40.00%
After tax cost of debt =		5.26%

In summary, Bimini's after-tax cost of debt is 5.26 percent in order to provide a 10.49 percent return to the holders of bond C and 3.85 percent to the investors in bond D.

Convertible Debt

Convertible bonds are bonds that are convertible into equity. A convertible bond is a hybrid security combining a debt and an equity instrument (the call option to purchase stock). When corporate managers consider the cost of debt and equity, they should separate the two components embedded within the convertible bond issue. Often, the debt portion is considered within the weight of debt while the equity portion is considered in the weight of equity.

For example, assume that another firm, ICG, Inc., plans to offer convertible bonds to finance the construction of a factory. The firm wants to estimate its cost and weight of debt to use when estimating its WACC after issuing the additional debt. ICG issued $1 million in bonds three years ago that have a current market value of $1.1 million. The firm also has $2 million in market value common stock outstanding. The firm's marginal tax rate is 40 percent. The following summarizes the current and expected additional debt.

	Book Value	Market Value	Years to Maturity	Coupon (%)
Bond Issue A	$1,000,000	$1,100,000	7	6.00
Convertible Bond Issue B	1,000,000	950,000	10	4.25

ICG expects to sell Convertible Bond Issue B at 95 percent of par and the YTM on similar nonconvertible securities is currently 10 percent. The YTM on Issue A is 4.31 percent and the expected YTM on the convertible bond is 10 percent, not 4.89 percent. Using 4.89 percent ignores the benefit provided by convertibility. Also, the total $950,000 should not be counted as debt. Instead, the financial manager should estimate the equity and debt components embedded within the market value. First, this requires estimating the value of the bond component. Using the coupon of 4.25 percent, 10 years to maturity, and 10 percent interest rate, the bond component should be worth the following:

	Par	Years to Maturity	Coupon	YTM	Value
Convertible Bond Issue B	$1,000,000	10	4.25%	10.00%	$646,687.39

After estimating the value of the straight debt, the financial manager should remove the value of the equity component by subtracting the value of the straight debt from the total value of the issues.

Total Value	Bond Component	Option Component
$950,000	$646,687	$303,313

Next, the financial manager should estimate the cost and percentage use of debt and adjust for the tax shield.

	Amount	Percent Total	Cost (%)	Weighted Cost (%)
New Debt	$1,100,000.00	0.63	10.00	6.30%
Current debt	646,687.39	0.37	4.89	1.81
Before tax cost of debt =				8.11%
After tax cost of debt =				4.87%

The resulting weights of equity and debt are as follows:

	Current	New	Total	Weight (%)
Debt	$1,100,000	$646,687	$1,746,687	43.13
Equity	2,000,000	303,313	2,303,313	56.87

Component Cost Estimation: Preferred Stock

The cost of preferred stock is the return required by investors for holding this form of investment. In the case of noncallable, no-maturity-date, and fixed-dividend preferred stock, the required rate of return can be estimated as:

$$k_p = \frac{D_p}{P_p} \tag{18.8}$$

where

k_p = Cost component (required return on) of preferred stock;
D_p = Dividend paid on the preferred stock; and
P_p = Price of the preferred stock.

Recall that Bimini has $500,000 in preferred stock outstanding. Assume that Bimini pays a dividend on preferred stock of $50,000 a year. The resulting k_p is 10 percent = $50,000/$500,000. Having examined the methods used to calculate each component cost (debt, equity, and preferred stock), the chapter now presents a unifying example.

COMPREHENSIVE EXAMPLE OF ESTIMATING THE WACC

Bimini wants to estimate its WACC. Management provides the following information: The firm's equity has a beta of 1.25; the current risk-free rate on a long-term government bond is 5 percent; and the current expected return on the stock market is 10 percent. Bond issue C has 10 years to maturity, pays an annual coupon of 8 percent, and has a yield of 10.49 percent. Bond issue D has 25 years to maturity, pays an annual coupon of 7 percent, and has a yield of 3.85 percent. The firm has 10,000 shares of preferred stock with a market value of $50 that yields 10 percent. The firm's current marginal tax rate is 40 percent. The following summarizes the book and market values of debt, equity and preferred stock.

Issue	Book Value	Market Value
Stock Issue A	$250,000	$1,000,000
Stock Issue B	300,000	500,000
Bond Issue C	1,000,000	850,000
Bond Issue D	200,000	300,000
Preferred stock Issue A	500,000	500,000
Total	$2,250,000	$3,150,000

Using the cost and weight of each component, the WACC is calculated as follows:

Component	Cost (%)	Weight (%)	Weighted Cost (%)
Cost of debt	8.76	36.51	3.20
Cost of equity	11.25	47.62	5.36
Cost of preferred stock	10.00	15.87	1.59
		WACC =	8.86

Thus, WACC = 8.76% $(1 - 0.40)(0.3651) + 11.25\%\ (0.4762) + 10.00\%\ (0.1587) =$ 8.86%.

COST OF CAPITAL FOR A PROJECT

For simplicity, some companies apply their overall cost of capital to all investment projects. Financial theory recommends, however, using a different hurdle rate for projects with different levels of risk (Damodaran, 2001; Baker and Powell, 2005; Brealey, Myers, and Allen, 2006; Pratt and Grabowski, 2008). In principle, the duration and risk of the financial securities used to estimate the WACC should match that of the FCFs being discounted (Koller, Goedhart, and Wesseles, 2005). If the chosen projects and the firm share the same risk profile, a firm should use its overall cost of equity as the overall cost of equity of the project. However, several problems may result from a firm using its overall WACC to estimate the value of its capital budgeting projects. For example, a firm with a low WACC, which embodies the average risk of firm's projects, would tend to choose risky projects (i.e., projects with high IRRs). Over time this tendency would increase the firm's overall riskiness and would lead to a higher cost of borrowing at the firm level and, eventually, a drop in shareholders' value. To illustrate, an oil refinery is inherently less risky than oil drilling and exploration. Faced with the option to expand into oil drilling using its current firm-level WACC, the refiner would choose to engage in the drilling activity. However, this activity would increase the firm's overall riskiness. When the refiner returns to the capital markets to raise additional capital for refining, the price it has to pay for capital would likely increase. This process could continue until the firm's cost of capital rises to the point at which the firm can no longer feasibly invest in refining activities.

Exhibit 18.3 illustrates the relationship between project returns, risk, and the firm-level WACC. The firm-level WACC is constant across the spectrum of projects. This would lead the firm to accept all projects with IRRs above its WACC, while rejecting all projects with IRRs that are below its WACC. However, how should the firm treat the investment in an expansion and renovation of a store? Undertaking such a project might result in a low return, one that will in many cases be lower than the firm's WACC. However, without renovation and expansion the firm will be unable to remain competitive.

One method that firms employ to combat most problems associated with using a single cost of capital is to use different discount rates for each project type

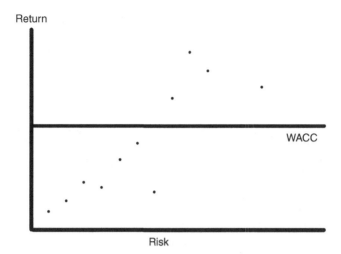

Exhibit 18.3   Constant Non-Project-Adjusted WACC
Note: This exhibit shows that a firm having projects with returns (IRRs) greater than its WACC would accept them if the firm uses its firm-level WACC to make capital budgeting decisions and would reject those with returns (IRRs) below its WACC. However, the firm should consider project risk when making this decision. If the firm does not consider project risk, it tends to select more risky projects, which over time increase the total risk level of the firm.

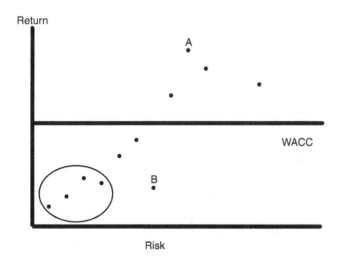

Exhibit 18.4   Graph of Expansion and Renovation Opportunities
Note: The figure contains a grocer's expansion and renovation opportunity set with the renovations circled. If the firm uses its firm-level WACC to make capital budgeting decisions, it would reject all renovations and would accept only the more risky expansions. For example, the firm would accept projects whose returns are greater than its WACC (e.g., Project A), and reject those projects whose returns are less than its WACC (e.g., Project B).

or division. According to Emery, Finnerty, and Stowe (2007), firms often use five separate risk classes to eliminate the problems associated with using a single cost of capital. The authors also suggest that using three classes is valuable in alleviating the problems with using a firm-level WACC alone. Consider the case illustrated in Exhibit 18.4, which shows a grocer's entire location expansion and renovation opportunity set. The circled projects are renovations of current locations, while the other data points represent expansion to new locations. In this case, each renovation project has low risk and low return. However, Project B is an expansion to a new location, and when appropriately discounted, has a negative NPV.

Assuming no capital rationing, a firm should accept all the value-enhancing projects and should reject value-destroying projects such as Project B. Management could use the adjusted WACC method to estimate the present value of the maintenance projects. In this case, the firm may accept a low IRR project, if discounted at a lower WACC. This method allows the firm to have some control over the WACC it uses to estimate a project's present value. However, with this control comes a level of subjectivity and increased error. Additionally, some projects may be difficult to classify and may fall outside the predefined categories.

Another method that firms use to adjust the WACC is based on a project's beta. If the firm is considering a new project, it could adjust the beta used to estimate the cost of equity based on the project's riskiness and not on the firm's overall beta. For example, if the firm's beta is 1.25 and the project's beta is 1.75, the financial manager could use the beta of 1.75 to estimate the cost of equity when calculating the WACC used to estimate the project's present value. As Exhibit 18.5 illustrates, the WACC used should more closely match the project's risk.

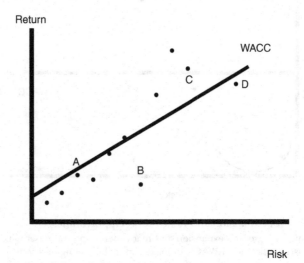

Exhibit 18.5   Adjusted Project Level WACC Estimation
Note: Projects A through D represent projects with different levels of risk. If the firm uses its firm-level WACC to select projects, it would select the more risky projects and reject the less risky projects. By adjusting the WACC (hurdle rate) using project-level risk profiles, the firm can overcome this tendency. As illustrated, the hurdle rate should increase as project risk increases.

For example, Bimini decides to diversify its business by investing in a commercial aircraft business besides its current hotel and gaming services. Bimini has a tax rate of 40 percent and a current debt-to-equity ratio of 25 percent, applicable for both divisions. The financial manager decides to use the pure play approach to estimate betas for each division. The *pure play approach* is a method of estimating a project's beta by identifying several publicly traded companies in the same or similar line of business as the proposed project and determining their betas.

First, before calculating a pure play beta for each business, the financial manager should identify comparable publicly traded firms involved in the same business as each of the firm's divisions. Second, calculating the current beta for each division involves computing the average of current betas of the chosen comparable firms. Third, the financial manager calculates the unlevered beta for each division, taking into account the average debt to equity ratio for the group of firms in each business. The following is the formula for an unlevered beta.

$$\text{Unlevered Beta}_{\text{division}} = \frac{\text{Current Beta}_{\text{division}}}{1 + (1 - \text{Tax Rate})(\text{Average Debt-to-Equity for the Industry})} \quad (18.9)$$

Finally, the levered beta is calculated using the current market values for debt and equity and the current debt-to-equity ratio. Bimini's unlevered beta is the value weighted average of the unlevered betas of each business, using the proportion of firm value derived from each business as weights. Using the average 25 percent for the debt-to-equity ratio for the group of firms in each industry, the user can calculate a levered beta and a cost of equity for each division as shown in Exhibit 18.6.

$$\text{Unlevered Beta}_{\text{division}} = \frac{\text{Levered Beta}_{\text{division}}}{1 + (1 - \text{Tax Rate})(\text{Average Debt-to-Equity})} \quad (18.10)$$

Therefore, in analyzing projects in the commercial aircraft business, the financial manager should use 9.60 percent as the cost of equity.

Exhibit 18.6   Cost of Equity by Business Segment

	Hotel/Gaming Services	Commercial Aircraft	Firm
Unlevered beta	1.25	0.80	0.98
Debt-to-equity ratio	25.00%	25.00%	25.00%
Levered beta	1.437	0.920	1.127
Risk-free rate	5.00%	5.00%	5.00%
Risk premium	5.00%	5.00%	5.00%
Cost of equity	12.19%	9.60%	10.64%

This exhibit shows the betas and cost of equity of each business segment as estimated and compared to the firm's cost of equity.
Adapted from Damodaran (2001).

COST OF CAPITAL IN AN INTERNATIONAL CONTEXT

To increase shareholder wealth, companies look for profitable investments and focus on policies that reduce the cost of capital for those projects. Internationalizing the company's cost of capital is one such policy. Therefore, integration or segmentation of international financial markets has implications for deriving the appropriate cost of capital. But no agreement exists between academics and practitioners on how to estimate the cost of capital in an international context. If the project is in a developed country, that economy is likely to be integrated into the global economy and projects with similar risks are likely to have similar costs of capital. When markets are imperfect, international financing may lower the company's cost of capital if cheaper financing sources are available in different markets. When countries are not integrated into the global economy, country factors often play an important role. Hargis and Mei (2006) find that country risk differences matter because there is a lower degree of diversification of the emerging markets to world goods and financial markets. They find that global discount rates explain 55 percent of the variation of country discount rates and industry discount rate variation explains 78 percent of country discount rates.

In the CAPM framework, the discount rate should capture each risk premium as long as these risks are nondiversifiable for the investors. Because the variance of cash flows might differ, the cost of capital should reflect these differences despite having identical expected cash flows from projects in the two countries (Pratt and Grabowski, 2008). In an emerging markets context, investors typically face greater nondiversifiable risk because these markets are rarely integrated. The nondiversifiable risk is also known as *systematic risk*, which is the portion of an asset's risk attributable to market factors that affect all firms such as war, inflation, and international incidents. Harvey (2004) shows a significant negative relationship between political, financial, and economic risks and the implied cost of capital for emerging markets. Lower ratings (higher risks) are associated with higher expected returns and higher implied costs of capital.

In practice, financial managers use various ad hoc approaches of which many have questionable theoretical and empirical validity (Harvey, 2001). In the majority of models, which are mainly variations of a global CAPM, the cost of capital is increased to account for "country risk" while the proxy for the market becomes the global market portfolio. Illiquid equity markets, a short history for equity markets, and a small number of traded stocks make calculating a company's systematic risk difficult. Studies show that when analyzing a stock of an international firm from an emerging market due to low correlations between emerging markets and developed markets, the beta is very low (Harvey, 1995a, 1995b). This raises many questions about the validity of the global CAPM model and its use for estimating the cost of capital in a global context.

Mishra and O'Brien (2005) study the implied cost of capital estimates for individual stocks from 16 developing countries and find that global beta explains differences in the implied cost of capital. Other theoreticians and practitioners include additional adjustment factors, such as sovereign yield spread and country credit ratings, to compensate for the low estimated beta (Erb, Harvey, and Viskanta, 1996; Hauptman and Natella, 1997; Damodaran, 1999). Although government policies, legal and regulatory structure, accounting standards, and market conditions all affect the cost of capital in a particular country, cross-country differences in the cost of capital are disappearing as capital markets become more integrated. Ideally, the financial manager should incorporate all systematic country-specific factors in the expected cost of capital and the company-specific factors in the cash flows of the project evaluation process. Given the increasing globalization of markets, using a global industry beta relevered to the firm's target capital structure is recommended to accurately determine a firm's true risk in an emerging market.

Financial managers calculate the global cost of capital using different methods and perspectives. Common data providers include Morningstar (Ibbotson), Duff and Phelps, Bloomberg, Thomson Reuters, Compustat, Value Line, Capital IQ, and Barra. While the concepts applied to developed markets and emerging markets are similar, the application can differ. When choosing the data sources for the cost of capital, the financial manager should pay attention to the measurement of the risk-free rate, appropriate time period, and size effect for the equity risk premium, industry premium, company-specific factors, and beta choices including levered or unlevered, frequency, periodicity, and adjustment factors.

SUMMARY AND CONCLUSIONS

Estimating the cost of capital provides the critical link that enables converting a stream of expected cash flows into an estimate of present value. This allows for informed pricing decisions and comparisons of one investment opportunity against another for regulatory purposes and corporate valuation. Estimating the cost of capital requires applying solid methodologies to determine the value drivers captured by market pricing based on current economic and financial information.

Business schools expose students to various models and apply these models in a classroom setting. However, when users try to apply them to real business problems, they often encounter many challenges. Knowing where and how to find critical information and how to apply it in a timely manner using an economically sound model is often the difference between a successful and unsuccessful decision. Data availability and quality are as important as the models used. Because the cost of capital is not directly observable, the financial manager must derive it from the return investors expect to get from a firm's securities. Under a DCF model, the value of any asset is the present value of future expected cash flows (e.g., dividends, coupon and face value for bonds, and FCFs) discounted at the appropriate discount rate.

Estimating the WACC requires determining the cost of each capital component and its corresponding weight. This is also the project's cost of capital when the project's risk is similar to that of the firm's average project. When a project's risk differs from the average or normal risk of the firm's capital project, the financial manager should adjust the discount rate to reflect the project's riskiness.

DISCUSSION QUESTIONS

1. What are the guidelines for choosing the risk-free rate?
2. Reconcile the choice between using the realized historical risk premium versus a forward-looking risk premium when estimating a project's cost of equity.

3. An analyst makes the following statement: "A firm should add the total capital raised in a convertible bond issue to its debt balance when estimating the cost of capital and should ignore the equity portion until the bonds have been converted, at which time the firm should add the proportion of equity issued to the total amount of its equity capital." Assess this statement.

4. A manager contends that a firm should use historical or book weights when estimating a firm's WACC because they are easily observable and can guide the estimation process. Provide a counter to this argument for a rapidly growing firm that raises large amounts of external capital. Would the answer change for a well-established firm that does not expect to raise capital?

REFERENCES

Anderson, Ronald, Steven Byers, and John C. Groth. 2000. "The Cost of Capital for Projects: Conceptual and Practical Issues." *Management Decision* 38:6, 384–393.

Ang, Andrew, and Jun Liu. 2004. "How to Discount Cashflows with Time-Varying Expected Returns." *Journal of Finance* 59:6, 2745–2783.

Baker, H. Kent, and Gary E. Powell. 2005. *Understanding Financial Management: A Practical Guide*. Malden, MA: Blackwell Publishing.

Bancel, Franck, and Usha R. Mittoo. 2004. "Cross-Country Determinants of Capital Structure Choice: A Survey of European Firms." *Financial Management* 33:4, 103–132.

Bartholdy, Jan and Peare, Paula. 2001. "The Relative Efficiency of Beta Estimates." Available at http://ssrn.com/abstract = 263745 or doi:10.2139/ssrn.263745.

Bierman, Harold Jr. 1993. "Capital Budgeting in 1992: A Survey." *Financial Management* 22:3, 24.

Blume, Marshall E. 1971. "On the Assessment of Risk." *Journal of Finance* 26:1, 1–10.

Blume, Marshall E. 1975. "Betas and the Regression Tendencies." *Journal of Finance* 30:3, 785–795.

Brealey, Richard A., Stewart C. Myers, and Franklin Allen. 2006. *Principles of Corporate Finance*, 8th ed. Boston: Irwin McGraw-Hill.

Brigham, Eugene R., and Phillip Daves. 2010. *Intermediate Financial Management*. Mason, OH: South-Western Cengage Learning.

Brounen, Dirk, Abe De Jong, and Kees C. G. Koedijk. 2004. "Corporate Finance in Europe: Confronting Theory with Practice." *Financial Management* 33:4, 71–101.

Bruner, Robert F., Kenneth M. Eades, Robert S. Harris, and Robert C. Higgins. 1998. "Best Practices in Estimating the Cost of Capital: Survey and Synthesis." *Journal of Financial Practice and Education* 8:1, 13–28.

Claus, James, and Jacob Thomas. 2001. "Equity Premia as Low as Three Percent? Evidence from Analysts' Earnings Forecasts for Domestic and International Stock Markets." *Journal of Finance* 56:5, 1629–1666.

Copeland, Tom, Tim Koller, and Jack Murrin. 2000. *Valuation: Measuring and Managing the Value of Companies*, 2nd ed. New York: John Wiley & Sons.

Courtois, Yves, Gene Lai, and Pamela Peterson. 2008. "Cost of Capital." In Michelle R. Clayman, Martin S. Fridson, and George Troughton, eds. *Corporate Finance: A Practical Approach, 127–169*. Hoboken, NJ: John Wiley & Sons.

Damodaran, Aswath. 1999. "Estimating Equity Risk Premiums." Working Paper, New York University.

Damodaran, Aswath. 2001. *Corporate Finance Theory and Practice*. Hoboken, NJ: John Wiley & Sons.

Damodaran, Aswath. 2009. "Equity Risk Premiums (ERP): Determinants, Estimation and Implications—A Post-Crisis Update." Available at http://ssrn.com/abstract = 1492717.

Daves, Phillip, Michael Ehrhardt, and Robert Kunkel. 2000. "Estimating Systematic Risk: The Choice of Return Interval and Estimation Period." *Journal of Financial and Strategic Decisions* 13:1, 7–13.

Daves, Phillip E., Michael C. Ehrhardt, and Ronald E. Shrives. 2004. *Corporate Valuation: A Guide for Managers and Investors.* Mason, OH: Thomson South-Western.

Dimson, Elroy, Paul Marsh, and Mike Stanton. 2002. *Triumph of the Optimistics.* Princeton, NJ: Princeton University Press.

Emery, Douglas, John Finnerty, and John Stowe. 2007. *Corporate Financial Management,* 3rd ed. Upper Saddle River, NJ: Prentice Hall.

Erb, Claude, Campbell R. Harvey, and Tadas Viskanta. 1996. "Expected Returns and Volatility in 135 Countries." *Journal of Portfolio Management,* 22:3, 46–58.

Fabozzi, Frank. 2000. *Fixed Income Analysis for the Chartered Financial Analysts Program.* New Hope, PA: Frank Fabozzi Associates.

Fama, Eugene F., and Kenneth R. French. 2002. "The Equity Premium." *Journal of Finance* 57:2, 637–659.

Fernandez, Pablo. 2009. "The Equity Premium in 150 Textbooks." Available at http://papers .ssrn.com/sol3/papers.cfm?abstract_id = 1473225.

Fernandez, Pablo, and Javier del Campo. 2010. "Market Risk Premium Used in 2010 by Analysts and Companies: A Survey with 2,400 Answers." Available at http:// papers.ssrn.com/sol3/papers.cfm?abstract_id = 1609563.

Gitman, Lawrence J., and Vincent A. Mercurio. 1982. "Cost of Capital Techniques Used by Major U.S. Firms: Survey and Analysis of Fortune's 1000." *Financial Management* 11:4, 21–29.

Gitman, Lawrence J., and Pieter A. Vandenberg. 2000. "Cost of Capital Techniques Used by Major US Firms: 1997 vs. 1980." *Financial Practice and Education* 10:2, 53–68.

Graham, John R., and Campbell R. Harvey. 2001. "The Theory and Practice of Corporate Finance: Evidence from the Field." *Journal of Financial Economics* 60:2–3, 187–243.

Graham, John R., and Campbell R. Harvey. 2006. "The Equity Risk Premium: Evidence from the Global CFO Outlook Survey." Available at http://ssrn.com/abstract = 871105.

Hargis, Kent, and Kianping Mei. 2006. "Is Country Diversification Better than Industry Diversification?" *European Financial Management* 12:3, 319–340.

Harvey, Campbell R. 1995a. "Predictable Risk and Returns in Emerging Markets." *Review of Financial Studies* 8:3, 773–816.

Harvey, Campbell R. 1995b. "The Risk Exposure of Emerging Markets." *World Bank Economic Review* 9:1, 19–50.

Harvey, Campbell R. 2001. "12 Ways to Calculate the International Cost of Capital." Working Paper, Duke University.

Harvey, Campbell R. 2004. "Country Risk Components, the Cost of Capital, and Returns in Emerging Markets." Available at http://ssrn.com/abstract = 620710.

Hauptman, Lucia, and Stefano Natella. 1997. "The Cost of Equity in Latin America: The Eternal Doubt." Credit Suisse First Boston, Equity Research, May 20.

Ibbotson, Roger G., and Peng Chen. 2003. "Long-run Stock Returns: Participating in the Real Economy." *Financial Analysts Journal* 59:1, 88–98.

Koller, Tim, Marc Goedhart, and David Wesseles. 2005. *Valuation: Measuring and Managing the Value of Companies.* Hoboken, NJ: John Wiley & Sons.

Mishra, R. Dev, and Thomas J. O'Brien. 2005. "Risk and Ex-Ante Cost of Equity Estimates of Emerging Market Firms." *Emerging Market Review* 6:2, 107–120.

Oblak, David, and Roy J. Helm Jr. 1980. "Survey and Analysis of Capital Budgeting Methods Used by Multinationals." *Financial Management* 9:4, 37–41.

Poterba, James M., and Larry H. Summers. 1995. "A CEO Survey of U.S. Companies Time Horizons and Hurdle Rates." *Sloan Management Review* 37:1, 43–53.
Pratt, Shannon, and Roger J. Grabowski. 2008. *Cost of Capital: Applications and Examples*, 3rd ed. Hoboken, NJ: John Wiley & Sons.
Ryan, Patricia A., and Glenn P. Ryan. 2002. "Capital Budgeting Practices of the Fortune 1000: How Have Things Changed?" *Journal of Business and Management* 8:4, 355–364.
Siegel, Jeremy. 2002. *Stock for the Long Run*, 3rd ed. New York: Irwin.
Stanley, Marjorie, and Stanley Block. 1984. "A Survey of Multinational Capital Budgeting." *Financial Review* 19:1, 36–54.
Stowe, John, Thomas Robinson, Jerald Pinto, and Dennis McLeavey. 2007. *Analysis of Equity Investments: Valuation*. Hoboken, NJ: John Wiley & Sons.

ABOUT THE AUTHORS

Octavian Ionici is an Executive-in-Residence Professor of Finance and the Director of the Financial Services Lab at the Kogod School of Business, American University. His research interests focus primarily on financial modeling, corporate valuation, and real options. His research has appeared in journals such as the *Review of Business, Journal of Emerging Markets, International Journal of Business* and *Finance Research*, and *International Journal of Applied Decision Sciences*. He holds a B.S. in Economics from the Bucharest Academy of Economic Studies, an M.A. in Financial Economics from American University, and a Ph.D. in Finance from the Bucharest Academy of Economic Studies.

Kenneth Small is an Associate Professor of Finance at Coastal Carolina University. He currently holds the Marshall Butler Professorship in Finance. His research has appeared in the *Journal of Behavioral Finance, CPA Journal, Journal of Economics and Finance, Journal of Emerging Markets, Corporate Finance Review*, and others. He is a Chartered Financial Analyst (CFA) and a Certified Financial Planner (CFP). He previously was a faculty member at Loyola University in Maryland. He was recently selected as the university-level Mentor/Advisor of the Year after being nominated as Professor of the Year. He holds an M.A. in Economics from the University of Tennessee, an M.B.A. from Texas A & M International University, and a Ph.D. in Finance from the University of Tennessee.

Frank D'Souza is an Assistant Professor of Finance at Loyola University Maryland. His research interests are in corporate finance, derivatives, corporate governance, and behavioral finance. His research has been published in scholarly Journals such as *Corporate Governance: An International Review, International Journal of Business and Finance Research*, and *University of Pennsylvania Journal of Business Law*. He has also been awarded Outstanding Paper awards for his presentations at the SWFA and the IBFR conferences. He holds an M.B.A. from St. Cloud State University and a Ph.D. from Oklahoma State University.

Using the Capital Asset Pricing Model and Arbitrage Pricing Theory in Capital Budgeting

S. DAVID YOUNG
Professor of Accounting and Control, INSEAD

SAMIR SAADI
Ph.D. Candidate, Queen's University

INTRODUCTION

Estimating the opportunity cost of capital is one of the most critical financial issues facing managers. The most common tool for evaluating this issue is the capital asset pricing model (CAPM) along with its competitor, the arbitrage pricing theory (APT). After decades of research, much debate remains as to the validity of either model to estimate the cost of equity capital. Most of the literature on the CAPM focuses on its predictive power, the appropriate parameter inputs, and beta estimation techniques.

Given the aim of the chapter and space limitations, the chapter avoids the formal mathematical proofs of these models, which can be found in any standard text on asset pricing, but discusses the assumptions and conditions needed for these models to hold. The discussion reveals that unlike the APT and multifactor models, the CAPM continues to be the dominant tool for corporate use in estimating the cost of equity.

The rest of the chapter is organized as follows. The next section presents the CAPM followed by a section that considers the model's theoretical extensions. The chapter then discusses the challenges involved in using the CAPM. The next section discusses the biases associated with the empirical testing of the CAPM and is followed by a section that presents the APT, including a brief discussion on recent developments regarding new risk factors. The final two sections describe current practice in the field and present a summary and conclusions.

THE CAPITAL ASSET PRICING MODEL

Over the past five decades, the CAPM and the APT have come to dominate the asset pricing literature. Developed almost simultaneously by Sharpe (1964) and

Lintner (1965), the CAPM is widely considered to be one of the most important developments in financial economics. The CAPM not only became popular with academics but also attracted the attention of practitioners because it provided a simple and intuitive approach to pricing risk. Like any equilibrium model, the CAPM is heavy on assumptions, some of which are highly unrealistic. These assumptions, which are also required for mean-variance efficient portfolio theory to hold, include the following:

- Investors are single-period price takers, are risk-averse, and have the objective of maximizing the utility of terminal wealth.
- Investors have homogenous expectations of the probability distribution of security returns.
- There are no taxes, transaction costs, or other market imperfections.
- Information is freely available to investors.
- Investors have a large number of marketable assets, all of which are perfectly divisible.
- A risk-free asset exists and investors can borrow and lend at this rate.
- Investors select portfolios based solely on the mean and variance (risk) of expected returns. To ensure that this assumption holds also requires postulating that security returns follow a normal distribution. This assumption is motivated by the fact that, with a normal distribution, the first and second moments are fully determined.

Although the above assumptions are highly restrictive, the basic predictions of the CAPM are shown to hold even when most of the patently unrealistic assumptions are relaxed. In any case, a theoretical model is an abstraction of a noisy, complex reality, and should be evaluated based on how well it describes or predicts, not on the realism of its assumptions. In fact, the main attraction of the CAPM is that it provides a simple and practical approach to the mechanical complexity of the Markowitz portfolio model (Markowitz, 1952). Thus, the CAPM's assumptions should not be the major issue as long as the model is sensible.

In its basic version, the CAPM may be written as follows:

$$E(R_i) = R_f + [E(R_m) - R_f]\beta_i \qquad (19.1)$$

where $E(R_i)$ is the expected rate of return on asset I; R_f is the risk-free rate; $E(R_m)$ is the expected rate of return on the market portfolio; and β_i (beta) is the measure of risk, defined as the scaled covariance of the asset's return with the return on the market portfolio:

$$\beta_i = \frac{Cov(R_i, R_m)}{Var(R_m)} \qquad (19.2)$$

Exhibit 19.1 is a graphic representation of the CAPM from Equation 19.1 with beta on the x-axis and expected rate return on the y-axis. The line starting from R_f is called the security market line (SML). According to the CAPM, all assets should plot along the SML. Thus, the CAPM provides required returns for all risky assets

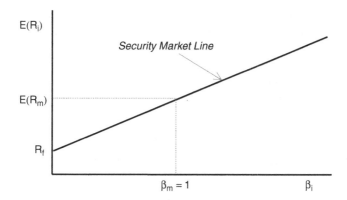

Exhibit 19.1   The Capital Asset Pricing Model

Note: This is a graphic representation of the CAPM with beta on the x-axis and expected rate return on the y-axis. The line starting from R_f is called the security market line (SML). According to the CAPM, all assets should plot along the SML if the market is in equilibrium.

based solely on a linear relationship between that asset's expected return and its volatility relative to that of the market (i.e., beta).

A central point to note is the type of asset risk that matters in the CAPM framework. Empirically, the return on any asset can be written as a linear function of market return:

$$R_i = a_i + b_i R_m + \varepsilon_i \tag{19.3}$$

where a_i is a constant and ε_i is a random error term independent of market return. Since a_i has a zero variance and ε_i is independent of market return, the asset return variance can be written as:

$$Var(R_i) = \sigma_i^2 = b_i^2 \sigma_m^2 + \sigma_\varepsilon^2 \tag{19.4}$$

Equation 19.4 indicates that the variance, which measures total risk, can be split into two parts: systematic risk, $b_i^2 \sigma_m^2$, and unsystematic risk. *Systematic risk*, known also as nondiversifiable or market risk, is the risk that applies to all assets. It can be caused by political or economic events, changes in interest rates, or unexpected inflation, among other things. Because such events affect the returns of all assets, investors cannot eliminate the resulting risk by holding diversified portfolios. *Unsystematic risk*, however, is specific to an individual asset and hence can be diversified away. For this reason, it is also known as diversifiable or asset-specific risk.

According to the CAPM, only systematic risk should matter to investors. Investors will not be compensated for bearing unsystematic risk because they are assumed to hold diversified portfolios that eliminate such risk. The CAPM defines systematic risk as β_i (beta). An inference from Equation 19.2 is that the beta of the market is 1.0. An asset with higher volatility (higher systematic risk) than that of the market has a beta greater than 1.0, while beta is less than 1.0 for an asset with less volatility (less systematic risk) than the market. Given that only systematic risk is compensated, an asset's required return is nothing but that asset's systematic risk (β_i) times the market risk premium ($E(R_m) - R_f$), which measures the additional returns required by investors to hold a risk-bearing asset instead of the risk-free asset.

In short, the CAPM provides an intuitive way to quantify the trade-off between risk and expected return. Because a company's beta can be measured as the covariance between the return on common stock and the market index, managers can use the CAPM to directly estimate the cost of equity capital. Despite this intuitive appeal, the CAPM is currently more controversial than ever. The remainder of the chapter discusses the concerns raised regarding the validity of the CAPM. These concerns have led to, among other things, the development of a competing model, the arbitrage pricing theory (APT).

THEORETICAL EXTENSIONS OF THE CAPM

In a seminal paper, Rubinstein (1973) shows that a firm should undertake a project if the expected rate of return of the project is greater than the appropriate risk-adjusted discount rate for the project, also known as the *hurdle rate*, with the discount rate revealed by the CAPM. This is equivalent to the discount rate being equal to the expected rate of return of a security with the same risk as the project. If the project has the same risk as the firm as a whole, then the appropriate beta to use is that of the firm.

Similar to Rubenstein (1973), several theoretical papers use the CAPM to develop capital budgeting criteria (e. g., Hamada, 1969; Stapleton, 1971; Bierman and Hass, 1973). As shown by Litzenberger and Budd (1970) and Senbet and Thompson (1978), the proposed criteria are all equivalent to those in Rubenstein. But most importantly, this stream of literature suggests that all the assumptions under which the CAPM is derived must hold in order for the CAPM to be useful in valuing and selecting projects. However, as expressed above, almost all of the model's assumptions are violated in the real world. For this reason, several papers have proposed theoretical extensions of the CAPM that relax some of the model's most unrealistic assumptions.

The Risk-Free Asset

One of the most critical CAPM assumptions is that investors can borrow and lend at the risk-free rate. The risk-free asset is the starting point for the linear relationship between expected return and systematic risk. It allows investors to ignore the characteristics of individual assets and instead form portfolios combining the riskless asset and the market portfolio in ways that reflect their risk aversion. However, several early researchers questioned the very existence of a riskless asset. Black (1972) solved the problem by suggesting an alternative CAPM using short selling as a proxy for the risk-free asset. The new proxy is a portfolio that is not necessarily risk-free (i.e., minimum variance) but is uncorrelated with the market portfolio—that is, a portfolio with zero beta. If $E(R_z)$ is the expected rate of return on the zero-beta portfolio, Black's model can be written as:

$$E(R_i) = E(R_z) + [E(R_m) - E(R_z)]\beta_i \qquad (19.5)$$

Black's adaptation of the CAPM provides important insights about the validity of the standard CAPM. First, beta remains the appropriate measure of systematic risk. Second, even in the absence of a risk-free asset, the relationship between expected return and systematic risk remains linear when there are no restrictions on short selling. However, this assumption is itself unrealistic. A recent example is the unanticipated ban on the short sale of shares of designated financial sector companies ordered on September 18, 2008, by the U.K.'s Financial Services Authority, the Securities and Exchange Commission, and the Ontario Securities Commission. A few days later, the financial authorities in Australia, Taiwan, and the Netherlands imposed a similar ban. These actions arose amid an unparalleled seize-up in global credit markets caused by, among other factors, the collapse of Lehman Brothers, which generated defaults and write-downs throughout the system.

Another shortcoming related to the risk-free asset is that even if it exists, borrowing and lending at the risk-free rate is unlikely to be possible for all investors. In the real world, most investors can lend but not borrow at the risk-free rate. Relaxing the equality of lending and borrowing rates and providing free access to the riskless asset affects the intercept, the slope, and the linearity of the CAPM.

Taxes and Heterogeneous Expectations

The basic CAPM model treats taxes as irrelevant. Yet, in the real world, investors face different tax rates and, generally, dividends are taxed at higher rates than capital gains. This implies that investors in higher tax brackets will require higher returns on assets with higher dividend yields. Brennan (1970) develops an after-tax version of the CAPM that accounts for the effect of different tax rates on dividends and capital gains. The model suggests that expected return is a function of the risk-free rate, beta, and dividend yield. Interestingly, Brennan concludes that beta is still the appropriate measure of systematic risk and that the linearity of the risk-return relationship continues to hold.

Both the CAPM and Modern Portfolio Theory (MPT) rest on a necessary yet unrealistic assumption stating that investors have homogenous expectations of risk and return. This assumption ensures that all investors have the same optimal risky efficient portfolio and merely allocate their capital between the risk-free asset and the optimal risky asset. Under heterogeneous expectations, investors have different efficient frontiers and therefore may have different optimal risky portfolios. Even more importantly, when the homogeneity assumption is relaxed, the market portfolio is not necessarily efficient, thereby rendering the CAPM untestable.

Other Theoretical Extensions of the CAPM

The CAPM is a single-period model in that it assumes all investors have identical time horizons. However, investors have different investment horizons rather than a single-period buy-and-hold strategy. Merton (1973) introduces a model that extends the one-period CAPM to a continuous-time version, known as the intertemporal CAPM, where asset returns follow a lognormal distribution instead of a normal distribution.

CHALLENGES TO USING THE CAPM

Starting in the late 1970s, the asset pricing literature uncovered several problems calling into question the validity of the CAPM as applied in practice. This section provides a discussion of these challenges.

The CAPM Is an Expectational Model

To test the reliability of the CAPM, researchers are compelled to use historical returns. Hence, they do not test investors' expectations. Instead, they use historical data that must mix realizations and expectations. Because the CAPM is an expectational model, this approach casts doubt on empirical tests and ultimately the usefulness of the resulting betas for estimating the cost of equity capital.

Several papers in the empirical literature claim that ex-post returns might not be a good proxy for a firm's cost of equity. For example, Stulz (1999) and Hail and Leuz (2006) show that ex-post returns not only capture differences in a firm's cost of equity but also reflect the shocks to a firm's growth opportunities, differences in expected growth rates, and changes in investors' risk aversion. Simply put, ex-post returns are exceedingly noisy, leading several observers to conclude that realized returns are a poor measure of expected returns (Pástor, Sinha, and Swaminathan, 2008). Fama and French (1997) assert that expected returns estimated from ex-post returns are imprecise because of the uncertainty of the factor (risk) premiums and the imprecision in the factor loading estimates.

The Model Tells Little about How to Define Its Components

The CAPM states that a stock's expected returns are a function of the risk-free rate, the firm's beta, and the market risk premium. The model is silent, however, about what should be the risk-free asset and how to precisely compute the latter two components. Also, the CAPM says nothing about how these measures change over time and what time interval to use to estimate them. For instance, computation of beta requires deciding on the proxy for the market portfolio, the measurement intervals used within the holding period, and the form of the market model used. Several studies show that different choices for each factor lead to nontrivial differences in estimating beta and, thereby expected returns. Young and O'Bryne (2001) offer practical examples.

Knowing the incremental return that shareholders require to hold risky equities rather than the risk-free asset is central to corporate finance and investment. The equity (or market) risk premium is a key determinant of this required return. In effect, it represents the "price" of risk. While some but not universal agreement exists on the proxy for the risk-free asset (e. g., government bills or bonds) and the market portfolio (e. g., the S&P 500 in the United States, the FT All Shares in the United Kingdom, and the CAC40 in France), debate continues to rage regarding the appropriate market risk premium. The market portfolio is typically proxied by a portfolio that includes all stocks traded in the United States. A three-month U.S. Treasury bill is commonly considered to be a good proxy for the risk-free asset. Mehra and Prescott (1985), who report an equity premium in the United

States over the period 1889 to 1978 of about 6.18 percent, largely triggered the debate. They show that such a premium is too large to be rationalized by standard asset pricing models. This finding led to a score of studies trying to explain this puzzle.

As later studies show, estimates for the historical risk premium are highly contingent on the time period under study. For example, Siegel (1992) documents an equity premium of only 1.99 percent during 1800 to 1888. When he includes more recent data, Siegel (1998) finds that the average equity risk premium over treasury bills is about 4.1 percent during 1802 to 1998 but 8.6 percent during 1926 to 1998. Mehra (2003) updates Mehra and Prescott (1985) and reports a premium of 6.9 percent, 8.0 percent, and 7.8 percent for the periods 1889 to 2000, 1926 to 2000, and 1947 to 2000, respectively.

Dimson, Marsh, and Staunton (2003) examine equity risk premiums in 16 countries over the period 1900 to 2002. The authors report a "world" equity premium of 5.1 percent computed using 92 overlapping decades. Their results change significantly, however, when they split the sample into two nonoverlapping periods. Along these lines, Fama and French (2002) report that the equity risk premium declined in the United States post–World War II. Claus and Thomas (2001) document a similar declining pattern around the world.

Although the use of historical data over long time periods is the standard approach to computing the equity premium, the overwhelming evidence of changing spreads between equity returns and risk-free assets casts doubt on the reliability of such methods. One concern is that the so-called *equity risk premium puzzle* is just an artifact of this approach (Damodaran, 2008). Some contributors to the academic literature such as Benninga and Sarig (1997) recommend alternative, forward-looking methods but such methods are not widely practiced.

Several papers use a survey approach to gauge equity risk premiums. Although potentially biased, surveys provide some useful insights on what investors, managers, and academics believe to be the appropriate risk premium. For instance, in one of the first such studies on the magnitude of the equity risk premium, Welch (2000) surveyed 226 financial economists and reports an average estimate of 6.7 percent for one- to five-year time horizons and about 7 percent for a 10-year time horizon. Still, Welch documents a wide range of estimates as low as 2 percent and as high as 13 percent. The survey results of Graham and Harvey (2008) show that, on average, chief financial officers think that a reasonable equity risk premium is about 3.8 percent with a median of 4.2 percent.

More recently, Fernandez (2009a) surveyed 1,403 finance and economics professors from 38 countries about the equity risk premium they use to calculate the required return to equity in 2008. The author reports an average rate of 6.3 percent in the United States, 5.9 percent in Australia, 5.5 percent in the United Kingdom, 5.4 percent in Canada, and 5.3 percent in Europe. Fernandez documents the lowest premium for Belgium (4.1 percent) and the highest for India (10.5 percent). Interestingly, he finds that equity risk premiums tend to vary widely not only across professors within the same country, but also within the same institution. Finally, Fernandez (2009b) examines 150 widely used textbooks in corporate finance and valuation, and finds that the recommended equity risk premiums range from 3 percent to 10 percent.

CAPM and Anomalies

The results from early tests of the CAPM were largely positive, with researchers reporting evidence consistent with the mean-variance efficiency of the market portfolio (Black, Jensen, and Scholes, 1972; Fama and MacBeth, 1973). However, by the late 1970s, the market anomalies literature began to surface. In the context of the mean-variance frontier, anomalies can be thought of as characteristics of individual companies that can be used to group assets such that the resulting portfolios have a higher ex-post Sharpe ratio (a measure of returns adjusted for total return variability) than that of the market proxy. In other words, investors can form portfolios that seem to outperform the market on a risk-adjusted basis.

Early anomalies include the price/earnings (P/E) effect (Basu, 1977) and the size effect (Banz, 1981). Basu finds that the market portfolio appears not to be mean-variance efficient relative to portfolios formed on the basis of a firm's P/E ratio. Firms with low P/E ratios appear to have higher returns than predicted by the CAPM. Similarly, Banz shows that low market capitalization firms have higher returns than predicted. This line of research implies that investors could "beat the market" by investing in low P/E or low market capitalization (cap) stocks. Reinganum (1981) confirms Banz's findings but rejects Basu's by showing that the P/E effect is, in fact, a small-cap effect. However, financial economics do not consider the size effect a daunting challenge to the CAPM because small firms constitute only a small fraction of the total market capitalization in the United States.

Fama and French (1992) find that the relation between beta and average return disappears over the 1963 to 1990 period. On the other hand, the univariate relationship between average return and size, leverage, earnings-to-price, and book-to-market (B/M) (the book value of equity to the market price of equity) is strong. In multivariate tests, the negative relation between size and average return and the positive relation between B/M and average return are robust to the inclusion of other variables. According to Fama and French, beta does not explain all the cross-section of average stock returns, and the combination of size and book-to-market seems to absorb the roles of leverage and earnings-to-price in average stock returns, at least during the 1963 to 1990 period. In further work, Fama and French (1996) present a three-factor model:

$$E(R_i) - R_f = b_i \left[E(R_m) - R_f \right] + s_i E(SMB) + h_i E(HML) \qquad (19.6)$$

where $E(SMB)$ is the difference between returns on a portfolio of small stocks and large stocks, and $E(HML)$ is the difference between returns on a portfolio of high and low book-to-market stocks. Although Fama and French (1992, 1996) reject the CAPM, their three-factor model still includes the CAPM beta (or the market beta) as the latter does have some explanatory power. In other words, the market beta still provides a partial but incomplete description of an asset's risk.

Several studies show that the B/M effect is caused by mispricing and is not a result of the ratio acting as a risk factor (Stein, 1996; Piotroski, 2000; Mohanram, 2005). For instance, LaPorta, Lakonishok, Shleifer, and Vishny (1997) report evidence consistent with investors underestimating future earnings for high B/M stocks and overestimating future earnings for low B/M stocks.

As Da, Guo, and Jangannathan (2009) show, the B/M anomaly is really a within-industry rather than across-industry effect. They also show that the B/M effect is highly correlated with financial leverage and capital expenditure (Capex), which is a proxy for real options available to the firm. Da et al. (p. 23) conclude that their results are "consistent with the view that the [B/M] effect is to a large extent due to the nature of the real options available to a firm, since it is reasonable to expect financial leverage to be related to firm's real options in the event of financial distress, and Capex to proxy for a firm's growth options."

Ferson, Sarkissian, and Simin (1999) argue that returns on portfolios constructed using stock attributes may appear to be useful risk factors even when the attributes are completely unrelated to risk. Last, Da et al. (2009) show that, when they use Hoberg and Welch's (2007) aged-beta approach, the CAPM outperforms the Fama-French three-factor model in explaining the average returns on a CAPM-beta-sorted portfolio during the 1932 to 2007 period. Da et al. conclude that little empirical evidence exists to warrant the abandonment of the CAPM as a tool for calculating the cost of equity capital.

DeBondt and Thaler (1985) report that stocks with low returns in a three-to-five year period have higher subsequent returns than stocks with high returns over the same period. This anomaly is sometimes referred to as a *contrarian effect*. On the other hand, Jegadeesh and Titman (1993) find that recent past winners (portfolios formed on the previous year's returns) outperform recent past losers, leading to a *momentum effect*. Fama and French (1996) test these competing effects using their three-factor model and find no abnormal performance from the long-term reversal strategy of DeBondt and Thaler. They attribute the observed anomaly to the similarity of past losers and small distressed firms. On the other hand, Fama and French cannot explain the short-term momentum effects found by Jegadeesh and Titman. The estimates of abnormal returns are strongly positive for short-term winners. Several studies show that evidence on the momentum effect seems to persist, but may reflect predictable variation in risk premiums that are not yet understood (e. g., Easley, Hvidkjaer, and O'Hara, 2010).

BIASES IN TESTING FOR THE VALIDITY OF THE CAPM

In a seminal paper, Roll (1977) argues that the empirical problems associated with the CAPM may be caused by difficulties in implementing valid tests of the CAPM, rather than resulting from theoretical shortcomings of the model. In particular, Roll contends that the model is empirically untestable because a true market portfolio is not empirically observable. Hence, since tests of the CAPM did not and cannot use the true market portfolio, they should not be considered as tests of the CAPM, but rather tests of whether the index portfolio chosen was ex-post efficient.

Although empirical work documents anomalies that signal economically important deviations from the CAPM, there is little theoretical motivation for the firm characteristics studied in the literature. In fact, a strong possibility exists that the evidence against the CAPM is overstated because of data-snooping and sample selection biases. *Data-snooping* refers to the biases in statistical inference that result from using information from data to guide subsequent research with the same or related data.

Lo and MacKinlay (1990) illustrate the potential magnitude of data-snooping biases in a test of the standard CAPM. They consider cases in which the characteristic used to group stocks into portfolios is selected not from theory but from previous observations of mean stock returns using related data. Comparisons of the null distribution of the test statistics with and without data-snooping suggest that the magnitude of the biases can be immense. To limit the biases, Lo and MacKinlay suggest using data from different time periods or on different samples.

Sample selection biases can arise when data availability leads to certain subsets of stocks being excluded from the analysis. For example, Kothari, Shanken, and Sloan (1995) maintain that data requirements for studies looking at B/M ratios lead to failing stocks being excluded and a resulting survivorship bias. Because the failing stocks would be expected to have low returns and high B/M ratios, the average return on high B/M stocks would have an upward bias. They argue that such bias is largely responsible for the results of Fama and French (1992, 1993).

THE ARBITRAGE PRICING THEORY

By the late 1970s, many academics were convinced that the CAPM failed to explain the cross-section of expected returns and suggested that one or more additional factors may be required. The result was two main alternatives to the standard CAPM: the arbitrage pricing theory (APT) developed by Ross (1976) and based on arbitrage arguments, and the international capital asset pricing model (ICAPM) developed by Merton (1973) and based on equilibrium arguments. This section focuses on the APT.

The APT is more general than the CAPM in that it allows for multiple risk factors. In fact, the CAPM is a special case of the APT that occurs when the market rate of return is assumed to be the single relevant factor. Unlike the CAPM, the APT does not require identifying the market portfolio. Also, the only assumption in the APT is that markets are competitive and frictionless. The theory provides an approximate relation for expected asset returns with an unknown number of unidentified factors:

$$R_i = E(R_i) + b_{i1}f_1 + \cdots + b_{ik}f_k + \varepsilon_i \tag{19.7}$$

where R_i is the random rate of return on the ith asset; $E(R_i)$ is the expected rate of return on the ith asset; b_{ik} is the sensitivity of the ith asset's returns to the kth factor; f_k is the mean zero kth factor common to the returns of all assets; and ε_i is a random zero-mean error for the ith asset. The APT can also be written in matrix format:

$$R_i = a + BF_{ki} + \varepsilon_i \tag{19.8}$$

where R_i is the $(N \times 1)$ vector of excess returns; B is the $(N \times k)$ matrix of factor sensitivities; and F_{ki} is the $(k \times 1)$ vector of factor portfolio excess returns.

The major problem with the APT is that it does not specify the nature of the underlying factors that influence security returns. Financial economists have employed several approaches to handle this issue. The statistical approach consists of using factor or principal components analysis to build factors from a comprehensive set of asset returns. The factor analysis involves a two-step procedure: (1) Estimate the factor sensitivity matrix and the disturbance covariance matrix, and (2) use these estimates to construct measures of the factor realizations. The principal components analysis reduces the number of variables without losing too much information in the covariance matrix. The objective is to reduce the dimension from N asset returns to K factors. The principal components serve as the factors. The first principal component is the normalized linear combination of asset returns with maximum variance. The second principal component is the normalized linear combination of asset returns with maximum variance for all combinations orthogonal (i.e., independent) to the first principal component, and so on.

Another approach specifies macroeconomic and financial market variables that are thought to capture systematic risks in the macroeconomy such as unexpected changes in interest rates and inflation. The study by Chen, Roll, and Ross (1986) is a good example of this approach. They argue that in selecting factors one should consider forces that will explain changes in the rate used to discount future expected cash flows and forces that influence expected cash flows. The authors propose a five-factor model including: (1) maturity spread (i.e., the yield spread between long- and short-term interest rates for U.S. government bonds); (2) expected inflation; (3) unexpected inflation; (4) industrial production growth; and (5) the default premium (i.e., the yield spread between high- and low-grade corporate bonds). Chen et al. find that aggregate consumption growth and oil prices have no incremental effects beyond the five factors and therefore exclude them from the model.

A third approach is to specify characteristics of firms that are likely to explain differential sensitivities to systematic risks and then form portfolios of stocks based on these characteristics. Firm characteristics shown to be empirically important include the market value of equity, P/E ratios, and B/M ratios. The general finding is that factor models including a broad-based market portfolio such as an equal-weighted index do a good job in explaining the cross section of returns. However, because these characteristics have been identified largely through empirical analysis, their importance may be overstated.

Indeed, users of the APT-inspired models should be aware of two serious dangers that arise when choosing factors to fit existing data without regard to economic theory. First, the models may overfit the data because of data-snooping bias. In this case, the model will have little or no value in predicting future asset returns. Second, the models may capture empirical regularities that are due to market inefficiency or investor irrationality. In this instance, they may continue to fit the data but will lead to Sharpe ratios for factor portfolios that are too high to be consistent with a reasonable underlying model of market equilibrium. Deriving a factor structure from an equilibrium model can mitigate both problems.

Another issue with the APT is that it does not specify the number of factors to include in the model. For the model to be useful, the number of factors (k) should be reasonably small. In empirical work, financial economists have handled this lack of specification in several ways. One approach is to repeat the estimation and testing of the model for a variety of values of k and observe if the tests are sensitive to increasing the number of factors. For example, Lehmann and Modest (1988) present empirical results for 5, 10, and 15 factors. Their results display minimal sensitivity when the number of factors increases, suggesting that five factors are adequate. A second approach is to test explicitly for the adequacy of k factors using a likelihood ratio test. Roll and Ross (1980) use this approach and conclude that three or four factors are adequate.

RECENT DEVELOPMENTS: DOES INFORMATION ASYMMETRY MATTER TO THE COST OF EQUITY?

Whether information asymmetry affects the cost of equity capital remains controversial. Information asymmetry arises when differing capital market participants are not equally well endowed with information. For example, managers may have information about their firm's risks and future cash flows that investors do not. Asymmetries can also arise between investors and market makers. According to the CAPM and the APT, individuals are compensated only for bearing systematic risk. Information asymmetry should not be priced because all relevant information is assumed to be reflected in the stock price at all times. According to Easley, Hvidkjaer, and O'Hara (2002), this static view of market efficiency may be inconsistent with the dynamic of new information arrival. Further, when stocks have differing levels of public and private information, uninformed investors face information risk when trading with informed traders (Easley and O'Hara, 2004). The literature is, however, inconclusive on whether such a risk can cause price disequilibrium and, if so, whether it can be diversified away (Hughes, Liu, and Liu, 2007; Core, Guay, and Verdi, 2008; Easley, Hvidkjaer, and O'Hara, 2002, 2009).

Empirical tests to determine whether such risk matters face stiff criticism regarding the reliability of the proxies, particularly in the absence of any theoretical model pricing information risk. The absence of an adequate proxy has led to mixed results and generated controversy. For instance, Easley et al. (2002, 2009) report evidence supporting the Easley and O'Hara (2004) model. Using a measure of private information known as the probability of information-based trading (PIN) to proxy for information asymmetry, they find that PIN is positively and significantly related to average stock returns. Developed by Easley, Kiefer, O'Hara, and Paperman (1996), PIN infers the probability that a trade is based on private information using high-frequency data trading. However, Duarte and Young (2009) cast serious doubts on these findings. Decomposing PIN into two components—one related to information asymmetry and one related to illiquidity—they find that only the illiquidity component is priced. Similarly, Aktas, de Bodt, Declerck, and Van Oppens (2007) report evidence against the use of PIN as a proxy of information risk. Moreover, their study, among others, stresses the convergence problem encountered when estimating PIN for a stock with a large number of trades because the likelihood function does not converge to a maximum for such stocks.

USING THE CAPM AND THE APT IN PRACTICE

For nearly 50 years, there has been an ever-increasing volume of survey-based studies that examine corporate finance practices including capital budgeting and cost of equity estimation. A review of the literature suggests that, over time, these practices have gradually aligned more closely with finance theory. This section provides a discussion of the results reported from survey-based studies on corporate use of the CAPM and multifactor models.

Gitman and Vandenberg (2000) examine cost of capital estimation techniques in large U. S. firms using the same survey instrument from an earlier study (Gitman and Mercurio, 1982) and find an increase in the popularity of the CAPM over time. In particular, they find 93 percent of firms using the CAPM in 1997 in contrast to only 30 percent in 1980. Interestingly, Gitman and Vandenberg (2000) report that less than 1 percent of respondents report using the APT.

One capital budgeting survey of U. S.-based companies, conducted by Graham and Harvey (2001), shows that the CAPM is the most popular approach for estimating the cost of equity, with 73.5 percent of respondents indicating that they always or almost always use it. Multifactor approaches rank third behind average stock returns. When asked about sources of risk to consider other than market risk, the respondents highlight interest rate risk, exchange rate risk, business cycle risk, and inflation risk. But only interest rate risk, size, inflation risk, and foreign exchange rate risk seem to be taken into account when estimating discount rates.

A survey of European firms by Brounen, De Jong, and Koedijk (2004) shows that although the CAPM is less popular in Europe than in the United States (with a level of usage ranging from 34 percent to 56 percent), it is still the most popular method in the United Kingdom, the Netherlands, Germany, and France. Truong, Partington, and Peat (2008) report that the CAPM is the most widely used approach by Australian public firms. While 72 percent of these firms use the CAPM, only 1 percent indicates using the Fama-French three-factor model while no firm reports using the APT.

In a 1991 survey of large Canadian firms, Jog and Srivastava (1995) report that managers tend to rely more on subjective judgment than on formal models when computing the cost of equity, with 30.2 percent of respondents reporting the use of such approaches. Accounting return on equity and the CAPM are ranked second (12.9 percent) and third (9.5 percent), respectively.

More recently, Baker, Dutta, and Saadi (2009), who expand and update Jog and Srivastava's survey, find that while the CAPM has become more popular among Canadian public firms, it is still less popular than subjective judgment. In fact, 60.3 percent of respondents report using judgment often or always, compared to 52.3 percent using the cost of debt plus an equity premium and only 36.8 percent of Canadian firms indicating the use of the CAPM. Roughly 7 percent of firms report using multifactor models. Using judgment is even more pronounced in smaller Canadian firms. This finding is consistent with the capital budgeting literature suggesting that smaller firms tend to use less sophisticated methods when estimating their cost of capital (see, for instance, Brounen et al., 2004).

To summarize, the results from survey-based research indicate that the CAPM continues to be widely used in the field. Multifactor models are much less popular and are rarely used in practice. The growing popularity of the CAPM among managers is consistent with the increasing volume of academic studies that support the use of the model to estimate the cost of equity. Da et al. (2009) provide a review of this literature.

SUMMARY AND CONCLUSIONS

There is much statistical evidence against the CAPM. Despite this evidence, the model remains a widely used tool in corporate finance. Also, much controversy exists on how to interpret this evidence. Some observers argue that multifactor models should replace the CAPM, while others contend that the evidence against the CAPM is overstated due to various biases. Still others claim that no risk-based model can explain the anomalies of stock market behavior, which leads to the need for behavioral models. Practitioners are largely immune to such debates. Because of its undeniable intuitive appeal and relative ease of use, the CAPM continues to be the dominant approach to calculating the cost of equity capital.

DISCUSSION QUESTIONS

1. Why have multifactor asset-pricing models failed to become popular with practitioners?
2. Does the equity risk premium (expected, not ex post) vary from country to country? Why or why not?
3. Is the equity risk premium likely to increase or decrease in the future? Why?
4. Building on Roll's (1977) critique, will financial economists ever be able to appropriately test the CAPM? Why or why not?
5. Because using the true market portfolio is impossible, the CAPM does not provide an accurate estimate of a firm's or project's cost of equity capital. Hence, should practitioners adjust their cost of equity capital when using the CAPM and, if so, how?

REFERENCES

Aktas, Nihat, Eric de Bodt, Fany Declerck, and Herve Van Oppens. 2007. "The PIN Anomaly around M&A Announcements." *Journal of Financial Markets* 10:2, 169–191.

Baker, H. Kent, Shantanu Dutta, and Samir Saadi. 2009. "Corporate Finance Practices in Canada: Where Do We Stand?" Working Paper, Queen's University.

Banz, Rolf W. 1981. "The Relationship between Return and Market Value of Common Stocks." *Journal of Financial Economics* 9:1, 3–18.

Basu, Sanjay. 1977. "Investment Performance of Common Stocks in Relation to Their Price-Earnings Ratios: A Test of the Efficient Market Hypothesis." *Journal of Finance* 12:3, 129–156.

Benninga, Simon, and Oded H. Sarig. 1997. *Corporate Finance: A Valuation Approach.* New York: McGraw-Hill.

Bierman, Harold, and Jerome E. Hass. 1973. "Capital Budgeting Under Uncertainty: A Reformulation. " *Journal of Finance* 28:1, 119–129.

Black, Fischer. 1972. "Capital Market Equilibrium with Restricted Borrowing." *Journal of Business* 45:3, 444–454.

Black, Fischer, Michael C. Jensen, and Myron Scholes. 1972. "The Capital Asset Pricing Model: Some Empirical Tests." In Michael C. Jensen (ed.), *Studies in the Theory of Capital Markets*, 79–121. New York: Praeger.

Brennan, Michael J. 1970. "Taxes, Market Valuation and Corporate Financial Policy." *National Tax Journal* 23:4, 417–427.

Brounen, Dirk, Abe de Jong, and Kees C. G. Koedijk. 2004. "Corporate Finance in Europe: Confronting Theory with Practice." *Financial Management* 33:4, 71–101.

Chen, Nai-Fu, Richard R. Roll, and Stephen A. Ross. 1986. "Economic Forces and the Stock Market." *Journal of Business* 59:3, 383–404.

Claus, James, and Jacob Thomas. 2001. "Equity Premia as Low as Three Percent? Evidence from Analysts' Earnings Forecasts for Domestic and International Stock Markets." *Journal of Finance* 56:5, 1629–1666.

Core, John E., Wayne R. Guay, and Rodrigo S. Verdi. 2008. "Is Accruals Quality a Priced Risk Factor?" *Journal of Accounting and Economics* 46:1, 2–22.

Da, Zhi, Re-Jin Guo, and Ravi Jagannathan. 2009. "CAPM for Estimating the Cost of Equity Capital: Interpreting the Empirical Evidence." Working Paper 14889, National Bureau of Economic Research.

Damodaran, Aswath. 2008. "Equity Risk Premiums (ERP): Determinants, Estimation and Implications." Working Paper, New York University.

DeBondt, Werner F. M., and Richard H. Thaler. 1985. "Does the Stock Market Overreact?" *Journal of Finance* 40: 3,793–805.

Dimson, Elroy, Paul Marsh, and Mike Staunton. 2003. "Global Evidence on the Equity Risk Premium." *Journal of Applied Corporate Finance* 15:4, 8–19.

Duarte, Jefferson, and Lance Young. 2009. "Why Is PIN Priced?" *Journal of Financial Economics* 91:2, 119–138.

Easley, David, and Maureen O'Hara. 2004. "Information and the Cost of Capital." *Journal of Finance* 59:4, 1553–1583.

Easley, David, Søren Hvidkjaer, and Maureen O'Hara. 2002. "Is Information Risk a Determinant of Asset Returns?" *Journal of Finance* 57:5, 2185–2222.

Easley, David, Søren Hvidkjaer, and Maureen O'Hara. 2010. "Factoring Information into Returns." *Journal of Financial and Quantitative Analysis*, forthcoming.

Easley, David, Nicholas M. Kiefer, Maureen O'Hara, and Joseph Paperman. 1996. "Liquidity, Information and Less Frequently Traded Stocks." *Journal of Finance* 51:4, 1405–1436.

Fama, Eugene F., and Kenneth R. French. 1992. "The Cross-Section of Expected Stock Returns." *Journal of Finance* 47:2, 427–465.

Fama, Eugene F., and Kenneth R. French. 1993. "Common Risk Factors in the Returns on Stocks and Bonds." *Journal of Financial Economics* 33:1, 3–56.

Fama, Eugene F., and Kenneth R. French. 1996. "Multifactor Explanations of Asset Pricing Anomalies." *Journal of Finance* 51:1, 55–84.

Fama, Eugene F., and Kenneth R. French. 1997. "Industry Costs of Equity." *Journal of Financial Economics* 43:2, 153–193.

Fama, Eugene F., and Kenneth R. French. 2002. "The Equity Premium." *Journal of Finance* 57:2, 637–659.

Fama, Eugene F., and James D. MacBeth. 1973. "Risk, Return, and Equilibrium: Empirical Tests." *Journal of Political Economy* 81:3, 607–636.

Fernandez, Pablo. 2009a. "Market Risk Premium Used in 2008 by Professors: A Survey with 1,400 Answers." Working Paper, University of Navarra. Available at SSRN: http://papers.ssrn.com/sol3/papers.cfm?abstract_id=1344209.

Fernandez, Pablo. 2009b. "The Equity Premium 150 Textbooks." Working Paper, University of Navarra. Available at SSRN: http://papers.ssrn.com/sol3/papers.cfm?abstract_id=1473225.

Ferson, Wayne E., Sergei Sarkissian, and Timothy T. Simin. 1999. "The Alpha Factor Asset Pricing Model: A Parable." *Journal of Financial Markets* 2:1, 49–68.

Gitman, Lawrence J., and Vincent Mercurio. 1982. "Cost of Capital Techniques Used by Major U.S. Firms: Survey and Analysis of Fortune's 1000." *Financial Management* 11:4, 21–29.

Gitman, Lawrence J., and Pieter A. Vandenberg. 2000. "Cost of Capital Techniques Used by Major U. S. Firms: 1997 vs. 1980." *Financial Practice and Education* 10:2, 53–68.

Graham, John R., and Campbell R. Harvey. 2001. "The Theory and Practice of Corporate Finance: Evidence from the Field." *Journal of Financial Economics* 60:2–3, 187–243.

Graham, John R., and Campbell R. Harvey. 2008. "The Equity Risk Premium in 2008: Evidence from the Global CFO Outlook Survey." Working Paper, Duke University. Available at SSRN: http://papers.ssrn. com/sol3/papers.cfm?abstract_id=1162809.

Hail, Luzi, and Christian Leuz. 2006. "International Differences in the Cost of Equity Capital: Do Legal Institutions and Securities Regulations Matter?" *Journal of Accounting Research* 44:3, 485–531.

Hamada, Robert S. 1969. "Portfolio Analysis, Market Equilibrium and Corporation Finance." *Journal of Finance* 24:1, 13–31.

Hoberg, Gerard, and Ivo Welch. 2007. "Aged and Recent Market Betas in Securities Pricing." Working Paper, Brown University.

Hughes, John S., Jing Liu, and Jun Liu. 2007. "Information Asymmetry, Diversification, and Cost of Capital." *Accounting Review* 82:3, 705–730.

Jegadeesh, Narasimhan, and Sheridan Titman. 1993. "Returns to Buying Winners and Selling Losers: Implications for Stock Market Efficiency." *Journal of Finance* 48:1, 65–91.

Jog, Vijay, and Ashwani K. Srivastava. 1995. "Capital Budgeting Practices in Corporate Canada." *Financial Practice and Education* 5:2, 37–43.

Kothari, S. P., Jay Shanken, and Richard G. Sloan. 1995. "Another Look at the Cross-Section of Expected Stock Returns." *Journal of Finance* 50:1, 185–224.

La Porta, Rafael, Josef Lakonishok, Andrei Shleifer, and Robert Vishny. 1997. "Good News for Value Stocks: Further Evidence on Market Efficiency." *Journal of Finance* 52:2, 859–874.

Lehmann, Bruce N., and David M. Modest. 1988. "The Empirical Foundations of the Arbitrage Pricing Theory." *Journal of Financial Economics* 21:2, 213–254.

Lintner, John. 1965. "The Valuation of Risk Assets and the Selection of Risky Investments in Stock Portfolios and Capital Budgets." *Review of Economics and Statistics* 47:1, 13–37.

Litzenberger, Robert H., and Alan P. Budd. 1970. "Corporate Investment Criteria and the Validation of Risk Assets." *Journal of Financial and Quantitative Analysis* 5:4, 395–418.

Lo, Andrew W., and Craig A. MacKinlay. 1990. "Data-snooping Biases in Tests of Financial Asset Pricing Models." *Review of Financial Studies* 3:3, 431–468.

Markowitz, Harry. 1952. "Portfolio Selection." *Journal of Finance* 7:1, 77–99.

Mehra, Rajnish. 2003. "The Equity Premium: Why Is It a Puzzle?" *Financial Analysts Journal* 59:1, 54–69.

Mehra, Rajnish, and Edward C. Prescott. 1985. "The Equity Premium: A Puzzle." *Journal of Monetary Economics* 15:2, 145–161.

Merton, Robert C. 1973. "An Intertemporal Capital Asset Pricing Model." *Econometrica* 41:5, 867–887.

Mohanram, Partha. 2005. "Separating Winners from Losers among Low Book-to-Market Stocks using Financial Statement Analysis." *Review of Accounting Studies* 10:2–3, 133–170.

Pástor, Lubos, Meenakshi Sinha, and Bhaskaran Swaminathan. 2008. "Estimating the Intertemporal Risk-Return Tradeoff Using the Implied Cost of Capital." *Journal of Finance* 63:6, 2859–2897.

Piotroski, Joseph D. 2000. "Value Investing: The Use of Historical Financial Statement Information to Separate Winners from Losers." *Journal of Accounting Research* 38: (supplement), 1–41.

Reinganum, Marc R. 1981. "A New Empirical Perspective on the CAPM." *Journal of Financial and Quantitative Analysis* 16:4, 439–462.

Roll, Richard. 1977. "A Critique of the Asset Pricing Theory's Tests' Part I: On Past and Potential Testability of the Theory." *Journal of Financial Economics* 4:2, 129–176.

Roll, Richard R., and Stephen A. Ross. 1980. "An Empirical Investigation of the Arbitrage Pricing Theory." *Journal of Finance* 35:5, 1073–1104.

Ross, Stephen A. 1976. "The Arbitrage Theory of Capital Asset Pricing." *Journal of Economic Theory* 13:3, 341–360.

Rubinstein, Mark E. 1973. "A Mean-Variance Synthesis of Corporate Financial Theory." *Journal of Finance* 28:1, 167–181.

Senbet, Lemma W., and Howard E. Thompson. 1978. "The Equivalence of Mean-Variance Capital Budgeting Models." *Journal of Finance* 33:2, 395–401.

Sharpe, William F. 1964. "Capital Asset Prices: A Theory of Market Equilibrium under Conditions of Risk." *Journal of Finance* 19:3, 425–442.

Siegel, Jeremy J. 1992. "The Equity Premium: Stock and Bond Returns since 1802." *Financial Analysts Journal* 48:1, 28–38.

Siegel, Jeremy J. 1998. *Stocks for the Long Run.* New York: Irwin.

Stapleton, Richard C. 1971. "Portfolio Analysis, Stock Valuation and Capital Budgeting Decision Rule for Risky Projects." *Journal of Finance* 26:1, 95–117.

Stein, Jeremy. 1996. "Rational Capital Budgeting in an Irrational World." *Journal of Business* 69:4, 429–455.

Stulz, René. 1999. "Globalization, Corporate Finance, and the Cost of Capital." *Journal of Applied Corporate Finance* 12:3, 8–25.

Truong, Giang L., Graham Partington, and Maurice Peat. 2008. "Cost-of-Capital Estimation and Capital Budgeting Practice in Australia." *Australian Journal of Management* 33:1, 95–121.

Welch, Ivo. 2000. "Views of Financial Economists on the Equity Premium and on Professional Controversies." *Journal of Business* 73:4, 501–537.

Young, S. David, and Stephen F. O'Byrne. 2001. *EVA and Value-Based Management—A Practical Guide to Implementation.* New York: McGraw-Hill.

ABOUT THE AUTHORS

S. David Young is Professor of Accounting and Control at INSEAD, where he has been since 1989. He holds a Ph.D. from the University of Virginia and is a Certified Public Accountant (United States) and a Chartered Financial Analyst. His published work includes articles in a wide range of academic and professional journals including several recent articles in *Harvard Business Review* and the *Journal of Applied Corporate Finance.* He is also the author or co-author of several books including *EVA and Value Based Management: A Practical Guide to Implementation; The Rule of Experts: Occupational Licensing in America; Attracting Investors: A Marketing Approach to Finding Funds for Your Business; Profits You Can Trust: Spotting and Surviving Accounting Landmines;* and *Financial Reporting and Analysis: A Global Perspective.* He has also served as an advisor to several European, Asian, and North American companies, mainly on aspects of value-based management.

Samir Saadi is currently a finance Ph.D. candidate at Queen's School of Business and visiting researcher at INSEAD. His research interests include executive compensation, mergers and acquisitions, and dividend policy. He has published in finance and applied economics journals including the *Journal of International Financial Markets, Institutions and Money, Journal of Multinational Financial Management, Journal of Theoretical and Applied Finance,* and *Review of Financial Economics.*

He also participated in several finance conferences such as the Financial Management Association, Eastern Finance Association, European Financial Management Association, and Southern Finance Association. Mr. Saadi is the recipient of several prestigious awards and scholarships from Social Sciences and Humanities Research Council of Canada (SSHRC), Europlace Institute of Finance (EIF), and American Finance Association (AFA).

CHAPTER 20

Financing Mix and Project Valuation

Alternative Methods and Possible Adjustments

AXEL PIERRU
Senior Economist, IFP Energies nouvelles

DENIS BABUSIAUX
Adjunct Professor, IFP School

INTRODUCTION

Various methods are available for valuing investment projects. However, project valuation is necessarily based on an implicit or explicit assumption about the project's financing mix that can influence the choice of the method used. In general, analysts value investment projects under the assumption that the firm must comply with an overall debt ratio at a company level, at least for all projects belonging to a given risk class. Research indicates that 80 percent of firms have some form of target debt-to-value ratio and that the acceptable range of values around the target is tighter for larger firms (Graham and Harvey, 2001). When the firm targets a predefined debt ratio, the standard hypothesis, which ensures the convergence of the conventional project-valuation methods, is that each year the project's debt ratio and the firm's target debt ratio are equal. Historically, the consistency of conventional project-valuation methods has been substantiated by comparing them in pairs (e.g., Boudreaux and Long, 1979; Chambers, Harris, and Pringle, 1982). This chapter proposes a unique formulation from which these methods could be derived and demonstrates the equality of their net present values (NPVs) and the consistency of their internal rates of return (IRRs) in a straightforward manner.

In certain cases, for instance, when the project studied is financed by project finance, the firm directly targets absolute debt amounts expressed in dollars over the project's life. The project-valuation procedure then differs from that used when the firm targets a debt ratio in that the analysis must take the targeted predetermined debt schedule into account. The chapter also emphasizes that several possible definitions of a loan can be associated with a project and discusses their respective relevance for project valuation. The viewpoint of industry practitioners is also examined.

The last part of the chapter deals with free cash flow (FCF) adjustments that extend the field of application of the standard (after-tax) weighted average cost of capital (WACC) method. First, discounting FCFs at the firm's after-tax WACC relies on the assumption that every year the interest cost immediately generates a proportionate tax shield. This assumption is usually violated when some interest costs are not paid but capitalized. The chapter includes a simple FCF adjustment that compensates for this violation. Second, a multinational firm investing in various countries may take advantage of the fact that some of its subsidiaries have local access to loans for which the after-tax cost is lower than can be obtained elsewhere. Existing disparities in the tax treatment of interest paid can therefore lead the multinational firm to seek an optimal allocation of its debt capacity among its various projects. In this context, a generalized version of the standard WACC method has to be used.

CONVENTIONAL PROJECT VALUATION METHODS

Consider a firm whose investment projects all belong to the same risk class and are financed using loans contracted at the same annual interest rate, r. Interest payments are assumed to be deductible from taxable income and generate tax shields at the corporate tax rate, θ. The firm complies every year with a (predefined) target debt ratio, w, on a consolidated basis at the firm's level. The firm's cost of equity is k_e. Management is considering a project that would generate the after-tax operating cash flow, F_t where t denotes the differing years. The after-tax operating cash flow, also called *free cash flow* (FCF), is the project's cash flow before any financial claims are paid. For tax purposes, the taxable income used is defined as the earnings before interest and taxes (EBIT), which means that the FCF includes no interest tax shields. The project's lifetime extends from year 0 to T. D_t then denotes the amount of outstanding debt associated with the project at the end of year t (with $D_t = 0$ when $t \geq T$ and $D_{-1} = 0$). All these data, like those that follow, are expressed in nominal dollars.

Standard WACC Method

This method discounts the project's FCFs at the firm's after-tax WACC, denoted i, where $i = w(1 - \theta)r + (1 - w)k_e$. A standard WACC calculation reflects the viewpoint of the firm's department that is in charge of project evaluation and for which all financing-related data are already included in calculating the discount rate. The project's NPV is therefore:

$$NPV = \sum_{t=0}^{T} \frac{F_t}{(1+i)^t} \tag{20.1}$$

A variant of the standard WACC method is used to compare economic and financial analysis. This is the economic value added (EVA) method in which the discount rate is the same as the one employed with the standard WACC method but which replaces the cash flow used above with an economic profit for each year.

Instead of considering the initial investment as a cash flow, each year the EVA method subtracts the depreciation amount and an opportunity cost equal to the discount rate multiplied by the investment book value from the FCF. The present value of a project's annual EVA stream is equal to the NPV that would be computed with the standard WACC method.

Equity Residual Method

As shown by Chambers et al. (1982), the equity residual method, which is also known as the "cash flow to equity method" (e.g., Oded and Michel, 2007), values the project under study from the invested-equity perspective. The cash flows available for distribution to the shareholders (i.e., each year, the FCF minus the principal repayment and the after-tax interest payment) are those considered in the analysis. All loan flows and associated interest tax shields are then included in calculating equity cash flows. The discount rate employed is that of the shareholders, that is, the cost of equity. From the shareholders' perspective, the project's NPV is:

$$NPV = \sum_{t=0}^{T} \frac{F_t + D_t - (1 + (1 - \theta)r) D_{t-1}}{(1 + k_e)^t} \tag{20.2}$$

Babusiaux and Pierru (2009) suggest a variant of the equity residual method that they call the "displaced equity method." This method adopts the point of view of shareholders who consider the full project's value and not only their invested equity. From this perspective, the debt amount associated with the project every year is treated as if it replaces an equivalent amount of equity, which would otherwise be tied up in the project. The shareholders' reinvestment of this displaced equity yields a return equal to their cost of equity, k_e. This cost of equity is herein viewed as an opportunity cost because the displaced amount of equity is implicitly assumed to be invested in other assets with a similar risk for the shareholders. This equity displacement remains hypothetical in the sense that the cost-of-equity rate considered here is that corresponding to the project's financial structure under study.

In other words, in any year $t - 1$, the outstanding amount of debt D_{t-1} is merely viewed as a means of "freeing up" an equivalent amount of equity that is immediately invested by the shareholders for one year at the equity rate of return, k_e. The cash flow yielded by this investment in the following year is $(1 + k_e) D_{t-1}$. The actual gain for the shareholders in year t is given by the difference between this cash flow and the sum of the after-tax interest payment and debt repayment:

$$(1 + k_e) D_{t-1} - (1 + (1 - \theta)r) D_{t-1} = (k_e - (1 - \theta)r) D_{t-1} \tag{20.3}$$

Therefore, in the displaced equity method, the shareholders' cash flow in year t is:

$$F_t + (k_e - (1 - \theta)r) D_{t-1} \tag{20.4}$$

This cash flow can also be interpreted as the sum of the FCF and the savings on the capital charge since using D_{t-1} costs $(1 - \theta)r D_{t-1}$, whereas tying up the same amount of equity would cost $k_e D_{t-1}$. With the displaced equity method, the project's NPV is:

$$NPV = \sum_{t=0}^{T} \frac{F_t + (k_e - (1 - \theta)r) D_{t-1}}{(1 + k_e)^t} \qquad (20.5)$$

Babusiaux and Pierru (2009) demonstrate that the equity residual method and the displaced equity method always yield the same NPV and IRR. Furthermore, to value a given project, the displaced equity method only requires knowledge of the schedule of the amounts of outstanding debt associated with the project. Every year, the displaced equity cash flow is the project's FCF adjusted in a very simple way. Clearly, when the expected outstanding debt amounts are known, using the displaced equity method is an easy way to calculate a project's NPV because it does not require explicitly computing the equity residual cash flows.

Numerical Illustration
Assume the project under study has an expected life of 6 years with an investment outlay of $220 million being spent in year 0. The project's after-tax operating cash flow (FCF) is assumed to remain constant and equal to $50 million each year from year 1 to year 6. This project is partly financed by a loan of $100 million contracted in year 0 at an annual interest rate of $r = 6$ percent. Interest is paid annually and the full principal is repaid at the end of year 6 in a single payment. Interest payments are deductible from the project's taxable income, which is subject to the tax rate of $\theta = 35$ percent. The cost of equity, k_e, is assumed to be 12 percent.

The cash flows from both equity perspectives are given in Exhibit 20.1. Because the firm repays the full principal at maturity, FCF is adjusted every year in the same way with the displaced equity method. Both equity perspectives give the same NPV ($18.90 million) and return on equity (19.9 percent).

Exhibit 20.1   Displaced Equity and Equity Residual Cash Flows ($ millions)

Year t	0	1 to 5	6
Free cash flow F_t	−$220.0	$50.0	$50.0
Outstanding debt at the end of the year D_t (with $D_{-1} = 0$)	100.0	100.0	0.0
Displaced equity cash flow $F_t + (k_e - (1 - \theta)r) D_{t-1}$	−220.0	58.1	58.1
Equity residual cash flow $F_t + D_t - (1 + (1 - \theta)r) D_{t-1}$	−120.0	46.1	−53.9

This exhibit illustrates a project with a 6-year expected life involving an investment outlay of $220 million during year 0. The project's after-tax operating cash flow is estimated to be $50 million each year from year 1 to year 6. This project is partly financed by a loan of $100 million contracted in year 0 at an annual interest rate of $r = 6$ percent with interest paid annually, and the full principal is repaid at the end of year 6. Interest payments are deductible from the project's taxable income, which is subject to the tax rate of 35 percent. The cost of equity, k_e, is assumed to be 12 percent. Cash flows are from displaced equity and equity residual perspectives.

Arditti-Levy (BTWACC) Method

Arditti and Levy (1977) suggest that the cash flows to be discounted are equal to the sum of the FCFs and interest tax shields (tax savings due to the deduction of the interest payments from the taxable income) in each year. The discount rate used is the firm's before-tax weighted average cost of capital (BTWACC), or $wr + (1 - w)k_e$. According to the BTWACC method, the project's NPV is:

$$NPV = \sum_{t=0}^{T} \frac{F_t + \theta r\, D_{t-1}}{(1 + wr + (1 - w)\,k_e)^t} \qquad (20.6)$$

In particular, international oil companies, which are subject to important disparities in the tax treatment of interest paid, use this method. Each country has its particular petroleum tax code and the deduction of interest payments is often defined through specific contracts such as production sharing agreements. In this case, determining the after-tax cost of debt is not straightforward, which historically prompted the use of the BTWACC method in the oil and gas industry (this point is, however, further discussed later when a generalized version of the standard WACC method is presented).

As Babusiaux (1990) suggests, another way to describe the BTWACC cash flows is to observe that the cash flow in year t is the sum of the flows received (or spent) by the shareholders, the equity cash flow, $F_t + D_t - (1 + (1 - \theta)r)\,D_{t-1}$, and the debtholders, $(1 + r)\,D_{t-1} - D_t$. In this manner, the method reflects the viewpoint of the company's fund suppliers. Note that the cash flows considered in the Arditti-Levy method are the same as those considered in the capital cash flows approach suggested by Ruback (2002).

CONSISTENCY OF METHODS UNDER THE TARGET-DEBT-RATIO ASSUMPTION

In a straightforward manner, this section proves the consistency of all conventional project-valuation methods when the firm targets a predefined debt ratio.

Project Value and Project Contribution to Firm Debt Capacity

The economic value of the project at the end of year t, denoted as V_t, is equal to the sum of the present values at year t of the FCFs generated by the project after year t. Each year, the project's economic value represents the increase in the firm's value as a result of the project. When the project's debt is included in the calculation of the debt ratio targeted by the firm, the project's contribution to the firm's debt capacity is equal each year to the product of its economic value and the firm's target debt ratio. As a result, the standard hypothesis, which ensures the convergence of the conventional project-valuation methods, is that each year the project's debt ratio and the firm's target debt ratio are equal with the former being defined with respect to the project's value. The concept of a project's economic value also has another practical interest: It represents the minimum cash amount at which the firm is willing to sell its stake in the project.

The project's value V_t at the end of year t is accordingly expressed as follows:

$$V_t = \sum_{s=t+1}^{T} \frac{F_s}{(1+i)^{s-t}} \qquad (20.7)$$

Or, equivalently, as:

$$V_t = (1+i)\,V_{t-1} - F_t \qquad (20.8)$$

In particular, the project's NPV is equal to $V_0 + F_0$, with:

$$V_0 + F_0 = \sum_{t=0}^{T} \frac{F_t}{(1+i)^t} \qquad (20.9)$$

A Simple General Formula

Let a be a (discount) rate of any value. As Pierru and Feuillet-Midrier (2002) show, the project's NPV can be reformulated as follows (with $V_{-1} = 0$ by convention):

$$\sum_{t=0}^{T} \frac{F_t}{(1+i)^t} = \sum_{t=0}^{T} \frac{F_t + (a-i)\,V_{t-1}}{(1+a)^t} \qquad (20.10)$$

Equation 20.10 shows that a project's NPV can be obtained by discounting the FCFs at a rate different from the discount rate i that should normally be used; this is valid provided the FCFs are adjusted. Every year, this adjustment is equal to the difference between the two discount rates times the project's value in the previous year. As the following subsections show, each of the conventional project-valuation methods (standard WACC method, equity residual method, and Arditti-Levy method) corresponds to a specific choice of the discount rate a, which immediately ensures their consistency.

Equality of the NPVs

Assume that in each year t the loan D_t associated with the project complies with the firm's target debt ratio w, i.e., $D_t = w\,V_t$. In other words, the loan considered represents the project's actual contribution to the firm's debt capacity. Under this assumption, Equation 20.10 can then be written:

$$\sum_{t=0}^{T} \frac{F_t}{(1+i)^t} = \sum_{t=0}^{T} \frac{F_t + \left(\frac{a-i}{w}\right) D_{t-1}}{(1+a)^t} \qquad (20.11)$$

Standard WACC Method
If $a = i$, both the left-hand and right-hand sides of Equation 20.11 correspond to the project's NPV given by the standard WACC method, with FCFs discounted at the after-tax WACC.

Equity Residual Method
Assume that $a = k_e$. Then since $a - i = w\,(k_e - (1 - \theta)\,r)$, Equation 20.11 becomes:

$$\sum_{t=0}^{T} \frac{F_t}{(1+i)^t} = \sum_{t=0}^{T} \frac{F_t + (k_e - (1 - \theta)\,r)\,D_{t-1}}{(1 + k_e)^t} \qquad (20.12)$$

The right-hand side of Equation 20.12 is the project's NPV with the displaced equity method (see Equation 20.5). Since both equity perspectives yield the same NPV, the project's NPV computed with the equity residual method is therefore equal to that calculated with the standard WACC method.

Arditti-Levy Method
Now set $a = wr + (1 - w)\,c$. Then $a - i = wr\theta$. Equation 20.11 gives:

$$\sum_{t=0}^{T} \frac{F_t}{(1+i)^t} = \sum_{t=0}^{T} \frac{F_t + \theta r\,D_{t-1}}{(1 + wr + (1 - w)\,k_e)^t} \qquad (20.13)$$

According to Equation 20.13, the project's NPV is equal to the sum of the FCFs and interest tax shields discounted at the BTWACC. The standard WACC method and the Arditti-Levy method therefore yield the same NPV.

Consistency of the IRRs

Equation 20.10 also offers a single formulation of the consistency of the IRRs determined with the various methods. To obtain this formulation, Equation 20.10 has to be rewritten from the standpoint of the capital amount remaining due each year t rather than the project's value. This still nonrepaid capital amount is defined by taking the project's IRR as the cost of capital.

Let K_t be the capital amount not yet repaid at the end of year t and let IRR_{wacc} be the IRR obtained with the standard WACC method. It follows that:

$$K_0 = -F_0,$$
$$K_T = 0,$$
$$K_t = (1 + IRR_{wacc})\,K_{t-1} - F_t. \qquad (20.14)$$

Note that the nonrepaid capital amount coincides with the project's value when the project's NPV is zero.
In year 0, by definition:

$$K_0 + F_0 = \sum_{t=0}^{T} \frac{F_t}{(1 + IRR_{wacc})^t} = 0 \qquad (20.15)$$

Equation 20.10 can be rewritten as follows (with $K_{-1} = 0$ by convention):

$$\sum_{t=0}^{T} \frac{F_t}{(1 + IRR_{wacc})^t} = \sum_{t=0}^{T} \frac{F_t + (a - IRR_{wacc})K_{t-1}}{(1+a)^t} = 0 \qquad (20.16)$$

where a is a rate of any value.

Assume that in each year t the amount D_t of the loan associated with the project is such that $D_t = wK_t$. In other words, the project's debt ratio, $\frac{D_t}{K_t}$, in the sense of Linke and Kim (1974), is assumed to be equal to the firm's debt ratio, w. Equation 20.16 then becomes:

$$\sum_{t=0}^{T} \frac{F_t + \dfrac{a - IRR_{wacc}}{w} D_{t-1}}{(1+a)^t} = 0 \qquad (20.17)$$

Return on Equity

First set $a = \frac{IRR_{wacc} - w(1-\theta)r}{1-w}$. Equation 20.17 then gives:

$$\sum_{t=0}^{T} \frac{F_t + \left(\dfrac{IRR_{wacc} - w(1-\theta)r}{1-w} - (1-\theta)r \right) D_{t-1}}{\left(1 + \dfrac{IRR_{wacc} - w(1-\theta)r}{1-w} \right)^t} = 0 \qquad (20.18)$$

Equation 20.18 clearly defines $\frac{IRR_{wacc} - w(1-\theta)r}{1-w}$ as being the IRR obtained with the displaced equity method (which is the same as the return on equity yielded by the equity residual method). If IRR_e denotes the project's return on equity, then:

$$IRR_{wacc} = w(1-\theta)r + (1-w) IRR_e \qquad (20.19)$$

According to Equation 20.19, the project's IRR is a weighted average of the project's return on equity and the after-tax cost of debt.

Now consider the decision to accept or reject a given project. With the standard WACC method, the project is undertaken if its IRR_{wacc} is greater than the firm's discount rate, i. With the equity residual method, the project is undertaken if its return on equity, IRR_e, is larger than the firm's cost of equity. Comparing Equation 20.19 to that defining the WACC:

$$i = w(1-\theta)r + (1-w)k_e \qquad (20.20)$$

IRR_e is greater than k_e, if and only if, IRR_{wacc} is greater than i. Both approaches therefore lead to the same decision.

Note that the assumption made here about the debt ratio is not the same as that considered when analyzing the consistency of NPVs. However, both assumptions are equivalent for a project whose NPV is zero. In real life, loans that are apparently associated with projects generally do not comply with the above debt-ratio assumption. This point is discussed later in the chapter at some length. When, however, the capital initially borrowed is a proportion w of the investment cost and this loan is repaid over a period close to the project's life, Equation 20.19 may be considered as a correct approximation of the relationship between returns.

Return under the BTWACC Method
Now set a equal to $IRR_{wacc} + w\theta r$. Equation 20.17 then gives:

$$\sum_{t=0}^{T} \frac{F_t + \theta r\, D_{t-1}}{(1 + IRR_{wacc} + w\theta r)^t} = 0 \tag{20.21}$$

According to Equation 20.21, $IRR_{wacc} + w\theta r$ is the project's IRR obtained with the BTWACC method, denoted as IRR_{btwacc}.
Replacing IRR_{wacc} according to Equation 20.19 gives:

$$IRR_{btwacc} = wr + (1 - w)\, IRR_e \tag{20.22}$$

The IRR obtained with the Arditti-Levy method is therefore a weighted average of the return on equity and the interest rate on debt. Since the method's discount rate is $wr + (1 - w)k_e$ (i.e., the firm's BTWACC), IRR_{btwacc} is greater than the BTWACC discount rate, if and only if, IRR_e is greater than k_e. The Arditti-Levy method therefore leads to the same decision as the equity residual method and, consequently, the standard WACC method. As previously noted, Equation 20.22 often provides a correct approximation of the relationship between rates of return when the amount borrowed is the proportion w of the investment cost.

THE ADJUSTED PRESENT VALUE APPROACH

Myers (1974) defined the project's adjusted present value (APV) as the present value of its FCFs plus that of its interest tax shields. In this approach, the present value of the FCFs is determined by discounting them at the firm's unlevered cost of equity, denoted as ρ, that accounts for the operating risk. The rate ρ is the cost of equity that the firm would have if all its projects were financed with equity only (i.e., no debt).

When the firm directly targets (absolute) debt amounts expressed in dollars throughout the project's life, the interest tax shields that then have no exposure to the operating risk have to be discounted at the debt's interest rate. The project's APV is then:

$$APV = \sum_{t=0}^{T} \frac{F_t}{(1 + \rho)^t} + \sum_{t=0}^{T} \frac{\theta r\, D_{t-1}}{(1 + r)^t} \tag{20.23}$$

By contrast, when the firm targets a predefined debt ratio, the interest tax shields are exposed to the operating risk because every year they are proportional to the debt amount that itself is dynamically maintained as a proportion of the firm's value. Thus, under the target-debt-ratio assumption, both FCFs and interest tax shields are ultimately exposed to the operating risk, and the APV is no longer given by Equation 20.23.

Consider a Miles and Ezzell (1980, 1985) world where the amount of interest paid in year t is known with certainty at the end of year $t - 1$ (i.e., a year before, when D_{t-1} is known). In other words, due to the expectation revision process, the interest tax shields expected in year t are exposed to operating risk during $t - 1$ years. According to Miles and Ezzell (1985), in year 0 the project's APV is therefore:

$$\sum_{t=0}^{T} \frac{F_t}{(1+\rho)^t} + \frac{\theta r\, D_{t-1}}{(1+r)(1+\rho)^{t-1}} \tag{20.24}$$

More generally, the project's value V_t at the end of year t is expressed as follows (with $V_T = 0$):

$$V_t = \sum_{s=t+1}^{T} \frac{F_s}{(1+\rho)^{s-t}} + \frac{\theta r\, D_{s-1}}{(1+r)(1+\rho)^{s-t-1}} \tag{20.25}$$

According to Equation 20.25, V_t and V_{t+1} are linked by the following equation:

$$V_t = \frac{V_{t+1} + F_{t+1}}{1+\rho} + \frac{\theta r\, D_t}{1+r} \tag{20.26}$$

By assuming that the firm targets the debt ratio w, it follows that $D_t = w V_t$ and Equation 20.26 gives:

$$V_t = \frac{V_{t+1} + F_{t+1}}{1 + \rho - w\theta r \left(\dfrac{1+\rho}{1+r}\right)} \tag{20.27}$$

By solving the recurrence Equation 20.27:

$$V_t = \sum_{s=t+1}^{T} \frac{F_s}{\left(1 + \rho - w\theta r \left(\dfrac{1+\rho}{1+r}\right)\right)^{s-t}} \tag{20.28}$$

According to Equation 20.28, the project's APV, equal to $V_0 + F_0$, is therefore:

$$APV = \sum_{t=0}^{T} \frac{F_t}{\left(1 + \rho - w\theta r \left(\dfrac{1+\rho}{1+r}\right)\right)^{t}} \tag{20.29}$$

The denominator in the right-hand side of Equation 20.29 corresponds to the adjusted-discount-rate formula, $\rho - w\theta r \left(\frac{1+\rho}{1+r}\right)$, derived by Miles and Ezzell (1985) for the firm's WACC.

Harris and Pringle (1985) have proposed that all interest tax shields be treated as risky and discounted at ρ under the target-debt-ratio assumption. The project's APV is then:

$$APV = \sum_{t=0}^{T} \frac{F_t + \theta r D_{t-1}}{(1+\rho)^t} \qquad (20.30)$$

The project's value, V_t, at the end of year t is now expressed as follows (with $V_T = 0$):

$$V_t = \sum_{s=t+1}^{T} \frac{F_s + \theta r D_{s-1}}{(1+\rho)^{s-t}} \qquad (20.31)$$

and

$$V_t = \frac{V_{t+1} + F_{t+1} + \theta r D_t}{1+\rho} \qquad (20.32)$$

By replacing D_t with $w V_t$:

$$V_t = \frac{V_{t+1} + F_{t+1}}{1+\rho - w\theta r} \qquad (20.33)$$

By solving the recurrence Equation 20.33, the project's APV given by Equation 20.30 is also equal to:

$$\sum_{t=0}^{T} \frac{F_t}{(1+\rho - w\theta r)^t} \qquad (20.34)$$

As shown by Taggart (1991), the adjusted discount rate $\rho - w\theta r$ appearing in Equation 20.34 can be considered a continuous-time version of the formula derived by Miles and Ezzell (1985). Note that according to Equation 20.30, the firm's BTWACC should be equal to its unlevered cost of equity ρ.

PITFALLS WHEN APPLYING PROJECT-VALUATION METHODS

A project valuation is necessarily based on an implicit or explicit assumption about its financing mix. This assumption potentially influences the choice of the valuation method used and the resulting project's NPV. Making this assumption may be a source of pitfalls.

To clarify this, Pierru (2009) introduces several possible definitions of a loan that can be associated with a project and discusses their respective relevance for project valuation. This clarification is consistent with financial theory and practice, which distinguish two possible cases for a project's financing: (1) The firm targets a predefined debt ratio and the project's debt schedule is included in calculating this target debt ratio; or (2) the firm targets absolute debt amounts (i.e., in dollars) over the project's life. Both cases involve distinctly different project valuation procedures.

For the first case, two distinct types of loan can be associated with the project under study. To illustrate this point, take the example of a project in the oil and gas upstream sector. In many countries, the permitted amount of interest tax shields on such a project depends on the amount invested in the project. For example, Pierru and Babusiaux (2008) report that in Norway, where the tax rate on an oil-field project is 78 percent, comprised of an ordinary income tax plus a special petroleum tax, interest paid to lenders is fully deductible from taxable income provided that the amounts borrowed do not exceed 80 percent of the investment made in the project. For fiscal purposes, an "apparent loan" (and its corresponding repayment schedule) is therefore attributed to the project. Although contracted to finance the project considered, this loan is usually guaranteed by the firm, consolidated with other corporate-finance loans and included in calculating the debt ratio targeted by the firm.

To calculate the project's taxable income, the fiscal authorities deduct the interest paid on this apparent loan. However, the project's actual contribution to the firm's debt capacity is likely to differ from the amount of the apparent loan. This contribution corresponds to a "theoretical loan" that can also be associated with the project. Every year, the amount of this theoretical loan satisfies the debt ratio targeted by the firm with respect to the project's value (this corresponds to the assumption $D_t = wV_t$ in the previous sections). If the amount of the project's apparent loan is less than the amount of the project's theoretical loan, one should consider that the firm compensates for this difference by issuing more corporate bonds or by increasing the amount of another project's apparent loan (i.e., by borrowing more somewhere else). Note that subsidized loans and financial (capital) leases are other instances of apparent loans that have to be included in calculating the firm's target debt ratio even though they are usually attributed to specific projects and are contingent upon the amount invested in these projects.

The apparent loan is likely to have a repayment schedule reflecting corporate practice (for example, repayment in uniform annuities), whereas the theoretical loan does not. Nevertheless, if analysts used the equity residual method to determine the project's equity value, considering the (realistic) repayment schedule of the apparent loan would be incorrect. The project's equity value should be calculated by considering the theoretical-loan repayment schedule. Industry practitioners, however, usually employ the standard WACC method, not the equity residual method, because the value of the WACC remains constant throughout time. Note that a generalized version of the standard WACC method that should be used by multinational firms is introduced later in the chapter.

For the second case, a predetermined stream of debt cash flows (i.e., the debt repayment schedule directly targeted by the firm) is associated with the project. This may happen in various instances such as when the project is the firm's sole project (at least in a given class of risk) or when it is financed by project finance (i.e., with limited or nonrecourse loans). The project's equity value can then be calculated by considering this stream of debt cash flows and applying the equity residual method, as is usually done in practice. To do so, the operational viewpoint usually adopted by industry practitioners views the project's cost of equity as being the minimum return-on-equity value required by the firm to undertake the project under the assumptions made about its financing (i.e., given the cost, amount, and repayment schedule of the project's debt). In other words, industry practitioners implicitly consider that the project's cost of equity remains unchanged over the project's lifetime.

On the contrary, the financial literature argues that a project's cost of equity is susceptible to change over time when dollar amounts of outstanding debt are targeted. For instance, Inselbag and Kaufold (1997) derive a formula showing this is consistent with the APV approach, while Ruback (2002) similarly produces such a formula consistent with the capital asset pricing model (CAPM) approach. The project's value must then be computed following a delicate and complex process rendering the equity residual method nonoperational.

According to Esty (1999), sponsors typically use the equity residual method to value equity investments in project finance deals. Inselbag and Kaufold (1997, p.122) state that the equity residual method is "popular among certain practitioners, particularly those involved in real estate investments, leveraged buyout, leveraged leasing and project finance transactions." Babusiaux and Pierru (2009) note that, in the energy industry, return on equity is one of the profitability criteria usually used to assess capital-intensive projects. For practitioners, assuming a constant cost of equity and using the equity residual method or the displaced equity method is an easy and pragmatic way of estimating a project's equity value. To compute the project's value, they do not resort to the standard WACC method because this would require them to recalculate the value of the WACC every year. Finally, another way of calculating the project's value is using the APV approach, by applying Equation 20.23, but this requires the analyst to know the unlevered cost of equity.

ADJUSTING FOR CAPITALIZED INTEREST COSTS

Discounting FCFs at an after-tax WACC relies on the assumption that every year the interest cost immediately generates a proportionate tax shield. This assumption is usually violated when some interest costs are not paid but capitalized. For instance, in many countries, capitalized interest costs are depreciated according to the same rule as that applied to the project's capital expenditures, and they therefore generate deferred tax shields. The project's FCFs have to be adjusted as shown by Pierru and Babusiaux (2010) to offset this violation.

WACC and Capitalized Interest: A Simple Adjustment

Consider that, for the project under consideration, construction requires t years and production starts in year $t + 1$. No interest payment occurs before the start of production and all interest costs generated until year t are therefore capitalized. Let C_s $(s = 0, \ldots, t - 1)$ be the outstanding debt in year s whose interest costs in year $s + 1$ are capitalized (with $C_{-1} = 0$ by convention). The project's NPV is then as follows:

$$\sum_{s=0}^{t} \frac{F_s - \theta r C_{s-1}}{(1+i)^s} + \sum_{s=t+1}^{T} \frac{F_s + \sum_{k=0}^{t-1} \theta A_{s,k}(r C_k)}{(1+i)^s} \qquad (20.35)$$

where $A_{s,k}(r C_k)$ is the depreciation amount in year s resulting from the capitalization of interest costs $r C_k$ in year $k+1$.

Equation 20.35 has a straightforward interpretation: Discounting the firm's FCFs at the rate i relies on the assumption that every year the firm's total interest cost (i.e., the interest produced by the loan amount that satisfies the firm's target debt ratio) generates an interest tax shield at rate θ, whereas the interest cost $r C_{s-1}$ does not produce any tax shield in year s. Consequently, to remain consistent with the WACC, lost interest tax shields are deducted from the project's FCF every year during construction, and tax shields generated by the depreciation of capitalized interest are added to the project's FCF every year during production. In both cases, the adjustment made compensates for the departure from the assumption that every year the firm's total interest cost immediately generates a proportionate tax shield. The valuation Equation 20.35 therefore further generalizes the standard WACC method. For projects where capitalized interest costs produce no tax shields (i.e., $A_{s,k}(r C_k) = 0$ in every year s), the adjustment simply consists of subtracting the lost interest tax shields from the FCF for every year during construction.

Note that the FCF adjustment only accounts for the fiscal treatment of capitalized interest. In countries where, for fiscal purposes, capitalized interest costs are treated like interest payments (i.e., they are directly deducted from the firm's taxable income), no adjustment is required. Since the target debt ratio has to be satisfied, every dollar of interest capitalized simply replaces a dollar of debt that otherwise would have been contracted. Paying one dollar of interest and borrowing one dollar of debt simultaneously is equivalent to capitalizing this dollar. The capitalization of interest costs then has no impact on the firm's value.

Numerical Illustration

A firm is studying a project in which capital investments are spent over three years: $250 million in year 0, and $375 million in years 1 and 2. The project's FCF is assumed to remain constant and equal to $200 million every year from year 3 (start of production) to year 10 (end of the project's life). Every year (from year 0 to year 2), the project's investments are financed 40 percent by loans contracted at the annual interest rate $r = 6$ percent. Until the end of year 2 (here $t = 2$), interest costs are capitalized and, for fiscal purposes, depreciated in a straight-line way from year 3 to year 7. The interest costs produced from year 3 on are paid and (immediately) deducted from the project's taxable income (subject to a tax rate equal to 35 percent). All these loans are consolidated with the firm's debt and are hence included in its target debt ratio calculation. The WACC used by the firm to discount its FCFs is $i = 9$ percent. All data are expressed in nominal dollars.

Exhibit 20.2 gives the project's FCFs adjusted for capitalized interest costs, as well as all intermediate calculations. The capitalized interest costs amount to

Exhibit 20.2 Lost Interest Tax Shields, Depreciation Tax Shields, and Adjusted FCFs ($ millions)

Year t	0	1	2	3 to 7	8 to 10
Free cash flow F_t	−250.00	−375.00	−375.00	200.00	200.00
Loan contracted in year t	100.00	150.00	150.00		
Outstanding debt whose interest costs are capitalized C_t	100.00	256.00			
Capitalized interest costs in year t rC_{t-1}		6.00	15.36		
Lost interest tax shields in year t $\theta r C_{t-1}$ $(t = 1, 2)$		2.10	5.38		
Tax shield from depreciation of capitalized interest costs in year n $\sum_{k=0}^{1} \theta A_{t,k}(rC_k) = \theta\left(\frac{rC_0 + rC_1}{5}\right)$ $(t = 3, \ldots, 7)$				1.50	
Adjusted free cash flow	−250.00	−377.10	−380.38	201.50	200.00

$6 million in year 1 (with $C_0 = \$100$ million) and $15.36 million in year 2 (with $C_1 = 100 + 150 + 6 = \$256$ million). The resulting annual depreciation amount (from year 3 to year 7) is therefore:

$$\frac{6 + 15.36}{5} = \$4.28 \text{ million.}$$

According to Equation 20.35, the present value of the adjustments for capitalized interest costs is:

$$-\frac{0.35 \times 0.06 \times 100}{1.09} - \frac{0.35 \times 0.06 \times 256}{1.09^2} + \sum_{t=3}^{7} \frac{0.35 \times 4.28}{1.09^t} = -\$1.54 \text{ million.}$$

The project's NPV is therefore $20.5 million.

VALUATION OF THE MULTINATIONAL FIRM'S PROJECTS: THE GENERALIZED ATWACC METHOD

This section presents a generalized version of the standard WACC method, called the *generalized ATWACC method*, which should be used by a multinational firm facing disparities in the tax treatment of interest paid across different taxing environments.

The Case of the Multinational Firm Facing Various Tax Rates

Consider a multinational firm subject to different tax schemes across varying countries. For the sake of simplicity, assume that all the firm's investment projects belong to the same risk class (e.g., they are all oil-field development projects) and are financed using loans contracted at the same annual interest rate, r. The firm's cost of equity is still denoted as k_e. Further assume that each project u generates a given stream of FCFs that goes from year 0 to year T. The FCF at year t of project u is denoted as $F_{u,t}$. At each year t, the taxable income of project u is subject to a specific tax rate, denoted as $\theta_{u,t}$.

Consider a predefined target debt ratio, still denoted as w, with which the multinational firm must comply. The firm may, however, want to allocate to a project loans representing more (or less) than the portion corresponding to its target debt ratio w (which must be satisfied at company level). In fact, debt financing giving rise to tax shields in a given country depends on the investments made in that country. For example, apparent loans, as previously defined, are usually associated with oil-field development projects. Further, tax rules, such as those related to the deductibility of interest payments, and applicable tax rates can vary greatly from one project to another in the oil-and-gas exploration and production sectors. The multinational firm must therefore seek an optimal allocation of its debt across projects and across countries.

Optimal Allocation of Debt among Various Projects

In theory, each year the firm must allocate the loans in increasing order of their after-tax cost $(1 - \theta_{u,t})r$ where $\theta_{u,t} = 0$ if the interest payments are not deductible from the taxable income. When the total amount of loans available at company level (in compliance with the target debt ratio) is fully used up, the after-tax cost of the last loan allocated will correspond to the firm's marginal cost of debt. If the firm's debt capacity were increased by a dollar, this dollar would be contracted at this marginal cost (on an after-tax basis). Denote the tax rate that applies to the taxable income of the project to which this last loan is allocated as θ. At company level, the firm's marginal after-tax cost of debt is therefore $(1 - \theta)r$ (subsequently assumed to be constant over time).

The Firm's Discount Rate: The Weighted Average of the Firm's Marginal Financing Costs

In accordance with standard microeconomic reasoning, the firm uses its marginal cost of capital as its discount rate. As the firm maintains its debt ratio equal to a predefined target debt ratio, the composition (debt and equity) of the last dollar of capital raised by the firm satisfies this target debt ratio. The firm's marginal cost of capital is therefore a weighted average of the firm's marginal after-tax cost of debt and its cost of equity. In the standard case where the firm faces only a single tax rate, determining the firm's marginal after-tax cost of debt is not an issue because it is the same for all projects. Here, the after-tax cost of debt actually paid depends on the project considered. Because of the resulting optimal debt allocation between projects, the firm's marginal after-tax cost of debt is $(1 - \theta)r$. The discount rate to be used is a WACC computed on a marginal basis. However, unlike the standard case, this WACC discount rate, computed as the weighted average of the firm's marginal financing costs, is not equal to the weighted average of the firm's average financing costs (that which would be obtained by considering the average after-tax cost of debt). As a result, the cash flows of all the projects must be discounted at the same rate, i, defined as follows:

$$i = w(1 - \theta)r + (1 - w)k_e \tag{20.36}$$

The use of a single discount rate by the firm implies that the cost of equity is the same for all projects, regardless of their debt ratio, which may appear to contradict some traditional results of finance theory. In fact, this assumption is justified here by the existence of the constraint of compliance with the target debt ratio at company level. This constraint "connects" the projects and results in no differentiation in their cost of equity. Pierru (2008) proves this result by considering the firm's value as the sum of the APVs of its various projects.

NPV of a Project

The NPV of project u is given by the following formula:

$$NPV = \sum_{t=0}^{T} \frac{F_{u,t} + (\theta_{u,t} - \theta)r D_{u,t-1}}{(1 + i)^t} \tag{20.37}$$

where $D_{u,t-1}$ is the outstanding amount at the end of year $t-1$ of the debt (i.e., apparent loan) allocated to project u (with $D_{u,-1} = 0$ by convention).

The cash flow attributed to the project under consideration is therefore equal to the sum of the project's FCF and an interest-tax-shield differential for each year. The economic interpretation of this differential is as follows: At each year $t-1$, compliance with the firm's target debt ratio w implies that, if loan amount $D_{u,t-1}$ could no longer be allocated to project u, it would then be allocated to the project with the firm's marginal after-tax cost of debt. The corresponding after-tax interest payment would then be $(1 - \theta)r D_{u,t-1}$, instead of $(1 - \theta_{u,t})r D_{u,t-1}$. Therefore, project u generates the following reduction of after-tax interest payment:

$$(1 - \theta)rD_{u,t-1} - (1 - \theta_{u,t})rD_{u,t-1} = (\theta_{u,t} - \theta)r D_{u,t-1} \tag{20.38}$$

Additional Remarks on the Use of the Method

From a practical standpoint, the generalized ATWACC method is easy to use because calculating the projects' cash flows does not depend on the debt ratio targeted by the firm. Babusiaux and Pierru (2001) have also proposed an adaptation of the BTWACC method, consistent with the generalized ATWACC method. This method is difficult to implement because calculating the project's cash flow requires knowledge of the project's debt ratio each year.

Even if allocation of the debt across projects takes into account qualitative or strategic considerations, the generalized ATWACC method remains applicable. Indeed, users do not need to explicitly define the allocation of debt, they have only to determine the firm's marginal (after-tax) cost of debt. Furthermore, the method proposed reverts to the standard WACC method when applied to projects subject to a tax rate similar to that used to define the firm's marginal after-tax cost of debt. Note also that the BTWACC method may be viewed as a specific case of the generalized ATWACC method, one in which the firm's after-tax marginal cost of debt is equal to the before-tax interest rate (i.e., $\theta = 0$). The focus thus far has been on the computation of a project's NPV. Of course, other criteria that are used in practice, such as the IRR, profitability index, and discounted payback period, can also be computed with the generalized ATWACC method.

Numerical Example

Consider a firm using the generalized ATWACC method that computes its discount rate with the following data (expressed in nominal dollars): $k_e = 12$ percent, $r = 6$ percent, $\theta = 35$ percent, and $w = 40$ percent. The firm's marginal after-tax cost of debt, which is determined by the firm's central services as previously described, is therefore:

$$(1 - 0.35)\,6\% = 3.9\%$$

According to Equation 20.36, the discount rate used by the firm is thus equal to 8.76 percent.

The company is studying an investment project that involves bringing an oil field into production. The earnings produced by this project are subject to a tax rate, θ_u, of 78 percent, constant throughout time. Assume that the fiscal system is a concession that allows deductibility of the interest payments from the taxable income.

The project under study has a lifetime of 7 years, the investment outlay ($200 million) being spent in year 0. The FCF (i.e., revenue minus operating expenses, royalties, and tax on earnings before interest) is equal to $40 million each year from year 1 to year 6 and equal to $18 million on year 7. The project is partly financed by an (apparent) loan of $160 million contracted in year 0 at an annual interest rate of 6 percent. The loan reimbursement is assumed to be "as fast as possible" as is often the case in practice.

The first step is to compute the schedule of debt reimbursement. Each year, the outstanding debt amount will decrease by an amount equal to the difference

Exhibit 20.3   Debt Repayment Schedule ($ millions)

Year	0	1	2	3	4	5	6	7
Outstanding debt at the end of the year	160.00	122.11	83.72	44.83	5.42	0.00		
Free cash flow		40.00	40.00	40.00	40.00	40.00	40.00	40.00
After-tax interest payment		2.11	1.61	1.11	0.59	0.07		
Principal repayment		37.89	38.39	38.89	39.41	5.42		

Exhibit 20.4 Cash Flow with the Generalized ATWACC Method ($ millions)

Year	0	1	2	3	4	5	6	7
Investment	200.00							
Free cash flow		40.00	40.00	40.00	40.00	40.00	40.00	18.00
Interest-tax-shield differential		4.13	3.15	2.16	1.16	0.14		
Cash flow	−200.00	44.13	43.15	42.16	41.16	40.14	40.00	18.00

This exhibit shows that a project's cash flow is computed by adding this interest-tax-shield differential to the FCF.

between the FCF and the after-tax interest payment (the tax rate considered being 78 percent, the effective project's tax rate). The results are given in Exhibit 20.3.

Each year, the differential of interest tax shields is obtained by multiplying the outstanding debt amount at the end of the previous year by:

$$(0.78 - 0.35)\,6\% = 2.58\%$$

The project's cash flow is computed by adding this interest-tax-shield differential to the FCF. The results are given by Exhibit 20.4.

The generalized ATWACC method yields a negative NPV of −$0.21 million.

To compare this value with that obtained with a nonrigorous computation, now assume that the firm uses the BTWACC method. The discount rate is then computed on a before-tax basis:

$$(0.4 \times 6\%) + (0.6 \times 12\%) = 9.6\%$$

With the BTWACC method, every year, the project's cash flow is obtained by adding the full interest tax shields to the FCF, as in Exhibit 20.5.

The resulting NPV is then $1.94 million. This (positive) value is incorrect because here the project's debt ratio is not equal to the debt ratio targeted by the firm, which precludes the use of the BTWACC method. Babusiaux and Pierru (2005) provide additional numerical illustrations of the generalized ATWACC method.

Exhibit 20.5 Cash Flow with the BTWACC Method ($ millions)

Year	0	1	2	3	4	5	6	7
Investment	200.00							
Free cash flow		40.00	40.00	40.00	40.00	40.00	40.00	18.00
Interest tax shield		7.49	5.72	3.92	2.10	0.26		
Cash flow	−200.00	47.49	45.72	43.92	42.10	40.26	40.00	18.00

This exhibit shows that with the BTWACC method, every year, the project's cash flow is obtained by adding the full interest tax shields to the FCF.

SUMMARY AND CONCLUSIONS

Various methods are available to evaluate an investment project. Each of them involves a specific definition of the cash flow and discount rate used. These methods (i.e., the standard WACC, BTWACC, equity residual, displaced equity, and APV with certain assumptions) lead to the same decision if the project's debt ratio remains equal to the firm's target debt ratio throughout the project's life.

In practice, the most widely used method is the standard WACC method, which allows the firm to separately consider the financing decisions and the investment decisions. This amounts to assuming that, every year, the loan associated with the project satisfies the firm's target debt ratio, with respect to the project's value.

The existing disparities in tax rates and in tax treatments of interest paid can lead a multinational firm to seek an optimal allocation of its debt capacity among its various projects. As a result, for fiscal purposes, an apparent loan and its corresponding repayment schedule may be attributed to each project. The generalized ATWACC method can then be used to value the firm's projects in a consistent manner. Where financing a project has no influence on the firm's debt capacity (nonrecourse project finance, for instance), a return-on-equity calculation using the equity residual method (or the displaced equity method) is the recommended approach.

DISCUSSION QUESTIONS

1. An international oil company is studying an oil-field development project in Norway. In this country, interest payments are deductible from the taxable income. Because the local tax rate is especially high, the after-tax cost of debt is less than in other countries. Could the project be valued using the equity residual method?

2. A company uses the BTWACC method to assess investment projects. Its management has set the value of the discount rate. Analysts are currently studying a project that would be partly financed by a loan whose interest rate is still unknown. They carry out a sensitivity analysis and find that the higher the interest rate, the greater is the project's IRR. Discuss whether this finding is surprising.

3. An analyst within a company computes a project's NPV from the shareholders' perspective. In evaluating the project, the analyst uses the company's 12 percent cost of equity capital. The analyst first uses the equity residual method, and then checks the results with the displaced equity method. Both give the same NPV. The analyst also determines the project's return on equity. Surprisingly, the analyst finds that the two cash flow streams do not yield the same return. Why?

4. Management is assessing an investment opportunity that takes place in a country where the company currently has no activity. This project is expected to generate a negative taxable income during several early years, which would cause the postponement of interest tax shields. How should the management take this into account if the company uses the standard WACC method to value its projects?

5. A company targets a debt ratio of 40 percent. Recently, analysts within the company have assessed a project with both standard WACC and equity residual methods. To apply the latter, analysts considered that the capital borrowed amounted to 40 percent of the project's investment cost. When carrying out sensitivity analyses, the analysts observed that both methods lead to the same conclusion within a large range of assumptions about the selling price of the products, the market share, and other parameters. However, the NPVs obtained with the two methods sometimes differ markedly. Why?

REFERENCES

Arditti, Fred D., and Haim Levy. 1977. "The Weighted Average Cost of Capital as a Cutoff Rate: A Critical Analysis of the Classical Textbook Weighted Average." *Financial Management* 6:3, 24–34.

Babusiaux, Denis. 1990. *Décision d'investissement et Calcul Économique dans l'entreprise*. Paris: Economica.

Babusiaux, Denis, and Axel Pierru. 2001. "Capital Budgeting, Investment Project Valuation and Financing Mix: Methodological Proposals." *European Journal of Operational Research* 135:2, 326–337.

Babusiaux, Denis, and Axel Pierru. 2005. *Corporate Investment Decisions and Economic Analysis. Exercises and Case Studies*. Paris: Editions Technip.

Babusiaux, Denis, and Axel Pierru. 2009. "Investment Project Valuation: A New Equity Perspective." *Engineering Economist* 54:2, 101–108.

Boudreaux, Kenneth J., and Hugh W. Long. 1979. "The Weighted Average Cost of Capital as a Cutoff Rate: A Further Analysis." *Financial Management* 8:2, 7–14.

Chambers, Donald R., Robert S. Harris, and John J. Pringle. 1982. "Treatment of Financing Mix in Analyzing Investment Opportunities." *Financial Management* 11:2, 24–41.

Esty, Benjamin C. 1999. "Improved Techniques for Valuing Large-Scale Projects." *Journal of Project Finance* 5:1, 9–25.

Graham, John R., and Campbell R. Harvey. 2001. "The Theory and Practice of Corporate Finance: Evidence from the Field." *Journal of Financial Economics* 60:2–3, 187–243.

Harris, Robert S., and John J. Pringle. 1985. "Risk-Adjusted Discount Rates—Extensions from the Average-Risk Case." *Journal of Financial Research* 8:3, 237–244.

Inselbag, Isik, and Howard Kaufold. 1997. "Two DCF Approaches for Valuing Companies under Alternative Financing Strategies (and How to Choose Between Them)." *Journal of Applied Corporate Finance* 10:1, 114–122.

Linke, Charles M., and Moon K. Kim. 1974. "More on the Weighted Average Cost of Capital: A Comment and Analysis." *Journal of Financial and Quantitative Analysis* 9:6, 1069–1080.

Miles, James A., and John R. Ezzell. 1980. "The Weighted Average Cost of Capital, Perfect Capital Markets and Project Life: A Clarification." *Journal of Financial and Quantitative Analysis* 15:3, 719–730.

Miles, James A., and John R. Ezzell. 1985. "Reformulating Tax Shield Valuation: A Note." *Journal of Finance* 40:5, 1485–1492.

Myers, Stewart C. 1974. "Interactions of Corporate Financing and Investment Decisions—Implications for Capital Budgeting." *Journal of Finance* 29:1, 1–25.

Oded, Jacob, and Allen Michel. 2007. "Reconciling DCF Valuation Methodologies." *Journal of Applied Finance* 17:2, 21–32.

Pierru, Axel. 2008. "Financing and Valuation of a Marginal Project by a Firm Facing Various Tax Rates." *Frontiers in Finance and Economics* 5:2, 56–71.

Pierru, Axel. 2009. "'The Weighted Average Cost of Capital Is Not Quite Right: A Rejoinder." *Quarterly Review of Economics and Finance* 49:4, 1481–1484.

Pierru, Axel, and Denis Babusiaux. 2008. "Valuation of Investment Projects by an International Oil Company: A New Proof of a Straightforward, Rigorous Method." *OPEC Energy Review* 32:3, 197–214.

Pierru, Axel, and Denis Babusiaux. 2010. "WACC and Free Cash Flows: A Simple Adjustment for Capitalized Interest Costs." *Quarterly Review of Economics and Finance* 50:2, 240–243.

Pierru, Axel, and Elisabeth Feuillet-Midrier. 2002. "Discount Rate Value and Cash Flow Definition: A New Relationship and its Implications." *Engineering Economist* 47:1, 60–74.

Ruback, Richard S. 2002. "Capital Cash Flows: A Simple Approach to Valuing Risky Cash Flows." *Financial Management* 31:2, 85–103.

Taggart, Robert A. 1991. "Consistent Valuation and Cost of Capital Expressions with Corporate and Personal Taxes." *Financial Management* 20:3, 8–20.

ABOUT THE AUTHORS

Axel Pierru is a senior economist at IFP Energies nouvelles (France). Dr. Pierru holds a Ph.D. in economics from the Panthéon Sorbonne University (Paris). He has research and teaching interests in the areas of corporate finance, operational research, and energy economics. Dr. Pierru has published articles in various academic journals, including the *Quarterly Review of Economics and Finance, Frontiers in Finance and Economics, Engineering Economist, European Journal of Operational Research, Optimal Control Applications and Methods, Louvain Economic Review, Energy Economics, Energy Policy, OPEC Energy Review*, and *Revue Economique*. With Denis Babusiaux, he has co-authored *Corporate Investment Decisions and Economic Analysis, Exercises and Case Studies*.

Denis Babusiaux is a former director at the IFP (France) and has teaching and research interests in capital budgeting and energy modeling. He graduated from the Paris School of Mines and holds a Ph.D. in economics. He is a former adjunct professor at the University of Pennsylvania and a past president of the French affiliate of the International Association for Energy Economics.

PART VII

Special Topics

CHAPTER 21

Capital Budgeting for Government Entities

DAVINA F. JACOBS
Senior Economist, Fiscal Affairs Department, International Monetary Fund

INTRODUCTION

Capital budgeting for government entities has multiple roles. For example, capital budgeting serves as an instrument of fiscal policy to improve the net worth of government, particularly in the area of economic infrastructure, and as a vehicle for economic growth and development. This is usually achieved through greater reliance on debt than on such conventional sources of financing as taxation. In this context, *capital budgeting* refers to budgets that are self-contained and separate from the budget for recurrent expenditures. The term *investment budget* is sometimes used to emphasize the importance of public investment to promote economic growth. These two concepts are similar and distinct from the concept of a *development budget*, which includes expenditures that are unrelated to investment. According to Webber (2007), governments introduce capital budgets to serve all these objectives, singly or collectively, depending on the context. In some cases, attention has focused on capital budgets as a way to reduce deficits caused by an excess of recurrent expenditures versus revenues.

Notwithstanding the seeming virtues of capital budgets, opinions continue to be divided, as they have been during the past seven decades, about their utility in governments. In the present context in which some of the more advanced countries have budgetary surpluses and use them to reduce levels of government debt, there is little incentive to revive the debate about the need for capital budgets. In the developing world, however, where many governments operate on the edge of financial instability, the debate about capital budgets and their equivalents continues.

A key challenge in government budgeting is to define an appropriate balance between current and capital expenditures. Budgeting for government investment also remains poorly integrated into the formal budget preparation process in many countries. Experience shows that in the absence of properly organized capital budgets, governments resort to borrowing without due consideration of the sustainability aspects, assets are inadequately maintained, and major projects suffer from overall poor management and performance.

Premchand (2007) argues that the establishment of capital budgets could not necessarily have prevented these poor results. Moreover, the issue arises as to whether capital budgets promote an improved process of decision making and an overall management culture that permits continuing attention to the government's net worth, particularly for countries continuing to depend on debt finance as a major instrument of budgetary resources. Thus, an important topic is to consider whether capital budgets provide an improved framework for allocating, using, and accounting for government resources.

This chapter provides an overview of the evolution of past and current budgeting practices by government for capital budgets. It also offers a comparison between the budget practices between low-income countries (LICs) and more advanced countries. Additionally, it highlights possible solutions for use by government entities wanting to ensure more efficient capital budgeting practices in low-income countries denoted here as LICs (Gupta, Schwartz, Tareq, Allen, Adenauer, Fletcher, and Last, 2008).

AN OVERVIEW OF GOVERNMENT CAPITAL BUDGETING PRACTICES

Sarraf (2005) describes the different methods used to identify "capital" and how a government's consumption and investment activities should be separately recorded in government budget records and statistics. Governments around the world may define "capital" in different ways. The World Bank (2006, p. 84) notes that "capital spending is generally about physical assets with a useful life of more than one year." But it also includes capital improvements or the rehabilitation of physical assets that enhance or extend the useful life of the asset (as distinct from repair or maintenance, which ensures that the asset is functional for its planned life).

Capital spending is sometimes equated with *investment* or *development spending*, where expenditures have benefits extending years into the future. Under this definition, governments may include physical assets for government use (e.g., office buildings), physical assets of a public good nature that also enhance private sector development (e.g., roads and water systems), and intangibles (e.g., education and research). Distinguishing between investment and noninvestment expenditures can be difficult. If investment spending receives favored treatment in the annual budgeting process, nearly all spending, whether recurrent or not, ends up being classified as investment. Every government establishes some arbitrary cut-off point to distinguish capital from current expenditures. For budgeting purposes, the relevant distinction is between capital and current (or operating) expenditures. *Current expenditures* are purchases of assets to be consumed within one year, regardless of expenditure size. Small expenditures (e.g., less than US $25,000) are regarded as current, regardless of the fact that the monies could be consumed over a period longer than one year.

The existence of different definitions of capital does not necessitate a dual budgeting system. Separate data on government consumption and investment can be maintained within a unified government budget. This chapter focuses mainly on government investment. However, some of the most common and serious problems with government capital budgeting can arise from its interface with current spending.

There has also been increasing interest in recent years in rules limiting the budget balance and the total level of government debt. The European Union (EU) reinforced these developments in the 1990s by the conditions for membership in the Monetary Union, which put limits on budget deficits and the total level of debt. These have been now succeeded by the Stability and Growth Pact, which limits the level of government sector deficit. Some countries such as the United Kingdom and Germany have or are developing explicit links or rules between the level of net government investment and the level of government debt. This may include the so-called "golden rule," which specifies that increases in the stock of government debt should not exceed net government investment.

The German Constitution mandates the golden rule and a balanced budget. However, a law was passed in 1967—at a time when government investment was still widely seen as an instrument for controlling unemployment—allowing exceptions for federal and state governments where more investment is considered justified by macroeconomic conditions. This exception has been applied in Germany many times. Spackman (2002) compared this exception with the example of The Netherlands, which applied the golden rule between 1927 and 1958. In 1997, the U.K. government introduced a policy under which the budget is balanced over the economic cycle, with no exceptions, and a target is set for the level of government debt.

Control of government debt is at least as important in low-income countries as it is in developed economies. However, the first priority of LICs is to develop reliable measures of government assets and especially liabilities. Information on capital assets and liabilities should ideally be monitored. In fact, some LICs have found establishing some form of the golden rule helpful.

The Evolution of Capital Budgeting Practices

Budgeting for capital expenditures has evolved over the decades and its importance has varied over time. Premchand (2007) identifies six discernible stages of changes in government capital budgeting practices. The first stage is the Great Depression years during which efforts mainly focused on designing ways to ensure economic recovery. At the time, most governments did not favor borrowing for financing capital outlays, except for emergencies. In a cautious approach, Sweden introduced a capital budget that was to be funded by government borrowing and used to finance the creation of durable and self-financing assets that would contribute to an expansion of net worth equivalent to the amount of borrowing. This so-called investment budget found extended application in other Nordic countries in the following years.

The second stage took place during the late 1930s when the colonial government in India introduced a capital budget to reduce the budget deficit by shifting some items of expenditures from the current budget. Some believed that introducing this dual-budget system would provide a convenient way to reduce deficits while justifying a rationale for borrowing.

The third stage, which occurred during the 1940s to 1950s, is characterized by the growing importance attached to capital budgets as a "vehicle" for development plans. Partly influenced by Soviet-style planning, many LICs formulated comprehensive five-year plans and considered capital budgets the main impetus for economic development (Tarschys, 2002). Where capital budgets did not exist, a variant known as the *development budget* was introduced.

The fourth stage reflects the importance of economic policy choices on the allocation of resources in government. According to Premchand (2007), governments applied quantitative appraisal techniques on a wider scale during the 1960s, leading to more rigorous application of investment appraisal and financial planning.

In the 1960s and 1970s, a common view was that government budget allocation, including investment expenditures, could be largely reduced to a "scientific" process by systems such as planning, programming, and budgeting systems (PPBS) or even zero-based budgeting (ZBB). The term PPBS is still sometimes used to describe any well-balanced, analytically based approach to planning expenditure programs. However, PPBS was originally presented as a way of deriving by rigorous analysis the "optimal" allocation of expenditure. At the "planning" stage, systems analysis identified objectives and potential solutions. "Programming" applied economic techniques such as cost-benefit analysis to existing and potential new policies. "Budgeting" applied the results of this analysis to derive annual budgets. ZBB was a later experiment, which applied a rather similar, comprehensive logic to individual programs.

Spackman (2002) argues that this belief in the application of scientific processes in budgeting turned out to be misguided for three main reasons. One reason was that finding the best way forward for governments depends not only on analysis but also on pragmatism and politics. Second, the information demands were equivalent to those required to run a centrally controlled economy. Third, the implied power structure within government was that of central control, not delegated authority and local initiatives.

The fifth stage saw a revival of the debate about the need for a capital budget in government, particularly in the United States. Along with the growing application of quantitative techniques during the 1960s came the view that introducing a capital budget could be advantageous. But this view did not gain much support. A U.S. President's Commission (1967, p. 9) investigating budget concepts in the United States concluded that a capital budget "would seriously distort the budget as a decision-making tool" and could lead to greater outlays on bricks and mortar, and, as a result, current outlays on services could suffer. The commission rejected the use of separate capital budgets and the introduction of accrual accounting in government accounts. *Accrual accounting* is an accounting methodology under which transactions are recognized as the underlying economic events occur, regardless of the timing of the related cash receipts and payments. The introduction of accrual accounting, which did not make any progress in the United States until the early 1990s, would have meant the division of expenditures into current and investment outlays.

Meanwhile, Sweden, which had made pioneering efforts in the 1930s, undertook a review of its budget system in the early 1970s. Sweden found that excessive focus on capital budgets would need to be adjusted by recognizing that the overall credibility and creditworthiness of a government depends more on its macroeconomic policy stance and less on its net worth. This shift in emphasis contributed to a decline in the popularity of using the capital budget until the late 1980s, when it came to be revived in a different form. By then, government officials recognized that the management of government finances required a new approach, which was the application of accrual accounting.

During this sixth stage, partly because of the experiences of Australia and New Zealand, a renewed push by international financial institutions occurred to introduce accrual budgeting and accounting. These ideas found a foothold in the United States, where advocates held the view that the absence of a distinction between investment outlays and ordinary or current outlays led to unintended neglect of infrastructure or accumulated assets. Ensuring proper asset maintenance, which may be as important as asset creation, required a division of outlays into current and capital outlays, as a part of day-to-day budget management.

CURRENT GOVERNMENT CAPITAL BUDGETING PRACTICES

The practices of countries in budgeting for capital vary considerably, revealing several categories. The first category includes those countries that observe the distinction between current or operational and capital budgets.

Premchand (2007) emphasized that, given tradition and considerable diversity in country experience, another important issue is the purpose served by a capital budget. In considering this important issue and in seeking an answer to the most important question (that of whether capital budgets provide a better framework for allocating resources and, specifically, for determining long-term public investments), one must recognize that the level of economic development in countries can also influence the development of changes in practices in capital budgeting.

Capital Budgeting in Developed Countries

Dual budgeting originated in European countries, but in those countries it lasted only for a short period. It was introduced in the late 1930s in order to help governments ensure that they used borrowed resources only for capital expenditures. After World War II, as governments relaxed their use of borrowed funds, budgets became integrated. The change in approach reflected several factors. These factors included massive postwar reconstruction work and increased recurrent expenditures as well as the acceptance of the Keynesian model of linking government spending and the size of the budget deficit and borrowing requirements to both fiscal and monetary determinants and the business cycle. Moreover, the realization soon became clear that the need to reap a return—whether financial, social, or economic—applied to the entire spectrum of government spending. Hence, regardless of their financing sources, a government's recurrent spending and capital investment together could produce results, provided the context is one of overall macrofiscal balance.

While few developed countries now maintain totally separate budgets, the extent and form of budgetary integration—particularly the management of capital spending—still differs substantially in some instances. For this reason, effective integration of current and capital budgets is perhaps best measured qualitatively by the extent to which the current and investment spending decisions of the government are "well balanced" in the sense of being logically consistent with, and mutually supportive of, a given policy framework or set of policy objectives. In practice, this means that the services for which government departments and spending agencies are responsible are delivered as effectively and efficiently as possible, given the budget resources available.

A few examples of unsatisfactory balances between current and capital spending can be highlighted, many of which can be found in the education sector, such as having many teachers but too few or poor-quality classrooms and teaching facilities. Although many administrations in developed countries may not consciously seek to optimize the current/capital spending balance, they nonetheless aspire to achieve consistency and efficiency within the context of their ongoing resource allocation and budget management decisions. In fact, getting the right balance between current and capital spending across the whole range of budget activities depends substantially on the quality of budget planning systems and capabilities. While these issues may involve a much wider range of factors than simply the extent of budgetary integration per se, an unified budget generally makes developing better systems, policies, and capabilities in these areas easier.

Capital Budgeting in Low-income Countries

As set out in Webber (2007), in many countries, separate current and capital budgets—that is, a "dual budget" process—have their origins in the public finance management policies and structures established by colonial administrations. These administrations clearly distinguished between the recurring operational costs involved in maintaining a narrow range of government services and the "developmental" expenditures needed from time to time to establish new facilities or new administrative functions. Limitations on local revenue-raising capacity meant that approval for major capital expenditures often required special budgetary provisions including referral to the home treasury or supervising colonial authority.

Dual budgeting did not disappear, however, with the departing colonial administrations. The continued separation of current and development budgets also appealed to the new administrations in that it enabled them to separate the ongoing costs of government and the associated raising of current revenues from ambitious new development plans and their associated financing needs. Development assistance donors have reinforced this separation over the years through their traditional preference for funding of "development" activities, while at the same time shying away from the "consumption spending" associated with current expenditures. This traditional view of current expenditures as being of lesser economic importance or merit has diminished in recent years, especially within the multilateral institutions, though it is still evident in the chronic underfunding of some government services.

During the 1960s, LICs' nascent institutions of political and economic management tended to adopt the technical practices of the western democracies. Many countries in Africa, Latin America, and the Middle East adopted national development planning, which had European roots and was still being practiced in Belgium, France, and Spain. Inexperienced finance ministries could not carry out the new tasks of medium-term development planning and capital project appraisal, so governments set up planning, development, or economic affairs ministries for the purpose. In practice, the new ministries soon became responsible for the identi-fication, appraisal, budgeting, and even accounting and reporting of investment budgets in an initial but major and lasting step toward dual budgeting.

Frequently, finance and development ministries issued their own separate bud-get circulars, and the dual approach to budgeting also took root in the government entities. Politically visible gaps in physical infrastructure, and then capital project supremacy in government budgeting, helped to create new financial power bases. This left the finance ministries responsible for budgeting civil service salaries and the needs of some small government ministries with minimal operational expen-ditures. Lack of coordination between the finance and planning or development ministries may also have reflected differences between their ministers and/or heads of state who, in some cases, exercised *de facto* control of investment decisions and their funding. Such settings made introducing consolidated budget presenta-tion and classification systems difficult. Moreover, as discussed by Sarraf (2005), some substantial but unforeseen recurrent costs evolved from the expansion of investment projects.

The use of public investment programs (PIPs) in the 1980s, as promoted by the World Bank and other donor agencies, saw the introduction of more coordi-nated project selection and appraisal processes. Though PIPs replaced individual project appraisal, this intensified the dynamics of dual budgeting. Moreover, addi-tional donor support to recurrent developmental and humanitarian expenditures created further coordination problems with governments' traditional recurrent budgets.

Both before and during the PIP era, governments emphasized calculating the recurrent spending that capital projects would need after their completion, but in practice finance ministers were uninformed and reluctant or financially unable to provide the necessary funds. The lack of provision for recurrent funds added to the concerns that had already been created by the organizational separation of the two budgets. Some may argue that the main reason for underbudgeting of recurrent expenditures for completed capital projects was, and still is, general fiscal stress in LICs. But a counterargument is that the fiscal stress could have been projected before initiating the projects. Alternatively, other spending priorities could crowd out the claims of these projects on recurrent budgets. Both arguments point to the lack of coordination between recurrent and development budgets.

The main impact of a dual budgeting system on budget execution and reporting occurred through capital or recurrent projects financed by donors. Donor financing usually required governments to keep separate accounts for domestic counterpart funds and to deposit such funds along with donor funds in special bank accounts, outside the purview of central treasuries or accountants-general. These special accounts, mainly in commercial banks, were governed by flexible spending rules and often bypassed the national budget systems, undermining the objective of comprehensive government accounting, banking, and cash management coverage. Moreover, to ensure the availability of funds for recurrent expenditures of selected capital projects, government authorities created expedients such as extrabudgetary funds and trust accounts, whose transactions were subject to separate accounting and banking rules. This contributed to weaker reporting and delays in closing government accounts, due to the difficulty of reconciling government accounting records with government banking transactions. Although in most countries central treasury offices and accountants-general issued circulars requiring line ministries to report their transactions, these reports were not complete or timely in practice.

Government authorities also created special project management units in line ministries, dealing with the accounting and banking of the cash components of external loans and grants, as well as with government counterpart funds. Because these recurrent and capital transactions were not classified in terms of the object of expenditures, in practice, the decision to itemize expenditures was entrusted to line ministries in the course of budget execution. Several line ministries did not use the government standard object classification that was used for traditional recurrent expenditures, thereby multiplying the accounting and reporting problems.

Since the late 1990s, new financial assistance policies and instruments such as poverty-reduction strategy papers (PRSPs), the monitoring of sector-wide poverty-reducing expenditures, and budget support approaches have been changing the dynamics of donor/client relationships. Moreover, several donors have substantially increased their financing of recurrent expenditures in response to urgent needs in health, education, and other sectors in poor countries. The new approaches have implications for consultations, conditionality, and data requirements, and for technical assistance to support an integrated approach to recurrent and development outlays. Public expenditure reviews (PERs) were originally known as *public investment reviews*, and reflected the World Bank's theory that capital investment would drive growth in developing countries. However, PERs have now clearly moved toward more intra- and intersectoral analyses, combining both recurrent and development expenditures, and, where data are available, reviewing the joint impact of both types of spending on budgetary outcomes including economic growth, poverty reduction, and asset maintenance. But while most LICs have at least begun using medium-term expenditure frameworks (MTEFs) to replace five-year national plans and government investment programs, their annual programming and budgeting of recurrent and development operations still tend to be carried out by separate organizations.

Some LICs have merged their finance ministries with their planning or development ministries but others are slow in doing so. In many developing and transition countries, finance ministries have traditionally been much weaker than planning ministries, which have benefited from close relations with the World Bank and other aid providers. The organizational separation of planning and finance ministries has become institutionalized in culture and politics in several countries. Political concerns about eliminating a ministerial portfolio, combined with institutional revivalism between the two ministries at the institutional level, persist in many LICs. Governments may mitigate the political concerns associated with eliminating a ministerial portfolio if they use their authority to create as many alternative cabinet posts as they want—say, for example, creating a ministerial post for environment or splitting the ministry of trade and industry into two.

Today, the integration of recurrent and development budgets in LICs has become a necessity because:

- Government borrowing is no longer limited to capital expenditures.
- Only an integrated analysis of recurrent and development expenditures can identify those poverty-reducing expenditures that have immediate impact

(e.g., social transfers and targeted subsidies, and some other social expenditures) or an indirect impact through accelerating economic growth.
- Part of external concessional credits and the bulk of donor grants are used for recurrent expenditures, supplementing the government's recurrent budget.
- Recurrent costs of capital projects continue to be ignored, even after several decades of experience, in part because of lack of coordination between two separate budgets.

GOVERNMENT CAPITAL PROJECT APPRAISAL METHODS

Changes in attitudes toward capital project appraisal (CPA) methods have been broadly similar to those toward higher level government planning and budgeting. In the 1960s and early 1970s, great hopes were placed on CPA techniques such as cost-benefit analysis (CBA) (in which nonmarketed outputs are explicitly valued in monetary terms) as a way of deciding scientifically the optimal level and distribution of investment. Experience shows that for most areas of public investment this was unrealistic. Even in those areas where a useful scope for such scientific analysis exists (notably transport, where time and injury risks can be valued), some major impacts, on the environment, for example, usually cannot be valued. In the great majority of public policy areas, such as law and order, defense, employment, regional, industrial, education, health, or public administration, explicitly valuing outputs is rarely possible.

Capital Project Appraisal in Government Entities

According to Spackman (2001), CPA centers on comparing a potentially wide range of options. In contrast, project evaluation of projects compares a narrower range of options, one of which will eventually be executed. Thus, as part of an ongoing asset management process in government, project evaluation should be considered as a necessary follow-up to the project appraisal phase.

CPA in government could be considered as an economic analysis of the costs and benefits that might be generated by the proposed government investment options. These may include alternative locations, size, design, or timing of a new or renovated prison, hospital, or defense establishment, for example, and especially the alternative (or the opportunity costs) of not undertaking the investment. In principle, the appraisal includes all costs such as those involving using the capital asset throughout its lifetime. It should also include a sensitivity analysis, legislative and environmental impacts, and possible impacts on other sectors.

Examples of activities for which new capital project proposals need to be appraised include:

- Estimation of potential demand and definition of the level, type, and standard of service the new asset is to provide.
- New or replacement capital projects such as whether to undertake a project, whether to undertake it now or later, and on what scale and in what location, and to determine the degree of private sector involvement.

- The use or disposal of existing assets such as whether to sell or replace existing facilities by new ones, or relocate facilities or operations elsewhere, or to contract out, or market test, operations.

Ideally, CPAs should always include an assessment of whether the project would provide "value for money." This may sometimes be wholly in financial terms (e.g., in comparing the costs of different ways of providing the same output). More often, CPAs entail some factors that can be quantified but not valued (e.g., the impact of water purification plant on health benefits), or that cannot even be quantified (e.g., environmental concerns), and about which explicit judgments have to be made.

CPAs should also include an analysis of the budgetary implications of a proposal over time. This may need to include an analysis for the government sector as a whole as well as for the spending department or agency. The information provided by this, or by the examination of other institutional constraints, may determine the final decision. However, a budgetary or financial appraisal, or any other appraisal of some specific aspect of the proposal, should never be seen as an alternative to an "economic appraisal." They are complementary.

The Treasury Board of Canada, within the Canadian Ministry of Finance (2010), has developed a useful "checklist" for consideration during CPA and evaluation processes, which includes the following aspects set out on their website: (1) the clarity of the objectives; (2) the choice and definition of the options; (3) the estimation of costs and benefits; (4) valuation issues; (5) an assessment of project risk and uncertainty; (6) the net present value (NPV) calculation; (7) a presentation of the results; and (8) the evaluation itself.

Are CPA Procedures Getting "Any Better"?

According to a recent report prepared by Laursen and Myers (2009), the quality of CPA practices across countries is difficult to compare. In most of the EU countries, the results of the CPA process do not necessarily determine the decision about which projects will go forward, and the system still allows wide political discretion in selecting individual projects. Although CBA is a standard component of project appraisal in all countries, especially for EU-funded projects, the quality of the analysis is typically not independently reviewed and the resulting analysis is not necessarily an important factor in project selection. Various projects could generate positive economic benefits, assessing their relative value-for-money rate. Moreover, project appraisal processes in the EU countries give much less attention to business case justification, project management arrangements, risk mitigation, and procurement strategies than is the case in the United Kingdom or Ireland.

The existing EU guidelines on CBA for CPA provide a strong technical toolkit for the EU countries to use, but the above-mentioned report highlights some areas of concern. The report notes that sensitivity analysis is generally performed as part of the CBA, but it may not affect whether a project goes forward. In Slovenia, for example, a motorway project included analysis to assess the risk of lower benefits and higher costs. With only a 5 percent increase in project costs or a 10 percent decrease in benefits, the NPV for the bypass project would turn negative and the internal rate of return (IRR) would fall below the common discount rate.

Nevertheless, construction of the project began in 2001. Furthermore, little evidence suggests that CPA methodologies incorporate explicit analysis of alternative options.

In the United Kingdom and Ireland, central coordinating ministries such as the Treasury play a much more assertive role in managing the government investment process than in most other EU countries. Although its interventions are very selective, the U.K. Treasury is heavily involved in the overall transport strategy and high-level planning and controls. The level of involvement in specific transport projects varies widely, depending upon the scale and funding complexity of the project. The U.K. Treasury issues general guidelines for project appraisal and evaluation. Responsible departments have further developed these guidelines such as when the Department of Transport issued, with Treasury approval, its own guidelines.

While CBA has traditionally been a core component of CPAs, the United Kingdom has refined the approach to include risk adjustments and distributional aspects. The U.K. "Green Book" provides basic principles on appraisal and evaluation, as well as specific conventions such as the choice of discount rates (United Kingdom Treasury, 2009). Additionally, the "Green Book" often describes the process of project appraisal and evaluation as stages of a broad policy cycle that some departments and agencies formalize in the acronym ROAMEF (Rationale, Objectives, Appraisal, Monitoring, Evaluation and Feedback). CPAs should provide an assessment of whether a proposal is worthwhile, and clearly communicate conclusions and recommendations. The essential technique is option appraisal, whereby government intervention is validated, objectives are set, and options are created and reviewed by analyzing their costs and benefits.

Requirements for Effective CPA Procedures

In many countries, "readiness" of the project to move forward can become a more important consideration than its strategic or economic value. As the abovementioned EU study by Laursen and Myers (2009, p. 15) notes that, "the flow of EU money has shifted the emphasis from appraising projects to managing a project portfolio." Given that EU funding lapses after a predetermined period, governments face pressure to make sure that they have a group of projects ready to begin. This can have the effect of creating a perverse incentive in that governments fear losing these funds if they cannot spend them. Apparently, spending the money on suboptimal projects is better than risking loss of the funds and having no project. Inevitably, some preparations take longer than expected once the funds are available. In some countries, frequent delays in projects occurred, for example, because of the difficulties with obtaining land acquisition rights. This may in turn increase the incentive to promote projects where land rights have already been acquired, rather than those that carry high economic returns.

CPAs can include checks and balances to ensure sound principles are being applied. In some countries the staged external review of large projects provides an important measure of quality control, and this can be especially important in early stages. For the past few years, the U.K. Transport Department has used the standard central government *Gateway Process,* which applies to all types of major investment projects. This process sets out the stages of the review (gateways): strategic assessment, business justification, delivery strategy, investment decision, readiness for service, operations review, and benefits realization. External review before projects start is a tool also used for quality assurance. Additionally, special reviews have helped identify the main causes contributing to the systemic underestimation of project costs.

In summary, a number of general requirements for effective CPAs can be defined:

- Providing well-informed and open-minded consideration of alternative options, against well-defined policy objectives.
- Taking proper account of opportunity costs (so that the use of labor, for example, is normally recognized as a cost, and not seen instead as a benefit).
- Addressing any "optimism bias" so as to ensure the proper calculation of all overall costs.
- Considering factors that cannot be explicitly valued in money terms as well as those that can.

This contrasts with what is often performed as CPAs in LICs, which is a cost analysis of an already well-defined proposal. The capacity of some LICs to undertake such an analysis is often strong, whereas the capacity for economic analysis, to question initial proposals, might be weaker. In conclusion, efficient prioritization and selection of capital projects also remain key issues for countries to consider. Jacobs (2008) identifies the main aspects that should be taken into account. The following section sets out some general conclusions for improving capital budgeting in government entities.

LESSONS LEARNED IN IMPROVING CAPITAL BUDGETING PRACTICES IN GOVERNMENT ENTITIES

Progress in integrating recurrent and capital budgets in some less-advanced countries has been very limited. One factor that helps to maintain the status quo of separate budgets is antiquated economic development theory, which emphasizes capital spending for faster economic growth. Another factor is institutional incentives. Donor practices have also tended to reinforce dual budgeting practices. Donors have traditionally focused on capital investments. A desire to attract donor funding gives a country a strong incentive to maintain a separate development budget process. Recent shifts toward donors' provision of budget support over project aid and multidonor involvement in financing recurrent expenditures may increasingly change that incentive. The failure to ensure resources for ongoing maintenance of capital investments gives some agencies an incentive to seek earmarked or extrabudgetary revenues (e.g., road funds). As an added consequence of separate budgets, some ministries pursue activities through the development budget that would otherwise be treated as recurrent spending, due to the budgetary incentives that are at work. Finally, as identified by Sarraf (2005) and Webber (2007), the simple dynamics of separate ministries for finance and for development or planning, with their own domestic constituencies, and governments' general reluctance to reduce the number of ministerial portfolios, also work against the integration of recurrent and development budgets.

Key Benchmarks for Capital Budgeting Improvements

Some practical recommendations for achieving budget integration in LICs would appear to be useful. In summary, Jacobs (2008) offers the following benchmarks for budgeting of government capital. These recommendations may only be attainable over the medium term.

Determining the Resource Envelope

- Capital expenditure decisions should be based on a consolidated budget approach, incorporating all revenues and expenditures, in particular foreign-financed projects and extrabudgetary funds with investment activities.
- Capital expenditure decisions should be based on a medium-term budget perspective.
- Decisions about capital expenditures should be taken in the context of a hard budget constraint. There should be explicit ceilings for guarantees and commitments beyond the budget year.
- Governments should have clear policies about which capital expenditures should be (1) financed by the budget, (2) realized through public-private partnerships, and (3) handled by government or private enterprises. These policies should reflect the cost structure of the activities and the possibilities for user-financing, as well as political priorities.

Efficient Prioritization and Selection

- The budget calendar and the procedures for integration of capital expenditures in the budget must be clear, transparent, and stable. Development and analysis of capital investment proposals should largely be completed before the budget preparation process starts.
- All projects should be subject to cost-benefit analysis. If the subjection of all projects to CBA is too costly, the focus could primarily be on the larger projects, while using a simplified methodology for smaller projects.
- A government investment agency, with strong links to the Ministry of Finance, should prepare guidelines for project development and analysis. This agency should review project proposals to ensure that they are adequately prepared and analyzed, and should have the authority to reject projects that do not meet the established technical standards.
- The Ministry of Finance should give the cabinet recommendations for which investment projects should be realized within the available resource envelope. Ministries should compete for investment funds based on the net social value and political priority of their investment proposals.
- The decision to implement an investment project should be independent of the financing and procurement modalities for the project. Private–public partnerships (PPPs) can improve risk allocation, but the benefits must be substantial to compensate for increased financing and transaction costs. Decisions regarding PPPs should be an integral part of the budget process, and PPP arrangements should be fully disclosed in budget documents.

Efficient Implementation
- Rules for budget adjustments should give incentives for realistic initial capital cost estimates. Cost overruns during project implementation should be partly covered by reallocation within ministries' existing budgets. Ministries should be allowed to retain part of any real cost reductions.
- Capital investment project proposals should only be considered when they include a detailed disclosure of the expected operating costs, indicating how these will be accommodated within existing resource envelopes or making an explicit proposal for additional financing of the operating costs.
- Capital investment project proposals should only be considered after the ministry has explained how it will fully cover the maintenance of its existing capital stock.
- Governments should avoid excessive targeting of capital expenditures for budget cuts. Decisions on budget cuts should be based on the medium-term budget and take full account of future expenditure pressures as a result of underfunding.
- There should be project completion reports for all capital expenditure projects. These should form the basis for cross-sectoral analysis, methodology development, and continuous improvements in the investment process.

SUMMARY AND CONCLUSIONS

In summary, an effective capital budgeting process should form an integral component of a sound overall budgeting system. A well-designed public financial management system supports each aspect of the system, including capital spending. Good multiyear planning furthermore supports overall fiscal balance, with more stable spending patterns for ministries and programs, and for their capital planning and execution. Good budget execution and procurement will enable timely, within-budget completion of projects (assuming good program and project management). Dorotinsky (2008) states that financial management information systems will support the financial and program management needs of the executive, ministries of finance and economy, spending ministries, and program managers. In addressing these aspects, governments should continuously aim to improve not only their capital budgeting processes, but also their public financial management systems overall. The earlier recommendations for achieving budget integration in some less-advanced countries could be critical for success. However, obtaining the necessary results could take governments several years.

DISCUSSION QUESTIONS

1. Sarraf (2005) and Webber (2007) explain the existence of "dual budgets" in many countries as part of the public financial management structures established by colonial administrations before the 1960s. Why did these dual budgets continue to function even after the demise of the colonial powers in low-income countries?

2. How can LICs achieve improvement in their capital budgeting practices, and what would be the most crucial for success?

3. Discuss the need for clear rules and procedures in the appraisal of government capital projects.

4. Provide a brief overview of the stages of change in government capital budgeting practices.

REFERENCES

Canadian Ministry of Finance. 2010. "Capital Appraisal and Evaluation Checklist." Available at http://www.tbs-sct.gc.ca/pubs_pol/dcgpubs/tbm_122/siglist-eng.asp.

Dorotinsky, William. 2008. "Capital Budgeting and Public Financial Management—Parts I & II." Available at http://blog-pfm.imf.org.

Gupta, Sanjeev, Gerd Schwartz, Shamsuddin Tareq, Richard Allen, Isabell Adenauer, Kevin Fletcher, and Duncan Last. 2008. *Fiscal Management of Scaled-up Aid*. Washington, D.C.: International Monetary Fund.

Jacobs, Davina F. 2008. "A Review of Capital Budgeting Practices." IMF Working Paper, WP/08/160. Washington, DC: International Monetary Fund.

Laursen, Thomas, and Bernard Myers. 2009. *Public Investment Management in the New EU Member States: Strengthening Planning and Implementation of Transport Infrastructure Investments*. Washington, D.C.: World Bank.

Premchand, Agripudi. 2007. "Capital Budgets: Theory and Practice." In Anwar Shah, *Budgeting and Budgetary Institutions*, 89–108. Washington, D.C.: World Bank.

Sarraf, Feridoun. 2005. *Integration of Recurrent and Capital "Development" Budgets: Issues, Problems, Country Experiences, and the Way Forward*. Washington, D.C.: World Bank.

Spackman, Michael. 2001. "Public Investment and Discounting in European Union Member States." *OECD Journal on Budgeting* 1:1, 213–260.

Spackman, Michael. 2002. "Multi-Year Perspective in Budgeting and Public Investment Planning." Working Paper, OECD Global Forum on Sustainable Development, Paris.

Tarschys, Daniel. 2002. "Time Horizons in Budgeting." *OECD Journal on Budgeting* 2:2, 77–103.

United Kingdom Treasury. 2009. *Green Book*. Available at http://www.hm-treasury .gov.uk/data_greenbook_index.htm.

U.S. President's Commission. 1967. *Report of the President's Commission on Budget Concepts*. Washington, D.C.: U.S. Government Printing Office.

Webber, David. 2007. "Integrating Current and Development Budgets: A Four-Dimensional Process." *OECD Journal on Budgeting* 7:2, 93–107.

World Bank. 2006. *Ukraine: Creating Fiscal Space for Growth: A Public Finance Review*. Report No. 36671-UA. Washington, D.C.: World Bank.

ABOUT THE AUTHOR

Davina Frederika Jacobs joined the Fiscal Affairs Department of the International Monetary Fund (IMF) as an economist in 1999. Before joining the IMF, she served for five years in the South African Ministry of Finance's Budget Office and another seven years as economist in the South African Central Advisory Services (CEAS). She has authored several working papers while at the IMF. Her interests span widely across the public policy and public financial management sector field with previous work focusing on fiscal indicators of sustainability, medium-term fiscal and budgetary frameworks, governance issues, budget classification, gender budgeting, and capital budgeting. She is also a regular blogger in the IMF's Public Financial Management Blog, available at http://blog-pfm.imf.org. Dr. Jacobs received a B.Com, Hon. B. Com, and an M. Com in Economics from the University of the Orange Free State, and D. Com in Economics from the University of Pretoria.

Decision Making Using Behavioral Finance for Capital Budgeting

YURI BIONDI
Tenured Research Fellow, French National Center of Scientific Research,
Ecole Polytechnique of Paris

GIUSEPPE MARZO
Tenured Research Fellow, University of Ferrara, and Professor of Business
Economics and Management, University of Ferrara

INTRODUCTION

Accepted methods of capital budgeting are based on the neoclassical assumptions of individual rationality (Ross, 2004) and profit maximization by the business firm. Individuals are then assumed to make their decisions according to the discounted utility model (DUM), formalized by von Neumann and Morgestern (1947) or Savage (1954). They then revise their subjective expectations according to Bayesian rules that ensure the progressive convergence of revised expectations to the "true" probability of events and values. Because risk cannot be priced under this approach (i.e., its price turns out to be zero), the neoclassical framework of analysis further assumes that individuals are risk averse. In a similar vein, the business firm is assumed to be a "slot machine" that discounts future net cash inflows against present net cash outflows where capital budgeting decisions are concerned.

When the clash between theory and reality (and practice) is measured against this peculiar conceptual framework, the most widespread response repeats the "as if" developed by Friedman (1953) and his methodological unrealism. Accordingly, all that matters are the implications of one theory, not the overarching representation of reality upon which such theory is based. This paradoxically leads to a world in which reality is expected to comply with a theory that is unrealistic by definition, which is then understood as the best of the possible worlds: the world that normatively should be attained and the framework with which actors should comply to achieve that world.

Methodological unrealism combined with DUM is not the only approach provided by social scientists interested in financial decision making. According to Fransman (1994), theoretical pluralism has eventually been the driver for human

knowledge development. Simon (1978) has championed the critique of methodological unrealism and the development of an alternative conceptualization. In his
Nobel lecture, Simon stresses numerous logical fallacies in Friedman's (1953) reasoning. By taking the example of falling bodies, Simon (p. 495, fn. 1) concludes: "We
can use [the simple law, ignoring air resistance] to predict the path of a body falling
in a vacuum, but not the path of one falling through the Earth's atmosphere." Accordingly, unrealistic theorizing does not seem the most appropriate method for
driving the construction of parachutes and airplanes. Is it then appropriate as the
foundation for developing financial decision making when confronted with ignorance, hazard, and economic organizational dynamics, realistic features of practice
that are not incorporated under the DUM?

Simon's (1978) Nobel lecture disagrees with accepted doctrine and refers to
the longstanding tradition in the institutional area of economic thought criticizing
the neoclassical assumptions of "individual rationality" and the firm as a "slot
machine." Veblen (1898, pp. 73–74) describes and stigmatizes the neoclassical representation of the human mind as follows: "the hedonistic conception of man is
that of a lightning calculator of pleasures and pains, who oscillates like a homogeneous globule of desire of happiness under the impulse of stimuli that shift him
about the area, but leave him intact. [...] Spiritually, the hedonistic man is not a
prime mover." In the same line of reasoning, Commons (1934, p. 244) called our
historical epoch "the Age of Stupidity." Indeed, Commons argues that people are
not the rational creatures that the Enlightenment had suggested in the eighteenth
century. Rather, Commons (p. 682) held that "man is a being of stupidity, passion,
and ignorance," not to mention guile, theft, and treason.

Concerning the special environment of the business firm, Shubik (1993) contends that actual accounting systems are neglected by neoclassical theorizing. According to the latter, Shubik (p. 74) states:

> Firms are not institutions. Production is described by production correspondences
> available to all who have the resources. It is as though the only items necessary to
> bake a cake were the ingredients and a recipe (free to and immediately understood
> by all). The firm as an entity with an internal organization and a management with
> goals of its own is not included in this abstraction.

On the contrary, Shubik (1993, p. 77) notes that accounting systems factually
are quantifying devices employed in ongoing economic organizations, "directed
towards helping governments and firms to cope with ongoing problems of day
to day and year to year decision-making. First and foremost, accounting of all
varieties has had to grapple with the dynamics of both the firm and government." These accounting systems integrate the institutional structure of production
(Biondi, Canziani, and Kirat, 2007).

Drawing upon this institutional economic perspective, this chapter aims at
disentangling the contribution of the behavioral and institutional approaches to
financial decision making. Both individual decision making and the institutional
rules framing the capital budgeting processes take place in specific organizational
contexts. Behavioral approaches address individual processes of knowledge discovery, treatment, and revision. Institutional approaches deal with cultural, social, and regulatory structures that frame and shape those individual processes.

The rest of the chapter reviews the contribution of each approach along three complementary organizational dimensions and related patterns of research. First, the cognitive dimension introduces a more comprehensive and realistic understanding of the working of the human mind in the context of financial decision making. Second, the organizational dimension explores this decision making in the specific socioeconomic contexts where that decision-making process takes place. Third, the institutional dimension subsumes alternative criteria of decision making that can be taken as a reference according to these behavioral and organizational perspectives.

COGNITIVE DIMENSION

The hypothesis of rationality imposes a peculiar framework on analysis and is based upon various cognitive assumptions. In particular, it requires the complete and timely availability of all the relevant information required to "do the right thing" and the revision of previous decisions and expectations according to Bayesian rules.

By contrast, behavioral research tries to overcome this framework that is fraught with unrealistic tenets and misleading representations of the human mind. It investigates the actual modes of decision making and essentially distinguishes two orders or levels of knowledge that are mobilized to perform the financial decision. From one side, individuals hold, process, and update a specific set of individual worldviews, which are peculiar representations based on their perception of the contextual situation where the decision has been made. From the other side, they apply heuristics and rules of thumb in order to choose among alternative lines of action that are envisioned according to those worldviews.

The Representativeness and Availability Biases

Numerous cognitive biases, documented by Tversky and Kahneman (1982, 1983) and Tversky, Slovic, and Kahneman (1990), among others, affect an individual's decision making. For example, probabilities that individuals assign to an event are influenced by the "representativeness" of that event. Individuals evaluate the probability of an event depending on similarities of that event with well-known classes, disregarding evidence about the underlying probabilities. Consequently, they usually find patterns in random data based on the similarity of those random walks with some nonrandom pattern. People are also affected by the so-called "law of small numbers," which is the tendency to believe that even small-sized samples should reflect the properties of the parent population. For example, if five heads are generated out of five tosses of a fair coin, then people think that tails are due, in order to balance the 50/50 base-rate probability of a fair coin toss.

The "availability bias" acts through recalling similar events from the decision-makers' memory. The easier is the recollection of an event, the higher will be the probability assigned to its occurrence. Researchers also find that people make estimates starting from an initial value (anchoring) and then adjusting it in order to find out the final answer over a series of trials and errors (known as anchor-and-adjust) (Kahneman, Slovic, and Tversky, 1982). Such a bias can affect estimations in cash flows representations.

The Prospect Theory of Kahneman and Tversky

Cognitive biases depart from assumptions of individual rationality and need to be understood from a distinctive framework of analysis. Kahneman and Tversky (1979) develop "prospect theory" in order to take into account the individual decision making as it is factually performed. Through the analysis of individual responses to several prospective games, they find that individuals are affected by the "framing effect." Different ways of presenting the same problem lead to different decisions. Before them, Slovic (1972) demonstrates the existence of such an effect by studying the decisions of medical therapies chosen by individuals in different contextual frames. Benartzi and Thaler (1999) further show the relevance of this framing effect in which subjects systematically judge a share of common stock as riskier when its returns are presented on a weekly basis than when presented on a yearly basis. Weekly volatility is usually greater than yearly volatility, but subjects cannot distinguish between the weekly and the yearly contexts.

According to the new framework of analysis, individual choice is made on the basis of both a "value function," which tabulates the value assigned to a prospect comprising a series of expected payoffs, and a "weighting function" associated with the weight assigned to probabilities associated with those payoffs. In particular, every prospect's value is a function of a reference point, usually the status quo or an aspiration level, with respect to which the prospect's payoffs are coded as gains or losses. The value function is S-shaped, generally concave for gains and convex for losses, and is steeper for losses than for gains. Depending on how the decision is presented, an individual frames the value function in terms of gains or losses with respect to his or her own reference point. The decision maker displays a gain-seeking behavior or a loss-avoiding behavior if the alternative decision is put on the loss side or, respectively, on the gain side. Contrary to practiced DUM, not only do individuals fail to show a unique and positive relationship in the risk-return relationship (subsumed by compound discounting), but they also tend to change the direction of this relationship depending on the way they frame decisions.

Cognitive Biases in Intertemporal Choices

Biases in intertemporal choices are similar to those shown by prospect theory and are well documented. Thaler (1981) and Lazaro, Barberan, and Rubio (2002) provide evidence of persistent deviations and anomalies relative to DUM such as the "common difference effect," the "absolute magnitude effect," and "delay-speedup asymmetry."

Concerning the common difference effect, the "stationary property" of DUM assumes that, given a preference relation between the alternatives $(x; t)$ and $(y; t^*)$ with $y > x$ and $t^* > t$, such a relation still holds when the dates of occurrence of the alternatives are increased by a common time interval, that is, between $(x; t + n)$ and $(y; t^* + n)$. This assumption does not hold in practice as shown in Thaler (1981). Olsen (1993) and Cropper, Aydede, and Portney (1992, 1994) find similar results. This implies that the discount rate appears to decrease as a function of the time delay, implying a hyperbolic or simple discounting formula.

Concerning the absolute magnitude effect, large monetary amounts are less discounted than small ones, proportionally speaking (Thaler, 1981; Benzion, Rapoport, and Yagil, 1989; Chapman and Elstein, 1995). In particular, delay–speedup asymmetry, which constitutes a classic framing effect, implies an asymmetric preference between speeding up a loss and delaying a gain (Loewenstein, 1988). A greater amount is then required to compensate for delaying an incoming reward from t to $t + n$ than for anticipating (speeding up) a loss by the same interval from $t + n$ to t. Loewenstein finds that the former appears to be about two to four times greater than the latter. The two combined imply a discount rate that varies with the size and sign of expected payoffs.

On this basis, Loewenstein and Prelec (1992) systematize intertemporal biases affecting individual choices into a behavioral model of intertemporal choice. Their model is reference-point based and relies, as does prospect theory, on both a discount function and a value function. It includes asymmetry in intertemporal switches, framing effects, effects of prior expectations on choice, higher than market-based discount rates estimated from purchases of consumer durables, and nonmonotonic optimal benefit plans. In particular, the model predicts the tendency to cut investment when profit is lower than anticipated.

The Problems with Dynamic Revision of the Knowledge Basis

Further criticisms of the classic model concern the process of revising decisions or expectations taken on the basis of DUM. Dohmen, Falk, Huffman, Marklein, and Sunde (2009) provide empirical evidence that individuals neither apply Bayesian rules when they revise their knowledge basis nor do their decisions approximate the results provided by those rules. Other studies such as Epstein, Noor, and Sandroni (2010) try to formalize this kind of non-Bayesian updating. In particular, Walliser and Zwirn (2001) suggest distinguishing two orders of probabilities that drive distinctive kinds of revision: one concerns single events (revising) and another concerns wholes of events (updating probabilities of probabilities). In the case of extraction of colored balls from one box, the first-order probability concerns the extraction of one red (black) ball, while the second-order probability concerns the very presence of red (black) balls in the box. Drawing upon the implications of the "law of small numbers," this framework of analysis may be applied to the occurrence of rare events. Rare events seldom occur over time and tend to disappear from individuals' memory. This might lead them to wrongly "update" their worldviews by excluding the very possibility of such events, thus neglecting all the consequences of their rare but still possible occurrence.

ORGANIZATIONAL DIMENSION

This research explores the decision-making process in the specific economic environment where it takes place, whether a business or nonbusiness firm. According to Anthony (2007, p. 208),

> to be consistent with the profit maximization premise, a firm should invest in new assets whenever the return from the investment is equal to or greater than the marginal cost of capital, provided that there is no other available investment opportunity which will permit an even greater return. In theory, therefore, the businessman is supposed always to know his marginal cost of capital, and he is

supposed to know about and evaluate all other investment opportunities every time a project is presented for consideration. [...] Evidently, businessmen take a much less complicated approach; they set up criteria such as maximum payback or minimum acceptable return, which if things work out as anticipated will ensure a satisfactory profit. This leads to quite different working rules from those prescribed by the economists; indeed, the difference in the literature between articles by economists and articles by practical businessmen on this subject is so great that it is difficult to believe they are writing about the same problem.

From the behavioral perspective, the main topics in this area are the representation of expected cash flows for the investment project, the incorporation of optimism and overconfidence biases, and the possibility for an escalation of commitment to a failing course of action related to the sunk cost effect.

The Representation of Expected Cash Flows

Many authors (Hogarth and Makridakis, 1981; Pinches, 1982; Scott and Petty, 1984; Mukherjee, 1987; Kaplan and Ruback, 1995; Strand, 1999) claim that accepted theory is mainly focused on the methodologies and techniques of valuation, while too little attention has been given to both estimating and forecasting expected cash flows. Cash flow forecasting practices potentially contain major cognitive biases, especially those known as optimism and overconfidence. The relevance of these two biases is, however, at issue. While some authors propose a systematic increase in the risk-adjusted discount rate for cash flows (Miller, 1987) in order to offset the biases, others disagree and criticize the methodology of the analysis itself (Brown, 1974; Miller, 1978).

A survey by Kaplan and Ruback (1995) shows that experts' forecasts deviate no more than 10 percent from the realized value of transactions. However, Hribar and Yang (2006) provide evidence that overconfident chief executive officers (CEOs) are more likely to undermine their own forecasts of earnings and to issue point forecasts (that is, forecasts that are based on a single value instead of a range). Also, the forecasts of overconfident CEOs have a narrower range. The findings of these studies suggest that experts may create forecasts that are as biased as behavioral finance scholars maintain.

While optimism can be understood as the increase of the mean of expected values, overconfidence produces a reduction of the expected variance of these values. Optimism translates into the overvaluation of expected inflows as well as the undervaluation of expected outflows (Hogarth and Makridakis, 1981). Kahneman and Lovallo (1993) show that optimism in estimates usually comes from the fact that decision makers isolate the actual problem from its contextual situation. Decision makers neglect future opportunities, past experiences, and available statistics. This brings them to behave optimistically, in spite of analyzing past and prospective data. Weinstein (1980) finds that the degree of desirability, perceived probability, personal experience, perceived controllability, and stereotype salience may influence the degree of optimistic bias. Puri and Robinson (2007) show that optimism is related to numerous work and life choices. For example, more optimistic people work harder, expect to retire later, are more likely to remarry, invest more in individual stocks, and save more. The authors also find that while moderate optimists have reasonable financial behavior, those who are overly optimistic generally behave in an imprudent way.

Overconfidence and representativeness biases can influence the capital budgeting processes. According to Kahneman et al. (1982, p. 8), predictions of future prices (or profits) depend on insensitivity to predictability and are subject to the representativeness bias: "If the description of the company is very favorable, a very high profit will appear most representative of that description; if the description is mediocre, a mediocre performance will appear most representative." According to Kahneman and Riepe (1998), the human mind appears to work as a pattern-seeking device. This leads decision makers to give a rational meaning to events that can actually be random. For example, even though the following two sequences derived from tossing a coin—HHHTTT and HTHTTH (where H stands for heads and T for tails)—have the same probabilities, the second sequence is perceived to be more random than the first one.

The Optimism Bias

Controlling for optimism in cash flows representations is performed either in audit analysis, when forecasted cash flows are compared to actual, or by asking users of cash flow estimations if they feel cash flows are optimistically forecasted. Pohlman, Santiago, and Markel (1988) conduct a survey of the Fortune 500 companies and find a significant difference between forecasted and actual cash flows, even though the differences might result from factors other than optimism such as agency costs and accidental events. They also find that defining the figures that an unbiased estimator would predict is difficult. Marshall and Meckling (1962) confirm the presence of optimism bias after making a Bayesian correction of prior estimates to account for unexpected events at the time of forecasting.

Statman and Tyebjee (1985) design an experiment based on a previous study by Cyert, March, and Starbuck (1961) to verify that users of estimates are aware that they may be optimistically biased. The authors find that many users believe that estimates are systematically biased towards optimism and the seniority of users is positively correlated with such a belief. In particular, users with more than three years of experience tend to overly correct their estimations. In their survey of Fortune 500 companies, Pruitt and Gitman (1987) find that analysts' capital forecasts are optimistically biased and managers adjust estimates downward to offset such upward bias. Statman and Tyebjee confirm that more experienced people tend to adjust estimates to compensate for optimism. Ascher (1993) reviews several project appraisals undertaken by the World Bank and finds that forecasted return rates are optimistically biased and are therefore higher than actual realized rates of return.

Some models try to capture such optimistic bias. For example, Heaton (2002) develops a model with overoptimistic managers and efficient capital markets. According to the model, if managers believe that the firm is undervalued in capital markets, they may either underinvest if financial outsourcing is required, or overinvest in negative net present value (NPV) projects, even if they are still assumed to act in shareholders' interest. Thus, a mix of under- and overinvestment can exist independent of any agency cost or opportunistic behavior. Tyebjee (1987) shows that managers more engaged in new product development projects are usually more optimistic and that, during the planning process, they hold some "illusion of control," that is, the tendency to believe that controlling or having an influence on outcomes is possible, even if this is not true (Langer, 1982).

Glaser, Schäfers, and Weber (2008) further analyze the phenomenon by focusing on all senior managers instead of a single manager's behavior. The authors find that when managers are optimistic, they increase their exposure to company-specific risk when transacting company stocks and invest more. Their evidence also shows that managerial optimism increases their investment–cash flow sensitivity. Similarly, Lin, Hu, and Chen (2005) find that in firms confronted with higher financing constraints, optimistic management implies higher investment–cash flow sensitivity.

The Overconfidence Bias

The overconfidence bias is related to the representativeness heuristic. Representativeness occurs when the decision makers feel that the decision problem in which they are engaged is similar to other issues with which they have already dealt. Overconfidence can be rooted in individuals' personality (Schaefer, Williams, Goodie, and Campbell, 2004) or generated by contingent situations. Langer (1982) analyzes the role of the "illusion of control," which involves a false faith in personal capabilities. Langer distinguishes among skill-based situations, when a causal relationship exists between skilled behavior and performed result, and lucky situations, where good luck plays the major role. Because subjects can frame lucky situations as skill-based situations, they wrongly believe that they have the situation under control.

Decision makers are sometimes overconfident because they no longer exactly remember what they thought at the moment of valuation. Using hindsight, decision makers seek to justify what they did and thus rationalize any previous decision (this is the so-called hindsight bias). Radzevick and Moore (2008) contend that people are more confident when their own side is strong and this feeling is independent of the strength of the competition. They link this effect to the fact that people have better information about their own side than the other side. By contrast, Moore and Cain (2007) show that overconfidence is not as universal as it is often supposed to be. Their paper presents evidence that people usually feel below average on difficult skill-based tasks.

Empirical researchers have investigated overconfidence bias in corporate executive decision makers. Ben-David, Graham, and Harvey (2007) find evidence that executives are overconfident. Companies with overconfident CEOs use lower discount rates for investment valuation, finance projects using more debt, and use proportionally more long-term debt. CEOs are also less likely to pay dividends. Malmendier and Tate (2005a, 2005b) find similar results. Camerer and Lovallo (1999) show evidence of the effect of overconfidence on start-up investments. Cooper, Woo, and Dunkelberg (1988) survey 2994 entrepreneurs and find them to be optimistic and overconfident. Entrepreneurs see very favorable prospects, with 81 percent of the interviewees viewing the odds of success as 7 out of 10 or better and 33 percent perceiving such odds as 10 out of 10. The authors also document that entrepreneurs believe that they can control their own destiny, the "control illusion" effect. Cooper et al. further find that past experience does not mitigate this perception.

Continuing this line of inquiry, Ucbasaran, Westhead, Wright, and Flores (2010) find that entrepreneurs do not appear to adjust their optimism for past business failures. Koellinger, Minniti, and Schade (2007) find that subjective and often biased perceptions have a crucial impact on new business creation across all the countries in their sample. They report that the national environment with its social and cultural underpinnings plays a significant role. Further, their evidence shows a negative correlation between overconfidence and the survival chances of nascent entrepreneurs.

The Sunk Cost Effect

The way decisions makers represent sunk cash flows can also lead to flaws in their analysis. Sunk costs are expenses made in the past that cannot be recovered. Such costs should not affect the valuation of a project under the DUM model. This treatment is commonly covered in standard finance texts. In particular, sunk costs should not affect the decision whether undertaking, continuing, or stopping the project. Because sunk costs do not influence a project's future cash flows, the analyst should ignore them in performing the valuation of the investment. However, sunk costs affect differential cash flows from continuing or stopping the project. If the firm stops a project, sunk costs should be accounted for as losses, and the manager in charge of that project would be accountable for them.

Contrary to DUM theory, many studies provide evidence that decision makers often consider sunk costs in making their decisions (Arkes and Blumer, 1985; Kogut, 1990; Roodhooft and Warlop, 1999). Fantino (2004) argues that poor decision making is often the result of the misapplication of rules and principles that have led to effective decisions in the past. This especially applies to the base-rate fallacy, which refers to the tendency to ignore background information in favor of case-specific cues in assessing the probability of an event, and the sunk cost effect. Roodhooft and Warlop show that sunk costs are relevant in the make-or-buy decision even after controlling for other opportunistic and relational variables.

Keasey and Moon (2000) perform experiments that confirm the sunk cost effect. Specifically, their evidence shows that subjects are more likely to continue a bad project if they have already made a prior investment. Fellner (2009) studies the decision to terminate a project. He finds that the sunk cost effect affects executives and project managers differently and that the scale of the project is unrelated to the perception of failure. Parayre (1995), adopting a constructive critical perspective, develops a theoretical model that shows the conditions under which the sunk cost effect can be a successful precommitment strategy. In sum, under conditions of limited knowledge, Arrow (1974, p. 6) notes that "the past is relevant because it contains information which changes the image of the future; the probabilities which govern future actions are modified by observations on the past. It follows that present decisions with implications for the future are functions of past values of variables as well as present values."

Dealing with Opportunity Costs

Cash flow representation should also deal with opportunity costs. *Opportunity cost* is the value or return a decision maker gives up by choosing one alternative rather than another. In the DUM approach, opportunity cost is an important element for choosing alternative investment opportunities that is captured through the use of solely incremental cash flows in valuation. Psychological studies, however, find that the consideration of opportunity costs in valuation is often absent or disvalued (Chenhall and Morris, 1991; Casey, 1994).

Kahneman, Knetsch, and Thaler (1986, 1990, 1991) study the behavior of subjects asked to set a price for buying or selling a predefined widget. As expected, selling prices are usually greater than buying prices. In setting the prices, incurred costs associated with actual cash outflows are valued more than opportunity costs. This problem of incorporating opportunity costs relates to the so-called "endowment effect," which states that an asset is valued more if it is already held by the valuing subject. Thaler (1980) argues that even though opportunity and out-of-pocket costs should receive the same treatment according to DUM theory, subjects actually provide very different valuations for them.

The Escalation of Commitment to a Failing Course of Action

The escalation of commitment to a failing course of action is a well-known phenomenon that refers to continued investment in a project when expected future results are negative and suggest abandoning it. Researchers such as Staw (1974, 1976) have studied this phenomenon since the 1970s. It is now recognized as a major pitfall in the control of an investment project. This phenomenon is related to the sunk cost effect. According to self-justification theory (Festinger, 1957; Staw and Fox, 1977; Brockner, 1992), individual responsibility, especially when formalized in organizational terms, can push the person in charge to continue a project despite negative expected results. Individual commitment is usually rewarded and is judged as a characteristic of a reliable human being. The choice of pursuing a failing course of action can then result from the inability of decision makers to free themselves from the social norms in which they are embedded (Staw, 1981).

Another explanation for escalation is rooted in prospect theory (Kahneman and Tversky, 1979). Individuals are loss-averse in the loss side, especially when they deal with alternatives characterized by high expected losses and low probable positive results (the loss aversion bias). This is, of course, a potential source of the commitment escalation effect since the attempt to avoid the high expected losses leads individuals to choose the continuation of the project. In this way, their loss and failure will be delayed and they can go on hoping to eventually generate positive outcomes in the future. Finally, specialization can provide another explanation for the commitment escalation effect (Williamson 1985, 1991; Zardkoohi, 2004). Because the value of specialized and project-specific resources is greater when they are employed by the undertaken project than elsewhere, the abandonment of a failing project contrasts with the preservation of the project-specific value of those resources.

INSTITUTIONAL DIMENSION

Under DUM, criteria such as NPV and internal rate of return (IRR) are considered as the only appropriate criteria when making capital budgeting decisions. The biases discussed in the prior sections suggest that alternative criteria incorporating cognitive and organizational dimensions may be desirable. In fact, traditional practitioner criteria such as payback period or a preference for financial slacks have been treated as heresy or stupidity and dismissed on the grounds of failing to meet DUM criteria.

However, ease of understanding and implementation are important features for adopting a capital budgeting methodology. In a survey conducted on the capital budgeting methods adopted by Fortune 500 companies, Burns and Walker (1997) show that ease of use is of paramount importance in choosing between capital budgeting methods. Easiness can then be considered as a meta-criterion for evaluating capital budgeting projects. Other factors that influence the choice of decision criteria include familiarity with valuation methods; the comprehensibility of different methods; and the ease of data gathering and calculation. As a result, "crude" but simpler methodologies can survive competition from sophisticated but overcomplicated techniques.

Alternative Rationales

This section explore three topics offering rationales for departing from accepted models of investment valuation: (1) the adoption of hurdle rates for investment project valuation and selection; (2) the adoption of selection criteria that are second-best criteria or absolutely suboptimal criteria in the light of the DUM approach, such as payback period; and (3) a generalization of discounting based on different rates for discounting and replacing cash flows from investment projects.

Hurdle Rates and Capital Budgeting

Some studies find that firms use discount rates higher than a theoretically "correct" rate such as one based on the capital asset pricing model (CAPM) (Summers, 1987; Kaplan and Atkinson, 1988; Drury, 1990). They argue that such errors can compromise the firms' competitiveness due to an underinvestment phenomenon resulting from using artificially higher rates. A discount rate that is too high can also be detrimental for firm continuity.

Identifying an appropriate discount rate may involve several potential problems. For example, even if decision makers agree on using the CAPM to determine the cost of a firm's equity, the calculation of such a rate can result in different figures depending on the econometric tools and measures applied during the calculation process. According to several studies, the range of discount rates may be very large and vary between 4.5 and 6 percent (Copeland, Koller, and Murrin, 1991), 6 to 8 percent (Brealey, Myers, and Allen, 2006), 2 to more than 8 percent (Jagannathan and Meier, 2002), and –10 to 20 percent (Shefrin, 2007).

Welch (2000) documents how economists do not share a common perspective on discounting. The use of differing hurdle rates can then depend on (and be justified on the basis of) the application of different models by firms and researchers. The comparative validity of the differing models is still at issue from a theoretical perspective. A useful example to illustrate this idea is the so-called "beta-dead" strand of research. Fama and French (1992, 1993) criticize the ability of the beta approach to efficiently reflect the relevant systematic risk of a security. They do this by showing its ineffectiveness in predicting assets' returns.

The authors then argue for better explanatory factors related to fundamental analysis and accounting information such as the market-to-book ratio. Stein (1996) still supports using the CAPM for rational capital budgeting, but different perspectives on the effectiveness of beta can translate into different approaches to calculating the discount rate.

The use of hurdle rates (or discount rates higher than theoretically correct ones) might also be treated as a pragmatic response to overoptimism and overconfidence biases in cash flows estimation. Some authors such as Hogarth and Makridakis (1981), Statman and Tyebjee (1985), and Pohlman et al. (1988) find a systematic overvaluation of the expected cash flows accruing to investment projects. In this case, adopting higher discount rates is a crude way to compensate for such upward estimates. This type of adjustment may create two alternative kinds of problems. First, decision makers may then be confident of having corrected both optimism and overconfidence, while these biases could still persist. Second, if the overestimation of cash flows by managers is a heuristic tool for incorporating the value of embedded real options that are not explicitly valued, then the higher discount rate can offset the greater value assigned to the project's expected but unincorporated cash flows (Busby and Pitts, 1998).

External or internal financial rationing is a further justification for using hurdle rates. In the case of external rationing, hurdle rates operate as a substitute for the profitability index. For example, Mukherjee (1991) highlights that a hurdle rate is more understandable than other criteria of project selection such as the profitability index. Concerning internal financial rationing, hurdle rates might operate as a mechanism of organizational control in order to balance information asymmetries (Antle and Eppen, 1985; Arya, Fellingham, and Glover, 1998). When information is asymmetrically available within a firm, the divisions proposing an investment project are usually better informed on the likely profitability of the project than their headquarters. Because divisions may then aim to retain resource slacks, headquarters may react by adopting an internal system of financial rationing. In such a context, hurdle rates are detached from project risks and serve as a tool for allocating financing among the firm's divisions by taking into account opportunistic slack behavior.

Departing further from DUM assumptions, hurdle rates may also be a tool for dealing with dynamic sustainability or continuity of the firm (Marzo, 2007). Finance theory and the CAPM are essentially static in the sense that they assume market pricing takes into account all possible future contingencies. Static approaches assume implicitly that markets are complete, as did the original Arrow and Debreu (1954) model. However, complete markets for any future contingency only exist in theory. A firm applying the CAPM (or any other market-based calculation of project risk) could obtain, at best, only the maximization of static efficiency that neglects other alternative options different from those actually available.

To make a decision that is consistent over time (dynamic perspective), firms should consider that current prices could not (and actually do not) integrate any possible future use of every present and future resource. Such deficiency is firmly related to the fact that innovation takes place in firms, not in markets, and its value depends on inner specificities and structures (or systems) that supersede the market price system. To take into account future opportunities originated by such a firm-specific environment, management can use hurdle rates to constrain current proposals and therefore save current cash funds for future projects still under development. This behavior can be even more pronounced if the firm expects to suffer from financial constraints such as a lack of cash availability in the future. In sum, hurdle rates can act appropriately as internal tools for valuing and selecting investment projects, especially under intertemporal financially constrained conditions.

Valuing Investment Projects by Payback Period

The DUM approach claims that compounded or discounted cash flow (DCF) techniques (not only NPV and IRR but also those based on real options analysis) are the optimal criteria for valuing and selecting investment. In particular, in the simplest situation of a project that does not embed real options, the NPV method is assumed to define the value of the project. Surveys show that although DCF techniques are increasingly employed during the last few decades, corporate management still uses other DUM suboptimal methods or "rules of thumb" (Sangster, 1993; Graham and Harvey, 2001).

In particular, behavioral finance scholars such as Shefrin (2007) argue that using the payback period criterion reflects the decision makers' cognitive errors, linked to their inability to learn how to correctly value investment projects. In fact, the role of this method should not be undermined. Even if using the payback period derives from a low level of managerial sophistication, it may also be useful in some circumstances.

First, suppose that a firm is comparing two alternative investment projects, A and B, with the same NPV. If the two projects are evaluated by using the "right" risk-adjusted rate of return, the firm should be indifferent to choosing A or B. However, the cash flow profiles of the two projects may differ over time. For example, project A's lower cash flows are expected to occur at more near future periods, while B's higher cash flows are expected to take place at more distant future periods. The manager may then effectively apply the payback period as a way of dealing with future financial constraints or uncertainties, on the basis that estimates for the distant future are in principle less reliable and more subject to disappointment and hazard. Therefore, project A dominates B because its value is less exposed to the remote future.

Second, the above discussed hurdle rate approximation of the optimal exercise of a "wait-and-see" option can be translated in terms of the payback period (Boyle and Guthrie, 1997; McDonald, 1999). Accordingly, given the stochastic process of the project's cash flows, when the maximum value of the option is approaching, the payback period of the investment declines relative to the past, making the payback period an acceptable heuristic for valuing the investment alternative.

Finally, the payback period is a way to cope with cash or budget constraints because it ranks projects in terms of their speed in refunding the investor. That is, payback shows the length of time needed for cash inflows to cover the initial outflows incurred by the investment project.

A Generalization of Discounting under Multiple Discount Rates

Investment valuation criteria ultimately relate to the fundamental relationship between investment decision making and time. The DUM approach was developed to fit competitive market pricing and conditions that are assumed to clear the financial market or put the economic system into general equilibrium. However, such an approach may be at odds with viable rules under conditions of ignorance, hazard, and organizational dynamics.

All financial decisions implicitly deal with the future. Discounting is a practical method to account for the timing of the investment projects that have to be assessed, resulting in two measurement outcomes: a conventional measure for net economic value, and a comparative ranking of different opportunities at disposal.

The discounting approach incorporates the time element of the project in its cash inflows and outflows to rank the different opportunities. The value of this element contributes to frame the current decision into an understanding of the future states of the ongoing activity. Thus, discounting is expected to enhance the decision makers' understanding of time horizons.

There are different views about discounting. The DUM approach adopts a market basis and stresses only a positive compound discounting rate. Samuelson (1976, pp. 473–474) defines this rate both as the *"market* standard of performance" and the *competitive* opportunity rate for inside investment projects. Welfare economics questions the level of the discount rate in the case of welfare choices involving the "claims of posterity." Some industrial economists such as Hayes and Garvin (1982, p. 70) further criticize the logic underlying compound discounting and argue that

> An over-reliance on analytic techniques like discounting future cash flows leads managers to defer critical investments in the capital stock on which their companies depend. Such techniques and the assumptions on which they rest, claim these authors, inevitably bias managers against investment and thus short-change the future of American industry.

Following the same line of reasoning, Porter (1998, p. 466), speaking about corporate investment and industrial time horizons, criticizes the American capital investment system and stresses the need to "evaluate investments in two stages—first, determining the asset positions needed for competitiveness and second, evaluating exactly how to achieve those positions." According to Porter (p. 439), every investment has to cope with special conditions related to corporate goals and organizational principles, senior management intervention, and capital allocation and investment monitoring systems. From this perspective, investment valuation criteria are important in affecting the corporate investment decision-making process. Within the firm, running the business is then the priority. Corporate management is called to make investment valuation suitable for the special context and needs of the firm. From the same perspective, Shackle (1967, p. 99) suggests considering money as "not useful in itself," but as "a store of strategic power."

Within the firm, the view of the financial process of investing provided by the DUM approach appears to be incomplete. This approach is especially concerned with a market basis and general competitive conditions under complete and perfect markets. It neglects, therefore, the special economics of relational economic contexts that cope with the specifics of the business firm. Samuelson (1976, p. 473) once called the critique of discounting the "bogey of compound interest." Scared by the bogey, decision makers would be unable to cope with the future of the ongoing activity since the preference for today is computed only by a negative compound weight on future states. The bogey leads to neglecting the financial process of investing that is concerned with real time and context. Investment opportunities could then be misevaluated and the whole investment information treating process may be biased when decision makers operate under the compound discounting scheme.

Recent advances in relational contracting and behavioral finance support and expand that earlier critique:

- According to Baker, Gibbons, and Murphy (2001, 2002) and Biondi, Canziani and Kirat (2007), markets and firms should be understood as two different economic environments. Managerial tasks in the firm require judgment and knowledge of the specifics of complex situations. The firm as a relational economic context must provide its special way to coordinate these tasks because they cannot be controlled by outside market arrangements. In short, firms must have management and related decision-making rules because their governance cannot replicate the market. In particular, this managerial coordination allows firms to improve on market outcomes. Inside investment projects can have better returns of reference than the outside returns from market alternative replacements.
- Recent developments in behavioral finance fostered by Kahneman and Tversky (1979) stress the need for a double choice in the investment decision-making process: a weighting function that establishes the weights for each expected result and a value function that ranks the expected results themselves (Kahneman and Riepe, 1998; Frankfurter and McGoun, 1999; Marzo, 2002).
- The influential works of Loewenstein and Thaler (1989), Loewenstein and Prelec (1992), and Laibson (1997) argue for simple or hyperbolic discounting coupled with a behavioral approach to economic individual preferences.

Notwithstanding, decision makers are accustomed to considering rules based on compound discounting (either present value or IRR) as the benchmark for their investment decisions. A new interpretation of discounting seems to be required to bridge the gap between the recent theoretical insights and widespread practices. The new interpretation may generalize valuation rules to the relational economic context that frames all those investment projects to be assessed.

What is, therefore, the actual meaning of discounting? Decision makers look at discounting to estimate the value of timing and to establish some conventional criterion to compare internal (that is, firm-specific) investment opportunities. Under this scheme, a single measurement is called to summarize each investment project in order to portray a vast collection of operations, conditions, risks, and results in a simple and effective way. From this perspective, discounting is expected to provide the shortcut method to obtain such a measure. The discounting measurement process is consistent with the statistical notion of the mean of the cash flows sequence, whose weight must be established according to the decision-makers' perspectives and to the ongoing continuity (and future conditions) of the whole business activity.

Every business activity constitutes a special relational economic context. Its decision makers receive information through numerous channels that treat and reduce that information by various ways and under special conditions. Discounting is one of the information-treating devices that allows decision makers to rank and choose investment opportunities. Because this process is laden with ignorance, hazard, and dynamics, the information provided is typically blurred or filtered information, meaning that some aspects of the information may be obscured or lost.

In this context, the DCF-based approach attempts to deliver information in a form that permits only one rational conclusion. However, the information generating process actually affects the decision. In fact, empirical researchers deny that common measures such as NPV and IRR play a clear-cut role in choosing between alternative investment projects (Sangster, 1993). Investment issues are so critical that they require judgment and knowledge of the specifics involving complex and dynamic activities. The information-filtering process only provides some pieces of information that are relevant and reliable to make decisions. Decision makers have still recourse to various measures including payback and accounting rate of return that are harshly criticized by advocates of the DUM approach. Investment valuation criteria based on DCF analysis are widespread and influential. Yet, decision makers also use criteria based on alternative approaches, including some that are theoretically incompatible with DUM, to gather relevant information about each investment opportunity. All these investment valuation criteria are then more complement than substitute, and together provide a better picture of the project scope and implications.

This appears to be the spirit of discounting as an information-treating device in actual investment decision making. One particular flaw of the DCF scheme deserves to be overcome. As Baldwin (1959, pp. 98–99) claims:

> It is to one critical assumption underlying the usual procedure [of present value and IRR] that I take strong exception. The future receipts and payments are reduced to their present value by discounting them at the same rate as that which the proposed investment is estimated to provide. In other words, management assumes that, for the period between the base point and the time when the funds are spent or collected, the funds are, or could be, invested at the rate of return being calculated for the proposal. This is simply not true. Indeed, it is only by coincidence that the two would be at all alike.

According to recent theoretical developments, every business activity generates a special financial process, which produces inside returns that are expected to improve on the outside returns from alternative replacements. As an information-treating device involved in this process of investing, discounting can no longer neglect time and context. It has to account for these different returns of reference instead of one unique rate in order to take into account the replacement structure of future inflows. In particular, a generalization of discounting may apply to the conventionally established cash flow pattern in which the actual replacement mix is comprised of replacements at compound interest, at simple interest (bonds and so on), or has a more complex return structure. Following this line of reasoning (Biondi, 2010), the generalization provides a family of financial measures based on at least two discount rates of reference, one for inside investment (y) and another for outside replacement (i), represented as:

$$\sum_{t=0}^{n} f(1+i; 1+y; t; a_t) \cdot a_t \text{ or, in a continuous time: } \int_{0}^{n} f(y; i; t; a_t) a_t dt \qquad (22.1)$$

where $a_0 \ldots a_n$ = the cash flow sequence for the investment project; y = the discount rate for outflows (negative cash flows); and i = the discount rate for inflows (positive cash flows). This formulation may be further generalized to multiple rates over time instead of one constant rate for the entire period, and to expected measures for each flow: $E_t(a_t)$. This generalization differs from the usual approach based on compound discounting alone:

$$\sum_{t=0}^{n} (1+i)^{-t} \cdot a_t \quad \text{or} \quad \int_{0}^{n} e^{-i \cdot t} \cdot a_t dt. \qquad (22.2)$$

The difference between NPV and IRR based on compound discounting ultimately rests on the different assumptions about the replacement (reinvestment) rates and term structure. In the case of NPV, the replacement is assumed to be made at the discount rate, while in the case of IRR, it would be made at the same rate as IRR. Thus, the generalized approach vindicates the return-based measures like IRR and logically unifies discounted values and discounted rates of return. Usual measures with one unique discount rate for investment and replacement, as well as other measures based on compound (exponential) or simple (hyperbolic) discounting, become special cases of the generalized function $f(y;i;t;a)$. This function declares the underlying discounting logic and describes the relationship between inside investments and time horizons applied by decision makers to compare inside investment opportunities. A change in the replacement rate clearly modifies the project's return, but it does not modify its comparative ranking. Further studies on the relevant properties of $f(y;i;t;a)$ may be developed. For example, Rubinstein (2000) suggests a function where the discount factor f_t is decreasing in t and increasing in a_t (the larger the sum of money at stake, the higher (closer to 1) is the discount factor). She suggests a procedural rationality approach framed with nonexpected utility theory (see also Kahneman and Riepe, 1998; Frankfurter and McGoun, 1999).

The DUM approach assumes that the project's investment rate and the replacement rate are the same, and this would be true under a perfect capital market. Yet, if capital markets are imperfect and firms are conditioned by capital rationing, this approach will lead to under (over) valuing the discounted value of low (high) return projects. This is because the cash inflows from the projects are reinvested at the same rate as the cash outflows, while the actual rates of reference differ. For instance, by assuming that the rate of reference for discounting is the investment rate, the usual IRR over (under) values investment projects with high (low) rate of return. This implies that cash flows from projects with high (low) return will be reinvested at a higher (lower) rate, hence leading to over (under) valuation of the project. The usual approach fails to consider more realistic reinvestment opportunities available to the firm and may mislead the capital budgeting process, especially when ranking alternative investment projects.

SUMMARY AND CONCLUSIONS

The accepted approach to capital budgeting leaves decision makers without appropriate guidance because it ignores the cognitive, organizational, and institutional dimensions of their decision. This chapter has summarized alternative perspectives addressing these specific dimensions. Together, they suggest generalizing the current approach based on DCF analysis to provide decision makers with alternative ways to assess investment opportunities under more realistic approaches driven by behavioral and institutional finance.

DISCUSSION QUESTIONS

1. What are the basic tenets of prospect theory? Why is this theory so important for behavioral finance?
2. Which cognitive and organizational biases affect the representation of cash flows to be employed in capital budgeting?
3. What is the role of hurdle rates in behavioral capital budgeting?
4. Is the hypothesis of one unique discount rate for financing and investing appropriate for capital budgeting? How can this hypothesis be generalized?

REFERENCES

Anthony, N. Robert. 2007. "The Trouble with Profit Maximization." In Yuri Biondi, Arnaldo Canziani, and Thierry Kirat. *The Firm as an Entity: Implications for Economics, Accounting, and Law*, 201–215. New York and London: Routledge.

Antle, Rick, and Gary D. Eppen. 1985. "Capital Rationing and Organizational Slack in Capital Budgeting." *Management Science* 31:2, 163–174.

Arkes, Hal R., and Catherine Blumer. 1985. "The Psychology of Sunk Cost." *Organizational Behavior and Human Decision Processes* 35:1, 124–140.

Arrow, Kenneth J. 1974. "Limited Knowledge and Economic Analysis." *American Economic Review* 64:1, 1–10.

Arrow, Kenneth J., and Gérard Debreu. 1954. "The Existence of an Equilibrium for a Competitive Economy." *Econometrica* 22:3, 265–290.

Arya, Anil, John Fellingham, and Jonathan Glover. 1998. "Capital Budgeting: Some Exceptions to the Net Present Value Rule." *Issues in Accounting Education* 13:3, 499–508.

Ascher, William. 1993. "The Ambiguous Nature of Forecasts in Project Evaluation: Diagnosing the Over-Optimism of Rate-of-Return Analysis." *International Journal of Forecasting* 9:1, 109–115.

Baker, George, Robert Gibbons, and Kevin J. Murphy. 2001. "Bringing the Market Inside the Firm?" *American Economic Review* 91:2, 212–218.

Baker, George, Robert Gibbons, and Kevin J. Murphy. 2002. "Relational Contracts and the Theory of the Firm." *Quarterly Journal of Economics* 117:1, 39–84.

Baldwin, H. Robert. 1959. "How to Assess Investment Proposals." *Harvard Business Review* 37:3, 98–104.

Benartzi, Shlomo, and Richard H. Thaler. 1999. "Risk Aversion or Myopia? Choices in Repeated Games and Retirement Investments." *Management Science* 45:3, 364–381.

Ben-David, Itzhak, John R. Graham, and Campbell R. Harvey. 2007. "Managerial Overconfidence and Corporate Policies." Available at http://ssrn.com/abstract==890300.

Benzion, Uri, Amnon Rapoport, and Joseph Yagil. 1989. "Discount Rates Inferred from Decisions: An Experimental Study." *Management Science* 35:3, 270–284.

Biondi, Yuri. 2010. "Cost of Capital, Discounting, and Relational Contracting: Optimal Return and Duration Criteria for Joint Investment Projects." *Applied Economics*. Forthcoming. Available at http://ssrn.com/abstract=1330587.

Biondi, Yuri, Arnaldo Canziani, and Thierry Kirat, eds. 2007. *The Firm as an Entity: Implications for Economics, Accounting and Law.* New York and London: Routledge.

Boyle, Glenn W., and Graeme A. Guthrie. 1997. "Payback and the Value of Waiting to Invest." Available at http://ssrn.com/abstract==74.

Brealey, Richard A., Stewart C. Myers, and Franklin Allen. 2006. *Principles of Corporate Finance.* Boston: McGraw-Hill.

Brockner, Joel. 1992. "The Escalation of Commitment to a Failing Course of Action: Toward Theoretical Progress." *Academy of Management Review* 17:1, 39–61.

Brown, Keith C. 1974. "A Note on the Apparent Bias of Net Revenue Estimates for Capital Investment Projects." *Journal of Finance* 29:4, 12-15.

Burns, Richard M., and Joe Walker 1997. "Capital Budgeting Techniques among the Fortune 500: A Rational Approach." *Managerial Finance* 23:9, 3–15.

Busby, Jerry S., and C. G. C. Pitts. 1998. *Assessing Flexibility in Capital Investment. A Guide to Applying Real Options Principles in Investment Appraisal.* London: CIMA.

Camerer, Colin, and Dan Lovallo, 1999. "Overconfidence and Excess Entry: An Experimental Approach." *American Economic Review* 89:1, 306–318.

Casey, Jeff T. 1994. "Buyers' Pricing Behavior for Risky Alternatives: Encoding Processes and Preference Reversals." *Management Science* 40:6, 730–749.

Chapman, Gretchen B., and Arthur S. Elstein. 1995. "Valuing the Future: Temporal Discounting in Health and Money" *Medical Decision Making* 15:4, 373–386.

Chenhall, Robert, and Deigan Morris. 1991. "The Effect of Cognitive Style and Sponsorship Bias on the Treatment of Opportunity Costs in Resource Allocation Decisions." *Accounting, Organizations and Society* 16:1, 27–46.

Commons, R. John. 1934. *Institutional Economics. Its Place In Political Economy.* New York: Macmillan.

Cooper, Arnold C., Carolyn Y. Woo, and William C. Dunkelberg. 1988. "Entrepreneurs' Perceived Chances for Success." *Journal of Business Venturing* 3:2, 97–108.

Copeland, Tom, Tim Koller, and Jack Murrin. 1991. *Valuation: Measuring and Managing the Value of Companies.* New York: John Wiley & Sons.

Cropper, Maureen L., Sema K. Aydede, and Paul R. Portney. 1992. "Rates of Time Preference for Saving Lives." *American Economic Review* 82:2, 469–472.

Cropper, Maureen L., Sema K. Aydede, and Paul R. Portney. 1994. "Preferences for Life Saving Programs: How the Public Discounts Time and Age." *Journal of Risk and Uncertainty* 8:3, 243–265.

Cyert, Richard M., James G. March, and William H. Starbuck. 1961. "Two Experiments on Bias and Conflict in Organizational Estimation." *Management Science* 7:3, 254–264.

Dohmen, Thomas, Armin Falk, David Huffman, Felix Marklein, and Uwe Sunde. 2009. "The Non-Use of Bayes Rule: Representative Evidence on Bounded Rationality." ROA Research Memorandum Series, ROA-RM-2009/1 February. The Netherlands: University of Maastricht. Available at http://www.roa.unimaas.nl/resmem.htm.

Drury, Colin. 1990. "Counting the Cost of AMT Investment." *Accountancy* 105:1160, 134–137.

Epstein, Larry G., Jawwad Noor, and Alvaro Sandroni. 2010. "Non-Bayesian Learning." *The B.E. Journal of Theoretical Economics* 10:1 (Advances). Available at http://www.bepress.com/bejte/vol10/iss1/art3.

Fama, Eugene F., and Kenneth R. French. 1992. "The Cross-Section of Expected Stock Returns." *Journal of Finance* 47:2, 427–465.

Fama, Eugene F., and Kenneth R, French. 1993. "Common Risk Factors in the Returns on Stocks and Bonds." *Journal of Financial Economics* 33:1, 3–56.

Fantino, Edmund. 2004. "Behavior-analytic Approaches to Decision Making." *Behavioural Processes* 66:3, 279–288.

Fellner, Gerlinde. 2009. "Illusion of Control as a Source of Poor Diversification: Experimental Evidence." *Journal of Behavioral Finance* 10:1, 55–67.

Festinger, Leon. 1957. *A Theory of Cognitive Dissonance*. Stanford: Stanford University Press.

Frankfurter George M., and Elton G. McGoun. 1999. "Ideology and the Theory of Financial Economics." *Journal of Economic Behavior and Organization* 39:2, 159–177.

Fransman, Martin. 1994. "Information, Knowledge, Vision and Theories of the Firm." *Industrial and Corporate Change* 3:2, 1–45.

Friedman, Milton. 1953. *Essays in Positive Economics*. Chicago: University of Chicago Press.

Glaser, Markus, Philipp Schäfers, and Martin Weber. 2008. "Managerial Optimism and Corporate Investment: Is the CEO Alone Responsible for the Relation?" Available at http://ssrn.com/abstract==967649.

Graham, John R., and Campbell R. Harvey. 2001. "The Theory and Practice of Corporate Finance: Evidence from the Field." *Journal of Financial Economics* 60:2–3, 187–243.

Hayes, H. Robert, and Garvin A. David. 1982. "Managing as If Tomorrow Mattered." *Harvard Business Review* 60:3, 70–79.

Heaton, J. B. 2002. "Managerial Optimism and Corporate Finance." *Financial Management* 31:2, 33–45.

Hogarth, Robin M., and Spyros Makridakis. 1981. "The Value of Decision Making in a Complex Environment: An Experimental Approach." *Management Science* 27:1, 93–107.

Hribar, Paul, and Holly Yang. 2006. "Does CEO Overconfidence Affect Management Forecasting and Subsequent Earnings Management?" Available at http://ssrn.com/abstract==929731.

Jagannathan, Ravi, and Iwan Meier. 2002. "Do We Need CAPM for Capital Budgeting?" *Financial Management* 31:4, 55–77.

Kahneman, Daniel, and Dan Lovallo. 1993. "Timid Choices and Bold Forecasts: A Cognitive Perspective on Risk Taking." *Management Science* 39:1, 17–31.

Kahneman, Daniel, and Mark W. Riepe. 1998. "Aspects of Investor Psychology." *Journal of Portfolio Management* 24:4, 52–65.

Kahneman, Daniel, and Amos Tversky. 1979. "Prospect Theory: An Analysis of Decision under Risk." *Econometrica* 47:2, 263–292.

Kahneman, Daniel, Jack Knetsch, and Richard H. Thaler. 1986. "Fairness and the Assumptions of Economics." *Journal of Business* 59:4, S285–S300.

Kahneman, Daniel, Jack Knetsch, and Richard H. Thaler. 1990. "Experimental Tests of the Endowment Effect and the Coase Theorem." *Journal of Political Economy* 98:6, 1325–1348.

Kahneman, Daniel, Jack Knetsch, and Richard H. Thaler. 1991. "Anomalies: The Endowment Effect, Loss Aversion and the Status Quo Bias." *Journal of Economic Perspectives* 5:1, 193–206.

Kahneman, Daniel, Paul Slovic, and Amos Tversky. 1982. *Judgment under Uncertainty: Heuristics and Biases*. Cambridge: Cambridge University Press.

Kaplan, Robert S., and Anthony A. Atkinson. 1998. *Advanced Management Accounting*, Englewood Cliffs, NJ: Prentice Hall.

Kaplan, Steven, and Richard S. Ruback. 1995. "The Valuation of Cash Flow Forecasts: An Empirical Analysis." *Journal of Finance* 1:4, 1059–1093.

Keasey, Kevin, and Philip Moon. 2000. "Sunk Cost Effects: A Test of the Importance of Context." *Economics Letters* 66:1, 55–58.

Koellinger, Philipp, Maria Minniti, and Christian Schade. 2007. "'I Think I Can, I Think I Can': Overconfidence and Entrepreneurial Behavior." *Journal of Economic Psychology* 28:4, 502–527.

Kogut, Carl A. 1990. "Consumer Search Behavior and Sunk Costs." *Journal of Economic Behavior and Organization* 14:3, 381–392.

Laibson, David. 1997. "Golden Eggs and Hyperbolic Discounting." *Quarterly Journal of Economics* 112:2, 443–477.

Langer, Ellen J. 1982. "The Illusion of Control." In Daniel Kahneman, Paul Slovic, and Amos Tversky, (eds.), *Judgment under Uncertainty: Heuristics and Biases*, 230–238. New York: Cambridge University Press.

Lazaro, Angelina, Ramon Barberan, and Encarnacion Rubio. 2002. "The Discounted Utility Model and Social Preferences: Some Alternative Formulations to Conventional Discounting." *Journal of Economic Psychology* 23:3, 317–337.

Lin, Yueh-hsiang, Shing-yang Hu, and Ming-shen Chen. 2005. "Managerial Optimism and Corporate Investment: Some Empirical Evidence from Taiwan." *Pacific-Basin Finance Journal* 13:5, 523–546.

Loewenstein, George F. 1988. "Frames of Mind in Intertemporal Choice." *Management Science* 34:2, 200–214.

Loewenstein, George F., and Drazen Prelec. 1992. "Anomalies in Intertemporal Choice: Evidence and an Interpretation." *Quarterly Journal of Economics* 107:2, 573–597.

Loewenstein, George, and Richard H. Thaler. 1989. "Anomalies: Intertemporal Choice." *Journal of Economic Perspectives* 3:4, 181–193.

Malmendier, Ulrike, and Geoffrey A. Tate. 2005a. "Does Overconfidence Affect Corporate Investment? CEO Overconfidence Measures Revisited." *European Financial Management* 11:5, 649–659.

Malmendier, Ulrike, and Geoffrey A. Tate. 2005b. "Who Makes Acquisitions? CEO Overconfidence and the Market's Reaction." *Journal of Financial Economics* 89:1, 20–43.

Marshall Andrew, and William Meckling. 1962. "Predictability of the Costs, Time, and Success of Development." In National Bureau of Economic Research, ed. *The Rate and Direction of Inventive Activity: Economic and Social Factors*, 461–476. Princeton: Princeton University Press.

Marzo, Giuseppe. 2002. "La relazione tra rischio e rendimento: Proposte teoriche e ricerche empiriche" ("The Risk-Return Relationship: Theories and Empirical Evidence"), *Serie Working Papers del Dipartimento di Economia Aziendale*, Università degli Studi di Brescia 22.

Marzo, Giuseppe. 2007. "Economics and Finance of the Firm as an Entity." In Yuri Biondi, Arnaldo Canziani, and Thierry Kirat, eds. *The Firm as an Entity: Implications for Economics, Accounting, and Law*, 317–347. London and New York: Routledge.

McDonald, Robert L. 1999. "Real Options and Rules of Thumb in Capital Budgeting." In Michael J. Brennan and Lenos Trigeorgis, eds. *Project Flexibility, Agency and Product Market Competition*, 13–33. London: Oxford University Press.

Miller, Edward M. 1978. "Uncertainty Induced Bias in Capital Budgeting." *Financial Management* 7:3, 22–28.

Miller, Edward M. 1987. "The Competitive Market Assumption and Capital Budgeting Criteria." *Financial Management* 16:4, 22-28.

Moore, Don A., and Daylian M. Cain. 2007. "Overconfidence and Underconfidence: When and Why People Underestimate (and Overestimate) the Competition." *Organizational Behavior and Human Decision Processes* 103:2, 197–213.

Mukherjee, Tarun K. 1987. "Capital-Budgeting Surveys: The Past and the Future." *Review of Business and Economic Research* 22:2, 37–56.

Mukherjee, Tarun K. 1991. "Reducing the Uncertainty–Induced Bias in Capital Budgeting Decisions—A Hurdle Rate Approach." *Journal of Business Finance and Accounting* 18:5, 747–753.

Olsen, Joseph A. 1993. "Time Preference for Health Gains: An Empirical Investigation." *Health Economics* 2:3, 257–265.

Parayre, Roch. 1995. "The Strategic Implications of Sunk Costs: A Behavioral Perspective." *Journal of Economic Behavior and Organization* 28:3, 417–442.

Pinches, George E. 1982. "Myopia, Capital Budgeting and Decision Making." *Financial Management* 11:3, 6–19.

Pohlman, Randolph A., Emmanuel S. Santiago, and F. Lynn Markel. 1988. "Cash Flow Estimation Practices of Large Firms." *Financial Management* 2:2, 71–79.

Porter, E. Michael. 1998. *On Competition.* Cambridge, MA: Harvard Business University Press.

Pruitt, Stephen W., and Lawrence J. Gitman. 1987. "Capital Budgeting Forecast Biases: Evidence from the Fortune 500." *Financial Management* 16:1, 46–51.

Puri, Manju, and David T. Robinson. 2007. "Optimism and Economic Choice." *Journal of Financial Economics* 86:1, 71–99.

Radzevick, Joseph R., and Don A. Moore. 2008. "Myopic Biases in Competitions." *Organizational Behavior and Human Decision Processes* 107:2, 206–218.

Roodhooft, Filip, and Luk Warlop. 1999. "On the Role of Sunk Costs and Asset Specificity in Outsourcing Decisions: A Research Note." *Accounting, Organizations and Society* 24:4, 363–369.

Ross, Stephen A. 2004. *Neoclassical Finance.* Princeton: Princeton University Press.

Rubinstein, Ariel. 2000. "Is It 'Economics or Psychology'?: The Case of Hyperbolic Discounting." Working Paper 00-21, Tel-Aviv University, The Foerder Institute for Economic Research.

Samuelson, Paul A. 1976. "Economics of Forestry in an Evolving Society." *Economic Inquiry,* 14:4, 466–492.

Sangster, Alan. 1993. "Capital Investment Appraisal Techniques: A Survey of Current Usage." *Journal of Business Finance and Accounting* 20:3, 307–331.

Savage, Leonard J. 1954. *The Foundations of Statistics.* New York: John Wiley & Sons.

Schaefer, Peter S., Cristina C. Williams, Adam S. Goodie, and W. Keith Campbell. 2004. "Overconfidence and the Big Five." *Journal of Research in Personality* 38:5, 473–480.

Scott, David F., and J. William Petty. 1984. "Capital Budgeting Practices in Large American Firms: A Retrospective Analysis and Synthesis." *Financial Review* 19:1, 111–123.

Shackle, George L. S. 1967. *The Years of High Theory: Invention and Tradition in Economic Thought 1926–1939.* Cambridge: Cambridge University Press.

Shefrin, Hersh. 2007. *Behavioral Corporate Finance.* New York: Irwin/McGraw-Hill.

Shubik, Martin. 1993. "Accounting and Its Relationship to General Equilibrium Theory." In Yuri Biondi, Arnaldo Canziani, and Thierry Kirat, eds. *The Firm as an Entity: Implications for Economics, Accounting, and Law,* 73–81. New York and London: Routledge.

Simon, A. Herbert. 1978. "Rational Decision Making in Business Organizations." *American Economic Review* 69:4, 493–513.

Slovic, Paul. 1972. "Psychological Study of Human Judgment: Implications for Investment Decision Making." *Journal of Finance* 27:4, 779–799.

Statman, Meir, and Tyzoon T. Tyebjee. 1985. "Optimistic Capital Budgeting Forecasts: An Experiment." *Financial Management* 14:3, 27–33.

Staw, Barry M. 1981. "The Escalation of Commitment to a Course of Action." *Academy of Management Review* 6:4, 577–587.

Staw, Barry M. 1974. "Attitudinal and Behavioral Consequences of Changing a Major Organizational Reward: A Natural Field Experiment." *Journal of Personality & Social Psychology* 29:6, 742–751.

Staw, Barry M. 1976. "Knee-Deep in the Big Muddy: A Study of Escalating Commitment to a Chosen Course of Action." *Organizational Behavior and Human Performance* 16:1, 27–44.

Staw, Barry M., and Frederick V. Fox. 1977. "Escalation: Some Determinants of Commitment to a Previously Chosen Course of Action." *Human Relations* 30:5, 431–450.

Stein, Jeremy C. 1996. "Rational Capital Budgeting in an Irrational World:" *Journal of Business* 69:4, 429–455.

Strand, Sverre. 1999. "Forecasting the Future: Pitfalls in Controlling for Uncertainty." *Futures* 31:3–4, 333–350.

Summers, Lawrence H. 1987. "Investments Incentives and the Discounting of Depreciation Allowances." In Martin Feldstein, ed. *The Effects of Taxation on Capital Accumulation*, 295–304. Chicago: University of Chicago Press.

Thaler, Richard H. 1980. "Toward a Positive Theory of Consumer Choice." *Journal of Economic Behavior and Organization* 1:1, 39–60.

Thaler, Richard H. 1981. "Some Empirical Evidence on Dynamic Inconsistency." *Economics Letters* 8:3, 201–207.

Tversky, Amos, and Daniel Kahneman. 1982. "Judgment Under Uncertainty: Heuristics and Biases." In Daniel Kahneman, Paul Slovic, and Amos Tversky, eds. *Judgment under Uncertainty: Heuristics and Biases*, 84–98. Cambridge: Cambridge University Press.

Tversky, Amos, and Daniel Kahneman. 1983. "Extensional Versus Intuitive Reasoning: The Conjunction Fallacy in Probability Judgment." *Psychological Review* 90:4, 293–315.

Tversky, Amos, Paul Slovic, and Daniel Kahneman. 1990. "The Causes of Preference Reversal." *American Economic Review* 80:1, 204–217.

Tyebjee, Tyzoon T. 1987. "Behavioral Biases in New Product Forecasting." *International Journal of Forecasting* 3:3–4, 393–404.

Ucbasaran, Deniz, Paul Westhead, Mike Wright, and Manuel Flores. 2010. "The Nature of Entrepreneurial Experience, Business Failure and Comparative Optimism." *Journal of Business Venturing*. Forthcoming.

Veblen, Thorstein. 1898. "Why Is Economics Not an Evolutionary Science?" *Quarterly Journal of Economics* 12:4, 373–397.

Von Neumann, John, and Oskar Morgestern. 1947. *Theory of Games and Economic Behavior.* Princeton: Princeton University Press.

Walliser, Bernard, and Denis Zwirn. 2001. "Change Rules for Hierarchical Beliefs." Paris School of Economics (PSE) Working Paper. Available at http://www.pse.ens.fr/walliser/pdf/wz10.pdf.

Weinstein, Neil D. 1980. "Unrealistic Optimism about Future Life Events." *Journal of Personality and Social Psychology* 39:5, 806–820.

Welch, Ivo. 2000. "Views of Financial Economists on the Equity Premium and on Professional Controversies." Available at http://ssrn.com/abstract==171272.

Williamson, E. Oliver. 1985 *The Economic Institutions of Capitalism: Firms, Markets, Relational Contracting.* New York and London: Free Press.

Williamson, E. Oliver. 1991. "Comparative Economic Organization: The Analysis of Discrete Structural Alternatives." *Administrative Sciences Quarterly* 36:2, 269–296.

Zardkoohi, Asghar. 2004. "Response. Do Real Options Lead to Escalation of Commitment?" *Academy of Management Review* 29:1, 111–119.

ABOUT THE AUTHORS

Yuri Biondi is a tenured research fellow of the French National Center of Scientific Research (CNRS) at the Ecole Polytechnique of Paris and affiliated professor at the CNAM of Paris. He is editor-in-chief of *Accounting, Economics and Law—A Convivium* (published by The Berkeley Electronic Press) and editor of *The Firm as an Entity: Implications for Economics, Accounting and Law* (Routledge, 2007). His research interests include economic theory and economics, accounting, and finance of business and nonbusiness organizations. He graduated from Bocconi University of Milan, University of Lyon, University of Brescia, and Sorbonne University of Paris.

Giuseppe Marzo is a tenured research fellow of Business Economics and Management at the University of Ferrara and a Professor of Business Economics and Management at the University of Ferrara. He is a member of the Advisory Board of *Accounting, Economics and Law—A Convivium* and the co-editor of *Visualising Intangibles: Measuring and Reporting in the Knowledge Economy* (Ashgate, 2007). His interests are in the fields of real options theory, business finance, behavioral finance, intangible assets valuation, and the methodology of finance. He received his Ph.D. from the University Ca' Foscari of Venice.

CHAPTER 23

Merger and Acquisition Pricing: The Valuation of Synergy

RAINER LENZ
Professor of International Finance, University of Applied Sciences, Bielefeld

INTRODUCTION

Globalization and economies of scale effects fuel corporate merger activities in nearly every sector. Nevertheless, empirical studies show that most mergers and acquisitions (M&As) are unsuccessful and destroy shareholders' wealth. In hindsight, finding that the acquirer paid too high a price relative to the achieved synergy is reasonably straightforward. Which methods can a manager use for the valuation of future synergy effects, and how can the value of synergy be incorporated into merger pricing? If the firm's management had a clear picture of the relationship between the takeover premium being paid and the expected synergy gains, it could potentially avoid making some irrational decisions.

The valuation of synergy is vital to the success of any merger. Given current valuation methodologies and the complexity of the task, valuing synergy is also the most challenging element of M&A pricing. Conventional valuation methods assume that sales figures and the market share of the acquiring company are easily transferable within the new entity. Current synergy practices also assume that amalgamating various corporate functions will produce substantial cost reductions. The key component missing from current methodologies is the failure to analyze every corporation as a complex system containing various elements and relationships. If a merger constitutes such a delicate system, analysts cannot accurately forecast the outcome measured in turnover and profit by simply aggregating key financial figures.

The goal of this chapter on M&A pricing is to go beyond the simplicity of current methods in order to develop a methodology better suited for evaluating synergy effects. The first step is to create a model for benchmarking the success of a merger. This valuation model links the takeover premium paid at the beginning to the needed synergistic return. The next step is to propose a new method for valuing synergy, which uses traditional capital budget instruments and integrates elements from both the framework of knowledge management and sociological system theory. This holistic approach provides an innovative solution for the complex problem of M&A pricing and could enhance the success rate of mergers.

TYPES OF MERGERS AND SYNERGY

The terms *merger* and *acquisition* are often used synonymously despite slight differences. If two companies of similar size agree to unite as one new single corporation to explore the benefits of larger economic scale, it is called a merger. In this sense, mergers do not often occur in practice. An acquisition typically occurs when a larger company takes over a smaller one. The stock of the acquired company ceases to exist, while the stock of the acquiring company continues to trade in the market. Acquisitions are more common than mergers in today's globalized and highly competitive markets. The distinction between a merger and an acquisition helps to identify which company is acting and which one is reacting, but has less relevance for the pricing process. The creation of synergy effects through the formation of a new single economic unit is highly important and often determines the success of a merger. Firms can attain different types of synergy effects through various types of mergers. In general, M&As are categorized in three different types of integration:

- *Horizontal integration* is a merger of two forms in the same business (e. g., two competitors).
- *Vertical integration* is a combination of two businesses at different points on the value chain (e. g., a supplier and its customer).
- *Conglomerate mergers* are the combination of companies in unrelated lines of business (e. g., a manufacturer and an insurance company).

Economies of scale are the most common motive for horizontal mergers (Gorton, Kahl, and Rosen, 2009). Producing a higher number of goods with the same fixed costs leads to a decline in average costs per unit. This strategy focuses mainly on cost-cutting effects. In horizontal mergers, all corporate functions such as treasury, marketing, sales, production, administration, and research are duplicated and provide the opportunity to combine functions and to scale down working staff and management. Additionally, savings could result from sharing central facilities such as headquarters, top management, and information technology. Eccles, Lanes, and Wilson (1999) note that these kinds of cost savings are sometimes called "hard synergies," which should signal the high level of certainty that they materialize. The basic assumption of this approach is that the market share and turnover of the companies will increase, while the sum of the costs will decrease.

Some view financial synergies as a special case of the economies of scale effect. Clearly, a merger between firms increases the volume of refinancing by debt or equity capital. Sometimes higher volume opens doors to financial markets for corporate bonds or asset-backed securities. Commercial banks regularly request for securitization a minimum volume of debt or assets due to the high transaction costs of this process. In this regard, a merger could eventually lower refinancing costs as bond market yields are lower than bank loan rates at the same level of credit risk. A broader access to bond markets could shift the company's financing structure toward a higher share of debt, which subsequently leads to lower average costs of finance. Hence, a decline in the firm's weighted average cost of capital (WACC) should result from this alteration. Conversely, a higher debt-to-equity ratio may deteriorate the firm's credit rating and results in additional interest expenses. Consequently, the overall effect of a merger on the firm's financing condition remains unclear.

Revenue enhancement is second on the list of merger motives after cost-cutting effects (Eccles et al., 1999). Revenues of combined firms can be leveraged by cross selling existing products through new distribution channels or using the new strength in distribution power for placing new products with higher profit margins. All these effects are hard to predict as the customer base of the acquired firm is not a fixed variable. Some customers will avoid buying products from the merged company if they fear an increasing economic dependence on one supplier. Additionally, market conditions could change as remaining competitors may react in response to an acquisition. Generally, revenue enhancement strategies take more time to show results than cost-cutting decisions do; but, on the other hand, their positive impact on corporate earnings is long lasting and not a one-time occurrence.

The incentive for vertical mergers is primarily to gain greater control in the value chain (Fan and Goyal, 2006). The reasons for taking over supplier firms may include ensuring a certain quality standard in input goods, receiving specific technology know-how in producing strategically valuable input materials, or synchronizing operating activities of suppliers with producers of final goods. While in past decades companies found outsourcing various types of production and services efficient, some have observed a contrary trend in recent years (Sikula, Kim, Braun, and Sikula, 2010). Automobile manufacturers serve as a good example of vertical mergers. The use of defective materials by suppliers to manufacturers of automobiles causes most recalls from automotive producers (Murphy, Winter, and Mayne, 2003). The guarantee of a certain quality of automobile causes current producers to reintegrate former outsourced production parts in a reverse trend.

Some justify conglomerate mergers by contending that diversification across business lines helps maintain the current level of earnings, reduces uncertainty of future profit development, and, therefore, stabilizes a long-term growth path. Such diversification decreases unsystematic risk and leads to reduced volatility. This diversification effect can be achieved by adding a sufficient number of assets to the portfolio. However, Markowitz's (1952) portfolio theory is based on the assumption of unrestricted market liquidity, which is present for tradable financial market assets such as stocks and bonds. This precondition is not present for the assets underlying conglomerates, as transaction costs and the market liquidity of buying or selling companies or real investments are not comparable to financial market assets. Shareholders will not pay a premium for firms that diversify because they could do that on their own much more efficiently. Thus, conglomerate mergers tend to misallocate scarce funds by subsidizing investments with poor growth opportunities for the sake of reducing the overall business risk of the conglomerate.

THE SUCCESS OF MERGERS AND THE VALUATION OF SYNERGY PREMIUMS

The failure rate for mergers is astonishing with more than half failing to provide any notable increase to shareholders' wealth. Researchers have coined this phenomenon the "post-merger underperformance puzzle" (Antoniou, Arbour, and Zhao, 2006). The benchmark for success in a merger has to be clearly defined to have a discussion about failure rates. Brealey, Myers, and Allen (2007) define a merger as successful when the postmerger value of the integrated firm is higher than the sum of the paid acquisition price for the acquired firm and the value of the acquiring firm before the merger. Therefore, assuming that firm A would choose to merge with firm B, success could be defined as follows:

$$V_C^0 > P_B^0 + V_A^0 \tag{23.1}$$

where

V_C^0 = Value of the combined firm AB in period 0
P_B^0 = Acquisition price for firm B in period 0
V_A^0 = Value of firm A in period 0

Defining success in this way has the advantage of enabling application of well-known investment criteria such as net present value (NPV). Consequently, investments with a positive NPV can be deemed a success. The sum of the acquisition price and value of firm A could be interpreted as the payout in period 0, and the value of the combined firm C should be seen as the present value of a future return on investment (V_C^0).

Only synergies, such as economies of scale, can lead to returns on investments that justify a merger or acquisition. Typically, *synergy* is defined as a benefit that occurs when the value of the combined firm C exceeds the collective values of the separate entities. In general, synergy effects are of central importance in nearly every scientific discipline. Expressions such as mutualism, win-win situations, critical mass, co-evolution, threshold effects, and non-zero-sum games are used to capture the underlying sense of what a synergy is in practice (Corning, 2003). The total synergy value resulting from a merger equals the difference between the combined firm's value and the sum of each individual firm's value (Equation 23.3).

$$V_C^0 > V_A^0 + V_B^0 \tag{23.2}$$
$$S_C^0 = V_C^0 - (V_A^0 + V_B^0) \tag{23.3}$$

where
V_C^0, V_A^0, and V_B^0 are as previously defined
S_C^0 = Value of the synergy in total in period 0

The acquisition price frequently exceeds the value of firm B, due to the additional premium paid to firm B's shareholders. Selecting the market capitalization of a company as a benchmark for corporate value, the acquisition price per share is in many cases 40 to 60 percent higher than the actual share price (Moeller, Schlingemann, and Stulz, 2005). For obvious reasons, shareholders of firm B will not sell or exchange their shares if they cannot realize a higher price relative to that prevailing in the stock market. Therefore, the premium can be seen as an incentive given to shareholders to part with their existing stock. The acquiring company is willing to pay the requested premium to shareholders because it expects a much greater synergistic return to result from the merger. Consequently, the premium payout to the seller could be interpreted as the seller's anticipated synergy premium (Equation 23.4). The buyer's synergy premium is merely the difference between the total synergy and seller's premium (Equation 23.5).

$$P_B^0 = V_B^0 + S_{SP}^0 \tag{23.4}$$

$$S_C^0 - S_{SP}^0 = S_{BP}^0 \tag{23.5}$$

where

P_B^0 = Acquisition price in period 0
V_B^0 = Value of firm B in period 0
S_{SP}^0 = Seller's synergy premium in 0
S_{BP}^0 = Buyer's synergy premium in period 0

The success of any merger requires that the NPV of the buyer's synergy premium be at least slightly positive. Rewriting Equation (23.1), success of a merger can be defined as follows:

$$V_C^0 - \left(V_A^0 + V_B^0\right) - S_{SP}^0 > 0 \tag{23.6}$$

Even though a positive buyer's synergy premium fulfills the criterion for a successful merger, the terms may not be equitable for both sides. As the primary risk taker in the merger, shareholder A should receive at least the equivalent synergy premium as shareholder B. Taking such a fair value criterion into account, the total synergy outcome from a merger for a given period should be twice as high as the premium paid for the acquisition of firm B. The calculation of the total synergy premium should also incorporate the time value of money and any risk that the synergies will not crystallize through an appropriate discount rate.

$$S_C^T = \left[2 * \left(P_B^0 - V_B^0\right)\right] * (1 + r)^T \tag{23.7}$$

The following considerations allow for the development of a benchmark, which can be used to accurately assess the success of a merger. The postmerger value of the integrated firm has to be equal to or greater than the sum of the firm values A and B and the total synergy premium. The value of a merger can then be measured either in the present or future, as long as both figures are taken at the same point in time. Hence, the benchmark of success could be formalized at the time when the merger happens as in Equation (23.8) or at a point in the future as in Equation (23.9).

$$V_C^0 - \left(V_A^0 + V_B^0\right) - \left[2 * \left(P_B^0 - V_B^0\right)\right] \geq 0 \tag{23.8}$$

$$V_C^T - \left[\left(V_A^0 + V_B^0\right) * (1 + r_f)^T\right] - \left[2 * \left(P_B^0 - V_B^0\right) * (1 + r)^T\right] \geq 0 \tag{23.9}$$

where
V_C^0, V_A^0, V_B^0, and P_B^0 are as previously defined
r_f = Risk-free interest rate
r = Risk-adjusted interest rate
T = Fixed point of time in future

DIFFERENT ELEMENTS—DIFFERENT PRICING

The definition of success shows that any M&A pricing should contain three elements: (1) valuation of the acquired corporate system B and the acquiring corporate system A; (2) valuation of the new corporate system C; and (3) the division of the synergy premium between the buyer and the seller. The new firm C should be valued independently from the pricing process of corporations A and B, as synergies will only arise if the two economic systems merge and form a new single unit. Consequently, throughout the pricing process, treating corporation C as a new economic system is essential. Given this logic, the precise value of corporation C cannot be determined by the sum of A and B plus some synergy.

Systems theory provides a holistic view of what transpires during the merger process and offers a guideline for acquisition pricing. This approach views a corporation as a complex economic system of interdependent elements and relationships. A company is an open system, insofar as it exists in a mutual relationship (input and output relationships) to its environment. Every element in a firm is organically linked with one another in the firm's system of organization, corporate culture, organizational routines, and activities (Gupta and Ross, 2001). Sales, turnover, and profit are directly correlated to the regular interaction of interrelated groups of activities within a corporate system. Mergers disrupt this harmonic balance by removing and adding certain elements and corporate functions. As a direct result of this modification, the measurable output in the form of sales, revenue, and turnover also varies substantially. The merger of two intricate systems leads to creating a new corporate system, firm C, with its own distinctive elements and relationships. Any valuation of such a system, given its uniqueness and individuality, requires a separate pricing process.

Output categories such as sales, turnover, profit, or earnings before interest and taxes (EBIT) are completely intertwined within corporate systems, which frequently interact with one another. Relationships between variables can also be illustrated using mathematical functions. Therefore, the profit of firm A is directly correlated to a corporate system function "$f(a_1, a_2, a_3...)$" with its variables 'a', which symbolize corporate units such as sales, production, and finance. Subsequently, the expected profit of the new entity C is the outcome of the corporate system function of C with its merged corporate functions of system A and system B. Functional relationships between variables 'a' and 'b' within the new corporate system C are unique and not linked by simple value additivity.

$$\text{Profit A} = f(a_1, a_2, a_3, a_4....) \tag{23.10}$$

$$\text{Profit C} = f(a_1 b_1, a_2 b_2, a_3 b_3, a_4 b_4, ...) \tag{23.11}$$

Exhibit 23.1 illustrates this way of thinking in system categories.

The valuation process of firms A and B differs markedly from the valuation process of firm C. Pricing firms A and B is made slightly easier given their existing systems and assuming the elements and relations within the systems will not be modified or split. With the process of performance unaltered, valuation of A and B can be found in various sources of codified and publicly available information, such

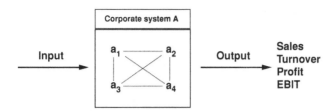

Exhibit 23.1 The Corporate System
Note: A company is an open system as it exists in a mutual relationship (input and output relationships) to its environment. Every element (symbolized by a1...a4) in this corporate system is organically linked with one another and embedded in the corporation's system of organization, culture, routines, and activities. Output figures such as sales, turnover, and profit are directly correlated to the regular interaction of interrelated groups of activities within the corporate system.

as turnover and EBIT, located in balance sheets and business reports. No additional knowledge of the corporate system function is required for the valuation of A and B.

Contrary to this, firm C constitutes a unique corporate system. Hence, its valuation requires additional internal information concerning the relations and elements within the system. Without an existing system in place, a performance projection of system C could only be derived from internal and system-specific knowledge about the elements and relationships of system A and system B. Codified knowledge about the performance of firm C in the form of balance sheets or business reports does not exist. Furthermore, codified knowledge pertaining to A and B is less applicable due to an absence of value additivity. Therefore, any pricing of firm C uses system-specific knowledge of A and B in order to develop a vision about the interaction of elements and interrelations in the new system C, as well as all future performance processes.

This new approach to valuing mergers refers to the theory of knowledge management, which distinguishes between two forms of knowledge: implicit and explicit knowledge (Polanyi, 1967). Applied to the merger problem, revenue, sales, turnover, earnings, and profit are the outcomes of a system and could be interpreted as explicit information. Information about relationships between the single elements within a corporate system could be called the tacit or implicit knowledge. Explicit and implicit elements of knowledge are complementary and are not considered mutually exclusive (Nonaka and Takeuchi, 1997). This principle of knowledge management, applied to the identification of synergy sources in a merger, can lead to a more holistic view of corporate value. Recognizing tacit knowledge also contributes to identifying synergy.

The Valuation of the Existing Corporate Systems A and B

Based on the assumption that a corporation continues to operate independently, both economically and legally, after the acquisition, sources of publicly available codified information such as business reports and balance sheets could be used for the purpose of valuation. To determine a fair value for the potential acquisition candidate, analysts use a wide range of valuation techniques and methods. These methods, with their specific assumptions, often produce differing values, despite sharing common characteristics. These methods generally fall under three categories: (1) asset-oriented approaches, (2) income-oriented approaches, and (3) methods based on multiples and ratios.

Asset-oriented Approaches

The starting point for any asset-oriented approach is the balance sheet as a tabular representation of a firm's assets and liabilities at a particular point in time (Aluko and Amidu, 2005). The simplest technique available to any investor is to calculate the book value, also known as shareholder's equity, or the net worth of a company. Because book values of assets and liabilities reported on the balance sheet rarely reflect their current market values, investors often make necessary adjustments toward current market prices. Occasionally, when market values are not readily attainable for specific assets or are distorted, replacement costs of assets should be viewed as a proxy variable.

The obvious weakness of the asset-oriented approach is its backward orientation. Hence, book values of a balance sheet reflect only past performance based on historical revenues and costs, while the valuation of any investment requires a projection of future cash flows. Asset-oriented approaches are incapable of deriving future-oriented information directly.

Income-oriented Approaches

This technique is future-oriented and calculates the current value of the firm based on projected earnings or cash flows. The most common approach, the discounted cash flow (DCF) method, uses free cash flow (FCF) derived from corporate financial statements as a benchmark for financial performance. FCF measures the cash generated by a business regardless of the financial structure. Future FCF for the planned period is then discounted by a risk-adjusted rate. The risk-adjusted rate, known as the WACC, reflects investors' opportunity costs. The estimated value of the target company is obtained by summing all discounted FCFs, plus the discounted terminal value. As Brealey et al. (2007) note, the terminal value or horizon value defines the value of the company by the end of the analyzed period.

$$\text{DCF value} = \sum_{t=1}^{T} \frac{FCF_t}{(1+r)^t} + \frac{TV_T}{(1+r)^T} \qquad (23.12)$$

where

> FCF = Free cash flow
> r = Discount rate (or WACC)
> TV = Terminal value
> t = Period of time

Forecasting implies a degree of inaccuracy. A change in certain key assumptions or estimated variables, such as the discount rate, the growth rate, and capital requirements, can widely alter DCF values. Equally critical is the forecasted terminal value, as it often contributes above 50 percent to the total NPV.

Methods Based on Multiples and Ratios

Analysts often use multiples in financial markets. For example, they may determine the fair value of a share by comparing the firm's individual financial ratio to the average ratio of firms in the same industry segment. The basic principle underlying these methods is the *law of one price*, which states that in competitive markets identical goods sold in different countries must sell for the same price, ignoring transaction costs. Applied to the valuation problem, this "law" states that corporations operating in the same industry segment with identical sales revenues, earnings, and equal assets should have the same value. Based on this principle, a relationship between corporate value and some corporate performance variables such as earnings, turnover, or cash flow can be calculated for firms within a specific industry segment.

Therefore, any valuation by the multiple market approach is based on the general assumption that the corporate value is a linear function of the deviation of the firm's specific variable (e. g., assets, sales, and revenues) from the defined market standard. Despite this, practice often exhibits subtle differences that are of substantial importance. One would then expect value estimations based on multiples to lack accuracy, particularly when individual firms differ markedly from the market average. Empirical studies confirm this assessment (Lie and Lie, 2002).

Based on a sample of more than 700 firms engaged in acquisitions during 1990 to 2001, Mukherjee, Kiymaz, and Baker (2004) show that 49.3 percent of respondents prefer the DCF method, followed by 33.3 percent for the combination of the DCF approach plus market multiple analysis. Although the survey does not ask explicitly about the use of asset-oriented approaches, about 5 percent of respondents indicate using additional methods. Each method surveyed refers to external information and fails to use internal information generated by individual analysis. However, traditional methods of evaluation are justifiable if firms continue to maintain existing corporate structures while operating independently after the merger.

The Valuation of the New Corporate System C

The valuation process of synergies is analogous to corporate risk management in some respects. For example, both focus on business processes analysis, are future-oriented, deal with uncertainty, and aggregate all information about risks and synergies into a single overall figure. The difference is that synergies are the chance or the positive result of an uncertain definite event. Synergy and operational risk can be seen as two sides of the same coin in that the risk of a merger is that expected synergies fail to materialize. The task of corporate risk management is identifying the risks inherent in the different steps of a business process, selecting a set of variables, providing an estimate for the likelihood and severity of operational risk, and designing a control mechanism. Applying this general structure of risk management to valuing synergies leads to a distinction with the following phases: identification, documentation, integration planning, and evaluation.

The Identification of Synergy

Identifying potential synergy effects requires a solid understanding of the strengths and weaknesses of the business processes of corporate systems A and B in order to develop a vision about the future performance of system C. Synergy is neither a given resulting from the possession of resources nor inherent in tangible or intangible corporate assets. In a merger, synergy is the result of amalgamating existing resources of firm A and B in a uniquely redesigned combination. The unification of resources to maximize value is a business process. Consequently, the identification of synergy requires considering a corporation from a new perspective as an organized system of business processes. The primary focus must be on business processes as a key indicator for the ability of an organization to deliver its products or services in a timely and efficient manner. Any business process contains three key dimensions:

1. *Human resources.* Human resources are the most important intangible corporate asset. Due to specialization, only a few key personnel are likely to have specific knowledge about business processes and their interactions with other people and systems within the firm.
2. *Technology.* Technology is most broadly defined as the entities, both material and immaterial, created by applying mental and physical effort to achieve some value. This definition includes tools and machines as well as business methods, software, or techniques to solve specific problems.
3. *Organization.* Corporate business processes are embedded in peculiar corporate organization characterized by hierarchy levels, decision-making lines, functions, and culture.

The identification of synergy in a merger begins with a comparison of those business processes for firm A and B that are similar in regard to its efficiency, strengths, and weaknesses. The superior technology, the better organization, and better trained human resources are adopted by firm C. Furthermore, the identification of synergy implies the "reengineering of business processes" as first used in Hammer (1990), as it combines and organizes given resources in a new way to realize an added value. Davenport (1993, p. 2) defines *business process reengineering* as "term process innovation, which encompasses the envisioning of new work strategies, the actual process activity and the implementation of the change in all its complex technological, human and organizational dimensions."

How could this identification process materialize? The optimal solution would be a Web-based 3-D visualization of all business processes of firm A and B on split screens. This visualization of corporate business processes on parallel computer screens would enable discovering points of overlap for comparison and developing new business processes with existing resources. However, despite the tremendous progress made in interactive Web applications in recent years, this kind of 3-D visualization of all corporate business processes is still unrealized. Nevertheless, this ideal solution could lead to a potential breakthrough in the amount of information and documentation necessary to identify synergy effects. Central business processes that involve employees, suppliers, and clients from both firms have to be documented in a map. The data then have to be edited with information about human resources, job descriptions, and organization diagrams. Because "hidden" system-specific information is not codified in documents, it is time-consuming to generate and requires the physical presence of analysts within the systems. The documentation phase is followed by an assessment of the organizations' strengths and weaknesses, which enables analysts to identify potential opportunities—especially technological and human resource openings. Performance targets and benchmark results involved in the merger contribute to the redesign of existing business processes. Afterwards, a process vision is developed by selecting strategic relevant business processes for reengineering and subsequently formulating a prototype for the new business process design after the merger.

Integration Planning for Redesigned Business Processes

After the business processes of the new corporate system C are identified, designed, and prototyped, the planning phase for implementation of the new business concept can begin. This step involves detailed planning on how to incorporate resources (human resources, technology, and organization) from corporate systems A and B into operation within the new system C. Evaluation of the new system C requires that planning for the postmerger integration starts before the closure of the merger, otherwise returns and integration are impossible to calculate. Synergies have to be clearly defined and transformed into measurable integration targets. Similar to project management, this includes the definition of various targets measured in concrete figures, a breakdown in milestones and deadlines, work plans, and target completion dates. Integration planning must project which corporate functions (e. g., marketing, treasury, and information technology) are involved in reaching this target and which manager will assume leadership throughout the integration process. Integration planning cannot be performed in a top-down approach because of the complexity involved and minimal staff backing. The highest priority should be the incorporation of staff members into the planning process during the primary stages of integration. Staff involvement, combined with transparent corporate communication, is crucial for reaching strategic goals. The result of integration planning is a detailed roadmap laying out the accomplishments needed in each area of the company, individual responsibilities, and completion dates (Bruner, 2004).

Dumay (2004) criticizes this way of process thinking as a purely technocratic management perspective of organization, which mainly ignores the central role of management within organizations. According to Dumay (p. 17), "In such a view, organizations are the means to accomplish the objectives of the organization's owners. These objectives are embedded within a corporate strategy that is realized by business processes." To negate this criticism, integration planning has to pay equal attention to nontechnical organizational elements such as social structure, rules of conduct, corporate culture, communication, and participants in order to facilitate the restructuring of business performance processes. This is in line with the concept of "human due diligence," supported by Harding and Rouse (2007), which gives priority to structural and cultural aspects of corporate organization. However, since the implementation of a new corporate organization leads to an increase in costs with the transformation of existing social structures, reporting lines, and corporate cultures, it should be accounted for in the evaluation process.

The Valuation of Corporate System C

Following the identification of synergy effects and integration planning, the new corporate system C is no longer a black box for evaluation. On the contrary, the box is filled with expert knowledge concerning the future system of business processes and its implementation given the existing resources of systems A and B. In general, the value of an asset is derived by its capacity to generate cash flows. The preceding work of mapping and redesigning business processes visualizes the way to achieve value within a corporate system. The investment appraisal method that is applied must make use of this information pool by forecasting the net cash flows from projected single business processes, incorporating a risk assessment regarding the underlying uncertainty of key variables for cash flow forecasts, and quantifying the systemic risk because business processes within a corporate system are naturally correlated.

A simple DCF approach, such as the NPV method, is incapable of processing the risk and return information in an appropriate manner because the risk is typically solely incorporated in the discount factor. The discount factor contains a risk-free interest rate, which reflects the time value of money, and a risk premium to reflect the investor's rate of return for investment opportunities with similar risk (opportunity costs). The risk premium has to be interpreted as a premium for systematic (market) risk, not for unsystematic (project) risk. For example, the beta factor in the often employed WACC explicitly incorporates this risk into the discount rate. Thus, the specific risk of the investment project (unsystematic risk) should be represented by a modification of the cash flow variables within the present value formula.

Corporate finance textbooks such as Brealey et al. (2007), often propose three methods to account for the underlying risk of cash flow forecasts in the present value formula: sensitivity analysis, scenario analysis, and Monte Carlo simulation. The wealth of information generated by the analysis of existing corporate systems and the developed vision of the future system allows for the use of all three methods of risk-return analysis, and each approach can deliver valuable information for the merger decision. Sensitivity analysis provides investors with an idea of the major risk factors. Scenario analysis addresses what happens if anything goes wrong or if everything works out to be optimal. Monte Carlo simulation provides a complete risk-return profile of all possible outcomes and utilizes all given information. Additional calculation costs for employing all three methods seem to be negligible relative to the added value of information.

Corporation C exists as a vision of projected operational processes combined with a plan for its implementation. The starting point for the evaluation is a cash flow forecast for each operational process involved with the value chain. Besides operational processes, the corporate system includes management processes and other supporting processes, which govern and facilitate the general operation of the system. Because these processes are not directly involved in generating cash, their value has to be incorporated as variable or fixed costs in the cash flow forecast of operational processes. The cash flow forecast of modified or unchanged operational processes may use available information about revenues and costs of existing operational processes in systems A and B. Obviously, cash flow forecasts for the newly designed processes of system C

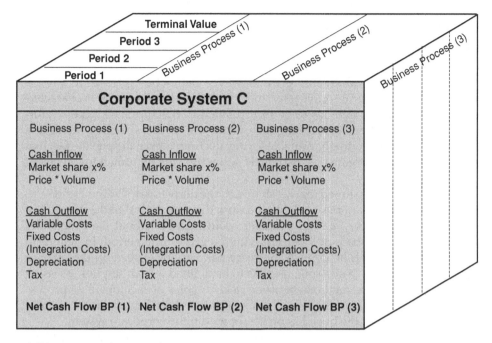

Exhibit 23.2 Evaluation of Corporate System C

Note: A corporate system exists of input and output relationships with its environment. These mutual relationships are documented as a network of internal business processes. Every business process generates a net cash flow per period of time. The present value of corporate system C is the sum of net cash flows for all operational business processes discounted for each period.

have a higher degree of uncertainty because analysts must project revenues and costs.

The cash flow forecast for each (operational) business process is performed in detail for three to five periods and concludes with the calculation of a *terminal value*, which is the discounted value of all future cash flow beyond a given date (Exhibit 23.2). Assuming that cash flows will continue to grow indefinitely at a constant rate after the projected horizon of three to five years, the cash flow stream is then termed a growing perpetuity and can be calculated as a present value of an infinite geometric series. The results of integration planning determine the timeline for revenues and integration costs for each process. Finally, the net cash flow result of one business process 'n' is discounted for each period 't' and summed up for all business processes to achieve a present value for all future net cash flows of corporate system C (Equation 23.13).

$$V_C^0 = \sum_{n=1}^{N} \sum_{t=1}^{T} \frac{NCF_t^n}{(1+r)^t} \tag{23.13}$$

where

$V_C^0 =$ Value of the combined firm in period 0
$NCF_t^n =$ Net cash flow of business process n in period t

r = Discount rate (WACC)
n = Number of business processes
t = Period of time

Outcomes of the evaluation process, however, cannot be expressed in a single present value figure because the assessment of future developments is character- ized by uncertainty, which has to be incorporated in the appraisal model. Infor- mation and transparency concerning the overall risk and its specific sources in a merger project are exceedingly valuable for any decision maker, despite the fact that the assumed risk environment is extremely subjective due to human involvement (see Exhibit 23.2).

For example, the assumed market share and the derived sales volume and sales prices for each period are risk variables because they are critical to the viability of the project. In such cases, a sales manager could be asked about the probability of reaching a market share of x percent within a given time period. In general, a probability function can be defined for every risk variable, based on the opinion of experts. Afterwards, a systemic risk has to be defined, which implies assessing the correlations for interrelations between risk variables of each business process in each period, risk variables of each business process between observed periods, and variables between the business processes within the corporate system.

The result of the risk analysis is a risk-return profile of the merger project, which can be shown by using a diagram. In the case of a scenario analysis, the risk-return profile consists of a few points, which may signal the probability of worst, medium, or best case scenarios. Monte Carlo simulation provides the most thorough analysis by using a full picture display to show all possible risk and return combinations. A cumulative probability distribution, which implies arranging the present value results in ascending order, conveys the degree of probability for an expected project result (Savvides, 1994). At this stage of evaluation, the beforehand formalized definition of success could be used as a benchmark (Equations 23.8 and 23.9). The probability that firm C's present value exceeds the sum of present values of firm A and firm B and the defined total synergy premium should be in excess of 50 percent. The ultimate decision for a merger is, however, contingent upon the investor's appetite for risk. The risk-return profile merely provides transparency for the investor's risk attitudes. The risk-return data could be enhanced by calculating an expected value and several ratios such as the *expected loss ratio*, which measures the expected loss relative to the merger's overall expected NPV.

The Use of External versus Internal Evaluation Teams

A final issue involves who should perform the extensive data and process mining in the identification phase of evaluation. In general, there are four possible choices: (1) an internal management team of the acquirer (firm A); (2) an internal management team composed of firm A and B; (3) an external private audit company; and (4) an external public audit institution. For selecting the most appropriate type of inquiring unit, four determinants should be considered.

First, investigation teams must cope with numerous information problems. For example, such problems include asymmetric information, evaluation processes with contrasting points of view, and internal process information, which is not fully documented. Nevertheless, any information deficiencies can be minimized by including management staff from firms A and B.

Second, the merger directly affects each employee of firm A or B. Fears and concerns about job security or redesigned functions often permeate the merger process, culminating in the loss of highly skilled personnel to a competitive labor market. Merger situations are often characterized by individual uncertainties and a state of persistence, which burden the overall company performance. Human resource involvement from both A and B early in the merger process can be interpreted as a preemptive move to create trust and credibility. However, the personal and deep involvement of investigators could block the view for the restructuring of existing or for the development of new business processes. For this purpose, one needs to take a look from a distance. Investigation teams, irrespective of being insiders or outsiders, require a straightforward corporate communication of the overall vision for the merger by publishing progress reports. Corporate communication is critical in determining the level of collaboration between the corporate staff of both companies.

Third, under conventional due diligence, the primary focus is restricted to the target acquired company. However, information must also be requested from the acquiring company A to obtain more accurate and reliable synergy effects. The identification of synergy continuously entails the analysis of two business models of varying strengths and weaknesses because a merger of companies implies the fusion of two complex systems with diverse elements and relations. There can be some doubt whether internal investigation teams have the needed extraordinary degree of reflexivity, i.e., knowing their company's own strengths and weaknesses, comparing them with those of the target company, and developing a vision for the combined corporate system.

Fourth, the targeted visualization and analysis of all important business processes unlock the vault to the most valuable resource a company owns: its intellectual property. Comparable to the source code used to design software, visualization and analysis can tell how to combine resources to achieve value. Product piracy in the sense of illegal reproduction of products leads to considerable losses in sales and profit. Nevertheless, pirates still must devise a way to replicate production. In the case of a merger, the acquiring company exposes all of its safeguarded business processes, similar to a chef's cooking recipes, which detail each ingredient and the production processes involved. Knowledge of business process is the highest form of intellectual property a corporation possesses and must be protected by the highest security measures possible. In regard to protection of intellectual property, the use of an external public audit institution acting as a trust broker within a merger process should be worth considering as an alternative to private audit companies.

SUMMARY AND CONCLUSIONS

The high failure rate of mergers provides a constant stimulus to examine the common practice of merger pricing and the underlying theoretical appraisal models. The preceding review of the merger problem presents several solutions to increase the success rate of mergers.

The chapter views any premium paid, in addition to the market price of the target firm, as a seller's premium for future synergy effects. The acquiring firm's shareholders invariably bear the risk when any payout occurs, while the share- holders of the target firm bear much less risk. Consequently, the acquiring firm's shareholders request an equivalent synergy premium to that of the seller. Taking these aspects into account, the message for managers is that the acquiring firm should only pay a premium if a reasonable expectation exists that the total synergy effect to be realized in the future is at least twice as high as the premium plus risk-adjusted compound interest.

A merger constitutes a new corporate system C, to be built up by the fusion of complex corporate systems A and B, with diverse elements and relationships. Codified knowledge taken from balance sheets and business reports provides a sufficient data basis for evaluation if the performance processes of the existing corporate system remain unchanged. However, mergers are implemented with the intention of improving or modifying existing processes as well as installing new ones. Therefore, investors have to open the "box" to gain an inside view and to generate system internal information. Further complicating matters is that system "box C" does not yet exist. Therefore, any pricing of firm C should use system- specific knowledge of A and B to develop a vision about the future performance processes and interactions in the new system C.

This view of a merger process has several implications. For example, under conventional due diligence, the primary focus is restricted to the acquired company. Identifying the synergy effects under the system-based method requires a two-way perspective to analyze the strengths and weakness of each firm's business model. Thus, investors require an extraordinary degree of reflexivity in order to know their company's own strengths and weaknesses, to compare them with those of the target company, and to develop a vision for the combined corporate system.

Due diligence teams require new actors with a diverse set of skills. Teams con- sisting of individuals who have considerable experience and solid understanding of each firm's core business are needed. The investment appraisal is dependent on expert knowledge. Synergy assessments performed by risk managers may lead to further changes in the value because of the similarities that exist with corporate risk management.

To generate system internal information, corporations must reveal safely guarded business processes in order to conduct the necessary data mining. In this sense, a merger process is a collaborative effort waged by each firm involved. Hos- tile takeovers are synonymous with information asymmetry because uninformed investors acquire "black boxes" with incomplete knowledge about the contents. The identification phase and integration planning begin after each contract has been notarized, confirmation of payment has occurred, and ownership has been transferred. In this case, payment should come in the form of equity, as opposed to cash, so that new shareholders will share both the value and the risk of the merger transaction (Rappaport and Sirower, 1999).

In conclusion, the pricing process needs a radical change. Because synergy ef- fects crystallize through an innovative or superior combination of given corporate resources, pricing begins with identifying the given processes, followed by devel- oping a vision of future business processes, then engaging in integration planning. Expert knowledge of future business processes (i.e., system internal information) provides the foundation for the cash flow forecasts and any additional uncertainty (unsystematic risk) should be explicitly incorporated into the pricing model.

DISCUSSION QUESTIONS

1. Define the term "synergy" for M&A activity and explain why synergy is the most important variable in M&A pricing.

2. Discuss whether horizontal, vertical, and conglomerate merger types involve different types of synergy.

3. How is success of a merger defined in general? Taking into account a fair distribution of the total synergy between shareholder groups A and B, what does "success" mean?

4. Explain why conventional methods of corporate valuation (asset-oriented and income-oriented approaches) are not very well suited for valuation of the merged company C. Use the concepts of *system theory* and *value additivity* as well as *implicit* and *explicit knowledge* in the explanation.

5. Describe the different steps in the valuation process of company C based on a system theoretical approach.

6. Explain the role of due diligence teams in an M&A.

7. What impact does the new approach on pricing process and due diligence have?

REFERENCES

Aluko, Bioye T., and Abdul-Rasheed Amidu. 2005. "Corporate Business Valuation for Mergers and Acquisitions." *International Journal of Strategic Property Management* 9:3, 173–189.

Antoniou, Antonios, Philippe Arbour, and Huainan Zhao. 2006. "How Much Is Too Much: Are Merger Premiums Too High?" Available at http://ssrn.com/abstract = 884244, 1–22.

Brealey, Richard A., Stewart C. Myers, and Franklin Allen. 2007. *Corporate Finance*, 9th ed. New York: McGraw-Hill.

Bruner, Robert F. 2004. *Applied Mergers Acquisitions*. Hoboken, NJ: Wiley Finance.

Corning, Peter. 2003. *Nature's Magic: Synergy in Evolution and the Fate of Humankind*. New York: Cambridge University Press.

Davenport, Thomas. 1993. *Process Innovation: Reengineering Work through Information Technology*. Boston: Harvard Business School Press.

Dumay, Mark. 2004. "The Theoretical Impact of Process Thinking on Information Systems Development." Available at http://arxiv.org/abs/cs/0409037v1.

Eccles, Robert G., Kersten L. Lanes, and Thomas C. Wilson. 1999. "Are You Paying Too Much for That Acquisition?" *Harvard Business Review* 77: 4136–146.

Fan, Joseph P. H., and Vidhan K. Goyal. 2006. "On the Patterns and Wealth Effects of Vertical Mergers." *Journal of Business* 79:2, 877–902.

Gorton, Gary, Matthias Kahl, and Richard J. Rosen. 2009. "Eat or Be Eaten: A Theory of Mergers and Firm Size." *Journal of Finance* 64:3, 1291–1344.

Gupta, Oliver, and Goran Ross. 2001. "Mergers and Acquisitions through an Intellectual Capital Perspective." *Journal of Intellectual Capital* 2:3, 297–309.

Hammer, Michael. 1990. "Reengineering Work: Don't Automate, Obliterate." *Harvard Business Review* 68:4, 104–112.

Harding, David, and Ted Rouse. 2007. "Human Due Diligence." *Harvard Business Review* 85:4, 124–131.

Lie, Erik, and Heidi J. Lie. 2002. "Multiples Used to Estimate Corporate Value." *Financial Analysts Journal* 58:2, 44–54.

Markowitz, Harry M. 1952. "Portfolio Selection." *Journal of Finance* 7:1, 77–91.

Moeller, Sara B., Frederik P. Schlingemann, and René M. Stulz. 2005. "Wealth Destruction on a Massive Scale? A Study of Acquiring-Firm Returns in the Recent Merger Wave." *Journal of Finance* 60:2, 757–781.

Mukherjee, Tarun K., Halil Kiymaz, and H. Kent Baker. 2004. "Merger Motives and Target Valuation: A Survey of Evidence from CFOs." *Journal of Applied Finance* 14:2, 7–24.

Murphy, Tom, Drew Winter, and Eric Mayne. 2003. "Insourcing." *Ward's Auto World* 39:5, 44–48.

Nonaka, Ikujiro, and Hirotaka Takeuchi. 1997. *The Knowledge-Creating Company: How Japanese Companies Create the Dynamics of Innovation.* Oxford: Oxford University Press.

Polanyi, Michael. 1967. *The Tacit Dimension.* New York: Anchor Books.

Rappaport, Alfred, and Mark L. Sirower. 1999. "Stock or Cash? The Trade-Offs for Buyers and Sellers in Merger and Acquisitions." *Harvard Business Review* 77:6, 147–158.

Savvides, Savvakis C. 1994. "Risk Analysis in Investment Appraisal." *Project Appraisal* 9:1, 3–18.

Sikula, Andrew, Sr., Chong W. Kim, Charles K. Braun, and John Sikula. 2010. "Insourcing: Reversing American Outsourcing in the New World Economy." *Supervision* 71:8, 3–9.

ABOUT THE AUTHOR

Rainer Lenz has taught international finance at the University of Applied Sciences, Bielefeld, Germany for 10 years. He also has extensive working experience as an investment banker and as an economic adviser to a German MP. His fields of research are monetary and exchange rate policy and risk-return analysis of capital market instruments. He has published several articles on financial topics that have appeared in banking journals and newspapers. He holds a diploma in Economics from the University of Bonn and has a Ph.D. degree from the University of Karlsruhe. His visiting academic positions include the American University in Washington, D.C., the Universidad Iberoamericana, Puebla, Mexico, and the University of West Florida in Pensacola, Florida.

CHAPTER 24

Multicriteria Analysis for Capital Budgeting

FERNANDO R. FERNHOLZ
Associate Professor of the Practice, Duke University

INTRODUCTION

Firms often make capital budgeting decisions based on more than one criterion because decision makers need to consider multiple objectives or other factors. Hence, analysts and managers should know the methodologies for systematic and simultaneous consideration of multiple criteria when making important investment decisions. The discussions in this chapter aim to help analysts and decision makers explore these multicriteria methodologies to rank, select, and decide whether to invest in proposed investment projects, to expand capacity and/or the operations of existing projects, or to optimize a portfolio of investments.

This chapter incorporates recent research and practice on multicriteria analysis (MCA) and multiattribute analysis to expand the decision-making tools, approaches, techniques, and considerations that are traditionally used. The chapter first presents the concept and motivation for using MCA analysis, followed by a discussion of the basic methodology and some methodological issues. It then concludes with some examples of applications and further issues for consideration as they relate to capital budgeting.

This chapter builds on the discussion in earlier chapters of the well-accepted and commonly used single review criteria for decision making, such as net present value (NPV), internal rate of return (IRR), and specific financial measures such as debt ratios and after-tax net cash flows. In general, MCA analysis assumes that the goals of shareholder wealth maximization and other value functions for decision makers hold for capital budgeting decisions. Using MCA enables decision makers to consider the factors leading to the achievement of the firm's stated objectives.

THE CONCEPT OF MCA

MCA is neither new nor mysterious. Intuitively or formally, individuals use this kind of analysis, for example, when they buy an automobile and simultaneously consider and weigh the factors of safety, functionality, cost, and appearance. Two people may include the same factors but value them differentially; hence they may leave the dealership satisfied with the selection of very different kinds of automobiles. Decision makers, especially in larger organizations, need a systematic approach to capital investment decisions to help them achieve the firm's stated goals, communicate their decisions effectively to stakeholders, and attain some level of objectivity in their decision making. While the need for some level of subjective valuation in decision making remains, using more comprehensive analytical tools can help improve the process.

MCA is analysis based on methodologies that use an array of criteria systematically to guide capital investment decision making, usually among a relatively small number of discrete alternatives. Using MCA is justified because it allows decision makers to simultaneously consider different criteria that can contribute to estimating an expanded objective "value" for a firm. With an expanded objective value, a firm develops and examines a "value index" for the analysis of net benefits that can go beyond pure monetary considerations. For example, besides the wealth maximization summarized by expected NPVs, a firm might also want to consider environmental and social variables that can have long-term implications for the commercial value of the investments under evaluation. These values can reflect social or political perspectives. The analysis and decision making might include some subjective judgments and correspond to some increased "value" for the owners that cannot easily be expressed in pure monetary terms. New environmental regulations and market preferences as a result of more scientific information made available through time, for example, could affect the profitability and sustainability of a proposed investment.

To clarify this concept, assume that two new lines of production and sales, A and B, produce new products for the "green" energy market. In the process of deciding on the production line in which to invest, the owners may want to reduce harmful environmental impacts such as pollution, while also creating jobs with certain skills in the local communities. Although each new line of production may contribute a similar amount to the firm's net worth, one (A) may be more profitable but less environmentally friendly and employ fewer people than the other (B). In this case, the following question arises: Will the decision makers consider the potential trade-off in terms of the different attributes of the two proposed lines of production, which allow one line to be traded for the other, up to a certain amount in terms of NPV impact? If the second line of production (B) is less efficient in market terms than (A), but is better in terms of the environmental and labor impacts, how heavily should the decision maker weigh these factors to reflect the value they create for the owners, given their differential impact on long-term sustainability and profitability? MCA allows examining the methodologies and developing a "value objective function" to answer such questions.

Some Real-World Challenges

While using MCA has its benefits, some limitations are associated with selecting a project using this technique. Two basic limitations are: (1) the uncertainty that the decision maker faces given inadequate information about the future, and (2) the possibility that the social, environmental, or political values captured might change. Hence, decision makers sometimes use subjectivity when interpreting results and have to adapt and experiment in order to update their information base.

Decision makers often do not have all the relevant information needed to assess and optimize capital decisions. This point is important to remember given that capital budgeting decisions often require a substantial investment of resources. In the "ideal" paradigm of decision making (Bell, Raiffa, and Tversky, 1989), collecting relevant information and evidence is a critical part of the choice process. Seldom, however, do decision makers have complete information that allows them to fully optimize their choices. As noted in Bell et al. (p. 19), Herbert Simon questions the usefulness of choice as a metaphor for describing and interpreting human behavior as "normative models" (for complex decision making), which "might attempt to rationalize the search and quitting process in terms of subjective expected utility maximization in which time and physical and emotional effort are included as part of the utility calculus."

Companies and institutions such as banks have been using and perfecting multiattribute analysis for such areas as judging credit risk before making loan decisions. Although banks have developed sophisticated specifications and weights for the parameters they have determined using past data, they regularly update the parameters and experiment with modifications to the specifications and weights. Brealey and Myers (2003) offer examples of techniques and applications when they discuss multiple discriminant analysis (MDA) for calculating weights for relevant variables (such as earnings before interest and taxes, sales-to-total assets, market value, equity-to-book value of debt, retained earnings-to-total assets, and working capital-to-total assets) in order to separate good from bad credit prospects in bank loan decision making. Today, lending and other financial institutions are using modified versions of the technique developed initially by Altman (1993) that uses Z-scores with minimum thresholds.

In practice, decision makers need to review and consider additional decision criteria because both conditions and knowledge about the impact of relevant attributes change over time. Further, corporations may change their own set of primary and secondary objectives, which have implications for the decision criteria and their weights.

ELEMENTS OF MCA AND DECISION MAKING

Triantaphyllou (2000) and Pomerol and Barba Romero (2000) discuss the following elements that contribute to effective multicriteria decision making.

Decision Space

Most MCA for decision making in business and finance deals with discrete decision spaces for which the methods discussed here are appropriate to help find optimal solutions. This facilitates the analysis because complex decision spaces with continuous values for inputs and outputs require mathematical programming with multiple objective functions. Linear programming with objective functions subject to constraints is applicable more to operation decisions. In some cases, decision makers can use linear programming to determine the scale of an investment if they can make and measure changes on a continuous basis. In this case, they could frame the objective function using NPV as the single criterion for decision making.

Alternative Capital Budgeting Decisions

The number of alternative courses of action for a decision is defined as finite and relatively small in total number. In other words, decision makers can use the methodology for problems that can be defined with some degree of simplicity and clarity to an (m) number of alternative courses of action.

Simplification and Validity

Decision makers use simplifications to represent a model of reality. They seek an efficient model for decision making that is clear and understandable for the users from the assumptions to the final results. There is both art and science in developing and using these methods for each organization.

Decision Criteria

The decision maker tries to define and elicit some attributes of each possible alternative that allow the analyst and decision maker to compare goals, expected results, and relative costs and then to rank them using some of the methodologies described below. The number of criteria to be used will also be finite and relatively small in number (n).

Decision Weights

Most methods described here require adopting a system of weights to assign relative importance to each criterion used and to develop an index of value (aggregation rules) for the decision maker. In the example of "green" production lines below, the decision maker could assign, for instance, the following weights to three key factors: 50 percent to profitability considerations, 30 percent to environmental concerns, and 20 percent to labor considerations.

Decision Matrix

The decision matrix for MCA analysis incorporates information about the number of different alternatives to be considered and assigns one row to each alternative and one column for each criterion that is important for decision makers to consider. For each alternative, the analyst or the decision maker uses indicators of output or performance relative to each criterion. Examples of numerical values could be rates of return in percent, NPV in dollars, number of workers to be employed, and amount of pollution that could be generated. Based on expert opinion and surveys, the decision matrix could include qualitative information (e.g., extremely high, very high, high, low, very low, and extremely low) in some cases. As discussed below, qualitative information can be mapped from the performance or decision matrix to the scoring or index mapping for further analysis.

On top of the decision matrix is a row with the explicit weights assigned by decision makers, which could be through a process of negotiation, to each criterion, from 1 to (n). Exhibit 24.1 shows a simple decision matrix that uses the example discussed earlier, with three alternatives (m) to be considered and three decision criteria (n).

Exhibit 24.1   The Elements of the Decision Matrix

Investment alternatives: A1, A2, A3

Criteria	C1 Efficiency	C2 Labor	C3 Environmental Impact
Weights	w1	w2	w3
Attributes of each alternative (from A1 to A3)			
A1	a11	a12	A13
A2	a21	a22	A23
A3	a31	a32	A33

Note: The example above illustrates how three alternatives (A1, A2, and A3) could be ranked according to values for each criterion (C1, C2, and C3).

In a properly constructed matrix of evaluation, the decision maker would translate the attributes a(ij) to an index valuation i(ij) or the score indexes for each alternative and criterion, and use the maximization rule to select the most desirable alternative under these assumptions. Exhibit 24.2 illustrates this matrix.

METHODS OF MCA AND DECISION MAKING

This section focuses on three important methods—the weighted sum method, the weighted product method, and the analytical hierarchy process method—that are particularly important to decision makers dealing with capital budgeting.

The Weighted Sum Model

The weighted sum model (WSM) can be applied to a multidimensional problem by converting the attributes in each dimension and criterion of analysis into an aggregated index of valuation. The WSM is probably the most commonly used method in MCA. An important rule in the WSM is to select, using well-specified values for the weights w(i) and the scores or indexes i(ii), the alternative that maximizes the product of the row index values times the vector of weights from w1 to w3:

Choose A(i) that maximizes: $\sum i(ij)w(j)$; from $j = 1$ to n; for each $i = 1$ to m

$$(24.1)$$

Exhibit 24.2   The Score or Index Matrix

	C1	C2	C3
I(A1)	i11	i12	i13
I(A2)	i21	i22	i23
I(A3)	i31	i32	i33

Note: The values calculated in the decision matrix are normalized to scores in this matrix.

The example that follows considers that all alternatives (A1 to A3) have passed the test of having a positive NPV, but at different amounts. For simplicity, this case is not concerned with budget constraints but rather with the aggregate and multiattribute value of each alternative. The NPVs reflect dollars; labor represents different levels of employment generation for the region (in thousands of jobs, for example); and the environmental value represents levels of pollution, where the value accepted by the decision makers is better for a lower level of pollution per alternative, everything else being the same.

Normalization Rules for Generation of Value Indexes

Relatively simple rules are used to convert the attribute or results of each alternative, expressed in different dimensions (for example, dollars, employment numbers, and pollution levels), to an index of "values" for each category or criterion. For instance, for both the efficiency and employment generation criteria, the decision maker divides the a(ij) values by the maximum within the column; for example, for the highest NPV, the index is $2.00/2.00 = 1.00$, which is also the maximum ratio. The other indexes then follow in the same manner: $1.80/2.00 = 0.90$ and so on. The same procedure is applied in this simple example for the labor criterion column. Both the NPV and labor criteria would then be consistent with the idea that higher index values reflect higher objective "values" for decision makers. For the environmental results and criterion column, the index must be transformed using an appropriate mathematical transformation such as the following suggested procedure: Divide one (or use the reciprocal) by the ratio of the value a(i3) to the minimum $[\min[a(13), a(23), a(33)]]$ of the range, which in this case is -10. So the first value $i(13) = 1/[(-20)/(-10)] = 0.50$, and so on. The analysis can also use other consistent transformations. Exhibit 24.3 reflects the results of this process.

The numerical results, for total scores, are the sum of the products of each row cell i(ij) with each column cell w(j). For example, for the first alternative, the total score is $0.85 = 1.0(0.5) + 0.83(0.3) + 0.50(0.2)$. This example shows the total score for each alternative, as they result from the product of the indexes times the corresponding weights (added across the row). In this example, alternative B is the most desirable or "valuable" in terms of the definitions adopted in this case. From a narrow financial profit sense, alternative A is more desirable using the single NPV rule. After the analysts and decision makers agree on the methodology in principle, the ranking of the alternatives in comparative terms where the symbol ">" means "better than" is B > A > C.

Sensitivity Analysis

Sensitivity analysis can be used for WSM and the other methods. It is used to see if choosing some other combination of weights changes the ranking. In the first case shown in Exhibit 24.4, a range of values for weight 1 (wealth maximization being the most important one) is employed and the decision maker can observe the changes in ranking. If weight w1 changes from 0.20 to 0.80, keeping weight w2 equal to 0.30, but making weight w3 equal to the difference of $(1 - w1 - w2)$, the relative ranking for B does not change, although for the second place, when w1 is higher than 0.70, C > A.

In another example of changes in the labor column, with b(22) changed from 12 to 14 and C(32) from 9 to 12, the decision maker can explore different values for

Exhibit 24.3 Example of the Application, Decision Matrix D1, and Corresponding Score Matrix SM1

Panel A. From the Matrix D1

	NPV	Labor	Environment
A	2.00	10	−20
B	1.80	12	−15
C	1.50	9	−10

Panel B. The Score or Index Matrix SM1

	w1 0.5	w2 0.3	w3 0.2		Vector of weights	Total Scores
Alternatives						
A	1.00	0.83	0.50	w1	**0.5**	**0.85**
B	0.90	1.00	0.67	w2	**0.3**	**0.88**
C	0.75	0.75	1.00	w3	**0.2**	**0.80**

Note: This example shows that higher index values reflect greater objective "values" consistent with the value function of decision makers. The calculation shows that alternative B would be the preferred option. The process of scoring has to be consistent with the value function of decision makers.

the NPV of alternative A, in this case the relative attribute a(11) (See Exhibit 24.5). In this manner, the decision maker can assess the sensitivity of ranking to changes in the value of a(11) while changing the value for b(22) to 14 and c(32) to 12.

The ranking does not change for values of a(11) that include 1.6 to 2.2 (See Exhibit 24.6). The same results are obtained if the same original values for the labor column are used.

Sensitivity analysis in this example shows some degree of consistency in the ranking of the alternatives, with B consistently ranked as the preferred alternative. The basic ranking for B has not changed for values of a(11) from 1.6 to 2.2, even in the presence of changes in b(22) and c(32). In the last case, though, C > A is valid for a(11) values that range from 1.60 to 2.1, which is different from the first discussion of B1. Given the parameters of this small example, even under variation in weights and attributes with a certain range of values, alternative B is consistently better

Exhibit 24.4 Sensitivity of Total Scores in SM1 to Different Values of the Weight W1

Sensitivity to W1

Alternatives	0.2	0.3	0.4	**0.5**	0.6	0.7	0.8
A	0.40	0.55	0.70	**0.85**	1.00	1.15	1.30
B	0.41	0.57	0.73	**0.88**	1.04	1.20	1.35
C	0.28	0.45	0.63	**0.80**	0.98	1.15	1.33

Note: This exhibit tests whether some combination of weights changes the ranking of the alternatives. The base case is reflected in bold. For all values of W1 from 0.2 to 0.8, B remains the preferred alternative as it consistently has the higher value ranking.

Exhibit 24.5   Example of the Application, Decision Matrix D2, and Corresponding Score Matrix SM2

Decision Matrix: D2

	NPV	Labor	Environment
A	2	10	−20
B	1.8	14	−15
C	1.5	12	−10

Score or Index Matrix: SM2

	w1 0.5	w2 0.3	w3 0.2	Vector of Weights	Total Scores
A	1.00	0.71	0.50	0.5	**0.81**
B	0.90	1.00	0.67	0.3	**0.88**
C	0.75	0.86	1.00	0.2	**0.83**

Note: This exhibit shows that ranking of alternatives can change with different values used for labor. Alternative B still has higher scores, followed by alternative C, then A. The values for the attributes for labor have changed. Alternative B still has higher scores but C follows A in this case.

than the other two choices if the decision maker is only interested in finding the best alternative.

The Weighted Product Method

The weighted product method (WPM) is a method of ranking and selection similar to the WSM, where the total scores are obtained by multiplying the relative ratios of the attributes (if all the values are expressed in the same dimension) or the ratios of the indexes for pairwise comparison. The ratios are raised to the power of the weight before the multiplication; for example, to obtain the relative weighted ratio of one alternative over the other:

$$R(A/B) = \prod \text{ for } (i\,(aj)\,/\,i\,(bj))^{\wedge}\,w\,(j) \text{ from 1 to n} \tag{24.2}$$

Exhibit 24.6   Sensitivity to One of the Attributes (a11)

Sensitivity to a(11)

	1.6	1.7	1.8	1.9	**2**	2.1	2.2
A	0.76	0.79	0.81	0.81	**0.81**	0.81	0.81
B	0.93	0.93	0.93	0.91	**0.88**	0.86	0.84
C	0.87	0.87	0.87	0.85	**0.83**	0.81	0.80

Note: This exhibit shows that the ranking of alternatives does not change despite variations in values for labor. Over the range given, alternative B is still the preferred alternative, followed by C and then A in the range of values 1.6 to 2.0 for a(11).

Exhibit 24.7   Score Matrix under the Weighted Product Method

The Score or Index Matrix S2

	w1	w2	w3		Weighted Product Method (WPM)		
	0.5	0.3	0.2		Relative Ratios		
Alternatives					A	B	C
A	1.00	0.83	0.50	A		1.06	0.96
B	0.90	1.00	0.67	B	0.94		0.91
C	0.75	0.75	1.00	C	1.04	1.10	

Note: This exhibit shows the weighted ratios of alternatives A, B, and C and the consistency of a higher ranking for alternative B, followed by C, and then A.

where i(aj) are the index score values for alternative A; i(bj) are the index score values for alternative B; while w(j) are the agreed weights for each criterion j (from 1 to n); and π is the symbol for multiplication. In the example here, the ratio is: $R(A/B) = [(1.00/0.90)^{0.5}][(0.83/1.00)^{0.3}][(0.50/0.67)^{0.2}] = 0.94$, which is reflected in the matrix of results under column A in relation to row B shown in Exhibit 24.7.

Using the same procedure, the relative ratios for each alternative in relation to the others are obtained by going down each column. For example, for alternative B, R(B/A) in relation to A is 1.06 and R(B/C) in relation to C is 1.10. Using this procedure, Exhibit 24.8 shows that the same ranking as before is obtained: B > A > C.

Within the WPM, a simplified version is to raise each index value by the weight of the criterion and multiply the resulting values across the row for each alternative. In this case, only the values of the indexes i(ij) are used to obtain the product, raising each index to the weight w(j) first and multiplying the results for each column, times the values of all the other columns in each row (for each alternative). The formula for each product is used as:

$$P(A(i)) = \prod i (aj)^{\wedge} w (j), \text{ for } j = 1 \text{ to } (n) \tag{24.3}$$

Exhibit 24.8   Simplified Product Method

	Total	
	Scores	**Ranking**
A	0.82	2
B	0.87	1
C	0.79	3

Note: This exhibit shows that the ranking of the alternatives using the simplified product method is consistent with that using the previous methods. With the simplified product method, the ranking of alternatives does not change with B being the highest, followed by A, and then C as in SM1.

For example for alternative B, $P(B) = (0.90)^{0.5}(1.00)^{0.3}(0.67)^{0.2} = 0.87$. Again, the same ranking as before is obtained: B > A > C.

The Analytic Hierarchy Process Method

The analytical hierarchy process (AHP) method is similar to the WPM described above, in that it moves from expected attributes or results of each alternative in several dimensions to the index scores using some particular normalization procedures. The methodology elicits expert evaluation in numerical terms based on quantitative and even qualitative information associated with each alternative. One way to express the relative scores for each criterion is to normalize the rankings (previously done using a different method), expressed in fractions, such that the total addition of index scores i(ii) for all alternatives and for each criterion is equal to one (revised AHP method). Once this transformation has been accomplished, the numerical application is similar to the WSM and the example presented above. Exhibit 24.9 presents an example of the AHP method.

The ranking of projects is the same as before with B > A > C. The sensitivity analysis for this method also shows that the ranking does not change for different values of the weight W1, with similar results to the sensitivity analysis above.

The results of the sensitivity analysis show that the ranking (B > A > C) does not change for weights of W1 that range from 0.20 to 0.80, as was the case before (See Exhibit 24.10). While B is the dominant alternative in all cases here, the relative ranking of A > C changes for W1 greater than 0.5.

Exhibit 24.9   Example of Analytical Hierarchy Process Method, Matrix D1

Attributes of each alternative (from A1 to A3)

	NPV	Labor	Environment	Scores Environment
A	2.00	10	−20	0.50
B	1.80	12	−15	0.67
C	1.50	9	−10	1.00

The Score or Index Matrix

	w1	w2	w3		
	0.5	0.3	0.2		

Alternatives				Vector of weights	Total Scores
A	0.38	0.32	0.23	w1	0.5	0.33
B	0.34	0.39	0.31	w2	0.3	0.35
C	0.28	0.29	0.46	w3	0.2	0.32
$\sum$ i(ij)	1.00	1.00	1.00	[100%]		

Note: The exhibit shows that the AHP method uses index scores in selecting among alternatives. The sum of scores has been normalized to be equal to 100 percent for each column. Alternative B has the highest total score and is the preferred option.

Exhibit 24.10   Sensitivity to W1 under the AHP Method

Sensitivity to W1							
	0.2	0.3	0.4	0.5	0.6	0.7	0.8
A	0.149	0.21	0.27	0.33	0.39	0.45	0.51
B	**0.153**	**0.22**	**0.28**	**0.35**	**0.41**	**0.48**	**0.54**
C	0.098	0.17	0.25	0.32	0.40	0.47	0.54

Note: This exhibit shows that despite differing values for weight W1, alternative B maintains the higher ranking and is the preferred choice. The higher ranking for B is maintained for values of the weight W1 from 0.20 to 0.80.

ROBUSTNESS OF RESULTS OF MCA METHODS

A potential criticism of the MCA methods is the degree to which the rankings can be reversed and even biased, depending on (or as a function of) the weights, the robustness and expected value differences in the attributes, and the methodology of normalization used to convert attribute values (decision matrix) into the indices (score index matrix). If conflicting criteria exist such as profitability versus environmental impacts, the weights or value of benefits and costs for each of the alternatives considered can possibly be biased. Cases may exist where the results are close and where further analysis and discussion might be needed to arrive at the desired ranking and selection. In relation to contradictory attributes such as benefits and costs in the same decision matrix, proponents can argue that agreement exists on a transparent method to compute NPVs. In the case of monetary benefits and costs, the problem of contradictory attributes can be avoided. Nevertheless, exploring possible cases where MCA might lead to some contradiction in ranking is important.

Triantaphyllou and Baig (2005) address the issue of consistency and the robustness of results among the WSM, WPM, and AHP including some variants such as the multiplicative AHP model. The main objective of their research has been to test the probability of reversal of the ranking obtained with these methods as a function of the number of alternatives and the number of criteria used. In their study, the decision-making matrix includes conflicting attributes of benefits and costs. To test the robustness of the results, the authors test a simulation model that includes alternatives (m) from 3 to 21 and criteria (n) from 3 to 21 using random simulation.

Some key results merit discussion. To test consistency in selecting the best alternative, the ideal results would be low or zero contradiction. The contradiction rate is defined as the percentage times that the benefits-to-cost ratio versus the benefits less cost approach yields different ranking results. Using random simulation, Triantaphyllou and Baig (2005) test the different MCA methods detailed above by estimating the percent probability of ranking reversal that represents the contradiction rate. For the WSM and simple AHP methods and with the lowest number of alternatives (3) and number of criteria (3), the contradiction rate as defined here is less than 6 percent. If the number of alternatives increases to 21 but the same number of criteria (3) is maintained, the rate of contradiction can increase to more than 25 percent for the WSM and AHP methods. A combination of a high number of alternatives (21) with the high number of criteria (21) results in some decrease in the contradiction rate to about 13 percent. While the ranking contradiction results to select the best alternative method are on the low side, the full sequence of ranking the results for potential contradictions are slightly less robust.

Triantaphyllou and Baig (2005) conduct tests to estimate if any relative position of the ranking sequence among the alternatives can change depending on the number of alternatives chosen and criteria for selection. They find that the contradiction rate can increase to 10 percent for (3) alternatives and (3) criteria from 6 percent in the case described above. These contradiction rates only apply to the WSM, AHP, and revised AHP methods. There is no contradiction in ranking when applying the multiplicative AHP method or the WPM. The rate of contradiction for multiplicative methods is 0 percent.

A review of the academic literature including Triantaphyllou (2001) and Triantaphyllou and Baig (2005) reveals that decision makers can use MCA methods as a learning and decision making (or support) tool with some degree of confidence based on the robustness of the ranking results. At the same time, they need to be cautious about interpreting and using MCA methods. Organizations using similar tools can improve the efficacy of the decision-making processes by gradually incorporating more information and precision in relation to the attributes for each alternative and by reviewing regularly the weights after realizing the results of previous decisions. The consistency of the results tends to increase through time. These organizations are observed to improve performance in decision making and in subsequent phases of the capital budgeting cycle. Hobbs (1986) offers additional insights into experimentation with MCA methods.

Efficiency Criteria, Other "Value" Considerations, and Sensitivity Analysis

The relative performance of the narrow efficiency criterion can be illustrated using the first two columns of decision matrix D1 shown in Exhibit 24.11 using, for example, only NPV and one additional dimension such as labor. The analysis in relative terms is very similar regardless of changes in the dimensions or units used

Exhibit 24.11 Example of Rankings under the Efficiency Criterion

Attributes of Each Alternative (A, B, and C)

	Investment	Labor	Wage	Labor Cost	Revenue	Net Revenue/ Period	PV of the Perpetuity	NPV	Rank
A	−1000	10	20	−200	230	300	3000	2,000	1
B	−1600	12	20	−240	274	340	3400	1,800	2
C	−1100	9	20	−180	206	260	2600	1,500	3

Note: This exhibit shows that using NPV to measure efficiency and an additional dimension such as labor generation may result in a different ranking of the alternatives compared to earlier examples. In this case, alternative A is the preferred option. The ranking corresponds to the maximization of NPV rule. Under labor generation alone, the higher ranking would correspond to B.

by the decision maker to reflect the investment costs, revenues, and expenditures as well as the NPV. As in the example shown in Exhibit 24.11, there are three potentially successful investment choices (e.g., they all pass the NPV positive test). At the same time, all three are associated with different levels of employment generation as a result of using alternative technologies. The three different projects are labeled as A, B, and C. The same discount rate of 10 percent is used to evaluate all three. The efficiency ranking of the three projects as measured by the NPV results can be calculated using the present values of the investment and labor cost and assuming that present values of the yearly revenues can be converted using a perpetuity formula (present value = fixed annual cash flow/discount rate. The present value of investment for each alternative, with cost of labor as the only yearly input cost, can be converted to present values using the perpetuity formula and gives the efficiency ranking of the three projects as measured by the NPV results. Exhibit 24.11 shows the calculation of efficiency attributes of the three projects, labor demands, and costs. The first ranking along the NPV criterion shows that alternative A is the preferred option.

The NPV is calculated by adding the present value of the perpetuity (e.g., $3,000 for project A), less the investment costs, expressed in present values (or −$1,000 for project A), giving a total expected value of NPV of $2,000. Given the parameters for projects B and C, the order of the rank is project A followed by B and C or A > B > C. The company making the decision is also concerned about the net generation of employment. This could be the result of political anxieties about high unemployment in the area, county, or country where the firm expects to locate these investments. Taking only the employment generation dimension into account, the decision maker would conclude by examination that project B would generate more employment (12 units) than A or C.

At this point, the decision maker may want to explore the following question: Are there circumstances and considerations under which the company would augment the results of the NPV criterion (maximization of wealth) with the net employment generation criterion in order to achieve a combined objective of wealth maximization with employment creation? In a pure competitive economy, this question might not seem relevant because the underlying assumption is that market mechanisms allocate resources and factors of production, resulting in the allocation of different factors of production (e.g., land, capital, and labor) up to their net contribution to the profitability (bottom line) of alternative investment activities. Nevertheless, the company making the investment may want to consider social goals (such as employment generation or labor-related goals) before reaching a decision. Implicitly, the prevalence of unemployment could be considered a source of risk (e.g., theft of property, social unrest due to unemployment, and political or regulatory disfavor) or a source of diminished purchasing power for the local market. In a single-dimension analysis and in a particular context and country, the potential negative effects of unemployment could be considered either by using a risk-adjusted discount rate when calculating the NPV, or by factoring in expectations of additional expenditures or lower revenues in a regular cash flow analysis. Another perspective that could emerge in particular settings with high unemployment is the necessity to explicitly take this dimension into consideration when seeking licensing for the investment from local or state authorities, who in turn might place employment generation as a top priority. Exhibit 24.12 shows two

Exhibit 24.12   The Scoring Indexes and the Calculation of an Aggregate Value

Scoring Matrix: Dividing Each Value by the Maximum in Each Column (Expressed in Percent)

	Scores for Efficiency	Weight W1	Score for Labor Employment	Weight W2	Sum of Scores	Rank
A	100.0	0.8	83.3	0.2	96.7	1
B	90.0	0.8	100.0	0.2	92.0	2
C	75.0	0.8	75.0	0.2	75.0	3

Note: This exhibit shows possible ways to organize scoring and ranking of the three alternative projects (A, B, and C), according to efficiency and employment generation. For an initial set of weights of 0.80 (W1) and 0.20 (W2), the weighted rank is the same as in Exhibit 24.11.

possible ways to organize the scoring and ranking of the three projects: scoring according to efficiency and to employment generation.

For the efficiency dimension, for example, the decision maker divides the NPV (of project A) by the maximum NPV (project A) of all comparable projects and expresses the ranking in percent. This continues in the same way with the NPV values of projects B and C, which give a percent partial score of efficiency of 90.0 (B) and 75.0 (C). For the labor employment dimension, the decision maker could proceed in the same way, with the highest score for project B that generates or uses 12 units of labor, and this results in a 100 percent partial score and the lowest for project C that would only generate nine units of employment and thus would obtain a score of $9/12 = 75.0$. Exhibit 24.13 shows this calculation, as well as the aggregation of the two scores using initial weights of 0.80 (W1) for efficiency and 0.20 (W2) for employment generation. Exhibit 24.13 shows sensitivity analysis for this example, with weights for efficiency (W1) changing from 0.30 to 0.80.

The upper part of Exhibit 24.13 shows that initially applying higher weights to the criterion for wealth contribution (or the financial efficiency criterion) with the complement of a lower weight for the employment generation criterion replicates

Exhibit 24.13   For Some Range in the Values of W1, the Ranking Is the Same as the Ranking with the Pure Efficiency Criterion

Sensitivity to Weight W1 where Weight W2 is the complement to 1 or W2 = 1.0 − W1

	Total Score	0.30	0.35	0.40	0.45	0.50	0.55	0.60	0.65	0.70	0.75	0.80
A	96.7	88.3	89.2	90.0	90.8	91.7	92.5	93.3	94.2	95.0	95.8	96.7
B	92.0	97.0	96.5	96.0	95.5	95.0	94.5	94.0	93.5	93.0	92.5	92.0
C	75.0	75.0	75.0	75.0	75.0	75.0	75.0	75.0	75.0	75.0	75.0	75.0

Note: This exhibit shows sensitivity analysis among the alternative options with changing weights (0.30 to 0.80) for efficiency (W1). Once the weight for efficiency decreases to a value of 0.60, the ranking changes: B ranks first, followed by A, and then C.

the same ranking as the NPV ranking. Thus, the sequence would still be A > B for values of W1 higher than 0.65.

In principle, the question is: Are there possible and plausible values for which the ranking might change if other considerations or criteria are simultaneously undertaken for decision-making purposes? The mechanics of such a question are explored by changing the relative weights (W1 and W2) given to the first criterion on efficiency and the two on employment generation potential. From the sensitivity analysis that follows the initial ranking, the impact of different weights given to efficiency considerations (W1) and to employment considerations (W2 = 1 – W1) is revealed. The NPV criterion and the weighted criterion coincide up to weights W1 of about 0.65 (or 65 percent) and with 0.35 (35 percent) for W2.

The decision maker should not expect in many circumstances with relatively high weights given to the efficiency (e.g., NPV) criterion for ranking that high departures from wealth maximization decisions will occur. On the other hand, a combination of a narrower range for the values for the NPVs and employment generation could put the scores closer together or flip the initial rankings. Further analysis and discussion would be needed in such cases.

APPLICATIONS OF MCA METHODS

A review of the existing literature on the use of MCA methods for capital decision making seems to indicate that the MCA methodology is used more for projects in the public sector. This is understandable considering the multiple goals of public sector agencies. The private sector, by contrast, is increasingly concerned with achieving not only primary but also secondary goals, as well as with recognizing the factors that affect long-term sustainability and, lately, environmental considerations that might affect corporate valuation of investments through time. Hence, many corporations use these methodologies. For large-scale capital investments, MCA is an especially valuable tool for both the public and private sectors. Consequently, analysts and decision makers should be familiar with the approaches and be aware of the limitations of the tools.

MCA methodologies are used for a range of capital budgeting decisions on issues of finance, infrastructure, and social projects. For example, Steuer and Na (2003) have compiled a total of 265 references for multiple criteria decision making (MCDM) techniques applied to problems and issues in finance. Most of the articles in the survey refer to cases of investment decision problems. Almost 25 percent of the references are for MCDA and AHP. The most cited reference concerns general programming and multiple objectives programming that use linear and nonlinear optimization techniques to find solutions to issues related to capital budgeting, portfolio selection, and commercial bank management. A much lesser used technique is multiattribute utility theory (MAUT), which uses various mathematical tools for assessing preferences (value function) and ranking alternatives.

Firms often use MCA in the selection, design, and operation of infrastructure projects. Turskis, Zavadskas, and Peldschus (2009) use linear, nonlinear, and particularly logarithmic methods of normalization to arrive at the score matrix. They also use four different methods of ranking that lead to the agreed "best" investment solution in the choice of construction design. Firms have successfully used different MCA methods in plant location decision making (Brimberg and

ReVelle, 2000). Hobbs, Chankong, Hamadeh, and Stakhiv (1992) as well as Hobbs and Meier (2000) apply MCA methodology for investments in the water sector and the environment. Shianetz, Kavanah, and Lockington (2007) use MCA methods for the assessment of tourist destinations and projects. MCA also guides decisions for manufacturing technology investments (Tan, Lim, Platts, and Koay, 2006a, 2006b). Hajkowicz and Collins (2006) examine 113 papers that use MCA methods for water management and find heavy usage of MCA for water policy evaluation, strategic planning, and infrastructure selection. Saaty and Vargas (1994) discuss using the AHP method in technological, economic, political and social environments. Dyer and Sarin (1979) discuss value functions and multiattributes. Sandahl and Sjogren (2003) discuss the use of MCA methods vs. traditional NPV and single-criterion methods by Sweden's larger corporations. Sarabando and Dias (2009, 2010) present the results of evaluations starting with qualitative information matrices to arrive at the ranking of alternative investments using the MCA method.

IMPLEMENTING MCA: SOME KEY CONSIDERATIONS

The effective use of MCA requires organizational support and commitment from the top. If the agency is shifting from other forms of analysis to support investment decisions, this means that new processes must be accepted and learned (Ray and Triantaphyllou, 1999).

Incorporating MCA into Organizational Practice

MCA, like any other tool, has to be rooted in the organizational practice and culture of a company or agency because capital budgeting decisions are not separate from other functions in the organization. Aksoy, Butler, and Minor (1996) outline some common characteristics that can facilitate adopting MCA. These factors include ease and use, its understanding and acceptance within an organization, perceived usefulness, and the time and cost of implementation.

Management should invest time and care to ensure that the process of setting up the MCA system—the formulation of alternatives and ranking used by the organization—is done well because these factors affect the ability of managers to both formulate and implement projects effectively. Similar to other management systems or tools, much depends on the support of the organization and leadership for MCA to be effectively implemented.

MCA, Organization, and People

Various parties are involved in setting up and using MCA methods and systems including decision makers, analysts, promoters or supporters of the system, external vendors for systems, and consultants from within or outside the organization (Pomerol and Romero, 2000). Once the system is in place, managers involved in design and implementation become the key actors.

A key group, which may be the main initiator of an MCA program, consists of the decision makers or leaders in the organization. Key decision makers may have limited time to devote to the detailed process of evaluating capital budgeting projects. Still, they need to be able to appreciate the assumptions and key conditions for the MCA and to be ready to build support and address initial resistance to changing processes. Especially in the initial stage, leaders need to be involved at the different organizational levels to ensure that incentives exist for managers to adopt the new system and to encourage their interest and participation. Relevant executives of a company need to formulate or agree on the set of criteria to use that corresponds to the underlying values and goals of the corporation and the related weights assigned. As the transparency of the MCA process increases for the team involved, so does the quality of the output, advice, decision making, and even implementation that emerges from the system. Transparency itself may be another challenge, depending on corporate culture and context.

Analysts and their support team of managers, consultants, and suppliers are the ones who craft the MCA process and need to perform their roles with coordination and flexibility. They need to respond to the firm's needs and to recognize that a learning curve exists in applying these methods. Promoters of MCA methods need to think about the internal and external conditions, incentives, perspectives, and motivations for a successful and sustainable implementation of MCA systems. Hammond, Keeney, and Raiffa (1998) offer a practical guide to decision making.

Future Direction

In the complex global economy, both the public and private sectors are increasingly likely to use MCA systems. This increase in usage is likely to occur by using one system of choice or by incorporating MCA into a much bigger program of selection elements. Technology plays an important role in making MCA systems user friendly. Several software programs are currently available or under development. Some are based on spreadsheet applications and platforms, while others require special software installation and expertise.

SUMMARY AND CONCLUSIONS

MCA is a set of methodologies that can aid decision makers in the capital budgeting process. This is particularly so in cases involving multiple objectives, regulatory conditions, or other valuation factors for the decision makers involved. Several commonly used methods are WSM, WPM, and AHP. Technological developments such as easy access to comparative information (electronic databases) and the ability to share methodological applications and examples across the organization and in different locations facilitate the introduction, use, and participation by important stakeholders.

Organizations have successfully implemented MCA when they have planned and carefully considered the main elements that are important in capital budgeting decisions such as the goals or values that each alternative can bring to the decision makers and the corresponding criteria and weights. Decision makers agree on these elements at the outset of the process. This does not mean, however, that they should not change the criteria in light of dynamic conditions in market preferences, technologies, and better research and information systems. Decision makers need to provide guidance for the successful implementation of MCA systems.

The systems in place need to be credible and acceptable. Ultimately, the system must be directed by decision makers and cannot be fully automated. Active research is taking place into the methodologies and results of applications of MCA methods. Investors need to test and adapt MCA methods, plus the other methods discussed in this book, to their specific company needs and environments.

DISCUSSION QUESTIONS

1. Multicriteria decision-making tools appear more relevant for use in the public versus the private sector. What reasons might help explain this discrepancy?
2. What is the relationship between the NPV criterion and MCA?
3. What are some advantages for investors if they consider other effects of their investment other than a purely monetary return? Consider the case of investments in new transport technology projects.
4. In terms of process, what requisites or factors are important to start implementing the MCA methodology for private sector investment decisions?

REFERENCES

Aksoy, Yasemin, Timothy W. Butler, and Elliott D. Minor III. 1996. "Comparative Studies in Interactive Multiple Objective Mathematical Programming." *European Journal of Operational Research* 89:2, 408–422.

Altman, Edward I. 1993. *Corporate Financial Distress and Bankruptcy*. New York: John Wiley & Sons.

Bell, David E., Howard Raiffa, and Amos Tversky. 1989. *Decision Making*. Cambridge: Cambridge University Press.

Brealey, Richard A., and Stewart C. Myers. 2003. *Principles of Corporate Finance*. New York: McGraw-Hill.

Brimberg, Jack, and Charles S. ReVelle. 2000. "The Maximum Return-on-Investment Plant Location Problem." *Journal of the Operational Research Society* 51:6, 729–735.

Dyer, James S., and Rakesh K. Sarin. 1979. "Measurable Multiattribute Value Functions." *Operations Research* 27:4, 810–822.

Hammond, John S., III, Ralph L. Keeney, and Howard Raiffa. 1998. *Smart Choices: A Practical Guide to Making Better Decisions*. Boston: Harvard Business School Press.

Hajkowicz, Stefan, and Kerry Collins. 2006. "A Review of Multiple Criteria Analysis for Water Resource Planning and Management." *Water Resources Management* 21:9, 1553–1566.

Hobbs, Benjamin F. 1986. "What Can We Learn from Experiments in Multi-objective Decision Analysis?" *IEEE Transactions. On Systems Management and Cybernetics* 16:3, 384–394.

Hobbs, Benjamin F., Vira Chankong, Wael Hamadeh, and Eugene Stakhiv. 1992. "Does Choice of Multicriteria Method Matter? An Experiment in Water Resource Planning." *Water Resources Research* 28:7, 1767–1779.

Hobbs, Benjamin F., and Peter M. Meier. 2000. *Energy Decisions and the Environment: A Guide to the Use of Multicriteria Methods*. Norwell, MA: Kluwer Academic Publishers.

Pomerol, Jean Charles, and Sergio Barba Romero. 2000. *Multicriterion Decisions in Management: Principles and Practice*. Boston: Kluwer International Series.

Ray, Thomas, and Evangelos Triantaphyllou. 1999. "Procedures for the Evaluation of Conflicts in Rankings of Alternatives." *Computers and Industrial Engineering* 36:1, 35–44.

Saaty, Thomas L., and Luis G. Vargas. 1994. *Decision Making in Economic, Political, Social and Technological Environments with the AHP*. Pittsburgh, PA: RWS Publications.

Sandahl, Gert, and Stefan Sjogren. 2003. "Capital Budgeting Methods among Sweden's Largest Groups of Companies—The State of the Art and a Comparison with Earlier Studies." Working Paper, School of Economics and Commercial Law, Goteborg University.

Sarabando, Paula, and Luís C. Dias. 2009. "Multiattribute Choice with Ordinal Information: A Comparison of Different Decision Rules." *IEEE Transactions on Systems, Man, and Cybernetics, Part A*, 39:3, 545–554.

Sarabando, Paula, and Luís C. Dias. 2010. "Simple Procedures of Choice in Multicriteria Problems without Precise Information about the Alternatives' Values." *Computers & Operations Research* 37:12, 2239–2247.

Schianetz, Karin, Lydia Kavanagh, and David Lockington. 2007. "Concepts and Tools for Comprehensive Sustainability Assessments for Tourism Destinations: A Comparative Review." *Journal of Sustainable Tourism* 15:4, 369–389.

Steuer, Ralph E., and Paul Na. 2003. "Multiple Criteria Decision Making Combined with Finance: A Categorized Bibliographic Study." *European Journal of Operational Research* 150:3, 496–515.

Tan, Kim Hua, Chee Peng Lim, Ken Platts, and Hooi Shen Koay. 2006a. "An Intelligent Decision Support System for Manufacturing Technology Investments." *International Journal of Production Economics*, 104:1, 179–190.

Tan, Kim Hua, Chee Peng Lim, Ken Platts, and Hooi Shen Koay. 2006b. "Managing Manufacturing Technology Investments: An Intelligent Learning System Approach." *International Journal of Computer Integrated Manufacturing*, 19:1, 4–13.

Triantaphyllou, Evangelos. 2000. *Multi-Criteria Decision Making: A Comparative Study*. Boston: Kluwer Academic Publishers.

Triantaphyllou, Evangelos. 2001. "Two New Cases of Rank Reversals when the AHP and Some of Its Additive Variants Are Used That Do Not Occur with the Multiplicative AHP." *Multi-Criteria Decision Analysis* 10:1, 11–25.

Triantaphyllou, Evangelos, and Khalid Baig. 2005. "The Impact of Aggregating Benefit and Cost Criteria in Four MCDA Methods." *IEEE Transactions on Engineering Management* 52:2, 213–226.

Turskis, Zenonas, Edmundas Kazimieras Zavadskas, and Friedel Peldschus. 2009. "Multi-criteria Optimization System for Decision Making in Construction Design and Management." *Engineering Economics* 1:61, 7–17.

ABOUT THE AUTHOR

Fernando Fernholz joined the Sanford School of Public Policy at Duke University in 2001. He worked with the Harvard Institute for International Development from 1985 until moving to Duke. He teaches graduate and undergraduate courses on economics, public finance, and international development. He is the co-director of the Program of Project Analysis and Risk Management (PARM) at Duke University. He has worked as an advisor to private and public sector organizations and governments in different countries around the world. His research and advisory services interests include capital budgeting, concession contracts, privatization, economic growth and development, education, health and nutrition, public debt, local government finance, and infrastructure. Professor Fernholz headed his own consulting, construction, and data processing companies before he moved to academia. He has a Master of Civil Engineering from the RWTH Aachen in Germany, MPA from the Kennedy School of Government, and a Ph.D. in Economics from Boston University.

Answers to Discussion Questions

CHAPTER 2   CORPORATE STRATEGY
AND INVESTMENT DECISIONS

1. In the emergence state, incumbent firms may undertake irreversible investments that allow them to commit credibly to a specific strategy; an example is the building of a large idle capacity. Such commitments may prevent further entry in the industry, as potential entrants fear that incumbents will compete aggressively by expanding production in the event of new entry. This strategy may reduce the amount of entry in the industry in the emergence state or it could speed up the transition to the growth stage. To value such investments properly, the present value of the strategic advantage conferred by the investment must be taken into account. This can be done, for example, by modeling sales growth as falling less dramatically over time than it would in case no such investment is undertaken.

2. If markets are efficient, capital will always flow to its most profitable use and thus corporate allocation of capital cannot add value. Thus, a necessary condition for the corporate allocation of capital to add value is the existence of frictions in financial markets. In less than perfect capital markets, some businesses may have difficulties raising capital. For example, markets may not understand the logic of complex and innovative businesses. Asymmetric information can also be a reason, as managers may have sensitive information that is unavailable to outside investors. Businesses without tangible assets may also find borrowing difficult because they have little collateral. In such cases, conglomerates may alleviate some of these problems and thus can tap capital markets more easily. Furthermore, conglomerates may use the internally generated funds (i.e., retained earnings) from their divisions to engage in *winner picking*, which is the practice of transferring funds from divisions with high cash flows but poor investment opportunities to divisions with low cash flows but good investment opportunities.

3. The resource-based theory of the firm is a version of the traditional economics of competition. Perfect competition implies little or no profits (or "normal" profits). Monopolists, on the other hand, have "extraordinary" profits. However, monopoly power only survives if firms have some resources that are unique. Firms that aim to remain profitable in the long run should invest in and protect their unique resources, which are assets that are not easily available to competitors. The resource-based view implies that firms should consider only projects that are related to their crucial assets. Firms' long-run strategic decisions are affected by management's ability to identify crucial assets and the set of projects that are complementary to these crucial assets. Under the nexus-of-contracts view, most stakeholders are protected by bilateral contracts with the firms' equity holders, who own the firm in the sense that they have residual cash flow rights. In practice, this

view suggests that managers should aim to maximize the market value of shareholders' equity. These two views are complementary. The resource-based view is concerned with the sources of value creation (the unique resources), while the nexus-of-contracts view is concerned with the division of value (i.e., how shareholders and other stakeholders should be compensated).

4. Due to the presence of network externalities, in some markets only a few dominant standards may survive. An important strategic issue in these markets is whether formerly independent firms should coordinate their efforts. Although competing firms are usually not allowed to jointly fix prices or restrict production on antitrust grounds, they are usually allowed to cooperate on technology development and adoption. Because cooperation is paramount for sustaining high profit levels in the industry, a firm may choose one of three possibilities: (1) to compete fiercely hoping to win the standards battle; (2) to cooperate with competitors in developing a common standard; or (3) to eliminate competition by fully integrating with current competitors. Which option is the preferred one depends on various factors such as the division of surplus among firms in the industry, the value of synergies from coordination, and the structure of incentives inside each firm.

CHAPTER 3   CORPORATE GOVERNANCE AND INVESTMENT DECISIONS

1. To explain investment cash flow sensitivity, some authors consider asymmetric information theory, which supposes that the information is not equally distributed between managers and suppliers of external finance, and others refer to agency theory. An assumption of asymmetric information theory is that managers act in the best interests of existing shareholders and external investors cannot assess the quality of investment projects. Therefore, these investors require a premium that leads to a higher cost of external financing. Such a situation may have two implications. First, managers will prefer internal funds to finance new projects. This implies a positive relationship between the availability of cash flow and investment. Second, in some cases, managers will prefer to underinvest rather than to look for new investors. Consequently, investment cash flow sensitivity can be a symptom of underinvestment. According to agency theory, however, managers are assumed to take actions that are not in shareholders' interests. To increase their power, managers undertake the highest level of investment. As a result, they may use a firm's free cash flows in unprofitable projects. Investment cash flow sensitivity is then a symptom of overinvestment.

2. Managers may prefer to invest in projects with short-term performance for several reasons. First, a nontrivial part of executive compensation is often based on short-term accounting performance. Therefore, to increase their compensation, managers might focus on reporting good short-term accounting profits. Second, managers concerned with their careers might invest in projects with short-term profits. In both cases, managers might have a short horizon and therefore might be reluctant to undertake projects that generate profits only in the long run.

3. Career concerns are the main reason that induces managers to herd other managers in their investment decisions. In that way, bad performance would be attributable to a common negative shock and not to the manager's own decisions. Therefore, firms would be less likely to fire the manager when performance does not meet expectations.

4. Theoretically, the board of directors plays an important governance role. Yet, the empirical literature is inconclusive as to whether the board is effective in reducing investment

distortions. Board members might be ineffective for two major reasons. First, the chief executive officer (CEO) may control the information received by the board, which affects the board's judgment. Second, board members may care about their careers and prefer not to be in conflict with the CEO.

5. The presence of large shareholders in the firm has a positive enhancement effect by monitoring managers in order to attenuate the overinvestment of free cash flows. More-over, these activist shareholders can spend time and effort to provide information about investment projects and therefore reduce underinvestment problems stemming from asymmetric information. However, these large shareholders also have a negative en-trenchment effect. When their shareholdings exceed a certain level, underinvestment and overinvestment problems can be exacerbated.

CHAPTER 4   MEASURING INVESTMENT VALUE: FREE CASH FLOW, NET PRESENT VALUE, AND ECONOMIC VALUE ADDED

1. Following the proof in Equation 4.14, start with FCF/(1 + A-TWACC) and substitute in [P-TWACC − k_D(Tax Rate)(D/V)] for A-TWACC. Execute the following algebraic steps:

$$V = FCF/[1 + P\text{-}TWACC - k_D(Tax\ Rate)(D/V)]$$
$$V[1 + P\text{-}TWACC - k_D(Tax\ Rate)(D/V)] = FCF$$
$$V(1 + P\text{-}TWACC) - k_D(D)(Tax\ Rate) = FCF$$
$$V = [FCF + k_D(D)(Tax\ Rate)]/(1 + P\text{-}TWACC) = CFA/(1 + P\text{-}TWACC)$$

2. The CFA calculation includes the tax savings from interest and the A-TWACC also includes the tax benefit of interest in its calculation (recall A-TWACC = P-TWACC − k_D(Tax Rate)(D/V)). Consequently, using both metrics in a valuation can be construed as double counting the tax benefit of interest within the cash flow and the discount rate.

3. The constant discount rate used in the basic textbook version of NPV is a summary discount rate, call it "z," for all the different rates that apply to the different cash flows through time. Assuming discount rates are larger the farther into the future the cash flow occurs, "z" will overdiscount early cash flows and underdiscount later cash flows to arrive at the same NPV figure as the associated dynamic NPV version. Thus, "z" is like the yield to maturity for a bond in that a bond's cash flows are also discounted at different rates depending upon maturity, yet the yield to maturity is a single summary discount rate applied to all of the bond's cash flows to produce the correct bond price.

4. The scale issue occurs when simply changing the debt financing to equity financing for converting CFA to FCF without considering that the project may not be as large should the debt financing not have been available. Consequently, the smaller nondebt project's cash flows (i.e., the all-equity version of the project) will most likely decrease by more than just the tax savings on interest relative to the associated CFA for the larger scale debt financed project.

5. When there is no debt, FCF and CFA are the same because the tax savings from interest is zero. P-TWACC and A-TWACC are also equal because once debt is taken out of the capital mix, both calculations equal the cost of equity (k_E in Equations 4.11 through 4.14).

6. Accelerated depreciation will initially reduce NOPAT more than when NOPAT is cal-culated with straight-line depreciation. The trend will eventually reverse with the

straight-line depreciation version of NOPAT being less than the accelerated depreciation version of NOPAT. Following Exhibit 4.5, the practice should be to convert depreciation to the straight-line method when calculating EVA.

CHAPTER 5   ALTERNATIVE METHODS OF EVALUATING CAPITAL INVESTMENTS

1. Liquidity often matters more to smaller versus larger firms because the firm may be able to accept only a few large projects (or possibly only one) at any given point in time. By using PB to emphasize liquidity initially, a small firm can grow and meet short-term obligations. Eventually the growth could lead to a firm being large enough to consider multiple projects with some projects being long-term oriented and worthy of more detailed analysis such as using net present value (NPV).

2. Myers (1977) contends that by using too much debt, a firm becomes short-term oriented in order to meet short-term debt obligations. The firm may have to forego longer-term projects that add value because these projects may not generate sufficient liquidity in the short term.

3. Fisher's rate of return (FROR) is the discount rate that sets the NPV of both of the projects equal to each other.

4. Multiple IRRs can occur when net cash inflows and net cash outflows occur at different points in time throughout the project's life. Each time the cash flow stream switches sign, a new IRR potentially emerges. That is, a project with unconventional cash flows (i.e., a project with more than one change in sign of the cash flows) may potentially have as many IRRs as changes in sign.

5. Because the cash flows change sign twice, the project can potentially have two IRRs. In the example, the project's IRRs are 10 percent and 20 percent.

6. The MIRR must agree with an associated NPV analysis because the NPV, calculated as a PI, is embedded in the MIRR calculation. Consequently, whenever NPV > 0, MIRR > k because PI > 1. Whenever NPV = 0, MIRR = k because PI = 1. Whenever NPV < 0, MIRR < k, because PI < 1.

CHAPTER 6   CAPITAL RATIONING FOR CAPITAL BUDGETING

1. Agency costs in capital budgeting are overinvestment and understating future performance. Overinvestment occurs because managers prefer to control larger rather than smaller assets. Therefore, they engage in investments though other alternatives (e.g., investment in other divisions or outside the firm) in order to achieve a high return. These opportunity costs are agency costs because principals who engage in overinvestment are unaware of the opportunity costs as a result of information asymmetry. Understating future performance could lead to wrong investment decisions, which could then lead to agency costs. Managers have incentives to lower expectations on future performance so that their performance goals are not too difficult to reach. Capital rationing leads to a relative comparison of different projects so that only the most promising projects receive funding in the capital budget. Overinvestment is thus reduced. Further, competing with projects for capital makes an understatement of future performance unattractive because that would increase the likelihood that a project will not receive funding.

2. The major benefit of capital rationing is reduced agency costs. At the same time such a more competitive setting can harm the firm's culture and lead to an atmosphere of

distrust. Further, strong competition could provide managers with incentives to manipulate their performance outlook or at least present a biased performance outlook. Firms need to find a way that ensures both low agency costs in the process of capital budgeting and an acceptable level of competition within the firm so that manipulation and other obtrusive actions do not arise.

3. In organizations with homogeneous divisions, competitive capital rationing can help to ensure that only the best projects receive funding so that firm value is increased and money is not "wasted" on projects that provide lower performance than others. In organizations with heterogeneous divisions, competitive capital rationing can lead to difficulties because some divisions generally have lower performance outlooks than others due to the nature of their business. However, some level of competition can help to improve performance and can provide managers with incentives to choose the best projects. Although comparisons between projects are less possible with heterogeneous divisions, a firm could benefit from a more competitive spirit.

4. One stream of the literature assumes that lying and misrepresenting information to a superior does not incur any personal costs or disutility (e.g., bad conscience). Thus, individuals engage in lying to the maximum level as soon as a small incentive exists to do so. Another stream of the literature compares an individual's motivation to lie to the motivation to provide effort. Similar to effort with an increasing cost function (cost of delivering effort), authors of that stream of literature argue that individuals lie up to a certain point where lying becomes too costly. Individuals reach this point when they lie so much that the bad feelings of doing so (the "cost") loom larger than the benefits that could be gained by lying. A third stream of the literature expects that the level of lying is proportional to the level of competition. That is, individuals lie more within a more competitive setting. The theoretical argument here is that the surroundings provide individuals with an excuse to lie. Individuals blame a competitive setting for their drop in ethical standards ("I had to misreport as otherwise, I would not have a chance.").

5. The three main streams in the literature on individual behavior in competitive settings rely on several assumptions. With multiple rounds, individuals create a reputation. Thus, over multiple rounds, the likelihood that someone discovers misreporting over time increases. This possible threat to damaging a person's reputation reduces the likelihood that an individual would lie to the maximum due to the small incentives. Much of the behavior described in the literature on honesty in combination with competition is based on information asymmetry that decreases over time.

CHAPTER 7 ANALYZING FOREIGN INVESTMENTS

1. Ensuring the success of a foreign investment project requires the support of all major business functions. In the preparation phase ("setting the scene"), the financial function is already involved, for example, with capital expenditures. The investment sum may be large, especially with financial firm startups. The financial calculations in the information management phase can be done with spreadsheets that analysts have used before. However, contacting the financial experts periodically may be useful and increase their involvement in the project. In the risk management phase, financial experts will ask for hedge strategies and other measures that may limit risks. They will also have a voice in the decision making.

2. The statement may be true but easily modeling the complications of foreign investments may be very difficult. Sensitivity analyses and scenario analyses may therefore be helpful in obtaining an understanding of the expected outcomes and their reliability.

3. U.S. firms are generally allowed to use less conservative depreciation practices than German firms are. Hence, U.S. firms will have fewer tax shields from depreciation than their counterparts. The payback period of their investments is therefore generally longer.

4. The financial director in question appears to be more interested in a local view than in the parent firm's view on earnings. As a rule, shareholders would disagree with this director. However, the director may have made the statement because the local government blocked funds or because taking a local view was necessary to convince the authorities of good intentions.

5. The responses involving the attractiveness of this investment from the subsidiary's and parent's viewpoint follow.
   A. The annual CFs are LTO 7.5 million – (LTO 0.6 million + LTO 2.2 million + LTO 1.6 million + LTO 0.9 million) = LTO 7.5 million – LTO 5.3 million = LTO 2.2 million. The annual local profit is LTO 2.2 million – LTO 1 million = LTO 1.2 million. The annual ROI is LTO 1.2 million/LTO 10 million = 12 percent. The PV of the operational CFs is LTO 1.2 million × 5.650 = LTO 6.78 million. The NPV for the subsidiary is LTO 6.78 million – LTO 5.00 million = LTO 1.78 million.
   B. NBB gets ("blocked") dividends and fees and it provides the investment sum. The FV of the dividends is LTO 1.2 million × 3.106 = LTO 3.727 million. The PV is (LTO 3.727 million × 0.3122 =) LTO 1.1635 million × 0.7 = LTO 0.815 million. The PV of the fees is LTO 0.6 million × 5.650 = LTO 3.390 million. The project's NPV is LTO 0.815 million + LTO 3.390 million – LTO 5.00 million = LTO – 0.80 million. The NPV in AUD must be calculated as follows: the PV of the dividends is A$ 3.727 million × 0.7/3.0 = A$ 0.870 million. The PV of the fees is A$ 0.6 million × (0.8929/2.1 + 0.7972/2.2 + 0.7118/2.3 + 0.6355/2.4 + 0.5674/2.5 + 0.5066/2.6 + 0.4523/2.7+ 0.4039/2.8 + 0.3606/2.9 + 0.3220/3.0) × 0.7 = A$ 0.6 million × 2.133 × 0.7 = A$ 0.896 million. The investment outlay is A$ 5 million/2 = A$ 2.5 million. Thus, the NPV is A$ 0.870 million + A$ 0.869 million – A$ 2.5 million = A$ – 0.76 million. The project should therefore be rejected.

CHAPTER 8   POSTCOMPLETION AUDITING OF CAPITAL INVESTMENTS

1. PCA has the potential to aid a company in avoiding previous mistakes and to identify systematically successful processes that can be repeated in future projects. Specifically, it can help companies to improve the accuracy of underlying assumptions and goals in their planning material. PCA feedback can enhance the development of proposals for new projects, improve the understanding of key factors affecting investment projects, and develop knowledge related to strategy formulation. Additionally, PCA can be conducive to improving capital investment processes in general.

2. By definition, formal PCA occurs after the initial investment is completed when the project is operational (compared with the monitoring of the implementation phase of an investment). Hence, making changes after commissioning an investment can be too late. Also, the triggers for change are likely to come from alternative mechanisms such as routine reporting and informal discussions.

3. Alternative people for conducting PCA include those with prior involvement with the investment projects or individuals fully outside the firm. Individuals with prior involvement have detailed knowledge about the project. However, there is a risk that due to information asymmetry, they could present the outcome subjectively or even be tempted

to use their information advantage to manipulate figures or exaggerate performance estimations. External persons would enhance the objectivity of PCA, but they may lack knowledge about the project. One potential solution to enhance accuracy and objectivity of PCA would be to use hybrid teams, that is, to connect people from the business unit making the investment with outside resources.

4. With regard to performance measurement of a completed investment, companies have various "non-PCA" means available to help them acquire a sense of whether the targets of an investment project are being met. These means include formal systems for routinely following up key production figures as well as sales and profit centers. Control mechanisms such as visiting investing sites, presentations, and discussions can be formally arranged for investment control purposes, but typically they seem to be more informal. Major perceived benefits from PCA within companies are related to organizational learning. PCA does not have exclusivity in achieving the organizational learning benefits that are suggested to accrue from this approach. Specifically, the use of central expertise and experienced internal resources appears to be important for transferring and sharing capital investment experiences within a company. The existing alternative means to achieve the benefits suggested for PCA may discourage adoption of PCA. Specifically, smaller companies without major capital investments may perceive the existing means to be sufficient for their purposes. Furthermore, existing alternative means among the PCA adopters may affect the degree of sophistication of the PCA system. In other words, smaller companies that have less capital investments do not necessarily pay so much attention to the sophistication of PCA design.

CHAPTER 9   CAPITAL BUDGETING TECHNIQUES IN PRACTICE: U.S. SURVEY EVIDENCE

1. The survey method of research has some inherent shortcomings that require the researcher to be extremely careful when designing the survey instrument or deriving conclusions based on survey responses. Some of the major shortcomings are as follows. First, a small percentage of the survey population usually responds to a survey. Because a large percentage of the population chooses not to respond, this potentially introduces nonresponse bias. Thus, the researcher faces the task of showing that respondents and nonrespondents belong to the same population. Second, the person who completes the questionnaire may be unknown. Therefore, the possibility exists that this person might not be fully familiar about the survey topic, rendering the input obtained less meaningful. Third, questions should be framed in such a fashion as not to be leading (reflecting the researcher's bias) or subject to misinterpretation. If questions are not carefully prepared, conclusions based on survey-based results are less reliable. Fourth, the possibility exists that academic jargon differs from that used or understood by respondents, who are often practitioners. Finally, comparing and synthesizing the results of multiple surveys may be difficult because choices given to the same or a similar question could vary among surveys

2. Practitioners suggest that developing ideas into a full-blown proposal is more difficult yet more critical than later stages such as project selection or project auditing because the main input for a project's worth is developed in this stage. If cash flow estimates are done improperly, the ultimate decision regarding a project might turn out to be wrong. The selection stage is the most extensively researched area in capital budgeting surveys over the past five decades. Survey questions focus on whether firms, especially large firms, have adopted discounted cash flow techniques.

3. Surveys point out several deviations that vary from theory. For example, traditional theory suggests the following: (1) net present value (NPV) is superior to the internal rate of return (IRR) primarily because of its ability to select among competing projects the one that adds most value to the firm; and (2) using the payback period method should be discouraged primarily because it does not consider the time value of money. However, surveys consistently show that the IRR tends to be more popular with practitioners and firms continue to use the payback method as a selection technique.

4. Theory suggests that a firm should accept all positive NPV projects because implementing these projects should increase value to the firm. Therefore, when the management foregoes an otherwise positive NPV project, it falls short of fulfilling its goal of maximizing the wealth of shareholders. Capital rationing occurs when there is a limit to the amount that a firm can invest in projects regardless of the opportunity for profitable projects. Consequently, a firm operating in a capital rationing environment has to forego some positive NPV projects. Thus, in theory, capital rationing runs counter to the goal of shareholder wealth maximization.

5. Capital rationing might result from either external suppliers of funds limiting the amount available to a firm or the firm itself limiting the amount it wants to invest. Most surveys appear to indicate that capital rationing is internally imposed. Various explanations have been offered to justify internal capital rationing. Two major explanations are rooted in the interfirm and intrafirm information asymmetry. The first explanation suggests that senior managers impose capital rationing to discourage junior managers from making an unduly optimistic forecast relative to a project's true worth. The second explanation is based on the information asymmetry between senior managers and the external capital market. Senior managers impose capital rationing because they believe that this information asymmetry problem causes external financing to be costly.

6. A comprehensive analysis of survey results on capital budgeting suggests that the gap between traditional capital budgeting theory and actual practices has narrowed over the last few decades. In the development stage, most firms agree that cash flows are the appropriate cost-benefit data. Many firms estimate cash flows in a manner consistent with theory including consideration of opportunity costs as well as inflation. In the selection stage, the use of DCF techniques as a primary selection tool has increased, while the use of the payback period method as the primary selection tool has declined. Firms compute the cost of capital in keeping with theory and appear to recognize risk differences among projects and adjust for the risk accordingly, albeit on an ad hoc basis. Several major gaps remain between capital budgeting theory and practice. For example, firms sometimes apply their cost of capital as the hurdle rate for non-average-risk projects. This is especially evident in the Graham and Harvey (2001) survey in which the authors report that many firms use a company-wide discount rate when evaluating cross-border projects. Also, in the postaudit stage, firms continue to rely on short-term measures such as return on investment when evaluating managerial performance.

CHAPTER 10   ESTIMATING PROJECT CASH FLOWS

1. A project's NPV indicates whether the project generates sufficient future cash inflows to provide a return that exceeds the firm's hurdle rate. A positive NPV indicates that the project's return exceeds the firm's hurdle rate, while a negative NPV indicates that the project's return is lower than the firm's hurdle rate. A project's IRR measures the return generated by the project and is the discount rate at which the project NPV equals zero. A project that generates an IRR that is positive, but lower than the firm's hurdle rate, would result in a negative NPV.

2. Including the tax consequences of future cash flows in a DCF model will generally decrease the project's NPV. Tax payments reduce future net cash inflows, resulting in a lower NPV. Future cash inflows result in increased future cash outflows in the form of payments to federal, state, and local taxing authorities. Tax benefits arising from depreciation deductions over the project life generate tax savings, which are included in DCF models as cash inflows. However, depreciation benefits are typically less than the increased tax payments associated with future cash inflows. Additionally, the sale of an asset at the end of the project period has tax consequences. If the expected proceeds are greater than the asset's tax basis, cash outflows in the form of additional tax payments must be included in the DCF model. If expected proceeds are lower than the asset's tax basis, cash inflows in the form of tax savings must be included in the DCF model.

3. Three methods commonly used to adjust for project risk are as follows:

   • *Increase the discount rate used in DCF models.* Increasing the discount rate is consistent with finance theory of risk-return trade-offs. That is, higher risk investments must generate higher returns to justify the assumption of the additional risk. Firms using this method adjust their costs of capital upward to a level that is appropriate for perceived project risk.

   • *Shorten the project life.* Shortening the project life accounts for the uncertainty inherent in any forecast. Capital budgeting makes many assumptions; among them is that the firm will realize the cash flows during the expected project period. Projects that generate positive NPVs after reducing the expected project life are more likely to generate returns that exceed the firm's hurdle rate than are projects for which NPVs go from positive to negative when the life is shortened. Firms can use this method as a sensitivity analysis by determining the minimum life needed to achieve a positive NPV.

   • *Sensitivity analysis.* Sensitivity analysis includes "what-if" scenarios. This method addresses the extent to which increases in initial investment, decreases in future inflows, increases in future outflows, or decreases in the terminal value affect project returns.

4. Several possibilities exist to explain the use of the payback period method to evaluate investment opportunities. Research indicates that smaller firms and firms run by less educated or less sophisticated managers are more likely to use the payback period method than DCF methods. Research also indicates that many firms use the payback period method when making investment decisions involving the replacement of existing productive capacity. Larger firms run by better educated and more sophisticated managers are more likely to use the payback period as an initial screening method. Firms often reject potential investments with payback periods that exceed prescribed maxima before they invest resources to prepare DCF models.

CHAPTER 11   CAPITAL BUDGETING AND INFLATION

1. Consider the price of a computer. A reasonable statement is that the prices of computers have been constant or even decreasing in nominal terms. This suggests that in the presence of inflation, the prices of computers have been decreasing in real terms. Thus, assuming that the expected real increase in prices is zero is invalid.

2. With an expected inflation rate of 5 percent, the impact on the present value of the cash receipts is negative. With credit sales, customers have received the goods and will pay for them in the next year. In the presence of inflation, the delayed payment has a negative effect.

3. In the presence of inflation, the present value of the principal repayments decreases. The decrease in the present value of the principal repayment is exactly offset by the increase in the present value of the interest payments so that the NPV of the loan and loan repayment is zero. Thus, the present value of the interest payments increases. Because the present value of the interest payments increases, the present value of the tax savings from the interest payments also increases.

4. Since the annual depreciation allowances are not indexed to inflation, the present value of the annual depreciation allowances decreases in the presence of inflation. This means that the tax liability increases.

5. Calculating the real WACC with parameters in real terms results in the following:

$$WACC_{Real} = D\%(k_d)(1 - T) + E\%(k_e)$$
$$= 40\%(6\%)(1 - 20\%) + 60\%(10\%)$$
$$= 1.920\% + 6.000\% = 7.92\%$$

Calculating the nominal WACC results in the following:

$$K_d = 6\%(1 + 5\%) + 5\% = 11.30\%$$
$$K_e = 10\%(1 + 5\%) + 5\% = 15.50\%$$
$$WACC_{Nominal} = D\%(K_d)(1 - T) + E\%(K_e)$$
$$= 40\%(11.30\%)(1 - 20\%) + 60\%(15.50\%)$$
$$= 3.616\% + 9.300\% = 12.916\%$$

Using the Fisher relationship to obtain the "deflated" WACC, the value for the deflated WACC is 7.539 percent, which is lower than the value of the real WACC, which is 7.92 percent.

$$WACC_{Difference} = (12.916\% - 5\%)/(1 + 5\%) = 7.539\%$$

CHAPTER 12   BASIC RISK ANALYSIS TECHNIQUES IN CAPITAL BUDGETING

1. The CE results in the CE(NPV) and involves the following steps:
   - Forecast the cash flows for the project.
   - Assign the appropriate certainty equivalent factor (CEF) to its corresponding yearly cash flow.
   - Multiply the cash flow by its CEF to determine the certain cash flow.
   - Discount the cash flows at the risk-free rate, deduct the initial investment, and obtain the CE(NPV).

2. Calculating the RADR(NPV) involves the following steps:
   - Forecast the cash flows for the project.
   - Determine the risk-adjusted discount rate (RADR).
   - Discount the cash flows at the RADR, deduct the initial investment, and obtain the RADR(NPV).

   This method is related to the CAPM in that the CAPM can be used to determine the RADR. The CAPM has many disadvantages but arguably remains one of the theoretically sound methods to be used in the RADR(NPV).

3. Discounting the cash flows at 16 percent results in a NPV of $52,709. The CVs for years 1, 2, 3, and 4 are 0.11, 0.31, 0.33, and 0.30, respectively.

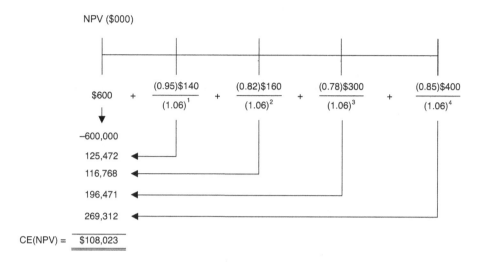

According to the normal NPV, the project should be accepted given its positive NPV of $52,709. The CE(NPV) of $108,023 indicates that risk adjusting the project makes it more attractive because it adds more value to the firm. Because the project has lower risk than suggested by using the WACC, the firm should accept the project.

4. The NPV and RADR(NPV) of each project are calculated as follows:

Project X
NPV @ 15% = $206,966
The RADR is calculated using the CAPM as follows:
$r_p = 7\% + 1.5(15\% - 7\%) = 19\%$
RADR(NPV) @ 15% = $152,892
Project Y
NPV @ 15% = $207,620
The RADR is calculated using the CAPM as follows:
$r_p = 7\% + 2(15\% - 7\%) = 23\%$
RADR(NPV) @ 23% = $90,122

Although both projects have highly similar and positive NPVs, the RADR(NPV) indicates that Project X is preferable to Project Y.

5. The two methods are related, use the same inputs such as cash flows, and should theoretically be subject to the same judgment biases. If all inputs are applied consistently, the CE and RADR methods should produce the same NPV.

CHAPTER 13 CAPITAL BUDGETING WITH POLITICAL/COUNTRY RISK

1. Political risk often refers to doing business abroad, leading to additional risks not present in the domestic environment. These additional risks emanate from various country differences in economic structures, policies, sociopolitical institutions, geography, and currencies. As such, reaching a conclusive definition of political risk is difficult because of

the multiplicity of the sources of risk, the complexity of their interactions, and the variety of social sciences involved.

2. The advantages and disadvantages of each technique are summarized in the following table.

Techniques	Advantages	Disadvantages
Comparative techniques	Useful in the screening process	Lacks an objective theory for parameter selection
		Uses an arbitrary distribution of weights
		Adopts the same grid for all countries
Analytical techniques		
Special report approach	Focuses on one country at a time, low cost, and rapid implementation	Subjective, partial, and lacks a scientific analysis
Probabilistic approach	Applies to complex situations	Difficult to calculate the appropriate probabilities
Sociological approach	Makes individualizing the analysis possible	Difficult to apply in a comparative context
Multicriteria approach	Provides a decision-support tool	Subjective (based on the analysts' judgment)
Expert systems approach	Relies on quantitative and qualitative information	Requires expensive information
Econometric techniques	Is objective	Relies on historical information (backward looking)

3. To incorporate political risk in the capital budgeting process, the analyst has to adopt two steps: (1) identify and assess the risk using one or a combination of risk assessment techniques, and (2) translate the assessment with the discounted cash flow format. Three methods are available for including political risk in the NPV framework: (1) adjust the required rate of return to reflect the incremental political risk, (2) adjust downward the expected cash flows, and (3) evaluate the project's NPV without the political risk, quantify the political risk separately, and then subtract the quantified political risk from the project's NPV.

4. Accounting for political risk in the CAPM requires using an international market index denominated in a convertible currency. The systematic risk obtained from the modified CAPM captures the political risk. Several modified CAPMs that account for political risk have been developed. For example, Ibbotson Associates estimates the required rate of return using the world CAPM and then adds a risk premium estimated from the past performance of the country's market. Clark (1991, 2002) develops a macro CAPM to estimate the country political risk by developing a world macroeconomic index. The main feature of Clark's CAPM model is that the estimated risk-adjusted return is not constrained by the existence of certain markets or an estimation of their integration or degree of segmentation. Clark's model estimates both the country beta and the project beta with respect to the country index. The overall beta is the product of the country beta with the project-specific beta.

5. Political risk is measured as the value of an insurance policy that reimburses all losses resulting from the political event or events in question. Clark (1998) models political events as a Poisson jump process because they occur intermittently, at discrete intervals, and generate an actual loss. In this model, explicit loss-causing events are distinguished from ongoing change and are represented by geometric Brownian motion. Clark (1997) provides an example of how to estimate the risk premium.

CHAPTER 14   RISK MANAGEMENT IN PROJECT FINANCE

1. Although different alternatives are available to control and mitigate risks (retention and insurance), the use of the network of contracts revolving around the SPV is probably the most effective. Contracts can be designed to incentivize the counterparties responsible for a specific risk to avoid it and its effects on project cash flows. If this risk emerges, the counterparty will be called to pay liquidated damages to the SPV. In this way, the project is protected against negative events that could hamper the ability of the venture to repay operating costs, debt service, and dividends. Corielli, Gatti, and Steffanoni (2010) argue that an effective use of nonfinancial contracts (NFCs) can lower the credit spread required by lenders and allow sponsors to use a higher debt-to-equity ratio for the financing of the project.

2. Project sponsors decide to invest money in a project finance transaction based on the comparison between the IRR_{equity} and their weighted average cost of capital (WACC) in a manner similar to what happens for normal corporate finance settings. Internal rate of return (IRR) is the same criterion that banks use to evaluate the funding of a project with debt. In this case, the IRR is calculated by comparing the cash outlays due to debt drawdowns with the repayment implied by the agreed amortization schedule. However, the same IRR can be generated by different time profiles of cash flows, and the criterion cannot detect if the cash available for debt service (the unlevered free cash flow) in a given year is strictly higher than the debt service agreed to for that specific year. Cover ratios are designed for this purpose and are supplemental criteria that banks use to decide whether to provide funds for the project.

3. Cover ratios are financial covenants set by banks in terms of minimum and sometimes average values to protect themselves against unexpected unlevered free cash flow shortfalls. The minimum value is a direct function of cash flow volatility: The higher the expected volatility, the higher is the minimum level of the various cover ratios required by banks. Because implementing an effective risk management analysis can mitigate cash flow volatility, risk management has a direct influence on cash flows. The more effective the risk analysis and risk allocation, the lower is the level of the minimum debt service cover ratio (DSCR) and the loan life cover ratio (LLCR) required by lenders.

4. In principle, shareholders should use the value of free cash flow to equity (FCFE) when calculating the IRR_{equity}. This is natural when FCFE equals dividends paid (a common situation in standard corporate finance settings). In project finance, dividends can differ from FCFE for two reasons. First, shareholders must comply with the request of banks to provide money to debt reserve accounts and such money is then unavailable to pay out in dividends. Second, shareholders could face the dividend trap every time the depreciation of fixed assets in the profit and loss statement is higher than the value of principal repayments in the statement of cash flows of the SPV.

CHAPTER 15   RISK SIMULATION CONCEPTS AND METHODS

1. The range of NPV values decreases from (–$1,365,928 to $2,044,706) to (–$942,970 to $1,749,476) when correlation between the price and variable cost exists.

2. Comparing Panel A of Exhibits 15.4 and 15.6, the distribution with the lower variance (Exhibit 15.6) has more probability at the mean when compared to Exhibit 15.4. Consequently, the answer is the probability of the mean actually occurring lowers as the variance increases.

3. In Exhibit 15.3, the probability is between 20 percent and 25 percent (i.e., somewhere between the 75th percentile and 85th percentile). In Exhibit 15.5, the probability is between 10 percent and 15 percent (i.e., somewhere between the 80th percentile and 90th percentile).

4. Looking at Panel C of Exhibit 15.3, the variable with the largest magnitude regression coefficient is the variable cost per unit in the first year.

5. Looking at Panel C of Exhibit 15.5, the variable with the largest magnitude regression coefficient is the variable cost per unit in the first year. When comparing the regression coefficient with Exhibit 15.3, the magnitude has increased by about 30 percent, implying that the existence of correlation between the price and the variable cost has increased the influence of variable cost on the NPV.

6. The "compact" pro forma model allows the user to vary the number of finite cash flows (i.e., the duration of the project).

CHAPTER 16   REAL OPTION ANALYSIS: INTRODUCTION

1. The "under-investment" problem occurs when a firm theoretically has too much debt forcing the firm to prefer shorter-term projects that generate liquidity to service the debt over longer-term projects that can allow the firm to grow in the future.

2. Management discretion can potentially reduce losses and increase gains throughout the life of the project which increases the value of the project.

3. A series of small investments increases the value of the project because the initial decision to invest can be re-evaluated every time a new investment is made in the future. This allows the potential to end a project before fully committing all capital to the project or perhaps scaling up the investment in the project because the project has potential for additional less risky gain.

4. The firm will use an option to expand when an increase in operations will generate additional profit to meet additional demand. The firm will use an option to contract when a decrease in operations will save money by not generating excess capacity due to reduced demand.

5. By recognizing where management flexibility is valuable, management can create flexibility in contracting or in how a project is implemented to generate value even when the value cannot be specifically quantified. In other words, merely creating real options can be valuable even when a value cannot be calculated.

6. A rainbow option is when multiple options are available at a point in time within a project or throughout time within a project. Generally, one cannot value all of the options, but should consider the existence of all of the options when making a decision.

CHAPTER 17   APPLICATIONS OF REAL OPTIONS ANALYSIS

1. The discount rate for an entire risky project is an inappropriate discount rate for individual future cash flows within the project because individual cash flows have different risk attributes than the project as a whole. Some cash flows are safer while others are riskier than the entire project. This is similar to how individual securities within a portfolio have different risk attributes than the risk of the entire portfolio.

2. The futures/forward price is the current price (or value) of the project appreciated by the risk-free rate. When determining a project's current price or value using DCF analysis, the option valuation using risk-neutral pricing contains the DCF valuation within the risk-neutral probability structure. This is inappropriate because the futures/forward price is used to construct the risk-neutral probability distribution.

3. Initially, there is value to waiting. The NPV of waiting is $1.02 million = [($12/(1.08) − $10]/(1.10) versus the NPV of executing immediately $0.91 million = [$12/(1.10)] − $10. If there is no volatility (i.e., keeping the discount rate at 10 percent), no value exists to waiting. The NPV of waiting is $0.83 million = [$12/(1.10) − $10]/(1.10) versus the NPV of executing immediately $0.91 million = ($12/1.10) − $10.

4. Because there is a cost, the mine will not open or close immediately, because the option to do so would need to have sufficient value to trigger opening or closing. If the mine is losing money, it will not close until pending losses are larger than the cost of closing and possibly even larger than the cost of closing, depending on the volatility creating a valuable option to wait. If the mine is closed and the economic conditions allow for profitable operation, the mine will not open until pending profits are larger than the cost of opening and possibly even larger than the cost of opening, depending on volatility creating a valuable option to wait. Consequently, the mine can still operate at a loss under this scenario.

5. If the option to expand is valuable, then the "opposing" option to abandon will not be highly valuable, because it is unlikely to be exercised.

6. No, the value of the options in a rainbow option are generally less than the sum of the options valued independently of the rainbow option. This results from the interaction between the options within the rainbow option. This situation is similar to a portfolio of securities whose sum of individual security volatilities are more than the volatility of the portfolio given diversification benefits.

CHAPTER 18   COST OF CAPITAL: AN INTRODUCTION

1. The most used approach to choosing a risk-free rate is to equate it to the yield to maturity (YTM) on an outstanding long-term Treasury security. The choice of the maturity of the bond depends on the length of the cash flow being discounted. For example, the firm should use shorter maturities for evaluating capital budgeting projects having a shorter life, but a long-maturity bond is a reasonable choice for valuation of companies or business units. Courtois, Lai, and Peterson (2008) suggest matching the length of the investment to the length of the appropriate risk-free rate. For example, a 30-year investment should be matched to the 30-year government bond yield. The correct risk-free rate is the rate as of the valuation date, not the average rate of a historical data set.

2. In the standard historical approach, the difference between actual returns earned on stocks over a long time period and actual returns earned on Treasury bonds is calculated to determine an average equity risk premium. Estimations of the equity risk premium based on extrapolations of historical data are risky and biased (Damodaran, 2009). Questions remain about the length of the period to use, the use of a short-term or long-term risk-free government bond, the appropriate underlying market index to use, and the choice of arithmetic or a geometric mean. The historical approach does not consider what the market anticipates as the risk premium. Under the forward-looking approach, the equity risk premium is derived from prevailing market valuations. By assuming that the current market value is equal to the fair value, the financial manager can determine the cost of equity capital and, therefore, the implied equity risk premium. Unfortunately, this approach involves many challenges to constructing a fundamental valuation model. Because the goal is to arrive at a reasonable estimate, this requires using past and current methodologies that incorporate all available information at the time of analysis and being aware that investors have different expected risk premiums due to different expectations of equity cash flows and growth rates.

3. The analyst is incorrect. The firm should consider the convertibility of the newly issued bonds. The proportion of debt and equity in the issue should be allocated to the firm's total debt and equity. If the total amount of the issue is considered debt, the firm's weight of debt will be higher and the weight of equity will be lower than its true amount. Given that the cost of equity is generally higher than the cost of debt, the firm will incorrectly estimate a lower cost of capital than when using the correct weights.

4. Using historical or book weights in the estimation process often provides an incorrect estimate of a firm's cost of capital. The greater the amount of raised capital, the more likely the capital structure will change and render the historical weights invalid. When calculating the expected cost of capital, either target or market value weights should be used because they reflect the expectations of the investors, and market value closely reflects how a company has to raise new capital. The financial manager should use target weights, especially if the firm is expected to retire securities over the forthcoming period. As firms age, their positive cash flows tend to increase, which allows the firm to retire debt and equity that it used to grow the business.

CHAPTER 19   USING THE CAPITAL ASSET PRICING MODEL AND ARBITRAGE PRICING THEORY IN CAPITAL BUDGETING

1. Multifactor asset-pricing models are much harder to use than the CAPM for several reasons. First, debate exists over how many factors are appropriate and how those factors are priced. Second, uncertainty exists about whether any improvement in helping corporate managers understand their firms' systematic risk offsets the cost of the added complexity required by multifactor models. The intuitive nature of the CAPM and the presence of only one risk factor simplify explaining the CAPM versus multifactor asset-pricing models to nonfinance managers.

2. Ex ante, there should be no difference in the equity risk premium across countries. This can be understood by considering systematic versus unsystematic (diversifiable) risk. From the perspective of the global capital markets, the risk of any one country is largely offset by asset price movements in other countries. For example, the country-specific risk of investing in Brazil is largely offset by the risk of investing in China or the United States. Thus, even if one country has greater total risk than another, the

incremental risk is diversifiable, leaving only systematic risk. In other words, the market risk premium should be the same across all countries. The systematic risk across countries will differ, but only because each country has its own unique distribution of industries and different industries have different betas. The market risk premium, however, should be the same.

3. Any answer to this question is speculative, but the equity risk premium is likely to decrease due to competitive forces in the capital markets. This process, however, could take a very long time.

4. Roll (1977) argues that the CAPM is empirically untestable because a true market portfolio is not empirically observable. Researchers cannot use the true market portfolio for several reasons. First, the market portfolio has to include all financial and nonfinancial assets in the economy. Second, some assets that should be included in the portfolio have unobservable characteristics. Third, the true market portfolio may include international assets if international capital markets are open and asset prices conform to an international version of the CAPM. Thus, researchers are unlikely to be able to use a proxy of the true market portfolio that is on the mean-variance efficient frontier. Consequently, from Roll's perspective, the CAPM can never be tested. Whether financial economists can surmount this hurdle is largely a matter of conjecture.

5. According to several empirical studies, the CAPM's estimate of cost of equity capital is biased upward for firms with high betas but biased downward for firms with low betas. As a result, managers of high-beta firms could erroneously reject profitable projects, while managers of low-beta firms could mistakenly accept unprofitable projects. Hence, managers should consider adjusting CAPM's estimates toward the economy-wide mean (i.e., $\beta = 1$) in order to avoid over-rejection or overacceptance of projects.

CHAPTER 20 FINANCING MIX AND PROJECT VALUATION: ALTERNATIVE METHODS AND POSSIBLE ADJUSTMENTS

1. Using the equity residual method may be correct in two cases: (1) when the funding of the project has no impact on the financing mix of other projects, and (2) when a company targets a fixed debt ratio and the project's debt ratio is equal to the firm's target debt ratio. Because borrowing in Norway is less expensive than in other countries, the project's debt is probably greater than that satisfying the firm's target debt ratio. If such is the case, although it would correctly take into account the Norwegian tax specificities, the equity residual method would associate an excessive financial leverage effect with the project. This leverage effect would not be relevant because a project's debt ratio greater than that targeted by the firm must be compensated by smaller debt ratios for other projects. Here, the correct approach would be to use the generalized ATWACC method.

2. Using the BTWACC approach is correct only if the data used to compute the cash flows are consistent with those used to determine the discount rate (defined as a before-tax weighted average cost of capital). Changes in the interest rate of the loan imply changes in the value of the discount rate. When the interest rate is higher, the internal rate of return (IRR) is greater because the tax shields included in the project's cash flows are larger. However, this does not mean that the project is more profitable, since the IRR must then be compared to a higher discount rate.

3. When correctly applied, both methods yield the same return on equity. When using the displaced equity method, the analyst probably calculated the cash flows associated with a cost of equity of 12 percent. This is correct when computing the project's net present

value (NPV). However, when determining the project's return on equity by zeroing its NPV, the analyst must consider the cost of equity as an unknown variable (appearing in the cash flow formula). Usual IRR functions in spreadsheets cannot be used when using the displaced equity method.

4. The method is similar to that proposed in this chapter for capitalized interest costs. When the taxable income is negative, the free cash flows (FCFs) should be decreased by the lost interest tax shields. The FCFs should be increased by these tax shields when they are recovered (losses are assumed to be carried forward until the taxable income becomes positive).

5. The creation of value corresponding to a project's positive NPV increases the firm's debt capacity. A loan amounting to 40 percent of the investment cost does not take this into account. Borrowing 40 percent of the sum of the investment cost and NPV would represent the project's actual contribution to the firm's debt capacity. Under this assumption, both methods would yield similar NPVs and the same NPV if the project's debt ratio remains constant throughout time. In other words, if the firm borrows "only" 40 percent of the investment cost, it does not use the full leverage effect from which the project should benefit. For this reason, the equity residual method yields a lower NPV than the standard WACC method.

CHAPTER 21   CAPITAL BUDGETING FOR GOVERNMENT ENTITIES

1. The separation of current and development budgets appealed to the new administrations following colonial administrations in that it enabled them to separate the ongoing costs of government and the associated raising of current revenues with ambitious new development plans and their associated financing needs. Development assistance donors have further reinforced this separation over the years through their traditional preference for funding of "development" activities, while being cautious about funding "consumption spending" associated with current expenditures. This traditional view of current expenditures as being of lesser economic importance or merit has diminished in recent years, although it is still evident in the chronic underfunding of some government services.

2. Jacobs (2008) offers the following benchmarks to consider when aiming to improve the capital budgeting process in LICs:
   - *Determine the appropriate resource envelope:* All capital expenditure decisions should be based on a consolidated budget approach, incorporating all revenues and expenditures, in particular foreign-financed projects and extrabudgetary funds with investment activities. Capital expenditure decisions should be based on a medium-term budget perspective. Decisions about capital expenditures should be taken in the context of a hard budget constraint with explicit ceilings for guarantees and commitments beyond the budget year. Governments should have clear policies regarding which capital expenditures should be financed by the budget, realized through public-private partnerships, and handled by government or private enterprises.
   - *Efficient prioritization and selection*: The budget calendar and the procedures for integration of capital expenditures in the budget must be clear, transparent, and stable. Development and analysis of capital investment proposals should largely be completed before the budget preparation process starts. All projects should be subject to cost-benefit analysis (CBA). If the subjection of all projects to CBA is too costly, the focus could first be on the larger projects, while using a simplified methodology for smaller projects. A government investment agency, with strong links to the Ministry of Finance, should prepare guidelines for project development and analysis. This

agency should review project proposals to ensure that they are adequately prepared and analyzed, and have the authority to reject projects that do not meet the established technical standards. The Ministry of Finance should give the cabinet recommendations for which investment projects should be realized within the available resource envelope. Ministries should compete for investment funds based on the net social value and political priority of their investment proposals. The decision to implement an investment project should be independent of the financing and procurement modalities for the project.

- *Efficient implementation*: Rules for budget adjustments should give incentives for realistic initial capital cost estimates. Cost overruns during project implementation should be partly covered by reallocation within ministries' existing budgets. Ministries should be allowed to retain part of any real cost reductions. Capital investment project proposals should only be considered when they include a detailed disclosure of the expected operating costs, indicating how these will be accommodated within existing resource envelopes or making an explicit proposal for additional financing of the operating costs. Capital investment project proposals should only be considered after the ministry has explained how it will fully cover the maintenance of its existing capital stock. Governments should avoid excessive targeting of capital expenditures for budget cuts. Decisions on budget cuts should be based on the medium-term budget and take full account of future expenditure pressures as a result of underfunding. Finally, there should be project completion reports for all capital expenditure projects. These should form the basis for cross-sectoral analysis, methodology development, and continuous improvements in the investment process.

3. Capital project appraisals (CPAs) can include checks and balances to ensure that sound principles are being applied. In some countries, the staged external review of large projects provides an important measure of quality control, and this can be especially important in early stages. Various general requirements for effective CPAs could be defined, including the following:
    - Providing well-informed and open-minded consideration of alternative options, against well-defined policy objectives.
    - Taking proper account of opportunity costs (so that the use of labor, for example, is normally recognized as a cost, and not seen instead as a benefit).
    - Addressing any "optimism bias" so as to ensure the proper calculation of all overall costs.
    - Considering factors that cannot be explicitly valued in money terms as well as those which can.

4. Premchand (2007) identified the following six stages of changes in government capital budgeting practices.
    - *First stage.* During the Great Depression years efforts were mainly focused on economic recovery. Government borrowing for financing capital outlays, except for emergencies, was not favored.
    - *Second stage.* In the late 1930s, the Indian government introduced a capital budget in order to reduce the budget deficit. This was done by moving some expenditure items from the current budget. This dual-budget system provided a justifiable method to reduce deficits while justifying a rationale for borrowing.
    - *Third stage.* The period in the 1940s and 1950s could be seen as the time when the use of capital budgets became important for economic growth and the framing of economic development plans. Partly influenced by Soviet-style planning, many low-income countries formulated comprehensive five-year development plans and considered capital budgets as the main driver for economic development (Tarschys, 2002). Where capital budgets did not exist, a variant known as the *development budget* was introduced.

- *Fourth stage.* This reflects the importance of economic policy choices on the allocation of government resources. In the 1960s governments applied quantitative appraisal techniques on a wider scale, leading to more rigorous application of investment appraisal and financial planning (Premchand, 2007).
- *Fifth stage.* A revival of the earlier debate about the need for governments to make use of a capital budget could be noted, especially in the United States. Along with the growing application of quantitative techniques during the 1960s came the view that introducing a capital budget could be beneficial to society. But this view did not gain much support. A president-appointed commission rejected the use of separate capital budgets and the introduction of accrual accounting in government accounts. Meanwhile, Sweden found that excessive focus on capital budgets would need to be adjusted by a recognition that the overall credibility and creditworthiness of a government depend more on its macroeconomic policy stance and less on a government's net worth. This shift in emphasis contributed to a decline in the use of the capital budget until the late 1980s. By then, government officials recognized that the management of government finances required a new approach, and this approach was the application of accrual accounting.
- *Sixth stage.* The successful experiences of the Australian and New Zealand governments of the introduction of accrual budgeting and accounting led to a renewed push by international financial institutions for the importance of capital budgeting. These ideas were advocated in the United States, where the view was that the absence of a distinction between investment outlays and ordinary or current outlays could lead to unintended neglect of infrastructure or accumulated assets. Ensuring proper asset maintenance, as well as asset creation, required a division of outlays into current and capital outlays as a part of daily budget management.

CHAPTER 22   DECISION MAKING USING BEHAVIORAL FINANCE FOR CAPITAL BUDGETING

1. Kahneman and Tversky's prospect theory tells a very different story on risky decision making than standard finance and economics. It recognizes that individuals are affected by the "framing effect" because different ways of presenting the same problem lead to different decisions. Individuals make their decisions after having coded decision problems as gains or losses with respect to a reference point. From this codification, a "value function" arises, which tabulates the value assigned to a prospect comprising a series of expected payoffs, and a "weighting function" is associated with the weight assigned to probabilities associated with those payoffs. The value function is S-shaped, generally concave for gains and convex for losses, and is steeper for losses than for gains. The reference point seems to coincide with the status quo, but a shared theory on how it is determined is unavailable. The importance of prospect theory for behavioral finance is reflected in the numerous cognitive biases it can take into account, and in the different risk-return relationship it proposes with respect to traditional theory.

2. The representation of cash flows is affected by optimism, overconfidence, and the way such representation deals with sunk costs and opportunity costs. While optimism can be understood as the inflation of the mean of expected values, overconfidence produces a reduction of the expected variance of these values. Studies on the way sunk costs are embedded in the representation of cash flows demonstrate that decision makers often take into account such costs, even though standard finance theory prescribes ignoring them in decision making. The role of sunk costs can be one cause of the escalation of

commitment to a failing course of action, which is the tendency to continue a project even if it would be better to stop it. Finally, decision makers often inappropriately consider opportunity costs. The endowment effect occurs when the valuation of opportunity cost depends on whether the decision maker is on the buying or selling side.

3. Standard finance theory advocates using the CAPM to discount a project's expected cash flows. Studies on the practice of business finance demonstrate that using rates higher than CAPM-based rates is very common. Even though the rationale for this evidence could be found either in the difficulty of determining the correct risk premium to be employed when adopting CAPM or in causal errors, many reasons can be advanced to interpret such a behavior from a behavioral perspective. Hurdle rates could represent a way to offset optimism and overconfidence in the representation of cash flows. Hurdle rates could also represent a way for dealing with the combination of uncertainty and capital rationing: They would operate as a substitute for the profitability index, thereby helping in choosing the more profitable investments. Finally, high hurdle rates could prevent actual investments in order to save money for future investment opportunities. This way such rates would operate as a rule of thumb for taking into account the possible expansion of the opportunity set a firm deals with in the future.

4. Approaches that assume complete and perfect financial markets stress only one positive compound discounting rate, defined both as the market standard of performance and the competitive opportunity rate for firm-specific investment projects. Such unrealistic approaches have been criticized by welfare economics (defending the claims of posterity) and by business economists and professionals concerned with the myopia that those approaches imply. In particular, they neglect the special relational economics that fits with the specifics of the business firm and its investment process. Recent advances in institutional and behavioral finance support and expand this critique, allowing the generalization of the received discounting approach. Different forms of discounting (including simple or compound discounting) can then be understood as statistical means of the expected investment project's cash flow sequence. These forms can be subsumed in new investment valuation criteria based upon multiple discount rates (at least one for investment and another one for replacement) and can be adjusted for discount rate term structure.

CHAPTER 23   MERGERS AND ACQUISITIONS PRICING: THE VALUATION OF SYNERGY

1. In an M&A context, synergy occurs when the value of the combined firm C exceeds the collective values of the separate entities A and B. The total synergy value resulting from a merger equals the difference between the combined firm value and the sum of each individual firm value. The realized synergy should be seen as the return on investment of an M&A. The higher the possible future returns on investment, the more investors are willing to pay for the acquisition of an asset. Therefore, the assessment of future synergy affects today's acquisition price.

2. The three major merger types are horizontal, vertical, and conglomerate. Horizontal mergers can lead to the economies of scale effect (cost-cutting effects), financial synergies, and revenue enhancement by cross-selling effects. Synergies in vertical mergers generally involve control of the supply chain, which may include quality control and just-in-time production. Although conglomerate mergers involve a diversification effect, this is not a synergy effect. Markets should not pay a risk premium for unique risk because investors can reduce this risk by diversifying their financial assets.

3. An investment in a merger is successful if the value of the combined firm C is higher than the sum of the acquisition price for firm B and the value of firm A compared at the same point in time. Therefore, the total synergy value realized by the merger has to be higher than the acquisition premium paid to shareholders of the acquired company B. Taking into account a fair distribution of the total synergy value between shareholders of companies A and B, the total synergy value should be twice as high as the premium paid for the acquisition of firm B for a given time period.

4. Based on a system theoretical approach, a corporation is a complex economic system of elements and interrelationships that depend upon each other. Every element in a firm is organically linked with one another in the firm's system of organization, corporate culture, organizational routines, and activities. Sales, turnover, and profits are directly correlated to the regular interaction of activities within a corporate system. A merger constitutes a new corporate system, C, with diverse elements and interrelationships. Conventional valuation methods assume that sales figures and market shares of corporations A and B are easily transferable to the new entity C, and the outcome of a merger could be accurately forecasted by simply aggregating key financial figures. However, because the profit of C is not just the sum of A's and B's profits, there is no value additivity property. As a new corporate system, company C requires, given its uniqueness and individuality, a separate pricing process. As the merged company C does not exist yet, no codified (explicit) information, which could be taken from balance sheets or business reports, is readily available. Therefore, any pricing of firm C should use system-specific (implicit or tacit) knowledge of A and B to develop a vision about the future performance processes and interaction of elements in the new system C. Conventional methods cannot be used for valuation of firm C as these methods are solely based on codified information and assume value additivity.

5. The system theoretical approach contains three elements: identification of synergy, integration planning for redesigned business processes, and the valuation of net cash flows from projected business processes. The identification of synergy begins with analyzing similar business processes of firms A and B regarding their efficiency and strengths and weaknesses. The new firm C should adopt the superior technology, the better organization, and the more skilled human resources. The identification of synergy also implies business process reengineering, in a way that new business processes are developed based on a reassembling of the given technology, knowledge, and expertise of human resources. Integration planning transforms the identified synergies into measurable integration targets. Similar to project management, integration planning includes the definition of various targets measured in concrete figures, a breakdown in milestones and deadlines, work plans, and target completion dates. Hence, integration planning determines which corporate functions (e.g., marketing, treasury, and information technology) are involved in reaching this target and which managers will assume leadership throughout the integration process. The corporate system C exists as a vision of projected business processes combined with a plan for implementation. The valuation starts with a cash flow forecast for each operational process involved in the value chain of firm C for a given time period. Afterwards, net cash flow results of one business process "n" are discounted for each time period "t" and summed up for all business processes to arrive at a single present value for all future net cash flows of corporate system C. This valuation should be complemented by risk management tools (e.g., sensitivity analysis, scenario analysis, and Monte Carlo simulation) because key variables of the cash flow projection are faced with high uncertainty and the business processes within a corporate system are naturally correlated.

6. Due diligence teams have to deal with the following issues: the need for system internal information, information asymmetry, various principal-agent problems, and the security

of intellectual property. Internal due diligence teams gathered by experts from firms A and B can generate system internal information and overcome the information asymmetry problem, but are affected by principal-agent problems and have difficulties securing intellectual property. Purely external teams do not have the internal knowledge necessary to generate system internal data and may have conflicts of interest in making the deal. If the deal is completed, fees for external audit are often high and further consulting for integration planning and implementation is needed. Success in a merger requires close collaboration of management teams and, therefore, the development of trust. Given this logic, the involvement of a public external audit institution acting as a trust broker within the merger process could be an alternative worth considering.

7. A radical change is needed for the pricing process. First, a payment of a merger premium for shareholders of the acquired firm is only justified if a reasonable expectation exists that the total synergy to be realized is at least twice as high as the paid premium plus risk-adjusted compound interest. Second, the value of synergy has to be explicitly incorporated into pricing models by using system-specific knowledge of A and B in order to develop a vision of corporate system C with its future business processes. Using a system theoretical approach, due diligence requires a two-way perspective of investors as both business models, the acquiring and the target company's model, continuously have to be analyzed and compared regarding strengths and weaknesses. For this kind of due diligence, experts with a diverse set of skills, vast experience, and solid understanding of each firm's core business are needed. The investment appraisal of synergy effects depends on expert knowledge.

CHAPTER 24 MULTICRITERIA ANALYSIS FOR CAPITAL BUDGETING

1. In the public sector, projects often have multiple objectives, whereas the private sector tends to focus on maximizing shareholder wealth as the main objective. Private sector capital investments may directly or indirectly affect the economy and society. Hence, there is a growing trend to systematically take these impacts into consideration. Decision makers in both the private and public sectors can use MCA methods to incorporate more information into the decision process and to address various forms of risk and opportunity.

2. The NPV criterion is still critical. Companies can use MCA methods if they want to add more considerations when comparing similar capital decisions that generate positive returns but have different effects such as on society and the environment. Using the MCA versus traditional NPV methods may lead to different rankings of projects. This could be the case especially if the value that such projects create to the firm's owners is of paramount importance. MCA expands the information provided by the NPV criterion.

3. MCA can incorporate risk information into the decision-making process and input or output variables that include other dimensions beyond a purely monetary return and those that could change through time. MCA methods might offer additional insights to decision makers. The evaluation of capital investments in new transport technology that is undergoing rapid transformation might need to include considerations beyond financial return measures such as their environmental impact or fuel resource use. Using MCA enables the decision maker to incorporate expected changes in regulatory regimes and expected preferences by customers in a transparent manner.

4. Important factors needed to initiate the application of MCA methodology for private sector investment decisions include the following: support from decision makers, a culture of learning by doing, a willingness to try new methodologies, and a gradual approach that initially uses relatively simple decision-making and scoring matrices. MCA methods have to be understood as a learning tool for analysts and decision makers in the organization. The process can be refined with improved result, once MCA methods have some degree of use and acceptance.

Index

Printed in the United States
By Bookmasters